Base Ecumenism

Shapers of Ecumenical Theology Series
Series Editor: Jesudas M. Athyal

Praise for *Base Ecumenism*

Raimundo Barreto's *Base Ecumenism* is a monumental achievement: not only a comprehensive and accessible account of Latin American ecumenical contributions by a polyglot historian at the height of his powers, but also a wide-ranging, visionary retelling of the ecumenical movement that provides fresh and compelling insight into its renewed urgency. This essential work not only serves its stated purpose as a thorough account of major ecclesiological, ethical, theological, and epistemological developments out of Latin America over the past century; it also offers a persuasive reorientation to what Christian ecumenism is, where it comes from, and why it should matter in the world today.

—Aaron T. Hollander, associate director, Graymoor Ecumenical and Interreligious Institute, and author of *Saint George Liberator: Hagiography and Resistance in the Modern Mediterranean*

In studies on the rise and development of the modern ecumenical movement, Latin America has been widely neglected. Thus, Raimundo Barreto's new book, focusing on Latin American initiatives and their impact on the reshaping of the ecumenical ideal in the course of the twentieth century, fills a painfully felt lacuna. *Base ecumenism*, as distinguished from hierarchical organizational structures, is the key term of his analysis, as he pays special attention to lay activities, grassroots initiatives, independent communities, and interfaith coalitions. In doing so, he opens new perspectives also on the formation of the ecumenical movement in other world regions. An urgently needed, fresh approach to our understanding of current global ecumenism.

—Klaus Koschorke, emeritus chair of Early and Global History of Christianity, University of Munich

In this book, Raimundo Barreto reclaims the ecumenical spirit from captivity through an alliance of confessionalist Eurocentric and post-communist nationalist Orthodox churches. Locating himself in Brazilian "base ecumenism" and diasporic theological discourses in the US, he maps out an alternative history of the ecumenical movement and paves future roads for an intercultural ecumenism beyond the Geneva impasse.

—Volker Küster, author of *The Many Faces of Jesus Christ: Intercultural Christology*

This comprehensive work eloquently delves into the unique contributions of Latin America to modern ecumenical theology, illuminating the profound impact of grassroots movements on the global ecumenical landscape. It meticulously explores how the epistemic shift toward recognizing the poor as central theological partners transformed both the region and the broader ecumenical dialogue. By highlighting these pivotal developments, the book underscores the vital role of base ecumenism in fostering new forms of *koinonia* and creating paths for inclusive and equitable theological discourse to address contemporary global challenges.

—Vladimir Latinovic, lecturer, University of Tübingen

Base Ecumenism calls attention to the multiple irruptions of the Global South from the in-between spaces of imperial and colonial systems of western, northern Christian missions. In decolonial manner, it exposes the vinculum between geopolitical and religious interests prevalent in ecumenical movements, yet also the collective struggle in Latin American churches against domination that led to a shift in consciousness from non-personhood to historical and political subjectivity. Before the reader, structures that seemed irreversible begin to crumble as democratic ideals and commitments to social change rooted in the Latin American milieu spread through transnational networks, creating a sense of *oikumene* as interdependence and connectedness.

—Elaine Padilla, professor of philosophy and religion, and Latinx/Latin American studies, University of La Verne

This book is an important analysis of the new Latin American theology: the development of liberation theology and the relationship of the diversity of ecumenical ecclesiastical theologies. Raimundo Barreto, professor at Princeton Theological Seminary, has become a crucial international theologian and also a magnificent writer. I recommend the reading and serious consideration of this excellent book.

—Luis N. Rivera-Pagán, Henry Winters Luce Professor Emeritus of Ecumenics, Princeton Theological Seminary

Base Ecumenism fills a glaring gap in studies of the ecumenical movement. Dr. Barreto brings to the forefront grassroots expressions of ecumenism and solidarity with the poor in Latin America and demonstrates the significant global impact of such local movements. The book emanates a spirit of ecumenism and plurality in its consideration of Latin American Catholic, Protestant, and Pentecostal contributions and in its attentiveness to marginalized subjects—including the role of women, sexuality, and interreligious relations. This enlightening study is a must-read for anyone interested in the past, present, or future of Christian ecumenism.

—Deanna Ferree Womack, associate professor of the history of religions and interfaith studies, Candler School of Theology, Emory University, and author of *Protestants, Gender and the Arab Renaissance in Late Ottoman Syria*

Redolent not only of erudition but also of vision, Barreto's work opens the aperture on ecumenics more widely than any recent work I know of. Invigorated by Latin American perspectives, *Base Ecumenism* breaks through the constraints of the faith-and-order church-centric paradigm and shows how an inclusive dialogue with extra-Christian voices will enrich us all. *Base Ecumenism* will have a global readership, not least in World Christianity circles, where the author is regarded as a path-breaker extraordinaire.

—Richard Fox Young, professor emeritus of the history of religions, Princeton Theological Seminary

Base Ecumenism

Latin American Contributions to Ecumenical Praxis and Theology

Raimundo C. Barreto

FORTRESS PRESS
MINNEAPOLIS

BASE ECUMENISM
Latin American Contributions to Ecumenical Praxis and Theology

30 29 28 27 26 25 1 2 3 4 5 6 7 8 9

Library of Congress Control Number: 2024031477 (print)

Cover art by Cerezo Barredo
Cover design: Savanah N. Landerholm

Print ISBN: 978-1-5064-3014-0
eBook ISBN: 978-1-5064-3015-7

Para Eliã, Caio, Cauã e Lulu, amores
e inspiração da minha vida.

CONTENTS

Abbreviations xi

Shapers of Ecumenical Theology Series xv

Acknowledgments xxiii

Preface xxvii

1. A Changing Ecumenism 1
   Idea and Organization of the Book 11
   The IMC: The First Embodiment of the Ecumenical Dream 14
   Tambaram: Rethinking the Relationship between Christianity and Other Religions 27
2. The Rise of Latin American Ecumenism 35
   The Committee on Cooperation in Latin America (CCLA) and the Panama Congress 40
   Latin American Protestantism Comes of Age 52
3. The Shortcomings of the Liberal Project and the Rise of the Third World 69
   Protestantism Discovers Its Latin Americanness 79
   The Third World as a New Theological Locus 83
4. The Rise of Liberation Christianity among Latin American Protestants 93
   Latin American Protestants and the Liberation Turn 97
   The WSCF and the Student Christian Movement in Latin America 103
5. Toward a World-Oriented Ecumenism 117
   Moving Beyond the Responsible Society Framework 117
   Looking for Alternative Spaces for a World-Oriented Ecumenism 132
   The Formation of ISAL 145
   The Latin American Evangelical Conferences (CELA) 156

6. Catholic Action and the Roots of Base Ecumenism 167
Catholic Action and Worker Priests in Latin America 169
Evolution and Change in Latin American Catholic Action 176
The Brazilian JUC 184
JUC and Popular Action: The Revolutionary Turn in the Brazilian Catholic Action 193

7. Vatican II and the Birth of the Church of the Poor 207
The Latin American Church Prior to the Vatican II 207
The Church of the Poor and the Pact of the Catacombs 219
The Reception of Vatican II in Latin America: The Joint Pastoral Program in Brazil 232

8. CEBs, Medellin, and the Dawn of Liberation Theology 237
The "Faithful, Creative, and Selective Reception" of Vatican II in Latin America 237
Justice, Peace, and the Poverty of the Church in the Medellin Documents 243
Comunidades de Base and the Rebirth of the Church in Latin America 251

9. The Rise of Base Ecumenism 273
CEBI and the Popular Reading of the Bible 273
The Ecumenism of the CEBs 280
Contributions from Puebla 283

10. The Global Impact of Base Ecumenism 297
Ecumenismo de Base: Globalization from Below 297
Paulo Freire, the WCC, and the Globalization of the *Pedagogy of the Oppressed* 306

11. The Globalization of the Third World Project and the Ecumenical Movement 315
EATWOT and the World Forum on Theology and Liberation (WFTL) 315
Pope Francis and the Globalization of Hope from Below 352

12. For an *Oikoumenē* in Which Many Worlds Coexist 367
Toward an Ecumenism of the Spirit 372
A World in Which Many Worlds Fit 384

Bibliography 389

Index 415

ABBREVIATIONS

ABB	—	Aliança de Batistas do Brasil (Alliance of Brazilian Baptists)
ACAS	—	Associação de Cristãos Acadêmicos (Association of Academic Christians)
ACB	—	Ação Católica Brasileira (Brazilian Catholic Action)
AP	—	Ação Popular (Popular Action)
ASEL	—	Acción Social Ecuménica Latinoamericana (Latin American Ecumenical Social Action)
CCLA	—	Committee on Cooperation in Latin America
CEB	—	Confederação Evangélica do Brasil (Protestant Confederation of Brazil)
CEBs	—	Comunidades Eclesiais de Base (Ecclesial Base Communities)
CEDI	—	*Centro Ecumênico de Documentação e Informação* (Ecumenical Center of Information and Documentation)
CEI	—	Centro Ecumênico de Informação (Ecumenical Center of Information)
CELA	—	Conferencia Evangélica Latinoamericana (Latin American Evangelical Conference)
CELADEC	—	Comisión Evangélica Latinoamericana de Educación Cristiana (Evangelical Latin American Commission on Christian Education)
CELAM	—	Consejo Episcopal Latinoamericano (Latin American Episcopal Council)
CESE	—	Coordenadoria Ecumênica de Serviço (Ecumenical Coordination of Social Service)
CESEEP	—	Centro Ecumênico de Serviços à Evangelização e Educação Popular (Ecumenical Center for Services to Evangelization and Popular Education)
CLADE	—	Congreso Latinoamericano de Evangelización (Latin American Evangelization Congress)

CLAI — Consejo Latinoamericano de Iglesias (Latin American Council of Churches)
CNBB — Conferência Nacional dos Bispos do Brasil (National Conference of Bishops of Brazil)
CONIC — Conselho Nacional de Igrejas Cristãs do Brasil (National Council of Christian Churches)
CPC — Centros Populares de Cultura (Popular Cultural Centers)
CPT — Comissão Pastoral da Terra (Pastoral Land Commission)
CWME — Commission on World Mission and Evangelism
DEI — Departamento Ecuménico de Investigaciones (Ecumenical Research Department)
EIG — Evangélicas pela Igualdade de Gênero (Evangelical Women for Gender Equality)
EATWOT — Ecumenical Association of Third World Theologians
FMP — Frente de Mobilização Popular (Front of Popular Mobilization)
FTL — Fraternidad Teológica Latinoamericana (Latin American Theological Fellowship)
IMC — International Mission Council
IPB — Igreja Presbiteriana do Brasil (Presbyterian Church of Brazil)
IPI — Igreja Presbiteriana Independente do Brasil (Independent Presbyterian Church of Brazil)
ISAL — Iglesia y Sociedad en América Latina (Church and Society in Latin America)
ISEDET — Instituto Superior de Estúdios Teológicos (Higher Institute of Theological Studies)
JAC — Juventude Agrária Católica (Catholic Agrarian Youth)
JCB — Juventude Católica Brasileira (Brazilian Catholic Youth)
JEC — Juventude Estudante Católica (Catholic Student Youth)
JIC — Juventude Independente Católica (Catholic Independent Youth)
JOC — Jeunesse Ouvrier Catholique (Youth Catholic Workers); in Portuguese, Juventude Operária Católica

JUC — Juventude Universitária Católica (Catholic University Youth)
LEAL — Literatura Evangélica Latinoamericana (Latin American Evangelical Literature)
MCP — Movimentos de Cultura Popular (Movements of Popular Culture)
MEB — Movimento de Educação de Base (Movement of Base Education)
MST — Movimento dos Trabalhadores Rurais Sem Terra (Landless Workers' Movement)
REPAM — Red Eclesial Pan-Amazónica (Pan-Amazonian Ecclesial Network)
RIBLA — Revista de Interpretación Bíblica Latinoamericana (Latin American Journal of Biblical Interpretation)
SCM — Student Christian Movement
SRSI — Setor de Responsabilidade Social da Igreja (Church's Sector of Social Responsibility)
UCEB — União Cristã de Estudantes do Brasil (Christian Student Union of Brazil)
UETC — União de Estudantes para o Trabalho de Cristo (Union of Students for the Work of Christ)
UFCO — United Fruit Company
ULAJE — *Unión Latinoamericana de Juventudes Evangélicas* (Latin American Evangelical Youth Union)
UNE — União National de Estudantes (National Student Union)
UNELAM — Comisión Provisional pro Unidad Evangélica Latinoamericana (Provisional Commission for Latin American Evangelical Unity)
WCC — World Council of Churches
WMPM — World Meeting of Popular Movements
WSCF — World Student Christian Federation
YMCA — Young Men's Christian Association
YWCA — Young Women's Christian Association

SHAPERS OF ECUMENICAL THEOLOGY SERIES

While the history of the modern ecumenical movement is often traced back to the World Missionary Conference in Edinburgh in 1910, it has its roots in lay movements such as the Student Christian Movement, the Young Women's Christian Association and the Young Men's Christian Association where Christians from different confessions and denominations came together to pray, study the Bible, and share their concerns on social issues. The Faith and Order and the Life and Work movements arose out of the inspiration of the Edinburgh Conference, which showed the possibility of churches working toward unity on other matters. The World Council of Churches (WCC) was born out of bringing the Faith and Order and Life and Work movements and the Missionary movement together (although the Missionary movement formally joined the WCC later at the WCC New Delhi Assembly in 1961).

From the beginning, however, there were individuals and initiatives from all over the world that built up the ecumenical movement. At the Edinburgh Conference the most pertinent challenges on the need for ecumenism came from the Chinese and Japanese delegates (there were seventeen Asians in a twelve-hundred-delegates meeting). V. S. Azariah of India addressed the overwhelmingly Western audience and said, "You have given your bodies to be burned. We ask for love, give us *friends*," thus setting in motion a process that would make *oikoumeme* truly a movement of the whole inhabited earth.[1] The deliberations at Edinburgh stimulated scholarly interest in non-Western cultures and religions, leading to a long process of discussions that continued at the missionary conferences in Jerusalem (1928), Tambaram (1938), and beyond.

[1] For a detailed discussion, see Wesley Ariarajah's "Contribution of Asian Participants to the Edinburgh 1910 Conference," in *Power, Politics and Plurality: Essays by S. Wesley Ariarajah*, ed. Marshal Fernando (Colombo, Sri Lanka: Ecumenical Institute for Study and Dialogue, 2016), 271–284.

In the decades that followed the Edinburgh Conference, individuals and initiatives from Asia, Africa, Latin America, and other parts of the world went on to shape the ecumenical movement at various levels. There were also local and regional initiatives that molded the ecumenical movement such as Base Ecumenism in Latin America, indigenous theologies from Africa, theologies of the marginalized and subaltern people from Asia, the Urban and Rural Mission, Interreligious Dialogue, and several such trends from around the world. Underlying all of these movements was the theological basis of a common understanding about the unity of the churches around the world and the vision of building up a just and participatory community. As the policy statement of WCC put it, the "ecumenical process which led to the formation of the WCC was not only a response to the gospel imperative of Christian unity. It was also an affirmation of the call to mission and common witness and an expression of common commitment to the search for justice, peace and reconciliation in a chaotic, warring world divided along the lines of race, class and competing national and religious loyalties."[2]

Within this larger context Fortress Press has undertaken the publication of a series of volumes on the theme "Shapers of Ecumenical Theology." These books highlight the ecumenical vision of some of the individuals and initiatives that shaped modern ecumenical theology and introduce readers to the formation and development of ecumenical theology in the twentieth century. Each volume of the series contains a representative selection of key figures, movements, and writings, cutting-edge commentary, and detailed introductory and concluding articles. The focus of the series is a guided study of a selection of some pivotal ecumenical figures and their writings but also important initiatives that have shaped the ecumenical movement over the past century. The series has a broad ecumenical reach, and the history of modern ecumenism is evaluated in the context of postmodernity and postcoloniality. Consequently, these books not only address the key developments in ecumenical theology during the last century but also include an emphasis on their implications for our times and for the future. The books are expected to be used

[2] The Policy Statement on "Common understanding and vision of the WCC (CUV)" adopted by the Central Committee of the World Council of Churches in September 1997.

as textbooks enabling the students to read the original authors of modern ecumenical theology. Throughout, key themes and issues that drove ecumenical reflection in the last century are addressed in the series.

Let me mention three areas the books in the series will focus on.

Christian Unity

Apart from the Mainline Protestant churches that have traditionally been seen as the primary constituency of ecumenical institutions, modern ecumenical theology was shaped by confessional diversity with an openness to include diversity even where mutual differences seemed profound. In this context, the Orthodox confession should perhaps be mentioned first as fellowship with the Orthodox churches contributed immensely to the self-understanding of the ecumenical movement. Most of the Eastern Orthodox churches that had not joined the WCC in the beginning became part of the Council at the New Delhi Assembly. Even before the Assembly there were discussions to revise the basis of WCC. In response to the demand of the Eastern Orthodox churches, the Christocentric affirmation in the basis was revised and set in a Trinitarian setting. The New Delhi Assembly also set in motion a long-term study on the theological questions involved in the full integration of the Orthodox communion in the WCC. "Recognizing the central importance given in the Orthodox tradition to the conciliar process in the church of the early centuries, the assembly recommended that a study be undertaken of the councils of the early church and their significance for the ecumenical movement."[3]

Another major Christian group, the Pentecostals too have contributed tremendously to shaping ecumenical theology, especially at the grassroots level and among the most vulnerable sections in Asia, Africa, and Latin America, where Pentecostalism has experienced a

[3] Konrad Raiser, "Orthodox contribution to the WCC" (public lecture at an international symposium on "Orthodox theology and the future of ecumenical dialogue: perspectives and problems," in Thessaloniki, Greece, June 3, 2003), accessed May 1, 2024, http://www.oikoumene.org/en/resources/documents/wcc-programmes/ecumenical-movement-in-the-21st-century/member-churches/special-commission-on-participation-of-orthodox-churches/orthodox-contribution-to-the-wcc.

vigorous growth.[4] The Joint Consultative Group between Pentecostals and the World Council of Churches "determined that a study of discipleship and formation would allow the group to move from a convergence agenda—addressing the nature of the church—to a learning agenda in which an exchange of models can strengthen the churches' witness in the world."[5]

The shared vision of ecumenism between the Roman Catholic Church (RCC) and the member churches of WCC too "continues to engage churches and others everywhere in concrete action through its Pilgrimage of Justice and Peace."[6] A Joint Working Group of the WCC and the Vatican was established to monitor, further, and promote the relationship and cooperation between the RCC and the WCC and its member churches. In more recent times, Pope Francis, with his deep sensitivity toward environmental threats and critical views on the international economic order and the plight of refugees, immigrants, and the poor, has emerged as a willing partner of the ecumenical movement in reshaping the parameters of Christian unity and witness.

There can thus be little doubt that the ecumenical movement, a global effort to realize the biblical vision of the one body of Christ, has been one of the most important developments in Christianity over the past hundred years. Thanks to the ecumenical vision, Catholic, Orthodox, Protestant, and Pentecostal Christians now make common witness to Christ in various parts of the world. Issues that once caused tension among Christians have been resolved through dialogue. Participation in the ecumenical movement has also helped churches of different traditions and cultures to forge a broad commitment to reject racism, to stand in solidarity with the poor and the marginalized, to care for the environment, and to strive together for peace. Underlying this ecumenical endeavor is the vision that the quest for

---

[4] In the concluding chapter of this book the author discusses how Latin America is one of the landscapes where Pentecostalism has experienced an expressive boom in the past few decades.

[5] "WCC and Pentecostals discuss discipleship and formation in California" (April 11, 2017), accessed May 1, 2024, https://www.oikoumene.org/en/press-centre/news/wcc-and-pentecostals-discuss-discipleship-and-formation-in-california.

[6] "Pope Francis to visit the World Council of Churches this Summer," World Council of Churches, March 2, 2018, accessed May 1, 2024, http://www.oikoumene.org/en/press-centre/news/pope-francis-to-visit-the-world-council-of-churches-this-summer.

unity is God's will that has a universal dimension and embraces the human community and all of God's creation. "Church unity is vital to the health of the church and to the future of the human family."[7] Integral to Christian unity is a deep commitment for justice. A commitment to the unity and renewal of the church needs to be held together with an absolute commitment to the reconciliation of God's world. As Philip Potter put it in his 1977 address to the WCC central committee, "The whole burden of the ecumenical movement is to cooperate with God in making the *oikoumene* an *oikos*, a home, a family of men and women, of young and old, of varied gifts, cultures, possibilities, where openness, trust, love and justice reign."[8]

Perspectives from the South

Beyond the confessional unity of the churches and the acknowledgment of God's work in the world, the books in this series also recognize the shifting center of gravity of world Christianity to the Global South. We include here the pioneering role played by the ecumenical movement in challenging a Eurocentric theology and ecclesiology by highlighting the perspectives of the colonized and marginalized people in Asia, Africa, and Latin America. In particular, this series recognizes the pivotal role played by the liberation struggles of the oppressed people in shaping ecumenical theology during the last one hundred years. Although Base Ecumenism, as the 'ecumenism of the people,' originated in Latin America, it has had important ramifications in other parts of the world as well. As Raimundo C. Barreto put it, base ecumenism has not only been an important force transforming and revitalizing interchurch and interfaith relations, but it also offers fresh notions of ecumenicity, which are particularly relevant to recent scholarly attempts to reexamine ecumenical relations in the era of world Christianity.

There were also other grassroots-level theological initiatives that played a role in the shaping of ecumenical theology. Among theological initiatives that emerged from Asia, Dalit theology has contributed considerably to this process. Dalit theology emerged from the conviction

[7] The Policy Statement, "Common understanding and vision of the WCC."

[8] John Briggs, Mercy Amba Oduyoye, and Georges Tsetsis, eds., *A History of the Ecumenical Movement* vol. 3, *1968–2000* (Geneva: WCC Publications, 2004), 53.

that traditional Christian theology was largely based on the perspectives of the dominant class and caste, and consequently did not represent the life situations of the marginalized communities such as the Dalits. "This non-representative character of traditional theology raised serious questions about the credibility of the Christian faith when the Indian Church itself became predominantly Dalit in membership."[9]

With one in every four Christians living in sub-Saharan Africa, and with a rediscovery of the significance of indigenous African religions and spirituality in the life of the church, the role of the religions and cultures of the African continent for the Christian world is being widely recognized. There are also the realities of indigenous ecumenical theological expressions, such as Minjung theology from Korea, Burakumin theologies from Japan, the womanist theologies, the theology of struggle from the Philippines, homeland theology from Taiwan, and so on. This Fortress series recognizes the fundamental paradigm shift in the ecumenical agenda from a decisively non-Western perspective.

These books therefore respond to a growing interest in viewing ecumenical theology from the perspective of the Global South. In particular, they examine the impact of selected ecumenical theologians and movements on theological formation through a detailed review of their history and thought as expressions of ecumenical theological engagement with unity and justice. The underlying concern here is that theologizing in Asia, Africa, and Latin America occurs in a context of multireligiosity, on the one hand, and rampant poverty and social inequality on the other. Therefore, religiosity and a commitment for justice and peace have been at the center of the ecumenical theology that emerged there.

Theologizing from the Margins

Ecumenism is about responsible action with regard to "the whole inhabited earth." From the beginning, the ecumenical movement

---

9 "New Challenges for Dalit Theology," Jesudas M. Athyal, "The Changing Face of the Indian Society...And the New Challenges for Dalit Theology" (Presented at the International Consultation on 'Dalit Theology and A Theology of the Oppressed' held at the Gurukul Lutheran Theological College, Chennai, November 13–15, 2004), accessed May 1, 2024, https://jmathyal.tripod.com/id1.html.

has been affirming that unity takes place in the struggle for justice. It is the recognition that ecumenism demands a quest for the realization of justice for the sake of unity; it ties together faith and justice. One significant concept of modern ecumenical theology, therefore, is the perspective from the margins. The marginalized are those people who are pushed out of the mainstream to the periphery—those sidelined in the social, political, cultural, and religious life of the mainstream society. Ecumenism is a search for the people in the margins, for the most vulnerable sections of the society. As D. T. Niles put it, "the ecumenical vision revealed indeed God's pilgrim people on the center and frontier of the church and the world."[10]

This series of books also recognizes that ecumenical theology should be prophetic in form and content. Prophetic ecumenism contains both the powerful word to unmask situations of injustice and the powerful word to announce what is possible. "Ecumenism should bear witness to this word, as a sign of resistance and at the same time as anticipation of what is hoped. The ecumenical movement can never be silent; bold words are an integral part of ecumenism. The attempt to arrive at consensus can turn to be an abdication of the prophetic duty."[11] These books, we hope, portray ecumenical theology as the message that can unmask situations of injustice and affirm the message of unity and peace.

Base Ecumenism: Latin American Contributions to Ecumenical Praxis and Theology

It is in this historical and theological background that Fortress Press has initiated the publication of a series of volumes on the theme, "Shapers of Ecumenical Theology." These timely books highlight key ecumenical trends and their relevance for the contemporary church. Since so much scholarly attention has been given to theologians from North Atlantic countries, this series emphasizes theological voices from other parts of the world.

---

10. Ninan Koshy, *A History of the Ecumenical Movement in Asia*, vol. I (Hong Kong: CCA, APAY, WSCFAP, 2004), 30.

11. Ninan Koshy, "Ecumenism: Perspectives from the Margins" (lecture, August 14, 2012).

We are happy to publish in the Shapers of Ecumenical Theology series this book by Raimundo C. Barreto, titled *Base Ecumenism: Latin American Contributions to Ecumenical Praxis and Theology*. Paying special attention to initiatives such as "the popular reading of the Bible" and the Latin American understanding of macro-ecumenism, this book highlights the agency of women, racially minoritized groups, and the youth in recent developments in the ecumenical world, thus making a key contribution to ecumenical discussions from the context of the majority world. The book moves from revisiting grassroots ecumenical developments in Latin America—such as the church and society movement (1950s) and the Base Christian Communities (1970s)—to the concept of "base ecumenism," while also engaging independent and Pentecostal communities, as well as interfaith coalitions in a religiously plural Latin America. Furthermore, the book presents base ecumenism as comparable to similar ecumenical initiatives in the history of the modern ecumenical movement, arguing that it contributes fresh and renewing ecumenical insights important for ecumenical formation in this era of world Christianity.

With rare clarity, the author discusses ecumenical initiatives that emerge from the people—from the bases—in conversation with interchurch ecumenical work. The book discusses the important ecumenical developments of base ecumenism which, although originated in Latin America, have important ramifications for the broader ecumenical movement.

Let me acknowledge the support of Fortress Press in the publication of this volume. Fortress Press hopes to partner with ecumenical institutions and publishing houses in a wide range of countries so that the books in this series can be available to people around the world at an affordable price. The series serves as introductory readers, providing a great opportunity for scholars, pastors, students, and lay Christians to engage with firsthand texts of the pioneers of ecumenical theology. It is our hope and prayer that this series of books will be received well by ecumenical people around the world.

Jesudas M. Athyal
(Editor of the Series)

ACKNOWLEDGMENTS

This book is the product of several years of work and numerous conversations, trips, conferences, lectures, and class discussions. The project started with an invitation from Jesudas Athyal, during an ecumenical gathering of the National Council of Churches in the United States, to contribute a volume to the Fortress Press series Shapers of Ecumenical Theology. I am deeply grateful for his kind invitation and continuous support as the general editor of the series and acquisition editor at Fortress Press. I am particularly grateful to his close reading, comments, and suggestions for the manuscript. While benefiting from his excellent editing and ecumenical expertise, I take full responsibility for the content of this book.

The support from Princeton Theological Seminary, primarily through a sabbatical leave, allowed me time for archival and field research, which was crucial for this project's completion. The PTS Class of 1955 awarded me two back-to-back research grants, which I used to visit archives in the World Council of Churches in Geneva, the Burke Library at Columbia University, and the Benson Latin American Collection at the University of Texas. Professional development funding from Princeton Theological Seminary and a budget for ecumenical representation as Chair of the Committee on Christian Unity and Interfaith Relations of the American Baptist Churches were also crucial to enable my participation in various ecumenical and interfaith gatherings in the United States and other parts of the world, including Brazil, Colombia, Cuba, England, Germany, Norway, and Switzerland. The time spent respectively in the WCC collections and the Burke Library archives at Columbia University was particularly precious. I will always be indebted to the expertise and generosity of the staff in those two archives. This book also benefits from the author's access to the information system of the Brazilian National Archives.

As I traveled for my research, I enjoyed the hospitality of several friends. My colleague and friend Claudio Carvalhaes, professor of worship at Union Theological Seminary, generously hosted me in his home as I spent time in the archives of Burke Library. During my visit to the Benson Latin American Collection, Dean David Jensen kindly hosted me in a state-of-the-art guest apartment at Austin Theological Seminary. My brother Ronaldo Barreto and his family equally welcomed me into their home as I worked for a few weeks in Bahia, Brazil. During those days, pastor Moises Alves, my good friend of blessed memory, graciously offered an office I could work from. I am equally grateful to pastor Waldir Martins Barbosa for the invitation to participate in the CEBI Bahia State Seminar on Social Rights, Faith, and Politics on May 5–7, 2017. That immersion in a CEBI seminar was highly informative and enlightening.

More recently, I spent time in the archives of the Archdiocese of São Paulo, where I depended on the expertise of Jair Mongelli Junior to access a wealth of documents kept at the archdiocese. Teresa Ribeiro kindly shared her vast network as a journalist and president of the Paulo Freire Popular Institute, connecting me with critical players in the Latin American ecumenical scene, including Frei Betto and Father Júlio Lancellotti. Likewise, I am indebted to the Protestant faculty of the University of Bonn, especially Matthew R. Robinson and Dean Cornelia Ritcher, for the opportunity to spend time on campus as an International Fellow in fall 2023. This period in Germany was crucial for the conclusion of this book.

I cannot forget to thank Kenneth Henke and Brian Shetler, former and current Special Collections and Archives curators at Princeton Theological Seminary, and Kate Skrebutenas, former reference librarian at PTS. They facilitated access to resources, which would have been challenging to put my hands on otherwise. In addition to them, Jeremy Wallace, Assistant Director for Research and Public Services at the Wright Library, also provided fantastic support whenever I needed access to resources not available at the Wright Library. I am deeply indebted to these and other library colleagues for their exceptional dedication and professionalism.

During the long period I worked on this manuscript, I had a number of research assistants. Among them, I must mention Steve Santos Belo, Melissa Martin, and Stephen Di Trolio, for their diligent work sifting potentially relevant resources in the Wright Special Collections to prepare this manuscript. I am particularly grateful to Stephen Di Trolio for his precious assistance with the index.

This book is only possible due to uncountable exchanges in the classroom and conferences on ecumenism and world Christianity. Some of those conversations took place in meetings of the World Council of Churches, the North American Academy of Ecumenists, Ecclesiological Investigations Network, the *II Seminário de Teologia Ecumênica na América Latina: História, Hermenêutica e Método*, and *Teaching Ecumenism in the Context of World Christianity* convened by the Ecumenical Institute at Château de Bossey. My contributions to some of those conversations have appeared in articles and book chapters I have published in recent years, also informing a great deal of my work in this book.

The American Baptist Churches entrusted me in the past seven years to represent them in several ecumenical forums, including the National Council of Churches USA, the World Council of Churches, the Global Christian Forum, and the Baptist World Alliance. Prior to that, years of involvement in the conception, formation, and development of the Aliança de Batistas do Brasil, the first ecumenical Baptist denomination in Brazil, along with other grassroots movements in that country, put me in touch with numerous faces of base ecumenism.

Finally, I am and will always be deeply indebted to Eliã, my life partner, and my three beloved children, Caio, Cauã, and Luana.

Despite my work competing for my presence, they have continuously filled me with unmerited love, understanding, and support. To all who directly or indirectly contributed to the making of this book, including those not mentioned above, *muito obrigado*, from the bottom of my heart.

PREFACE

The Shapers of Ecumenical Theology series introduces scholars to the formation and development of modern ecumenical praxis and theology, offering a solid study of pivotal ecumenical leaders and movements in the twentieth century. This volume adds to the series by unearthing specific contributions from Latin America to the modern ecumenical movement, interrogating the ways Latin American ecumenism emerged, developed, and changed, and considering how peculiar developments in the region have contributed to enrich the ecumenical movement more broadly.

The book underscores, in particular, ecclesial and theological developments stemming from the turning of Latin American Christianity to the poor as new theological subjects in the second half of the twentieth century. Such an epistemic turn to the poor had a revolutionary impact, transforming those often regarded as 'nonpersons' into historical subjects, and their social loci into crucial sites of enunciation, thus bringing new perspectives to the theological task. Through that move, the poor, or, sociologically speaking, the " 'nonpersons'—that is, those who are not considered to be human beings with full rights, beginning with the right to life and to freedom in various spheres"—were now regarded as crucial agents in the process of liberation.[1] As an implication of that epistemic move, the poor, those who have been forcibly pushed to the margins, became subjects with a critical role to play not only in their own liberating struggles but also in the interpretation of the Christian faith and of the world.[2]

The rise of those who were heretofore absent as historical subjects represents what Gustavo Gutiérrez depicted as "the irruption

[1] Gustavo Gutiérrez, *A Theology of Liberation*, 15th Anniversary Edition (Maryknoll, NY: Orbis Books, 2019 [1988]), xxix, Kindle.

[2] By absent, Gutierrez means "of little or no importance, and without the opportunity to give expression themselves to their sufferings, their comraderies, their plans, their hopes." Gutiérrez, *A Theology of Liberation*, xx.

of the poor into our history."[3] Such an irruption has an ecumenical dimension, since it represents an expansion of the horizons of the *oikoumenē*, which must now include those whose personhood and dignity have been often denied. This book seeks to understand not only the impact of such a social, cultural, theological, and epistemic turn in the context of Latin American ecumenism, revisiting movements and ideas born in the ecumenical experience in that continent, but it also underscores its significance for the broader ecumenical movement, particularly since the final decades of the twentieth century.

Interpreting the impact of the turn to the poor beyond liberationist lenses (that is, also as a decolonial turn), this book emphasizes not only its political and economic dimensions, but also the cultural and epistemic ones, paying attention to delinking strategies from ways of being and knowing that have perpetuated colonial structures of power. Thus, such a project is not only about deconstructing and dismantling power asymmetries but also about re-creating, reimagining, and reexisting in other possible ways.[4]

Focusing on the multifaceted expressions of the phenomenon Latin Americans call *ecumenismo de base* or base ecumenism, this book considers the subjectivity of new theological, social, cultural, and political actors whose voices were particularly noticed in ecumenical circles in the 1960s and their contributions to an enlarged understanding of ecumenicity.[5] These subjects represent

---

[3] Gutiérrez, *A Theology of Liberation*, xx.

[4] Or, as Mignolo and Walsh put it, "not only resisting." Walter D. Mignolo and Catherine E. Walsh, *On Decoloniality: Concepts, Analytics, Praxis* (Duke University Press, 2018), 120, Kindle. See also Raimundo Barreto and Roberto Sirvent, eds., *Decolonial Christianities: Latin American and Latinx Perspectives* (Cham, Switzerland: Palgrave MacMillan, 2019), 1–21.

[5] By choosing this expression, I am indebted, among others, to Gerhard Tiel, who describes *ecumenismo de base* as an alternative to official ecumenism. Whereas the latter focuses on the unity of the church, the former focuses on the unity of humanity, thus putting an accent on common practices rather than on doctrinal dialogue. Base ecumenism is, therefore, a Third World originated ecumenism, which has as its starting point not the Christian confessions but the sociopolitical problems at the root of the suffering of those pushed to the margins of society. Consequently, not only its starting point is different but its priorities and methods are also distinct. Thus, in base ecumenism, the poor is a hermeneutical-historical category used in three distinct but complementary ways: (1) The poor is the other, the colonized

the possibility of being and thinking otherwise, bringing to the fore the need to pay attention to those who have been excluded, pushed away. This deepening and enlarging of the ecumenical table is crucial for the actualization of the ecumenical movement to meet new challenges and for the construction of an ecumenical path that can lead toward a more sensible conviviality in the contemporary world, thus creating new forms of koinonia that are more effective in taking difference seriously and addressing persisting asymmetries of power.[6]

Ecumenismo de base—or base ecumenism—is an expression commonly used in Portuguese and Spanish as a reference to grassroots ecumenism in the Latin American context. It refers to the ecumenism that stems from the irruption of the poor. While grassroots ecumenical initiatives exist in other parts of the world, perhaps in no other continent has such a popular ecumenical perspective been as widely influential as in Latin America, especially since the rapid expansion of the *comunidades eclesiales de base* (CEBs) in the 1970s and 1980s, which mobilized important sectors of church and society in response to the troubling experiences of widespread violence against the impoverished majority of the Latin American peoples at a time when military dictatorships and protracted civil wars proliferated in the region.

The CEBs and similar expressions of *ecumenismo de base* that emerged in connection with them forged what the 2021 Brazilian Ecumenical Fellowship Campaign deftly depicted as "organized

---

whose culture and ways of life have been at least partially destroyed and who have reinvented new ways of subsistence in response to the colonial genocide; (2) the poor are also referred to as a social class, as those who are oppressed and dispossessed by a dominant class; and (3) the poor are those pushed away, dehumanized, expelled from the halls of humanity and from human systems (work, housing, rights, health care, education, etc.), thus the propriety of Gutiérrez's reference to the nonperson. Consequently, the rise of concepts such as the church as the people of God and the church of the poor, which will be discussed later, become particularly significant. Ecclesiastical ecumenism and base ecumenism are not mutually exclusive. Nevertheless, at times they might be at odds with each other. See Gerhard Tiel, *Ecumenismo na Perspectiva do Reino de Deus: Uma análise do movimento ecumênico de base* (São Leopoldo, Brazil: Editora Sinodal, 1998), 13–17.

6 For the possibility of mapping new futures that challenge dominant epistemologies, see Otto Maduro, *Maps for a Fiesta: A Latina/o Perspective on Knowledge and the Global Crisis* (New York: Fordham University Press, 2015).

love,"[7] becoming an important incubator of major social movements.[8] Over the years, base ecumenism has taken different shapes and forms, helping to organize communities, which, although composed mostly by Christians, are not limited to the confines of Christianity, and which operate with an emphasis on transformative social action.

This book sheds light on the radical ecumenicity that stems from the liberation Christianity at the origins of this phenomenon. Taking into consideration the epistemic and ontological demands that the rise of world Christianity presents contemporary ecumenists with, this book interrogates base ecumenism not only as a critical movement shaping the broader ecumenical movement but also as an anticipation of and contribution to the renewal of ecumenism in a world filled with deep differences and persistent rifts and conflicts that threaten not only the continuation of human life but also the well-being of the planet.

Every author has a journey that informs how they interpret the sources with which they interact. The best one can do as they engage

---

[7] The Ecumenical Fraternity Campaign (known simply as *Campanha da Fraternidade*) is a thematic ecumenical annual campaign in Brazil, which highlights specific emphases that help coordinate ecumenical activities on the national level during the ecclesial year. It also aims to educate church and society and renew the call for the responsibility Christians have to promote and enhance life. Although the campaign originated as a Catholic initiative, it is currently organized jointly by CNBB (National Conference of Bishops of Brazil) and CONIC (National Council of Christian Churches). See CNBB Sul 3, "Fraternidade e Diálogo: Compromisso de Amor," Formação, Campanha da Fraternidade Ecumênica 2021, accessed October 3, 2022, https://anec.org.br/wp-content/uploads/2020/10/CAMPANHA-DA-FRATERNIDADE-2021.pdf.

[8] In an interview with the author, Frei Betto said that, according to the current President of Brazil and founder of *Partido dos Trabalhadores* (PT)—the Brazilian Workers' Party—Luiz Inácio Lula da Silva, the CEBs were more critical for the foundation of PT than the workers' unions, because of CEB's capillarity at the time of the party's creation (1980). Frei Betto, interview conducted by the author on October 11, 2023, São Paulo, Brazil. Betto, the short name by which Carlos Alberto Libânio Christo is known, is a Dominican Friar and former director of the student sector of Catholic Action in Brazil, who was arrested by the military government in the early 1970s, tortured, and sentenced to four years in prison. His physical and moral courage as a survivor of such tragic experiences has turned him into a living icon of Latin American liberation theology. Among his many writings, one can find the letters he wrote from his prison cell in Carlos Alberto Libânio Christo: *Against Principalities and Powers: Letters from a Brazilian Jail* (Maryknoll, NY: Orbis Books, 1977).

in scholarly research is to be truthful to what they see in the sources they access, and honest in how they listen to texts and subjects they engage with. Yet, at the end of the line, there is always a situated subject, an interpreter conditioned by personal and communal experiences, memories, affections, and socioeconomic and cultural circumstances. The experiences that constitute me as a human being and the memories I cultivate in my life journey necessarily impact how I engage this topic.

I am a diasporic Latin American scholar of world Christianity working in United States academia. I also identify as an ecumenist, that is, someone interested in examining ecumenical relations, networks, and organizations on the local, national, and international levels. Furthermore, I have been involved as a practitioner in ecumenical work for many years. What initially attracted me to the ecumenical movement was, ironically, the anti-ecumenism of the Brazilian Baptist church I grew up in—a denomination highly influenced by Southern Baptist theology and missiology. I began to reject the exclusivism characteristic of that narrow perspective in my youth. Years later, I encountered others who dared to experiment with a different kind of faith, and who, in the process, became open to engage and embrace different cultural and religious traditions. In the 1990s, progressive Catholics and Protestants in Brazil encouraged me to dream of safe spaces where those pushed away from their churches could find refuge. As a result of that, in 2005, I actively took part in the creation of *Aliança de Batistas do Brasil* (ABB), a small ecumenical Baptist network founded in the economically impoverished Northeastern part of Brazil and at the ecclesial margins of existing Baptist denominations in the country. In the years following its creation, the ABB affiliated itself with some national and continental ecumenical bodies, including *Conselho Nacional de Igrejas Cristãs* (National Council of Churches in Brazil, -CONIC), *Coordenadoria Ecumênica de Serviço* (Ecumenical Service Coordination,- CESE), and the *Consejo Latinoamericano de Iglesias* (Latin American Council of Churches,- CLAI), becoming the first Brazilian Baptist denomination to be formally involved in the ecumenical movement.

Since I moved to the United States, I have served as representative of the American Baptist Churches (ABCUSA) in various ecumenical bodies and chaired the ABCUSA Committee on Christian Unity and Interfaith Relations (CCUIR) until recently. In that capacity, I have collaborated with the National Council of Churches, USA (NCCUSA), and the World Council of Churches (WCC), being elected to serve on the WCC Central Committee in the 11th WCC Assembly in Karlsruhe, Germany (2022). Whereas this journey places me at the center of the insider/outsider dilemma, I mention these experiences simply to name the privileged access I have had over the years, which informs my interpretation of certain dynamics within the ecumenical movement and of the materials I read in the preparation of this book.

While ecclesiastical and interecclesiastical structures advancing ecumenical relations remain critical, new ecumenical spaces beyond those established within ecclesiastical structures are also increasingly important for the ecumenical challenges emerging this century and must be considered more closely. They can be concomitantly signs of ecumenical crisis and renewal, being particularly attuned to crucial issues dividing Christians and other humans today, which cannot be understood exclusively on the basis of confessional differences. Race, ethnicity, gender, sexuality, culture, migration, intolerant and authoritarian ideologies, economic disparities, and environmental concerns are critical contemporary areas for global and local ecumenical agendas, which require both responses orchestrated on the world stage and prompt local engagement. Difference around these matters, which is often asymmetrical, deeply impacts interfaith and intra-faith relations these days. The nuanced forms of difference and discord stemming from such a fast-changing religious landscape demand renewed ecumenical imagination.

In the same way as the plethora of grassroots organizations that compose the World Social Forum have repeatedly declared to hegemonic world structures that another world is possible, grassroots ecumenical organizations and other popular ecumenical networks emerging in response to new threats to life in the contemporary world are also loudly stating that other ways of being ecumenical are not only possible but urgently necessary. Contemporary ecumenism must address the drastic separations stemming from colonialism, patriarchy, sexism, racism, and global capitalism, which continue to separate people, constituting persistently open wounds.

In response to these growing demands, this book revisits the development of ecumenical Christianity in Latin America, examining its impact on ecumenical praxis and discourse both in the region and around the world. Its goal is to shed light on contemporary ecumenical possibilities stemming from the major demographic, cultural, and epistemological shifts brought about by, among other things, the rise of world Christianity.

Raimundo C. Barreto
Bonn, Germany
October 27, 2023

1

A CHANGING ECUMENISM

The modern ecumenical movement is the product of a particular historical juncture. As Dale Irvin rightly notices, the ecumenical instruments conceived in connection with the 1910 World Missionary Conference in Edinburgh emerged under the influence of "lingering memories of Christendom East and West."[1] Likewise, the ecclesiastical bodies that came together to form the ecumenical movement in the twentieth century were haunted by "the spectre of Constantine." In Irvin's words,

> [T]he churches or communions that formed the Ecumenical Movement in the 20th century . . . were mostly the descendants of Protestant communions that had formed along state lines in Europe and, although disestablished, continued to align themselves with the dominant culture and its political and social life, in North America.[2]

In fact, the modern missionary movement that created the early conditions for the rise of the ecumenical movement was shaped in the context of a colonial Christendom imposed on colonized lands and peoples around the world "in the name of the gospel of the Crucified."[3] That is one of the facets of the colonial matrix of power at the roots of a hierarchized global order, which continues to inform economic, political, racial, cultural, gendered, and even religious power structures in the world today.[4]

---

[1] Dale Irvin, "Specters of a New Ecumenism: In Search of a Church 'Out of Joint,'" in *Religion, Authority, and the State: From Constantine to the Contemporary World*, ed. Leo D. Lefebure (New York: Palgrave Macmillan, 2016), 3–32 (17).

[2] Irvin, "Specters of a New Ecumenism," 20.

[3] Enrique Dussel, "Epistemological Decolonization of Theology," in *Decolonial Christianities: Latinx and Latin American Perspectives*, New Approaches to Religion and Power, ed. Raimundo Barreto and Roberto Sirvent (New York: Palgrave MacMillan, 2019), 25–42 (32).

[4] See Walter D. Mignolo, "Introduction: Coloniality of power and de-colonial thinking," *Cultural Studies* 21:2–3 (2007): 155–167 (156). See also

Starting with the imperial Iberian expansion of the late fifteen and early sixteenth century, a global hierarchy of power with Europe at its top and other continents ranked against that backdrop sedimented a new world order, which inventively took new forms as many of the former colonies started to give birth to new modern nations in Asia-Pacific, Africa, Latin America, and the Caribbean. This persistence of a hegemonic organization of power formed in the colonial era, which continued after the end of colonial administrative systems, is what decolonial theorists call coloniality. Coloniality, in other words, refers to the enduring legacy of colonialism in the modern world-system. As Nelson Maldonado-Torres explains, "while colonialism is typically considered to be a political arrangement that has existed since time immemorial, coloniality refers to the logic, culture, and structure of the modern world-system."[5] Part of the task of this book is to shed light on the colonial impact in the shaping of the ecumenical instruments created in the twentieth century, while also examining how grassroots ecumenical initiatives such as *ecumenismo de base*, forged in formerly colonized nations, can function as decolonial counterparts, thus contributing to the reimagination of the ecumenical movement in the twenty-first century.

While the modern ecumenical movement can be traced to as far back as at least the beginning of the nineteenth century, the single most formative event that put into motion the process of institutional embodiment of the ecumenical ideal in the twentieth century was the World Missionary Conference of Edinburgh in 1910. Some critical ecumenical instruments of the twentieth century began to be conceived in that gathering and in subsequent initiatives and events that followed it. Edinburgh 1910 was a conference filled with militant language intended to bring the Western missionary goal of spreading the Christian faith throughout the world and establishing Christianity as a world religion to fruition. Christian unity was understood in that context as a prerequisite for missionary success. The evangelization of the world in this generation was Edinburgh

Anibal Quijano, "Coloniality and Modernity/Rationality," *Cultural Studies* 21:2–3 (2007): 168–178.

[5] Nelson Maldonado-Torres, "On the Coloniality of Human Rights," *Revista Crítica de Ciências Sociais* [online], 114 (2017), DOI: https://doi.org/10.4000/rccs.6793, accessed on October 25, 2021.

1910's key slogan and remained a missionary emphasis for most of the twentieth century.

Even though Edinburgh 1910 was not the first world missionary conference, it was the most representative event of an ongoing movement for Christian unity that had been taking form in previous decades among Protestant mission agencies, Bible societies, and student and youth Christian movements. Such a concern for Christian unity was particularly noted in the missionary fields in the Global South. The evangelistic impetus of that movement was centrifugal, moving from its perceived center (Christendom) to the parts of the world outside that center (mission fields), its peripheries (heathendom), targeting especially non-Christian (non-Western) peoples, and often operating in conjunction with the colonial apparatus. Brian Stanley explains the colonial overtones in Edinburgh 1910 as follows:

> Edinburgh 1910 was conceived as a great deliberative council of the Church Protestant that would prepare its missionary armies to launch a concerted and final onslaught on the dark forces of heathendom that still ruled supreme beyond the frontiers of western Christendom. Those who responded with quiet determination by committing themselves anew to this militant and intensely serious calling could, like the crusaders of the medieval age, be sure of the eternal blessing of God on their united endeavours. Crusading language was often implicit and occasionally explicit at Edinburgh.[6]

The Edinburgh Conference thus reflected both the reigning spirit of the Protestant field at the turn of the twentieth century and the Western colonial mindset informing world relations then. The self-identification of modern European empires as Christian had been sedimented through the colonial enterprise. The decolonial construct modernity/coloniality helps to explain the inseparable connection between modernity and colonialism and coloniality, underscoring how the political, economic, cultural, and religious aspects of the conquest and subsequent colonization that inaugurated the early stages of modernity were inevitably intertwined.

---

[6] Brian Stanley, *The World Missionary Conference, Edinburgh 1910* (Studies in the History of Christian Missions) (Grand Rapids, MI: W. B. Eerdmans, 2009), loc. 168–171, Kindle.

As Puerto Rican historian Luis N. Rivera-Pagán has deftly demonstrated, the conquest and subsequent colonization of the Americas was at the same time a political and a religious event.[7] As Rivera-Pagán notices, in one of his early letters reporting on his arrival at the Indies, Christopher Columbus (1451–1506) informed the Iberian monarchs who had commissioned him that he had "taken possession" of all the newly 'discovered' lands "on behalf of Your Highness with proclamation and extended royal banners."[8] Then, he urged Christendom to celebrate the "turning of so many people to our holy faith."[9] Later that same year, the Catholic monarchs instructed Columbus—now Viceroy of the Indies and Admiral of the Ocean Sea—to persuade the inhabitants of the islands to conversion to the Christian faith by all possible means.[10] Such correspondence reminds us that the tragic events of the conquest and the colonization that followed ultimately were part of a Christian enterprise financed by Christian monarchs and perpetrated by professing Christians, having as one of its explicit goals the Christianization of the people they encountered in their excursion. Since the lands they found were inhabited, it was also necessary to legitimize the decision to "take possession" of those lands. In the context of Christendom, that justification had to be articulated both theologically and legally.

Modern Western missionaries saw themselves as the bearers of the gospel to non-Western peoples, carrying along with the evangelistic mandate a civilizational one, which inferred the superiority of the Western Christian civilization in comparison to other cultures and traditions. The West, self-identified as the dominion of Christianity, designated the non-Western world as its missionary field. According to that worldview, the tasks of missionizing and colonizing were intrinsically intertwined.

---

[7] Luis N. Rivera-Pagán, *A Violent Evangelism: The Political and Religious Conquest of the Americas* (Louisville, KY: Westminster-John Knox, 1992).

[8] Cristóbal Cólon, *Textos y Documentos Completos*, ed. Consuelo Varela, *Nuevas Cartas*, ed. Juan Gil (Madrid: Alianza Editorial, 1995), 220. Cited in Luis N. Rivera-Pagán, *Essays from the Diaspora* (Mexico City: Publicaciones El Faro, 2002), 62.

[9] Christopher Columbus, "Letter of Columbus describing the results of his first voyage," in *The Journal of Christopher Columbus*, trans. Cecil Jane (New York: Clarkson N. Potter, 1960), 201. Cited in Rivera-Pagán, *Essays from the Diaspora*, 62.

[10] Rivera-Pagán, *Essays from the Diaspora*, 63.

In its discussion of the centrality of the missionary task, the Commission I of Edinburgh 1910 underscored that the primary missionary problem the church faced was "to ensure a vitality equal to the imperial expansion of the missionary programme."[11] The commission interpreted the evangelization of the world through an imperialistic lens, seeing the ultimate missionary goal as the conquest of the world for Christ. The coloniality of such a language was reinforced as the commission urged for the subduing of "the peoples of the non-Christian world."[12]

The modern ideal enshrined in the ecumenical instruments that began to be forged in the wake of that Edinburgh World Missionary Conference, therefore, stemmed from a Christendom that understood itself in connection with the expansion of the Christian empires throughout the world. Thus, the ecumenical ideal of overcoming internal divisions that began to inform the world missionary movement should contribute to "the application and extension of [Christian] doctrine and practices 'overseas.'"[13]

In the course of the twentieth century, Western perceptions of the non-Western world continued to be tainted by an ideology of Western superiority, often in the form of Christian and white supremacy.[14] According to such a worldview, Christianity was understood as superior to non-Christian (non-Western) religions, but also, in Christian circles, Western Christianity was perceived as superior to non-Western Christianity. In the first half of the twentieth century,

---

[11] World Missionary Conference, 1910. *Report of Commission I: Carrying the Gospel to All the Non-Christian World* (Edinburgh and London: Oliphant, Anderson & Ferrier/Fleming H. Hevell Company, 1910), 47.

[12] World Missionary Conference, 1910. *Report of Commission I.*

[13] Dale T. Irvin, "World Christianity: An Introduction," *The Journal of World Christianity* 1/1 (2008): 1–26 (17).

[14] As Khyati Y. Joshi shows, whiteness and Christianity have not only coexisted but also supported each other throughout the history of the United States, creating a white Christian privilege that continues to impact workplaces, classrooms, and the broader society. Although her work focuses more specifically on the American context, that same association is also identifiable in the contemporary ordering of the global society, still tainted with lingering colonial memories. For more, see Khyati Y. Joshi, *White Christian Privilege: The Illusion of Religious Equality in America* (New York: NYU Press, 2020), 2, 42. For the surge of a racialized global hierarchy, see Ramon Grosfoguel, "What is Racism?" *Journal of World-Systems Research* 22 (1): 9–15.

non-Western churches were referred to within ecumenical circles as "younger churches," even though Christian churches had existed in some African and Asian countries since the early centuries of the Christian era. The term "younger churches" was often used paternalistically, implying that non-Western churches (those in 'mission fields') needed the guidance and support of established Western churches in order to reach theological maturity and autonomy.

Whereas an incipient ecumenical movement inevitably reproduced the lingering colonial memories that shaped it, in the following decades that movement would undergo changes, often associated with the increasing participation of non-Western Christians in it. Although some initial signs of that ongoing transformation could be noticed in its embryonic stages as early as the 1920s, they became more apparent in the second half of the twentieth century.

Uruguayan theologian Julio de Santa Ana referred to the twentieth century as "the time of ecumenism in the history of Christianity."[15] Interpreting the ecumenical movement as the Christian response to the challenges of western modernity, Santa Ana saw it not merely as an exclusively Western phenomenon, but instead as an idea that took form, in particular, among young and lay Christians from diverse parts of the world.[16] At the same time that the burgeoning ecumenical movement started creating its institutions and instruments, significant demographic changes were concomitantly beginning to alter the face of Christianity around the world—changes that would be more drastically accentuated toward the end of the twentieth century.[17]

---

15 Julio de Santa Ana, "The Ecumenical Movement at the Crossroads," *Student World*, 2003/1: 11–23 (11).

16 Santa Ana, "The Ecumenical Movement at the Crossroads," 11–12.

17 Some of the books that brought popular attention to those changes include Justo L. González, *The Changing Shape of Church History* (St. Louis, MO: The Chalice Press, 2002); Phillip Jenkins, *The Next Christendom: The Coming of Global Christianity*, 3rd ed. (New York: Oxford University Press, 2011); Todd M. Johnson & Kenneth R. Ross, *Atlas of Global Christianity* (Edinburgh: Edinburgh University Press, 2009); Paul Kollman, "Understanding the World-Christian Turn in the History of Christianity and Theology," *Theology Today*, 2014, vol. 71(2), 164–177; Klaus Koschorke, "New Maps of the History of World Christianity," *Theology Today* 71/2 (2014):178–191; Lamin Sanneh, *Disciples of All Nations: pillars of World Christianity* (New York: Oxford University Press, 2008); and Andrew Walls, *The Cross-Cultural Process in Christian History: Studies in the Transmission and Appropriation of Faith* (Maryknoll, NY: Orbis Books; Edinburgh: T&T Clark, 2002).

Despite their small numbers at the time, in the decades following Edinburgh 1910, representatives from non-Western churches increasingly contributed to shaping the emerging twentieth-century ecumenical instruments. Although their presence can be noted already in the World Missionary Conference, its impact was more clearly felt for the first time in the Tambaram expanded meeting of the International Missionary Council in 1938, as I will discuss later. As Global South voices began to articulate their own views of the ecumenical ideal more intentionally, their impact on the ecumenical movement became inevitable.[18]

Between Edinburgh 1910 and the turn of the twenty-first century, Christianity underwent a drastic demographic change. As Andrew Walls put it, "the most striking feature of Christianity at the beginning of the third millennium is that it is predominantly a non-Western religion."[19] Such a transformation in the world Christian movement impacted ecumenical relations significantly.

---

[18] The use of the terms "Third World" and "Global South" throughout this book is intentionally ambiguous and interconnected. The meaning attributed to each of them overlaps and the latter cannot be fully comprehended without the history of the former. My usage follows the work of thinkers such as Andre Gunder Frank, L. S. Stavrianos, and Vijay Prashad, for whom the idea of the "Third World" relates to the expansion of global capitalism and intentional acts of underdevelopment as well as to the articulation of a tradition of protest and creative action in response to that. This is what Prashad calls "the third world project." See Vijay Prashad, *The Darker Nations: A People's History of the Third World* (NewYork/London, NY/UK: The New Press, 2007) and *The Poorer Nations: A Possible History of the Global South* (London and New York: Verso, 2012), L. S. Stavrianos, *Global Rift: The Third World Comes of Age* (New York: William Morrow & Co., 1981), and Andre Gunder Frank, *Latin America: Underdevelopment or Revolution: Essays in the Development of Underdevelopment and the Immediate Enemy* (New York and London: Monthly Review Press, 1969). Whereas the Third World Project, whose starting point is often associated with the Bandung Conference (1955), was suppressed by the mid-1970s, the idea of the Global South crafted at the beginning of the twenty-first century to reflect a new geopolitical arrangement after the end of the Cold War ironically inherited some of the same ambiguity seen in its predecessor. Although not necessarily articulated as a project, the Global South contains similar elements of resistance articulated through local and transnational grassroots movements. For the articulation of this connection, see Alina Sajed, "From the Third World to the Global South," *E-International Relations*, July 27, 2020, https://www.e-ir.info/2020/07/27/from-the-third-world-to-the-global-south/. Accessed by the author on July 10, 2023.

[19] Andrew F. Walls, "Eusebius Tries Again: The Task of Reconceiving and Re-visioning the Study of Christian History," in *Enlarging the Story: Perspectives on*

Among other things, this new world Christian demographics forces us to rethink what we mean by words such as *ecumenicity* and *ecumenism*. Who has a seat on the ecumenical table and who is still left out? Furthermore, the new configuration of world Christianity has helped many of us realize that some of the important issues driving the ecumenical agenda of the twenty-first century are different from those that brought the modern ecumenical movement into existence in the beginning of the twentieth century. As Walls deftly noted, the ecumenical issues of this century "no longer relate to confessional and denominational issues." Instead, many ecumenical issues of today have more to do with "how African and Indian and Chinese and Korean and Hispanic and North American and European Christians can together make real the life of the body of Christ."[20] A keen interpreter of the significance of the demographic shift in world Christianity, Walls became aptly aware that cultural differences in a world where numerous cultures and religious traditions coexisted more closely than ever before would be at the center of contemporary conflicts within and outside Christian communities.

The progress made in the understanding of gender identities and sexuality in different parts of the world in the past few decades is another important matter generating new demands today for deeper ecumenical reflection and intentional conversations. Such conversations are taking place not only in the west but also in multiple contexts around the world.[21] Some of the learning one can acquire

---

Writing Christian World History, ed. Wilbert R. Shenk (Maryknoll, NY: Orbis Books, 2002), 1.

[20] Andrew F. Walls, *The Cross-Cultural Process in Christian History: Studies in the Transmission and Appropriation of Faith* (Maryknoll, NY: Orbis Books, 2001), 57, 69. While Walls is cited here, one cannot forget that scholars such as José Miguez Bonino also challenged the limits of the ecumenical movement since the 1970s. See, for instance, his essay "A Latin American Attempt to Locate the Question of Unity," Consultation on Faith and Order, Salamanca, 1973, in *The Ecumenical Movement: An Anthology of Key Texts and Voices*, 2nd ed., ed. Michael Kinnamon (Geneva: WCC Publications, 2016), 95–98.

[21] The search for theological perspectives that can generate more affirming practices toward LGBTQIA+ Christians and others is not an exclusive privilege of liberal Christians in the Global North. In recent years, Latin America, for instance, has experienced a considerable growth of welcoming and affirming churches. Ana Ester Pádua Freire highlights two Christian welcoming and affirming Christian networks in Brazil, one Protestant and the other Catholic—respectively, *Evangélicxs pela*

in these conversations among and within various Christian communities around the world can contribute to the advancement of a new moral imagination, which can potentially help improve mutual understanding, thus promoting a culture of embrace as that which is represented in the South American Indigenous social philosophy known as *buen vivir* or life in harmony.[22]

Another significant rift in the contemporary world that has informed ecumenical relations since the 1950s is the grim global apartheid between the rich and the poor. As Thomas C. Schelling puts it,

> We live in a world that is one-fifth rich and four-fifths poor; the rich are segregated into the rich countries and the poor into the poor countries; the rich are predominantly lighter skinned and the poor darker skinned; most of the poor live in "homelands" that are physically remote, often separated by oceans and great distances from the rich. Migration on any great scale is impermissible. There is no systematic redistribution of income. While there is ethnic strife among the well-to-do, the strife is more vicious and destructive among the poor.[23]

Such an indictment reminds us of the significance of economic and racial justice for contemporary ecumenism. After all, one of the most consequential divisions the modern/colonial world created was the

Diversidade (Evangelicals for Diversity) and the *Rede Nacional de Grupos Católicos LGBT* (National Network of Catholic LGBT Groups). See Ana Ester Pádua Freire, "Marginal Desire and Unsubmissive Transit Between the Center and the Margin of Christianity: Two Brazilian Cases," in *Alterity and the Evasion of Justice*, eds. Deanna Womack and Raimundo C. Barreto, eds., *Alterity and the Evasion of Justice: Explorations of the "Other" in World Christianity*, World Christianity and Public Religion Series, vol. 5 (Minneapolis: Augsburg Fortress Press, 2023), 220. For a similar conversation in the African context, see Adrian van Klinken, *Kenyan, Christian, Queer: Religion, LGBT Activism, and Arts of Resistance in Africa* (University Park: Pennsylvania State University Press, 2019).

[22] Monica Chuji, Grimaldo Reginfo, and Eduardo Gudynas, "Buen Vivir," in *Pluriverse: A Post-Development Dictionary*, ed. Ashish Kothari et al (New Delhi, India: Tulika Books, 2019) 111–114.

[23] T. C. Schelling, "The Global Dimension," in *Rethinking American Security*, ed. Graham Allison and Gregory F. Treverton (New York: Norton, 1992), 196–210 (200), quoted in Richard Falk, *On Human Governance: Toward a New Global Politics* (University Park, PA: Penn University Press, 1995), 51.

racialization of the "line of the human," an imaginary line dividing between the human and those whose humanity is questioned or dismissed. Such a line is often constructed through "racial markers," which produce a global hierarchization of peoples and cultures. [24]

The scandalous disparity in the distribution of income and wealth in the contemporary world reflects the impact of the racialized power structures that emerged in connection with the modern European colonial expansionism. Schelling's sharp denunciation of the imbalance in the distribution of wealth evinces that such a racialized hierarchy of power did not go away with the end of colonization. Instead, it has increased with the sharper globalization of capital and continues to inform contemporary economic, political, educational, and religious structures around the world.

The cultural, social, epistemological and ontological shifts that follow the reconfiguration of world Christianity have created new moral and theological demands, calling for the rethinking of the ecumenical ideal, which must be freed from those lingering colonial memories. While twentieth-century ecumenical instruments remain significant and have shown the capacity to adapt and change in light of new realities and times, new mechanisms and structures are needed to tackle the walls separating Christians in particular, humans more generally, and life as a whole today.

Adopting analytical insights from world Christianity and decolonial scholarship, this book examines the development of the ecumenical movement from 1910 onward through a Latin American lens. In other words, it approaches global ecumenical events through the perspectives and experiences of ecumenical Latin American Christians, while also placing the development of Latin American ecumenism vis-à-vis international events, players, and networks. In this tale of mutual influence, the local or indigenous is always considered in light of broader exchanges through transnational networks, and the global is never constructed in hegemonic fashion, in ways that erase local perpectives, values, and identities.

Base ecumenism, therefore, functions as a people's story of ecumenism through a Latin American lens, paying special attention to the ideas and motivations of people and movements whose voices and thinking have been largely muted in dominant ecumenical narratives.

[24] Grosfoguel, "What is Racism?," 10.

At the same time, it takes the international circulation of ideas and influences that inform those local players seriously. Consequently, it sees the ecumenical movement as open and ever changing, pointing to new possibilities still in the making and taking into account the new configurations of world Christianity, which, as Irvin aptly noticed, are already boosting a new kind of ecumenism, which is "no longer bound to territorial definitions of sovereignty" and is consequently creating possibilities to move beyond the ecumenical movement's lingering imperial memories. These new ecumenical structures resembling the "fluid assemblages of cross-border networks often coalescing around specific local issues but with trans-local or transnational (global) consequences" must receive greater scholarly attention.[25] Standing as a challenge to hegemonic perspectives in ecumenical historiographies, this book contributes to the reimagination of ecumenicity; that is, what it means to be ecumenical in today's world.[26]

Idea and Organization of the Book

The remainder of this chapter begins to tell that story, highlighting the origins of the engagement of non-Western churches with ecumenical instruments such as the International Missionary Council (IMC) and their gradual impact on the ecumenical movement. The IMC, the first permanent ecumenical instrument in the twentieth century and the main predecessor of the World Council of Churches, provides an early example of how the increasing participation of non-Western Christians in the shaping of the twentieth-century ecumenical movement from its very inception was critical to the reshaping of the ecumenical ideal in the course of the twentieth century.

Building on the discussion about the earlier engagement of the so-called "younger churches" in incipient ecumenical circles in the remaining of chapter one, chapter two turns the reader's attention to the rise of ecumenical networks and early structures in Latin America. In response to the absence of Latin America in Edinburgh 1910, a coalition of mission agencies based in the United States formed the Committee on Cooperation in Latin America (CCLA),

[25] Irvin, "Specters of a New Ecumenism," 24–25.

[26] Irvin, "World Christianity," 18.

which organized the Edinburgh-inspired Latin American Congress on Christian Work in 1916, setting the stage for the coordination of Protestant missionary work in the region, which contributed decisively to the formation of incipient ecumenical networks and the rise of the first national and regional ecumenical instruments in the region.[27] In the course of the following decades, this movement led by North American mission agencies would undergo a significant change as more Latin American nationals were elevated to positions of leadership, voicing their priorities for an ecumenical agenda that they could call their own.

Chapter three examines the rise and impact of the Third World Movement on the Latin American ecumenical agenda in the 1950s and early 1960s, a time when a group of young Latin American ecumenical Protestants created youth movements increasingly focused on the social responsibility of the churches and the necessity of a more sensible public witness. Those movements are identified as the roots of an incipient liberation Christianity, which anticipated the rise of Latin American liberation theology. The chapter ends with an overview of the impact those developments in Latin America and other parts of the Global South had on the agenda of the 1966 World Conference on Church and Society, which demonstrates the rise of the Global South in ecumenical circles.

Chapters four and five offer an account of the liberation turn among ecumenically minded Latin American Protestants, discussing the role played by the Student Christian Movement and the rise of a world-oriented Latin American ecumenism in Protestant circles, which impacted the formation of national and regional ecumenical networks and international ecumenical discourse, with particular attention to their participation in the 1966 Geneva Conference on Church and Society.

Chapter six outlines the emergence of liberation Christianity within Latin American Catholicism, which laid the foundation for the growth of a base ecumenism, beginning with the expansion of Catholic Action in Latin America and the development of its various branches, especially those organized among young people, students,

[27] While Protestant missions had been active in Latin America for most of the nineteenth century, the CCLA created the conditions for more coordinated efforts toward their intent to evangelize the region.

and urban and rural workers. In Brazil, this development eventually led to the creation of Popular Action, a movement that played a crucial role in resisting the authoritarianism of the military dictatorship established in the country from 1964 onward.

Chapter seven shifts attention to the Second Vatican Council and the rise of the Church of the Poor, focusing on the articulation prior to and during the council of Latin American participants who not only intended to influence the council's agenda in the hope to bring the problem of widespread poverty to center stage, but who also started articulating the Latin American reception of the council, something that played a crucial role in the rise of Latin American liberation theology in the years that followed.

Chapters eight and nine expand on the previous chapter by discussing the faithful, creative, and selective Latin American reception of Vatican II, with especial attention to the Latin American Episcopal Conferences of Medellin 1968 and Puebla 1979, and the articulation of a multifaceted base ecumenism that took root in the region.

Chapter ten explores the global influence of base ecumenism, highlighting its impact on the worldwide ecumenical movement, with special attention to the WCC Department of Church and Society and Paulo Freire's advisory role in the World Council of Churches (WCC) in the 1970s. Freire, the mastermind behind the idea of popular education, served as a consultant for the educational program the WCC in Geneva from 1970 to 1980. During his years in Geneva, his ideas not only informed WCC documents but also circulated in various continents, especially Africa.

Chapter eleven continues the conversation about the global impact of base ecumenism by examining the Ecumenical Association of Third World Theologians (EATWOT) and the related World Forum on Theology and Liberation (WFTL). The latter part of this chapter discusses two cases in which the Third World Project influenced the global ecumenical agenda, first focusing on the World Council of Churches, in particular the Nairobi assembly in 1975, then discussing the influence of the Church of the Poor and the Argentinean theology of the people on pope Francis, particularly the way his papacy has contributed to bring critical concerns raised by Latin American liberation theology back to the global stage. Special attention is given to the document *Querida Amazonia* (2020), in which Francis makes a bold case for the integral conversion of the

Church, acknowledging the value of Indigenous peoples traditions and their ways of living in harmony with the planet as something Christians should learn from.

Finally, chapter twelve offers a concluding reflection on the transformation Latin American ecumenicity has undergone since the early 1900s and the envisioning of an *oikoumenē* inspired by the Latin American Indigenous imagination of a world in which many worlds fit, with particular accent placed on the coexistence of diverse knowledges and ways of knowing, and the dialogue of cultures. This chapter also discusses the role Latin American Pentecostalism is beginning to play in Latin American ecumenism, opening the ecumenical movement to new possible conversations.

The IMC: The First Embodiment of the Ecumenical Dream

The rise of the modern ecumenical movement resulted from a confluence of factors, a *zeitgeist*, a time when Christians in different parts of the world were longing for unity.[28] In particular, unity had become an aspiration of a number of Christians in the non-Western world who did not understand the need to replicate the Western Christian denominational divide in non-European contexts. A number of Protestant missionaries also dreamed of a united Christianity, which, in their view, would be able to conduct its world mission more effectively.

As early as 1806, British Baptist missionary William Carey (1761–1834) started sharing a vision for the organization of a World Missionary Conference, which he hoped could take shape as early as 1810. Carey also had a place in mind for that conference: the Cape of Good Hope, the site where different Protestant missions were stationed in South Africa. Such a conference would contribute to increased mutual understanding among different Christian missions. Nothing could be better for that than in-person conversations. As

[28] An earlier version of this section can be found in Raimundo C. Barreto, "The International Missionary Council: From Lake Mohonk 1921 to New Delhi 1961," in *Together in the Mission of God: Jubilee Reflections on the International Missionary Council*, ed. Risto Jukko (Geneva: WCC Publications, 2022), 31–58. Used with permission.

Carey put it, a few hours of conversations in person would have more effect on Christian relationships—and on the mutual efforts to understand each other's views—than "two or three years of epistolary correspondence."[29] Carey did not think of that conference as an isolated event. He wished to see such a gathering happening every ten years. Ultimately, his hope was that these gatherings would lead to the creation of "a general association of all denominations of Christians, from the four quarters of the world."[30] Carey's 'ecumenical' dream was driven, as it was the case with other missionaries, by the aspiration to evangelize the entire world.

Carey's dream of a world missionary gathering only materialized, though, years after his death, when British, Continental European, American, and Canadian mission societies decided to convene the first World Missionary Conference in London, in 1888, to celebrate the first centenary of modern Protestant missions.[31] With the success of the first World Missionary Conference, its organizers agreed to hold another similar event ten years later. Delayed by a couple of years, the second World Missionary Conference took place in New York, in 1900. Differently from its predecessor, the New York conference added the qualifier 'ecumenical' to its title, "not as claiming to be representative of all portions of the Christian Church, but because it represented mission work in all parts of the 'inhabited world.'"[32]

Like its predecessor, though, the New York Conference assumed that a follow-up meeting should take place within the next ten years. A General Committee to plan the next conference was named in 1907. The outcome of that planning, the 1910 World Missionary Conference in Edinburgh, would become a watershed for the ecumenical aspirations that had been shaping up in the previous century.

---

[29] See Klaus Koschorke, Frieder Ludwig, Marian Delgado, and Roland Spliesgart, eds., *A History of Christianity in Asia, Africa, and Latin America, 1450–1990: A Documentary Sourcebook* (Grand Rapids, MI: Wm. Eerdmans Publishing, 2007), loc. 1196, Kindle.

[30] Koschorke, Ludwig, Delgado, and Spliesgart, eds., *A History of Christianity*, loc. 1193–1194, Kindle.

[31] See World Missionary Conference, 1910, *The History and Records of the Conference Together with Addresses Delivered at the Evening Meetings* (Edinburgh and London: Oliphant, Anderson & Ferrier/Fleming H. Hevel Company, 1910), 4.

[32] World Missionary Conference, 1910, *The History and Records of the Conference*, 5.

Edinburgh 1910 became one of the most significant landmarks of the modern ecumenical movement. The ecumenical impetus that marked that conference had been incubated for decades through organizations such as the YMCA (Young Men's Christian Association, 1844), the Evangelical Alliance (1846), the YWCA (Young Women's Christian Association, 1854), and the WSCF (World Student Christian Federation, 1895). However, up to that point no global umbrella existed to coordinate all streams of ecumenical efforts forged in the previous century.

In contrast with the two previous world missionary conferences, Edinburgh 1910 set in motion a process of institutional embodiment of the conference's ideals and commitments. Among other things, the organizers envisioned the formation of a permanent body for international cooperation. The most significant step in that direction was the creation of a Continuation Committee composed of thirty-five members in the conference's aftermath "to carry forward the spirit of co-operation in the work of mission."[33] The conveners of Edinburgh 1910 envisioned an institutional instrument that could enable Protestant trans-denominational cooperation to fulfill the evangelistic mandate to the entire world in that generation. Such an effort stood in line with the generations-old perception of the Western churches as the bearers of the gospel for the rest of the world.

While the Edinburgh Continuation Committee was largely dominated by representatives from Western missionary societies and churches, China, India, and Japan ended up each with one representative in it. In the decade that followed, the Edinburgh Continuation Committee contributed to the formation of national continuation committees in a number of countries, including China, Japan, and Korea. Some of those national continuation committees would evolve later into national councils of churches, which would be critical for the shaping of the ecumenical movement in the coming decades.[34] Regardless of the varied forms they took, these emerging national ecumenical bodies would gradually engage in participation in various international ecumenical bodies in the following decades.[35]

---

33 Stanley, *The World Missionary Conference*, loc. 1400, Kindle.

34 Stanley, *The World Missionary Conference*, loc. 1402, Kindle.

35 The International Missionary Council was one of the most structured ecumenical instruments of the first half of the twentieth century. It was officially launched

Organized by Western missionary societies, Edinburgh 1910 was a consultation of mission agencies that escalated as never before the plan for a joint global missionary endeavor. Going beyond its predecessors, Edinburgh offered a concrete path for the ecumenical fulfillment of what was perceived as a missionary mandate. The Edinburgh Conference understood the church's missionary activity primarily in terms of planting "self-governing, self-supporting, and self-propagating Churches" all over the world.[36] Such a missionary goal could be more effectively achieved through collaborative efforts involving both Western missionary agencies and the growing non-Western churches in the parts of the world then perceived as "the mission field."

The growing attention to the so-called "younger churches" in the non-Western world, however, posed new questions about the nature of Christian relations and collaboration across colonial borders, raising new demands and challenges such as the need for the Western churches to acknowledge colonial wounds that directly impacted the lives of people and churches in the missionary fields. A number of young Christian leaders in non-Western churches understood the denominational divisions they inherited as a problem that belonged to the Western churches, and only hindered Christian evangelizing efforts in non-Western contexts. Consequently, they began to

---

during a missionary conference in Lake Mohonk, New York, in 1921. While its origins can be traced back to as early as 1920, the Life and Work Movement was only formally launched in 1925, at the Universal Christian Conference on Life and Work in Stockholm. Likewise, the Faith and Order Movement, initially proposed in 1910 to build ecumenical consensus and Christian unity, had its launching delayed by the first World War. After a preparatory meeting in 1920, it was formally launched at a conference in Lausanne, Switzerland, on August 3–21, 1927. It is worth remembering as well that, also in 1920, the Ecumenical Patriarchate of Constantinople made the first public appeal for the formation of a permanent organ of fellowship and cooperation of "all the churches," something along the lines of a "League of Churches," inspired by the post–World War I League of Nations. WCC Archives: http://archives.wcc-coe.org/Query/detail.aspx?ID=100399. For a brief historical overview of the World Conference on Faith and Order, see Odair Pedroso Mateus, "A Century of World Conferences on Faith and Order," *The Ecumenical Review* 75/2 (2023): 154–171.

[36] Kenneth Scott Latourette, "Ecumenical Bearings of the Missionary Movement and the International Missionary Council," in *A History of the Ecumenical Movement 1517–1948*, ed. Ruth Rouse and Stephen Charles Neil, 4th ed. (Geneva: World Council of Churches, 1993), 353–402 (358). Ideally, these churches would be undivided (359).

conceive ways to overcome those obstacles. In some cases, such efforts led to the formation of united churches, as it was the case in India. In others, such as in Latin America, they produced united seminaries, publishing houses, and hospitals. In a variety of ways, the aftermath of Edinburgh 1910 created the conditions for the rise of an ecumenical movement, which would operate on multiple fronts in the following decades.

The significance of the emerging ecumenical movement in the initial decades of the twentieth century was such that Archbishop William Temple depicted it as "the great new fact of our era."[37] Its impact was felt in different parts of the world. As US historian Kenneth Scott Latourette deftly noted, despite the central role that Western missionary agencies played in its inception, the ecumenical movement developed even more rapidly "in the lands of the younger Churches than in the West."[38] Such a development, however, must not be taken for granted.

In his magistral study of the third World Missionary Conference in 1910, Brian Stanley underscores that despite its ecumenical significance, the Edinburgh conference was not geographically representative of the world church. Protestant and Anglican foreign missionary societies dominated the conference. According to Stanley, "of the 1,215 official delegates, 509 were British, 491 were North American, 169 originated from continental Europe, 27 came from the white colonies of South Africa and Australasia, and only 19 were from the non-western or 'majority' world (18 of them from Asia)."[39] That unbalanced representation would slowly change with the demographic shift world Christianity would undergo, especially toward the second half of the twentieth century.

The initial signs of the impact such a demographic change would come to make on the incipient ecumenical instruments of the twentieth century began to be noticed with the growing participation of representatives from Global South churches in ecumenical missionary

---

[37] William Temple, *The Church Looks Forward*, New York: Macmillan, 1944, 2. Cited in *Understanding World Christianity: The Vision and Works of Andrew F. Walls*, ed. William R. Burrows, Mark R. Gornic, and Janice A. McLean (Maryknoll, NY: Orbis Books, Kindle Edition, 2011), loc. 2888, Kindle.

[38] Latourette, "Ecumenical Bearings of the Missionary Movement and the International Missionary Council," 363.

[39] Stanley, *The World Missionary Conference*, loc. 270–272, Kindle.

gatherings in the decades following Edinburgh 1910. The increasing representation of Christian leaders from formerly colonized parts of the world in ecumenical circles would eventually impact the ecumenical agenda. Although that impact of majority-world churches on ecumenical gatherings only became more noticeable in the second half of the twentieth century, it can be traced back to the 1920s, especially in connection with the International Missionary Council (IMC).

The Edinburgh Continuation Committee's plans to form an international committee that would serve as a permanent incarnation of the Edinburgh spirit were hampered due to World War I. During that time, an Emergency Committee was formed to address the tragic impact of the war and the increasing rift between German missions and American and British missionary societies, since the latter two took control of missionary fields previously under the auspices of the former. Amid such tensions, the plans for the creation of an International Committee for Mission Cooperation only resumed in 1920. Fears of centralization of power, though, led those planning the implementation of that new international Christian body to conceive it no longer as a committee but instead as an International Mission Council (IMC), which would enable decentralized and inclusive collaboration. The IMC was created in 1921.[40] In the course of a few years, it established itself as "the forerunner and the first comprehensive embodiment of the ecumenical movement."[41]

As the earliest institutional embodiment of the ecumenical movement, the IMC was the first ecumenical body to experience the impact of the growing participation of representatives from the "younger churches" in its rankings. In its inaugural meeting in Lake Mohonk, New York (1921), 7 of the 61 delegates from fourteen countries in attendance came from the majority world. Methodist historian William Richey Hogg, a pioneering "Professor of World Christianity" at Perkins School of Theology (1955–1987), identified those participants as follows:

---

[40] Latourette, "Ecumenical Bearings of the Missionary Movement and the International Missionary Council," 366.

[41] International Missionary Council, *The International Missionary Council: What It Is, What It Does* (New York: International Missionary Council, 1951), 2.

> Dr. S. K. Datta, from the National Missionary Council of India, Burma and Ceylon, and his colleague, a woman, Dr. Ma Saw Sa of Burma, added greatly to the meeting as did also Dr. (later bishop) Y. Y. Tsu, then a professor at St. John's University, Shanghai, and William Hung of the China Continuation Committee. From Japan came Hiromichi Kozaki, formerly president of Doshisha University, and Bishop Kogoro Uzaki of the Methodist Church, each representing the Japan Continuation Committee. Also present as coopted members, and because of their colour thought by some to represent the churches of Africa, were Dr. James E. K. Aggrey, a native of the Gold Coast but at the time a professor at Livingstone College, North Carolina, and Dr. Robert R. Moton, Principal of Tuskegee in Alabama.[42]

Like the Edinburgh Conference eleven years earlier, the Mohonk Lake gathering was for the most part a meeting of missionary agencies and their national partners. The formation of the IMC, though, had provoked a renewed conversation on matters of governance and representativity. The founders of the IMC understood the need to see it as an organ of cooperation without an executive power of its own, representing the collective will of national missionary agencies. Membership in the Council was limited to "missionary societies and boards, and the churches which they represent, and the churches in the mission field."[43] With offices in London and New York, and under the visionary leadership of John R. Mott (1865–1955)—and two regional secretaries, J. H. Oldham (1874–1969) and A. L. Warnshuis (1877–1958)—the IMC played a critical role in the formation of a worldwide Christian fellowship. Its first enlarged meeting took place in 1928 on the iconic Mount of Olives in Jerusalem. The agenda of that gathering included topics such as the Christian message to "non-Christian systems," religious education, the relationship between "younger" and "older" churches, international missionary cooperation, and the challenges of mission in relation to rural problems, industrialism, and race conflict.[44]

---

[42] William Richey Hogg, *Ecumenical Foundations: A History of the International Missionary Council and Its Nineteenth-Century Background* (New York: Harper, 1952), 203. The inclusion of the prominent African American leader Dr. Robert Russa Moton on that list is telling.

[43] Hogg, *Ecumenical Foundations*, 204.

[44] L. S. Albright, *The International Missionary Council: Its History, Functions and Relationships* (New York: The International Missionary Council, 1946), 11.

It is worth noting that, among other things, the Jerusalem enlarged meeting sought to promote a view of the task of international missionary cooperation that advanced the "interdependence of nations and races."[45] As John Mott explained it, Christianity was entering a new stage of international cooperation, which demanded the rethinking, restating, and reinterpretation of "the Christian message" in light of new challenges.[46] People from all "nationalities and races" were urged to cooperate, adding their intellectual resources to the task of evangelization in an increasingly international era.[47]

The conflation between nationalities and races as seen in Mott's writings reflected the Eurocentric problem of Christendom and a view of the world informed by Christian and white superiority. Mott's pioneering awareness of the racial problem in the incipient ecumenical movement, and his continuous work to promote a more inclusive religious transnational fellowship as head of the Young Men's Christian Association (YMCA) and chairman of the IMC, would render him the 1946 Nobel Peace Prize along with Emily Greene Balch, honorary international president of Women's International League for Peace and Freedom. Among the qualities highlighted to justify the awarding of Mott was his contribution to the struggle against racial discrimination:

> As general-secretary of the International Committee of the YMCA and president of YMCA's World Committee, Mott sought to advance understanding and reconciliation. He organized youth exchanges, set up study groups, and arranged international youth camps. Mott was at the same time a leading figure in the field of international Christian student and missionary cooperation, and took part during both World Wars in relief work for prisoners of war. He criticised the oppression of colonial peoples and was *a pioneer in the struggle against racial discrimination*.[48]

---

[45] John R. Mott, "The Future of International Missionary Cooperation," in *International Missionary Cooperation*, The Jerusalem Meeting of the International Missionary Council, March 24–April 4, 1928, vol. 7, ed. John R. Mott (New York: International Missionary Council, 1928), 3–48 (3).

[46] Mott, "The Future of International Missionary Cooperation," 4.

[47] Mott, "The Future of International Missionary Cooperation," 5.

[48] The Nobel Peace Prize, "John R. Mott—Facts," NobelPrize.org, Nobel Prize Outreach AB 2023, Wed. Nov 29, 2023, https://www.nobelprize.org/prizes/peace/1946/mott/facts/. Italics are mine.

Mott's emphasis suggests that some of the initial leaders of the ecumenical movement were aware of "the racial problem" that informed the relationship of American and European white Christians with the non-Western world. Willem Adolph Visser' t Hooft (1900–1985), the first president of the World Council of Churches (1948–1966), would note years later that many European and American churches had lost sight of "the supra-racial nature of Christianity."[49] Therefore, "From the perspective of the West, Christianity seemed to be the religion of the white man, and the coloured races seemed to represent the pagan world."[50] In other words, many Western Christians conflated not only race and nationality but also race and religion, conceiving Christianity as being primarily the religion of white Americans and Europeans while associating other religious traditions with non-white populations.

Seeking to avert such a situation, Mott saw Jerusalem 1928 as an opportunity to promote an expanded call for Christian unity aimed at bringing people from different nationalities and races into cooperation. The call for international cooperation stemming from that historical meeting—the first of its kind in the Middle East—intended, among other things, to represent the expression of a supra-racial Gospel, seen as essential for the effective witness of "the truly catholic nature of the Christian Church."[51] However, while Mott's words served as an aspiration for Christianity to overcome a racialized view of the world, the nascent ecumenical movement still replicated in many ways the white Christian superiority that was widespread at the time.

In an effort to move beyond the confines of Western Christianity, Mott portrayed the emerging ecumenical movement as an "interracial fellowship" through which people "of different racial groups entered into the marvelous power of genuine Christian fellowship."[52] An ecumenical fellowship of the proportions of the IMC should reflect the understanding that Christians are called to advance human reconciliation in a world deeply divided. In order to do that, they must overcome internal divisions, including those based on race.

---

49 W. A. Visser' t Hooft, *The Ecumenical Movement and the Racial Problem*, The Race Question and Modern Thought (Paris: UNESCO, 1954), 11.

50 Visser' t Hooft, *The Ecumenical Movement and the Racial Problem*, 12.

51 Mott, "The Future of International Missionary Cooperation," 7.

52 Mott, "The Future of International Missionary Cooperation," 9.

> Divisions among the Christians—denominational, national, racial—have ever been a stumbling block; but with the recent rapid shrinkage of the world these divisions have become more serious and intolerable than ever. [. . .] This stumbling-block must be removed.[53]

While the words found in documents of Jerusalem 1928 show some signs of rejection of the Eurocentric hegemony that had prevailed in modern missions, on the ground the situation was more complicated. As Deanna Womack keenly notes, Palestinian Muslim and Christian voices kept outside the gates of the conference were dismissed by the conference organizers, including Mott.[54] Womack's findings help us put those incipient signs of progress in perspective, as only one aspect of a more complicated story. While the significance of the inclusion of attention to racial discrimination in the ICM's understanding of ecumenical cooperation is laudable, the IMC leaders failed "to see and acknowledge the religious, cultural, or ideological 'other' just beyond our comfortable walls of protection."[55]

Having said that, it is still possible to affirm that the agenda of Jerusalem 1928 offered a significant contribution to expand the ecumenical ideal. Part of that progress can be credited to the larger representation of "younger churches" in that gathering in comparison to any previous ecumenical meetings. That small but significant progress resulted, among other things, from the extensive travels IMC leaders such as Mott and Oldham had made since the early 1910s. Those visits sparked the creation of national committees in various countries, which were conducive to the formation of a wide international network of national Christian organizations in Europe, North America, Africa, Asia, and the Middle East.[56] In the years prior to the gathering in Jerusalem, Mott visited China, the Philippines, Malaysia, the Netherlands, East Indies, Australia, Tasmania,

53 Mott, "The Future of International Missionary Cooperation," 9–10.

54 Deanna Ferree Womack, "A View from the Muslim Arabic Press, 1928: The International Missionary Conference in Jerusalem," *Exchange* 46 (2017): 180–205 (205).

55 Womack, "A View from the Muslim Arabic Press, 1928."

56 Hogg, *Ecumenical Foundations*, 214.

New Zealand, England, Holland, France, Switzerland, Hungary, and Poland.[57]

Although relatively small, Jerusalem 1928 had representatives from six continents. Fifty-one countries sent two hundred and fifty delegates to Jerusalem, with far greater participation from the "younger churches" than ever before. In addition to Africa, Asia, Australia, Europe, and North America, South America sent its first representatives to an IMC gathering. Moreover, the conference also counted with an unprecedented representation from Orthodox Churches and Christian youth movements.[58] According to Hogg, Jerusalem 1928 was "the first [truly] representative global assembly of Christians in the long history of the church,"[59] not only in light of the number of countries represented in that gathering but also because "nearly one-fourth (52) [of the delegates] represented younger churches."[60] The voices of those representatives from the "younger churches" did not go unnoticed. The conference report on religious education, for instance, included findings from preconference events held by the All-Indian Conference, the Ceylon Christian Council, the Chinese delegates, and the National Christian Council of Japan, along with recommendations and resolutions from an international conference on Christian education held in Africa.[61]

The greater plurality of voices at Jerusalem 1928 impacted the agenda of the meeting, which featured contributions from Asia and Africa, in addition to including themes that were also of concern for Latin American Christians, as chapter two will discuss, such as the concentration of land in the hands of a few, the rise of the labor

---

[57] Albright, *The International Missionary Council: Its History, Functions and Relationships*, 9ff.

[58] Albright, *The International Missionary Council: Its History, Functions and Relationships*, 10.

[59] Hogg, *Ecumenical Foundations*, 244.

[60] Hogg, *Ecumenical Foundations*, 245. Among them, Erasmo Braga, from Brazil; Cheng Ching-yi, T. C. Chao, Francis C. M. Wei, and David Z. T. Yui, from China; Jashwant Chitambar, K. T. Paul, S. K. Datta, and P. Ooman Philip, from India; Michio Kozaki and Kogoro Uzaki, from Japan; Helen Kim, from Korea; David Jabavu, from South Africa; and Sirwano Kulubya, from Uganda.

[61] International Missionary Council, *Religious Education, The Relation Between the Younger and the Older Churches*, vol. III of The Jerusalem Meeting of the International Missionary Council, March 24–April 4, 1928 (New York: International Missionary Council, 1928).

movement, the dominance of foreign capital, and migration.[62] The theme of Christian mission vis-à-vis racial conflicts was engaged mainly by representatives from the United States, South Africa, and the United Kingdom. The discussion was not limited to the issue of racism targeting black communities. Galen M. Fisher, the Executive Secretary of the Institute of Social and Religious Research and a former secretary of the YMCA in Japan, for instance, denounced racial discrimination against Asian-American immigrants in the United States and Canada,[63] highlighting discriminatory attitudes Japanese and Chinese immigrants experienced in North America such as widespread suspicion of Buddhist temples, fear on the part of white North Americans of interracial marriage, and outright racism.[64]

As he addressed the problem of interracial relations and anti-Asian sentiments, Fisher also highlighted the work of Christian organizations and churches promoting "inter-racial understanding,"[65] especially the Commission on International Justice and Goodwill of the Federal Council of Churches of Christ in America, "the chief agency promoting goodwill between Americans and Orientals."[66] Founded in 1914 in response to "anti-Japanese agitation and legislation in California," the Commission promoted studies on "the racial situation on the Pacific Coast," published multiple volumes on the topic, and "enrolled 2,000

---

[62] International Missionary Council, *The Christian Mission in Relation to Industrial Problems*, The Jerusalem Meeting of the International Missionary Council, March 24–April 4, 1928, vol. 5 (New York: International Missionary Council, 1928). Those themes emerged at the gathering mainly through the voice of American missionary Samuel Guy Inman, who articulated a justificative of the "rationale for missions in Latin America to the world missionary movement" in Jerusalem and Madras. See Carlos F. Cardoza Orlandi, "From Christian Continent to Mission Field: The Missional Discourse of the Committee on Cooperation in Latin America and Protestant Latin Americans Concerning the Missional Needs of Latin America (1910–1938)," (PhD diss., Princeton Theological Seminary, 1999), 9.

[63] Galen M. Fisher, "Relations Between the Occidental and Oriental Peoples on the Pacific Coast of North America," in *The Christian Mission in the Light of Race Conflict*, The Jerusalem Meeting of the International Missionary Council, March 24–April 4, 1928, Vol. 4 (New York: International Missionary Council, 1928), 118–174.

[64] Fisher, "Relations Between the Occidental and Oriental Peoples," 129.

[65] Fisher, "Relations Between the Occidental and Oriental Peoples," 133.

[66] Fisher, "Relations Between the Occidental and Oriental Peoples," 133.

citizens in a National Committee on American-Japanese Relations," among other initiatives.[67] Whereas the discussion of racial relations in Jerusalem 1928 deserves a chapter of its own, for the purpose of this book, it suffices to note that as it invited greater participation of Christians from all over the world, the IMC fostered some of the earliest ecumenical conversations on Christianity and race, a theme whose significance persists in ecumenical circles to this day.

J. H. Oldham, one of the three main IMC leaders at the time, had turned his attention to the relationship between Christianity and race since 1921. In 1924, he published a book called *Christianity and the Race Problem*, asking "whether the Christian Church has any contribution to make to the solution of the problems involved in the contact of different races in the world today," and what was the nature of that contribution.[68] The book was a direct outgrowth of his work in the Student Christian Movement (SCM) and the IMC, and became one of the documents that informed the preparations for the Jerusalem gathering.[69] Jerusalem 1928, thus, highlighted a theme that was receiving increasing attention in IMC circles, especially among representatives from the "younger churches" and minoritized ethnic and racial Christian communities in the North Atlantic.

Considering its catalyst agenda, one may concur with John Mott when he stated that Jerusalem 1928 "exerted a greater influence than that at Edinburgh in 1910" in the ecumenical agenda.[70] In particular, Mott was referring to the attention given at that meeting to the parity of the younger churches, and its unprecedented display of the "churches that had resulted from missionary labour in the preceding century in Latin America, Africa, Asia, and the Islands of the Seas."[71]

The impact of that meeting could also be felt in some developments that followed that conference, including: (1) the Five-Year

[67] Fisher, "Relations Between the Occidental and Oriental Peoples," 133.

[68] J. H. Oldham, *Christianity and the Race Problem* (London: The Student Christian Movement, 1924), 12.

[69] Hogg, *Ecumenical Foundations*, 233–234.

[70] John R. Mott, *Addresses and Papers of John R. Mott*, vol. V, page 667, cited by Hogg, *Ecumenical Foundations*, 253.

[71] Hogg, *Ecumenical Foundations*, 253.

Movement in China, under the leadership of Dr. Cheng Ching-Yi,[72] which promoted a surge in the membership of Chinese independent churches in the 1930s; and (2) the Kingdom of God Movement in Japan, led by Toyohiko Kagawa, which Hogg considered to be "one of the most effective undertakings ever launched by the Christian churches of Japan."[73]

In the decade following Jerusalem 1928, the IMC continued to solidify organizationally while also being forced to respond to important world crises such as the great economic depression, the Japanese occupation of Manchuria in 1931, and its offensive against China in 1937.[74] All these events informed the preparation for the second enlarged meeting of the IMC, which took place in Tambaram, India, in 1938.

Tambaram: Rethinking the Relationship between Christianity and Other Religions

The Tambaram enlarged meeting of the IMC was originally planned to take place in China. However, the full-scale Japanese invasion of China in 1937 turned impossible for the conference to be held there.[75] Thus, the 1938 gathering ended up happening in the village of Tambaram, near Madras, India. Four hundred seventy-one representatives from sixty-nine countries were in attendance. This was the first time that most of the representatives in an ecumenical gathering came from the "younger churches," including Oceania.[76] The impact of that Global South majority was visible in the discussions that took place at the conference. India and China had the largest

[72] For Dr. Cheng's own interpretation of the movement, see his article at the *International Review of Missions*, then published by the IMC. C. Y Cheng, "An Interpretation of the Five-Year Movement in China," *International Review of Missions* 20/2 (1931): 173–188.

[73] Hogg, *Ecumenical Foundations*, 255.

[74] Hogg, *Ecumenical Foundations*, 258ff.

[75] Hogg, *Ecumenical Foundations*, 288.

[76] Albright, *The International Missionary Council: Its History, Functions and Relationships*, 16. Tambaram also counted with the presence of members of other ecumenical bodies, including the World Conferences on Life and Work and on Faith and Order, and the Provisional Committee of the World Council of Churches, creating the opportunity for initial considerations about the future of the IMC in light of the emerging WCC. (17)

delegations. The Chinese delegation was led by a woman, Dr. Wu Yi-fang.[77] Despite the war, Japanese representatives were also present in Tambaram.[78] Furthermore, the Tambaram gathering counted with a good balance between clergy and laity, and greater representation of women than any previous ecumenical event.[79]

Concern with the "younger churches" remained central for the IMC as it approached Tambaram. In one of the early meetings to discuss the creation of the World Council of Churches, William Paton (1886–1943), who had succeeded Oldham as an IMC Secretary, was recommended to serve "as one of the general secretaries of the World Council of Churches, in an honorary capacity, with special concern for the relation of the Younger Churches to the World Council."[80] Paton would play a key contributing role to integrate the majority-world churches into the emerging WCC fabric. According to his biographer, Eleanor M. Jackson, his premature death was one of the causes for the delay of the integration of the IMC into the WCC.[81] The Tambaram conference, which he significantly contributed to shape, reflected his chief concern with the "growing development of the Younger Churches."[82] In Tambaram, as Latourette deftly noticed, "The Church was becoming world-wide."[83]

One of the ways the majority of the non-Western delegates influenced the ecumenical conversation in Tambaram can be seen in their responses to the Christian message prepared for that meeting. In anticipation of Tambaram 1938, Dutch missionary and historian Hendrik Kraemer was asked to write a book with the goal of expanding and deepening the conversation initiated ten years earlier in

---

77 Hogg, *Ecumenical Foundations*, 293.

78 Latourette, "Ecumenical Bearings of the Missionary Movement and the International Missionary Council," 369.

79 Hogg, *Ecumenical Foundations*, 291. Seventy-seven women were sent as delegates to Tambaram.

80 Albright, *The International Missionary Council: Its History, Functions and Relationships*, 18.

81 Eleanor M. Jackson, "Paton, William," in *Biographical Dictionary of Christian Missions*, ed. Gerald H. Anderson (New York: Simon & Schuster Macmillan, 1998), 519.

82 Albright, *The International Missionary Council: Its History, Functions and Relationships*, 17.

83 Latourette, "Ecumenical Bearings of the Missionary Movement and the International Missionary Council," 369.

Jerusalem on the Christian message for the non-Christian world.[84] According to Kraemer, his book should specifically state "the fundamental position of the Christian Church [. . .] towards other faiths, dealing in detail with the evangelistic approach to the great non-Christian faiths." Consequently, he stated, "Evangelism, or the witness of the Church in relation to the non-Christian faiths, has therefore to be the main concern of this book."[85]

Kraemer's book advanced two main theses: (1) the absolute uniqueness of the Christian revelation and (2) the view that "the relation between Christian revelation and other religions 'is not one of continuity, but discontinuity.'"[86] While not relegating all teachings of other religions as mistaken, Kraemer, in Barthian fashion, affirmed the superiority and uniqueness of the Christian revelation, concluding that "if one were to decide to follow Christ, he or she should make a clean break with their religious past."[87] While a number of participants in Tambaram endorsed Kraemer's views, a group of Indian theologians challenged the emphasis on discontinuity. As Joshua Kalapati notices,

> This Rethinking Christianity Group broadly argued that Indian philosophy, culture, and tradition could not be ignored by those engaged in Christian mission on Indian soil, and secondly, that the 'Kingdom of God' rather than 'church' would provide a better platform for defining and doing mission in the pluralist context of India.[88]

The Tambaram meeting ended up underscoring that one of the consequences of the widening of the ecumenical fellowship through the increasing participation of non-Western delegates was that their views and lived experience among people of other faiths would

---

[84] Hendrik Kraemer, *The Christian Message in a Non-Christian World* (New York: Harper & Brothers, 1938).

[85] Kraemer, *The Christian Message*, v.

[86] Joshua Kalapati, "Tambaram International Missionary Council Conference, 1938," in *The Oxford Encyclopaedia of South Asian Christianity*, ed. Roger E. Hedlund, Jesudas M. Athyal, Joshua Kalapati, and Jessica Richard (Oxford University Press, 2011), https://www.oxfordreference.com/view/10.1093/acref/9780198073857.001.0001/acref-9780198073857-e-0961?print.

[87] Kalapati, "Tambaram International Missionary Council Conference, 1938."

[88] Kalapati, "Tambaram International Missionary Council Conference, 1938."

contribute to open new possible interpretations of the Christian message for the world, challenging established Western assumptions. Kraemer failed to provide a basis broad enough to instill a more constructive relationship with other faiths. His approach to missions, highly suspicious of natural theology, led him to conclude that the relationship with other faiths was mostly characterized by discontinuity, and that "other religions offer no point of contact with the Christian faith."[89] Many of the Asian Christians in Tambaram, however, could not agree with that view.

The discussions around Kraemer's book were both tense and revealing. They forced the IMC to "rethink every theological presupposition upon which it acted."[90] Furthermore, those conversations reinforced the long aspiration on the part of non-Western Christians for a more egalitarian relationship between Western missionary agencies and increasingly autonomous churches and national agencies in the non-Western world.

For the Asian theologians who challenged Kraemer's thesis of radical discontinuity, more than theology was at stake. As M. M. Thomas explained fifty years later,

> Tambaram 1938 took place at a time when the churches of Asia were awakening to the need of a selfhood oriented to witnessing to Jesus Christ among Asian peoples who were themselves struggling for self-identity and for the renaissance of their nations in the world of nations.[91]

They saw the "march towards authentic Asian selfhood" as crucial for the future of the Asian churches. Thus, the challenge they posed to Kraemer's approach to other religions had both theological and moral implications. Most Asian churches represented in Tambaram were grappling with the formation of their own Christian identity in contexts where nationalist sentiments nurtured the transition from a colonial past to a desired emancipated future; a nation-building process that required their continuous participation in "dialogue

---

[89] Hogg, 295.

[90] Hogg, 295.

[91] M. M. Thomas, "An Assessment of Tambaram," *International Review of Mission*, 77/307 (1988): 390–397 (390).

with religions and secular faiths within that context."[92] Tambaram 1938 was forced, then, to consider the challenges of the non-Western contexts in which new Christian communities were forming as an opportunity for self-critique. As Hogg underscores, the Madras meeting "saw the church standing under God's judgment. Madras concentrated on the church but did not absolutize it."[93]

While the conference did not arrive at an overall consensus on the matter of the Christian message in non-Western cultures, it produced a final statement, which fairly represented the critical dialogue that had taken place in Tambaram. The bulk of that conversation is recorded in the first volume of the Madras Series, *The Authority of the Faith*.[94] The volume is composed of an essay by Kraemer on the topic of "continuity or discontinuity" and responses by T. C. Chao from China, D. G. Moses from India, Tao Fong from China, A. G. Hogg, a Scottish missionary teaching at the Madras Christian College at the time, K. Kartensein from Switzerland, Walter Marshall from the United States, and H. H. Farmer from England.

Reaffirming his position on the radical discontinuity between the Christian revelation and any other religious presuppositions, Kraemer concluded, in his contribution to the conference's final message, that little had been accomplished at that stage of the ecumenical movement in terms of a common understanding of how Christian revelation relates to other religions, asserting that "a patient endeavor to understand and probe each other's presuppositions and starting points" was needed.[95] Chao, by his turn, stated that there are different levels of revelation, which people from different religious traditions can experience.

---

[92] Thomas, "An Assessment of Tambaram," 397.

[93] Hogg, *Ecumenical Foundations*, 298.

[94] International Missionary Council, *The Authority of the Faith*, The Madras Series, Presenting Papers Based upon the Meeting of the International Missionary Council, at Tambaram, Madras, India, December 12–29, 1938 (New York/London: International Missionary Council, 1939).

[95] Hendrik Kraemer, "Continuity or Discontinuity," in *The Authority of the Faith*, 6. In regard to the comparative study of religions, he says, "We have to adopt the attitude of an attentive and teachable hearer to the data presented to us by this branch of research. Comparative religion, however, can and must never become our authoritative guide. Its proper function is to be our intelligent and much appreciated informant." (10)

> The almighty God and all-loving God being the Creator of the universe, we can safely say that nature and man, in different but progressive orders, reveal God and His divine character and power. Nature reveals His power and intelligence while humanity reveals, especially in the lives of sages and prophets, His love and righteousness. All the nations, with their various religions, have seen God more or less clearly, although the forms in which their visions have been clothed are incomplete, insufficient and unsatisfactory. In them and in Jesus Christ, God has been revealing Himself, the same self, to mankind.[96]

While affirming the uniqueness of the Christian revelation, Chao did not see it as standing in contrast with other forms of divine revelation in history. Similarly, Hogg interpreted the uniqueness of the Christian faith in terms of the content of the revelation it bears witness to. He adopted, however, a positive attitude toward people of other faiths, acknowledging that many Hindus he knew, including Mahatma Gandhi, although not Christians, were clearly not strange to the ways of God.[97] Another important voice in the conversation, D. G. Moses, highlighted the inexhaustibility of the nature of God, which no human being can ever fully apprehend. Whereas affirming the uniqueness of the Christian revelation, he made enough room for a broader understanding of divine revelation, underscoring the role of reason in its apprehension.[98]

Thus, although the uniqueness of the Christian message was generally affirmed in Tambaram 1938, the conference's findings acknowledged the "values of deep religious experience and great moral achievements" in non-Christian traditions, while still asserting that Christ alone "is the full salvation which man needs."[99] Tambaram also affirmed that "the Church is called to a fuller and more adequate understanding of other religious faiths as total systems of life,"[100] urging it to "appropriate" whatever in "traditional cultures

---

[96] T. C. Chao, "Revelation," in *The Authority of the Faith*, 36–37.

[97] A. G. Hogg, "The Christian Attitude to Non-Christian Faith," in *The Authority of the Faith*, 102–125.

[98] D. G. Moses, "The Problem of Truth in Religion," in *The Authority of the Faith*, 63–89.

[99] IMC, *The Authority of the Faith*, 194.

[100] IMC, *The Authority of the Faith*, 195.

may contribute to the enrichment of its life and that of the Church universal,"[101] and to cooperate with people of other faiths "in all good social and community movements."[102]

Despite its limitations, the fact that Tambaram 1938 fostered an honest conversation about the tensions involved in the relations between Christianity and other religions vis-à-vis the task of evangelization points to an early ecumenical openness to dialogue with other faiths propelled by voices coming for the most part from the majority world. Of the greatest significance in that conversation is that the dominant Chinese and Indian interpretations of the Christian message and the important questions they raised offered critical insights that would inform future ecumenical conversations. Among other things, Tambaram provided new self-critical perspectives on how Christians should relate to other religions. The insights Tambaram offered for that conversation stemmed mainly from the widening of the church's ecumenicity that came with greater presence and participation of delegates from non-Western churches. Despite its focus on "the Church," Tambaram created conditions for an ecumenism that moved beyond ecclesiocentric concerns. Social, economic, political, and cultural factors were taken into account in the multifaceted experience of the so-called "younger churches," pushing Tambaram to reconsider questions of identity and belonging in religiously plural contexts.

At the end of the day, Tambaram inadvertently created the occasion for a revaluation of the Protestant missionary mindset, and for the expansion of the ecumenical horizons in regard to Christianity's relationship with different religions and cultures. Furthermore, in search of greater inclusion, the most diverse ecumenical event ever held at its time pointed to emerging differences in the self-understanding of Christians around the world, which would later be critical as the presence of a rapidly changing and widening world Christianity became more evident in ecumenical circles in the later decades of the past century. As the preparations for the creation of the WCC progressed, the IMC played a central role in assuring "the full representation of the churches of Asia, Africa, Latin America and the Pacific Islands" in the incipient ecumenical council, which

[101] IMC, *The Authority of the Faith*, 196.

[102] IMC, *The Authority of the Faith*, 197.

would become the main instrument of the ecumenical movement in the second half of the twentieth century.[103]

The influence of voices from the Global South on the agenda of the ecumenical movement has only increased since the formation of the World Council of Churches in 1948. Although a comprehensive investigation of the instances in which ecumenical agendas have expanded or changed due to the influence of Global South Christians is beyond the scope of this book, in the following chapters the reader will encounter several instances in which those situations happened, especially in connection with the increasing participation of Latin America in the ecumenical movement from the 1960s onward.

103 World Council of Churches, *The World Council of Churches: Its Process and Formation* (Geneva: World Council of Churches, 1946), 8.

2

THE RISE OF LATIN AMERICAN ECUMENISM

As underscored in the previous chapter, the ecumenical aspiration at the roots of the modern ecumenical movement predated the 1910 World Missionary Conference in Edinburgh at least by a century. Yet, the Edinburgh conference is commonly identified as the origin of the instruments that shaped the ecumenical movement in the twentieth century. While Edinburgh 1910 was a key turning point in a still insipient ecumenical movement, that conference does not tell the whole story of the movement that took shape in its wake. One of the reasons for that is the exclusion of Latin America from that critical conference.[1] The basis for that exclusion was that the conference was aimed to discuss the evangelization of the non-Christian world, and Latin America, along with other regions such as Catholic Europe, were considered to be part of Christendom—thus "beyond the horizons of Christian mission."[2] As Brian Stanley points out, the exclusion of Latin America from the Edinburgh 1910 agenda reinforced the existing tendency in Western missionary agencies to identify the West with Christianity—or Christendom—and the East (the Orient, as the Europeans called it at the time) with "heathendom."[3] Latin America was neither one nor the other or, perhaps, a combination of both.

Furthermore, the inclusion of Latin America in a conversation about world evangelization would have upset the Catholic Church. The Anglicans, key players in Edinburgh 1910, did not want that to happen. So, to diffuse potential tensions, the masterminds of that conference decided to leave Latin America out of it. An unintended

---

1 Justo L González and Ondina E. González, *Christianity in Latin America* (New York: Cambridge University Press, 2008), 236, Kindle. Only one African native leader was in Edinburgh, and no one from the Christian communities in the Pacific Islands, the Caribbean, Latin America, and "the tribal peoples of Southeast Asia" attended the Edinburgh conference. Stanley, *The World Missionary Conference*, loc. 279, Kindle.

2 Stanley, *The World Missionary Conference*, loc. 281, Kindle.

3 Stanley, *The World Missionary Conference*, loc. 972, Kindle.

effect of that absence, though, was the accentuation of the already-existing sentiment among British and American evangelicals that Latin America was a "neglected continent." That was the view, in particular, of American Protestant missionary agencies.[4]

In response to that absence, a group of American mission executives led by Robert E. Speer organized informal meetings during the Edinburgh conference to discuss Protestant missions vis-à-vis Latin America. Those informal meetings "led eventually to a conference on missions in Latin America, which was ultimately held in New York in March 1913 under the auspices of the Foreign Missions Conference of North America, which established a permanent body to co-ordinate American Protestant work on the continent, the Committee on Co-operation in Latin America."[5] In the years that followed, the CCLA would take the lead in a number of initiatives seeking to advance the Protestant evangelization of Latin America. That collaborative missionary work would create the conditions for the rise of an incipient Latin American ecumenical network in the following decades.[6]

Protestant missions began to establish themselves in Latin America in the early decades of the nineteenth century. Protestant proselytism

---

[4] Stanley, *The World Missionary Conference*, loc. 1582, Kindle. The land currently known as Latin America has many Indigenous names. One of them is Abya Yala, "Mature Land, Living Land or Earth in Flourishing," as it is known by the Kuna People. As Beatriz Carrera and Zara Ruiz Ribeiro point out, the recognition of the name Abya Yala "is in itself a symbol of identity and respect for the roots of the native peoples." While for the most part using Latin America to refer to this region in this book, I occasionally use Abya Yala, acknowledging the Indigenous origins of the land and Indigenous continuous resistance to the genocide they have experienced over five centuries. See "Prólogo" in *Abya Yala Wawgeykun. Artes, saberes y vivencias de indígenas americanos,* ed. Beatriz Carrera Maldonado and Zara Ruiz Romero (Madrid: Acer-vos, 2016), 12.

[5] Stanley, *The World Missionary Conference*, loc. 3755–3757, Kindle. British evangelical missionaries offered a parallel response to the same situation through "the formation in 1911 of the Evangelical Union of South America (now Latin Link)," loc. 3790, Kindle.

[6] Wilfred Scopes, ed., *The Christian Ministry in Latin America and the Caribbean*. Report of a survey of the Evangelical Churches undertaken February to May, 1961 on behalf of the International Missionary Council (now the Commission on World Mission and Evangelism of the World Council of Churches) (Geneva/London/New York: Commission on World Mission and Evangelism of the World Council of Churches, 1962), 21.

of Catholics in a region controlled by the Roman Catholic Church was often the cause of tensions between Protestant missionaries and national Catholic hierarchies. Edinburgh 1910 sought to avoid such a tension by focusing exclusively on the evangelization of non-Christian lands. US Protestant missions, however, were not going to stop their work in the region. They had come to stay and were eager to compete for Latin American converts with the Catholic Church.

By the early 1900s, when the first ecumenical institutions began to emerge in the region, Protestantism was seeking to deepen its roots in a territory still strongly associated with Catholicism.[7] Adding to a Protestantism transplanted from Europe to Latin America throughout the nineteenth century through migration, mission-oriented Protestant churches were established in the region mostly through the work of US denominations in the second half of that century. Those emerging churches initially had limited appeal to Latin American natives, since their evangelism depended significantly on the literacy of the communities they intended to reach. In addition to that, the evangelized needed to show a rational understanding of the gospel, by deciding to break with what the missionaries portrayed as an idolatrous and promiscuous past in order to achieve salvation.

Furthermore, by the time the World Missionary Conference met in Edinburgh, a popular form of Protestantism was also emerging in the region: Pentecostalism. By the end of the twentieth-century, that popular Protestant Christian stream would be the fastest-growing form of Christianity in the continent.[8]

The arrival of Protestantism in Latin America did not happen in a vacuum. The late nineteenth century and early twentieth century also

[7] Dafne Sabanes Plou, "Latin America," in *A History of the Ecumenical Movement, 1968–2000*, vol. 3, ed. John Briggs, Mercy Amba Oduyoye, and Georges Tsetsis (Geneva: World Council of Churches, 2004), 565–589 (565).

[8] In 1909, a split in the Chilean Methodist Church gave birth to the first Pentecostal church in the continent, the Methodist Pentecostal Church. See Néstor O. Míguez, "Latin America," in *The Oxford Handbook of Ecumenical Studies*, ed. Geoffrey Wainwright and Paul McPartlan (Oxford, UK: Oxford University Press, 2021), 527–535 (528). In the next couple of years, American migrants from Sweden and Italy would independently establish the two first Brazilian Pentecostal churches, Congregação Cristã no Brasil (1910) and Assembleias de Deus do Brasil (1911). See Paulo Barrera Rivera, "Pentecostalism in Brazil," in *Handbook of Religions in Brazil*, ed. Bettina E. Schmidt and Steven Engler (Leiden, NL: Brill, 2016), 117–131 (118).

witnessed the rise of American empire, which stretched its reach and interests toward the southern part of the continent through the articulation of ideological justifications such as the Monroe Doctrine and the Manifest Destiny. Both ideologies instilled a new understanding of the US as a continental power, justifying its territorial expansion to the south and west, which culminated with the absorption of Spanish-speaking territories from the 1830s to the Spanish-American War in 1898, when the US took control of Cuba, Puerto Rico, the Philippines Islands, and Guam.[9]

Land speculation in Central America, the control of the Panama Canal, the building of railroads to transport bananas, and outright political and military intervention in southern neighbor countries altogether signaled the growing US imperial ambitions, preparing the way for US dominion over the Americas in the twentieth century. The *Pax Americana* established through the Treaty of Paris that formally put an end to the Spanish-American War,[10] created the conditions for the expansion of US economic and political interests south of the Mexico-US border. US-controlled fruit companies became major political actors, aggressively interfering with state policies in countries such as Costa Rica, Nicaragua, Honduras, Guatemala, Colombia, and Cuba to further private power and interests and limit state control in the territories where those companies owned huge tracts of land. In 1899, those fruit companies merged to form the United Fruit Company (UFCO). At its peak, the UFCO "owned more than 230,000 acres throughout the region and 112 miles of railroad."[11] The growing evangelistic ambitions of US missionary agencies toward Latin America at that historical juncture was, therefore, perceived by many in Latin America as one of the multiple faces of the southward expansion of the American empire.

All these things took place in a region that had undergone anti-imperial wars of independence for most of the nineteenth century. The unexpectedly successful Haitian Revolution against colonial French control in 1804 was followed by a sequence of independence movements throughout the continent. By the time Brazil declared its

[9] Juan Gonzalez, *Harvest of Empire: A History of Latinos in America*, second revised and updated edition (New York: Penguin Books, 2022), 30–31.

[10] Gonzalez, *Harvest of Empire*, 65.

[11] Gonzalez, *Harvest of Empire*, 65.

independence from Portugal in 1822, Chile (1810), Colombia (1810), Mexico (1810), Paraguay (1811), Venezuela (1811), Argentina (1816), Costa Rica (1821), El Salvador (1821), Guatemala (1821), Honduras (1821), Nicaragua (1821), Peru (1821), and Ecuador (1822) had all already freed themselves from the dominion of Spain.

In 1823, US President James Monroe (1758–1831) "declared the entire hemisphere off-limits to European colonialism but also implied that the new Latin American nations would be under U.S. tutelage and direction."[12] In the decades that followed, that doctrine legitimated US imperial ambitions. Its transcendental garment—the Manifest Destiny—first used to justify the US westward expansion, turned into a tool to support the US self-proclaimed leadership as the bearer of democratic values and economic progress in the Americas. As Justo and Ondina González point out, the Manifest Destiny would be used later "to justify repeated interventions in various Latin American countries—interventions depicted as part of a historic mission to defend and promote democracy throughout the hemisphere."[13] The combination of these doctrines suggests a mandate of political, economic, and religious/cultural dominion. US missionary agencies drew on that same transcendental garment, interpreting it, though, as a call to expand the Protestant faith throughout the continent.[14]

Considering the parameters of Edinburgh 1910, the Protestant evangelization of a territory already Christianized by the Catholic Church needed to be justified. As Costa Rican historian Arturo Piedra points out, John Mott played an important role in the articulation of such a justification, allying himself with those who saw Latin America as a Protestant mission field. For him, the Catholic Church had failed the task to evangelize Latin America. Affirming the moral and religious superiority of the Protestant faith and concerned with widespread "moral vices" such as alcoholism, Mott and his North American colleagues did not see any significant difference between the moral state of Latin America and that which

[12] González & González, *Christianity in Latin America*, 206–207.

[13] González & González, *Christianity in Latin America*, 207.

[14] Arturo Piedra, *Evangelización Protestante en América Latina: Análisis de las razones que justificaron y promovieron la expansión protestante 1830–1960*, Tomo I (Quito: CLAI, 2001), 120.

justified Protestant missions in Africa or Asia.[15] For them, Latin American Catholicism was for the most part nominal: "A great deal of paganism" persisted.[16]

The proper evangelization of the region depended on the work of Protestant missions. Since the previous Christianization of the region had not properly done the job, the "Protestantization" of the continent was imperative. The meetings of US missionary executives to discuss the Latin American situation in Edinburgh, then, set the stage for a coordinated response that would lead to major developments in Latin American Protestantism. Key for the success of that enterprise was cooperation among diverse Protestant mission agencies. The creation of the Committee on Cooperation in Latin America (CCLA) in 1913 and the organization of the Congress on Christian Work in Latin America in 1916 were critical steps toward that goal. By contrast, those events also became milestones for the rise of ecumenical Latin American Protestantism.

The Committee on Cooperation in Latin America (CCLA) and the Panama Congress

The response to the exclusion of Latin America from Edinburgh 1910 was twofold. On the one hand, British Protestant missionaries working with small agencies in countries like Peru, Argentina, and Brazil joined "forces to form the Evangelical Union of South America (EUSA)," giving birth to a European interdenominational mission initiative in the region.[17] Of greater consequence for the future ecumenical articulation in the continent, however, was the meeting of North American missionary agencies in New York City in 1913, which resulted in the creation of the Committee on Cooperation in Latin America (CCLA).[18] Samuel Guy Inman (1877–1965), who would serve as the first CCLA executive secretary for the coming twenty-five years (1913–1938), described its origins as follows:

[15] Piedra, *Evangelización Protestante en América Latina*, 121.

[16] Stanley, *The World Missionary Conference*, loc. 756 and 3755, Kindle.

[17] See Latin Link, "History," at https://latinlink.org.uk/about-us/history, accessed on Oct. 14, 2022. See also, Stanley, *The World Missionary Conference*, loc. 3790, Kindle.

[18] The CCLA was constituted by the various Protestant mission boards from the United States and Canada that sustained missionary work in Latin America.

> The failure of the World Missionary Conference to discuss the problems of Latin America, and the growing interest in these lands on account of the opening of the Panama Canal and other Pan-American developments, led the Foreign Missionary Conference of North America to appoint, in 1913, a committee to organize a small conference on Latin America. At this conference, held in New York in 1913, a committee was appointed to deal with questions of cooperation in Latin America. This committee was afterward enlarged by practically all the Boards working in Latin America officially appointing members of it.[19]

Inman, one of the key participants in that gathering, was aware of both the religious and political motivations informing that enterprise. It was clear for him that the CCLA embodied the United States's geopolitical and religious interests in Latin America. Such aspirations were more significant to their actions than any demands coming from Latin American peoples or churches themselves. Since no Latin American attended the World Missionary Congress in Edinburgh, the informal meetings that discussed Latin American missions during that congress included only British and North American missionaries. The founding meeting of the CCLA, in 1913 was also an exclusively North American missionary event. Beginning at the meetings in Edinburgh 1910, mission agencies interested in Latin America began to discuss the organization of a conference similar to the one in Edinburgh with a focus on Christian missions in the Latin American continent.[20]

The newly-founded CCLA elected Robert E. Speer (1867–1947), then the secretary of the Presbyterian Board of Foreign Missions, as its chairperson. Samuel Guy Inman, who had spent a decade as a missionary in Mexico, was chosen to be the executive secretary. In their respective capacities, these two men were the main conveners of the Congress on Christian Work in Latin America, which would take place in Panama City on February 10–19, 1916. The mission boards comprising the CCLA divided Latin America into specific

---

[19] Samuel Guy Inman, *Christian Cooperation in Latin America: Report of a Visit to Mexico, Cuba and South America, March-October, 1917* (New York: CCLA, 1917), 32.

[20] Erasmo Braga, *Pan-Americanismo: Aspecto Religioso* (New York: Missionary EducationMovement of the United States and Canada, 1916), 82.

areas of influence to coordinate and distribute their evangelizing responsibilities.

The coordinated action of the CCLA resulted in the significant growth in the number of missionaries connected with the CCLA in Latin American countries following the Panama Congress, and in the increasing ownership of land and properties in the region by mission boards. Whereas at the time of the Panama Congress in 1916 there were 777 North American missionaries in Latin America, five years later that number had increased to 1,066. Likewise, in 1916 these mission boards were estimated to own the equivalent of $6,494,762 in real estate in Latin America. Five years later, that estimated amount had grown to $9,789,649. That rapidly growing missionary investment in the region had an impact on the development of ecumenical collaboration, funding the creation of a number of united (across denominational lines) institutions in Latin America such as seminaries, colleges, hospitals, newspapers, bookstores, and literature.[21]

While Panama 1916 was an indirect outgrowth of Edinburgh 1910, it had no formal connection with the work of the Edinburgh Continuation Committee that had been created to coordinate the next steps of the work toward Christian international cooperation, as discussed in chapter one. Although the CCLA was organized by individuals who had close ties with the Edinburgh Continuation Committee, the Panama Congress was sponsored independently. Its similarity to the Edinburgh Conference, nevertheless, is undeniable. Panama 1916 even replicated the eight commissions of Edinburgh 1910.[22]

In contrast to the 1913 inaugural meeting of the CCLA in New York, the Panama Congress invited participants from different parts of Latin America. Eduardo Montero, a professor at the University of Uruguay and a member of the Montevideo's Young Men's Christian Association (YMCA), presided over the meeting. The main shapers of the Panama Congress, though, were Robert Speer, who chaired

[21] Committee on Cooperation in Latin America, *Committee On Cooperation in Latin America: Report for 1921* (New York: Committee on Cooperation in Latin America, 1921), 2–3.

[22] Hogg, "The Christian Attitude to Non-Christian Faith," 173.

the working sessions, John R. Mott, who chaired the business committee, and Samuel Guy Inman, who worked for more than a year preparing the structure and program of the congress.[23] Panama 1916 had three hundred and four official delegates. Half of them were Latin American natives. There were also delegates from the United States, Canada, England, Spain, and Italy, and nearly five hundred visitors (non-delegates attending the meetings).[24]

The Congress offered the first opportunity for Latin American nationals and foreign missionaries to come together to discuss Protestant cooperation in the region. Like Edinburgh 1910, this was a missionary congress with an initial emphasis on cooperation among mission agencies. However, it ended up contributing significantly to the birth of the initial Latin American ecumenical structures. Like Edinburgh 1910, the Panama Congress envisioned "a continuing organization to perpetuate the co-operative endeavor it had initiated." Instead of creating a Continuation Committee, though, it designated the CCLA to serve as the body that would play such a role.[25] In addition to coordinating the missionary efforts to meet the needs and demands of the Latin American people, the CCLA also articulated a "rationale for missions in Latin America to the world missionary movement."[26]

An important issue for the CCLA was to figure out how to deal with the Catholic Church in Latin America. Different tones were adopted in response to that question. Some Protestant missions in the CCLA rejected the idea of any Catholic participation in the Panama congress. The CCLA as a whole, however, sought to avoid the anti-Catholicism that characterized some US Protestant missions. The title of the Panama Congress, for instance, was changed as a concession on the part of its Protestant organizers to the Catholic Church. Originally, mimicking Edinburgh 1910, the title was supposed to be "The Latin American Missionary Conference." However, due to the efforts on the part of some leaders of the CCLA to avoid

---

23 Hogg, "The Christian Attitude to Non-Christian Faith," 173. It is worth noting, though, that this was just a temporary leadership. All the members of the CCLA at the time were from the United States or Canada.

24 Hogg, "The Christian Attitude to Non-Christian Faith," 173–174.

25 Hogg, "The Christian Attitude to Non-Christian Faith," 174.

26 Orlandi, "From Christian Continent to Mission Field," 9.

offending the Catholic Church, the title of the gathering was changed to "Congress on Christian Work in Latin America."[27]

Even though no Catholic representative attended the congress, Catholic leaders in the region were invited to join. The general sentiment was that all Christians were welcome in the efforts to complete the missionary task in Latin America and the Caribbean. Some of the congress organizers suggested that the CCLA gave the Catholic Church the same treatment some Christian missions had often given to Judaism. For them, the Protestant goal was not to destroy Catholic Christianity but to fulfill it.[28] Furthermore, the justification for pressing missionary cooperation in Latin America should focus not on converting Catholics but on reaching out to Latin American younger generations whom Catholic existing influence had failed to reach and who were, consequently, becoming increasingly secular. Likewise, concern with Christianizing the "unreached" Indigenous population was another key element in the agenda of the congress.[29]

From the perspective of the Catholic hierarchy, however, not only were Protestants unduly invading their territory (territorial occupation was an expression used in CCLA reports), but they also saw Protestant missions as part of the growing imperialistic designs of the United States in the region. The choice of Panama as the location of the congress two years after the inauguration of the Panama Canal suggested that the US empire was flexing its muscles. A generally negative—sometimes even belligerent—attitude towards the Iberian-Catholic culture was also perceptible among members of the CCLA. Even some apparently more open-minded leaders such as Inman, who was highly influenced by the social gospel and his long tenure as a missionary in Mexico, used warlike references in his articulation of "the task before the evangelical churches," seeking a more sustained missionizing strategy that would turn the CCLA and

[27] John H. Sinclair and Arturo Piedra Solano, "The Dawn of Ecumenism in Latin America: Robert E. Speer, Presbyterians, and the Panama Conference of 1916," *The Journal of Presbyterian History*, 77/1 (1999): 1–11 (6).

[28] Sinclair and Solano, "The Dawn of Ecumenism in Latin America," 4. To Catholic ears, though, the arrogance and sense of superiority implied in that kind of approach was similarly offensive.

[29] Committee on Cooperation in Latin America, *Christian Work in Latin America*, vol. 1 (New York: TheMissionary Education Movement, 1917), 13–14.

its regional committees into advanced posts to support and equip the rise of national churches.[30]

Inman, one of the key masterminds of Panama 1916, would later acknowledge the limits of the Pan-American ideal that had fueled the mission agencies behind the congress.[31] A Disciple of Christ's minister who had previously worked in Hell's Kitchen, Inman had a more nuanced view of the relationship between the United States and Latin America than several of his colleagues. Interested in the well-being of the whole person, he reflected on the different stages of Pan-Americanism: from Simón Bolívar, who promoted the idea of inter-American friendship, to the Monroe Doctrine, to the increasing use of dollar diplomacy and "big stick" policies on the part of the United States. In contrast, he urged for a better understanding of the South American peoples and cultures on the part of US missionaries and the elimination of the bravado attitude many in the US held in relation to their southern neighbors that had generated both economic and military coercion.[32]

The great novelty of the Panama Congress was that it offered a continental platform for Latin American leaders who were absent from previous conversations among mission agencies about the future of Latin America. The decisions made until that point about the task of the Protestant missions had rarely involved Latin American Christians. The Panama Congress created the opportunity for rising Latin American Protestant leaders to take a seat at the table and participate in the discussions about the future of Christianity in the continent. Panama 1916 also emphasized the training of national leadership.[33] For that purpose, Inman proposed the formation of ecumenical centers whose impact on the Christian work in the region, he believed, would be "impossible to estimate."[34] The Panama Congress operated under the premise that "the people must be reached through their own nationals."[35]

---

[30] Inman, *Christian Cooperation in Latin America*, 29–30.

[31] Samuel Guy Inman, *Problems in Pan Americanism* (New York: George H. Doran Company, 1921).

[32] Inman, *Problems in Pan Americanism*, 323ff.

[33] Inman, *Christian Cooperation in Latin America*, 21.

[34] Inman, *Christian Cooperation in Latin America*, 23.

[35] Inman, *Christian Cooperation in Latin America*, 24.

While missionaries such as Inman, Speer, and John A. Mackay (1889–1983) would continue to play prominent roles in the leadership of CCLA in the following years, bringing attention to Latin America in major international ecumenical gatherings, the Panama Congress was a watershed in the process of identifying Latin American leaders who could carry its vision forward. Those select national leaders would soon become the main faces and voices of the "neglected continent" in global ecumenical settings. Among those rising national leaders, some of the most prominent were Brazilian Presbyterian Erasmo Braga (1877–1932), Mexican Congregationalist Alberto Rembao (1895–1962), and Mexican Methodist Gonzalo Báez-Camargo (1899–1983). As Carlos Cardoza Orlandi underscores, these men became important "interlocutors between the Latin American religious context and the North American mission boards, CCLA, and the World Missionary Conferences of Jerusalem and Madras."[36]

After the Panama Congress, the CCLA asserted its position as a body "thoroughly representative of all the Christian forces of Europe and North America serving Latin America," which acted "as a continuation committee for the Congress."[37] By 1917, regional committees on cooperation had been organized in "Mexico, Cuba, Peru, Panama, Bolivia, Chile, Argentina (including Uruguay and Paraguay), and Brazil,"[38] and plans for united efforts on theological education and publication were underway in various Latin American countries. The CCLA had three secretaries. Inman continued to serve as its Executive Secretary, now joined by George B. Winton (Editorial Secretary), and Webster E. Browning (Educational Secretary for South America).[39]

In his extensive travel throughout Latin America after the Panama Congress, Inman offered a detailed picture of the prospects and challenges the Protestant work experienced in the region. Among other things, he noticed that one of the main challenges for Protestantism in Latin America was the largely held perception that it was a foreign religion, not only due to the growing presence of US and European

36 Orlandi, "From Christian Continent to Mission Field," 10–11.

37 Inman, *Christian Cooperation in Latin America*, 32.

38 Inman, *Christian Cooperation in Latin America*, 34.

39 Inman, *Christian Cooperation in Latin America*, 35.

missionaries in the region, but also because of the way many national leaders communicated it.

> A peculiarly interesting comment on this matter of the missionary's language was made to me by several Latin Americans when they pointed out the fact that often the native ministers, after long association with the missionaries, came to use much of the foreign order in their speaking. Several said that they could not enjoy the preaching of these native ministers because they used so many foreign forms. This, of course, contributes to the feeling that is largely held that Protestantism is a foreign religion and that those who embrace it are in a way denying their own country and identifying themselves with North America.[40]

This statement draws attention to long-existing sentiments among Latin Americans regarding a deeply ingrained influence of an Anglo-Saxon mentality on the diffusion of the Protestant faith in the region, even as national leaders were beginning to play more prominent roles. These tensions would later motivate initiatives among more national Protestants to affirm the "Latin Americanness" of the Protestant faith in the region. Inman himself saw the need for a Christian message that included the peculiarities of the Latin American culture. In response to what he heard during his 1917 tour of Latin America, Inman realized that it was important to affirm Christianity as a universal religion, which, therefore, included "the Latin American as well as the Anglo-Saxon, the Oriental and all other nations, to make up its perfect whole."[41] In order to overcome that perception of Protestantism as a foreign religion in Latin America, Inman encouraged the missionary boards represented in the CCLA to get more acquainted with the Latin American literature that addressed the problems faced in the region, and to form friendships with the leaders of the nations where they served.

According to the CCLA report of December 31, 1919, the Panama Congress gathered representatives from "more than fifty different organizations interested in the spiritual life of Latin America."[42] In

---

[40] Inman, *Christian Cooperation in Latin America*, 165.

[41] Inman, *Christian Cooperation in Latin America*, 165.

[42] Committee on Cooperation in Latin America, *Report of Committee on Cooperation in Latin America, Representing the American and Canadian Mission Boards*

the evaluation of that Committee, three years after the Congress, the work done since that important gathering had deeply changed the relationship between the missionary boards represented in the CCLA and Latin America. Previously a neglected continent, without "a union school, union paper or union administrative committee in all Latin America," the situation, according to the report, now looked different. By the end of 1919, "seven regional conferences were held in the important centers of Latin America immediately following Panama and aided in outlining a comprehensive program for the whole field."[43] At the time the report was published, the CCLA was developing a continental-wide program continent-wide, which included the formation of "[r]egional committees in each section of Latin America, whose officially appointed members come together to study the entire work of that field."[44] Likewise, it had also started a monthly review, "La Nueva Democracia," which would be published between 1920 and 1964, circulating throughout Latin America.

The Committee also established united-run periodicals in Mexico and Cuba, and united Protestant seminaries in Puerto Rico and Brazil, while planning new follow-up continent-wide conferences. Another type of action the CCLA engaged was the promotion of temperance campaigns in conjunction with national temperance societies. In addition to the efforts to produce publications in Spanish and Portuguese, the Committee also sought to gain greater visibility in the Anglophone world, with publications about its work appearing in important secular and religious newspapers and magazines, including the "New York Evening Post, Boston Transcript, the Outlook, the Survey, South American, Pan American Magazine, Pan American Review, Educational Foundations, Missionary Review of the World, World Outlook, Student World, Intercollegian, Missionary Year Book, Missionary Voice, Christian Work, Christian Century, Christian Evangelist and World Call."[45] In addition, the

---

Working in Latin America (New York: Committee on Cooperation in Latin America, 1919), 1.

[43] Committee on Cooperation in Latin America, *Report of Committee on Cooperation in Latin America*, 1.

[44] Committee on Cooperation in Latin America, *Report of Committee on Cooperation in Latin America*, 2.

[45] Committee on Cooperation in Latin America, *Report of Committee on Cooperation in Latin America*, 13.

Home Missions Council in the US asked the CCLA "to act as its committee on Spanish-speaking work in the United States." Such a move allowed the committee to give the Interdenominational Council on Spanish-Speaking Work in the United States the same status the regional committees formed in Latin American countries had in the CCLA structure.[46]

Another area that got increasing traction in the work of the CCLA was the lay ministry of women, as seen on the report of the Commission V "on Women's Work" at the Panama Congress.[47] This was the first report of the kind with a Latin American focus. Earlier mobilization of women in mission resulted in the organization of the Women's Union Missionary Society in New York City in 1861. Between then and 1874, most Protestant churches in the United States organized Women's Boards of Missions. A number of those women ended up serving as missionaries in Latin America. Among them, Melinda Rankin (1811–1888) and Frances S. Hamilton (?–1915) in Mexico, and Martha Watts (1848–1909) in Brazil.[48] The report of Commission V highlighted, among others, the work of Josefa Dominguez, "the heroine of Mexican independence," in the struggles for freedom in Latin America,[49] offering a glimpse into the diverse contributions women made to Latin American societies—including Indigenous women. Citing American author Charles M. Pepper's description of the Indigenous women in Bolivia, the report stated,

> The Indian woman in Bolivia occupies a plane on an equality with man. She has no lord and master like the North American Indian. She works, but he also must work. She accompanies him with the pack trains, all the while as she trudges along, twirling her spools, and winding the wool into yarn; it is rare to see her without her spools, unless she is weaving at the loom.[50]

---

[46] Committee on Cooperation in Latin America, *Report of Committee on Cooperation in Latin America*, 13.

[47] Committee on Cooperation in Latin America, *Christian Work in Latin America*, vol. 2 (New York: The Missionary Education Movement, 1917), 103ff.

[48] Committee on Cooperation in Latin America, *Christian Work in Latin America*, 115ff.

[49] Committee on Cooperation in Latin America, *Christian Work in Latin America*, 123.

[50] Committee on Cooperation in Latin America, *Christian Work in Latin America*, 137.

This early recognition of non-patriarchal societal models among certain Indigenous peoples in Abya Yala in this report is remarkable and rare.

Whereas one can easily find derogatory and inaccurate references to Indigenous peoples and cultures on CCLA reports, this report coming from Commission V, an all-women commission, portrayed Indigenous life in Latin America in a more positive light. Other CCLA reports coming from the same congress referred to the Indigenous populations as primitive, pagan, and barbarian.[51]

The report of Commission V also highlighted the role of Latin American women in education, identifying the need for schools to train deaconesses, Bible women, social workers, and teachers, among others, and pointing to possibilities of collaboration with existing Latin American schools. At the same time, it described the Protestant schools in Latin American countries as spaces for the education of women. Diverging from the conventional distance Protestants usually took from Catholicism in Latin America, the report highlighted three important Catholic schools—two in Santiago and one in Lima—which focused on girls' education. Commission V also noted that Latin Americans were developing their own educational system, that only few women benefited from higher education, and that *liceum* education appealed mostly to upper-class women, making ecumenical cooperation imperative to fill the gaps in literature, education, and social and evangelistic work in the region.[52]

Despite all the contributions the CCLA's conferences, initiatives and national committees made to the rise of Latin American ecumenism, it remained under the control of North American mission boards. Its headquarters were located in New York City. The geopolitical framework it operated with continued to be that of the Pan-Americanism "promoted by US bureaucrats" and "often denounced by progressive Latin American intellectuals, union leaders, nationalists, and left-leaning leaders at the time as a mechanism to improve and stabilize economic relations between Latin America

[51] See, for instance, Committee on Cooperation in Latin America, *Christian Work in Latin America*, volume 1 (New York: The Missionary Education Movement, 1917), 253.

[52] Committee on Cooperation in Latin America, *Christian Work in Latin America*, vol. 2, 193.

and the United States and secure the expansion of US interests."[53] Despite celebrating the rise of local churches and leaders, many of the CCLA-affiliated missionaries continued to describe them as immature, lacking proper biblical knowledge, being morally lax, or having a distorted understanding of sin,[54] perceiving themselves, by contrast, as morally and spiritually superior.

Whereas conservative Protestant missions in Latin America focused primarily on personal evangelism and conversion, ecumenical individuals and agencies influenced by the social gospel concentrated their efforts on education and the recruitment of Latin American elites. Such a strategy, they believed, would lead to significant social change in the long run. Those emphases and strategies, though, were not mutually exclusive. In most cases, Protestant missions included both the personal and the social dimensions of the evangelizing task in their agenda.

The more it was immersed in the Latin American context, the more the CCLA understood that the future of the Latin American churches depended on the rise of leaders "born and bred in Latin America."[55] However, because they considered that the moral and spiritual formation of those nationals was deficient, the mission agencies that formed the CCLA concluded that qualified Indigenous leaders were difficult to find. Therefore, they should develop such leaders themselves. They devised two main strategies to achieve that goal: (1) identify promising leaders in Protestant seminaries in Latin America and train them where they live; and (2) send promising students to North America or Europe for theological training.[56] The former was preferred. In the following two decades those national

[53] Rosa Bruno-Jofré, "To Those in 'Heathen Darkness': Deweyan Democracy and Education in the American Interdenominational Configuration—The Case of the Committee on Cooperation in Latin America," in *Democracy and the Intersection of Religion: The Reading of John Dewey's Understanding of Democracy and Education*, by Rosa Bruno-Jofré et al (Montreal and Kingston: McGill-Queen's University Press, 2010), 131–170 (134).

[54] Committee on Cooperation in Latin America, *Christian Work in Latin America*, volume 2, 230ff.

[55] Committee on Cooperation in Latin America, *Christian Work in Latin America*, 277.

[56] Committee on Cooperation in Latin America, *Christian Work in Latin America*, 282.

leaders would rise to prominence in ecumenical circles. Among other things, their ascendance to key positions of leadership would raise new tensions, reinforcing the clamor for the Latin Americanization of the Protestant churches in the region.

Latin American Protestantism Comes of Age

The Panama Congress was the first of a series of events that prompted sustained conversation about the relationship between gospel and culture among Latin American Protestants. Prominent Latin American Protestant leaders such as Erasmo Braga were interested in the merging between the Protestant faith and what he considered to be Latin American high ideals, dreaming of a Protestantism that would become a vital agent of social change and a channel for moral and political progress in the region.[57] While some of the initial work of the CCLA as envisioned by North American Mission Boards reinforced US imperialistic views toward Latin America, being ideologically molded through the lens of Manifest Destiny,[58] the CCLA gradually, though not necessarily wittingly, set in motion processes that would contribute to the rise of a Latin American Protestant consciousness within incipient ecumenical circles in the region. Two continental CCLA congresses followed Panama 1916, meeting respectively in Montevideo (1925) and Havana (1929).

As I have discussed elsewhere, the continental gatherings in Montevideo and Havana played a critical role in the process of "Latin-Americanization" of the Protestant institutions in the region.[59] The conversations they prompted forced emerging ecumenical Latin American leaders to face the inviability of an uncritical embracing of the Pan-American framework North American mission boards sought to advance in Panama 1916. Paradoxically, as Jean-Pierre Bastian points out, the young Latin American Protestant leaders that CCLA had invested in became privileged interpreters and embodied

[57] Julio Andrade Ferreira, *O Profeta da Unidade: Erasmo Braga, Uma Vida a Descoberto* (Petrópolis, Brazil: Vozes, 1975).

[58] Jean-Pierre Bastian, *Breve Historia del Protestantismo en America Latina* (Mexico City: Casa Unida de Publicaciones, 1986), 116.

[59] Raimundo C. Barreto, *Protesting Poverty: Protestants, Social Ethics, and the Poor in Brazil* (Waco, TX: Baylor University Press, 2023), 99–101.

expressions of Pan-Americanism.[60] Some of them naively endorsed an understanding of Pan-Americanism that did not fully consider its neocolonial implications, thus contributing to the view of Latin America and the Caribbean as "a virtual U.S. sphere of influence."[61]

Brazilian Presbyterian pastor Carlos Eduardo Pereira (1855–1923), one of the three Brazilian delegates to the Panama Congress, articulated a Pan-American agenda that emphasized the self-interest of other nations besides the United States. Pereira, who also attended CCLA-sponsored regional meetings in Lima, Santiago, Buenos Aires, and Rio de Janeiro in the wake of Panama 1916, was a controversial figure in the eyes of some North American missionaries. Representing a growing nationalist sentiment among certain sectors of Brazilian Presbyterianism, he opposed the subordination of Brazilian Presbyteries to American boards and advanced inclusive policies in the Presbyterian schools in Brazil to allow the participation of Catholics.[62] Paradoxically, he had been one of the fiercest voices questioning the hesitance of the organizers of the Panama Congress to criticize the Roman Catholic Church. His quarrel with US Presbyterian missionaries was at the center of the first schism within Brazilian Presbyterianism, with Pereira and his followers leaving the Presbyterian Church of Brazil, founded by American missionaries, to organize the Independent Presbyterian Church of Brazil under the banners of nationalism, autonomy, and anti-Masonry in 1903. In spite of that, Pereira supported the Pan-American agenda of the Panama congress. Although aware that such an agenda could be used to advance potential imperialistic interests instead of opposing it, he opted for subverting it by interpreting the Pan-Americanism proposed in Panama 1916 as a continental alliance for peace, democracy and freedom based on the common interests of all nations involved.[63] Accordingly, he defined Pan-Americanism as

---

60 Bastian, *Breve Historia del Protestantismo*, 11.

61 Gonzalez, *Harvest of Empire*, 43. As Gonzalez notes, Bolívar was "weary of the growing arrogance from North Americans." Before he died, he stated that "the United States seemed 'destined by Providence to plague America with torments in the name of freedom.'" Bastian, *Breve Historia del Protestantismo*, 11.

62 Paul E. Pierson, *A Younger Church in Search of Maturity: Presbyterianism in Brazil from 1910 to 1959* (San Antonio: Trinity University Press, 1974), 34–35.

63 Carlos Eduardo Pereira, *O Problema Religioso na América Latina: Estudo Dogmático Histórico* (São Paulo: Empresa Editora Brasileira, 1920), 145–146.

> [T]he affirmation of continental consciousness, which is gradually illuminating the light of freedom and progress; and the noble feeling of solidarity of the peoples of the Western Hemisphere, who babble peace and love, in this anguished moment, when an entire continent is drowning in the blood of a barbaric and fratricidal war.[64]

Pereira was not naive. He was fully aware of how that term had been largely interpreted in light of the Monroe Doctrine. By praising it as a pact based on continental altruism, informed by reciprocal "national interests and conveniences," he turned that idea on its head.[65]

Braga, on the other hand, adopted a view that was more aligned with US ideals. In his report of the Panama Congress, he identified his point of view as one coming from a South American Christian influenced by the evangelical, liberal, and democratic ideas professed by his parents. However, as someone who had lived in the company of Anglo-Americans for many years, Braga saw himself also "as a disciple and as a teacher at the work of the implementation, in Brazil, of the practical methods of American pedagogy."[66] Braga, a high school teacher in the state public schools of São Paulo, and a journalist, would later produce the *Série Braga* (1919), an educational series for elementary school, which was implemented on the national level and influenced Brazilian teachers and students for decades. *Série Braga* was a showcase of Braga's belief in the merging of Protestant values and Latin American ideals for societal change.[67] He understood the nationalist sentiments on the part of many in Latin America as well as their fear that US missionary efforts were advancing imperialistic interests in the region. Yet, he chose to believe in the promise of collaboration between what he called the Saxon and the Latin elements in the Americas.

> It is fair to hope that an intelligent approximation of the two elements in America will have excellent results, producing

64 Pereira, *O Problema Religioso na América Latina*, 143.

65 Pereira, *O Problema Religioso na América Latina*, 156.

66 Braga, *Pan-americanismo*, iv.

67 Ferreira, *O Profeta da Unidade*, 103ff.

> the correction of idiosyncrasies and the exchange of precious qualities.[68]

Accordingly, Braga recalled that Latin American liberals always "looked up to Washington, Franklin, Jefferson and Hamilton as the patriarchs of American democracy upon which they molded the constitutions of their nations."[69] He also saw "Monroeism" through a positive lens, describing it as a guarantee against the possibility of European imperialism.[70]

Despite his pro-American sentiments, Braga admitted that the Pan-American commercial framework born out of the Washington Conference of 1889 caused legitimate concerns among Latin Americans about the possibility that the new doctrine would bring with it the "germ of the northern eagle's dominance."[71] At the end of the day, though, Braga was convinced that the distorted views on both ends of the continent resulted from imperfect and unilateral knowledge, which should be overcome. He believed, for instance, in the benefits that North American schools and missions had brought to Latin America. In support of his optimism, Braga highlighted the palpable gains stemming from the presence of Protestant schools, hospitals, Bible societies, the YMCA, and the YWCA, among other existing organizations supported by foreign missionary societies in Latin America.[72]

He was mainly concerned with another sort of threat, though. Critical of a church-centered evangelicalism, which alienated the Protestant churches from national life, Braga advanced a view of Christian witness based on shared service to the community and the larger society, which contributed to the future of the burgeoning Latin American nations.[73] In his eagerness to see social progress in the southern part of the continent, Braga uncritically accepted the belief in the Anglo-American moral and religious superiority. According to him,

---

[68] Braga, *Pan-americanismo*, 10. Translation is mine.

[69] Braga, *Pan-americanismo*, 18.

[70] Braga, *Pan-americanismo*, 18.

[71] Braga, *Pan-americanismo*, 18.

[72] Braga, *Pan-americanismo*, 22–23.

[73] Erasmo Braga and Kenneth Grubb, *The Republic of Brazil: A Survey of the Religious Situation* (London: World Dominion Press, 1932), 130.

> The political history of Saxon America and its social development are inseparable from the religious principles that presided over the cradle of the great democracy. Much more than race and environment, the difference in religion explains, not only in the New Continent but also in the Old, how certain peoples are advanced in comparison to others in the organization of their national life, the superior aspirations of the popular soul, the comprehension and intelligence of law and civil liberties, generalized public instruction, the elimination of social evils, and a certain superiority of moral standard, despite everything that can be argued against individual cases of corruption and against certain repugnant aspects of collective life, which are inseparable from human imperfections.[74]

Although reinforcing the formula advanced by the CCLA of Anglo-Saxon, Protestant superiority, Braga avoided the possibility of merely embracing Anglo-Saxon values brought by US missions as substitutes for Latin American culture. Instead, he proposed a path of fulfillment, a complement or combination of values that could be achieved through education in the molds of what he called "North American pedagogy." Believing in the need to unite efforts to address the social maladies impacting the region, Braga advocated for a Christocentric Christianity—represented in the slogan "Christianity is Christ"—to correct the church-centeredness he saw as an obstacle for a more effective Christian witness.[75] He promoted a social Christianity whose ultimate goal was "the integral realization of the Reign of God."[76] In short, Braga advanced a proposal of Protestantization of Latin America, while paradoxically hinting at a Latin Americanization of Protestantism through the education of Latin American leaders and the combination of what he called Latin and Anglo-Saxon values.

As the economic crisis of the 1920s worsened the socioeconomic disparities in the continent, though, and labor unions, student movements and left-wing Latin American political leaders intensified nationalist protests against the expanding North American hegemony in the continent, the need to affirm the Latin American identity of Protestant Christians in the region became increasingly urgent. The

74 Braga, *Pan-americanismo*, 41.

75 Braga, *Pan-americanismo*, 68.

76 Braga, *Pan-americanismo*, 77.

Montevideo and Havana congresses sought to address that demand. As Bastian states, "The two congresses that happened during this period were concerned with this consciousness-raising regarding the need to articulate a Latin American Protestant response to the crisis."[77]

Looking at the three continental congresses through that lens, Montevideo 1925 can be seen as a congress of transition between Panama 1916 and Havana 1929. Although the leadership of Montevideo 1925 was in thesis in the hands of a Latin American, American missionaries were still the de facto leaders. Erasmo Braga was the chair of the Montevideo Congress. But Speer and Inman were the main masterminds of the event. In Montevideo, the Latin American presence and participation was considerably greater than in Panama. In preparation for that congress, a change in representation was proposed to increase participation of people "born and bred" in Latin America. In Panama, only 7 percent of the participants were born in Latin America. The goal in Montevideo 1925 was to make Latin Americans the majority. As Luiz Longuini Neto points out, such a goal was not achieved. Of the 165 congress delegates, only 45 were Latin Americans. Representatives of the American mission boards and foreign missionaries were still dominant. Nevertheless, the Latin Americans in attendance played more important roles in Montevideo than in Panama.[78] Although some addresses were in English, Spanish was, for the first time, the official language of a CCLA sponsored continental congress. Between 1916 and 1925, many Latin American Protestants had become more self-conscious and increasingly interested in understanding what it meant to be Christian in the Latin-American sociocultural milieu.

The contribution from Latin American participants to the Montevideo 1925 congress began to be felt prior to its opening session. The Latin Americans who participated in the preparatory committee helped shape the congress's agenda.[79] With Braga presiding over the meeting, the topic of education gained prominence in Montevideo. Although this topic was already present in Panama

[77] Bastian, *Breve Historia del Protestantismo*, 11. Translation is mine.

[78] Luiz Longuini Neto, *O Novo Rosto da Missão* (São Paulo: Ultimato, 2002), 99.

[79] Longuini Neto, *O Novo Rosto da Missão*, 98.

1916, this time it received extended attention, with a three-day continental conference on education taking place prior to the beginning of the congress.[80]

In Spanish, John Mackay, the Principal of Colegio Anglo-Peruano, in Lima, gave the opening address of the congress, highlighting the adaptability of "the fundamental principles of education" to different conditions and situations through three emphases. The first emphasis was pedagogical. In discussing it, Mackay underscored the centrality of the student in the educational process: "the school is for the pupil." The second emphasis was sociological. For Mackay, such an emphasis is important because "the pupil is educated for life." Finally, the third emphasis underscored what Mackay called the transcendental principle, "life is eternal."[81]

Mackay's contributions to the CCLA conversation on education—his student-centered pedagogy, in particular—turned the participants's attention to the practical demands of life. In his practice as an educator in Peru, Mackay had promoted that sort of student-centered education, seeking to adapt the school to meet students' needs and not the opposite. Opposing the traditional idea that one should be educated for a profession, Mackay aspired for an education oriented to the idea of "citizenship for life."[82] Finally, his emphasis on the transcendental principle reminded his audience that "true education does not limit thought but rather expands and stimulates it."[83] By emphasizing that life is eternal or for God, Mackay portrayed life as constantly evolving, not limited by religious or state institutions. Even what one could consider the spiritual dimension of his pedagogy aimed at helping students reach their highest potential as humans. Mackay saw the centrality of the devotion to Christ and to "the kingdom of God" as important to forge human beings with "sufficient resolution and the spirit of sacrifice to live and die for great human ends."[84]

---

[80] Longuini Neto, *O Novo Rosto da Missão*, 100. Longuini Neto attributes the amount of attention this topic received to Braga's influence as an eminent Protestant educator in Brazil.

[81] John Mackay Metzger, *The Hand and the Road: The Life and Times of John A. Mackay* (Louisville, KY: Westminster John Knox Press, 2009), 137.

[82] Metzger, *The Hand and the Road*, 137.

[83] Metzger, *The Hand and the Road*, 138.

[84] Metzger, *The Hand and the Road*, 138.

The centrality of education became key for the Protestant impact on Latin America in the twentieth century, as seen not only in the numerous Protestant schools, universities, and seminaries formed in the region, but also in the ecumenically coordinated effort following those congresses, which would reach its peak with the formation of the *Comisión Evangélica Latinoamericana de Educación Cristiana* (CELADEC) in 1962—a recommendation from the second Latin American Evangelical Conference (CELA II), in 1961.[85]

A product of the revolutionary stream of the Latin American ecumenical movement of the 1960s, CELADEC would drastically shift its initial interest in the development of programs for Christian education in ecumenical perspective to a more direct focus on popular education and communication; that is, communication with grassroots movements and other *setores populares* (grassroots sectors of society) throughout Latin America. By the mid-1970s, CELADEC would be engaging with labor unions, base ecclesial communities, women's groups, and peasant communities who were creating "their own forms and means of expression as part of their organizational, protesting and social practices."[86] Concomitantly, CELADEC gradually decentralized its own structure, turning attention to "a number of intermediary institutions or groups that generated media aimed at sharing information important for the popular sectors, working with them, supporting their practices, and producing materials (messages) aimed at advancing self-education."[87]

CEDALEC is a good example of the turn to the base, the popular, that this book highlights in the development of Latin American ecumenism, which took place in the second half of the twentieth century. Many of the institutions that ended up making that turn stemmed from churches and ecclesiastical structures related to the CCLA in the region. It represents one of the expressions of the change Latin American ecumenism experienced in the course of the following

[85] Evangelical Latin American Commission on Christian Education. See Longuini Neto, *O Novo Rosto da Missão*, 101. The word *evangélica*, literally "evangelical," in this context is the equivalent of Protestant.

[86] Maria Cristina Mata, "La Experiencia del Programa de Comunicación de CELADEC," *Chascqui: Revista Latinoamericana de Comunicación* 8 (1983): 76–79 (76).

[87] Mata, "La Experiencia del Programa de Comunicación de CELADEC," 76–79 (76).

decades as more Latin American ecumenical Protestants began to undergo an experience of *conscientização*,[88] gradually subverting the liberal mode of education initially propagated in CCLA circles, without, however, discarding emphases such as the student-centered approach Mackay proposed in Montevideo 1925. Later on, that model would add a Freirean component to promote the oppressed learner as the subject of their own liberation, and education as the collaborative task of popular communities formed by teachers/learners. Instead of developing its own educational programs in a top-down fashion, CELADEC, under the influence of Freire's popular education, supported educational projects emerging from the popular sectors of society—which, in Freire's language, was "the basis for a truly democratic pedagogy."[89]

The Montivideo Congress, formally titled "Congress on Christian Work in South America," was hosted at Hotel Pocitos on March 29 to April 8, 1925. Its North American sponsors described it as a truly South American congress based on the facts that the congress was chaired by a Brazilian, had Spanish as its official language, and developed themes chosen in conjunction with a group of Latin Americans who participated in the preparatory committee.[90] Since most conversations took place in Spanish and Portuguese, more Latin Americans felt encouraged to participate. The environment it created encouraged Latin Americans from different parts of the continent to take advantage of the opportunity they had to spend time together to coordinate visions and plans.

Furthermore, the Montevideo congress created a shared space where missionary and national voices could talk to each other. In the opening plenary session, which had Erasmo Braga and John

---

[88] Paulo Freire defined *conscientização*, as the raising of critical consciousness, which includes "an openness to understanding social structures as modes of domination and violence." See Paulo Freire, *Educação como Prática da Liberdade* (Rio de Janeiro: Paz e Terra, 1967), 15.

[89] Freire, *Educação como Prática da Liberdade*, 25. The Portuguese word Freire uses here is "base," which is the same word to translate the English words *base* and *basis*.

[90] Wilton M. Nelson, "En Busca de un Protestantismo Latinoamericano: De Montevideo 1925 a La Habana 1929,"" in *Oaxtepec 1978: Unidad y Misión en América Latina*, edited by Consejo Latinoamericano de Iglesias (San José, Costa Rica: CLAI, 1980), 31–44 (35).

Mackay as main speakers, Braga spoke in Portuguese, and Mackay in Spanish. Both were translated into English.[91] The two men not only had significant influence on the overall conversation in Montevideo but would soon become critical spokespersons for Latin America in the broader ecumenical movement. Years later, Mackay would be elected the third President of Princeton Theological Seminary and become a highly influential ecumenist in the twentieth century.[92] Braga, on the other hand, would exert great influence in the shaping of the ecumenical movement in Brazil, while serving as an interface connecting Brazilian churches and ecumenical organizations with the emerging international instruments of the broader ecumenical movement. Unfortunately, his declining health and unexpected death in 1932 prematurely interrupted what could have been an even more extraordinary ecumenical trajectory.

Braga, the Executive Secretary of the Brazilian Committee on Cooperation, was a catalyst for many ecumenical initiatives in Brazil, founding periodicals, newspapers, and seminaries, and representing Brazilian Protestantism before government authorities and the press.[93] He was also key in bridging between the Brazilian Protestant experience and worldwide movements working for Christian unity. As Paul Pierson once noted,

> His office, housed in the same building as the Bible Society, became the Brazilian representative of a number of North American and European based ecumenical and philanthropic organizations, including the Federal Council of Churches in the USA, the Commission on Faith and Order, and the Conference on Life and Work, as well as the CCLA and the International Missionary Council (IMC). He took an active role in a number of gatherings: the World Sunday School Convention in 1924; the Congress on Christian Work in South America in 1925, at which he presided; and the Jerusalem meeting of the IMC in 1928, becoming a member of the Executive Committee of the latter.[94]

---

[91] Dafne Sabanes Plou, *Caminhos de Unidade: Itinerário do Diálogo Ecumênico na América Latina* (São Leopoldo: CLAI/Editora Sinodal, 2002), 33.

[92] See, for instance, Samuel Escobar, "The Legacy of John Alexander Mackay," *International Bulletin of Missionary Research* 16/3 (1992): 116–122.

[93] Pierson, op. cit., 158.

[94] Pierson, op. cit., 159.

Pierson also mentions Braga's role as an interpreter of "ecumenical currents in world Christianity to his own nation and church," including the series of articles he published in *O Puritano*[95] outlining the history of the ecumenical movement and explaining the function of the IMC, his participation in the Conference on Life and Work in 1925, and his broader contributions to multiple international ecumenical bodies.[96]

Braga was a tour-de-force for the still insipient Latin American ecumenical movement. Despite frustrations with the recrudescence of denominationalism in his own country and the limits of his efforts to advance interdenominational Protestant theological education,[97] he continued to spread his ecumenical ideals until his premature death at the age of fifty-five.

In 1928, Braga participated in the IMC Conference in Jerusalem, being one of the few Latin Americans attending that gathering. Mackay delivered one of the short addresses of Jerusalem 1928. The title of his address was "The Power of Evangelism." The other two speakers delivering similar addresses were a representative from Persia and another from India. In his address, which focused on the South American continent, Mackay drew attention to the "unchurched masses" and the need to present the message of the Gospel in ways that are organic to the conditions in which people live. He identified two critical Latin American demands that merited attention: (10) The need to "create a new sense of sin" and (2) the need for a "fresh interpretation of the Cross and the crucified Christ."[98] Even though Braga did not speak at Jerusalem 1928, his presence was noted in the reports of the Committee of the 1925 Congress on Christian Work in South America, transcribed in the third volume of the Jerusalem IMC Conference report.[99]

---

95 The official periodical of the Brazilian Presbyterian church up to 1958.

96 Pierson, op. cit., 159.

97 Pierson, op. cit., 161–162.

98 John A. Mackay, "The Power of Evangelism: In South America," in *Addresses on General Subjects*, The Jerusalem Meeting of the International Missionary Council, March 24–April 8, 1928, vol. 8, International Missionary Council (New York/London: International Missionary Council, 1928), 90–93.

99 International Missionary Council, *The Relation Between the Younger and the Older Churches*, 192–194.

Braga was also involved with the organization of the third continental Congress on Christian Work, which met in Havana in 1929. That would be his last appearance on the continental ecumenical stage. Before his passing, he contributed to forming the *Federação das Igrejas Evangélicas do Brasil* (FIEB), the first Brazilian federation of Christian churches.[100] Two years after his death, FIEB merged with two other national Protestant ecumenical organizations—the Brazilian Committee on Cooperation that Braga had chaired since its inception and the *Conselho Evangélico de Educação Religiosa no Brasil*—to create the *Confederação Evangélica do Brasil* (CEB).[101] CEB would become the main institutional umbrella for ecumenical cooperation among Brazilian Protestant churches in the following decades.

Despite all his accomplishments, Braga represented the paradox of an incipient Latin American ecumenism that, in a search for its own identity, found itself torn between the shadows of a North American liberal mindset infused with a naive belief in the conversion of his native culture through education and the need on the part of Latin American Protestants to affirm their own societal values in order not to succumb to a new form of imperialism. While insisting on a binary cultural view that implied the superiority of the Anglo-Protestant culture over the Catholic Iberian-American culture, Braga was able to see positive elements in Latin American Catholicism, which, he believed, if infused with Protestant individualist and democratic values, could lead to progress. The shortcomings of the Protestant liberal aspiration in the following decades, as it sought to respond to drastic changes taking place in Latin American societies, would lead a new generation of Latin American ecumenical Protestants to seek for more radical transformation.[102] The next CCLA congress in Havana (1929) would embryonically anticipate those conversations.

The Havana Congress (1929) was originally planned to happen in Mexico City in 1926, to commemorate the tenth anniversary of Panama 1916. The Cristero War in Mexico, though, forced the

---

[100] Federation of Brazilian Evangelical Churches.

[101] Brazilian Evangelical Confederation.

[102] José Miguez Bonino, *Faces of Latin American Protestantism*, trans. Eugene L. Stockwell (Grand Rapids, MI: Eerdmans, 1995), 21.

organizers to change their plans. As they considered a new location,[103] the Association of Ministers in Havana offered to host the congress, also changing its name to *Congreso Evangélico Hispanoamericano de La Habana*.[104] This congress differed from the previous two in that an agreement was reached beforehand for the CCLA to function only as an advisory board. The responsibility for the congress's organization would fall on Latin American nationals. Planning committees were formed in each participating country. They distributed questionnaires and held preparatory discussions ahead of the congress. A steering committee formed by thirteen people redacted the final preparatory documents.[105]

A total of two hundred individuals participated in the Havana Congress, with 118 of them originating from Latin America. Finally, a CCLA-sponsored continental congress had a Latin American majority among its participants. Mexico had the largest delegation, followed by Cuba. Gonzalo Báez-Camargo, a thirty-year-old lay Mexican Methodist professor who had fought in the Mexican Revolution, was chosen to preside over it. The organizational structure of the Havana Congress was also different from the previous two. This time, there were three vice presidents: one from Cuba, one from Mexico, and a third one from Puerto Rico. Such a structure underscored the vitality of an emerging batch of capable Latin American Protestant leaders. As Orlandi aptly notices, this was "the most Latin American congress of the CCLA,"[106] not only for all the reasons already mentioned, but also because Latin American leaders "claimed the responsibility for the organization of the Congress."[107]

The program outline was also unique when compared with the two previous congresses. The Havana Congress was organized around four major emphases.[108] The first part of the program focused on evangelical solidarity. This emphasis stemmed from the influence of the growing number of Latin American Protestants increasingly concerned with Protestant participation in the

[103] Nelson, "En Busca de un Protestantismo Latinoamericano," 36.

[104] Nelson, "En Busca de un Protestantismo Latinoamericano," 36.

[105] Sabanes Plou, *Caminhos de Unidade*, 36.

[106] Orlandi, "From Christian Continent to Mission Field," 148. He is including here both the continental and the regional congresses.

[107] Orlandi, "From Christian Continent to Mission Field," 171.

[108] Longuini Neto, *O Novo Rosto da Missão*, 103.

development of *Latin Americanidad*, including the need for more consistent Protestant engagement with the social struggles of the Latin American peoples. That sort of concern would inform the rise of a renewed understanding of the Protestant faith in the Latin American milieu in coming decades. Among other things, the Havana Congress encouraged the formation of national federations and councils of churches, which up to that point only existed in a few Latin American countries.[109]

The second major focus of that congress was education. On this front, Havana 1929 sought to deepen the conversation started in Panama and expanded in Montevideo. One of the nuances added in Havana, however, was its attention to student and youth organizations. The importance of those movements would be ratified as they, especially from the 1950s onward, would serve as incubators for rising leaders who would play protagonist roles in church and society in the following decades.

Another area of attention the Havana Congress brought to the fore was social action. Even though the Montevideo Congress, four years earlier, had mentioned existing Latin American social movements, it did not articulate that interest. In Havana, such an emphasis resulted from a growing movement on the part of some Latin American Protestant leaders to distance themselves from North American paternalism.[110] This conversation highlighted themes such as the attitude of the churches in relation to the broader community, industrial and rural problems, the medical missionary work, and the action of women in the evangelical work.[111] The fourth programmatic emphasis advanced in Havana was literature, another theme that continued ongoing conversations started in Panama.

One of the most consequential conversations in this congress, though, centered on the nature of the relationship between "mother churches" (represented by mission boards and missionaries) and their "daughters" or "adolescent churches," a term Inman used in reference to the national Latin American churches.[112] As highlighted

---

109 Sabanes Plou, *Caminhos de Unidade*, 36.

110 Longuini Neto, *O Novo Rosto da Missão*, 104.

111 Longuini Neto, *O Novo Rosto da Missão*, 104.

112 Longuini Neto, *O Novo Rosto da Missão*, 104.

in the previous chapter, increased concern with the relationship between "older" and "younger" churches had been a major topic of conversation in Jerusalem 1928.

In Havana 1929, a number of Latin American delegates were suspicious of missionary complicity with American imperialism. Some missionaries, in paternalistic fashion, continued to question the capacity of the Latin American churches to govern themselves and be financially independent. Others were concerned with the rebellious and revolutionary spirit some nationals exhibited.[113]

The Havana Congress became a milestone in the coming of age of Latin American Protestant ecumenism. Despite the above-mentioned tensions, there was no drastic rupture but serious dialogue and continuous negotiations. In his report as President of the congress, Báez-Camargo indicated that the Latin-Americanization of Protestantism was at the center of the Havana Congress's agenda, being

> [. . .] the result of a deep awareness and conviction, both in missionaries and in Latin Americans, that the kingdom of God would progress more quickly if the latter come to the fore as directors and managers of the work, while the former occupy the position of advisers and assistants; was the result of an agreement carried out on entirely friendly guidelines.[114]

The tensions between foreign missionaries and Latin American Protestant nationals continued to impact the development of Latin American ecumenism in the decades to come. In Havana 1929, Latin American national delegates insisted on efforts to overcome "a certain North American hegemony over the Latin Americans" still common in Protestant circles. Instead of drastically breaking with the missionary agencies, though, they turned to the three-self formula as a healthier strategy to move forward: "Our purpose is to achieve self-support, self-governance, and self-propagation without breaking with the spiritual communion of the universal church," the Congress affirmed.[115]

---

[113] Nelson, "En Busca de un Protestantismo Latinoamericano," 40.

[114] Gonzalo Báez-Camargo, *Hacia la Renovación Religiosa en Hispanoamérica* (Mexico City: Casa Unida de Publicaciones, 1930), 137. Cited by Orlandi, "From Christian Continent to Mission Field," 172.

[115] As cited by Longuini Neto, *O Novo Rosto da Missão*, 104.

Inman, who was still the CCLA executive secretary in 1929, saw that gathering as a critical transitional moment for Latin American Christianity.

> I believe I am not wrong if I say that in all modern missionary work this is the first congress at which the transition from a mission-centered movement to a church-centered movement takes place. Havana thus takes on a special significance for the missionary work, not only in Latin America, but also in other parts of the world.[116]

His statement points to the significance of that gathering to the ecumenical movement as a whole. The Havana Congress represents a moment in the history of Latin American Christianity in which the modern church-mission border was blurred. Latin American Protestants firmly pursued having their own voice on the table while trying to avoid driving mission partners away. Conversations between foreign missionaries and national Latin American leaders, which had been taking place since Panama 1916, reached a turning point in Havana. In other words, the Havana Congress marked a point of no return in the process of Latin-Americanization and nationalization of the insipient Latin American ecumenical work (still exclusively Protestant), thus initiating a long journey toward the development of an autochthonous theological language that could impact Latin American society more broadly.

In the aftermath of the Havana Congress, the articulation of Latin American Protestant cooperation paradoxically seemed to slow down. The call for the formation of a Latin American Federation of Churches heard in Havana did not materialize anytime soon. A couple of decades would separate Havana 1929 from the next round of continental ecumenical gatherings in Latin America.[117] In the meantime, however, the shaping and strengthening of national ecumenical structures continued to happen in a steady pace. Cooperation between the CCLA and emerging national and continental ecumenical initiatives never stopped. Between Havana 1929 and

---

116 Samuel Guy Inman, *Evangelicals at Havana* (New York: CCLA, 1929), 148. Cited by Sabanes Plou, *Caminhos de Unidade*, 40.

117 The next continental conference would only happen in 1949, with the first Conferencia Evangélica Latinoamericanas (CELA), in Buenos Aires.

CELA I, in 1949, some mission boards were integrated into national councils or federations of churches—a practical outcome of the proposal advanced in Havana.

While this pioneering period of Latin American ecumenism marked the rise of a Latin American consciousness within national and regional emerging ecumenical bodies, those bodies still largely depended on the North American liberal project, which continued to associate social progress with the Protestantization of Latin American societies. On the other hand, the majority of Latin American Protestants embraced a conservative evangelical Christianity that was more concerned with the salvation of individual souls than with the transformation of the social conditions in which most Latin Americans lived.

In the complex development of an increasingly diverse Protestant movement in Latin America, those leaning towards ecumenical cooperation under the umbrella of the ecumenical movement remained a marginal minority within a Christian segment that in itself was a religious minority—since the absolute majority of all Latin American Christians remained Catholic. Despite being a numerical minority, they would make significant contributions to change the way Protestants understood their role in relation to the larger society, creating movements that would lead to the rise of a Protestant stream of Latin American liberation theology—which, in the late 1960s would advocate for more drastic social change.

3

THE SHORTCOMINGS OF THE LIBERAL PROJECT AND THE RISE OF THE THIRD WORLD

In the first half of the twentieth century, the modern ecumenical movement was basically Protestant. In Latin America, that was also the case. The CCLA, a Protestant missionary cooperative hub, was the main organism supporting ecumenical work in the region for several decades. Even though the Havana Congress in 1929 approved the creation of a Latin American Protestant Federation, such a continental federation of churches would only begin to materialize in 1964 with the creation of the *Comisión Provisional pro Unidad Evangélica Latinoamericana* (UNELAM), a provisional body to promote church unity in the continent, which elected Uruguayan theologian Emilio Castro (1927–2013) as its first general secretary. Only in 1982, that regional ecumenical aspiration would take the form of a permanent council of churches with the creation of the *Consejo de Iglesias Latinoamericanas* (CLAI).[1] In contrast with the provisional nature of UNELAM, still a Protestant initiative, CLAI was a permanent ecumenical body that, although predominantly Protestant, also included Orthodox churches, in addition to several other Christian organizations from twenty-one Latin American countries.

In the aftermath of Havana 1929, the CCLA remained the main interecclesial body coordinating the ecumenical efforts within Latin America and the Latin American interaction with the broader ecumenical movement. In that capacity, it sent twenty-four representatives—most of them born in Latin America—to the International Missionary Council's expanded meeting in Madras, India, in 1938.[2] Likewise, it coordinated the participation of eight Latin

[1] UNELAM was the Provisional Commission for Latin American Evangelical Unity, whereas CLAI is the Latin American Council of Churches. See Sabanes Plou, *Caminhos de Unidade*, 59, 93.

[2] Plou, *Caminhos de Unidade*, 51.

American and Caribbean delegates in the second World Conference on Faith and Order, which met in Edinburgh, Scotland, in 1937.[3]

The presence of a Latin American delegation in the Faith and Order Conference in 1937 marked the beginning of a more consistent Latin American participation in the Faith and Order Movement, which would include important contributors to that commission. Someone of the stature of José Miguez Bonino (1924–2012), an Argentinean Methodist theologian who gained international notoriety for his contributions to liberation theology from the 1960s onward, spent many years of his life involved in the work of that commission. After attending the Faith and Order Conference in Lund, Sweden, in 1952, he served on the Faith and Order Commission between 1961 and 1977, being its regional chair for several years. Other Latin Americans have substantially contributed to the work of that commission, including Brazilian Presbyterian theologian Odair Pedroso Mateus (1955–), who was a member of the Secretariat of the World Council of Churches Commission on Faith and Order between 2007 and 2015, and served as the commission's Director from 2015 to 2022.

Despite the long story of Latin American participation in Faith and Order, for the most part Latin American Christians have shown greater interest in ecumenical engagement through mission initiatives—as represented initially by the IMC and, later, the WCC Commission on World Mission and Evangelism (CWME)—and, especially, in the peace and justice work represented by the Life and Work Movement. In contrast to Faith and Order, which is centrally concerned with examining the theological foundations for Christian unity and the social function of the Church,[4] the Life and Work Movement focuses on unity in service in response to the social maladies plaguing the world. Mass poverty, social, racial, gender and environment justice, conflict transformation, and peacebuilding are some of its emphases.[5] Since these are matters of life and death for so many people in Latin America and

[3] Alan Neely, "Protestant Antecedents of the Latin American Theology of Liberation" (PhD diss., American University, 1977), 81.

[4] Neely, "Protestant Antecedents of the Latin American Theology of Liberation," 79.

[5] Neely, "Protestant Antecedents of the Latin American Theology of Liberation," 92ff.

other parts of the world, it is understandable that a good amount of Latin American ecumenism has historically placed that sort of concern at the center stage.

The first Life and Work Conference met in Stockholm, Sweden, on August 19–30, 1925. This was also the first major international ecumenical gathering to include participants from Latin America. Marking the beginning of an international articulation of Christian social awareness, the main achievement of that conference was the establishment of a Continuation Committee to embody the movement's work and organize further conferences to "build relationships and establish means whereby Christian ethics could be applied to the social problems of modern life."[6] That Continuation Committee would give birth in 1930 to the Universal Council for Life and Work, which was put in charge of organizing the next Life and Work Conference.

Five Latin American delegates—who would also attend the Faith and Order Conference in Edinburgh—participated in the Universal Christian Council for Life and Work Conference in Oxford, England, on July 12–25, 1937. The two conferences were held within days from each other. Focusing on the theme "Church, State, and Community," the Oxford Conference addressed the problems of war, economic injustice, racial hatred, and the rise of nationalism (understood as an abuse of the gift of nationality).[7] The theme of the conference reflected the major crises and concerns of the time, including the increasing tensions in Germany, which reached the Council in 1934, when two competing delegations from the German Evangelical Church—the confessing branch, which had Dietrich Bonhoeffer as delegate, and the German National Churches, represented by Bishop Theodor Heckel—sought membership.[8]

Joseph Oldham, appointed head of the Advisory Commission on Research by the Life and Work Council, was the intellectual architect of Oxford 1937. A couple of years earlier, he released the book

6 Neely, "Protestant Antecedents of the Latin American Theology of Liberation," 95.

7 Universal Council for Life and Work, *The Message and Decisions of Oxford on Church, Community and State* (New York: Universal Christian Council, 1937), 10, 17.

8 Michael G. Thompson, *For God and Globe: Christian Internationalism in the United States between the Great War and the Cold War* (Ithaca, NY: Cornell University Press, 2016), 121.

Church, Community and State: A World Issue,[9] indicating the paraments to interpret the title of the forthcoming conference:

> [T]he proposed conference title, "Church, Community, and State," implied there was more at stake than the old question of church and state. Now the larger issues concerned nationhood, or rather, the very nature of the "community," his rendering of the word Volk. It was more than a German problem; it was, as the title of his work suggested, a world problem: "What place in God's purpose does the nation hold? What is the relation of the Church to the communal life with which its own life is inseparably intertwined?"[10]

The second Assembly of the World Council of Churches in Evanston (1954) would mark the moment when the ecumenical social agenda, especially its emphasis on the social responsibility of the church, would gain the attention of Latin Americans attending that gathering, being particularly influential in the rise of the Latin American Commission on Church and Society (ISAL), which will be discussed later.

The Latin American presence in the Life and Work Movement would be significantly more impactful in the World Conference on Church and Society (Geneva, Switzerland), July 13–24, 1966, which counted with the participation of 43 Latin American delegates—a gathering with a total of 338 officially participants. That Latin American delegation included people such as Emilio Castro (1927–2013), Orlando Fals Borda (1925–2008) and Julio de Santa Ana (1934–2023).[11]

Although still in an incipient fashion, Oxford 1937 was an important milestone for the development of an ecumenical social thought that offered a critique of the sinful nature of economic injustice, starting a conversation that would be critical for the formation of Latin American ecumenical thought in the 1950s. On that topic, the Message of the Conference stated the following:

---

[9] J. H. Oldham, *Church, Community and State: A World Issue* (New York & London: Harper and Brothers Publisher, 1935).

[10] Thompson, *For God and Globe: Christian Internationalism*, 121.

[11] Neely, "Protestant Antecedents of the Latin American Theology of Liberation," 105.

> In the economic sphere the first duty of the Church is to insist that economic activities, like every other department of human life, stand under the judgment of Christ. The existence of economic classes presents a barrier to human fellowship which cannot be tolerated by the Christian conscience. Indefensible inequalities of opportunity in regard to education, leisure, and health continue to prevail. The ordering of economic life has tended to enhance acquisitiveness and to set up a false standard of economic and social success.[12]

Concerns with race and racial discrimination, statehood, and nationalism, which dominated the agenda of that meeting, would become recurrent in the ecumenical movement. Because of World War II and the Cold War, the organization of further Life and Work conferences was postponed and some of the important conversations initiated in Oxford 1937 did not have an immediate follow up. The next major conference to have that sort of emphasis, planned under the auspices of the World Council of Churches (WCC), took place only in 1966. That conference aimed at responding to world conditions that had drastically changed since 1937, while also deepening some of its insights, which continued to be pursued through the structures of the newly formed WCC. Homer A. Jack, an American Unitarian Universalist pacifist and social activist who was in Geneva as an observer, reported that one of the conference participants carried a sign that read, "An impatient world challenges a complacent church."[13]

The 1966 World Conference on Church and Society was not simply another ordinary event in the tradition of Stockholm (1925) and Oxford (1937).[14] It also integrated post-World War II concerns to further ecumenical social thinking, taking into account social ethical concerns discussed in the three initial World Council of Churches assemblies: Amsterdam (1948), Evanston (1954), and New

---

12 Universal Council for Life and Work, *The Message and Decisions of Oxford*, 5.

13 Homer A. Jack, *Church and Society: Special Report* (Boston: Department of Social Responsibility, Universalist Unitarian Association, 1966), 2.

14 Although Geneva 1966 was not a life and work conference, through new structures and designs of the WCC, it expanded and deepened the legacy of the two life and work conferences mentioned earlier.

Delhi (1961).[15] The rapid changes happening in the second half of the twentieth century forced the churches to pay closer attention to the broader world and seek to understand it more thoroughly. As Mackay pointed out, the church should see itself as a world community. As such, its task was to "bind the world together."[16] One of the key problems the church had to wrestle with in that era was the cultural and civilizational disintegration of a world that "physically," that is, geographically, was increasingly interconnected. That physical unity, for Mackay, demanded the pursuit of spiritual unity to counter the process of disintegration.[17] World War II had escalated that awareness.

Furthermore, the post–World War II world saw the intensification of decolonizing struggles, as old European empires gradually lost their grip on formerly colonized people. Decolonization and liberation movements became pressing topics in ecumenical conversations. On the other hand, Eurocentric imperialism remained an issue to be grappled with.

The world in the wake of WWII was polarized between two major ideological blocks respectively led by the United States and the Soviet Union. To make the situation worse, amid such a global conflict, the Pandora's box of the catastrophic destructiveness of nuclear weapons had been opened.

Despite all potential for progress, the promises of economic growth and technological and scientific development that economic liberalism had propagated never materialized for the large majority of a rapidly increasing world population. Mass poverty became a reality increasingly common in various parts of the world. In response to those disparities and injustices, anti-colonial struggles and social revolutions caught the minds and thoughts of a large parcel of the

---

[15] M. M. Thomas and Paul Albrecht, "The Structure and Work of the Conference: An Introduction to the Report," in *Christians in the Technical and Social Revolutions of Our Time: World Conference on Church and Society, Geneva, July 12–26, 1966*, World Council of Churches (Geneva: WCC, 1967), 6.

[16] John A. Mackay, "Significant Trends Today in the Younger Churches of Mission Lands," Dec. 6, 1939, 1–4 (1). Introduction to Ecumenics—General Material (1938–1954). John Mackay Collection, Series IV—Princeton Theological Seminary Presidency, box 26.

[17] John A. Mackay, "The Church's Task in the Realm of Thought: Reflections on the Oxford Conference," *Princeton Seminary Bulletin* 31/3 (1937): 2–9 (4).

general public. In such a context, decolonizing movements began to organize trans-continentally. A remarkable moment in that development was the gathering of twenty-nine Asian and African political leaders for a Third World Conference in Bandung, Indonesia, in 1955, which marked the rise of the Third World project, indicating that peoples and nations that until then were considered subaltern subjects and communities decided to coordinate their struggles for rights and dignity on the world stage.

Many Latin Americans paid close attention to those developments that also informed revolutionary ideas catching fire particularly on university campuses across the continent. In 1966, four hundred sixteen government officials and political leaders from Africa, Asia and Latin America met in Havana for the First Solidarity Conference of the Peoples of Africa, Asia, and Latin America, which continued the Third World project started at Bandung. During that period, Latin American Christian students gradually engaged revolutionary social movements and networks. While committed to work with non-Christian partners, they wanted to understand the role Christians could play in a rapidly changing world. Discussions about the possibility of a more benevolent and just world order began to inform the agenda of ecclesial encounters in the region.

On the Protestant end, the first Latin American Consultation on Church and Society, in Huampaní, Peru, 1961, was a turning point in the development of a Latin American Protestant theology markedly committed to social change and justice. New theological questions were raised in the search for a deeper understanding of the conditions in which the impoverished masses of the continent lived and how to best respond to their plight. That consultation discussed themes that had also been raised in three national church and society consultations organized between 1955 and 1960 in Brazil, which not only focused on the social responsibility of the church but also the Latin-Americanization of Christianity, and the Christian insertion in the revolutionary process.[18]

---

[18] These consultations organized by the Sector of Social Responsibility of the Church of the Protestant Confederation of Brazil included participants from different countries in Latin American and beyond. See Barreto, *Protesting Poverty*, chapter 3.

On the Catholic end, similar concerns became increasingly part of the agenda of the Latin American Episcopal Council (CELAM), founded in 1955, and were central to the pastoral orientation that several Latin American bishops and priests would articulate more thoroughly in the wake of Vatican II.[19] By the early 1960s, Latin Americans were ready to play a more prominent role in global conversations taking place in ecumenical circles. The 1966 Conference on Church and Society represents one of the first major instances in which Latin American Christian voices were clearly articulated and heard on the global stage. As "one of the greatest Protestant (and Orthodox) gatherings in the twentieth century devoted to religious social action,"[20] this conference exemplifies how Latin American concerns and responses to injustice began to impact the ecumenical agenda at large.

Uruguayan Methodist theologian Emilio Castro, who would later be elected General Secretary of the World Council of Churches (1985–1992), was one of the speakers at that gathering, offering the conference's opening meditation.[21] Castro, who had become the first General Secretary of the recently founded UNELAM, also delivered a

[19] CELAM stands for Consejo Episcopal Latinoamericano. See Raimundo C. Barreto, "Vatican II, Medellin, and Ecumenism: A Brazilian Protestant Perspective," *Journal of World Christianity* 9/2 (2019): 187–202.

[20] Jack, *Church and Society: Special Report*, 1.

[21] Elected General Secretary of the recently formed Provisional Commission for Latin American Evangelical Unity (UNELAM), which he contributed to found, Castro would become a key Latin American ecumenical leader, articulating the organization of numerous events such as the Third Latin American Evangelical Conference (CELA III), which will be discussed later, and the UNELAM assembly in Oaxtepec, Mexico, 1978, which approved the creation of the Latin American Council of Churches (CLAI). On the global level, he actively participated in the Fifth WCC Assembly in Nairobi (1975), and in the efforts of the Christian Peace Conference (CPC) to promote "dialogue on cooperation and peaceful coexistence at the time of the Cold War." In 1972, he was appointed as Director of the Commission on World Mission and Evangelism (CWME). During his tenure with the CWME, his influence was felt in the WCC reaffirmation of its commitment to mission, especially in the 1982 document "Mission and Evangelism: An Ecumenical Affirmation," considered one of the most comprehensive statements by the WCC on mission. The top recognition of his global leadership came with his election as General Secretary of the WCC, a position he held from 1985 to 1992. In line with his previous work, his leadership in the WCC was marked by a dialectical synthesis of deep Christian spirituality and passionate commitment to justice, which contributed to open new possibilities for the

plenary talk about the contribution of the church to the transformation of Society. Several other voices from Latin America were heard in different plenary sessions, including Orlando Fals Borda, who delivered a brief but critical address to the gathering titled "Promise and Frustration in Social Change."[22] One of the conference plenary sessions focused exclusively on the theme "Christianity and Revolutionary Change in Latin America." Addresses by Candido Mendes de Almeida (1928–2022), a renowned Roman Catholic Brazilian lawyer and political scientist, Uruguayan Methodist pastor Hiber Conteris and Colombian Presbyterian theologian Gonzalo Castillo in that plenary session were "judged to be among the most thought-provoking of the conference."[23]

US Presbyterian theologian M. Richard Shaull (1919–2002), who had spent two decades in Latin America, being a critical player in the creation of the *Setor de Responsabilidade Social da Igreja* (SRSI) of the *Confederação Evangélica do Brasil*, delivered a plenary address titled "The Challenge and Relevance of Theology to the Social Revolutions of Our Time." In that address, Shaull challenged Christian theology to put itself in a position where it could offer those in the "revolutionary struggle of our times" resources of transcendence that contributed to the cultivation of creative imagination and the development of new ways to think about the challenges of our time.[24] Shaull's call for the churches to learn new ways to meaningfully engage the world articulated a Protestant prophetic heritage of Christian openness and participation in the world affairs that paralleled the Vatican II emphasis on *aggiornamento*. For Shaull, if churches and theologians were to play any role in what he defined as a revolutionary age, they needed to open themselves to think in new and creative ways; that is, thinking in historical fashion: "Churches and theologians must overcome the a-historical way of thinking which has dominated and

---

future of the council. See Carlos A. Sintado and Manuel Quintero Perez, *Emilio Castro: A Legacy of Passionate Ecumenism* (Geneva: WCC Publications, 2018), 7–8, 69ff.

[22] World Council of Churches, *Christians in the Technical and Social Revolutions of Our Time*, 36.

[23] World Council of Churches, *Christians in the Technical and Social Revolutions of Our Time*, 41.

[24] World Council of Churches, *Christians in the Technical and Social Revolutions of Our Time*, 25. For the Latin American influence on Shaull's theological thinking, see Barreto, *Protesting Poverty*, chapter 2.

which has prevented Christian involvement from being the explosive ethical factor it should be in history."[25]

Geneva 1966 made an important contribution to broaden the ecumenical agenda, as Christian leaders from Africa, Asia, Latin America, and the Middle East took the center stage to bring their own concerns to the ecumenical table. The conference counted with a number of lay Christians as speakers, and a prominent presence of young leaders and students. Furthermore, it made room for "a strong group of observers from the Roman Catholic Church" to participate, providing a special opportunity "for consideration of the larger ecumenical discussion on questions of Church and Society."[26]

Between Oxford 1937 and Geneva 1966, not only had the world significantly changed but the Ecumenical Movement had also undergone significant transformation. At the end of the 1937 conferences in Edinburgh (Faith and Order) and Oxford (Life and Work), a committee chaired by William Temple (1881–1944), composed of seven representatives of each movement (Faith and Order and Like and Work), met in London and recommended the merging of the Universal Christian Council for Life and Work and the Continuation Committee on Faith and Order into a new organization, a World Council of Churches (WCC). A Provisional Committee of the World Council of Churches was then established. After the end of World War II, the Council held its inaugural assembly in Amsterdam, Netherlands, being formally organized on August 22, 1948.[27]

In the same decades the world ecumenical movement solidified its structures, the coming of age of Latin American ecumenism was reaching a new stage. Between the Havana Congress in 1929 and the rise of ISAL in 1961, a group of Latin American ecumenical Christians gradually turned attention to the plight of the marginalized, the impoverished, the oppressed. That turn would not only change the face of Latin American Christianity but would also influence, in the long run, the broader ecumenical movement.

---

[25] World Council of Churches, *Christians in the Technical and Social Revolutions of Our Time*, 25.

[26] World Council of Churches, *Christians in the Technical and Social Revolutions of Our Time*, 42.

[27] See David P. Gaines, *The World Council of Churches: A Study of Its Background and History* (Peterborough, NH: Richard R. Smith, 1966), 161ff.

Protestantism Discovers Its Latin Americanness

In the years following the Havana Congress in 1929, new church councils, federations, and associations of Christian education were formed in various Latin American countries, and united theological seminaries were consolidated in Puerto Rico, Costa Rica, and Argentina. The formation of new national structures of cooperation represented an important step in the transition from the initial stages of ecumenism in Latin America—mostly led by foreign organizations—to a stage in which a self-conscious Latin American ecumenical movement began to take shape.[28]

Among the national initiatives that emerged in the 1930s, the creation of the Protestant Confederation of Brazil (CEB, *Confederação Evangélica do Brasil*) in 1934 was one of the most consequential.[29] The formation of CEB resulted from the merging of three ecumenical organizations: the Brazilian Committee on Cooperation, the Federation of Evangelical Churches, and the Evangelical Council of Religious Education in Brazil. Accordingly, its organizational structure comprised three councils, each of them focusing respectively on areas formerly under the auspices of those three organizations: (1) the Council of Churches; (2) the Council on Cooperation; and (3) the Council on Religious Education.[30] In addition to its work with the Brazilian churches and its representative role as a united Protestant voice on behalf of the churches taking stand on issues of common concern before the Brazilian society and government, the newly organized federation of churches liaised between Brazilian Protestant churches and emerging international agencies and forums, coordinating Protestant cooperative work on both the continental and the international levels. For instance, in 1935, CEB became directly affiliated with the IMC. Prior to that point, the relationship had been mediated through the CCLA.[31]

---

[28] See Luis E. Odell, "Fifty Years of Ecumenism in Latin America," in *The Growth of Interreligious Dialogue 1939–1989: Enlarging the Circle*, ed. Franklin H. Littell (Lewiston/Queenston/Lampeter: The Edwin Mellen Press, 1989), 95–111 (97).

[29] *Confederação Evangélica do Brasil* (CEB), *Relatórios: Biênio 1934–1936* (Rio de Janeiro: CEB, 1936), 1. Unless noted otherwise, the word *evangélica* "Evangelical" in the names of these councils or confederations of churches means "Protestant."

[30] *Confederação Evangélica do Brasil* (CEB), *Relatórios: Biênio 1934–1936*, 3.

[31] *Confederação Evangélica do Brasil* (CEB), *Relatórios: Biênio 1934–1936*, 10.

CEB also boosted social awareness and responsibility among Brazilian Protestant churches. Brazilian historian Wanderley Pereira da Rosa describes the formation of CEB as "the most ambitious Protestant initiative for the articulation of a Christian social ethics put at the service of the nation."[32] The commissions comprising the Confederation reflected an increasing concern with the presence of the church in the transformation of society. From its inception, for instance, CEB created a Commission on Ecumenism and Pacifism. Likewise, one of the three commissions composing the Council on Cooperation focused on social problems. By 1948, CEB had added a Commission on Literacy and another one to support war refugees.[33] The latter liaised with the Brazilian government and, starting in 1950, the United Nations High Commissioner for Refugees (UNHCR), to coordinate the reception of war refugees in Brazil, many of whom were Protestants.[34]

CEB's 1952–1954 Biennial Report refers to its assistance to the victims of a drought in the Brazilian northeastern states and to unemployed workers. That same report discusses CEB's consultative relationship with the United Nations through its Council on Inter-Ecclesial Relations.[35] It took, however, twenty years since its foundation for CEB to create a sector fully devoted to the "social responsibility of the church." The use of such a language emerged in 1955, when CEB created a Commission on Church and Society subordinated to its Department of Study and Documentation with the primary purpose of focusing "on the social responsibility of the Church and to carry out studies on the civic duties of evangelical Christians and their role not only in the life of the country, in general, and in its government, but particularly, their action in the industrial sector and in rural areas."[36]

---

[32] Wanderley Pereira da Rosa, *Por uma Fé Encarnada: Uma Introdução à História do Protestantismo no Brasil* (São Paulo: Editora Unida/Editora Recriar, 2020), 93.

[33] Confederação Evangélica do Brasil, *Relatórios: Biênio 1948–1950* (Rio de Janeiro: CEB, 1951), 6.

[34] Confederação Evangélica do Brasil, *Relatórios*, 49.

[35] Confederação Evangélica do Brasil, *Relatórios: Biênio 1952–1954* (Rio de Janeiro: CEB, 1955), 33.

[36] Confederação Evangélica do Brasil, *Relatórios: Biênio 1955–1956* (Rio de Janeiro: CEB, 1958), 21.

Waldo A. César (1923–2007), a lay Presbyterian leader in his early thirties, and later a tour-de-force in the shaping of the Church and Society Movement in Latin America, was named the executive secretary for that commission, which also had M. Richard Shaull, a missionary who taught at the Presbyterian Seminary of Campinas and worked with the *União Cristã dos Estudantes do Brasil* (UCEB),[37] as one of its members. These two men were the masterminds behind the work of the Commission on Church and Society from its inception.

The Commission on Church and Society emerged initially independently from CEB's structures. César was one of the Brazilians who attended the second WCC Assembly in Evanston (1954). Among other things, that gathering devoted a significant amount of time to discuss the Christian response to "social questions," with emphasis on "the responsible society in world perspective."[38] The Evanston Assembly created two study commissions in the WCC: a Commission on Responsible Society in World Perspective and the "Commission on International Affairs: Christians in the struggle for World Community."[39] Upon his return to Brazil, César gathered with Shaull and others to discuss the implications of Evanston for the Latin American situation. In response to those conversations, they created an independent Commission on Church and Society whose work would focus on the social responsibility of the churches. Later integrated into the Department of Study of the Protestant Confederation of Brazil, the Commission held a Consultation on the Social Responsibility of the Church, November 15–19, 1955, in São Paulo.[40] That was the first of four consultations that led a number of Brazilian ecumenical Protestants to immerse themselves in the Latin American revolutionary struggle.

The formation of the Commission on Church and Society was a milestone in the development of a burgeoning ecumenical movement in Latin America. The impact that Commission would have on Latin American ecumenism and on the broader ecumenical

---

[37] Christian Union of Students of Brazil.

[38] World Council of Churches, *Evanston Speaks: Reports from the Second Assembly of the World Council of Churches Evanston, Ill., U.S.A., August 15–31, 1954* (Geneva: WCC/SCM Press, 1954), 43ff.

[39] Benjamin Mays, "The Second Assembly of the World Council of Churches," Journal of Religious Thought 10, no. 2 (1953): 144–148 (146).

[40] Confederação Evangélica do Brasil, *Relatórios: Biênio 1955–1956*, 77.

movement—as exemplified at Geneva 1966—demonstrates the significance of mutual exchanges between global and local trends that have characterized the ecumenical movement. Very often global emphases and concerns are received and reinterpreted through local lenses, and, in return, Indigenous knowledge and initiatives are concomitantly internationalized.

Those local/global exchanges often bump fresh air into the ecumenical movement, thus promoting a spiritual crosspollination that prevents its ossification.[41] Certain common concerns and insights at particular moments in history—as it was the case with the emphasis on the social responsibility of the church in the 1950s—have traveled distances, inspiring Christians in different parts of the world. By contrast, those local Christians do not simply replicate the insights processed through international gatherings. Instead, they engage those thoughts through specific cultural lenses and sociohistorical experiences, not only making them their own but infusing new meanings into them. As they bring their own idiosyncrasies and insights to the ecumenical table, they impact, in return, broader interactions.

It is worth restating that the rise of social awareness among Latin American Protestants did not originate in Evanston 1954. In Evanston, however, a group of young Latin Americans found in the language of social responsibility the inspiration to start something new. In their response to the conversations in Evanston, they not only reinterpreted that language in light of their own context, but they also changed it, imagining other meaningful ways to address their own reality by adopting, for instance, the language of revolution and liberation—which, then, bounced back to worldwide ecumenical conversations as in the case of Geneva 1966.

A similar process would take place in the Catholic context vis-à-vis the Latin American reception and interpretation of the Vatican II, which would give birth to a new theological language that would impact Christians across the world. I will return to those

[41] Richard Shaull used the word "ossification" to encourage his US reformed tradition to engage Latin American liberation theology in dialogue, urging his North American mainline peers to look for new responses to the signs of the times. For Shaull, a tradition that repeats old answers in its responses to new challenges in a constantly changing world runs the risk of sclerosis and death. Richard Shaull, *The Reformation and Liberation Theology: Insights for the Challenges of Today* (Louisville, KY: Westminster/John Knox Press, 1991), 15.

developments in Catholic circles in later chapters. At this point, it suffices to say that these transformative processes of theological cross-pollination have impacted the very self-understanding of churches in contexts such as Latin America. In the process of reexamining their faith in light of particular cultural and sociohistorical experiences, Latin American Protestants in the mid-1950s were looking for new theological language. That search led them to engage not only with North Atlantic ecumenical partners, but also with secular and Catholic counterparts in Latin America and beyond.

The Third World as a New Theological Locus

The ecumenical instruments and networks that formed in the wake of Edinburgh 1910 were a creation of the Western churches. As Eritrean Lutheran theologian Yacob Tesfai puts it,

> The original home of the ecumenical movement is in the North. It was church leaders and churches of the North (or West) that were instrumental in founding and establishing the movement. The theologies and traditions of the churches of the North were decisive and predominant in it.[42]

That fact has been at the roots of tensions, contestations, and negotiations the ecumenical movement has been forced to face throughout its history and, in particular, since the second half of the twentieth century, a time when the participation of Christians from the Global South in the new ecumenical structures intensified.

Tensions between what Western missionary agencies used to call "younger churches" and those identified as "older churches" became more clearly noticeable in the years that followed the formation of the World Council of Churches in 1948. By the time the IMC Assembly met in Accra, Ghana, in the twilight of 1957, its delegates acknowledged the changing dynamic in mission relations. The North was no longer the home of missions, nor the South the mission recipient. Instead, they concluded, "The missionary movement has resulted in a new world Christian community; this has within itself the possibility

[42] Yacob Tesfai, "Ecumenism and 'the South': The Irruption of the Third World and Its Impact on the Ecumenical Movement," *Journal of Ecumenical Studies* 31/3–4 (1994): 332–344 (332).

of becoming a world-wide missionary community."[43] That realization justified the integration of the IMC into the WCC in 1961.

One of the working groups in Accra 1957 urged the churches represented in the IMC to root Christian witness in Indigenous cultural and social patterns, emphasizing the need for theological training that grounded the teaching of the Gospel "on indigenous flesh and expression."[44] Acknowledging that trend, the Accra gathering set up the Theological Education Fund "for the advancement of theological education in Asia, Africa and Latin America."[45] In the recommendation to its successor, the WCC Commission on World Mission and Evangelism (CWME), the delegates to the IMC gathered in Accra also stated that the time had come to leave the distinction between older and younger churches behind.

> Churches differ in resources and in opportunity for mission; but those differences are not in principle differences between "older" and "younger" churches. Within their fellowship in Christ, churches give and receive from one another in their missionary task; but such giving and receiving no longer takes place solely between "older" and "younger" churches. If they are churches, they are all alike called to mission.[46]

The integration of those formerly designated as mission fields into the worldwide church was meant to close the colonial abyss. There were no longer ways to justify the treatment of non-Western churches as missionary extensions of Western churches. All churches from anywhere in the world were supposed to be integrated into one broader world Christian fellowship. This growing conviction was reiterated in the 1961 report of the newly-formed Division of World Mission and Evangelism to the third WCC Assembly in New Delhi, India:

> Our temptation will be to think of the Division simply as the continuation of the interests of the International Missionary Council with emphasis on Asia, Africa and South America. We must resist

[43] International Missionary Council, *Minutes of the Assembly of the International Missionary Council*, Ghana, December 28, 1957 to January 8, 1958 (London, IMC, 1958), 85.

[44] International Missionary Council, *Minutes*, 23.

[45] International Missionary Council, *Minutes*, 53.

[46] International Missionary Council, *Minutes*, 90.

> this temptation. This is the Division of World Mission and Evangelism of the World Council of Churches. We are concerned not with three continents but with six. In co-operation with every department of the World Council and with the full resources of the Christian community in every land we must help the churches to confront men and women with the claims of Jesus Christ wherever they live.[47]

By the 1950s, the irruption of Global South churches began to impact the ecumenical instruments created in the initial decades of the twentieth century. To paraphrase the famous quote from William Temple cited earlier, world Christianity was becoming the *de facto* great new fact of this era. By the end of the first half of the twentieth century, the ecumenical movement was reexamining its self-understanding with increasing attention paid to the Christianities of the south. Along with that, one can see in those developments the rise of what Boaventura Sousa Santos calls "the epistemologies of the South;" that is, "the production and validation of knowledges anchored in the experiences of resistance of all those social groups that have systematically suffered injustice, oppression, and destruction caused by capitalism, colonialism, and patriarchy."[48] In the following decades, that process would give birth to various "theologies of the South."

While this coming of age of the Christianities of the South is still an unfinished project, one can argue that it can be traced back to the movements of political liberation and decolonization that began to mobilize transnationally in the 1950s. As formerly colonized, enslaved, and oppressed peoples rediscovered themselves as political and historical subjects, they also became epistemic agents, revitalizing traditional knowledges that had been pushed away, dismissed, ignored, and suppressed under colonial rule and rediscovering cultural and religious resources for the construction of another possible world.

---

47 International Missionary Council, *Minutes of the Assembly of the International Missionary Council,* November 17–18, 1961 and the First Meeting of the Commission on World Mission and Evangelization of the World Council of Churches, December 7–8, 1961 at New Delhi (Delhi, IMC, 1961), 30.

48 Boaventura de Sousa Santos, *The End of Cognitive Empire: The Coming of Age of Epistemologies of the South* (Durham and London: Duke University Press, 2018), 1.

Despite the improved conditions in the communication between missionary boards (such as those represented in the CCLA) and Christian leaders from the South, noticed, for instance, in the Havana Congress (1929), a fundamental abyss in the production of knowledge and power structures remained untouched. Change was only welcomed if it did not challenge Eurocentric concentration of power and privilege. In Geneva 1966, for example, some participants from the Global North were bothered by the "rebellious" spirit of the Latin American participants who dared to question their authority outwardly, reflecting the fear still present in the World Church and Society Conference that those loud voices from the South talking about revolution could go too far. For some participants, the voices of the youth and some speakers from the Global South sounded too radical.

Despite the fact that the increased presence of representatives from the Global South in ecumenical meetings and conversations was beginning to effect change in the ecumenical instruments, as Tesfai notices, there still remained a significant deficit in the presence of non-Western Christians "among the active players that shaped the movement and its agenda."[49] That demand would only be met when more people and nations broke free from colonialism and began to set their own agendas and priorities. Tesfai underscores, for instance, the irruption of the Third World, a phrase that EATWOT theologians have often used,[50] paraphrasing Gustavo Gutiérrez's important observation that "the participation of Christians in the process of liberation is simply an expression of a far-reaching historical event: the irruption of the poor."[51] A deeper renewal of the ecumenical movement demanded the rise of the poor in their midst. What is, then, the significance of the reference to "the Third World" for the ecumenical movement?

Gary Y. Okihiro offers a thought-provoking account of "Third World studies" as a field of study started at San Francisco State College in 1968, which was, however, aborted by the college administration

---

[49] Tesfai, "Ecumenism and 'the South,'" 332.

[50] EATWOT is the Ecumenical Association of Third World Theologians, organized during a meeting in Dar es Salaam, Tanzania, in 1976. See Virginia Fabella and Sergio Torres, eds., *Irruption of the Third World: Challenge to Theology* (Maryknoll, NY: Orbis Books, 1983).

[51] Gutierrez, *A Theology of Liberation*, xx.

and faculty and replaced with "ethnic studies."[52] In an exercise of imagination about a field that never was, Okihiro denounces the loss in the abandoning of Third World studies for ethnic studies, a field he believes remains undefined and susceptible to intellectual segregation and reduction to "identity politics."[53] By contrast, Okihiro affirms, Third World studies have a clearer subject matter, "society and the human condition broadly;" "the social formation or the forms and movements of society, its structure, relations, and changes over time;" and "power or agency and its articulations exhibited in the formations of race, gender, sexuality, class, and nation."[54] In other words, it integrates elements of liberation, decolonial and intersectional approaches. He describes Third World studies, therefore, as the theorizing of universal liberation "against all forms of oppression, material and discursive."[55] Instead of retreating into any sort of provincialism, it invites ample dialogue and engagement.

Okihiro's work retrieves memories of a concept that has been misused and depreciated.[56] While the term "Global South"—likewise, a heuristic concept that cannot be reduced to geography—can also be interpreted in subversive ways,[57] the phrase "Third World" invokes a historical memory of a political transformative project conceived by subjects often perceived as existing on the underside of history. The Third World was a movement with a coherent articulation of aspirations and demands from those who not only were economically and politically exploited but also intellectually deprived due to the suppression of their knowledge and the imposition of hegemonic ways of knowing from the North Atlantic.[58] The Third World project, therefore, had not only a political dimension but also an

---

52 Gary Y. Okihiro, *Third World Studies: Theorizing Liberation* (Durham and London: Duke University Press, 2016), 1.

53 Okihiro, *Third World Studies*, 2.

54 Okihiro, *Third World Studies*, 2.

55 Okihiro, *Third World Studies*, 14.

56 Being often associated with underdevelopment. Fabella and Torres, *Irruption of the Third World*, xii.

57 See, for instance, Sinah Theres Kloß, "The Global South as Subversive Practice: Challenges and Potentials of a Heuristic Concept," *The Global South* 11/2 (2017): 1–17 (4).

58 Walter D. Mignolo, *Local Histories/Global Designs: Coloniality, Subaltern Knowledges, and Border Thinking*, Princeton Studies in Culture/Power/History (Princeton, NJ: Princeton University Press, 2012), loc. 112, Kindle.

epistemological one. In general, it rejected the monopoly of capitalism and political absolutist claims, affirming instead an ethics of solidarity inspired by the Bandung spirit. At the same time, it advanced the vision of another possible order, reaffirming the humanity of those who were often treated as non-persons.[59]

The post–World War II world was drastically polarized between the Western capitalist empire (the First World), and the Eastern communist empire (the Second World). The nations struggling for autonomy in Asia, Africa, and Latin America were expected to fall in line, siding with one of the two major blocks. While that ideological divide inevitably impacted their political choices, a growing sense of the need for new spaces to coordinate the agency of those neglected by that binary global order was at the root of the organization of networks and movements that became known as the "Third World" project, to borrow an expression coined by Vijay Prashad.[60]

What united this group of non-aligned nations was the anti-colonial struggle. Together, they created several organizations to articulate their own hopes and demands. To reach their goals, they organized important conferences. As Prashad puts it, "In Bandung (1955), Havana (1966), and elsewhere, these leaders crafted an ideology and a set of institutions to bear the hopes of their populations. The 'Third World' comprised these hopes and the institutions produced to carry them forward."[61]

The Bandung Conference (1955) and the two follow-up gatherings in Cairo (1961) and Havana (1966) were the landmarks of a movement that combined economic, political, and cultural concerns. On top of the demands for "political equality on the world level," the Third World project advanced the creation of specific international platforms to address the demands of those who had been neglected by the existing polarized global order, focusing particularly on the United Nations.[62] They also advocated for "the redistribution of the world's resources, a more dignified rate of return for the labor power

---

[59] M. P. Joseph, *Theologies of the Non-Person: The Formative Years of EATWOT* (New York: Palgrave MacMillan, 2015), 13.

[60] Vijay Prashad, *The Darker Nations*, loc. 93, Kindle.

[61] Prashad, *The Darker Nations*, loc. 93, Kindle.

[62] Prashad, *The Darker Nations*, loc. 105, Kindle.

of their people, and a shared acknowledgment of the heritage of science, technology, and culture."[63]

As Prashad underscores, the Third World project represented a battle for the future, the dream for a more just world order. In their incessant struggle against colonialism, "the peoples of Africa, Asia, and Latin America dreamed of a new world. They longed for dignity above all else, but also the basic necessities of life (land, peace, and freedom)."[64] While this collective struggle for autonomy, freedom, and liberation was not capable of delivering the new world order they dreamed about, the hopes and dreams it sowed became pervasively inspirational among people struggling for liberation everywhere in the world.

In his Nobel Prize acceptance speech in 1964, Martin Luther King Jr. connected the ongoing African American civil rights struggles to the battles for independence taking place in Africa, Asia, and Latin America. For King, both were manifestations of a *zeitgeist*, the spirit of the times, which had been in a crescendo in the previous decade.

> Something within has reminded the Negro of his birthright of freedom, and something without has reminded him that it can be gained. Consciously or unconsciously, he has been caught up by the *Zeitgeist*, and with his black brothers of Africa and his brown and yellow brothers in Asia, South America, and the Caribbean, the United States Negro is moving with a sense of great urgency toward the promised land of racial justice.[65]

That *zeitgeist*, which one can also call the "Third World spirit," influenced a number of Global South Christian leaders, encouraging them to dream of a Christian Bandung.[66] Brazilian Catholic Archbishop

---

[63] Prashad, *The Darker Nations*, loc. 115, Kindle.

[64] Prashad, *The Darker Nations*, loc. 93, Kindle.

[65] Martin. L. King Jr., "Nobel Lecture," December 11, 1964, The Nobel Prize, https://www.nobelprize.org/prizes/peace/1964/king/lecture/.

[66] This reference to a "Christian Bandung" comes from Brazilian Archbishop Helder Camara, one of the most prominent interpreters of the Vatican II in Latin America. See Luiz Carlos Luz Marques, "As Circulares Conciliares de Dom Hélder," in *Dom Hélder Câmara: Circulares Conciliares*, vol. 1, eds. Luiz Carlos Luz Marques and Roberto de Araújo Farias (Recife, Brazil: Companhia Editora de Pernambuco, 2008), 52–70 (68). Bandung, Indonesia, was the location of the first intergovernmental Conference of Asian-African countries, in 1955, which is "widely regarded

Hélder Câmara (1909–1999) used this expression during Vatican II, as he sought to build a network of solidarity with bishops from Africa and Asia who also faced the cruelty of mass poverty and social exclusion. Another expression of a Christian Bandung would emerge later, with the creation of the Ecumenical Association of Third World Theologians (EATWOT), in 1976.

Such aspirations were also in display in a number of ecumenical initiatives between the 1960s and the 1980s that articulated the construction of global solidarity with the poor and the formation of international liberating networks. The articulation of those liberating hopes impacted the ecumenical movement on at least two fundamental levels: (1) It influenced its agenda and priorities, and (2) it informed its self-understanding and structures.

The Third World project embodied the articulation of hopes and aspirations from the margins, thus becoming a new locus of enunciation from where those who had been on the underside of modernity were now able to speak. In addition to its political significance, the Third World project had an epistemic meaning as it contributed to the formation of new ecologies of knowledge that stemmed from subaltern experiences of resistance of social groups systemically targeted by injustice and oppression.[67] For EATWOT theologians, for instance, the irruption of the Third World represented an ongoing project aimed at restoring life to its fullness. Such a view led them to rethink Christian theology and praxis,

---

as an important prelude to the nonaligned movement." Other gatherings with similar aspirations were organized on the level of the civil society. As Carolien Stolte points out, eleven days prior to the Bandung gathering, another conference took place in New Delhi, a popular, unofficial counterpart to Bandung. According to her, "In sharp contrast to Bandung, which was not open to the public, the nongovernmental nature of the Delhi conference enabled thousands of people to attend. Officially known as the Conference of Asian Countries on the Relaxation of International Tension (CRIT), it was heavily influenced by the growing peace movement of the early Cold War years." As Stolte highlights, in the next five years, the mobilization that followed the Delhi gathering gave birth to a number of additional conferences across Asia and Africa, which contributed to "the formation of the Afro-Asian People's Solidarity Organization (AAPSO) [. . .] in Cairo in December 1957." See Carolien Stolte, "'The People's Bandung': Local Anti-imperialists on an Afro-Asian Stage," *Journal of World History* 30/1–2 (2019): 125–156 (125–126).

[67] Boaventura de Sousa Santos, "Beyond Abyssal Thinking: From Global Lines to Ecologies of Knowledges," *Review (Fernand Braudel Center)* 30/1 (2007): 45–89.

underscoring the necessity to bring the knowledge production of the poor to the center stage.[68]

John Bennett referred to the 1966 Geneva conference as a "climatic event" describing it as an "event that marked the greatest participation of the third world up to that time in the life of the ecumenical community."[69] That meeting projected prophetic voices from the Third World to the global stage, giving them a platform to speak to the entire ecumenical movement. By doing that, it became one of the most critical global ecumenical gatherings of the twentieth century, with clear impact on the fourth WCC Assembly in Uppsala (1968), in which the influence of the Third World project was also clearly felt. M. M. Thomas, a crucial ecumenical prophetic voice from India and the chairperson of that conference, was later elected to moderate the WCC Central Committee. That conference was undoubtedly a milestone event. Through it the global ecumenical movement felt more clearly than ever before the impact of the irruption of the poor, the irruption of the Third World.[70]

---

[68] Fabella and Torres, xiii–xiv.

[69] John Bennett, "The Geneva Conference of 1966 as a Climactic Event," *The Ecumenical Review* 37/1 (1985): 26–33 (26).

[70] Bennett, "The Geneva Conference," 27.

4

THE RISE OF LIBERATION CHRISTIANITY AMONG LATIN AMERICAN PROTESTANTS

The liberation turn this chapter discusses precedes the rise of liberation theology and is larger than it. It is a turn that paved the way for a world-oriented ecumenism—a movement through which "the world" dislodged the churches as the center of ecumenical concerns. Michael Löwy discusses the rise of a liberation Christianity, which came to be before anything known as liberation theology had emerged. Referring to the latter, he asserts:

> Liberation Theology is a body of writings produced since 1970 by figures like Gustavo Gutiérrez (Peru), Rubem Alves, Hugo Assmann, Carlos Mesters, Leonardo and Clodovis Boff, Frei Betto (Brazil), Jon Sobrino, Ignacio Ellacuría (El Salvador), Segundo Galilea, Ronaldo Muñoz (Chile), Pablo Richard (Chile - Costa Rica), José Miguez Bonino, Juan Carlos Scannone, Ruben Dri (Argentina), Enrique Dussel (Argentina - Mexico), Juan Luis Segundo (Uruguay), Samuel Silva Gotay (Puerto Rico), to name only some of the best known.[1]

Relying on theologians such as Leonardo Boff, Löwy defines liberation theology as "the reflection of, and a reflection on, a previous praxis."[2] By contrast, he labels the liberating praxis at the origins of such a theological reflection "liberation Christianity."[3] According

[1] Michael Löwy, *The War of Gods: Religion and Politics in Latin America* (London/New York: Verso, 1996), 32.

[2] Löwy, *The War of Gods*, 32.

[3] While Löwy's English translator opted for the use of "liberationist" as the qualifier of that sort of Christianity while using "liberation" when it referred to theology, the Portuguese version of Löwy's book uses the word *libertação* (liberation) to qualify both the Christian praxis and the theology he refers to. I follow the Portuguese version here, using the word "liberation" as the qualifier for both the Christian liberating praxis seen in some social movements and the body of literature that stems from it (theology). See Michael Löwy, *O Que é Cristianismo da Libertação: Religião e Política*

to him, liberation Christianity emerged as a social movement in the 1950s and 1960s, prior to the rise of liberation theology.

> This movement involves significant sectors of the Church (priests, religious orders, bishops), lay religious movements (Catholic Action, Christian University Youth, Young Christian Workers), popularly based pastoral networks, ecclesial base communities (CEBs), as well as several popular organizations created by CEB activists: women's clubs, neighbourhood associations, peasant or workers' unions, etc.[4]

As a social movement, liberation Christianity is not limited by ecclesiastical boundaries. Instead, its "network goes well beyond the limits of the Church as an institution, however broadly defined."[5] Therefore, it impacts society at large. The exploration of liberation Christianity is critical for the understanding of a number of important social and historical phenomena, such as "the emergence of a new workers' movement in Brazil and the rise of the revolution in Central America (as well as, more recently, in Chiapas)."[6]

Löwy describes the liberation turn in Latin American Christianity as an outward turn toward the poor, the impoverished masses, and the world, vis-à-vis societal power structures and the huge asymmetries that create the conditions for mass poverty. Likewise, Richard Shaull referred to the radical call to be in the world and stand in solidarity with the poor through the analogy of a "church in the modern diaspora."[7] During the two decades he lived in Latin America, he saw movements such as the Student Christian Movement in Brazil as Christian koinonias shaped outside the confines of the institutional church for the transformation of the world. It was primarily in those spaces that one saw the rise of liberation Christianity.

The radical immersion in the struggle for justice that those movements represented was never under the control of ecclesiastical

---

na América Latina, 2nd ed. (São Paulo, Brazil: Editora Fundação Perseu Abramo/Expressão Popular, 2016).

[4] Löwy, *The War of Gods*, 32.

[5] Löwy, *The War of Gods*, 33.

[6] Löwy, *The War of Gods*, 32.

[7] Richard Shaull, "The Form of the Church in the Modern Diaspora," *The Princeton Theological Bulletin* 57/1 (1963): 3–18 (3).

institutions. On the contrary, they constituted borderline movements more attuned to those suffering the impact of an unjust social order than to the institutional church. Although those struggles for justice would sooner or later challenge priorities and commitments in the churches, they were intended to affect the entire social order. The fluid format liberation Christianity took through its engagement of social movements blurred the borders between church and society. Such a border-crossing movement unwittingly contributed to the intensification of tensions within church structures that understood that their role included the protection of those very borders.

Within Protestant circles, the main focus of this chapter, the rise of those modern diasporic Christian koinonias was not merely a consequence of the Latin-Americanization of Protestant Christianity discussed in the previous chapters. The growing involvement of ecumenical Christians in nationbuilding in Latin America and the ecumenical adoption of social agendas aiming at the transformation of the living conditions impacting the masses in the region marked the initial stages of a movement that gradually led to a deeper solidarity with the poor. That movement, though, still lacked language and conceptual tools to interpret the structural nature of the problems it intended to address. The responses it initially offered to the social and economic disparities that caught its attention became increasingly insufficient in light of the challenges it was presented with. A more drastic move was needed to enable those ecumenical Christians to properly respond to the grim situation of injustice they were called to engage. The liberation turn that took place in Catholic and Protestant circles—almost concomitantly and often independently—contributed to the formation of a movement, which set in course a series of developments that still informs Christian responses to multifaceted experiences of injustice, suffering, and persistent dehumanization.

Within Protestant circles, the rise of Latin American liberation Christianity in the mid-1950s and early 1960s took place mainly among an increasingly frustrated group of mostly lay and young Christians in search of theological language to understand themselves and their mission as Protestant Christians in Latin America. The Third World project—which, as described earlier, included post-WWII revolutionary and decolonizing movements and the critical thinking that emerged from them—was one of the inspirations for those Christian students and other youth Christian movements seeking to create Christian koinonias beyond the institutional confines of the churches they were affiliated with in an effort to work in solidarity with other social movements for the transformation of the world.

Amid such a process, the Third World project and its networks became a major inspiration, helping create a liberationist zeitgeist in the struggle for structural change and the realization of social justice for those undergoing different experiences of oppression. Lingering colonial structures, renewed forms of imperialism, and global capitalism were some of the faces of the structural injustice that needed to be collectively resisted and overcome. Labor, women, student, and youth movements of the day were on the frontline in that struggle. The Latin American liberation Christianity that began to take shape in the mid-1950s, thus, can be understood as an expression of the Third World spirit discussed in the last chapter.

As mentioned earlier, Protestants were a tiny religious minority in mid-twentieth-century Latin America, comprising less than 3 percent of the overall population. By contrast, Catholicism was the religion of more than 90 percent of all Latin Americans. Even by the early 1970s, Protestants were still less than 5 percent of the Latin American population.[8] Those Protestants involved in ecumenical conversations were at the fringes of that religious minority. That is one of the reasons why, even to this day, the liberation Christianity that emerged within Protestant circles in the late 1950s and early 1960s remains under examined. That lack of attention can be seen even in Löwy's reference to liberation Christianity. As a keen observer, Löwy mentions the *Junta Latinoamericana de Iglesia y Sociedad* (ISAL), founded in 1961, some developments in the WCC and, in the Brazilian case, the Protestant presence within CEBs' structures, to highlight the diverse composition of the liberation Christianity taking shape in Latin America.[9] However, for the most

[8] Pew Research Center, "Religion in Latin America: Widespread Change in a Historically Catholic Region," Nov. 13, 2014, https://www.pewresearch.org/religion/2014/11/13/religion-in-latin-america/#:~:text=in%20the%20priesthood.-,History%20of%20Religious%20Change,from%20the%20World%20Religion%20Database.

[9] Löwy, *O Que é Cristianismo da Libertação*, 14–15. ISAL stands for Latin American Board on Church and Society.

part, he places his attention on Catholic liberation movements, which are much better documented and which he knows more closely. The developments of that liberation Christianity within ecumenical Protestant circles deserves more attention given its significance both in the region and beyond. This chapter and the one that follows explain the developments leading to the rise of liberation Christianity within Latin American Protestant circles, which is at the roots of the surge of a Protestant stream of Latin American liberation theology toward the end of the 1960s.

Latin American Protestants and the Liberation Turn

In the years that followed Havana 1929, ecumenical Protestants organized a number of cooperative structures on the national level in different countries. The rise of those national initiatives would, in turn, renew the ecumenical articulations on the continental level in the years to come.

On the front of literature production, for instance, which had been a concern of mission-oriented discussions on cooperation since Panama 1916, and also of Bible Societies that operated uninterruptedly in Latin America since the second decade of the twentieth century,[10] united publishing houses were founded in Mexico City (1920) and Buenos Aires (1926). Those localized developments would be key for the organization by the CCLA of the first Conference on Literature, in Mexico City in 1941, which, by its turn, gave birth to the Latin American Committee on Christian Literature.[11]

Another conference, on the occasion of the twenty-fifth anniversary of the Latin American Biblical Institute in Costa Rica (1948), would result in the formation of Editora Caribe, one of the most important Latin American publishers in the twentieth century. Those developments contributed to the creation of *Literatura Evangélica Latinoamericana* (LEAL) in 1955. The steering committee for this new entity had representatives from fourteen countries, and ended up facilitating the publication and distribution of Protestant literature throughout the continent, also offering seminars of capacitation

[10] González and González, *Christianity in Latin America*, 209.

[11] Sabanes Plou, *Caminhos de Unidade*, 73–74.

and cataloguing services that would be critical to the development of Latin American Protestantism in the mid-twentieth century.[12]

Similarly, the CCLA continued to sponsor continent-wide cooperation projects in the areas of evangelization through radio broadcasting, the so-called "evangelism in depth" program and pastoral studies.[13] These developments, funded by US missionary agencies, stood in line with the liberal project that saw the success of the spreading of Protestant values and faith in Latin America as the route to the region's future.

Some of those developments, however, produced unintended consequences, contributing to significant change in the relationship of Protestantism with Latin America. Among them, the formation of youth and student organizations, which, through small local associations formed on university campuses throughout the region, created new autonomous spaces for the rise of a faith rooted in Latin America and in touch with the people's struggles in the region. In the 1950s, the Student Christian Movement (SCM) rose to become one of the most significant Protestant grassroots movements of the time and one of the earliest sites where a liberation turn would begin to take form within Protestant circles. Some of the young people who participated in the SCM were also involved in the effervescent secular student movement that concomitantly impacted the broader political scenario in the region. In Brazil, for instance, some Protestant students affiliated themselves and their organizations with the National Student Union (*União Nacional de Estudantes*, UNE), the national catalyst of what was at the time the largest and one of the most vibrant national student unions in the continent.

Youth and student Protestant organizations began to take form in Latin America in the 1920s.[14] The first national Protestant youth

---

12 Plou, *Caminhos de Unidade*, 75. LEAL stands for Latin American Evangelical Literature.

13 Plou, *Caminhos de Unidade*, 77.

14 See Sabanes Plou, *Caminhos de Unidade*, 49. The national youth unions or federations that began to take shape in the 1920s became the most significant lay expressions of the Protestant movement in Latin America in the first decades of the twentieth century. The YMCA and the YWCA began their work in the continent in 1880, with a South American Federation being stablished in 1914 for the coordination of the diverse YMCAs in South America. The nature, goals, and organization of their work, however, was much different from that of the federation and unions young

federation was formed in Argentina in 1926. Collaboration of those organizations of young Protestant Christians on the continental level, though, would only materialize fifteen years later through the creation of *the Unión Latinoamericana de Juventudes Evangélicas* (ULAJE) in 1941.[15]

Latin American national Protestant youth unions began to network in 1928 when young Chilean and Uruguayan Protestants attended a congress organized by the Argentinean Evangelical Youth Federation. That congress passed a resolution proposing the formation of a Latin American youth evangelical confederation. The idea continued to mature during a national congress held in Lima in 1934, which was followed by another congress coorganized by Protestant youth unions from Argentina and Uruguay in 1936.[16]

ULAJE's first Continental Youth Congress took place in Lima in 1941. The CCLA sponsored the event, publicizing it in the periodical *La Democracia*.[17] The main motivation for those incipient cooperative efforts among young Protestant leaders from multiple Latin American countries was the fulfillment of the evangelizing task. This was the vision that dominated the Lima congress.[18] The main achievement of that congress was the creation of ULAJE.

A second continental youth congress was held in Havana in 1946. The change of location to the Caribbean reflected the expansion ULAJE had experienced in its first five years of existence. The theme chosen to guide the second youth congress was "Christian Youth and Freedom."[19] ULAJE organized its third congress in Buenos Aires, in 1951. In that congress, Waldo César was elected as ULAJE's chairperson. In the years following that congress, César became one of the most important articulators of the Church and Society Movement in

Latin Americans began to organize locally and nationally in the 1920s throughout the continent. Therefore, the work of these two organizations stands beyond the scope of this analysis. For a glimpse at the work of YMCA and YWCA and its reception across the globe, see Harald Fischer-Tine, Stefan Huebner, and Ian Tyrrell, eds., *Spreading Protestant Modernity: Global Perspectives on the Social Work of the YMCA and YWCA, 1889–1970* (Honolulu: University of Hawaii Press, 2021).

[15] ULAJE initially stood for Latin American Union of Evangelical Youth. Later on, ULAJE replaced the word "evangelical" with "ecumenical." See Odell, "Fifty Years of Ecumenism in Latin America," 102.

[16] Sabanes Plou, *Caminhos de Unidade,* 114.

[17] Plou, *Caminhos de Unidade,* 115.

[18] Plou, *Caminhos de Unidade,* 116.

[19] Plou, *Caminhos de Unidade,* 116.

Latin America. In its fifth congress in 1956, which elected Uruguayan Methodist pastor Oscar Bolioli as its new General Secretary, ULAJE's commitment to social justice was sedimented. As Dafne Sabanes Plou underscores, at that time a growing number of young Latin American Protestants were seeking to develop a theological vision that encouraged greater participation on the part of the Protestant churches in the struggles for social change.[20] Such a vision became critical in the life of ULAJE. The more those young Protestants became aware of the social and political problems plaguing the region, the more opposition they faced within their own churches. Experiencing marginalization in their churches, some of those young Christians began to feel more comfortable navigating the secular arena. In response to the resistance faced within their denominations, a growing number of them sharpened their critique of the "institutional church," accusing it of hindering "a more dynamic relationship" with the popular processes taking place in the region.[21]

The 1950s were a time of social and political unrest throughout Latin America. In the wake of the Second World War, the United States wanted to affirm itself as "the supreme global power."[22] On the regional level, the US sponsored the Inter-American Treaty of Reciprocal Assistance (1947) and the creation of Organization of the American States (OAS) in 1948, with the declared purpose of regional economic cooperation and military protection for its members.[23] The outcome of those initiatives was the increased dominance of US economic and military interests in the region, deepening the political and economic troubles that already existed in the continent. As the major leader of a new global order, the United States asserted "its dominant position throughout the region as its primary commercial partner, and main economic source and provider of weapons."[24] The power asymmetry in the US relations with its Latin American neighbors was impossible to ignore. As Vijay Prashad notes, by the

---

[20] Plou, *Caminhos de Unidade*, 120.

[21] Plou, *Caminhos de Unidade*, 120.

[22] Edwin Williamson, *The Penguin History of Latin America*, Revised Edition (London, UK: 2009 [1992]), 346.

[23] Williamson, *The Penguin History of Latin America*, 346.

[24] Norman Rubén Amestoy, "De la crisis del modelo liberal a la irrupción del movimiento Iglesia y Sociedad em América Latina (ISAL)," *Teología y Cultura* 8/13 (2011): 7–26 (8).

mid-1950s the US already had a track record of interventionism and cracking down on anti-imperialist movements that was well-known in the region.

> Between 1900 and 1933, the U.S. military intervened to scuttle the national hopes of the people of Cuba (four times), the Dominican Republic (four times, including an eight-year occupation), Guatemala (once), Haiti (twice, including a nineteen-year occupation), Honduras (seven times), Nicaragua (twice), and Panama (six times).[25]

As the Cold War intensified, the US increased its efforts to maintain power over its Southern neighbors. Paradoxically, in the years following WWII, most Latin American countries still saw the US initiatives in the region through a positive lens. However, as US-backed developmentalist policies did not ameliorate the grave disparities and widespread poverty in Latin America, a growing number of Latin American leaders became more critical of US policies toward the region and started looking for alternatives. Agrarian reform was one of those measures many Latin American countries began to consider as a corrective to the huge concentration of land in the hands of small but powerful elites, which contrasted with the multitude of dispossessed. As mentioned earlier, by the mid-1940s, the United Fruit Company (UFCO) owned large swaths of land in Central America.[26] In Guatemala, for instance, one of the countries most plagued by foreign control of its lands, "2 percent of the land holders owned 72 percent of the arable land, and only a tiny part of their holdings was under cultivation."[27]

Agrarian reform aiming at the redistribution of idle land among impoverished and dispossessed peasant families was a political option under consideration in several Latin American countries, including Guatemala, where Jacobo Arbenz Guzmán, a young military officer who had a sweeping victory in the 1951 Presidential elections, vowed to redistribute "all idle lands to the peasants." Most of the 600,000 acres the UFCO owned in the country were not used. Arbenz

---

[25] Prashad, *The Darker Nations*, 106.

[26] Gonzalez, *Harvest of Empire*, 135.

[27] Gonzalez, *Harvest of Empire*, 136. Foreign control of the land contributed to the dislodging of a huge number of Mayans.

confiscated a hunk of those lands, offering $1.2 million as compensation to the North American company. The UFCO and the US State Department demanded a compensation of $16 million. Arbenz's refusal to abide by what he considered an overestimated compensation led CIA director Allen Dulles to convince President Dwight D. Eisenhower that Arbenz had to go. Dulles, a former partner of the United Fruit's main law firm in Washington, advised the US President to authorize the CIA to launch 'Operation Success,' "a plan for the armed overthrow of Arbenz, which took place in June 1954."[28]

The Organization of American States (OAS) rubber-stamped a resolution in support of the overthrow of a democratically elected president, justifying such an action with an unwarranted fear of "communist infiltration" in the southern hemisphere. Throughout the Cold War, "communism" became a catch-all word to justify military action and covert interventions on the part of the US against Latin American political leaders deemed a threat to national security. Following Arbenz's overthrow, Latin American leaders became even more suspicious of the intentions of the US government in the region and its responses to what they considered to be simply reformist measures such as land reform.[29]

United States interventionism in Latin America intensified in the later decades of the twentieth century, with the formulation of the national security doctrine. This doctrine dominated the US–Latin American relations until the 1980s, having devastating consequences in the region. Between the mid-1960s and the early 1990s, the US supported a number of military dictatorships and contributed to

---

[28] Gonzalez, *Harvest of Empire*, 137. Allen Dulles's brother, John Foster Dulles, was Eisenhower's Secretary of State and a leading figure in the Federal Council of the Churches of Christ, later the National Council of Churches in the USA, having cofound and chaired its Commission on a Just and Durable Peace. He was well known in ecumenical circles. He saw the United States as a Christian nation, and "believed strongly in the deployment of American force in defense of American interest and in defense of a wider peace." Mark Tooley, "John Foster Dulles, God & America," *Providence*, January 15, 2021, https://providencemag.com/2021/01/john-foster-dulles-god-america/. For more on the story of the Dulles brothers, see Stephen Kinzer, *The Brothers: John Foster Dulles, Allen Dulles, and Their Secret World War* (New York: Times Books, 2013). I am deeply grateful to Jesudas Athyal for drawing my attention to these connections.

[29] Amestoy, "De la crisis del modelo liberal," 9.

devastating civil wars. At its core, the national security doctrine enforced the annihilation of whoever was deemed a political threat to the US interests in Latin America.[30] As James L. Dietz suggests, American interventionism was articulated on the basis of the Monroe Doctrine.

> It is impossible that [foreign] powers should extend their political system to any portion of either continent without endangering our peace and happiness; *nor can anyone believe that our southern brethren, if left to themselves, would adopt it of their own accord.*[31]

In other words, the Monroe Doctrine presumed "that Latin American and Caribbean people neither have the right nor, apparently, the critical faculties to opt rationally and intelligently for an economic or political system not modeled on that of the United States."[32] Therefore, US economic and security interests—real or imagined—determined the boundaries of what was deemed acceptable as sovereign action on the part of Caribbean and Latin American states.[33] That imperial attitude on the part of the US toward its Latin American neighbors naturally contributed to the growth of nationalist and anti-imperialist sentiments in the region.

The WSCF and the Student Christian Movement in Latin America

In a context marked by the shadow of US imperialism in the 1950s, Latin American university students became one of the most active movements organizing for social reform at the time. The history of student mobilization in Latin America can be traced back to the First

[30] Daniel Feierstein, "National Security Doctrine in Latin America: The Genocide Question," in *The Oxford Handbook of Genocide*, ed. Donald Bloxham and A. Dirk Moses (Oxford, UK: Oxford University Press, 2010), 489–508.

[31] Gordon Connell-Smith, *The United States and Latin America: An Historical Analysis of Inter-American Relations* (New York: Halsted Press, 1974), 62, cited in James L. Dietz, "Destabilization and Intervention in Latin America and the Caribbean," *Latin American Perspectives* 11/3 (1984): 3–14 (4). *Italics* in Dietz's quote are mine.

[32] Dietz, "Destabilization and Intervention in Latin America and the Caribbean," 5.

[33] Dietz, "Destabilization and Intervention," 4.

International Congress of American Students held in Montevideo, Uruguay, in 1908. That event gathered participants from almost the entire continent.[34] However, as US interventions increased in the course of the twentieth century, a new and more politicized wave of student mobilization emerged organizing "against totalitarianism, authoritarian rule, and for democratization."[35] Those movements formed in university campuses across the continent stood in solidarity with labor movements, taking part in broader coalitions mobilizing for far more profound sociopolitical changes. The increasing political tensions in Latin America during the Cold War and the responses from vibrant secular students and labor movements made an indelible impact on Christian student movements in the region, both Protestant and Catholic.

As mentioned earlier, Protestant student organizations had existed in the region since the 1920s. As was the case with youth unions that emerged about the same time, they initially focused mostly on the need to cooperate for the sake of evangelizing other students. Those organizations received a boost from John Mott's visit to several Latin American countries in 1940.[36] Mott was one of the six students who founded the World Student Christian Federation (WSCF) in 1895, serving the organization, including as general secretary and later chair, for more than three decades.[37] Although taking on various other leadership roles in the ecumenical movement, his interest in the work of the WSCF never waned. One of the main motives behind his visit to Latin America and the Caribbean in 1940 was to arouse interest in the churches for the promotion of the Student Christian Movement (SCM).[38] As the SCM organized its networks in Latin America, its leaders opted for a decentralized strategy. Instead of forming a continental organism such as ULAJE to coordinate the

[34] Imanol Ordorika, "Student Movements and Politics in Latin America: A Historical Reconceptualization," *Higher Education* 83 (2022): 297–315, https://doi.org/10.1007/s10734-020-00656-6.

[35] Ordorika, "Student Movements and Politics in Latin America," 297–315.

[36] Sabanes Plou, *Caminhos de Unidade*, 122.

[37] Philip Potter and Thomas Wieser, *Seeking and Serving the Truth: The First Hundred Years of the World Student Christian Federation* (Geneva: WCC Publications, 1997), 13.

[38] Sabanes Plou, *Caminhos de Unidade*, 122.

movement in the region, they focused on supporting national student organizations.[39]

The WSCF had played a key formative role in the intellectual life of the broader ecumenical movement. In Latin America it was not different. As Alan Neely underscores, during the Life and Work Conference at Oxford in 1937, Ruth Rouse (1872–1956), who had been an active member of the Student Christian Movement and would later be a notable chronicler of the ecumenical movement, mentioned that there were not many faces in that conference that she did not recognize from her long association with the WSCF.[40]

Similarly, various Latin American students associated with the SCM would end up becoming key leaders in ISAL and the ecumenical movement more broadly.[41] Among others, Julio de Santa Ana and José Miguez Bonino, who would play major roles in the WCC, began their ecumenical lives in the SCM. Rubem Alves, one of the early proponents of Latin American liberation theology, also did.[42] Uruguayan Valdo Gallant, the first WSCF Secretary for Latin America, served as the WSCF General Secretary from 1961 to 1968. As Neely put it, these national student organizations functioned "as ideological incubators for the production of young Protestant Christians who were sensitive to the social and political implications of the Christian gospel and who subsequently became the foremost spokesmen of the ISAL movement in the 1960s."[43] Considering the size of its Christian student union, and its place as one of the first to affiliate with the WSCF in the region, the Brazilian experience of the SCM was among the most influential in the region.

---

39 Plou, *Caminhos de Unidade*, 123.

40 Neely, "Protestant Antecedents of the Latin American Theology of Liberation," 154.

41 Neely, "Protestant Antecedents of the Latin American Theology of Liberation," 156.

42 Alves's association with the SCM was highlighted at the 34th WSCF's General Assembly in 2008. He was a keynote speaker at a global Senior Friends Gathering held in tandem with that event. See WSCF, "Senior Friends rejoice in WSCF renewal," *Federation News*, Nov. 2008, https://www.wscf.ch/docs/resources/federation-news/WSCF_Federation_News_2008-11.pdf.

43 Neely, "Protestant Antecedents of the Latin American Theology of Liberation," 155–156.

Brazil's SCM was the largest and most active Christian student organization in the continent and one the first Latin America Christian student unions to officially affiliate with the WSCF, in 1954.[44] Brazil's SCM, known as *União Cristã de Estudantes do Brasil* (UCEB), was founded in 1926. It was then called *União de Estudantes para o Trabalho de Cristo* (UETC). Initially, it congregated mostly high school students.[45] Like other Christian youth organizations at the time, it aimed at equipping students to become missionaries in a society undergoing fast urbanization.[46] In 1940, another organization of students was formed—under the influence of the YMCA and the Protestant Confederation of Brazil (CEB)—to work exclusively with college and university students. The *Associação de Cristãos Acadêmicos* (ACA), another association of Christian students, organized through small local groups on university campuses across the country.[47] Upon UCEB's affiliation with the WSCF, the two organizations merged. UCEB became the acronym used to identify the national movement, while the acronym ACA began to be used to identify the local groups of students who regularly met on campuses across the nation.

In the 1940s, the main concerns of the Brazilian student Christian movement remained evangelistic and pastoral. Christian witness in the predominantly secular environment of the Brazilian universities and the identification of the Christian vocation of Protestant students were critical pastoral concerns for the student ministry of UCEB. The intensification of interactions with both the secular student movement in Brazil and the WSCF contributed to expand UCEB's understanding of the forms Christian witness could take in the Latin American context. On the international level, the General Committee of the WSCF created a Commission on Politics in 1946 "to stimulate the national SCM organizations to discuss political issues, to enhance their awareness of the Christian's responsibility

[44] Neely, "Protestant Antecedents of the Latin American Theology of Liberation," 155.

[45] See União Cristã de Estudantes do Brasil (UCEB), "Pequena História da UCEB," in *Cadernos da UCEB*, n.d. The M. Richard Shaull Papers, Wright Library, Princeton Theological Seminary. UCEB stands for Christian Student Union of Brazil, while UETC stands for Union of Students for the Work of Christ.

[46] Eduardo G. Faria, *Fé e Compromisso: Richard Shaull e a Teologia no Brasil* (São Paulo, Brazil: ASTE, 2002), 106.

[47] Faria, *Fé e Compromisso*, 106.

in regard to political problems, and to motivate them to become involved in the resolution of those problems."[48]

On the national level, since the organization of the *União National de Estudantes* (UNE), the Brazilian student national union, in 1937, a new space had emerged for university students to process fresh demands for political awareness and engagement. Since its inception, UNE organized annual congresses to "seek articulation with other progressive forces in society."[49] As the ACAs were inserted in the life of the Brazilian universities in important urban centers, these small groups of students became increasingly involved in the national struggles for justice. Initially alienated from those conversations, Protestant students gradually began to see their participation in the broader student struggle on local campuses as a significant aspect of their Christian witness.

Toward the end of the 1950s, UCEB consolidated its identity as a leading progressive Christian organization. Some of its students took on leadership roles in student academic centers in different states. The necessity to understand the nature of their engagement as Protestant Christians in those social struggles led UCEB students to look for theological language that could speak meaningfully to their reality.

A major turning point in the life of UCEB and in the Latin American SCM as a whole was the first Latin American Conference of Christian Students the WSCF organized in São Paulo, in July of 1952. That conference, which brought together Protestant students from various Latin American countries, reflected on the meaning of the Christian vocation in the Latin American context, urging its participants "to act in the diverse sectors of life in society and in the world Christian movement."[50] Reflection on the Christian attitude toward communism, a pressing matter those students were forced to face at the time in the Cold War Latin American context, was also prominent at that conference. The keynote speaker at the conference was Presbyterian missionary Richard Shaull.[51]

---

48 Faria, *Fé e Compromisso*, 157.

49 União National de Estudantes (UNE), "História da UNE," https://www.une.org.br/2011/09/historia-da-une/. Translation is mine. UNE stands for National Student Union.

50 Faria, *Fé e Compromisso*, 109.

51 Richard Shaull, *Surpreendido Pela Graça: Memórias de Um Teológo* (Rio de Janeiro: Record, 2003), 93.

After an eight-year tenure as a missionary in Colombia, Shaull had spent his furlough at Union Theological Seminary, New York, on a fellowship from the Board of Foreign Missions to study "the challenge of Communism and how to respond to it." Part of a team of missionaries brought to New York City for this study project, Shaull participated in weekly seminars led by Union professors Reinhold Niebuhr, John Bennett, and Searle Bates, engaging a variety of "political scientists, specialists on Marxism and communist movements, communist leaders from the US and abroad, missionaries from China and church leaders representing diverse approaches to communism."[52]

That intensive semester of studies at Union Theological Seminary prepared Shaull to engage the questions the Latin American students were asking in the WSCF conference. After a conversation with WSCF General Secretary Phillip Maury a day before the beginning of the conference, Shaull decided to stay in Brazil to support the work of UCEB. Maury strongly believed in UCEB's potential to respond "to a new generation of Protestants eager to deepen their faith and find their way as Christians in the world."[53] Shaull was equally impressed by the students he met—"especially by the Brazilians," he uttered. Reflecting on that encounter years later, he stated,

> [F]or the first time in my years in Latin America, I had found in the WSCF a world-wide community of men and women who shared my basic faith and theology, were committed to in-depth Bible study, were concerned about the vocation of Christians in the world, and were committed to express their faith in the midst of social struggles.[54]

While appreciative of the questions the Latin American students raised at the conference, Shaull thought that the focus on "communism" was misguided. For him, such a focus could become a distraction that would prevent them from examining the Latin American situation more thoroughly and from asking more fundamental questions. The conversation, in his view, should focus instead on the

[52] Shaull, *Surpreendido Pela Graça*, 74–75. According to Shaull, the participants in the seminars "were expected to identify the key issues being raised, work on them in small teams and produce a report of our conclusions at the end of the term." Shaull, 75.

[53] Shaull, *Surpreendido Pela Graça*, 94.

[54] Shaull, *Surpreendido Pela Graça*, 94.

revolutionary situation Latin Americans and other people around the world were experiencing.

While not everyone agreed on what should be the Christian relation to communism in Latin America, the dominant attitude in Protestant circles was defensive. For the most part, conversations on that topic in Latin American Protestant churches focused on refuting it on "biblical" grounds. Despite being critical of Marxism, Shaull was not interested in confronting it. He knew that despite its shortcomings, Marxism offered a compelling response to a systemic situation of injustice, and that its response appealed to many young people around the world—Latin Americans, in particular. In fact, he considered that the deficit of dialogue about the theme within most Protestant churches was a factor contributing to the exodus from the church of educated young Protestants involved in organizations such as UNE. That was the kind of crisis to which ULAJE had also been seeking to respond. The students involved in the SCM, though, were having those conversations not only in Christian circles but also on college campuses and other spaces.

In those conversations, Shaull became interested in developing a constructive Christian response to the social revolution taking place in the region so that the churches were not alienated from it. That is why more important than understanding "communism," it was to understand "revolution." Shaull was also aware that such a misleading focus on communism on the part of Latin American Christians stemmed from US missionary influence. In his presentations at the first Latin American WSCF conference, he stated,

> As we Americans peer into the mouth of the volcano, we see only the red fires of Communism and assume that it, and it alone, is the cause of all our trouble. Here is our first great mistake. Not Communism but Revolution is the fundamental fact we face; revolution which is worldwide, in fact, the first truly world-wide revolution in history, the first time that everywhere all institutions of the past seem inadequate and all things appear simultaneously and unprecedently out of joint. Communism has not caused this revolution, but has arisen as one of the most serious efforts to understand it and as the most powerful world force that has set out deliberately to direct it.[55]

[55] M. Richard Shaull, *Encounter with Revolution* (New York: Association Press, 1955), 3.

Shaull saw the worldwide revolutionary situation as a "revolt of the disinherited."[56] According to him, communism appealed to the disinherited because it offered three things: "(1) an explanation of what is happening and a solution; (2) a movement strong enough to achieve power and establish its solution; and (3) a total philosophy that gives a scientific and certain foundation for its program."[57]

While urging his peers to take that response to the revolutionary situation seriously and engage it constructively, Shaull argued that communism betrayed the goals of revolution because of its misguided understanding of humanity. He saw its program as inadequate. Its philosophy tended to become a straightjacket and its power corrupt.[58] Consequently, he deemed "communism" an insufficient response to the fundamental problems at hand. However, since communism did not cause those problems, the Christian focus needed to be brought back to the understanding of the fundamental issues at hand, which he identified as threefold: the economic problem of underdevelopment; the search for new political, social, and economic structures capable of establishing a more just society; and the question of moral and spiritual resources for Christian participation in the transformation of society.[59]

Shaull's lectures offered a programmatic statement for the work the Latin American Student Christian Movement would seek to do in the next decade. Besides anything else, those lectures contributed to change the terms of the conversation in ecumenical Protestant circles in the region. Shaull pointed to concrete possibilities for Christian participation in the Latin American revolutionary situation, and his young interlocutors took notice of that. He articulated an experience of spiritual renewal aimed at the transformation of society, which, while open to positively engaging with secular philosophies such as Marxism, highlighted its Christian distinctiveness. The theological language Shaull advanced allowed those students who were already engaging public discourse to identify common ground and vocabulary for Christians and non-Christians to form

---

56 Shaull, *Encounter with Revolution*, 4.

57 Shaull, *Encounter with Revolution*, 19.

58 Shaull, *Encounter with Revolution*, 35ff.

59 Shaull, *Encounter with Revolution*, 98ff.

coalitions to jointly address the common social reality they were seeking to change.[60] For him, revolution was the common ground to start such a conversation.

Accordingly, Shaull encouraged Latin American Protestant students to look for the sacred not in the confines of the institutions of the church but in the chaotic reality of life. Rubem Alves, who first met Shaull as a student at the Presbyterian Seminary of Campinas in 1953, shed light many years later on how he and his colleagues received the challenges Shaull posed to them. For him, the main challenge Shaull presented to them was the call to stop looking for the sacred in the internal gardens of the church and instead look for God in the daily struggles of the world, in the "eye of the hurricane."[61] According to Alves, Shaull did not conjure a revolution; he simply acknowledged its reality. The conditions of drastic social change in the mostly urban spaces in which those Latin American Protestant students lived in response to drastic social injustice were already revolutionary.

Shaull contributed a meaningful theological language that helped those Latin American Protestant students to interpret the reality in which they lived and discern a course of transformative action.[62] Whereas the dominant theological stream in Latin American Protestant churches at the time discouraged participation in worldly affairs, Shaull invited those students to go out and live in the world, where they could understand God's action and contribute to its

[60] Faria, *Fé e Compromisso*, 110.

[61] Rubem Alves, "O Deus do Furacão," in *De Dentro do Furacão: Richard Shaull e os Primórdios da Teologia da Libertação*, Richard Shaull (São Paulo, Brazil: Editora Sagarana; CEDI/CLAI, 1985), 19–24 (22).

[62] Alves, "O Deus do Furacão," in *De Dentro do Furacão*, 23. For Shaull, theologians should be immersed in the world, offering language to make sense of God's action in the world under changing circumstances and in light of the new challenges each generation of Christians faces. Such a task required theologians to listen carefully to the signs of the times. As Alves would say later, theology mattered as language because he saw language as a social fact. "It exists as 'creation,' as an expression of men's [sic] efforts to understand their experience as human beings." When Shaull emphasized the need for new theological language, he was calling for the articulation of a new interpretation of the Christian mission in Latin America vis-à-vis the lived experiences of those students, convinced that through such a creative language they would sow the seeds of alternative possible futures. Rubem Alves, *Dogmatismo e Tolerância* (São Paulo: Ed. Loyola, 2004), 165.

transformation. Theology was no longer something disconnected from the reality of life. Instead, as Alves asserted, it was supposed to be about living in the world.

Recalling those exchanges with Shaull in the 1950s, Alves asserted, "We desired to convert the world to the church. Shaull told us the opposite. The church should convert to the world; leave the inner garden and ride the wind . . ." [63] That moment represented the beginning of something new, the announcement of a new way of theologizing and being church. As Alves stated later,

> Well, Shaull. Without knowing, you started something new. And I hope you won't be offended if I call you patriarch, father of a nation. Or, if the name is too great for your humility, at least accept the title 'witness,' one who saw a new church being born and announced it.[64]

Alves was right. This was the beginning of a new path for the development of a Latin American theology. Although Shaull was not the creator of such a theology, he was an important instigator of a movement out of which such theologizing would emerge—at least its Protestant stream. He saw the potential for something new and fascinating taking form, as he referred to when speaking about his early Brazilian students in the Campinas seminary:

> I was convinced that creative theological development depended upon a dynamic ongoing dialogue between our heritage of faith and the contemporary human situation. This, I assumed, called for exploring new ways of becoming engaged with this heritage and a new pedagogy. I was fascinated by the possibility before a new generation to develop an authentically Brazilian theology, flowing out of reflection on the presence and power of God in the history and culture of Brazil. I felt certain that such theological creativity demanded serious involvement of seminary students in the life and struggles of their own people and was eager to encourage them to seek and draw on such involvement as they pursued their studies.[65]

---

[63] Alves, "O Deus do Furacão," in *De Dentro do Furacão*, 22.

[64] Alves, "O Deus do Furacão," in *De Dentro do Furacão*, 24.

[65] Shaull, *Surpreendido Pela Graça*, 113.

Some of those students, including Rubem Alves and João Dias de Araújo,[66] would be among the first to propose a Protestant liberation theology in Latin America. In his service as Acting General Secretary of UCEB, Shaull encouraged seminary students in Brazil to engage the SCM so they could be in touch with the effervescent reality of lay engagement as mediators of new church and society relations around the world.

According to Shaull, "When they [seminarians] took part in UCEB discussions, they were often surprised to discover how little they were in touch with the more dynamic developments taking place in Brazilian thought and society."[67] Uruguayan theologian Julio de Santa Ana (1934–2023), one of the most important Latin American ecumenists in the second half of the twentieth century, remembers the impact that his conversations with Shaull had on his theological formation when they first met at the *Instituto Superior de Estúdios Teológicos* (ISEDET), in 1953. A student at the time, Santa Ana recalls that in those years most leaders in Latin American Protestant churches thought that Christian witness demanded taking distance from the events of the world. Shaull helped him to change that view.

> Shaull was a master in showing us that doing theology is taking part in the struggles of our time, participating in history, because, only in it and from within it, it is possible to find God, and above all, to create conditions to listen to God's voice and even get to be an interpreter of God's Word.[68]

---

[66] Alves became a pioneering liberation theologian with the publication of his 1968 PhD dissertation "Toward a Theology of Liberation: An Exploration of the Encounter between the Languages of Humanistic Messianism and Messianic Humanism" in 1969. His book, written independently from that of Gustavo Gutiérrez, ended up published first. The two theologians met for the first time only in 1969 at a conference on theology and development in Cartigny, Switzerland. See chapter 11 for more on this encounter. Araújo, a contemporary of Alves at Princeton Theological Seminary, where he got a ThM degree in 1968, is largely unknown outside of Brazil. While some of his most important contributions were in the field of pastoral theology, he made important incursions in the development of a people's theology based on the praxis of the poor in Northeastern Brazil. See, for instance, João Dias de Araújo, *O Cristo Brasileiro: A Teologia do Povo* (São Paulo: ASTE, 2012).

[67] Shaull, *Surpreendido Pela Graça*, 119.

[68] Julio de Santa Ana, "Richard Shaull: Teólogo e Pioneiro Ecumênico—Um Testemunho Reconhecido," in *De Dentro do Furacão*, 33–39 (37).

Santa Ana also highlighted another important contribution Shaull offered to an incipient Latin American liberation theology: the primacy of praxis. Writing in the 1980s, at a time when the primacy of praxis had become a common practice in liberation theology, Santa Ana reflected on the challenges to understand it in the 1950s.

> Now, more than thirty years later, the thing has turned into a statement that no one questions (at least theoretically). At that time, however, this insistence seemed inappropriate, impertinent. It was a period when metaphysics counted in theological formation. Ideas that came "from above" were more important than those that emerged from confrontation with practice. Shaull insisted that in order to simply "say God" one must participate in our [human] historical situation. So only from the perspective of practice one could refer to knowing something.[69]

This important emphasis that Shaull began to advance in the mid-1950s was critical for the rise of base ecumenism. The praxis he encouraged then provided an incipient form of a new way of being church, which would become widespread with the rise of the Christian Base Communities or *Comunidades Eclesiales de Base* (CEBs) in the 1960s. While Shaull did not develop a theology of liberation himself, he pointed the way to it and contributed to its method. After he left Brazil, returning to the United States in 1962, Shaull ended up engaging with a full-fledged Latin American liberation theology in the 1980s. Such an encounter was not limited to the dialogues he continued to have with Latin American theologians. He was deeply impacted by his encounter with the Ecclesial Base Communities (Comunidades Eclesiais de Base or CEBs). What he learned from them and from the liberation theology that stemmed from their praxis changed him so drastically that he referred to it as a "second conversion,"[70] a transformative experience that drastically changed the way he read the Bible, learning to see it through the lens of "God's concern for the poor and Christ's proclamation of the advent of a

---

[69] Julio de Santa Ana, "Richard Shaull," 37–38.

[70] For a discussion of Shaull's three conversions, see Barreto, *Protesting Poverty*, chapter 2.

kingdom in which the poor and marginal will have a new life and a special place."[71]

In his Latin American immersion in the 1950s, Shaull also learned about the significance of the primacy of praxis. That awareness was at the root of the experiments he conducted with his students and colleagues in Campinas, giving birth to Christian koinonias outside institutional walls. Those Christian koinonias represented renewed forms the church could take in all spheres of life.[72] The most significant of those initiatives, in 1955, was called "Students in the Factory." Some of Shaull's students rented a home in an industrial area to live among industrial workers, work with them, and participate in their struggles.

> They found work in factories located in the area, became members of unions, mixed with workers at the entrance and exit of factories, and took part in community activities. [. . .] At dusk, and on weekends, they tried to systematize and reflect on their lived experiences—and how the themes and problems had affected them.[73]

Inspired by the Catholic worker-priest movement in France, those koinonias were formed in the cities of Campinas, São Paulo, and Rio de Janeiro. Concerned with the rapid industrialization Brazil was experiencing, especially in its southern urban areas, Shaull identified "ways to place some of his seminary students as workers in some factories in towns near Campinas during their summer vacations."[74] In its most enduring iteration, seven of Shaull's pupils rented a home

[71] Shaull, "Responding to the Challenge: Renewal and Re-Creation," *Freedom and Discipleship: Liberation Theology in an Anabaptist Perspective*, ed. Daniel S. Schipani (New York: Orbis Book, 1989), 147–158 (148).

[72] M. Richard Shaull, "The Present Life and Structure of the Church in Relation to Her Witness in Latin American Society," unpublished paper, 1959(?). The M. Richard Shaull Papers, Wright Library, Princeton.

[73] Shaull, *Surpreendido Pela Graça*, 121.

[74] Jovelino P. Ramos, "Wondering and Wandering with Dick Shaull," unpublished lecture (Herencia Lectures, Princeton Theological Seminary, October 9, 2015). Author's personal files. See also Theodore Gill, "CMI relembra a contribuição de Rubem Alves ao movimento ecumênico," *WCC News*, July 24, 2014, https://www.oikoumene.org/pt-pt/news/the-ecumenical-movement-remembers-rubem-alves-1933-2014.

in Vila Anastácio, São Paulo. The group's insertion in the day-to-day lives of the factory workers and their communal living in that setting created a renewed sense of the meaning of the gospel in their reality.

The hardening of the military dictatorship, which forced a number of UCEB's leaders into exile, contributed to the early end of those communal experiments, leading to the closing of UCEB in 1969. The impact UCEB had on the lives of those young leaders who took part in its ranks, though, remains a cherished memory of an era in which a still-incipient base ecumenism was tried by fire. That memory continued to inspire numerous other initiatives in the following decades.

The "Students in the Factory" program was an initiative jointly supported by the UCEB, the Brazilian Commission on Church and Society, and the Presbyterian Church of Lapa. While these experiments took place independently from the rising of the *Comunidades de Base* (CEBs) formed within Catholic circles in the mid-1960s, they significantly contributed to the earlier stages of a Latin American Protestant stream of theology of liberation, which not only advanced a proposal of social change but also promoted a deep rethinking of the way of being "church" in Latin America, pioneering what Leonardo Boff would call the reinvention of the church from the ground up.[75]

While the Protestant student-worker initiative took place at the margins of Brazilian Protestantism, supported only by a few Protestant congregations, the Catholic CEBs, by contrast, would be incorporated into the pastoral practice and institutions of the Latin American Catholic Church, as we will see later. As long as they found support among bishops and priests and a home in the archdioceses and parishes they were connected to, they flourished. Despite their differences, these experiments gave birth to a certain spirituality, a liberation Christianity, which not only remains alive and active in the region but which has also spread to other parts of the world, informing a number of other grassroots initiatives.

---

[75] Leonardo Boff, *Ecclesiogenesis: The Base Communities Reinvent the Church* (Maryknoll, NY: Orbis, 1992).

5

TOWARD A WORLD-ORIENTED ECUMENISM

Several students associated with the UCEB participated in the inception of the Brazilian Commission on Church and Society in 1955. The work of that commission contributed to expand the impact of the incipient liberation Christianity stirred up in SCM circles, giving birth to new fronts of ecumenical action throughout Latin America. In its continental articulation, a milestone for that movement was the creation in 1961 of the Latin American Commission on Church and Society (ISAL).

Upon its integration into the Protestant Confederation of Brazil (CEB), the Commission on Church and Society changed its name to *Setor de Responsabilidade Social da Igreja* (SRSI).[1] By the late 1950s, the SRSI had become the main face of a prophetic Brazilian Protestantism. In its origins, this commission was strongly influenced by the language of social responsibility borrowed from Evanston 1954. In subsequent years, though, already integrated into the structure of the Evangelical Confederation of Brazil (CEB), the SRSI organized four important conferences in Brazil, which showed an evolution of the language in the making of a Latin American ecumenical agenda for church and society.[2]

Moving Beyond the Responsible Society Framework

Between 1955 and 1962, the SRSI moved from a reformist approach to a more radical advocacy for social change that increasingly embraced a revolutionary framework. That development contributed to the rising of a Protestant liberationist theological language that would

[1] The Church's Sector of Social Responsibility.

[2] In *Protesting Poverty*, I discuss the four conferences SRSI held in Brazil between 1955 and 1962 in the context of the formation of the Brazilian ecumenical instruments. See Barreto, *Protesting Poverty*, chapter 3. The discussion that follows situates those conferences in the context of the broader developments in the WCC as well as vis-à-vis the rise of ISAL.

inform the work of the *Junta Latinoamericana de Iglesia y Sociedad* (ISAL) in the 1960s.[3] Formed in response to the growing ecumenical preoccupation with the social responsibility of the church in Evanston 1954, the Church and Society Movement in Brazil was a critical step toward the creation of ISAL.

Concerns with social issues and public witness were part of the ecumenical movement from its inception. The second Assembly of the World Council of Churches in Evanston (1954), though, embodied such concerns more thoroughly, giving the theme of social responsibility a prominent place in its agenda. The report submitted to that assembly on the topic "Evangelism: the mission of the church to those outside her life" stated:

> [W]herever Christians find themselves separated by caste, class, racial, or other barriers, they will boldly cross them, manifesting Christ's solidarity with the whole of mankind. In a divided world they will fulfill Christ's ministry of peace, manifesting in their own life the new mankind which has begun in Jesus Christ.[4]

Other reports shared in Evanston focused on issues of justice in response to racism and also to the economic asymmetries and widespread social injustice dividing the world. The Section III Report had the title "Social Questions: The Responsible Society in a World Perspective." Section IV focused on the topic "International Affairs—Christians in the Struggle for World Community," and Section V on "Inter-group Relations—The Church amid Racial and Ethnic Tensions."

The introduction to the Evanston report on the social issues brought unprecedented "attention to the problems facing the Churches in Africa, Asia, and Latin America," with particular emphasis on economic and political issues.[5] That report also addressed the situation of economic underdevelopment in large parts of the world as a crucial concern for the churches, reinforcing the need for "Christians to think about the responsible

---

[3] Latin American Commission on Church and Society. Later, ISAL became known simply as Iglesia y Sociedad en América Latina or Church and Society in Latin America.

[4] WCC, *Evanston Speaks*, 33.

[5] WCC, *Evanston Speaks*, 42.

society in a world perspective." The significance of that social turn is expressed in the following words in the introduction of the Section III Report:

> For the first time in an ecumenical document, here is an attempt to see the social problems of the various regions of the world as an inter-related whole. It is evident that in dealing with the problems of the economically under-developed countries the Churches of other countries are involved and have an important contribution to make. It may be hoped that the Evanston report in this respect will help to indicate the larger goals of Christian social responsibility today.[6]

Since the 1937 Life and Work Conference in Oxford, ecumenical conversations on social issues had privileged the ethical framework of responsibility, characteristic of a North-Atlantic Protestantism that saw itself as a privileged actor in the world. H. Richard Niebuhr and Reinhold Niebuhr contributed prominently to popularization of that concept. Both of them actively participated in the first WCC Assembly in Amsterdam (1948), where the term "responsible society" was first thematized.[7] Amsterdam 1948 defined the responsible society as the "society 'where freedom is the freedom of men [sic] who acknowledge responsibility to justice and public order and where those who hold political authority or economic power are responsible for its exercise to God and to the people whose welfare is affected by it."[8]

Responsibility was broadly understood as "a criterion by which we judge all existing social orders and at the same time a standard to guide us in the specific choices we have to make."[9] Christians were urged to live responsibly. In Niebuhrian terms, they were called "to live in response to God's act of redemption in Christ, in any society,

---

[6] WCC, *Evanston Speaks*, 45.

[7] WCC, *Evanston Speaks*, 48.

[8] WCC, *Evanston Speaks*. For the influence of the Niebuhr brothers on the ecumenical understanding of responsibility, see Gary B. MacDonald, "The Church and Social Responsibility: Contributions to Contemporary Social Ethics from the Ecumenical Social Method of the Oxford Conference on Church, Community, and State of 1937" (2019). Religious Studies Theses and Dissertations 12, https://scholar.smu.edu/religious_studies_etds/12.

[9] WCC, *Evanston Speaks*.

even within the most unfavourable social structures."[10] The novelty that Evanston 1954 brought to the ecumenical table was a broader approach to the economic and political nature of the social problems at hand, taking Africa, Asia, and Latin America into account. Another milestone at Evanston was the assembly's decision to create the Department of Church and Society, which became a powerful instrument for ecumenical study "on social questions, both in regard to the content of ecumenical thinking and to the organization of the continuing work."[11]

Was the framework of the responsible society concrete enough to help Latin American Christians as they responded to the challenges faced in their societies, though? The earliest critiques of the ecumenical emphasis on the responsible society pointed out the vagueness of the phrase. In an attempt to respond to that criticism, Evanston made an effort "to relate this idea to actual problems," opening up new lines of study of particular social questions African, Asian, and Latin American Christians were seeking to address.[12] Those conversations started prior to the assembly, in the preparation of the documents for Evanston 1954. M. Richard Shaull participated in those pre-assembly conversations. Evanston 1954 not only inspired the formation of the Church and Society Commission in Brazil in 1955 but was umbilically related to it, as Shaull's observations of the Brazilian reality were taken into account in the preparation of the documents for the Evanston assembly.

In Shaull's recollection of the events leading to the creation of the SRSI, he states that it all started when he met Waldo César on a trip to Rio de Janeiro in 1953. It did not take long for them to realize that they shared a common interest in doing something to awaken the church to its social responsibility. Following that encounter, they invited a number of individuals from Methodist, Presbyterian, and Baptist backgrounds to start an ecumenical effort to explore the Christian responsibility of Brazilian Christians toward the broader society. The group met on a regular basis and

---

[10] WCC, *Evanston Speaks.*

[11] WCC Central Committee, *Evanston to New Delhi, 1954–1961: Report of the Central Committee to the Third Assembly of the World Council of Churches* (Geneva: World Council of Churches, 1961), 46. This department was in charge of organizing the Geneva Conference on Church and Society in 1966.

[12] WCC Central Committee, *Evanston to New Delhi, 1954–1961*, 46.

was expanding when Shaull unexpectedly received a copy of the first draft of the document "The Responsible Society in World Perspective" in advance of the Second WCC Assembly in Evanston. In the letter that accompanied it, Paul Albrecht, who would later be elected Executive Secretary of the new WCC Department of Church and Society, asked Shaull to read and comment on that draft from a Latin American perspective. Glad to see the WCC's decentralized approach to the matter, Shaull promptly wrote Albrecht back. In his response, he expressed concern that the document only represented "a First World perspective which was somewhat different from the reality of our situation in Latin America." In his view, that survey "did not present an adequate picture of the real situation in much of Asia, Africa and Latin America, which was that of overwhelming poverty and exploitation." Furthermore, he also shared his perception that Latin America was a continent caught up in a revolutionary situation. Therefore, he affirmed, a "reflection on a 'responsible society' in Latin America might call for a quite different approach from that envisioned by Western Europeans and North Americans."[13]

To Shaull's surprise, Albrecht wrote him back immediately, thanking him for his critique of the draft and informing him that those comments would be considered as they moved forward. In the same letter, Albrecht asked Shaull to contribute a paper for a study on the "development of social action thinking," which would gather contributions from around the world. Shaull was initially reluctant to offer a Latin American perspective, as he was a North American missionary in Latin America. So, he encouraged Albrecht to find a Latin American to write that paper. In response, Albrecht told him that no Latin American had responded so far to his appeals and he was running out of time to gather that paper in time for the Evanston Assembly. Shaull ended up writing the paper. That contact with Albrecht initiated a long-term relationship between Shaull and the Church and Society program of the WCC. The more Shaull brought Latin America to the center of that conversation, the more he became critical of the original language of the program. He never disengaged, though, believing that his participation would help shape the newly formed program. Looking back into that decision, Shaull asserted,

[13] Shaull, *Surpreendido Pela Graça*, 174–175.

"From the beginning, I saw it as my task to show the WCC what was happening in Latin America; and to insist that this be considered in any study of Christian responsibility in society."[14]

Even more importantly, in his interactions with Albrecht, Shaull learned that the WCC Church and Society Department was planning a series of regional conferences to discuss the statement on social responsibility prepared at Evanston, launching an ampler discussion about the social responsibility of the churches, which engaged the situation experienced in each continent. Asked about the feasibility of holding a regional conference in Latin America, Shaull took the question to the Brazilian study group he and César had been meeting with, which strongly supported the idea. They made some conditions to join the initiative, though. First, they wanted the conference to be sponsored by an independent but representative group of lay individuals and church leaders. Second, they wanted the conference to happen in Brazil and for Brazilians. Third, they wanted to form a steering committee with Brazilians who were already thinking along the lines of the WCC proposal—thus avoiding that more conservative CEB leaders hijacked the event. Finally, they wanted to count on the knowledge and experience of representatives from other countries already involved in the work of the new department—preferentially not from the United States. The Brazilian starting point to that conversation would be "the awareness of the social revolution," whereas, those coming from other countries could present the WCC perspective "on the responsible society."[15] Those demands clearly set the tone of the conversation, which would give prominence to the voices and concerns of the local organizers, while putting them in a conversation among equals with WCC representatives and other international participants.

As all those conditions were met, the group started planning the consultation for November of 1955. In February of that same year, they organized the Brazilian Commission on Church and Society, which became the convener of the first Consultation on Church and Society in Latin America. Following that first consultation, the commission was integrated into the CEB's structure in December of 1955. The CEB Sector of Social Responsibilty (SRSI) organized three

14 Shaull, *Surpreendido Pela Graça*, 176.

15 Shaull, *Surpreendido Pela Graça*, 177.

subsequent consultations between 1957 and 1962. These consultations were extremely formative in the evolution of a Latin American Protestant ecumenical social thinking. They also informed the regional developments in church and society leading to the formation of ISAL.

The First Consultation on the Social Responsibility of the Church took place in the temple of a Presbyterian church in São Paulo. The recently formed independent Commission on Church and Society elected Benjamin Moraes as its chair and Waldo César as executive secretary. Shaull participated as one of its members. César carried out most of the preparatory work. The main expressed goal of the Church and Society Commission was to encourage "Brazilian Protestantism to analyze its role in the face of the Brazilian social reality."[16] Forty individuals—pastors, lawyers, professors, journalists, and a judge—representing nine churches participated in that First Consultation on Church and Society.[17] Its theme was "The Social Responsibility of the Church." Edgar de Vries and Paul Albrecht represented the WCC. Shaull highlighted two elements in that conference that merit attention. First, that was the first time when a significant number of individuals representing important Brazilian Protestant churches came to the realization that a conversation on the social responsibility of the church could no longer be avoided or delayed. Also, the presence of representatives from the WCC in the consultation brought up the question about the significance of the perspectives discussed in that small Latin American gathering to conversations

[16] "I Consulta: A Responsabilidade Social da Igreja," in José Bittencourt Filho, *Caminhos do Protestantismo Militante: ISAL e a Conferência do Nordeste* (Vitória: Editora Unida, 2014), 125. The late scholar of Brazilian Protestantism José Bittencourt Filho included the original documents from the four consultations the CEB's Sector of Social Responsibility organized between 1955 and 1962 in the appendices of this book. During the Military Dictatorship (1964–1985), raids were conducted in the CEB's offices and in the homes of the people in charge of the SRSI. During those raids, the military burned books and documents they considered subversive. The Rev. Carlos Alberto Correa Cunha, one of the secretaries of the *Conferência do Nordeste*, buried the documents he had in his backyard to hide them from the military. Once Cunha was able retrieve them, he gave them to his friend Bittencourt Filho. By publishing these documents, Bittencourt Filho turned the important memories of the Church and Society consultations he helped preserve accessible to more people.

[17] Faria, *Fé e Compromisso*, 122.

on the theme of Christian social responsibility taking place in other parts of the world.[18]

As for its contents, the consultation advanced a series of proposals on education for citizenship and political engagement (rejecting, though, the formation of Christian political parties), discussed the glaring social injustice characteristic of the modern world, and proposed a more constructive attitude toward Marxism, acknowledging the shortcomings of Christian public witness at the time and encouraging increased Christian participation in the social and political life of the country and in its social movements.

The Second National Consultation on Church and Society, the first organized in connection with CEB, took place in the Campinas Presbyterian Seminary in 1957. The theme of this consultation was "The Church and the Rapid Social Changes in Brazil."[19] This was a period when there was a push for national development under the leadership of President Juscelino Kubitschek (1956–1961). Despite the rapid urban growth and fast industrialization Brazil experienced during that period, the persistence and deepening of socioeconomic disparities and high living costs continued to raise questions about the shallow optimism of developmentalist discourses. That consultation sought to understand those processes more deeply, including the paradoxical implications of the industrialization boom.

Concerns with the life conditions of rural and industrial workers, the relationship between capital and work, and the protection of workers and peasants' unions and rights were some of the topics that consultation addressed as part of its concerted effort to advance an education for responsible citizenship. At a time of rapid social changes, the consultation concluded that one of the most important tasks for the churches was "to prepare the people for citizenship."[20] The second Church and Society Consultation reaffirmed the opposition to any sort of Christian overtake of political power, as implied in the rise of Christian political parties in the region. As citizens, there was a responsibility on the part of Christian individuals to

---

[18] Shaull, *Surpreendido Pela Graça*, 179.

[19] "II Consulta," in Bittencourt Filho, *Caminhos do Protestantismo Militante: ISAL e a Conferência do Nordeste*, 133.

[20] "II Consulta," in Bittencourt Filho, *Caminhos do Protestantismo Militante: ISAL e a Conferência do Nordeste*, 153.

fully participate in the life of the nation. As formative communities, it was part of the mission of the churches to educate for responsible citizenship. The consultation reiterated that "there is no evangelical vote" and that the evangelical (Protestant) church is not a political or economic system.[21]

In comparison with its predecessor, the boldest move this consultation made was to discuss agrarian reform as a necessary measure to create social and legal conditions for just development. The idea was to correct the old oligarchic concentration of lands perpetuating systemic unjust economic conditions in Brazil. For centuries, colonial monarchs distributed large lots of lands among friends of the crown. As Anthony Pereira highlights,

> Land in Brazil has traditionally been not merely a factor of production but a reward for service and proximity to power, as well as a foundation for the accumulation and maintenance of more power and privilege. This power includes the ability of large landowners to direct the legal and coercive apparatus of the state in their region. It also entails landlord control over and obligations to subaltern populations.[22]

Land reform has been a public debate for decades in Latin America. Most center-to-left Brazilian administrations have vowed to correct this glaring injustice. Peasant and rural workers' movements such as the Landless Workers' Movement (Movimento dos Trabalhadores Rurais Sem Terra, MST), founded in 1984, have continued that fight in recent decades, occupying idle *latifundia* and creating labor cooperatives to turn those idle estates into productive land. Until 2022, the MST had settled more than 370,000 families in 7.5 million hectares of land.[23] Powerful landowners have responded to those achievements with violence. Land conflicts are responsible for much of the violence against Indigenous and impoverished rural communities in Brazil.

---

[21] "II Consulta," in Bittencourt Filho, *Caminhos do Protestantismo Militante: ISAL e a Conferência do Nordeste*, 157.

[22] Anthony Pereira, "Brazil's Agrarian Reform: Democratic Innovation or Oligarchic Exclusion Redux?" *Latin American Politics and Society* 45/2 (2003): 41–65 (42).

[23] Friends of the MST, "What is the MST?" https://www.mstbrazil.org/content/what-mst.

The late 1950s and early 1960s were a period of significant mobilization around those issues. The rise of peasant leagues and rural workers' unions, particularly in Northeastern Brazil, bringing Marxists, Catholics, and Pentecostals together in the struggle for the rights of impoverished families of rural workers and for land reform, reflected grassroots efforts to reverse centuries of injustice. The military coup of 1964 suppressed that movement. The military regime that took over adopted land policies that only increased its concentration in the hands of a tiny elite.[24] In response to the violent crackdown against peasants and Indigenous peoples during the military dictatorship, the Catholic Church would create a Pastoral Land Commission (CPT) to serve the cause of rural workers and support their organization.[25]

Years prior to that, though, between 1955 and 1962, the SRSI showed an early awareness about the importance of the land struggle. Although a necessary topic, the organizers of the second SRSI consultation knew that its inclusion in the agenda of the event risked upsetting Brazilian elites and US partners, since conversations about land reform were often associated with the infiltration of communism. No wonder, following this consultation, the military began to surveil some leaders of the SRSI. According to Waldo César, in 1960, an agent of the Department of Political and Social Order (DOPS) reached out to him in private when the third consultation was in full session, interrogating him about the theme of the consultation.[26] The rise of the doctrine of national security, with its heightened suspicion of anything social and the Cuban Revolution in 1959 contributed to instill fear among both Latin American elites and the US government of talks about land reform anywhere in the region.

Two facts are noteworthy in the third consultation, which took place in 1960. First, the third national consultation on the social responsibility of the church sought to deepen the understanding of the presence and role of the Brazilian Protestant churches in the

---

24 Pereira, "Brazil's Agrarian Reform," 43.

25 Comissão Pastoral da Terra (CPT), "Histórico," https://www.cptnacional.org.br/sobre-nos/historico.

26 Waldo César, "Church and Society or Society and Church?" in *Revolution of Spirit: Ecumenical Theology in Global Context*, ed. Nantawan B. Lewis (Grand Rapids, MI: Eerdmans, 1998): 133–48 (138).

formation of the idea of a Brazilian nation—the idea of "nationality."[27] An evolution in the Brazilian Protestant social thought can be noted here. It was no longer necessary to justify the Protestant participation in the life of the nation. In the minds of the consultation planners, the need for contextualization of Brazilian Protestantism was no longer in question. It was time now to assess the meaning of Christian participation in the plural construction of nationality.

A second fact that deserves attention is that this meeting happened a year prior to the Second Latin American Evangelical Conference (CELA II) and the first Latin American Consultation on Church and Society, in Huampaní, Peru, 1961, which gave birth to ISAL.[28] As Wanderley Pereira da Rosa has noted, many of the participants of the SRSI consultation in 1960 attended that continental gathering a year later.[29] The evolution of the Protestant social thought emanating from the experience of Brazilian Protestants in the SRSI ended up impacting the formation of a continent-wide initiative with implications for the broader ecumenical movement.

The SRSI's brief but eventful journey culminated with its fourth consultation, this time in the city of Recife, the capital of the Northeastern state of Pernambuco, on July 22–29, 1962. Rosa describes this as the most important event that CEB ever carried. Undoubtedly, the Northeast Conference, as that consultation became known, was a landmark in the development of Latin American Protestant social and political theology.[30] By contrast, this consultation unfortunately also marked "the beginning of the end" of an era, the final stand for the SRSI, which would be dismantled in the wake of that gathering, in response to pressures coming from an increasingly conservative culture within and outside the Brazilian Protestant churches.[31]

The Recife gathering was the largest of the four SRSI consultations, with one hundred sixty participants representing seventeen Brazilian

---

[27] Waldo César, ed., *Presença da Igreja na Evolução da Nacionalidade* (Rio de Janeiro: CEB, 1960).

[28] CELA II and the first ISAL Consultation happened almost back-to-back, the former in Lima and the latter in Huampaní, just outside Lima.

[29] Rosa, *Por uma Fé Encarnada*, 116.

[30] Rosa, *Por uma Fé Encarnada*, 118.

[31] Bittencourt Filho, *Caminhos do Protestantismo Militante: ISAL e a Conferência do Nordeste*, 264.

states and sixteen Protestant denominations.[32] That consultation was more ecumenically representative than CEB itself. Despite its broader reach, Catholic representation remained notably absent. Whereas the SRSI team wanted to include Catholics among the invitees, the CEB leadership refused to accept it. They feared that if Catholics were involved, some Protestant churches would cut ties with CEB.[33]

Several things in the planning of this consultation deserve attention. The conference title, "Christ and the Revolutionary Process in Brazil" took notice of the revolutionary situation in Brazil and wrestled to understand the Christian task and responsibility in that setting. The title of the consultation also reflected the fact that a larger number of Brazilian Christians—facing increased repression—had given up on reformist hopes and were embracing the paradigm of revolution. In light of the elevated political tensions in the country, this event received unprecedented attention from both the media and politicians. Newspapers published sensationalist headlines such as "Christ present in the Brazilian crisis" or "Protestants propose a Christian revolution."[34] Brazilian Protestants, still a tiny religious minority, had never received that kind of attention before.

More than gaining public attention, the conference organizers also put themselves at the center of an important national debate as they invited notable Brazilian intellectuals to participate in the consultation. Thus, Protestant pastors such as Joaquim Beato (1924–2015), Almir dos Santos and João Dias de Araújo (1930–2014) were placed tête-à-tête with renowned Brazilian sociologists such as Gilberto

---

[32] Faria, *Fé e Compromisso*, 123. Rosa highlights the denominational diversity already present in the conference's local and national organizing committees, which included Methodists, Baptists, Congregationalists, Presbyterians, Lutherans, one Armenian Congregational, and also a representative from the Pentecostal church "O Brasil Para Cristo." See Rosa, *Por uma Fé Encarnada*, 118.

[33] "Entrevista com Waldo César," in Bittencourt Filho, *Caminhos do Protestantismo Militante: ISAL e a Conferência do Nordeste*, 504. While the SRSI had more cohesivity to advance its program, CEB imposed the limits of what could be done and who could participate. According to César, there was a moment prior to the conference when some leaders of CEB wanted to pull the plug on the entire consultation. The fact that the WCC funded the SRSI was probably one of the reasons why they did not succeed in shutting the conference down. "Entrevista com Waldo César," in Bittencourt Filho, *Caminhos do Protestantismo Militante: ISAL e a Conferência do Nordeste*, 501.

[34] César, "Church and Society or Society and Church?" 137.

Freyre (1900–1987) and Juarez Rubens Brandão Lopes (1925–2011), and economists of the stature of Celso Furtado (1920–2004) and Paul Singer (1932–2018) to reflect about the revolutionary process in Brazil and the Protestant participation in it.[35] Years later, Beato, who gave a plenary talk on the theme "The Prophets in Times of Social and Political Change," spoke about the importance of that moment:

> It was an important event. [. . .] Because it was the first time that Protestant groups could reflect about the social responsibility of the Christian, and the churches, at the highest level. We reflected not only, let's say, on the basis of a serious biblical and theological study, but also taking into consideration the positions of economists and sociologists such as Gilberto Freyre and Celso Furtado."[36]

Another important element in that conference was its location. This was the first time the SRSI planned a meeting in a Northeastern state. The Northeast has been a historically neglected and impoverished part of Brazil. At the same time, it is a place where many important social and cultural movements have started in the country. According to César, who, as the SRSI Executive Secretary, was at the center of the organization of the conference, the choice of Recife as the place to hold the conference turned its theme even more relevant. Although the Rio–São Paulo axis was considered the political and cultural center of the country, therefore, an area of greater influence, Recife, "the heart of the Northeast," had a particular appeal considering the theme of the conference, as it symbolized "the reality of the struggle between the past and a possible future in which the ownership of the land would not be in the hands of a few landlords."[37] In Recife, the consultation would also have the opportunity to be in touch with "the advance of social reforms and popular movements, among which the Peasant Leagues stood out."[38]

The preparatory process included visits to Recife and conversations with organized grassroots movements in advance of the

[35] "Entrevista com o Bispo Almir dos Santos," in Bittencourt Filho, *Caminhos do Protestantismo Militante: ISAL e a Conferência do Nordeste*, 461.

[36] "Entrevista com o Prof. Joaquim Beato," in Bittencourt Filho, *Caminhos do Protestantismo Militante: ISAL e a Conferência do Nordeste*, 467.

[37] César, "Church and Society or Society and Church?" 136.

[38] César, "Church and Society or Society and Church?" 136.

conference.[39] Common preparatory readings were distributed prior to the conference. Those documents shared in the preparatory stages of the conference included a paper authored by Shaull on the life and structure of the church vis-à-vis its witness in Latin American society, drawing attention to how the search for new forms of life and ecclesial structures had become a priority in Latin America and how that experience demanded attention from all. The document then turned to the need for Protestantism to update and indigenize its message "in order to intimately penetrate in the psychology, culture, and life of each Latin American, so Jesus can take a more Latin American form and bring the good news to each nation in the specific situation in which they find themselves."[40] Finally, Shaull urged the Brazilian Protestant churches to explore alternative forms of communal life. One suggestion he offered was the formation of small Christian communities within the larger context of plural "natural communities," where immersed Christian communities could serve as a "base for the orientation and direction for these other communities," creating spaces for these diverse groups to exist "in relation to one another and live the reality of unity which transcends all divisions of the world."[41] This proposal resembled the experiments the church and society movement had conducted earlier in Campinas, São Paulo, and Rio and also the new way of being church reflected in the emerging Catholic Christian or Ecclesial Base Communities (CEBs).

Rubem Alves submitted a paper with similar emphases. Discussing the form of the church in the current situation, Alves engaged Karl Barth's understanding of the humanity of God, talking about a God who accepts the totality of the human category and identifies

---

[39] In preparation for the Recife consultation, the steering committee traveled to the Northeastern states to visit with participants of the peasant leagues, dwellers of favelas, local pastors and priests, politicians, and intellectuals such as Celso Furtado. See Carlos Alberto C. da Cunha, "Um Padre Protestante, Músico e Poeta . . .," in *Memórias Ecumênicas Protestantes: Os Protestantes e a Ditadura, Colaboração e Resistência*, ed. Zwinglio M. Dias (Rio de Janeiro: KOINONIA Presença Ecumênica e Serviço, 2014), 102–108 (105ff).

[40] Richard Shaull, "Vida e Estrutura Atual da Igreja em Relação com seu Testemunho na Sociedade Latino-Americana," in Bittencourt Filho, *Caminhos do Protestantismo Militante: ISAL e a Conferência do Nordeste*, 265.

[41] Shaull, "Vida e Estrutura Atual da Igreja em Relação com seu Testemunho na Sociedade Latino-Americana," 269.

with "all the outcasts and wretched of the world."[42] Alves's paper advanced the idea of an incarnated church whose structure could not be rigid. Instead, it reflects as a mirror image of "what incarnation means in a dialogical form, i.e., in a form that makes the true encounter with the world in which we live possible."[43] In describing the world the church is called to dialogue with, Alves mentioned popular movements such as the peasant leagues, student movements, and rural and industrial workers' unions, pointing to a reality where power was dislodged from the hands of the bourgeoisie to new forms of social organizations. According to him, the church had to consider whether its structures, created for a society of slow social change, with the bourgeoisie at its center, would not become irrelevant if it did not engage such movements. To avoid that future, the Christian churches were challenged to discover new structural alternatives that can "speak to the contemporary situation, dialoguing with it and enabling the real presence of the Church in the world."[44]

These two preparatory papers advanced an ecclesiological contribution shaping up in Latin America in the early 1960s, which urged for the rethinking of existing ecclesiastical structures and would impact the ecumenical movement at large. Other preparatory papers circulated prior to the Northeast Conference addressed topics such as the Brazilian pre-revolution (Celso Furtado), the artist as a servant of humanity (Jacqueline Skiles), Christian ideology as the basis for the church's social action (Joaquim Beato) and the renewal of the church in history (W. A. Vissert' Hooft).

Despite the various instances in which this consultation can be distinguished from its predecessors, it must be paradoxically interpreted as standing in continuation with them. The Northeast Conference represented the apex of an ecumenical Protestant movement that would soon be suppressed. Its organizers considered it a success, and there were plans for follow-up. Tensions between the Confederation leadership and the SRSI had existed since the latter's inception, despite the fact that the SRSI was housed

[42] Rubem A. Alves, "A Forma da Igreja na Situação Presente," in Bittencourt Filho, *Caminhos do Protestantismo Militante: ISAL e a Conferência do Nordeste*, 277.

[43] Alves, "A Forma da Igreja na Situação Presente," 279.

[44] Alves, "A Forma da Igreja na Situação Presente," 281.

under a study department at CEB since 1955. Those tensions, however, had increased in anticipation of the Recife Conference. Despite those tensions, the general sentiment within the SRSI was that CEB would not interfere with its work. They were mistaken, though. After the Northeast Conference, the political situation in Brazil rapidly deteriorated. Prevalent theological and political conservative forces in the churches that formed CEB, along with increased pressure from sectors of the state, forced the dissolution of the SRSI within two years after that major consultation.

Looking for Alternative Spaces for a World-Oriented Ecumenism

In the wake of the Northeast Conference, CEB received another visit from government agents. According to César, upon his return from Recife to the CEB office in Rio, he realized that he no longer had a place within that structure.[45] In response to increased pressure, CEB suspended the SRSI activities and sacked its four secretaries: Waldo César, Domício Pereira de Matos, Jether Pereira Ramalho, and Francisco Pereira de Souza.[46] The military coup on March 31, 1964 only worsened the crisis.[47] CEB itself was discontinued in 1969. After the coup, some of the leaders of the Church and Society movement were forced to hide or leave the country. Rubem Alves, at the time a Presbyterian pastor in Lavras, Minas Gerais, was told that the military regime was coming for him. With help from Richard Shaull (now teaching at Princeton Theological Seminary) and Jaime Wright (1927–1999), he left the country to start his PhD work at Princeton Seminary.

Jovelino and Miriam Ramos also left for the United States. Others like Anivaldo Padilha and Paulo S. Wright joined Ação Popular (Popular Action), a revolutionary movement originally stemming

[45] Waldo César, interview with the author, Rio de Janeiro, Brazil, July 18, 2003.

[46] "Entrevista com Waldo César," in Bittencourt Filho, *Caminhos do Protestantismo Militante: ISAL e a Conferência do Nordeste*, 508.

[47] Jovelino Ramos, "Perseguições, Denúncias, Sofrimentos e Resistência—Depoimentos e Entrevistas," in *Memórias Ecumênicas Protestantes: Os Protestantes e a Ditadura, Colaboração e Resistência*, ed. Zwinglio M. Dias (Rio de Janeiro: KOINONIA Presença Ecumênica e Serviço, 2014), 25–35 (26).

from Juventude Universitária Católica (JUC).[48] Both of them were also forced to leave the country. Upon their clandestine return to Brazil, they were arrested and tortured. Padilha survived, while Wright was murdered by the military in 1973.[49] Zwinglio M. Dias and Waldo César were also briefly arrested by the regime and then left the country temporarily. Ivan Mota Dias, Zwinglio's brother, was tortured and murdered by the military regime in 1971 at age 29. Likewise, his body has never been found. This glimpse into stories of persecution, suffering, solidarity, and moral courage offers context to the challenges the Church and Society movement endured under Latin American authoritarian regimes backed by the US between the mid-1960s and early 1990s.[50]

Some of these individuals parted ways with their churches, in some cases for the rest of their lives. People like Alves, César, and Padilha were "denounced" to the military regime by leaders—at least in one case a pastor—from their denominations who collaborated with the military government. Under such circumstances, these individuals looked for alternative spaces to continue resisting the injustices impacting millions in the region. Some found a new home in the secular arena, either through the engagement with organizations such as the National Student Union (UNE), or by creating civil society organizations outside the confines of the church. Most of the former participants of UCEB and the SRSI, however, continued to promote the "ecumenism beyond the churches" they had discovered in their communal journey since the mid-1950s.[51]

Many of them continued to meet regularly in spaces beyond the reach of ecclesiastical institutions or the government. Waldo César

---

[48] Catholic University Youth. I will return to the Ação Popular movement in the next chapter.

[49] The military regimes that spread throughout Latin America from the 1960s to the early 1990s often tortured and killed dissidents. Often, their bodies would "disappear" so no one could be accountable for their deaths.

[50] For some of these memories, see Wanderley Pereira da Rosa and José Adriano Filho, eds., *Cristo e o Processo Revolucionário Brasileiro: A Conferência do Nordeste 50 Anos Depois (1962–2012)* (Rio de Janeiro: Mauad X, 2012); see also Zwinglio M. Dias, ed., *Memórias Ecumênicas Protestantes: Os Protestantes e a Ditadura, Colaboração e Resistência* (Rio de Janeiro: KOINONIA Presença Ecumênica e Serviço, 2014).

[51] César, "Church and Society or Society and Church?" 139.

recalls that when he was planning to create the journal *Paz e Terra* (which became one of the most important ecumenical publications in the region at the time), fearing that the dictatorship would be tapping his phone, he traveled from one town to another, sometimes across state borders, to speak with Catholic and Marxist interlocutors about his plan to create a truly ecumenical editorial board for the journal.[52] César and other individuals associated with the SRSI continued to look for alternative spaces to live out that vision of a world-oriented ecumenism.[53]

Paz e Terra emerged as an extraordinary initiative in response to the repression and censorship imposed on progressive movements by the military regime. As the military used communication tools to silence dissent and erase memory, *Paz e Terra* (published from 1966 to 1969) created an alternative space for counter-information for the purpose of resistance.[54]

Paz e Terra emerged from conversations between Waldo César and Luiz Eduardo Wanderley, a Catholic Marxist sociologist, when they worked together at CEI (*Centro Ecumênico de Informações*), another underground ecumenical space of resistance created by individuals previously associated with UCEB.[55] CEI existed between 1965 and 1974. After that period, the group of "former CEB leaders, pastors and lay people, theologians and students, youth and adults who identified with the ideals of Christian unity and socio-political responsibility" created the *Centro Ecumênico de Documentação e Informação* (CEDI),[56] seeking to adjust their response to the hardening of the dictatorship, which by the mid-1970s required not only counter-information but also proper documentation of human rights

---

[52] Waldo César, interview with Raimundo Barreto, Rio de Janeiro, July 18, 2003.

[53] Waldo César, "Um Ecumenismo Voltado Para o Mundo: Esboço Para uma História do Movimento Ecumênico no Brasil," *Contexto Pastoral* 26 (1995): 3–8.

[54] Magali do Nascimento Cunha, "A Revista Paz e Terra: um lugar da memória da comunicação religiosa, ecumênica e política no Brasil," *Horizonte*, 18/56 (2020): 513–541 (515).

[55] In 1964, CEI is the acronym for Centro Evangélico de Informação (Evangelical Center of Information). That name was changed to Centro Ecumênico de Informação (Ecumenical Center of Information) in 1965. Magali do Nascimento Cunha, "A Revista Paz e Terra: um lugar da memória da comunicação religiosa, ecumênica e política no Brasil," *Horizonte*, 18/56 (2020): 524.

[56] Cunha, "A Revista Paz e Terra," 524.

violations and concerted support to grassroot movements and pastoral action.[57]

CEDI's main publication, *Cadernos do CEDI*, offered resources for popular pastoral work, while a second magazine, *Aconteceu*, was dedicated to the accompaniment of the struggles of popular sectors of society. In 1994, as Brazil was in the process of rebuilding its democratic institutions, CEDI was reimagined, this time as *Koinonia—Presença Ecumênica e Serviço*, which continues to be a publication with distinct focus on "ecumenical solidarity," serving historically and culturally vulnerable populations throughout the country "in the process of social and political emancipation."[58] Several other ecumenical organizations also emerged in Brazil in these liminal spaces in the 1960s and 1970s. *Coordenação Ecumênica de Serviço* (CESE), an ecumenical agency for the protection of human rights and the promotion of peace and justice was founded in 1973.[59] Ever since, CESE has strengthened numerous "civil society organizations, especially grassroots organizations, engaged in the struggle for political, economic and social transformations that lead to structures in which democracy prevails with justice," being a catalyst to fund social projects in the peripheries of the great urban centers of Brazil.[60]

Presbyterian pastor Jaime Wright was one of CESE's founders and a key Brazilian religious leader in the 1970s. After the disappearance of his brother Paulo Wright, he worked tirelessly for the victims of political repression throughout Latin America. Courageously, he denounced torture and those who promoted it, supported the victims of torture, and carefully documented the systematic violations of human rights by the Brazilian military government. His name is often associated with two important events. First, along with Catholic Archbishop of São Paulo, Paulo Evaristo Arns and Henry Isaac Sobel, the rabbi at *Congregação Israelita Paulista*, Wright created an interfaith alliance to denounce the atrocities of the military regime. Among other things, in 1975, the three religious leaders organized an interfaith memorial ceremony in the wake of the regime's torture and

[57] CEDI is the Portuguese acronym for Ecumenical Center of Information and Documentation.

[58] See Koinonia's mission on its webpage: https://kn.org.br/quem-somos/sobre-koinonia.

[59] Coordination for Ecumenical Service.

[60] See CESE's webpage: https://www.cese.org.br/quem-e-a-cese/a-cese/.

assassination of Jewish journalist Wladimir Herzog. The memorial mass took place in the São Paulo Cathedral, which was surrounded by the police, thus becoming a symbol of resistance to and defiance of the authoritarian regime. That public act is considered a turning point in the Brazilian military dictatorship, which faded away until reaching a negotiated transition of the government back to the hands of the civil society in 1985.[61]

Also, along with Paulo Evaristo Arns, Wright produced the most complete documentation of the atrocities the Brazilian dictatorship committed against its adversaries, including the systemic use of torture and extrajudicial killing. With funds from the World Council of Churches, they documented thousands of charges against the military's abuses, gathering more than one million documents, which were taken to Geneva to be preserved. Furthermore, Wright contributed to build an international coalition to oppose the military dictatorship outside of Brazil. The summary of this initiative's findings was published later with the title *Brasil: Nunca Mais* (Brazil, never again), which includes the painful stories of hundreds of victims of the dictatorship.[62]

Another important ecumenical initiative that emerged in the 1970s was the *Centro de Estudos Bíblicos* (CEBI), an association created in São Paulo in 1979 with the goal of disseminating a new way of reading the Bible that took as its point of departure the social reality of the poor and their struggle for life. That method known as *leitura popular da biblia* (popular reading of the Bible) has been disseminated not only throughout Latin America, but also in other parts of the world. The movement was inspired by Paulo Freire's

---

[61] For an account of his life, see Derval Dasilio, *Jaime Wright: O Pastor dos Torturados* (Rio de Janeiro: Metanoia, 2012). The negotiated transition paradoxically included the assurance that no member of the military would be prosecuted for the many crimes committed on behalf of the military regime. The lack of accountability revived the wounds the families and descendants of the regime's victims have had to endure for decades.

[62] Paulo Evaristo Arns, *Brasil: Nunca Mais*, 10th ed. (Petrópolis: Editora Vozes, 1985). The documents were microfilmed and preserved in Geneva until 2011. They were then sent back to the Truth Commission created during the administration of President Dilma Rousseff—herself a victim of torture in the hands of the military in 1970. The collection of thousands of documents is available online: http://bnmdigital.mpf.mp.br/pt-br/.

popular education, drawing on the experience of the CEBs.[63] CEBI was founded by two Catholics and two Protestants: Carmelite biblical scholar Carlos Mesters (b.1931), Benedictine biblist and poet Agostinha Vieira de Mello (1926–2016), and the Protestant pastor Jether Pereira Ramalho (1922–2020), along with his wife Lucilia Ramalho (1948–2019).[64] Jether Ramalho, one of the four secretaries sacked from the Confederação Evangélica do Brasil (CEB) after the Northeast Conference, became one of the most prominent Latin American ecumenical voices in the last quarter of the twentieth century. He was one of the founders of ISAL, and of other popular ecumenical initiatives in the 1970s and 1980s.

Among others, Ramalho contributed to the creation of CEI and CEDI. When CEDI became Koinonia in 1994, he became the chief editor of the magazine *Tempo e Presença*. He was also involved in the work of CESEEP (Ecumenical Center for Services to Evangelization and Popular Education), and, despite being a Congregationalist, he became an adviser for the Catholic Base Ecclesial Communities (CEBs), which since the 1970s have included Protestant advisers and participants.[65] Among the many ecumenical activities he developed, Ramalho also served as a consultant for the WCC Commission on the Churches' Participation in Development's study "The Church and the Poor" led by Uruguayan theologian Julio de Santa Ana (1934–2023).[66] In that capacity, Ramalho was able to offer shelter to people being persecuted by the Brazilian military dictatorship. Among those individuals whom Ramalho helped was Brazilian educator Paulo Freire. Due to his many ecumenical connections, Ramalho mediated

---

[63] See Ira Shor and Paulo Freire, "What is the 'Dialogical Method' of Teaching?" *The Journal of Education* 169/3: (1987): 11–31.

[64] For more on the popular reading of the Bible, see Carlos Mesters, *Defenseless Flower: A New Reading of the Bible* (Maryknoll, NY: Orbis Books, 1989). A brief summary of the story of CEBI can be found on this link: https://cebi.org.br/historia/. See also a letter published by Carlos Mesters on the occasion of Jether Ramalho's passing: https://cebi.org.br/noticias/em-carta-frei-carlos-mesters-relembra-com-carinho-a-caminhada-com-jether-ramalho-na-fundacao-do-cebi/.

[65] For more on Ramalho, see José Ricardo Ramalho, ed., *Uma Presença no Tempo: A Vida de Jether Ramalho* (São Paulo: Oikos Editora, 2021).

[66] For more on that study, see Julio de Santa Ana, *Towards a Church of the Poor: The Work of an Ecumenical Group on the Church and the Poor* (Geneva: World Council of Churches, 1981). Julio de Santa Ana himself served as the general secretary of ISAL prior to becoming the studies coordinator in WCC Department for Development.

the process that culminated with a letter from the WCC inviting Freire to serve as a special consultant to its department of education, a role he played from 1970 to 1980.

CEBI has had a significant impact not only among Catholics but also on Protestant communities. Its communal method to read the Bible appeals, especially, to socially progressive evangelicals. A number of individuals affiliated with the Latin American Evangelical Fellowship (Fraternidad Teológica Latinoamericana, FTL) have been concomitantly associated with Revista de Interpretación Bíblica Latinoamericana (RIBLA), an academic hub for *leitura popular da Bíblia* in the continent, published by the Departamento Ecuménico de Investigaciones (DEI) in San José, Costa Rica.[67] Odja Barros, a Brazilian Baptist pastor and biblical scholar who has also embraced CEBI's ecumenical popular hermeneutics, has contributed to train grassroots agents throughout Latin America as local disseminators of the popular reading of the Bible. Moreover, she has contributed methodologically to the work of CEBI by incorporating a Latin American feminist perspective to its method.[68]

In 1970, Rubem Alves and other Protestant and Catholic theologians founded the Higher Institute of Theological Studies (Instituto Superior de Estudos Teológicos, ISET), in São Paulo, with support from the World Council of Churches. ISET sought to develop interdisciplinary research aiming "to understand the place of religion in Brazilian society." Alves was its first president, serving also as executive secretary until 1974, when Waldo César took over. Alves remained as president of the institute until 1978, being succeeded by sociologist Rubem César Fernandes. In 1973, ISET changed its name to Higher Institute of Religious Studies (Instituto Superior de Estudos da Religião, ISER) to make room for humanities and social sciences scholars. Through its numerous publications, including the journal *Religião & Sociedade*, created in 1977, ISER, which in 1982 changed its name again to *Instituto de Estudos da Religião* (Institute

[67] RIBLA was launched by DEI in 1988. Its first issue had the title "Lectura Popular de la Bíblia en América Latina: Una Hermenéutica de la Liberación." The editors of this first issue were Jorge Pixley, Pablo Richard, Elsa Tamez, and Neftalí Vélez.

[68] Her church is just one of the Latin American Protestant churches that have embraced the popular reading of the Bible. See Odja Barros, *Flores que Rompem Raízes: Leitura Popular e Feminista* (São Paulo: Editora Recriar, 2020).

of Religious Studies) has for more than five decades played a leading role in producing research on religion and society in Brazil.[69]

Considering the nature of its work over the years, ISER has become an academic institution with an important public voice, actively commenting on key events in the country's recent history. ISER Communications, created, in 1981, has been one of the means by which that voice is propagated. At the beginning of the *Diretas Já* Movement (a movement urging the end of the military dictatorship and presidential elections by popular vote in the early 1980s), ISER created a program called Advisory Group for Grassroots Organizations and Religious Entities, forming a network with other NGOs, universities, and international cooperation agencies to advance the important campaign for the redemocratization of the country.

Another example of the relevance of ISER to the broader society was its engagement with the United Nations Conference on Environment and Development (ECO 92) in Rio in 1992. ISER organized the Great Interreligious Vigil for World Peace, titled "A New Day for the Earth," bringing leaders from different religious traditions and ideologies together to advocate for the protection of the Earth. In addition to its many publications on the theme, ISER actively participated in the definition of "Agenda 21," a model of international public policy regarding environmental preservation, the Global NGO Forum, and the Creation of the Inter-Religious Movement (Movimento Interreligioso, MIR) in Rio de Janeiro.[70] All this social and environmental activism has taken place side-by-side with the continuous production of rigorous scholarship and reliable resources for the study of religion in Brazil, reflecting the ideal of engaged scholarship that Alves, César, and others championed in its early years.

A common characteristic distinguishing all these new ecumenical initiatives from the ones that existed prior to 1964 is that all the initiatives listed above include Catholics. Prior to 1964, the relationship between Catholics and Protestants in Brazil was almost nonexistent. Whereas some individuals in the UCEB and the SRSI occasionally sought to engage their Catholic counterparts, there was no institutional

[69] Despite this last name change, the institute has kept the same acronym, ISER, by which it is widely known.

[70] ISER, "Linha do Tempo ISER 50 anos," https://www.iser.org.br/linha-do-tempo/.

support for that, since denominational leaders affiliated with CEB did not want to risk backlash from their own churches. One of the few consistent efforts to promote Catholic-Protestant interaction in that period was mediated by Richard Shaull and Dominican Friar Bernardo Catão. Once a month, Shaull would take a group of UCEB students and Protestant seminarians to have soup with Catholic seminarians in the Dominican convent in the neighborhood of Perdizes, São Paulo. The monthly soup was followed by lively conversation between Protestants and Dominicans. As Dias, one of the students participating in that experiment, states, that "novelty [. . .] ended up generating a stir with the Protestant Churches in the city who found this relationship with Catholics an unacceptable absurdity!!"[71] Likewise, since Shaull was a US missionary and such missionaries were commonly associated with US political activism and interference in Latin America, the attitude toward him on the part of some Dominicans was also one of caution or even suspicion.[72]

On the brighter side, some of the long-term Catholic-Protestant relationships that began to be shaped in the joint efforts of resistance to the authoritarianism of the military regime that followed the 1964 coup d'état can be credited to these incipient and informal contacts. Furthermore, the institutional dislodgement the individuals associated with UCEB and the SRSI experienced after the Northeast Conference freed them to expand their ecumenical horizons and seek new ways to live out their faith beyond the vigilance of their denominations. Opting for the margins (or, often, pushed to them), these individuals transgressed beyond imposed conditions, moving out of "their place" to push back against oppressive boundaries (to borrow bell hook's insight). They turned marginalization and exile into liminal spaces where they could continue to produce counter-hegemonic discourses.[73] They turned imposed marginality into intentionally built marginal sites of resistance. Expounding on the significance of such a marginal locus of enunciation, hook states,

---

[71] Zwinglio Mota Dias, *Reencantamentos da Graça numa Favela Carioca: Memórias e Vivências de Zwinglio Mota Dias*, ed. Moisés Abdon Coppe (Juiz de Fora, MG: Editora Siano, 2021), 46.

[72] Author's interview with Frei Betto. São Paulo, Brazil, October 11, 2023.

[73] bell hooks, "Choosing the Margin as a Space of Radical Openness," *Framework: The Journal of Cinema and Media* 36 (1989): 15–23 (15).

> This site of resistance is continually formed in that segregated culture of opposition that is our critical response to domination. We come to this space through suffering and pain, through struggle. We know struggle to be that which is difficult, challenging, hard and we know struggle to be that which pleasures, delights, and fulfills desire. We are transformed, individually, collectively, as we make radical creative space which affirms and sustains our subjectivity, which gives us a new location from which to articulate our sense of the world.[74]

More than marginal, these spaces are also liminal, because what is marginal or marginalized is often pushed out across borders. In the case in question, many of the individuals pushed aside remained in contact with the religious traditions that they were in tension with, and their work, although from the margins, continued to impact those traditions—as they offered alternative understandings to their hegemonizing readings.

From various liminal locations, those marginal thinkers and activists were able to contribute in multiple ways to the ecumenical movement. Alves, for instance, voiced a question at a time of repression, authoritarianism, and submissiveness: "Where is the Church?" Under those circumstances, there were only two possible alternatives:

> Either we find it as an oppressed remnant within ecclesiastical structures, still trusting in the possibilities of the Reformation, or as a scattered people, dispersed sheep, yearning for new community structures that are expressions and instruments of love and freedom.[75]

Zwinglio Mota Dias, who was Alves's former student and parishioner in Lavras, Minas Gerais,[76] embodied a similar liminal existence, living between those two possibilities. While struggling with an authoritarian and repressive government in his country, this

---

[74] bell hooks, "Choosing the Margin as a Space of Radical Openness," 23.

[75] Rubem Alves, *Dogmatismo e Tolerância* (São Paulo: Ed. Loyola, 2004), e-pub, 249.

[76] Magali Cunha, "Lá se foi um pastor de verdade! Um tributo a Zwinglio Mota Dias," *Carta Capital*, https://www.cartacapital.com.br/blogs/dialogos-da-fe/la-se-foi-um-pastor-de-verdade-um-tributo-a-zwinglio-mota-dias/.

Presbyterian pastor and theologian expanded his ecumenical horizons, contributing to the development of ISAL and its journal *Cristianismo y Sociedad*, while exiled in Argentina and Uruguay, and, later, to the Commission on World Mission and Evangelism of the WCC. In the WCC, Dias was also active in the work of Urban Rural Mission, serving as moderator of its Advisory Group between 1985 and 1992.[77]

Dias moved across many other spaces. That constant border crossing impacted the way he understood his role as a Christian minister. In 1971, he was arrested by the military regime. The reason given by the military for his arrest was that they were searching for information about the whereabouts of his younger brother, "disappeared" on May 15, 1971.[78] In the months he remained in jail, Zwinglio Dias celebrated the eucharist with those imprisoned with him, most of whom were Catholic.

> During my stay at DOPS, I had an intense pastoral experience! The regime at this stage of my detention was much lighter as compared to DOI-CODI. We were about eight or ten prisoners who spent the day together in a kind of "living room" where we could talk, read, play cards, etc. Then we were put back in our cells at night. My being a pastor caught everyone's attention. There were many conversations about religion and politics and about Protestantism. None of them had a clear idea of what a Protestant church was. After some days of real religion and theology classes about my ecclesiastical tradition, I could see the [growing] interest in several of them reach the point where they asked me for "the celebration of a Mass!" I explained that I couldn't do that, but that we could celebrate the Eucharist—called, among Protestants, the Holy Communion—according to the rite of my church. As everyone agreed, we scheduled it for the next day during breakfast. Unfortunately, we didn't have wine or bread, so we agreed to use coffee and cookies as representations of the body and blood of Christ. This was a very touching moment, an expression of spirituality, faith,

[77] WCC News, "WCC celebrates life of Brazilian theologian and ecumenist Zwinglio Mota Dias," https://www.oikoumene.org/news/wcc-celebrates-life-of-brazilian-theologian-and-ecumenist-zwinglio-mota-dias.

[78] Dias, *Reencantamentos da Graça*, 58.

> and reassessment of our views regarding the reality of churches in the lives of the people.[79]

Once released from prison, still under threat, Dias wandered through Argentina, Uruguay (where, working at the headquarters of ISAL, he was almost arrested again after the 1972 military coup in that country), and ended up in Hamburg, in 1973, where he worked on his doctoral degree at Missionsakademiean der Universität Hamburg, writing a dissertation methodologically influenced by Paulo Freire on the crises and tasks of Brazilian Protestantism.[80] Upon his return to Brazil in 1979, Dias immersed himself in a deeply transformative pastoral ministry in a favela in Rio de Janeiro known as Morro do Alemão, where he served as the pastor of Igreja Presbiteriana da Vila Proletária da Penha for 22 years.[81]

In Vila Proletária da Penha, Dias implemented a pastoral praxis fully immersed in the problems of the community, putting the church's resources at the service of the broader community and implementing a missiological proposal centered on the church's participation in the community's social and political life.[82] Among the various initiatives the church engaged with, a project to legalize the ownership of homes for tens of thousands of people in Vila Proletária is worth noting, since most of the population in that neighborhood lacked official titles for the homes in which they lived. Dias also led the church in the development of a social education project, and helped found a local council of churches, which

[79] Dias, *Reencantamentos da Graça*, 60.

[80] Dias, *Reencantamentos da Graça*, 66. Dias's dissertation was published with the title *Krisen und Aufgaben im brasilianischen Protestantismus: e. Studie zu d. sozialgeschichtl. Bedingungen u. volkspädag. Möglichkeiten d. Evangelisation* (Bern, Frankfurt am Main, Las Vegas: Lang, 1978). In this analysis of the historical context of Brazilian society, Dias examined the ideological captivity of Brazilian Protestantism, which, he concluded, stemmed from its dependence on a theology imported from North America. In response, he advanced a view toward its renewing function vis-à-vis the impact of liberation theology—in particular, Paulo Freire's pedagogy, which he saw as critical for a renewed Protestant ecclesial practice rooted in the Brazilian sociocultural reality. During that period, he met Paulo Freire, who was still in Geneva as an education consultant for the WCC.

[81] Dias, *Reencantamentos da Graça*, 69.

[82] Dias, *Reencantamentos da Graça*, 74.

although short-lived, exemplified the ecumenical spirit that inspiried Dias's pastoral ministry.[83]

In that same spirit, his Presbyterian congregation developed relations with both Catholic base communities and African-derived religions in the community. The principle behind all those initiatives was the same:

> It was about changing the focus of attention and action of the local church: no longer thinking about itself, or trying to grow the number of followers and multiply its resources, but aiming at becoming an instrument of service to the proposals of the Reign of God. Thus, "evangelization" ceased to be a proselytizing action of a self-centered community and came to mean the provision of service, especially to the most vulnerable, and a testimony of communal life based on justice, love and compassion.[84]

Concomitantly, the church got involved in other actions for social change on the level of the city of Rio de Janeiro as well as on the national and international levels. One of those actions the church in Vila Proletária participated in was a national campaign Brazilian sociologist Herbert de Souza (Betinho) began in 1993 to eradicate hunger called "Citizenship Action against Hunger and Misery and for Life." The church joined the community association to form a local committee to fight hunger and participated in the First National Conference on Food Security, in Brasília (the national capital) in July 1994, along with representatives of the Community Association of Vila Proletária.[85]

One of the most emblematic pastoral actions Dias provided, though, was his support, from 1987 onwards, of a program aimed at protecting and promoting the rights of sex workers. The Non-Governmental Organization "DaVida – Prostitution, Civil Rights and Health," which Dias and Waldo César helped create and continuously supported, serving as treasurer and president for around ten years, was led by its founder and general secretary Gabriela Leite,[86] who also

83 Dias, *Reencantamentos da Graça*, 76–77.

84 Dias, *Reencantamentos da Graça*, 79.

85 Dias, *Reencantamentos da Graça*, 90–91.

86 In the 1970s, Gabriela Leite dropped out of college—she was a philosophy student in the prestigious University of São Paulo (USP)—and moved to Vila Mimosa,

founded the Brazilian Network of Prostitutes to advocate for their civil and health rights. In his role as a member of the Commission on World Mission and Evangelism of the WCC and of its Urban and Rural Mission Group, Dias mediated the affiliation of DaVida to this group and secured resources with the WCC to support the organization.

People like Ramalho, Dias, and César moved constantly between local and international spaces, contributing to the process of mutual ecumenical influence this book seeks to unveil. They also played leading roles in ISAL, which became the main Latin American umbrella of ecumenical action in the 1960s. Between 1961and 1975, ISAL was a critical space for ecumenical articulation in Latin America and the region's main interlocutor with the WCC.

The Formation of ISAL

Important ecumenical developments not only in Brazil, but also in Uruguay, Argentina, and other Latin American countries between 1955 and 1962 directly contributed to the formation of ISAL. It would be a mistake to deduct from the narrative above that ISAL was simply an expansion of the Brazilian SRSI. Nevertheless, the formation and development of that experience was a major factor in the rise and shaping of ISAL. The parallels between these two bodies are clear, as both represented the vanguard of the Latin American Protestant social thinking in the 1950s–1960s. The dismantling of SRSI in the beginning of the 1960s led a number of individuals associated with that program to find in ISAL their new home. Methodist pastor Almir dos Santos, who chaired the Northeast Conference in

Rio de Janeiro, where she worked as a prostitute. Concerned with the rights and health of sex workers, she created the National Network of Prostitutes in 1987. With support from Dias and César, among others, she organized six national gatherings of this network until her death in 2013. DaVida was the first social organization of national proportion to support sex workers, serving as a model for other organizations created later across the country. Leite gained notoriety in 2005, when she founded Daspu, a women's clothing brand whose income was used to support the rights of sex workers. Information was provided by Zwinglio Motas Dias via email on October 17, 2017. Some of it can also be found in a 2012 interview Gabriela Leite gave to *Revista Trip*: https://revistatrip.uol.com.br/homenageados/2012/gabriela-leite. Accessed on December 13, 2023.

1962, became the first president of ISAL in 1961. As soon as ISAL founded the journal *Cristianismo y Sociedad*, Waldo César became its representative in Brazil.

Conversations about the creation of a Latin American church and society board (junta) began at a meeting in Montevideo in 1957. Although the interest in the topic of the church's social responsibility had intensified in various Latin American countries, commissions on church and society emerged in only three of them during that period. The church federations in Argentina and Uruguay formed their respective commissions in 1957. In Brazil, as discussed earlier, a similar commission was formed in 1955, renamed later that year Setor de Responsabilidade Social da Igreja. In that preliminary encounter to discuss the formation of ISAL, there were also representatives from Chile, Colombia, and Peru.[87] Nevertheless, the intense seven years of church and society work in Brazil were particularly generative for the rise of ISAL.

Alan Neely (1928–2003), who served as a Baptist missionary in Cali, Colombia, identified the "'Section on Social Responsibility,' a division of the Protestant Confederation of Brazil, organized in the mid-1950s as a result of the influence of several persons who had been leaders in the national body of the Student Christian Movement," as one of the forerunners of ISAL. The other two were the Latin American Protestant youth movement and the "establishment in 1959 of a regional secretaryship for Latin America by the World Council of Churches' Division of Studies," which led to the publication and distribution of the bulletin "*Iglesia y Sociedad en América Latina*."[88]

Waldo César recalls that Luis Odell, the first Executive Secretary of ISAL, attended the SRSI's Northeast Conference and was fascinated by the work of the *Setor de Responsabilidade Social* in Brazil, affirming the "need to do something like this in the Latin American context."[89] They gathered with Julio de Santa Ana and Richard Shaull to organize ISAL. The creation of the journal *Cristianismo y Sociedad*

---

[87] Sabanes Plou, *Caminhos de Unidade*, 126.

[88] Neely, "Protestant Antecedents of the Latin American Theology of Liberation," 168.

[89] Waldo César, "O Itinerário de Vida de um Coração Ecumênico. . . Entrevista com o sociólogo Waldo A. Lenz César, um dos principais líderes ecumênicos protestantes do Brasil e da América Latina," in *Memórias Ecumênicas Protestantes*, 90–101 (95).

was also an outcome of those conversations. After the military coup in Brazil, César traveled to Montevideo, where he held meetings with other leaders of ISAL.[90] Concomitantly, he remained in contact with Shaull to identify people in the U.S. to help fund the emerging CEI.

The participants in the preparatory meeting for the launching of ISAL in 1959, in Brazil, identified the task of the upcoming consultation as to respond to "the growing concern manifest among Latin American Protestant Christianity to discover the best way to witness in the midst of a situation of constant transformation and continuing the study task already begun in countries such as Brazil, Uruguay and Argentina."[91]

The Latin American Protestant Consultation on Church and Society was scheduled for Huampaní, in the Lima surroundings, on July 23–27, 1961—thus five years prior to the WCC Conference on Church and Society in Geneva, 1966. Many of the participants in the ISAL Consultation also attended CELA II, the second Protestant conference in Latin America under the auspices of the CCLA, held in Lima, immediately after the end of the ISAL consultation. The two gatherings were organized independently from each other. While the ISAL Consultation represented a more autonomous and progressive incipient ecumenism, shaped in conversation with the SCM and the SRSI, CELA II was a gathering organized by official ecumenical instances led by the CCLA and various Latin American Protestant denominations.

The correlation between ISAL and the four conferences the SRSI organized in Brazil was evident. The agenda of an incipient ISAL infused the discussion about development and dependence with the language of revolution.[92] Realizing that an exclusive focus on development would limit the possibilities and impact of the movement, ISAL argued that the most critical challenge at hand was for Protestant Christians to participate in the Latin American revolutionary process.[93]

---

90. "When the coup happened [in Brazil], [Montevideo] was still a free place where we could take a breath." César, "O Itinerário de Vida de um Coração Ecumênico...," 90–101 (95).

91. Sabanes Plou, *Caminhos de Unidade*, 126.

92. Faria, *Fé e Compromisso: Richard Shaull e a Teologia no Brasil*, 125

93. Faria, *Fé e Compromisso: Richard Shaull e a Teologia no Brasil*, 125.

Fifty delegates from seventeen countries and fourteen denominations participated in the consultation convocated by the Church and Society Commissions from Brazil, Argentina, and Uruguay. Brazil, Argentina, and Mexico had the largest delegations. However, a diverse representation from the entire continent, from the Caribbean to Chile, was in attendance. Paul Albrecht, from the WCC, and W. Stanley Rycroft, the executive staff of the Board of Foreign Missions of the Presbyterian Church in the US and former executive secretary of the CCLA, served as consultants. Three US members of the CCLA and two missionaries stationed in Brazil also participated as observers.[94]

Among other things, the Huampaní consultation was important for the establishment of biblical and theological foundations for "the Protestant work in the field of social commitment."[95] It also played a critical role in the dissemination of an ecumenical theology and social thought in the region. As Neely points out,

> If one were obliged to choose the single most important agency which has served to disseminate the theological and social thought of the world ecumenical conferences, the organization known as 'ISAL,' i.e., the Latin American Committee on Church and Society, would doubtless be selected. Because it has functioned as the vanguard in the attempt to relate social responsibility and Christian theology, ISAL is the most significant though not the only Latin American antecedent to the Theology of Liberation.[96]

As in the case of the SRSI, ISAL interpreted the ecumenical language coming out of Evanston 1954 that emphasized the social responsibility of the church through the lens of the Latin American reality. It must be clear, though, that ISAL and its national counterparts were not merely disseminating an ecumenical theology received from Geneva. They interpreted it from the particular social and cultural conditions of Latin America and, in doing so, contributed

[94] The proceedings and conclusions of the consultation can be found in ISAL, *Encuentro y Desafío: La acción cristiana evangélica latinoamericana ante la cambiante situación social, política y económica* (Montevideo: ISAL, 1961).

[95] Sabanes Plou, *Caminhos de Unidade*, 127.

[96] Neely, "Protestant Antecedents of the Latin American Theology of Liberation," 165–166.

to expand and enrich ecumenical theology and social thought at large. ISAL's theological production is vast. Its main organism of theological diffusion, though, was the journal *Cristianismo y Sociedad*, founded in 1963.[97]

The Huampaní consultation was a Latin American initiative. As mentioned earlier, three national federations joined the call for this consultation. The CCLA was present only in consultative and observing roles. The organizing committee constituted in 1959 was formed by Latin American natives Luis E. Odell (Uruguay), Waldo A. César Lenz (Brazil), and Daniel D. Lurá Villanueva (Argentine). Its theme was the Christian social responsibility in Latin America in a context of growing popular desire for "freedom, progress, and social justice."[98] The consultation explored three areas of social responsibility: (1) Social responsibility in light of sociocultural changes; (2) Christian political action in Latin America; and (3) Christian preoccupation with progress and economic development.[99] Throughout the conference, working groups gathered to collaborate on these three areas.

Regarding the first emphasis, the consultation concluded that Latin America was experiencing significant sociocultural changes, with positive and negative implications. As those changes impacted the traditional structures of Latin American societies and seemed irreversible, the churches were urged to understand the nature of those changes and participate in that transformative process. The question the consultation asked regarding the role of the churches in those changes contains in itself a call for participation and exploration of how those changes could potentially announce the world to come.[100]

One potential form of participation was through the involvement in education on all social levels, beginning with literacy.[101] Considering the complexity of human problems, the churches were urged to attend to, in particular, rural and urban workers and prepare them to

[97] Federico Brugaletta, "Cristianismo y Sociedad (1963–1973). Protestantismo de Izquierda en la Historia Reciente de América Latina," *Catedral Tomada* 6/11 (2018): 236–263.

[98] Luis E. Odell, "Cronica," in *Encuentro y Desafío*, 13.

[99] Odell, "Cronica," 13.

[100] ISAL, *Encuentro y Desafío*, 27–28.

[101] ISAL, *Encuentro y Desafío*, 31.

better serve in cooperatives, unions, and associations, among others, acting as catalytic educational agents in the community.[102]

As for the prophetic participation of churches, communities, and individuals in the political life of the continent, the ISAL Consultation reinforced the concern already noted in the SRSI, discouraging corporate identification of churches with any political party. The Christian political participation Huampaní 1961 encouraged was that of individuals who were duly inserted in the political and social organizations that represented the broader communities they were part of.

The consultation called Christians to exert influence in areas such as social justice, morality in the public sphere, and resisting dictatorship, militarism, and clericalism, while alerting against importing democratic ideals from other places.[103] For the drafters of the consultation concluding documents, true democracy should guarantee, (1) ultimately, that power must reside with the people, (2) the need for effective democratic control of power, and (3) full human rights.[104]

According to its final document, the consultation supported a constructive Latin American nationalism, which included the "economic liberation of countries subject to the action of foreign interests" from imperialism.[105] Ultimately, Christian political participation in Latin America was encouraged for the sake of achieving social justice, an ideal described as having biblical and Christian origins.[106]

The third emphasis the ISAL consultation highlighted was the Christian preoccupation with development and economic progress. The main concern in this discussion was to assure the participation of the poor in the benefits of modern technology and economic progress, considering that such benefits were still the privilege of a few and that the state had the means to expand that ideal to all. The consultation named this emphasis "the revolution of rising hopes."[107] Protestant Christians were urged to understand and interpret the hopes, expectations, and demands from millions of impoverished ones, remembering that such hopes had been denied for too long.

102 ISAL, *Encuentro y Desafío*, 31.

103 ISAL, *Encuentro y Desafío*, 31.

104 ISAL, *Encuentro y Desafío*, 46.

105 ISAL, *Encuentro y Desafío*, 47.

106 ISAL, *Encuentro y Desafío*, 48.

107 ISAL, *Encuentro y Desafío*, 51.

One of the tasks at hand was to discern the work of Christ "in the economic and social changes" and in "the structural transformations" taking place in parts of Latin America.[108] Those economic changes were urgently necessary, considering the low quality of life many Latin Americans experienced, including widespread poverty and undernourishment. Inequality in the distribution of wealth was at the root of the problem. Therefore, economic development, the mantra of the late 1950s and early 1960s, was not enough. Such a growth "must be accompanied by new social structures based on the Christian understanding of justice in the distribution of wealth and income."[109]

Rapid urbanization and industrialization accelerated such inequality. The lack of working opportunities in rural areas forced millions to move to the cities in search of jobs and the promise of a better life. Instead of seeing the fulfillment of those promises, those who moved to urban centers ended up in human conglomerates in urban peripheries, "illiterate, in need of the qualification required for technical jobs, undernourished, uprooted," turning into what the consultation called "a forgotten proletariat."[110] In light of this grim reality, the consultation's main economic concern was "the establishment of systems that offer to each human being the opportunity to have a decent life and to flourish spiritually and culturally." For the church, the economic system cannot be an end in itself, but "a means to achieve a just and responsible society."[111] The ISAL consultation was not simply regurgitating the Northern Atlantic ecumenical understanding of the responsible society. Instead, as it interpreted such a concept in light of the concrete Latin American reality, it expanded its meaning, challenging Eurocentric assumptions.

The engagement with Marxist analytical tools in the conference documents did not mean the uncritical embracing of Marxism. While it challenged the predatory capitalism at the root of unjust living conditions, ISAL did not prescribe any particular economic system, arguing that the church should not fully identify with any specific system. Instead, it "must insist in the responsibility the government

[108] ISAL, *Encuentro y Desafío*, 51.

[109] ISAL, *Encuentro y Desafío*, 52.

[110] ISAL, *Encuentro y Desafío*, 53.

[111] ISAL, *Encuentro y Desafío*, 55.

has to adequately plan for economic development and the creation of the necessary industries to secure the fastest possible betterment of the general well-being of the population."[112]

At the same time, it recognized the situation of economic colonialism (dependence on foreign capital), which impacted the entire region, and the right of Latin American governments to control their natural resources, public goods, and basic industries. The guiding principle for Christian participation in the economic life was "to help all groups, regardless of race or religion, to participate in the development of the economic life."[113] This sort of advocacy for national control of wealth and resources and just distribution of goods would raise concerns among both Latin American denominational leaders and United States's observers.

Finally, the 1961 Consultation on Church and Society planned for future action towards (1) disseminating the concerns and aspirations of Christian witness in Latin American societies, according to the resolutions and recommendations of the First Latin American Evangelical Consultation on Church and Society; (2) stimulating and facilitating the creation of Commissions on Church and Society in Latin American countries through existing interdenominational national organizations; and (3) collaborating with existing national commissions on exchange of information and common publications, including the semestral bulletin "Iglesia y Sociedad en América Latina."[114]

In cooperation with national commissions on church and society in different countries, ISAL made a significant impact on the formation of Latin American ecumenical theology. After the military coup in Brazil and the dismantling of the SRSI, ISAL became the powerhouse for coordination of Christian participation in the revolutionary situation in Latin America.[115] Its influence was felt in various ways.

First, ISAL influenced the theological agenda in the region and beyond as one of the first Christian networks to use the emerging theory of dependence to address the theme of development.

[112] ISAL, *Encuentro y Desafío*, 55.

[113] ISAL, *Encuentro y Desafío*, 56.

[114] ISAL, *Encuentro y Desafío*, 60.

[115] Faria, *Fé e Compromisso*, 125. In the case of Brazil, some individuals formerly associated with SRSI informally formed a Brazilian section of ISAL.

Through its publications, the theological production of ISAL informed interdenominational conversations in various countries. The formation of a continental organization with a full-time general secretary—Luis E. Odell— also facilitated coordination and cooperation among the seven national commissions that constituted ISAL's initial base.

ISAL also uniquely contributed to sensitize Latin American Protestant churches regarding their social responsibility and understanding of their social and political action in the region. In response to its 1963 Consultation on Social Service and Social Action, which defined service as a key dimension of the proclamation of the gospel, ISAL created a secretariat to advise churches interested in developing social projects and work on social justice beyond paternalistic understandings of social service—often reduced to charity.[116]

Finally, the work of ISAL would also pave the way to expand ecumenical cooperation in the region to include Catholics. As Emilio Castro stated in 1971,

> ISAL is [. . .] a community that has transcended the limits of the Protestant confessions to be a hub where Catholics and Protestants come together, those who, as such, are deeply interested in giving a responsible testimony of their faith in light of the challenges that the problems of Latin American society present.[117]

ISAL was the first distinctively Latin American ecumenical body. It was formed by Protestant leaders who came out of the youth and student Christian movements of the 1950s—as it was the case with many other ecumenical leaders worldwide. Contributing to its distinctiveness was the fact that it created an ecumenical structure, which, although related to the churches, was relatively independent of top-down ecclesiastical structures compared to other existing ecumenical organisms at the time.

ISAL's distinctive Latin American voice was heard in the 1966 World Conference on Church and Society, in Geneva, which had

---

[116] Sabanes Plou, *Caminhos de Unidade*, 128–129.

[117] Emilio Castro, "Prologo," in *De la Iglesia y la Sociedad*, ed. Rubem Alves et al (Montevideo: Tierra Nueva, 1971), i–iii (iii).

Argentinean professor Mauricio López in its organizing committee.[118] That broader influence continued to be seen in the world stage through the important roles played by several individuals associated with ISAL not only in the shaping of liberation theology but also of ecumenical social thought and praxis. Such an influence has included over the years the work of people such as Julio de Santa Ana, José Miguez Bonino, Rubem Alves, Beatriz Melano Couch, Emilio Castro, Jether Ramalho, Ofelia Ortega, Jovelino Ramos, Anivaldo Padilha, Paulo Ayres Mattos, Zwinglio Mota Dias, Magali do Nascimento Cunha, Nancy Cardoso, Odair Pedroso Mateus and many other Latin American Protestants who, directly or indirectly, were impacted by the work of ISAL.

Richard Shaull who, although a US missionary, was both a participant in the making of ISAL and someone impacted by the theological praxis that emerged from it, was one of the first individuals in the North Atlantic to notice that the theology emerging in the revolutionary Latin American context in the 1960s represented a new starting point for theological thinking—one based on praxis in connection with the liberation of the oppressed.

> Perhaps this also suggests a new starting point for us today, confronted as we are by the silence of God and the crisis of all our theological concepts. We can no longer rely on moving forward in academic isolation analyzing old theological systems, developing them, and trying to translate them into contemporary terms. Our starting point must be situated in praxis, but a praxis of a very special nature: that which results from our own experience of exodus and exile by disassociating ourselves from the order of social oppression of which we are victims; moving hopefully towards a new promised land, towards the creation of a new order of social and personal existence.[119]

Stemming from a growing awareness among a group of Latin American protestants "of the new social reality that existed on their continent, namely, the awakening of the masses to their poverty, their illiteracy, their hunger, and more importantly to the causes and roots

---

118 Castro, "Prologo," 30.

119 Richard Shaull, "Iglesia y Teologia en la Voragine de la Revolución," in *De la Iglesia y la Sociedad*, 23–48 (34).

of their misery and suggesting," ISAL gave voice to "their unwillingness to continue living indefinitely under these conditions."[120] Such a move inevitably encountered resistance within the very ecclesiastical structures from which it emerged. The repressive political climate that began to spread in Latin America since the 1964 military coup d'état in Brazil exacerbated the opposition to the church and society movement in various Latin American countries. ISAL was forced to end its activities in 1973, the year Chile also experienced a brutal military coup that installed a right-wing dictatorship in the country which reverberated throughout the region.[121] While the dispersion of ISAL had a severe impact on the work it coordinated throughout Latin America, it did not prevent its associates from finding alternative ways to continue their ecumenically liberative work either through newly-formed ecumenical organizations such as DEI, CEI, CEDI, and CESE, among others, or through direct involvement in secular or Catholic-led social movements, which continued to resist the authoritarian political regimes that spread throughout the continent.

The conversations ISAL initiated in the 1960s with Catholic counterparts became a lasting contribution to the new ecumenical structures that were formed in the region later. With the end of ISAL, *Unidad Evangelica Latino Americana* (UNELAM), a Provisional Commission for Latin American Evangelical Unity, formed in 1963, became the main continental ecumenical umbrella, even though it never had the same level of autonomy that ISAL had.

An offspring of CELA II (1961), UNELAM proved to be an important step toward the formation of the Latin American Council of Churches (CLAI) in1982. While ISAL represents the Latin American contribution to a world-oriented ecumenism more closely connected to grassroots movements, UNELAM represents, more specifically, the efforts for an ecumenical journey that privileges the churches. While that process can be equally traced back to the Panama Congress, it results more directly from three important Latin American Protestant

[120] Neely, "Protestant Antecedents of the Latin American Theology of Liberation," 170.

[121] In 1975, there was an attempt to recreate ISAL with the name ASEL—Acción Social Ecuménica Latinoamericana (Latin American Ecumenical Social Action). But with the dispersion of its most significant leaders and minds, ASEL never had the same kind of impact ISAL had in the previous decade.

Conferences (CELA) sponsored by the CCLA, held between 1949 and 1969.

The Latin American Evangelical Conferences (CELA)

While the processes described in the earlier sections of this chapter were critical for the rise of an ecumenism turned to the world, the ecumenical significance of a simultaneous series of events continuing the conversations started at Havana 1929 cannot be ignored. The Latin American Protestant Conferences (CELA) took place during the same period the Church and Society Movement gained traction in the region. Some of the people involved in the planning of these conferences were also part of the Church and Society Movement. At the same time, these conferences represented the continuation of the efforts for unity initiated by the CCLA. As conferences that took place at a time of important transitions in the Latin American Protestant scene, a brief examination of them (CELA I, II, and III) can help clarify their significance for interchurch relations in the region.

As Thomas J. Ligget noted in 1959,

> By way of summary, we can say that in general the evangelical churches are projections of denominational structures of North American and European origin, that inter-church relationships now exist in many parts of Latin America through the regional and national Christian Councils, and that in a number of instances, there has been achieved a spirit of cooperation on the local level which has not been attained on the international level.[122]

The first of those conferences (CELA I) indicated an ongoing transition from relationships focusing on cooperation among mission boards to an ecumenism among Latin American churches. These conferences, although under the auspices of the CCLA, demonstrated the increasing desire for autonomy on the part of Latin American

[122] Thomas J. Liggett, *The Latin American Evangelical Church in Inter-Church Relationships: The Wider Responsibilities of the Evangelical Churches in Latin America*, Study Conference of the Committee on Cooperation in Latin America, Buck Hill Falls, PA, November 12–14, 1959 (New York: The Committee on Cooperation in Latin America, 1959), 13.

Protestant churches.[123] CELA I addressed the conflicts between Latin American leaders and mission boards during that transitional period. With the event of the three Congresses of Christian Action between 1916 and 1929, several councils or federations of Christian churches emerged in the continent. Others would take form in the 1950s. The CELAs became, then, a platform to help consolidate a growing Protestant self-awareness in the region.

CELA I continued to advance the process of Latin-Americanization of the Protestant churches displayed in Havana twenty years early. After the end of WWII, the National Evangelical Council of Mexico launched a convocation for a meeting originally planned for 1946. An organizing committee was formed, but the work to plan such a meeting demanded more time than originally expected. The IMC meeting in Whitby, Canada, in 1947 helped boost the plans, which materialized on July 18–20, 1949, in Buenos Aires, Argentina. Fifty-six delegates from fifteen Latin American countries (in addition to one from Spain, and two from the United States, along with forty-seven guests) gathered to reflect on the theme "Evangelical Christianity in Latin America."[124] The conference included delegates from eighteen Protestant denominations, being the most denominationally representative Protestant gathering ever seen in the region at that time. As Longuini Neto points out, this was the first continental ecumenical meeting in Latin America that counted with the participation of Pentecostal delegates.[125]

The conference was planned by Latin Americans. Argentinean Methodist Bishop Sante Uberto Barbieri was chosen to preside it. John Mackay, then President of Princeton Theological Seminary, and Marc Boegner, a French Protestant theologian representing the World Council of Churches (WCC), led the gathering's devotionals. The dominant voices at the conference were Latin American. CELA I focused on the theme of evangelization, boosted by the recognition of the growth of Protestantism in the region. Evangelism was the main motivating factor for Protestant unity and cooperation, even

[123] Liggett, *The Latin American Evangelical Church in Inter-Church Relationships*, 13.

[124] Longuini Neto, *O Novo Rosto da Missão*, 110–111; Sabanes Plou, *Caminhos de Unidade*, 94.

[125] Longuini Neto, *O Novo Rosto da Missão*, 110.

though themes such as world peace and the Universal Declaration of Human Rights were also on the agenda.[126]

The document, "Carta ao Povo Evangélico," an open letter from the conference to the churches in the region, sought to ease concerned minds by affirming that the kind of unity they were looking for did not seek an organic union but intended to manifest "the intimate spiritual unity we enjoy in Christ."[127] Most importantly, the letter unequivocally reaffirmed the Latin-Americanness of the Protestant churches in the region:

> Our evangelical churches, also called Protestant, spread across the continent and formed in their vast majority by Latin Americans and other ethnic types of our lands, are dignified and deeply rooted in their social environment. They are not exotic organizations, nor do they proclaim doctrines foreign to the pure gospel of our Lord Jesus Christ. We, the loving children of our countries, give thanks to God for them and seek to serve them loyally, desiring their progress in all orders, not with a view to a selfish predominance, which carries within itself the germ of its own destruction, but in the sense of Christ: "To serve," "to give life and give it abundantly." It is thus, as inspired by the love of Christ, that we strengthen the bonds of fellowship over all barriers of race, nationality or social status.[128]

Despite the lack of a concrete continuation strategy, CELA I laid the foundation for continued Latin American ecumenical cooperation.[129]

CELA II was held twelve years later, in Lima, Peru. That conference gathered more than two hundred participants from seventeen Latin American countries, with one hundred thirty official delegates. Six of the seventeen national delegations included Pentecostals.[130] The documents of CELA II show a more positive attitude toward the

[126] Longuini Neto, *O Novo Rosto da Missão*, 112.

[127] CELA I, "Carta ao Povo Evangélico," in Longuini Neto, 113–117 (114).

[128] CELA I, "Carta ao Povo Evangélico," 115.

[129] Sabanes Plou, *O Novo Rosto da Missão*, 99.

[130] José Miguez Bonino, "Hacia um Protestantismo Ecuménico: Notas para uma Evaluación Histórica del Protestantismo entre la I y II CELA (1949–1960)," in *Oaxtepec 1978*, 65–80 (69).

Catholic Church than the average Protestant views of that period. As Miguez Bonino noticed, instead of discussing the merits of Protestantism against the backdrop of Catholicism, this conference affirmed that all were "equally under the judgement of the Lord," and that Protestants were not guided by either aversion or attraction in their relationship with Catholics.

An unprecedented openness to dialogue seemed to be in the making, based on a "commitment to the truth."[131] Nevertheless, no Catholic representative participated in the conference, and no practical initiative towards Protestant-Catholic dialogue came out of it. At the end of the day, the progress seen in CELA II was that it hinted at a view of the Catholic Church, which did not portray it "as an adversary but in its internal diversity also as a possible interlocutor."[132]

Another perceptible change was that, in contrast to CELA I, the Lima conference sought to move beyond the liberal Protestant message that had prevailed in the CCLA since Panama 1916. Under that agenda, Protestants self-described as the bearers of progress for Latin America. CELA II, by contrast, based its understanding of the Latin American situation and the Christian mission on a Christology that emphasized the incarnation and lordship of Christ, interpreting the problems impacting the region not as resulting from its Catholic evangelization (as previous Protestant documents had implied) but as having multiple and complex causes.[133]

The Lima Conference discussed the economic and social problems impacting the region, including the unbalanced nature of industrial growth, widespread dehumanizing working conditions, unjust distribution of wealth, concentration of land (and the need for agrarian reform), the growing political awareness of the masses, and increased expectations for social change.[134] The analysis of the Latin American situation and the ways to solve its problems, though, were informed by a developmentalist perspective. CELA II spoke of social changes along the lines of educational reform, the expansion of the democratic

---

131 Bonino, "Hacia um Protestantismo Ecuménico, 77.

132 Bonino, "Hacia um Protestantismo Ecuménico, 77.

133 Bonino, "Hacia um Protestantismo Ecuménico, 76.

134 Bonino, "Hacia um Protestantismo Ecuménico, 78.

process, reconciliation among social classes, and reform of the international commerce.[135]

Reflecting its Christological accent, the theme of CELA II was "Christ, the Hope for Latin America." While the conference stood in continuation with CELA I, its organizers saw it as taking the process started in the 1949 gathering to the next stage. CELA II represented a movement coming of age, which affirmed not only its "evangelical conscience" but also "a new meaning of responsibility in a rapidly changing world."[136] As Benjamin Moraes described it,

> The evangelical councils and confederations that sponsor the II Conference are no longer incipient organizations from forty years ago that depended on non-Latin boards or bodies for their maintenance or guidance. They have long been established as a living expression of the very churches that constitute them and interpret the new mind of the forces that make up the ranks of Christ in Latin America.[137]

This increasingly autonomous Protestantism wanted to say that it had a message of its own to share with the Latin American people. Since Buenos Aires 1949, that message had been defined as Jesus Christ. However, by 1961, as Miguez Bonino underscored, the message had now become the fullness of Jesus. According to Miguez Bonino, that message was broader than either the conservative evangelical individualized Jesus or the liberal Protestant Jesus represented. CELA II portrayed a Jesus who was incarnated in the Latin American revolutionary situation. In Miguez Bonino's words, "Proclaiming Christ in Latin America means proclaiming him in the face of disorientation and the human search of our people."[138]

---

[135] Orlando Costas, "Uma Nueva Conciencia Protestante: La III CELA," in *Oaxtepec 1978*, 81–117 (82).

[136] Benjamin Moraes, "Lo Que Fue la Conferencia," in *Cristo la Esperanza para América Latina. Ponencias—informes—comentarios de la Segunda Conferencia Evangélica Latinoamericana, 20 de julio a 6 de agosto de 1961, Lima—Perú*, ed. Comisión II Conferencia Evangélica Latinoamericana (Buenos Aires: Confederación Evangélica del Río de La Plata, 1962), 11–15 (11).

[137] Moraes, "Lo Que Fue la Conferencia," 12.

[138] José Miguez Bonino, "Nuestra Mensaje," in *Cristo la Esperanza para América Latina*, 67–92 (85).

That conference called "believers to a prophetic ministry, a brave and decided participation in all community affairs," reminding them that, above all, "the Christian is an ambassador for reconciliation." Therefore, "Amidst all conflicts that agitate our peoples, where hate and desire for revenge intensify so easily, believers must be always ready to testify of a power that brings down all what divides humanity, making all one in Christ."[139] Although people like José Miguez Bonino, Emilio Castro, and Luis Odell, all involved in ISAL, were among the speakers and consultants of CELA II, this conference had its own identity in comparison to the meeting that happened just a few days earlier in Huampaní. CELA II can be better understood as a proponent of human dignity and reconciliation than of revolution and liberation.

Differently from its predecessor, CELA II formed a committee to start planning CELA III right away. The idea was to hold that conference in 1965 in Brazil. During those years, UNELAM, the recently founded Latin American Evangelical Union, in collaboration with the Brazilian Evangelical Confederation (CEB), would begin the preparatory work for CELA III. The 1964 military coup in Brazil and internal tensions between the increasingly conservative leadership of the post-Northeast Conference CEB and the more progressive leaders of UNELAM caused the postponement of CELA III until 1969. Several Brazilian Protestants, now living under a full-fledged military dictatorship, left the organization of the conference, which, at the invitation of the Federation of Evangelical Churches in Argentina, ended up meeting in Buenos Aires on July 13–19, 1969.[140]

This time, 206 representatives from 26 countries and 40 denominations and ecclesiastical organisms gathered to reflect on the theme "Debtors of the World," based on Romans 8:12[141] The conference explored "the obligation of Protestant churches to the diverse sectors of Latin America at a troubled time" of deep transformations throughout the region. The subthemes included (1) our debt and responsibility specifically as Latin American Protestants; (2) our Protestant debt in relation to the social, economic, and political transformations in Latin America; (3) our debt to the Latin American

139 CELA II, "Convocatória," in Longuini Neto, *O Novo Rosto da Missão*, 121–123 (121).

140 Longuini Neto, *O Novo Rosto da Missão*, 123–124.

141 Longuini Neto, 124.

women; (4) our debt to the Latin American youth; and (5) our debt to the Catholic community.[142]

The conference message articulated the debt theme in terms that resembled the emerging idea of integral or holistic mission, which identified "with the pains and hopes of the Latin American people," and which expressed "the same identification of Jesus Christ with his people in his pilgrimage to the cross; an intelligent and efficacious service in search of more just and human forms of social organization."[143] It is significant to highlight that two Catholic observers participated in CELA III. As Longuini Neto points out, the invitation extended to Catholic observers reciprocated the Catholic invitation for Latin American Protestants to send observers to the CELAM meeting in Medellin, Colombia, 1968.[144]

As Orlando Costas rightly stated, CELA III revealed a new Protestant conscience of itself, the Latin American social reality, and the Catholic Church.[145] In terms of the Latin American social reality, CELA III was able to offer a more contextually concrete analysis compared to its predecessors, using a more precise and committed socioanalytical language.[146] Consequently, it dared to face the root causes of the situation of underdevelopment in greater depth, pointing to the "socioeconomic imbalance" between the social classes. Furthermore, it called on the church to denounce the root causes of systemic injustice and those who are responsible for the struggles of the masses, and to replace "structures of oppression" with "humanizing structures."[147] One of the study commissions at CELA

---

[142] Longuini Neto, 124.

[143] CELA III, "Mensagem da Terceira Conferência Evangélica Latino-Americana," in Longuini, *O Novo Rosto da Missão*, 127–128. The language of identification with pains and hopes of the poor also resembles the preamble of *Gaudium et Spes*: "The joys and the hopes, the griefs and the anxieties of the men of this age, especially those who are poor or in any way afflicted, these are the joys and hopes, the griefs and anxieties of the followers of Christ." Pope Paul VI, *Gaudium et Spes: Pastoral Constitution on the Church and the Modern World*, Vatican, December 7, 1965, https://www.vatican.va/archive/hist_councils/ii_vatican_council/documents/vat-ii_const_19651207_gaudium-et-spes_en.html.

[144] CELA III, "Mensagem da Terceira Conferência Evangélica Latino-Americana," 127–128.

[145] Costas, "Uma Nueva Conciencia Protestante: La III CELA," 82.

[146] Costas, "Uma Nueva Conciencia Protestante: La III CELA," 82.

[147] Costas, 83.

III identified the presence of a "more conscient and revolutionary sector" in the church and its expectation that the church commit to the continental process of liberation.[148] It seemed clear at this point that the spread of a liberation Christianity throughout the continent and the news about the CELAM assembly in Medellin (1968), which will be discussed later, were already impacting the more official language and disposition of ecumenical Latin American Protestantism.

In addition to its invitation of Catholic observers, CELA III created a commission to work on the Protestant debt to Catholicism. That commission was aware of the changes taking place within the Catholic Church in the wake of Vatican II, among which "a new attitude towards other 'communities and ideologies,' Christian or not, its growing interest for the reading and diffusion of the Scriptures, and the brave commitment to the solution of the social maladies impacting various sectors of the Church."[149]

Seeking a better understanding of its religious, social, and cultural surroundings, the Protestant churches represented in Buenos Aires affirmed their commitment to witness Christ as a servant community, a church in the diaspora, a people on the way sharing in the struggles and anxieties of the world.[150] Affirming its incarnational mission, CELA III recalled John Mackay's *El Otro Cristo Español* to underscore the need for the Latin American Protestant churches to project the image of a Christ incarnated in all dimensions of life.[151] Embracing a liberating anthropology, CELA III paid particular attention to Latin American women, their situation and contributions in the region. One of its commissions examined, in particular, the situation of marginalization of women in Latin America. Two years earlier, UNELAM had held a consultation on the topic "The Role of Women in Church and Society." For Costas, this was the event that launched what later became a movement of women within Latin American Christianity.[152] Another emphasis of CELA III was the

---

148 Costas, 83.

149 Costas, 84.

150 Costas, 86.

151 John A. Mackay, *El Otro Cristo Español*, traducción de Gonzalo Báez-Camargo (México: Casa Unida; Buenos Aires: La Aurora, 1952). Costas, "Uma Nueva Conciencia Protestante: La III CELA," 87.

152 Mackay, *El Otro Cristo Español*, 88. The outcome of that consultation was published in Emilio Castro, ed., *El Rol de la Mujer en la Iglesia y en la Sociedad*

role of the Spirit empowering Christians to participate in the formation of a new humanity. According to Costas, this was the first Latin American Protestant conference that took seriously contributions coming from Pentecostalism, which has more recently become the largest and most representative group of indigenous Latin American Protestantism.[153]

Finally, CELA III not only revealed a new Protestant conscience in Latin America but also a divided one. The modern-fundamentalism controversy continued to impact Protestant life in the region, amplified by the Cold War, especially with the presence of US missionaries who sought to associate progressive developments in the ecumenical movement with communism. Along with that, there was a less extreme, although as important, discomfort among some conservative evangelicals with the concern with social justice in UNELAM and other ecumenical structures. As Costas notices, Herbert Mondey, a New Zealand missionary in Peru, in conjunction with some Pentecostals, planned to organize a "conservative invasion" of CELA III when the conference was still scheduled to take place in Brazil.[154] At that point, the Brazilian government was already surveilling some ecumenical leaders. That ideological element was key for the change of date and location of CELA III. The conservative dissatisfaction only spread, though, often instigated by missionaries such as C. Peter Wagner (1930–2016), who opposed the work of UNELAM, at the time coordinated by Castro, seeing it as a plan on the part of the WCC to bring the whole of Latin American Protestantism under its influence.[155]

In an effort to create an evangelical alternative to UNELAM, a congress sponsored by the Billy Graham Evangelistic Association

---

(Montevideo: UNELAM, 1968). Costas draws attention, in particular, to Beatriz Melano Couch's contribution to that volume. Couch, who studied with Mackay in Princeton and was involved in the formation of ISAL, was the first Protestant woman to hold a doctoral degree in theology and a pioneer in developing a women's theology in Latin America. See Beatriz Melano Couch, *La Mujer y la Iglesia* (Buenos Aires: Publicaciones El Escudo, 1973). Couch would also make an important contribution to the development of the Ecumenical Association of Third World Theologians (EATWOT), in the late 1970s and 1980s.

153 Mackay, *El Otro Cristo Español*, 91–92.

154 Mackay, *El Otro Cristo Español*, 92.

155 Daniel Salinas, *Latin American Evangelical Theology in the 1970's: The Golden Decade* (Leiden/Boston: Brill, 2009), 56.

(BGEA) was called to discuss the mission of the church in that same year. CLADE I, the Latin American Congress of Evangelization, was a numerical success, gathering 830 delegates and a total of 900 participants in Bogota, Colombia, on November 21–30, 1969, under the theme "Christian Action for a Continent in Crisis." Most of the individuals attracted to CLADE I did not feel fully represented in UNELAM or in the CELA conferences.

The tensions seen in CELA III, though, were not absent from CLADE I. This congress was perceived even by theologically conservative individuals as a product made in the United States for Latin America. Some of the theologians attending that congress scheduled a meeting in Cochabamba, Bolivia, in 1970, where they launched the *Fraternidad Teológica Latinoamericana* (FTL). As I show elsewhere, the FTL would become the main catalyst for a theologically conservative, yet socially progressive, evangelical movement.[156]

Base ecumenism results, to a significant extent, from the specific circumstances of Latin America during the period covered in this chapter. Beginning in Geneva 1966 and continuing in Uppsala 1968 and Nairobi 1975, the liberative language forged in that ecumenical turn to the world in Latin America and other parts of the Global South began to inform and shape the entire scope of the ecumenical movement. This chapter has discussed the preparatory conditions within Latin American Protestantism for the rise of a new theological language, which emerged from a growing self-awareness of the location from which Latin American Protestants interpreted the world and their faith, and the extent to which they engaged the situation of systemic injustice that limited the flourishing of their communities. While Latin American Protestants started to organize ecumenical structures as early as 1916, the more they engaged the reality of injustice in the region, and the more they perceived the resistance of the status quo to real and lasting social change, the more they felt the need to reinvent their ecumenicity, conceiving it increasingly in relation to broader solidarity with those who are disadvantaged, and instilling collaboration from the ground up with other sectors of society for transformative justice.

[156] FTL stands for Latin American Theological Fellowship. For my take on the formation of FTL and its significance, see Barreto, *Protesting Poverty*, chapter 4.

6

CATHOLIC ACTION AND THE ROOTS OF BASE ECUMENISM

If on the Protestant end Edinburgh 1910 can be considered the most generative event putting in motion a sequence of articulations that led to the rise of Latin American ecumenism, on the Catholic end, the Second Vatican Council (1962–1965) played that role. That does not mean, however, that Vatican II gave birth to liberation theology or to base ecumenism in Latin American Catholicism. Despite its significance, other global, regional, and local events and developments contributed to create a movement for the transformation of the Latin American Catholic Church in the 1960s—even though the process leading to that had been in the making for decades. Vatican II created the institutional conditions in the Catholic Church to allow the aspiration for change to materialize. But the Council itself was the result of changes already in course in the Church and the broader society in various parts of the world, including Latin America. This chapter focuses on the development of lay movements in Latin America, which prepared the way for the region's participation, interpretation, and creative reception of Vatican II.

Considering how closely the rise of liberation theology and the coming of age of a broader ecumenical impulse—among Catholics and Protestants—are interrelated, one can find the roots of a Catholic ecumenical awareness in the region in the formation of lay movements whose praxis contributed to the Latin American efforts to theologize solidarity with the poor and resistance to systemic oppression.[1] Starting in the mid-twentieth century, several Catholic movements began to form in conversation with Catholic theologies and experiences emerging in different parts of the world—including

[1] For a good overview of the diverse movements of resistance and solidarity that preceded the rise of a Latin American liberation Christianity in the twentieth century, see Pablo Richard, ed., *Raízes da Teologia-Latino Americana* (São Paulo, Brazil: Edições Paulinas, 1988).

France, Italy, and Belgium. Among the movements that would be critical to help shape contemporary Latin American Catholicism, the worker-priest movement, initiated in Marseille, France, in 1941, was key. As seen in chapter four, it also impacted the Protestant Church and Society movement. Other lay action-oriented movements that emerged even earlier in the twentieth century, in particular Catholic Action, also played a preparatory role in helping a conflicted Latin American Christianity to find its own theological voice in the latter part of the century.

While these movements prepared the way for the Latin American liberationist turn of the 1960s, Vatican II created the unique circumstances for the rearticulation of Catholic theology in the modern world on both the global and local levels, becoming critical for the theological renewal the Latin American Church would experience in the final decades of the past century. A number of Latin American bishops, priests, and lay activists planned the Medellin conference of 1968 in the wake of Vatican II inspired, among other things, by Pope John XXIII's encyclical *Mater et Magistra* (1961) and his reference to the impoverished countries, as he specifically stated in a radiophonic speech weeks away from the opening of the Council that the Church must present itself as the Church of all people; in particular, "the Church of the Poor."[2] That call for the Church to stand in solidarity with the impoverished masses of the world inspired the formation of "The Church of the Poor Group" during the second Vatican Council, among other efforts leading to a turn to the poor in the years that followed. That was not the only starting point for the rise of the Church of the Poor in Latin America, though. Combining the examination of regional and global events that contributed to rise of the Church of the Poor in Latin America, this chapter discusses specific developments that prepared the Latin American Church for Vatican II and for its reception, helping create the conditions for the rise of base ecumenism.

---

[2] See John XXIII, "*Nuntius Radiophonicus*," September 11, 1962, *Discorsi-Messaggi-Colloqui del Santo Padre Giovanni XXIII*, vol. IV, ed. Domenico Bertetto (Vatican: Tipografia Poliglotta Vaticana, 1962), 520–528. Spanish version available at https://w2.vatican.va/content/john-xxiii/es/messages/pont_messages/1962/documents/hf_j-xxiii_mes_19620911_ecumenical-council.html (Translation is mine).

Catholic Action and Worker Priests in Latin America

The most consequential lay Catholic movement in the first half of the twentieth century was Catholic Action. Its origins can be traced back to the rise of social Catholicism in the second half of the nineteenth century, and the delineation of a new social and economic Church teaching as depicted in Pope Leo XIII's encyclical *Rerum Novarum* (1891). Catholic Action only took the shape of a movement, though, in the beginning of the twentieth century, following Pope Pius XI's encyclical *Ubi Arcano Dei Consilio* (1922). Two main processes informed its formation and development. First, the Catholic Church's increased efforts to reclaim temporal authority, refusing to succumb to the privatized role secular modernity had asserted to religion. In other words, the incipient Catholic Social Doctrine was, among other things, meant to help the Church reassert its public relevance and "re-catholicize society."[3] Concomitantly, there was a renewed interest in the role the laity played in the Church's life and apostolate.

Efforts to include the participation of all Christians in the liturgy of the Church gained new impulse with Pope Pius X's *Motu Proprio* (1903), which affirmed the rising liturgical movement in the Catholic Church in the turn of the twentieth century. In it, the Church recognized the potential of lay organized movements to help advance its evangelizing mission in rapidly secularizing urban areas. In *Ubi Arcano Dei Consilio* (1922), Pius XI underscored the rise of clergy and lay organizations "formed to aid the missions in their manifold activities, both physical and moral, of the natural and the supernatural order, by the spreading far and wide of the Kingdom of Christ."[4] He specifically praised those organizations and movements formed under the name "Catholic Action," welcoming their work

[3] Ana Maria Bidegain, "From Catholic Action to Liberation Theology: The Historical Process of the Laity in Latin America in the Twentieth Century," *Working Paper # 48*, The Helen Kellogg Institute for International Studies, University of Notre Dame, 1985, 2, https://kellogg.nd.edu/sites/default/files/old_files/documents/048_0.pdf.

[4] The Holy See, *Ubi Arcano Dei Consilio: Encyclical of Pope Pius XI on the Peace of Christ in the Kingdom of Christ to our Venerable Brethren the Patriarchs, Primates, Archbishops, Bishops, and Other Ordinaries in Peace and Communion with the Apostolic See*, 11, https://www.vatican.va/content/pius-xi/en/encyclicals/documents/hf_p-xi_enc_19221223_ubi-arcano-dei-consilio.pdf.

and encouraging their further development "as the conditions of time and place seem to demand."[5] At the same time, keeping those initiatives under the control and direction of the clergy continued to be a concern. Accordingly, the development of Catholic action was often regulated by by-laws delimiting and systematizing its work under the tutelage of the Church.[6]

Catholic Action is broadly defined as "all apostolic activity performed by Catholics, with ecclesiastical approval."[7] It "is an organized and multiforme activity, performed by the laity in the field of social life, under the direct dependence of the ecclesiastic authority, with the end of Christianizing society."[8] Some of the criteria for its establishment are: (1) Catholic Action must be a response to an official call on the part of the Church. Therefore, it requires a mandate from the Catholic hierarchy, i.e., it must be authorized by the Church. Furthermore, (2) it must be "organized action," that is, an action in line with the unity of the Church, following the guidance of the *Sumo pontífice*. The concern with the unity and hierarchical organization of the Church was central to the Catholic involvement of the laity in its activities, which this chapter discusses.

Catholic Action has taken different shapes and forms in Latin America. In Brazil, it gave birth initially to the Men's Catholic Action, formed by single men aged thirty or more and married men of any age; the Women's League of Catholic Action for women over thirty and married women of any age; the Catholic Brazilian Youth for young men between fourteen and thirty years old; and the Youth Female Catholic, for girls of the same age group. The Catholic Brazilian Youth—Juventude Católica Brasileira (JCB)—formed its own subgroups: a) Benjamins Catholic Action, for children aged 8 to 12; and b) Aspirants of the Catholic Youth, for those between 12 and 14 years old.[9]

---

5 The Holy See, *Ubi Arcano Dei Consilio*, 11.

6 For the by-laws of the Brazilian Social Action, see J. B. Portocarrero Costa, *Ação Católica: Conceito, Programa, Organização* (Rio de Janeiro: Empresa Editora ABC Limitada, 1937), 17ff.

7 Luis Q. Calvimonte, *Orígenes de la Acción Católica en Córdoba: sus primeros diez años 1931–1941*, Cuadernos de História (Córdoba, Argentina: Junta Provincial de Historia de Córdoba, 1994), 8.

8 Calvimonte, *Orígenes de la Acción Católica en Córdoba*, 9.

9 See Portocarrero Costa, *Ação Católica: Conceito, Programa, Organização*, 18.

Other groups organized under the umbrella of Catholic Action would gain particular significance. Juventude Estudante Católica (JEC) was a student movement that reached mainly highschoolers. *Juventude Universitária Católica* (JUC) focused on college students, and *Juventude Operária Católica* (JOC) was a movement of young Catholic workers.[10] Another face of this movement was the *Juventude Agrária Católica* (JAC), the Catholic Young Agrarian Workers Movement. These specialized Catholic action groups were established in Brazil in the late 1940s, divided by gender, with separate female organizations coexisting with male-only counterparts. As these movements evolved in the 1950s and early 1960s, some of the female and male organizations merged.

Pope Pius XI is known as the Pope of Catholic Action. He saw the movement as instrumental for the insertion of the Apostolate of the Church in an increasingly secular world. In a letter to Brazilian Cardinal Sebastião Leme, the founder of the Brazilian Catholic Confederation, an organism created to coordinate the action of lay Catholics and its associations, the pope expressed his views on Catholic Action:

> As long as we have clearly defined our way of thinking about Catholic Action—namely in our first Encyclical "Ubi Arcanum Dei"—we are fulfilling the desire that you manifested to us during your recent stay in Rome, addressing our paternal word to you and to your brethren in the Episcopate. With this, we want to demonstrate once again the high concept we have of the collaboration that lay people can offer to the Apostolate of the Hierarchy, not only in defense of the truth and the Christian life threatened by so many snares, but also that they may be, in the hands of their shepherds, an effective instrument for ever greater religious and civil progress.[11]

Evangelization and civil progress were seen as the main goals for the renewed mobilization of the Catholic laity, and the two went hand-in-hand. Yet, some specialized sectors of Catholic Action went

---

[10] Portocarrero Costa, 18–19.

[11] Pope Pius XI, "Carta do Santo Padre Pio XI ao Exmo. Cardeal Dom Sebastião Leme e ao Episcopado Nacional," in Portocarrero Costa, *Ação Católica: Conceito, Programa, Organização*, 24. (Translation is mine.)

beyond the pope's expectation, becoming important catalysts for the awakening of greater social concern among young Catholics. Social action—a precursor of what would be later called social justice—was called for.[12] Exposure to those realities would also impact the journey of the priests overseeing the movement in the long run. As Uruguayan historian Ana Maria Bidegain points out, it was common for Catholic priests to have a seminary education that kept them distant from the realities of the world, out of "contact with the society in which they were required to exercise their ministry."[13] As the Catholic hierarchy struggled to regain the influence lost to secular ideologies in Latin American societies, these voluntary associations became important incubators of fresher ideas and lay leadership for church and society. As a greater number of younger priests engaged with lay realities and movements, they were awakened to the systemic nature of the problems they were called to address.

One of the earliest examples of that can be seen in the rise of the *Jeunesse Ouvrière Catholique* (Catholic Working Youth, JOC), which emerged initially in Brussels in 1924 through the initiative of a Catholic priest named Joseph Cardijn (1882–1967).[14] Raised in a Catholic working family, Cardijn undertook the task of closing the growing gap between the Church and the working class. His message affirmed an incarnate gospel capable of bringing sacrament, prayer, and social action together.[15] Cardijn made one of the most significant contributions to Christian praxis and theology in the first half of the twentieth century. He started a lay apostolate in factories, forming small communities of students, peasants, and their families who not only shared the Gospel in their own context but also directly participated in the transformation of the reality in which they lived.

Cardijn also made one of the most consequential methodological contributions to twentieth-century Christian theology through the formulation of the see-judge-act method, which influenced the work of JOC and, later, Latin American liberation theology. As Bidegain puts it,

---

12 Bidegain, "From Catholic Action to Liberation Theology," 2.

13 Bidegain, "From Catholic Action to Liberation Theology," 2.

14 Bidegain, "From Catholic Action to Liberation Theology," 6.

15 Bidegain, "From Catholic Action to Liberation Theology," 6.

> This method was supposed to start with concrete facts in the lives of the militants, analyze these facts into all the possible elements and evaluate them in light of the Gospel, and to act in accordance with the analysis and evaluation. That is to say that, at the same time, they would look for the working-class evangelization among them, by them and for them. It was essential to struggle for the defense of the interests of their own class.[16]

JOC was a young people's movement organized for and by workers. Priests functioned as advisers and coordinators.[17] The analytical method that emerged from this movement was empirically based. The problems its participants "encountered were to be scientifically assessed, properly considered, and only then was appropriate action to be taken."[18] In *Mater et Magistra* (1961), Pope John XXIII refers to the three stages of this method: "Firstly, one reviews the concrete situation; secondly, one forms a judgment on it in the light of these same principles; thirdly, one decides what in the circumstances can and should be done to implement these principles."[19] The principles of the social teachings of the Church were "brought to bear on practical problems," anticipating "the idea of theology as critical reflection on praxis so prominent in the writings of Gutiérrez, Assmann and Segundo."[20] The wide use of this tripartite approach to this day testifies to the broad influence that Cardijn and his see-judge-act method made on Christian theology and praxis in the twentieth century.

In Latin America, JOC initially focused mainly "on personal change, identity, and self-empowerment," although it was also interested in the transformation of the broader moral situation of society and in denouncing working conditions that dehumanized the workers.[21] The relation of Catholic Action with the worker's movement

---

[16] Bidegain, "From Catholic Action to Liberation Theology," 7.

[17] Gerd-Rainer Horn, *Western European Liberation Theology: The First Wave (1924–1959)* (Oxford, UK: Oxford University Press, 2008), 14.

[18] Horn, *Western European Liberation Theology*, 13.

[19] The Holy See, "*Mater et Magistra:* Encyclical of Pope John XXIII on Christianity and Social Progress," https://www.vatican.va/content/john-xxiii/en/encyclicals/documents/hf_j-xxiii_enc_15051961_mater.html.

[20] Alan Neely, "Liberation Theology in Latin America: Antecedents and Autochthony," *Missiology: An International Review* 6/3 (1978): 343–370 (353).

[21] Deborah Levenson-Estrada, *Trade Unionists Against Terror Book: Guatemala City, 1954–1985* (Chapel Hill: The University, 2008), 80, 81.

varied from place to place. Having started in Belgium, JOC expanded to several other countries, including France, in 1927, where it contributed to the organization of young agricultural workers in 1929, a movement that involved around 200,000 participants.[22] For several decades, various French Catholic Action subgroups developed studies, promoting "social weeks" to examine and discuss Catholic social teaching. These social weeks traveled from city to city like an "itinerant university."[23]

Another similar initiative loosely connected with social action was the *Missiens en Roulette* (trailer missions), through which teams of priests came on station wagons and trailers to an industrial community for three months, not only for the study of the Bible and the social and cultural problems but also for relief work. In addition to that, they supported and followed up on the work initiated by the Jocists.[24] At this juncture, the priests' apostolate, which tended to focus mainly on the parish, and the lay apostolate in the secular realm intersected. This proximity between the Church and the secular arena raised new challenges to the priests' comprehension of their responsibilities. Among other things, as they related to JOC and other Catholic Action groups, it became increasingly clearer for a number of them that the abyss between the Church and the proletarian masses was so deep that Jocists alone would not be able to overcome it. New mission strategies on the part of the priests themselves were necessary to advance that task.[25] The work-priest missions were supposed to fill that gap.

The first worker-priest missions emerged in France, in the 1940s, with the goal of reconnecting the Church and the working classes—which many in the Church considered to be the most de-Christianized sector of the French society.[26] Moving beyond their initial parish-centered strategies, the rising worker-priest

---

[22] Marie T. Dubalen, *The Worker Priests* (New York: Student League for Industrial Democracy, 1955), 12.

[23] Dubalen, *The Worker Priests*, 13.

[24] Dubalen, *The Worker Priests*, 13.

[25] Dubalen, *The Worker Priests*, 16.

[26] Dubalen, *The Worker Priests*, 16. The "dechristianization" of the proletariat was a growing challenge for the Church. Some industrial suburbs of Paris no longer had parishioners. As a contemporary observer noticed, in one of the industrial complexes in the observed area only four of nineteen thousand workers were practicing

missions formed a secular clerical body capable of immersing into the day-to-day reality of the working class, engaging the challenges they faced in the world. The Statute of the Mission of France described it as follows:

> The Mission of France is a secular clerical body under the French Episcopal jurisdiction destined to bring not only numeric help to the Dioceses in need of it, but also to accomplish an apostolic mission in the most dechristianized area, geographically and sociologically speaking. This task is to be assumed by the missionary clerics, specially prepared for problems of the contemporary world.[27]

While the original intention of the movement was to reconnect the workers to the Church, in practice the immersion of the priests in the secularized reality of the French working classes led many of them to distance themselves from the hierarchy of the Church. Not that these priests saw any contradiction between their priestly call and their work in the factories. On the contrary, they believed that real immersion in the reality in which the workers lived was the appropriate way to fully participate in their suffering. Such a solidarity and intimacy were expected to bring down the walls separating those works from the Church, as much as the infusion of prayer as a mystical dimension of work.[28] However, the more they participated in the workers' daily struggles and the more they spoke up on behalf of them, the more employers grew worried and complained about those priests to the Church.

In 1952, two worker-priests were arrested for taking part in a communist demonstration in Marseille. In a workers' strike in August 1953, worker-priests were once again vocally critical of the conditions in which their fellow workers had to live. The priests' participation in the struggles of the working class led them to take political stands in solidarity with those workers. The participation of worker-priests in campaigns for increased pay and improvement in the working conditions, often described by the press as unrests, caused the Vatican

---

Catholics. Robert F. Byrnes, "The French Priest-Workers," *Foreign Affairs* 33/2 (1995): 327–331 (327).

[27] Cited by Dubalen, 17.

[28] Dubalen, *The Worker Priests*, 24–25.

to suppress the movement.[29] In 1953, a seminary was closed at the order of the papal nuncio. Students were forbidden to work in industrial installations over the summer as they used to, and recruitment for the Paris Mission, one of the bases of the movement, was put on hold.[30] The seed of the movement, however, had already been sown. The growing suppression they faced at home was only matched by the growing interest in their ministry in other parts of the world.

By the early 1950s, stories about the worker-priest French experience were making waves among young Latin American Christians, inspiring both Catholic and Protestant workers, students, and seminarians to embrace a life of solidarity and commitment to industrial and rural working families based on the primacy of praxis, which took the struggle of impoverished classes seriously. Some Latin American priests engaged in the specialized sectors of Catholic Action began to experience a radical conversion to the world—to an ecumenism of life.[31] In the case of Brazil, JOC emerged in 1948, serving as a model for the creation of other specialized Catholic Actions.

Evolution and Change in Latin American Catholic Action

The developments abovementioned deeply impacted Latin American Catholicism. In dialogue with those experiences and ideas, Latin

---

[29] J. E. Flower, "Forerunners of the Worker-Priests," *Journal of Contemporary History* 2/4 (1967) 183–199 (184).

[30] Byrnes, "The French Priest-Workers," 329.

[31] In a recent address to the Joint International Commission for Theological Dialogue between the Catholic Church and the Eastern Orthodox Churches, Pope Francis refers to ecumenism of life as the dialogue of life that takes places in the day-to-day life among families and coworkers, for instance, who often experience together an ecumenism of suffering. That is, for him, the starting point of theological dialogue: "Theological ecumenism must therefore reflect not only on the dogmatic differences that emerged in the past, but also on the present experience of our faithful. In other words, the dialogue of doctrine must be theologically adapted to the dialogue of life that develops in the local, everyday relations between our Churches; these constitute a genuine locus or source of theology." The Holy See, "Address of His Holiness Pope Francis to the Joint International Commission for Theological Dialogue between the Catholic Church and the Oriental Orthodox Churches," Wednesday, June 23, 2022, https://www.vatican.va/content/francesco/en/speeches/2022/june/documents/20220623-dialogo-teologico.pdf.

American Christians—clergy and lay—developed their own movements, praxis, and theology. In the 1950s and 1960s, Latin American Catholicism saw the spread of Catholic Action and the worker-priest Movement. Learning from experiences in France and elsewhere, it produced something new, a theological movement based on a liberative praxis, which later would be known around the world as liberation theology.

Catholic Action started in Latin America in the 1920s in response to what was then called "the social question," which, since *Rerum Novarum*, had gained increasing significance in Catholic circles, including the affirmation of the right of workers to organize unions and fight for fairer wages and better working conditions. At the same time, Catholic Action emerged as a strategy to mobilize Catholic laity as the Church in Latin America struggled to regain influence it considered to have lost.[32]

Since the formation of the modern Latin American states in the nineteenth century, the broad influence the Church had on society in the colonial era decreased significantly throughout the region. As most of these new Latin American states established themselves as secular states, the Catholic Church had to compete with liberal and communist political parties, Protestant churches and secularizing values that had made into the constitutions of most Latin American countries, which often included separation of church and state. In this more pluralistic environment, Catholic societal influence could no longer be taken for granted. In such a context, Catholic Action became an important strategy for the Church to regain its place of privilege and authority in Latin American societies.

Catholic Action groups quickly popped up in multiple Latin American countries. Steadily they became spaces not only for Catholic activism but also for Catholic militancy.[33] Such a militancy took distinct political flavors and forms. While Catholic Action specialized groups tended to align with workers' unions and youth/student

32 See Acción Católica Peruana, *Primer Congreso Nacional* (Lima/Huampaní: Acción Católica Peruana, 1955), 27, 29–30.

33 Ney de Souza, *História da Igreja na América Latina* (Petrópolis: Vozes, 2022), 356. The material produced by the Peruvian Catholic Action to celebrate its twentieth anniversary in its first national congress in 1955 refers to its participants as "militants." Acción Católica Peruana, *Primer Congreso Nacional*, 1.

movements, in its initial years the broader Catholic Action in Latin America often aligned with fascist and traditionalist movements, electing the struggle to eradicate communist and secularist influences from Latin American societies as a chief objective. Both political philosophies were considered antichristian forces that needed to be defeated.[34]

A Manual of Catholic Action, published in Mexico in 1935, refers to Catholic Action as the rise of the secular apostolate in Latin America to combat the "paganization of society."[35] While any action in accordance with the principles of the Catholic faith could be broadly conceived as Catholic Action, in its inception in the region, more often than not, it denoted specifically activities "in favor of the Catholic religion."[36] Catholic Action's secular apostolate, therefore, depended on the Church hierarchy. Its chief goal was to re-Christianize society. To achieve that goal, members of Catholic Action were to instill a Christian conscience on every level of influence, bringing, in the language of Pius X, "all humanity under the empire of our Lord Jesus Christ."[37]

In 1922, Pius XI's *Ubi Arcano Dei* set the ideological basis for Catholic Action, describing it as "'divisions of an army' to prevent a greater retreat of the Church and prepare the reconquest of lost ground."[38] As Sergio Armando Cáceres Mateus underscores, Catholic Action emerged in Latin America in the wake of persistent efforts to implement an "uncompromising, ultramontanist and fundamentalist traditionalist Catholicism."[39] In such a context, it reinforced the most reactionary trends in the Church.

---

[34] González & González, *Christianity in Latin America*, 163. As González & González show, by the 1940s that role would be taken by "overtly political Christian Democratic parties as Catholics sought ways to put their faith into action in the political sphere."

[35] Luis Cirvadi, *Manual de Acción Católica: Volume I—Teoria*, 3rd ed. (Monterrey, Mexico: Pablo Cervantes, PBRO, 1935), 133.

[36] Cirvadi, *Manual de Acción Católica*, 30.

[37] Cirvadi, *Manual de Acción Católica*, 139–140. This is Cirvadi's paraphrase of Pope Pius X's encyclical *E Supremi* (1903).

[38] Ney de Souza, "Ação Católica, Militância Leiga no Brasil: méritos e limites," *Revista de Cultura Teológica* 14/55 (2006): 39–59 (42).

[39] Sergio Armando Cáceres Mateus, "La Acción Católica en la organización y puesta en marcha del Segundo Congreso Nacional Mariano de Colombia (1939–1946)," *Anuário de História Regional y de las Fronteras* 22/2(2017): 217–245 (222).

The Brazilian case is significant. As Ney de Souza puts it, "The initial role of Brazilian Catholic Action was to defend the values and Christian principles on the part of lay Catholics in the field of political activity."[40] The Brazilian Catholic Action (*Ação Católica Brasileira*, ACB) was created in 1935 under the auspices of the Dom Vital Center. Founded in 1922 by conservative Catholic lawyer Jackson de Figueiredo Martins (1891–1928) and Sebastião Leme da Silveira Cintra (1882–1942), the coadjutor archbishop of São Sebastião do Rio de Janeiro, this Center led the efforts to restore the prestige the Catholic Church felt it had lost since the promulgation of the Republican Constitution of 1891, becoming one of the most influential Catholic institutions in the country. In 1925, these two men led a campaign to amend the constitution and restore Catholicism as the official religion of Brazil. While they failed to achieve the intended result, under their leadership the Dom Vital Center became a powerhouse articulating Catholic political mobilization to defend conservative values.

After Figueiredo Martins's unexpected death in 1928, Leme found another exceptional lay collaborator in the figure of Alceu Amoroso Lima (1893–1983), a journalist, writer, and educator who had just returned to the Catholic faith that same year after living his young adult years outside the Church. Lima replaced Figueiredo Martins as president of the Dom Vital Center, assisting Leme in the formation of the Catholic Electoral League in 1933, an organization created to support the election of lay Catholics to political offices and encourage Catholic citizens to vote for candidates committed to Catholic values.

Brazil's national Catholic Action emerged in 1935.[41] Pius XI had encouraged Catholic Action to penetrate all dimensions of public life, although discouraging association with specific political parties.[42] Catholic individuals were free to affiliate with political parties or movements of which the Church did not disapprove. That was the

[40] Souza, "Ação Católica, Militância Leiga no Brasil: méritos e limites," 48.

[41] As Mário Antonio Betiato highlights, although the Brazilian Catholic Action was formally founded only in 1935, Dom Leme wrote a book titled *Catholic Action* in 1923 preparing the people for the renewal of the Church, which he asserted, was about to come. Mário Antônio Betiato, *Da Ação Católica à Pastoral da Juventude* (Petrópolis, Brazil: Vozes, 1985), 29.

[42] Murilo Mendes, "O Catolicismo e os Integralistas," *Anuário de Literatura* 9 (2001): 33–36 (34).

case of the *Ação Integralista Brasileira* (AIB), founded in 1932 by conservative journalist Plínio Salgado (1895–1975). Inspired by the Italian fascist movement,[43] AIB was not a political party per se, but a political movement that advanced an ultranationalist and traditionalist ideology. It promoted Catholic nationalism using the slogan "God, Country, and Family," popularized by Portuguese Prime Minister and strong man António de Oliveira Salazar (1889–1972), attacking those who rejected integralism as heretics, schismatics, apostates, and communists.[44] While President Getúlio Vargas (1882–1954) was not inclined to support the idea of turning Brazil back into a Catholic state, Salgado's ideas found support in important sectors of the Church.

AIB itself was not Catholic. It included Protestants and Kardecist spiritists among its affiliates. However, the majority of those involved in the movement was Catholic. Also, AIB significantly benefitted from the work of Catholic leaders such as Alceu Amoroso Lima through the Catholic Electoral League.[45]

Lima, formerly a liberal thinker, converted to Catholicism, embracing a conservative version of it that could be considered ultramontane. While he would change that position over the years, at the beginning of his tenure at the Dom Vital Center, he confessed that he was sympathetic to Integralism.

> Jackson de Figueiredo, however, would take posthumous action over me. With his death his influence would be completed. Dead, he would end up beating me at least for a while. This happened when I was invited to replace him as director of Centro Dom Vital. The feeling of responsibility, the tradition he left behind,

---

[43] Salgado visited Benito Mussolini and received money from Italy for the AIB in the mid-1930s. Also, when exiled from Brazil in 1939, he lived in Portugal under the authoritarian regime of António de Oliveira Salazar, whose precepts inspired him to support "Christian Democracy," [a political ideology] which led him to form "a new integralist party, the People's Representation Party (PRP, Partido de Representação Popular)" upon his return to Brazil in the early 1940s. See Leandro Pereira Gonçalves and Odilon Caldeira Neto, *Fascism in Brazil: From Integralism to Bolsonarism*, Routledge Studies in Fascism and the Far Right (London and New York: Taylor and Francis, 2022), ix, 45, 50.

[44] Mendes, "O Catolicismo e os Integralistas," *Anuário de Literatura*, 34.

[45] Gonçalves and Caldeira Neto, *Fascism in Brazil: From Integralism to Bolsonarism*, 8.

> the presence of common friends excited me. From then on, I moved in another direction, moving from the previous liberalism to an orthodox authoritarian position, based on the feeling of discipline and order. I was taken by the conviction that Catholicism was a right-wing position [. . .]. My articles on integralism date back to that time. I believed that integralism was a national political reaction of a unitary and authoritarian character, against the weakness of the State, regionalism and the class struggle, in favor of a strong State, national unity and corporate reform of the economy [. . .]. This was my position at the time, a markedly right-wing, anti-liberal, orthodoxly authoritarian position.[46]

Lima was the main collaborator of Leme in the creation of the Brazilian Catholic Action and its first president (1934–1945). He was also the president of the Dom Vital Center, the headquarters of the Catholic Reaction,[47] which sought for the Romanization of the Brazilian Church and society. At the beginning of his tenure, Lima saw clear affinities between the two, while strongly opposing initiatives such as the left-wing National Liberating Alliance of Carlos Prestes.[48] Because of his lay leadership in the Church, Lima ended up being nominated to the National Council of Education. His presence in that council signaled the influence of the Catholic Church on the federal government. Lima used that position to defend the role of religion in Brazilian education as "an antidote to the original sin

---

[46] Alceu Amoroso Lima, *Memórias Improvisadas: diálogos com Medeiros Lima* (Petrópolis, Brazil: Vozes, 1973), 120–121. As quoted by Rodrigo Augusto de Souza "A trajetória das ideias políticas de Alceu Amoroso Lima: da contrarrevolução ao modernismo católico (1928–1938)," *Cadernos de História da Educação* 20 (2021) 1–18 8).

[47] Catholic Reaction is the name given to a reactionary process that took place in Brazil and other parts of Latin America and Europe, in response to what was perceived as the abandonment of the traditional teachings of the Church. It opposed the influence of rationalism, empiricism and liberalism—often associated with skepticism and materialism—on Catholic clergy and laity. Holding a conservative political attitude, the movement strived to reaffirm the authority of the Church in the world and reclaim Catholic moral values as the proper response to the crisis of modernity. Ricardo Luiz de Souza, *A Reaçao Católica no Brasil: Instituição e Pensamento (1899–1945)* (Porto Alegre, Brazil: Editora da UFCSPA, 2023), 9ff.

[48] Carlos Roberto Jamil Cury, *Alceu Amoroso Lima* (Recife, Brazil: Fundação Joaquim Nabuco, 2010), 16.

that corrupts man [sic]."[49] In a book about the Christianization of the new era, he stated his counterrevolutionary position: "To those who want to regenerate the world through revolution, we counteroffer the regeneration of the world through religion."[50]

During those years, Lima's leadership of the Brazilian Social Action (ACB) instilled values derived from the social teachings of the Church in the lives of blue-collar workers, students, and the youth in general. Leme's death in 1942 and the end of Vargas's dictatorial regime (1937–1945) created new conditions for the democratization of the country. Reflecting those changes, since the late 1940s, the ACB entered a new phase in its history, slowly turning its focus to specialized groups such as JAC (Catholic Agrarian Youth), JUC (Catholic University Youth), JEC (Catholic Student Youth) and JOC (Catholic Workers Youth). Adopting the "see, judge, act" method to engage the concrete experiences of the sectors of society they were engaging,[51] these specialized groups became spaces that furthered rising democratic aspirations, preparing the way to the transformations that would take place in the popular sectors of Catholicism in the coming decades.

Lima himself reconsidered his antiliberal and counterrevolutionary militancy, returning to his early admiration of Jacques Maritain's integral humanism. He left the ecclesiastical machine in the mid-1940s to become an important journalist, writer, and critical observer of the Brazilian political scene. In the late 1940s and 1950s, he embraced Christian democracy, reimagining it through the lenses of Christian humanism.

In the 1960s, impacted by the transformations the Vatican II brought to Catholic thought and praxis, and engaging, among others, the ideas of Pierre Teilhard de Chardin (1888–1955), Lima came to support the social or base reforms implemented by President João Goulart (1919–1976), firmly opposing the military dictatorship that followed the 1964 coup.[52]

---

[49] Jamil Cury, *Alceu Amoroso Lima*, 20.

[50] Alceu Amoroso Lima, *Pela Cristianização da Idade Nova* (Rio de Janeiro, Brazil: Agir, 1946), 31, apud Rodrigo Augusto de Souza, "A trajetória das ideias políticas de Alceu Amoroso Lima: da contrarrevolução ao modernismo católico (1928–1938)," *Cadernos de História da Educação* 20 (2021): 1–18 (9).

[51] Cury, *Alceu Amoroso Lima*, 49.

[52] Alceu Amoroso Lima, *Revolução, Reação ou Reforma?*, 2nd ed. (Petrópolis, Brazil: Vozes, 1999), 6.

In the latter part of his life, Lima began to see the counterrevolution encamped by his former conservative allies as authoritarian and damaging to democracy. Consequently, he disavowed both his earlier reactionary commitments as well as the revolutionary violence some advocated for in 1964, proposing, instead, a reformist and democratic way forward: "Neither revolution nor reaction—reform."[53] By reform, he meant deep social and structural reform, devoid of the extremist processes he thought plagued Brazil during his lifetime. At that stage of his life, Lima believed that democracy should be not only liberal but also social, attending to the basic human needs of its constituents.

Among the various specialized Catholic Action groups that flourished since the early 1950s, JUC played a critical role in response to the social transformations taking place in Latin America. In the case of Brazil, the creation of the first Catholic University in the country in 1941 and of various other Catholic universities in the following years contributed to its flourishing. As Maria de Fátima Di Gregorio states, university students that transited in the specialized Catholic actions deepened their analysis of the national political situation, "redefining the identity of the lay groups that formed the Catholic left," while forming a united front to face the problems of the nation.[54] JUC would, therefore, establish itself as critical space where Catholic students would "discover the need for political commitment, reformist at the beginning [. . .] and later revolutionary—from 1959 onwards."[55]

In 1947, Lima left the national coordination of the ACB. Hélder Câmara, a Catholic priest from the Northeastern state of Ceará was tapped to become the adviser of the movement. In 1946, ACB received a letter from Pope Pius XI highlighting the significance of Catholic Action, particularly in a context of clergy scarcity, where fear abounded about potential dangers threatening the Catholic faith due to the quick changes in culture, science, and industry. Thus, the pope urged the strategic and organic articulation of the ACB as "the pacific

---

[53] Lima, *Revolução, Reação ou Reforma?*, 27.

[54] Maria de Fátima Di Gregorio, *História das Memórias do Movimento Social da Juventude Universitária Católica/JUC no Brasil dos Anos 50/60* (Curitiba, Brazil: Editora CRV, 2014), 54.

[55] Enrique Dussel, *História da Igreja Latino-Americana* (1930–1983), 2nd ed. (São Paulo, Brazil: Paulus, 1989), 15.

army of Christ."[56] In response to that letter, the Brazilian episcopate elaborated the bylaws of the ACB, which governed the movement until 1950, when bylaws for the emerging specialized Catholic Action groups were created, marking the transition to the second phase of the ACB—focused on the specialized groups.[57]

As the new national coordinator of Catholic Action, Câmara supported the specialized action groups, inspired by the French model.[58] The 1950s saw the rise of extremely dynamic specialized Catholic actions, which sought to implement Cardijn's see-judge-act method, thus expanding the ACB impact by penetrating specific sectors of the Brazilian society such as rural workers and families (JAC), students in general (JEC), urban workers (JOC), and university students (JUC).[59]

This stage of the ACB took Pope Pius XII's recommendation to turn every individual into an apostle of Christ in the social environment where they are to another level. The specialized groups sought to immerse themselves thoroughly into specific sectors of society. Those spaces were not empty, though. There were competing forces, including those coming from Marxist groups, which increasingly appealed to the imagination of young Latin Americans on university campuses and factory floors. While this resituating of Catholic Action in the 1950s took place in each specialized group, the following sections will focus on JUC, since in the 1950s the national student movement was one of most vibrant social movements in Brazil, exerting significant impact on the country's political life.

The Brazilian JUC

The rise of JUC and other specialized Catholic Action groups did not happen in a social or political vacuum. In the 1950s, Brazil, as

[56] Betiato, *Da Ação Católica à Pastoral da Juventude*, 34.

[57] Betiato, *Da Ação Católica à Pastoral da Juventude*, 34–35.

[58] Betiato, *Da Ação Católica à Pastoral da Juventude*, 36.

[59] Betiato, *Da Ação Católica à Pastoral da Juventude*, 38–39. In addition to those, JIC, the Catholic Independent Youth (Juventude Católica Independente), spread throughout forty-five archdioceses in the country, being responsible for the realization of important popular assemblies to discuss the problems young Brazilians were facing at the time. Betiato, *Da Ação Católica à Pastoral da Juventude*, 38. Since this group was less specialized than JAC, JEC, JOC, and JUC, this chapter does not devote much attention to it.

much of Latin America, was experiencing significant changes. The social effervescency of those years generated a mix of frustration and hope that contributed to the mobilization of young people—especially students and workers—eager to play a more decisive role in the struggle for a better society. The leading role students played during that period was remarkable. UNE, the *União Nacional dos Estudantes*, became one of the most active social movements in the country, catalyzing university students from all over Brazil to act together.

Formed at the I National Student Congress in Rio de Janeiro, in 1937, UNE initially convened congresses and coordinated with other progressive forces in Brazilian society to organize around causes impacting not only students but also the working classes and other vulnerable sectors of society. The first of those national mobilizations took place during World War II, when UNE vocally opposed Adolf Hitler's Nazi-fascism, putting pressure on President Vargas, who had chosen a position of neutrality. UNE confronted integralists who supported fascism and took advantage of the situation to seek "greater space to spread their ideology in the country."[60]

In the heat of the conflict, UNE executed its most dramatic plot when, in 1942, a group of students "occupied the headquarters of Clube Germânia, at Praia do Flamengo, 132, Rio de Janeiro, a traditional stronghold of Nazi-fascist militants." While one may not know whether that theatrical act had any impact on Vargas's decision or not, around the same time the occupation occurred, the Brazilian government officially entered the war, taking sides against Germany, Italy, and Japan. More symbolically yet was the fact that "that same year, President Vargas granted the occupied building of Clube Germânia to be the headquarters of the National Union of Students," making by decree-law "UNE official as an entity representing all Brazilian university students."[61]

In the following two decades, UNE would be actively involved in all aspects of the country's life, especially in the efforts to affirm

---

[60] União Nacional dos Estudantes (UNE), "História," https://www.une.org.br/memoria/historia/.

[61] União Nacional dos Estudantes (UNE), "História." See also José Luís Sanfelice, "A UNE na Resistência ao Golpe de 1964 e à Ditadura Civil-Militar," *Revista Simbio-Logias* 8/11 (2015): 127–143 (128).

the values of nationality, democracy and social justice. UNE's VIII National Student Congress in 1945 focused on two thematic axes: education and the national and world situation.[62] Regarding the first emphasis, the congress constituted "a commission to take suggestions for university reform to the Minister of Education, through the appointment of a student to the National Education Council." UNE also applied for funds to take its Literacy Caravan "to the interior of the country."[63] As for concerns with the national and world situation, UNE-affiliated students protested the authoritarian constitution of 1937 and lobbied the Ministry of Foreign Affairs to cut ties with Franco's Spain and Salazar's Portugal.[64]

Throughout the 1950s and 1960s, UNE's voice was heard in every major national debate, even though it never functioned as a unified bloc. UNE's leaders were affiliated to multiple political parties, from *União Democrática Nacional* (UDN), an economically liberal and morally conservative party supported by urban elites that feared communism and favored American imperialism, to *Partido Comunista Brasileiro* (PCB), also including center right and left parties such as *Partido Social Democrático* (PSD) and *Partido Trabalhista Brasileiro* (PTB). Consequently, UNE often had to navigate internal political tensions and negotiations.[65]

Consequently, UNE's public agenda was never steady. Depending on which party the elected President of UNE and its secretariat were affiliated with, UNE could lean toward either welfare-oriented reformist or more revolutionary approaches. By contrast, UNE's non-partisan nature reinforced its autonomy, making it a relevant voice capable of dealing with any political administration.

One constant in UNE's political contributions, though, was its nationalist inclinations. In 1950, UNE actively participated in the campaign to protect Brazil's sovereignty to explore its oil reserves

---

[62] André Luiz Rodrigues de Rossi Mattos, *Uma História da UNE: 1945–1964* (Campinas: Pontes Editores,2014), 52.

[63] Mattos, *Uma História da UNE: 1945–1964*, 52.

[64] Mattos, *Uma História da UNE: 1945–1964*, 53.

[65] As Sanfelice rightly puts it, "Within UNE, right-wing conservatives, socialists and communists, Catholic followers of the Youth Catholic University (JUC) and, in the 1960s, Popular Action (AP) trends clashed with each other." Sanfelice, "A UNE na Resistência ao Golpe de 1964 e à Ditadura Civil-Militar," 128. What could be added is that they also formed all kinds of coalitions.

against pressures from US-based oil corporations. Under President Vargas's *Estado Novo* (1937–1945), a period also known as the Third Republic, the exploration of oil was regulated by decree, being "of exclusive competence of the Federal Government," with "reserved refining to Brazilian natives." Vargas also established the National Oil Commission (CNP), which drafted a new oil legislation, considering its protection a matter of national security.[66]

Vargas advanced a form of state capitalism through which he intended to use the profit with the exploration of oil to favor Brazil's industrial development. Thus, that industry should remain under the guardianship of the state. His successor Eurico Gaspar Dutra (1946–1951), though, passed a new Oil Statute that allowed the participation of foreign capital in all phases of production. That new policy generated great debate in Brazilian society, leading to the nationalist campaign "The Oil is Ours," which opposed the control of oil exploration by foreign capital. UNE stood firm on the nationalist side of the debate, starting its own campaign for economic and political liberation in 1947. That was one of the first organized efforts to protect Brazil's natural resources and industries from the greedy attacks from the major international oil companies and the neocolonialism they represented.[67] The debate about oil production culminated with the creation of PETROBRAS in 1953, again under Vargas, who had returned to power, this time through the democratic vote. A mixed-capital oil company that has the Brazilian state as its majority owner, PETROBRAS, has become one of the largest energy companies in the world, uniquely contributing to the economic development of the country.[68]

---

[66] Mattos, *Uma História da UNE: 1945–1964*, 85.

[67] Mattos, *Uma História da UNE: 1945–1964*, 86–87.

[68] As the US participation in the scandal of the Carwash Operation in recent years in Brazil (with PETROBRAS as one of its main targets) shows, the issue about the national control of the exploration of Brazil's energy resources remains alive, and US government and energy companies continue to interfere, politically and economically, in Latin American domestic affairs to this day. See, for instance, Andrew Fishman et al, "'Keep it confidential': The Secret History of US Involvement in Brazil's Scandal-Wracked Operation Car Wash," *Intercept*, March 12, 2020, https://theintercept.com/2020/03/12/united-states-justice-department-brazil-car-wash-lava-jato-international-treaty/.

UNE also participated in the discussion of the National Education Guidelines and Bases Law (*Lei de Diretrizes e Bases da Educação Nacional* or LDB), advocated for education reform, fought for freedom of thought in schools and universities, and strived to keep schools and universities independent from the government. At a critical moment in Brazilian history, after Jânio Quadros's resignation from the presidency in 1961, as his military ministers planned to veto vice-president João Goulart from swearing in as the next president, UNE organized a national strike to guarantee Goulart's swearing in as dictated by the constitution.[69]

In 1963, in coordination with JUC and Popular Action, UNE sought to "deepen relations with worker unions and peasant leagues through the formation of a worker-student-peasant alliance" aiming to effectively integrate those groups into the Front of Popular Mobilization (*Frente de Mobilização Popular*, FMP), a united popular front to strive for a more just social order.[70] Such an alliance aimed to strengthen the struggle for national liberation. Although formalized only in 1963, FMP had already been at work organizing strikes to protect working families' rights and income, protesting the increased price of public transportation, and bringing popular movements together to protest the high living costs that led working families to experience food scarcity.

Perhaps the most important role UNE played in the defense of democracy came with its fierce opposition to the military dictatorship following the coup d'état on March 31, 1964. Prior to that, UNE played a prominent role defending constitutional democracy and protecting the rights of Brazilian citizens, as seen in the 1961 Campaign for Legality. During that campaign, UNE started using the slogan, "UNE has only one commitment: to fight for the people and for Brazil!"[71] While sometimes interpreted as a radicalization under communist influence, the agenda UNE embraced was in tandem with the Third World Movement discussed in chapter 3. That agenda included concerns with social justice, the curbing of

---

[69] Sanfelice, "A UNE na Resistência ao Golpe de 1964 e à Ditadura Civil-Militar," 129.

[70] Mattos, *Uma História da UNE: 1945–1964*, 236.

[71] Helgio Trindade, "A Legalidade e o Movimento Estudantil Brasileiro," *Anos 90*, 18/33 (2011): 129–164 (146).

economic abuses, just distribution of national wealth, land reform, national autonomy, self-determination of all peoples, freedom, and education for all.[72] Whereas such an agenda was often depicted by those in power as communist, UNE and its allies understood it as necessary steps for the protection of Brazil's national interests.

One of UNE's allies was Leonel de Moura Brizola (1922–2004), governor of Rio Grande do Sul, and one of the most important Brazilian political leaders of his generation. Speaking at a UNE conference in its headquarters in Rio de Janeiro, in 1961, three years before the coup d'état, Brizola made this point clear. Considering the significance of his speech—which, to my knowledge, has never appeared in English before—I translate a substantial piece of it here:

> I consider myself a free man, an emancipated man. Of the attributes I may have, independence is the one I cultivate the most, and I do so not just because of the imposition of temperament, but, above all, because I consider that public men from nations like Brazil absolutely need to think with the most absolute independence about the problems of their time and the problems of their country. It is a condition we cannot escape. It is imposed on us by the very fact that we experience the contradiction of two worlds, the antagonism of two systems that emerge dominant, between which we will have to choose our own path, compromising, in this choice, definitively, our destiny.
>
> Living under the pressure of this antagonism, we feel [. . .] the need to free our conscience from certain taboos and prejudices, from preconceived ideas and outdated conceptions. Liberation of conscience that allows us to reason beyond the contradictions and antagonisms that divide the world today; liberation of conscience that allows us to distinguish in the mass of information with which we are bombarded daily, always, what is a true idea or fact, from what is a prefabricated idea, or a fact manipulated to impress us.
>
> We reason like men who do not belong or do not surrender or sacrifice themselves to either of the two conflicting systems; we reason only in terms of Brazil, seeing only our land and our people, without fear, I repeat, of words and, above all, without attachment to solutions and formulas that must be maintained solely because

[72] Trindade, "A Legalidade e o Movimento Estudantil Brasileiro," 146–147.

> they were bequeathed to us or for the simple reason that they constitute a habit or a more or less established routine.
>
> When we defend a social system without applying our criticism to it and, therefore, becoming our conscious defense, we are not defending a system of human coexistence. The most accurate thing to say, in this case, is that what we are defending are the privileges that that system provides us with and that we wish to see perpetuated.
>
> This is an attitude of fear. It cannot be the attitude of a public man, or of the public men of a nation like ours who wish to overcome poverty, illiteracy, disease, and our situation as an underdeveloped country.
>
> If we have nothing to do with Russia, we must have the courage to say that we have nothing to do with the United States either. All we have is our own country, with the questions that worry us, with the problems that challenge us.[73]

For Brizola, the USA—Soviet Union binary was misplaced. The conversation should be distinctively about the protection of Brazil's national interests. His was a Third World agenda, in the sense advanced by Vijay Prashad (discussed in chapter 4). The fact that Brizola stated these powerful words at the headquarters of UNE shows how that movement was in tandem with those broader ideas.

In 1963, UNE expressed the need to get closer to other popular movements, affirming that the struggle for university reform was a struggle not simply in the interest of the students themselves but part of the broader struggle for the liberation of the people.[74] As José Luís Sanfelice deftly notices, ideologically, UNE positioned itself within the nationalist-reformist bloc, providing the basis for the reforms it expected President João Goulart to lead.[75] The fierce opposition to

---

[73] Leonel Brizola, "Conferência na UNE em 1961—o Brasil, os EUA e o Caso Cubano," conference delivered on June 16, 1961, reprinted in *Hora do Povo*, January 20, 2022, https://horadopovo.com.br/brizola-conferencia-na-une-em-1961-o-brasil-os-eua-e-o-caso-cubano/.

[74] UNE, "Luta atual pela reforma universitária (1963)," quoted in Mattos, *Uma História da UNE: 1945–1964*, 257.

[75] Sanfelice, "A UNE na Resistência ao Golpe de 1964 e à Ditadura Civil-Militar," 131.

that agenda, backed up by the United States, included not only the military but also civil and religious conservative organizations such as the Parliamentary Democratic Action (ADP) and the Brazilian Institute of Democratic Action (IBAD), in addition to businesspeople organized around the Institute of Research and Social Studies (IPES) and conservative Christians.

As for the last group, US and Brazilian conservative Catholics funded the "Marches of the Family with God and for Freedom," taking more than 400 thousand people to the streets in response to what they identified as the communist threat.[76] Anticipating the mobilization for a coup against Goulart, UNE sounded off the alarm about the need to follow the constitution and protect democratic freedom, calling the civil society to resist those intensifying authoritarian trends. The leading role UNE played in the democratic struggle caught the attention of the military, which targeted it when they came to power.

> The first action of the Brazilian civil-military dictatorship upon taking power in 1964 and deposing President João Goulart was to machine-gun and burn down the UNE headquarters at Praia do Flamengo, 132, on the fateful night of March 31st to April 1st. The extent of the discomfort that the military and conservatives felt towards the entity was clear. The dictatorship persecuted, arrested, tortured, and executed hundreds of Brazilians, many of them students.[77]

The military regime also removed UNE's legal status to be the organized representative of university students. From that point on, UNE was forced to operate illegally. Despite all suppression and persecution, UNE continued to resist, holding clandestine congresses and organizing marches and protests with other sectors of society. Some of those events were brutally repressed. In the wake of cultural and social revolutions around the world in 1968, in partnership with various Brazilian artists and intellectuals, UNE organized one of the most emblematic protests against the dictatorship, the

---

[76] Sanfelice, "A UNE na Resistência ao Golpe de 1964 e à Ditadura Civil-Militar," 131.

[77] UNE, "História."

"Hundred-Thousand-People March in Rio de Janeiro, calling for democracy, freedom and justice."[78]

A number of students involved in the work of UNE were tortured and killed during the dictatorship. Among them, Honestino Monteiro Guimarães, elected UNE's president in 1971, and an active member of *Ação Popular* (AP), was tortured and murdered after being arrested four times. His body was never returned to his family. The Brazilian government only disclosed the true cause of his death in 2013.[79]

Despite all those obstacles, UNE continued to play an important role resisting the dictatorship and contributing to the consolidation of the process of democratization in the eighties. With its legal status restored, UNE played a key role in the *Diretas Já* campaign of 1985, organizing rallies urging for the popular vote to choose the new president of the country after twenty-one years of dictatorship. While the campaign failed to get the intended outcome then, its vast popular mobilization became a watershed in the restoration of the Brazilian democratic institutions.[80]

This intense participation of students in the political life of the country took place not only in Brazil but throughout Latin America and in other parts of the world.[81] In fact, student participation in politics was nothing new in the continent. In 1918, a number of Argentinian students in Cordoba began a reform movement that spilled beyond its borders, impacting universities in Chile, Bolivia, Mexico, Cuba, and Peru.[82] In its legality campaign of 1961, a turning point for the organization, UNE mentioned the inspiration it got from the Cordoba reformist tradition.[83] UNE's twenty-fifth congress in 1962 counted with participants from Argentina, Dominican Republic,

---

78 UNE, "História."

79 UNE, "Presidentes," https://www.une.org.br/presidentes/honestino-guimaraes.

80 Another area of significance of UNE was its role as an incubator of political leadership. Some of the most important Brazilian politicians in the past forty years or so were affiliated with UNE at some point in their lives.

81 This phenomenon could be noticed, for instance, in countries like Argelia, Germany, Italy, the United States, Mexico, Colombia, Argentina, and many others. See Ruy Mauro Marini, "Os movimentos estudantis na América Latina," *Cadernos Cemarx*, 9 (2016): 89–104 (90).

82 Trindade, "A Legalidade e o Movimento Estudantil Brasileiro," 133.

83 Trindade, "A Legalidade e o Movimento Estudantil Brasileiro," 141.

the Soviet Union, and the International Union of Students (IUS)—which UNE had joined a year earlier. In 1966, at the Fourth Latin American Student Congress in Havana, students from twenty-two Latin American and Caribbean countries, including Brazil, founded the Latin American and Caribbean Continental Organization of Students. While a panoramic account of the student movement in Latin America and the Caribbean is beyond the scope of this book, the Brazilian case offers an important background for the reader to understand the nature of the impact JUC, as a Catholic Action specialized movement, had on the broader Brazilian student movement in the early 1960s.

JUC and Popular Action: The Revolutionary Turn in the Brazilian Catholic Action

Many of the critical developments UNE experienced between the 1950s and early 1960s were directly related to changes also happening in JUC, including those that led to the creation of Popular Action (*Ação Popular* or AP) in 1962.[84] These developments started with the participation of JUC students in the UNE Student National Congress of 1947, leading to the insertion of JUC leaders in UNE's leadership. In 1961, *jucista* Aldo Arantes was elected UNE's president, playing a significant role in UNE's revolutionary turn in the early 1960s.[85]

The early interest on the part of JUC in approaching UNE was motivated by the original Catholic Action call to instill all areas of society with Christian values and influence, turning each lay Catholic into an apostle. The initial intent was to "infiltrate" UNE and influence it as Christians.[86] The incipient participation of *jucistas* in UNE gatherings in the late 1940s did not draw much attention. Yet, in the following years, JUC became one of the critical political forces in the

[84] While this chapter focuses on the case of JUC, JOC, created two years earlier than JUC, also played a critical role as representative of the drastic transformation in Catholic thought and action in Latin America in the late 1950s and early 1960s. Among other things, JOC strengthened the ties between Latin American Catholic Action and the French Catholic thought. For more on that, see Ralph Della Cava, "Catholicism and Society in Twentieth-Century Brazil," *The Latin American Research Review* 11/ 2 (1976): 7–50 (41).

[85] Students affiliated with JUC were known as *jucistas*.

[86] Betiato, *Da Ação Católica à Pastoral da Juventude*, 62.

UNE secretariat, alongside socialists, communists, and representatives of the Republican Party.[87]

In 1948, JUC's presence at UNE as an organized group of Catholic students was noted for the first time, as two *jucistas* were elected to UNE's national secretariat.[88] Applying the see-judge-act method to the political situation of the country, many *jucistas* felt the need to engage organized collective efforts (as those under the UNE broader umbrella), seeking some level of structural change in the 1950s.[89] Among other things, during that decade, JUC gradually became involved in the struggle for university reform, which demanded not only greater investment to improve the quality of higher education but also more accessibility to higher education, something aligned with JUC's growing concern with the improvement of the living conditions of impoverished classes. In its struggle for social change, JUC perceived both "capitalism and communism as expressions of what it considered to be practical atheism, placing the two blocks in radical opposition to their evangelization goals."[90] Gradually, JUC established itself not simply as a religious movement but also as an increasingly important social movement in the country, making distinctive contributions to the social struggles it engaged with.

Although the turn to social justice marked the development of JUC in the late 1950s, it was only in its 1960 congress that its political turn became more "radical and definitive."[91] While praying together on a daily basis and interpreting their mission in Christian terms, these organized Catholic students occupied spaces where they could engage in social and political action on university campuses and beyond, becoming intentionally involved in the discussions of the major issues impacting the life of the nation at the time. As JUC developed its identity as a Catholic organization among university students, its witness far exceeded the confines of the institutional Church. That period of expansion of its insertion into the broader society put *jucistas* in regular contact with political parties and workers' unions. The expansion of JUC's horizons also led it to interact with the Popular

87 Mattos, *Uma História da UNE: 1945–1964*, 82.

88 Mattos, *Uma História da UNE: 1945–1964*, 84.

89 Betiato, *Da Ação Católica à Pastoral da Juventude*, 63.

90 Mattos, *Uma História da UNE: 1945–1964*, 97.

91 Marcio Moreira Alves, *A Igreja e a Política no Brasil* (São Paulo, Brasil: Editora Brasiliense, 1979), 125.

Cultural Centers (CPC, *Centros Populares de Cultura*) and the Movements of Popular Culture (MCP, Movimentos de Cultura Popular).[92] The more it immersed in the popular struggles, the more JUC took sides with left-wing movements and political parties, facing, in turn, stronger resistance from the hierarchy of the Church, which continued to support the conservative political powers.

Boosted by the success of the Cuban Revolution in 1959, JUC's tenth anniversary congress in 1960 renewed growing nationalist aspirations, while concomitantly generating in its opposers the fear of a communist invasion that US government and pro-American elites in the region contributed to cultivate. Just as in the case of the Church and Society Movement discussed earlier, JUC and other specialized Catholic Action movements began to think of the historical future of the region in revolutionary terms, something that was complicated to interpret within the limits of the traditional understanding of the Church's social doctrine.[93]

Although lay-oriented, Catholic Action, as discussed earlier, was a movement under the guidance and authority of the Church hierarchy. Despite its intended goal to renew the Church action in the world, such a role was inhibited by the Church's centralized and hierarchized structure. As Ralph Della Cava points out, under that model "the true mission of the laity [..] was to serve the institution of the Church."[94] Thus, while encouraging lay participation in the political life of the country, the Brazilian Social Action expected the laity to advance the interests of the institutional Church.

Even though such hierarchical structure did not go away in the 1950s, JUC and other specialized sectors of Catholic Action experienced a drastic transformation during that period thanks to their immersion in the rapid changes taking place in the Brazilian society. Cardinal Leme's successor in the ACB, Jaime Câmara (1894–1971) did not have his same administrative skills and interests as his predecessor.[95] Thus, he ended up placing his auxiliary bishop, Hélder Câmara (unrelated), as the national coordinator of the ACB. Câmara

92 Di Gregorio, *História das Memórias do Movimento Social da Juventude Universitária Católica/JUC no Brasil dos Anos 50/60*, 72–73.

93 Alves, *A Igreja e a Política no Brasil*, 126.

94 Della Cava, "Catholicism and Society in Twentieth-Century Brazil," 16.

95 Della Cava, "Catholicism and Society in Twentieth-Century Brazil," 30.

was supposed to be a safe choice by the conservative archbishop to keep the expanding apostolate of the ACB under control, considering his early conservative inclinations and the experience he had overseeing youth work, the labor movement, and communication in his home state of Ceará.[96]

Thanks to the influence of Alceu Amoroso Lima and Maritain's Christian humanism, though, Câmara became considerably lenient in his responses to more progressive junior priests and lay Christians leading the work of JUC and other specialized sectors of Catholic Action. In the course of his work with the ACB, he himself underwent a drastic change of mind regarding his early conservatism. Like Lima, perhaps even more radically than him, Câmara would undergo a radical conversion to solidarity with the poor as he expressed in his inauguration sermon as the Archbishop of Olinda and Recife, in April of 1964:

> Of course, loving everyone, I must, like Christ, have a special love for the poor . . . . There is no point in venerating beautiful images of Christ, I say, nor will it suffice for us to stop before the poor and recognize in them the disfigured face of the Savior if we do not identify the Christ in the human creature to be wrenched from underdevelopment. As strange as it may seem, I say that in the Northeast [of Brazil] Christ is called Zé, Antônio, Severino . . . "Ecce Homo": Behold the Christ, Behold the Man! He is the man who needs justice, who has the right to justice, who deserves justice.[97]

The change Câmara underwent in the early 1960s resulted, among other things, from his increasing involvement in popular movements such as the *Movimento de Natal*,[98] the *Movimento de Educação*

---

[96] Della Cava, "Catholicism and Society in Twentieth-Century Brazil," 32.

[97] Cited in José Ernanne Pinheiro, "Dom Helder Câmara como Arcebispo de Olinda e Recife (1964–1985)," in *Hélder, o Dom: Uma Vida que Marcou os Rumos da Igreja no Brasil*, ed. Zildo Rocha, 2nd ed. (Petrópolis, Brazil: Vozes, 1999), 77–87 (79). Translation is mine.

[98] The Natal Movement was a justice-oriented response from the diocese of Natal, Rio Grande do Norte, to "the drought industry," the political and economic use by politicians of the scarcity of water to manipulate public resources, preying on the abandonment of the population of impoverished municipalities to a state of mendicancy and famine. While the Church had been responding to that situation since 1953, assisting drought victims and trying to reduce "political interference in the application of money and distribution of food," beginning with the first Meeting

de Base,[99] the *Sindicatos Rurais*,[100] JAC, and the Liturgical Renewal Movement.[101] Câmara and other Catholic priests and bishops were not the engineers of a progressive movement within the Church. Instead, the more they interacted with young people involved in JOC and JUC, for instance, the more their understanding of the Latin American reality changed. More than ideological, the changes they experienced stemmed from compassion for the victims of a dehumanizing society that fed on inequality, whose leaders had become so dehumanized that they did not bother manufacturing famine.[102]

---

of Bishops of the Northeast, held in Campina Grande, on May 21st to 26th, 1956 under the auspices of the National Conference of Bishops of Brazil (CNBB), the Church started calling for the review of the federal policy regarding the recurrent droughts in the Northeast. The efforts led by Eugênio Sales, auxiliary bishop of Natal, and supported by Câmara as the national coordinator of ACB, to tackle the structural problems trigging hunger in the region, generated broader interest in the daily problems impacting tens of thousands of rural workers and families. Catholic youth associations, including JAC, along with other popular organizations and social movements, formed a coalition to "fight for the reform of structures [. . .] founding rural unions in the early 1960s" to organize local workers. See Alceu Ravanello Ferraro, *Igreja e Desenvolvimento: O Movimento de Natal*, ed. Renato Amado Peixoto, 2nd ed. (Natal, Brazil: Jovens Escribas, 2015), 21–33.

[99] Likewise, through the leadership role he played in the CNBB, Câmara, in 1961, launched the Movement of Base [or popular] Education (MEB) in partnership with the Ministry of Education and Culture (MEC). The concept of *educação de base* (base education) implied the idea of educating for change, which triggered a self-awareness that freed people from degrading social situations. Starting in 1962, MEB began to apply Paulo Freire's popular education method, which "interpreted illiteracy as a product of unequal social structures, and thus as an effect, and not a cause, of poverty. Freire proposed that educational processes operate toward the transformation of reality. In such a context, literacy was considered a tool to "enable critical examination and the overcoming of problems that affected people and communities." See UNESCO, *Youth and Adult Literacy in Brazil: Learning from Practice* (Brasilia, Brazil: UNESCO, 2009), 18, https://unesdoc.unesco.org/ark:/48223/pf0000162640. The first textbook MEB, published in 1963, was called "To live is to fight," exemplifying the implementation of Freire's method. See Movimento de Educação de Base (MEB), *Viver é Lutar* (Rio de Janeiro: MEB, 1963), https://www4.pucsp.br/cedic/meb/nas-salas-de-aula/arquivos-pdf/2-2-cartilha-viver-lutar.pdf.

[100] These included rural unions supported through the Natal Movement and the Peasant Leagues.

[101] Zildo Rocha & Daniel Sigal, eds., *Dom Hélder Câmara: Circulares Pós-Conciliares*, vol. III/Tomo I (Recife, Brazil: CEPE, 2012), 32.

[102] For a comparative analysis of three zones of drought and subsequent famine that decimated populations in India, Northern China, and Northeastern Brazil due to

The sharper their solidarity with the poor and the related demand for structural change became, the greater were the tensions between those youth Catholic movements and the sectors of the Church hierarchy that continued to associate those initiatives with communist infiltration, manufacturing fears that helped create the conditions for the coup d'état of 1964.[103] As the situation worsened, Câmara began to be attacked, receiving epithets such as "the red Bishop" or "a Fidel Castro in a cassock." His adversaries accused him of receiving money from communist sources to sponsor international trips, while the generals worked to keep him away from the media.[104]

If someone who was then an internationally acclaimed Catholic bishop faced such attacks, the fate of lay students working with JUC was worse. As it was the case with the Protestant SRSI, JUC did not survive the military coup. Many of its leaders and participants were forced to hide or flee the country to avoid being arrested, tortured, or even killed.

---

destructive policies enacted by ruling elites, see Mike Davis, *Late Victorian Holocausts: El Niño Famines and the Making of the Third World* (London/New York: Verso, 2001).

[103] That anti-communist fever was supported by United States agents. Among them, Robert S. Rapp, a missionary affiliated with the Independent Board for Presbyterian Foreign Mission (IBPFM), published a booklet in Portuguese to terrorize the Brazilian Protestant churches, accusing the Church and Society Movement associated with CEB of being infiltrated by communism. On the Catholic end, Father Patrick Payton, founder of the Holy Cross Family Ministries (HCFM) in the US, starting in 1959 and with help from the CIA, conducted the *Cruzadas do Rosário em Família* (Rosary Crusades in Family) in Brazil and other Latin American countries, escalating anticommunist fears among Catholics that created the social and cultural conditions for military interventions that followed. See Robert S. Rapp, *A Confederação Evangélica do Brasil e o Evangelho Social* (São Paulo, Brazil: Missão Bíblica Presbiteriana do Brasil, 1965); and Anderson José Guisolphi. "Os rosários precederam os coturnos: o anticomunismo nas Cruzadas do Rosário em Família na América Latina e os golpes civil-militares (1960–1964)," *Cadernos de História*, 21/33 (2019): 158–184.

[104] Joseph A. Page, "The Little Priest Who Stands UP To Brazil's Generals," *New York Times*, March 23, 1971, NYT Archives, https://timesmachine.nytimes.com/timesmachine/1971/05/23/91286597.pdf?pdf_redirect=true&ip=0. After the military coup, Câmara became one of the most known critical voices of the regime internationally. Inspired by Martin Luther King Jr. and Gandhi, he advocated for nonviolent resistance. At the same time, he dialogued with Marxists and supported those who gave up on the possibility of peaceful resistance and opted instead for armed revolution.

The deterioration of the relationship between the progressive sector of JUC and the Church hierarchy began long before 1964. JUC's closer involvement with the labor movement and Marxist groups on university campuses gradually immersed the Catholic student movement in the national political scene. That insertion in the struggle of the masses led JUC to a situation of gradual independence from the Church as the delineating lines of action for the movement were increasingly informed by broader social and political concerns that were not understood by many in the Church hierarchy.[105]

Frustration for not seeing the implementation of the social reforms they strived for led several *jucistas* to become increasingly sympathetic to revolutionary ideas. Those ideas were not only being discussed in UNE circles and the labor movement but also in conversations *jucistas* were having with their counterparts in places such as Argentina, Uruguay, and Colombia.[106] By that point, it was increasingly clear that JUC was internally divided. On the one hand, the Church, which had named priest Orlando Machado to facilitate the work of JUC nationally, was working hard to reassert its control of the movement. On the opposite end, priests and jucistas who had adhered to a liberationist or revolutionary approach to the struggle for rights, freedom, and justice were growing impatient.[107] In the eyes of many in the Church hierarchy, JUC had lost its original purpose, having become a left-wing organization associated with the ideas of Karl Marx and Paulo Freire.[108]

In 1959, as tensions were still building up, Father Almery Bezerra offered a study about the historical ideal, seeking to inspire JUC to define its political objectives ahead of the 1960 Congress. In that preparatory process, JUC deepened its understanding of "the Brazilian revolution," mostly informed by a democratic socialist framework.[109] The outcome of the 1960 congress, which counted five hundred participants from all over the country, signaled the

---

105 Di Gregorio, *História das Memórias*, 70.

106 Di Gregorio, 75.

107 Di Gregorio, 75, 81.

108 Di Gregorio, 85.

109 Haroldo Lima and Aldo Arantes. *História da Ação Popular: da JUC ao PCdoB* (São Paulo, Brazil: Editora Alfa-Omega, 1984), 28. The two authors were jucistas who became active at UNE (Arantes was elected UNE's president in 1961). Both were also founders of Popular Action.

victory of the progressive wing. Tensions continued to build, though, when, in 1961, JUC formed a coalition with the Brazilian Communist Party (PCB)[110] to elect the jucista Aldo da Silva Arantes as UNE's president, upsetting the Church hierarchy, which opposed Catholic Action's alignment with political parties. Arantes ended up being expelled from JUC due to the backlash from conservative sectors in the Church to his election.[111]

In the early 1960s, JUC's influence as an organized political force had significantly spread. The alliance with PCB around a reformist agenda dissatisfied both conservative clergy and revolutionary oriented jucistas. The latter ended up creating a movement called Popular Action (*Ação Popular*, AP) in 1962. As its founding document states, "Popular Action is the expression of a generation that translates into revolutionary action the fundamental options it assumed as a response to the challenge of our reality and as a result of a realistic analysis of the Brazilian social process."[112] Catholic in its origins and inspiration, AP saw itself initially as a Christian response to the Brazilian situation. Adopting revolutionary language, its initial orientation was nationalist. Facing fierce opposition from the Catholic hierarchy, though, which never accepted its mandate as legitimate, AP gradually became a political movement independent from the Church. Up to the 1964 military coup, AP coordinated its actions with JUC's political progressive sectors. Together, AP and JUC elected all UNE presidents between 1961 and 1964. During that period, several progressive Catholics abandoned Catholic Action and joined AP as the latter worked to implement the basic social reforms promised by President João Goulart.

After the 1964 military takeover, though, the new regime harshly suppressed JUC, arresting some of its leaders. The Church hierarchy remained silent. In the 1965 general assembly of the National Conference of Brazilian Bishops (Conferência Nacional dos Bispos do Brasil, CNBB), the tone of the bishops as they discussed specialized

---

110 Since the late 1950s, the Brazilian Communist Party (PCB) had relaxed some of the Marxist principles that had originated the party in 1922, adopting a reformist agenda. The dissatisfaction of many of its 50,000 members with the inefficiency of that kind of agenda led them to abandon PCB and create a new communist party, PCdoB (Partido Comunista do Brasil), in 1962.

111 Lima and Arantes, *História da Ação Popular: da JUC ao PCdoB*, 28.

112 "Documento-Base" (1963), as quoted in Trindade, *Anos 90*, 137–138.

social action was mostly of disapproval and condemnation of what they depicted as its deviations: "Today's specialized Catholic Action is committed to becoming so involved in political action that it has lost its former characteristics of 'spiritual formation.'"[113]

By contrast, others saw the political impulse in specialized Catholic Action as a lay response to the inability of the Church to give itself to the world, engaging the social problems in a non-self-serving manner. In 1961, Belgian-Brazilian priest and theologian José Comblin wrote an important essay underscoring the insufficiency of Catholic Action to respond vitally to the new challenges of a world that was in a process of emancipation.[114]

As Eduardo Hoornaert states, for being incapsulated in an overarching clerical system, Catholic Action was "incapable of being more than an instrument of preservation of this system inherited from the past."[115] In 1993, José Oscar Beozzo reinforced a similar view:

> All the "mandate" theology of Catholic Action, where lay people commit themselves and act not based on their vocation as baptized [Christians], but as auxiliary of the hierarchy's apostolate, tended to keep them in a minor position in the Church, closing the spaces for more autonomous social and political options.[116]

AP emerged as an independent alternative, seeking to fill the need for the incarnation of the Christian message of liberation through a wholly outwardly oriented praxis. AP was the creation of *jucistas* who wanted to radically stand in solidarity with popular movements like the Peasant Leagues, the Movement of Popular Culture, the Rural Unions and the Base Education Movement (MEB). Concerned with the AP's adoption of revolutionary language, the Church sought to limit what JUC could or could not do in their engagement of the

---

113 Alves, *A Igreja e a Política no Brasil*, 132. Only D. Hélder Câmara e D. Cândido Padim defended CA.

114 "The failure of Catholic Action?" (translation is mine). See Joseph Comblin, *Échec de l'Action catholique?* (Paris: Éditions Universitaires, 1961). Although his legal name was Joseph, having adopted Northeast Brazil as his home, he went by José.

115 Eduardo Hoornaert, "The Future of the CEBs," *Revista Eclesiástica Brasiieira* 51/201 (1991): 161–162 (161).

116 José Oscar Beozzo, "A Igreja no Brasil," in *A Igreja Latino-Americana às Vésperas do Concilio*, ed. José Oscar Beozzo (São Paulo, Brazil: Edições Paulinas, 1993), 46–75 (70).

social question.[117] The forceful attempt by the CNBB to submit JUC to its authority, including its efforts to dissolve JUC's leadership, provoked a harsh response from JUC, which by that time no longer saw itself as simply an extension of the hierarchy's apostolate. Those increasing conflicts, along with the military crackdown on the organization, and the departure of some of its most engaged members who opted for joining AP sealed the fate of JUC.

At the beginning, AP, although "inspired in the gospel for its actions," presented itself, at the same time "as socialist and revolutionary," a position that several young Catholic and Protestant Christians involved in social movements were increasingly finding themselves aligned with.[118] By the time of the 1964 coup, AP became a home for Catholics, Protestants (such as Paulo Wright and Anivaldo Padilha), and non-religious members of other social movements that were also being suppressed. Among its various initiatives, AP created the Movement Against the Dictatorship in 1966. This protest movement cried out for the restoration of the rule of law.[119]

Frustrated with the military systematic dismantling of dissenting political organizations, a number of participants in AP embraced armed resistance along with members of PCdoB—the communist party created in 1962, which had also gone underground in 1964. Throughout its existence, AP tirelessly supported other popular movements, seeking to promote what it described as a democratic and national revolution.[120] In 1972, AP officially merged with PCdoB, forming a Marxist-Leninist party.[121] After JUC's extinction in 1968, the only organized Catholic presence that remained active on university campuses were the incipient University Base Communities.

In the early 1980s, a movement called *Pastoral Universitária* emerged to fill that gap. In 1982, the National Service of Information (Serviço Nacional de Informação, SNI) of the Brazilian government produced a confidential report about the relationship between JUC and ENA (*Equipe Nacional de Articulação*), the emerging National

---

117 Beozzo, "A Igreja no Brasil," 70–71.

118 Beozzo, "A Igreja no Brasil," 71.

119 Souza, "Ação Católica," 61.

120 Souza, "Ação Católica," 52.

121 Lima and Arantes, *História da Ação Popular: da JUC ao PCdoB*, x.

Articulation Team formed to build a new national Catholic movement at the university called *Pastoral Universitária* (PU). The report mentioned the disappearance of JUC and the rise of AP, later turned into the Marxist-Leninist Popular Action (APML), as a preamble to the rise of ENA as a national team "leading the formation of the entity [PU], aiming to occupy the space opened with the deactivation of the JUC." That report reproduced the document ENA prepared in May of 1982, a bulletin titled "The Construction of the Movement," which was circulated and discussed among all groups involved in the creation of PU.[122] According to that bulletin, the main goal of PU was to restore an organized Catholic presence on university campuses.

The conversation about the creation of *Pastoral Universitária* started during the First National Encounter of Catholic University Students in 1978. For the planners of the movement, the freedom of each local group to organize itself ought to be respected, as long as the national unity of the movement was maintained. Although starting fresh as a new movement, PU intended to incorporate the JUC tradition. The document "A Construção do Movimento" begins with a historical justification for the new movement, acknowledging JUC's contributions to the Church and to the Brazilian society and explaining its dissolution in a way that, while highlighting the politization of the movement, named the Church hierarchy's support of the military coup in a self-critical examination of the political splits that contributed to the end of JUC.[123]

PU did not intend to create new groups. Its mission was to organize already-existing Catholic presence at the university, working with existing student organizations, including the Comunidades Universitárias de Base (CUBs), while also coordinating with the various regions of the CNBB—to avoid some of the problems JUC had faced. Whereas the creation of a unified movement was a priority,

[122] SIAN—Serviço Nacional de Informações, Agência Rio de Janeiro, Informe no. 158/119/ARJ/82, "Juventude Universitária Católica (JUC) e a Equipe Nacional de Articulação/ões (ENA)," Protocolo ACE no. 6964, September 28, 1982.

[123] Secretaria da Equipe Nacional de Articulação, "A Construção do Movimento: Justificativa Histórica, Referencial Teórico, Organização e Funcionamento," May 1982, Appendix document in "Juventude Universitária Católica (JUC) e a Equipe Nacional de Articulação/ões (ENA), 1," Protocolo ACE no. 6964, September 28, 1982.

the focus of PU was mainly pastoral, based on the need to respond to concrete personal and social demands.

In the early 1980s, a period when the Ecclesial Base Communities (CEBs) had already established a strong presence in Brazil, PU was interested in contributing to build up a Church committed to the liberation of all people. Accordingly, it should work "to enable greater commitment to the cause of a Church focused on the interests of the most humiliated and exploited." The liberation concern, which had been suppressed at the time of JUC's extinction, was returning even "with more force."[124]

The brief overview of JUC's journey offered above brings to light the long gestation of Christian popular movements learning to work for justice, which culminated with the rise of liberation theology in Latin America. That process started long before Vatican II. Despite the complications in the rise and development of Catholic Action, considering its early associations with integralism, this lay Catholic apostolic mission had a transformative impact on Brazilian society, being part of complex global dynamics that contributed to the formation of a liberating praxis and theology in the region.

The professed intention of Pius XI for Catholic Action was reinterpreted and negotiated in rapidly changing Latin American societies, giving birth to new forms of Christian movements, which, although resembling earlier movements in Europe and other parts of the world, became, by contrast, thoroughly Latin American, primarily responding to concrete realities and demands in that region, as the examples discussed in this section show.

As in the case of the Church and Society Movement discussed in the previous chapter, specialized Social Action movements turned themselves outwardly, prioritizing their service to the world—with particular attention to those victimized and dehumanized by systemic social injustices. While some of these movements drifted away from the institutional Church, they found their initial inspiration in the gospel, seeking to reflect core concerns from the Church social teachings, such as the emphasis on human dignity and the

---

[124] Secretaria da Equipe Nacional de Articulação, "A Construção do Movimento: Justificativa Histórica, Referencial Teórico, Organização e Funcionamento," 7. On page 6, the document refers to the intended impact of Pastoral Universitária on building a church of and for the poor, a grassroots church.

just treatment of the most vulnerable. As they sought to make sense of those things in concrete ways to effect social change, they found aid in secular social analyses—above all those inspired by Marxist critiques of capital. Focusing on practical responses of solidarity, different groups and individuals found distinct analytical tools to inform concerned action aiming at social change. For most participants of JUC in the 1960s, democratic socialism was the political philosophy that seemed to best enable them to act in accord with the social ideals they initially drew from the social teachings of the Church. The persistence of many in the Church to continue supporting authoritarian political powers that poisoned Latin America, made it difficult for many of those young thinkers and activists to remain in the Church. At the same time, a young generation of Latin American theologians who held their ears close to the ground would intensify their work interpreting the circumstances and Christian praxis seen in those youth movements and in the emerging CEBs in theological terms.[125]

That liberation Christian movement, which can be traced back to the late 1950s, resulted in the rise, a decade later, of one of the most influential theological movements of the second half of the twentieth century: liberation theology. The Catholic Church found itself at a historical juncture where it was no longer possible to avoid taking sides. When French journalist José de Broucker wondered in 1977 about the "radicalization" of specialized Catholic Action sectors in Latin America, asking Dom Hélder Câmara if the problem was the fact that the Church preferred a politics that united rather than one that divided, Câmara replied by pointing out that Broucker was forgetting that such an idealized neutrality was not possible: "[I]f we do not take the side of the oppressed, we take the side of the oppressors [. . .] Neutrality, in our case, especially in the regions and the sectors where injustices are the most glaring, is really impossible."[126] What was seen by some as a radicalization of the youth movements was understood by Câmara as an appeal

[125] I paraphrase here D. Helder Câmara's poem "Put Your Ear to the Ground," which appears at the beginning of chapter seven.

[126] Dom Hélder Câmara, *Les Conversions D'un D'UN Évêque* (Paris: Editions L'Harmattan, [1977] 2002), 109, https://www.perlego.com/book/3145204/les-conversions-dun-vque-entretiens-avec-jos-de-broucker-pdf.

to turn the social encyclicals into concrete instruments for the transformation of unjust realities.[127]

Being on the front line of the struggle for life in Latin America, members of specialized Catholic Action groups in the early 1960s were not afraid of taking sides with the oppressed—who, for them, included many people whose faces, names, and stories they were closely familiar with. The significant developments that took place between the 1950s and early 1960s impacted the Latin American Church more broadly, becoming formative to several Latin American bishops who participated in Second Vatican Council (1963–1965) and helping them to faithfully interpret it in light of the Latin American reality. It was not a coincidence that the Latin American Church offered one of the fastest organized receptions of the Council in any region. The events discussed in this chapter not only prepared Latin American Christians to quickly make sense of the Council vis-à-vis the social challenges in the region but also to contribute to the Council's outcome.

127 Câmara, *Les Conversions D'un D'UN Évêque*, 111.

7

VATICAN II AND THE BIRTH OF THE CHURCH OF THE POOR

Put your ear to the ground
and listen
hurried, worried footsteps,
bitterness, rebellion.
Hope hasn't yet begun.
Listen again.
Put your feelers.
The Lord is there.
He [sic] is far less likely
to abandon us in hardship
than in times of ease.[1]

The Latin American Church Prior to the Vatican II

In the decade preceding Vatican II, the Latin American Catholic Church struggled to reinterpret its role and mission vis-à-vis what was customarily referred to as "the social question."[2] As seen in the previous chapter, one of the questions that Latin American Catholics were dealing with then was the Christian call to participate in the struggles of the oppressed. It is not that the Latin American Church had ever been politically neutral. In fact, up to that point it had, for the most part, been the Church of the status quo. The process that some sectors of the Church (lay leaders involved in specialized social action, members of religious orders, and some priests and bishops) experienced, as they were immersed in the reality of the victims of systemic injustice, can be described as a conversion to the poor.

[1] Hélder Câmara, "Put your ear to the ground," in *Dom Hélder Câmara: Essential Writings*, Modern Spiritual Masters (Maryknoll, NY: Orbis Books, 2009), 95.

[2] José Miguez Bonino, "The Reception of Vatican II in Latin America," *Ecumenical Review* 37/3 (1985): 266–274 (267).

Perhaps no one exemplifies such a turn better than the Archbishop of Recife and Olinda, Hélder Câmara. As José de Broucker put it, "Dom Helder's itinerary is made of successive conversions [. . .] Conversion under the guidance of the Spirit is, for the Archbishop of Recife, the only way to be faithful."[3] Such a conversion produced, according to Câmara, "a special love for the poor."[4] That conversion to the poor was more than a change of course in his personal life and ministry. It molded the kind of change the Latin American Church was to experience in its priorities and commitments.

The experiences discussed in the previous chapter prepared the Latin American Church for the second Vatican Council. As José Oscar Beozzo points out, Latin America was "the only continent that, upon reaching the Council, already had a collegial episcopal structure, the Latin American Episcopal Council, CELAM, founded in Rio de Janeiro (RJ), in 1955."[5] Hélder Câmara and Manuel Larraín Errázuriz (1900–1966) took the lead in articulating the distribution of the Latin American bishops on the many commissions of the Council, also contributing names from other parts of the Global South to compose commissions.[6] In the years preceding the Council, those two men had gained prominence paving the way for the transformations the Latin American Church was to experience in the 1960s.

In Brazil, inspired by the developments he witnessed coordinating Catholic Action, Hélder Câmara, then the auxiliary bishop of Rio de Janeiro, played a critical role in the creation of the National Conference of Brazilian Bishops (CNBB) in 1952. During the First World Conference of the Laity in Rome, in 1950, Câmara noted that in the several presentations representatives from Brazil made on different themes, the conclusion was basically the same: "None of this will be possible or effective until there is a national conference of bishops in Brazil." Then, he concluded, "When I thought of a

---

[3] Câmara, *Les Conversions*, 14.

[4] Câmara, *Essential Writings*, 39. In his inaugural message to the people of Olinda and Recife in 1964, he stated, "At the last judgement, we shall all be judged by the treatment we have given to Christ, to Christ in the person of those who are hungry or thirsty, who are dirty, wounded, and oppressed," 40.

[5] José Oscar Beozzo, "Medellín: inspiração e raízes," *Koinonia*, https://www.servicioskoinonia.org/relat/202.htm.

[6] Câmara, *Les Conversions*, 152.

national conference, I envisaged a national secretariat as well which would serve all the bishops of the church of Christ incarnate in this land of Brazil."[7]

In that visit to Rome, Câmara discussed that idea with Monsignor Giovanni Batista Montini (1897–1978), then, the Vatican subsecretary of state. Not only did Montini welcome the idea and support Câmara's plans, but the two men initiated a friendship that would "become even more significant when Montini became Pope Paul VI."[8] CNBB was created in 1952, the same year Câmara became bishop. He was elected by acclamation as CNBB's first general secretary, a post he held for 12 years.[9] At that point, only in the United States, France, and Canada the Church had a national administration. That move was not only extremely significant for Brazil, considering its size and the influence of the Church in the country, but also for Latin America as a whole, since the Brazilian experience inspired the formation of the *Consejo Episcopal Latinoamericano y Caribeño* (CELAM) three years later.[10]

After creating CNBB, Câmara worked closely with Manuel Larraín Errázuriz, bishop of Talca, Chile, to plan the formation of CELAM.[11] They received authorization from the Vatican in 1954 and founded CELAM at the First General Conference of the Latin American Episcopate gathered on July 25–August 4, 1955, in Rio de Janeiro. The central concern leading to the creation of CELAM was the scarcity of priests and the need to coordinate efforts across Latin America for more effective fulfillment of the Church's apostolic vocation.[12]

Along with the need to work to increase priestly vocation, the conference raised awareness about the deep structural transformations taking place in the continent and the need for the formation of a Christian thought capable of informing society in the course of

---

[7] Câmara, *Essential Writings*, 47.

[8] Francis McDonagh, "Introduction: Dom Hélder in Context," in D. Hélder Câmara, *Essential Writings*, 11–36 (22).

[9] McDonagh, "Introduction: Dom Hélder in Context," 11–36 (22).

[10] The Episcopal Council of Latin America and the Caribbean.

[11] Fernando Berríos, "Manuel Larraín y la conciencia eclesial latinoamericana: Visión y legado de un precursor," *Teología y Vida* 50 (2009): 13–40 (13).

[12] Pius XIII, Pope. "Carta Apostólica 'Ad Ecclesiam Christi' Pio XII a los Obispos Latinoamericanos," Iª Conferencia General del CELAM, Rio de Janeiro (1955), https://www.celam.org/documentos/Documento_Conclusivo_Rio.pdf.

that process, calling for an "active presence of the Church, in order to influence the economic-social world" in three ways: "enlightenment, education, and action."[13] Accordingly, CELAM I, as that conference would be known, urged for an educational focus to disseminate the social doctrine of the Church as an "integral part of the Gospel and Christian morality," highlighting the role of Catholic Action.[14] Both bishops leading that effort in the years between CELAM I and Vatican II were not only firmly committed to that call but had been forged through the work they did coordinating Catholic Action in their respective countries.

Bishop Larraín studied philosophy in Santiago and theology at the Pontifical Gregorian University, in Rome, and was ordained in 1927. After his studies in Rome, he returned to Santiago, where he initially taught at the Pontifical Seminary, and later at the Catholic University. On August 7, 1938, he was consecrated a bishop, initially designated to assist Monsignor Carlos Silva Cotapos in Talca. After Cotapos's resignation in 1939, he became the titular bishop of the diocese of Talca, a function he performed until his tragic death in a car accident in 1966.

Between 1952 and 1962, Dom Larraín, as he was known, served as the associate coordinator of the Chilean Catholic Action and coordinator of the Interamerican Secretariat of Catholic Action.[15] His main pastoral concern resided on "the young people, the awakening of the laity, the redemption of the poor [. . .], the workers and the peasants."[16]

Larraín understood the need for bishops to fully immerse in all aspects of life. One of his main concerns was the living conditions of the impoverished majority of Latin Americans. Like Câmara, he understood that a bishop should be a servant of the people. For him,

---

[13] CELAM, "Declaración de los Cardinales, Obispos y demás Prelados Representantes de la Jerarquia de America Latina Reunidos em la Conferencia Episcopal de Rio de Janeiro (1955)," https://www.celam.org/documentos/Documento_Conclusivo_Rio.pdf.

[14] CELAM, "Declaración de los Cardinales, Obispos . . ."

[15] Manuel Larraín Errázuriz, *La Voz Profética de Don Manuel Larraín E. recopilación de discursos y escritos, textos integros* (Santiago, Chile: Ediciones Mundo, 1976), 7.

[16] Carlos Camus Larenas, "Presentación," in *La Voz Profética de Don Manuel Larraín E.*, 6.

the duty of the bishop "is to serve the great concerns and problems of the human community. He must be, to the extent of his strength, a builder of peace."[17]

In a continent like Latin America, that sort of pastoral approach would not allow for one to be silent, demanding critical analysis of the deep roots of the unjust situations preventing peace.[18] Thus, for Larraín, "the material and spiritual underdevelopment of the peoples that make up the so-called 'Third World'" was as serious and real a threat to life as a nuclear bomb, since misery, hunger, and illness caused as many deaths in the "Third World" as the total of deaths resulting from WWII.[19] Such a scandalous disparity motivated the Chilean bishop to look for "concrete and practical means of organization and cooperation, so that all resources are pooled, and all efforts are united in the purpose of realizing a true 'communion' among nations."[20]

Unsurprisingly, Larraín played a decisive role in the creation of CELAM, being elected its first vice president and, in 1964, its president, a function he performed only for a couple of years due to his untimely death. For many years, he also served as secretary of the Permanent Commission of the Chilean Episcopate and president of the Episcopate Commission for the Lay Apostolate, having an outstanding involvement in the Latin American congresses of Catholic Action and in the two world congresses of the lay apostolate, in Rome.[21]

Always looking for concrete responses to the challenges posed by poverty and injustice, Larraín advocated for agrarian reform, arguing that the concentration of land in the hands of a few was a problem of moral conscience that needed to be resolved. He invited peasants and urban workers in his diocese for face-to-face conversations, adopting a posture of humility, and carefully listening to their stories and concerns. Larraín saw Catholic Action as one of the greatest initiatives of his days, demanding both "holy

[17] Manuel Larraín Errázuriz, "Carta Pastoral: Desarrollo: éxito o fracasso em América Latina," *Veritas* 37 (2017): 205–232 (205). This pastoral letter was originally published in 1965.

[18] Errázuriz, "Carta Pastoral: Desarrollo: éxito o fracasso em América Latina," 206.

[19] Errázuriz, "Carta Pastoral," 206.

[20] Errázuriz, "Carta Pastoral," 207.

[21] Larraín Errázuriz, *La Voz Profética*, 8.

priests" and lay apostles to work together. To transform society, he would say, "we need apostles from it." Considering the immense task of the Catholic laity, he made it a priority to equip those "lay priests."[22]

Jesuit Alberto Hurtado, a close friend of Larraín's, distinguished Catholic action from temporal social action as two kinds of transformative Christian actions in the world:

> Catholic Action is the work of the laity acting under the hierarchy of the Church to Christianize people and institutions, while temporal social action is the work of lay people who, aware of their faith and in full harmony with it, act under their own responsibility, taking all the risks and dangers of the enterprise. Such is the labor field of unions, cooperatives, political parties.[23]

For Larraín, both types of action should happen side by side: "some will strive to baptize this world, and others to build it healthy, worthy of baptism. The two actions, the religious and the temporal, contribute to the creation of the world demanded by the principles of Gospel."[24]

As a member of the Lay Apostolate Commission, Larraín advanced both kinds of action, seeing the laity as indispensable missionaries "who establish continued contact between the world and the Church, the temporal and the eternal, the creative work and redemption."[25] He promoted a lay spirituality that sees life as a divine vocation and "the duty to the state as God's way," thus unifying the double task—profane and missionary—into a wholistic vocation, "the personal task of each one in the growth of the world and of the Church."[26]

Once open to the world, Christians are called to participate in the transformation of "the external conditions of life." Both the economic situation and the social environment that prevent the proletarian

---

[22] Errázuriz, *La Voz Profética*, 12.

[23] Alberto Hurtado, *Moral Social: Escritos inéditos del Padre Alberto Hurtado*, vol. 3., ed. P. Miranda (Santiago, Chile: Univ. Católica de Chile, 2003), 44. Cited by Berríos, "Manuel Larraín y la conciencia eclesial latino-americana," 21.

[24] Hurtado, *Moral Social: Escritos inéditos del Padre Alberto Hurtado*, 21.

[25] Larraín Errázuriz, *La Voz Profética*, 51.

[26] Errázuriz, *La Voz Profética*, 53.

redemption "must be redeemed."[27] For Larraín, Christians were called to work on economic and social reform to change the conditions that prevent the redemption of the worker.[28] He condemned the scandalous asymmetric distribution of wealth, advocating for a humanized property possession system, while criticizing the subservience of entrepreneurship to usury, which informed the demands of international capital. He encouraged Christian participation in workers' unions, urged for higher salaries, and envisioned a more humane and just society.

Larraín interpreted this turn to the world as an act of evangelization of the social structures of human life.[29] His theology of laicity was forged in conversation with the reality of urban and rural workers in Chile. The repeated encounter with such realities helped him see the gravity of social problems such as the relationship between the masses of rural workers and the land they cultivated, concluding that agrarian reform was a neuralgic theme for church and society in Latin America. Given his prophetic leadership and engagement in the struggles of the poor and marginalized, Larraín became a critical Latin American voice in the Second Vatican Council and its initial reception in Latin America.

Archbishop Hélder Câmara worked closely with Larraín in the formation of CELAM and in the Latin American preparation for Vatican II. Like Larraín, Câmara also emerged as a national Catholic leader through his work with Catholic Action, helping forge a Christian perspective inspired by the concept of the church of the poor, which the Vatican II would help popularize.[30]

As mentioned earlier, Câmara emerged in the Brazilian scene when, in the 1940s, he became the national coordinator of Catholic Action.[31] His experience advising Catholic Action in Brazil prepared him for the organization of both CNBB and CELAM. Between his ordination in 1931 and his participation in Vatican II, he experienced

---

[27] Errázuriz, *La Voz Profética*, 63.

[28] Errázuriz, *La Voz Profética*, 63.

[29] Luis Vaccaro Cuevas, "Monseñor Manuel Larraín, profeta desde el sur de Chile," *Revista Universum* 25/1 (2010): 188–202 (193).

[30] Câmara, *Essential Writings*, 47–48.

[31] Luiz Carlos Luz Marques & José Oscar Beozzo, "A Igreja do Brasil na Preparação do Vaticano II," *Horizonte* 9/24 (2011): 986–1009 (993).

multiple "conversions."[32] Initially infatuated with the integralism of Plínio Salgado and an understanding of the Church as the perfect society, Câmara gradually became sensitized by the reality of injustice and poverty he encountered in his pastoral journey. In his early work assisting the influent cardinal Sebastião Leme da Silveira (1882–1942), Câmara's main task was to "reestablish the visible presence and action of the Church in the social and political life of Brazil." In a short amount of time, he emerged as a key agent promoting the Church's participation in the acts of public life, thus becoming the main face of the Catholic Church in the National Council of Education.[33]

After Leme's death, Câmara began to engage popular movements, MEB, the Liturgical Movement, and the peasant leagues, assisting the work of specialized Catholic Action groups, especially JAC, JOC, and JUC.[34] After moving to Rio de Janeiro to assist Dom Jaime Câmara, he was put in charge of implementing religious education in Rio's public schools. During that period, Câmara organized the national secretariat of Ação Católica Brasileira (ACB). His repeated contact with the suffering of impoverished sectors of Brazilian society led him to gradually see the Church no longer as a perfect society but through the lens of its service to the poor.[35] His views on the need for a radical solidarity with the oppressed would mature throughout the 1950s, becoming central to his interpretation of the apostolic mission of the Church in the world, especially in societies as asymmetrical as those in Latin America.

Those evolving views informed Câmara's work in the CNBB and CELAM. The creation of CNBB was one of the most notable contributions he offered to the Brazilian episcopate.[36] The first conversations

[32] Carlos Josaphat, "Eclesiologia da Comunhão e da Sacramentalidade, da Colegialidade, da Participação e do Compromisso Social: 'A Igreja transmite o que ela é, o que ela crê,'" in *Helder, o Dom: Uma Vida que Marcou os Rumos da Igreja*, 2nd ed., ed. Zildo Rocha (Petrópolis, Brazil: Editora Vozes, 1999), 124–135 (131).

[33] José Comblin, "Prefácio," in Helder Câmara, *Vaticano II: Correspondência Conciliar: Circulares à Família do São Joaquim*, vol. 1/Tomo I. With an introduction and notes by Luiz Carlos Luz Marques (Recife, Brazil: Instituto Dom Hélder Câmara, 2004), xxi–xxxi (xxiii).

[34] See Barreto, "Vatican II, Medellin, and Ecumenism," 192.

[35] Ivanir Antônio Rampon, *O Caminho Espiritual de Dom Hélder Câmara* (São Paulo: Editora Paulinas, 2013), 30.

[36] Clement Isnard, "Dom Hélder e a Conferência dos Bispos," in *Hélder, o Dom*, 97–101 (97).

about forming CNBB took place in the General Secretariat of the Brazilian Catholic Action. With support of the apostolic nuncio, Câmara "began to promote Regional Bishops' Meetings" that led to the formation of CNBB in 1952.[37] As the first CNBB General Secretary, he used his platform to promote numerous initiatives attending to needs of the impoverished masses.

> In Rio, Dom Helder inaugurated a housing project for favela dwellers and set up an ongoing charitable drive for the needy. He soon gained international renown as "the bishop of the favelas." Dom Helder also lobbied the government for development programs to assist the masses. His prestige and growing political influence enabled him to become one of the principal advisers to President Juscelino Kubitschek (1956–1961), who promoted rapid industrial development through foreign investment, government stimulus, and the transfer of the national capital from Rio to newly built Brasilia. Dom Helder and the CNBB assisted Kubitschek in the effort to spread the benefits of development. For example, the bishops were instrumental in the foundation of an ambitious government program to bring industry and progress to the impoverished northeast.[38]

Throughout his journey, Dom Hélder, as Câmara was affectionally known in Brazil, found inspiration in groups that identified with the experience of the poor, including the French worker-priests, from whom he borrowed the phrase "The Church of Poverty and Service."[39] Following in their steps, Câmara and "other clergymen of his time adopted a spirituality of poverty and literally sought to live like the poor."[40] While tirelessly working to mobilize the clergy to serve the poor, he concomitantly "encouraged the laity to assert itself within the Church and to focus on questions of national importance."[41]

---

[37] CNBB, "Dom Hélder Câmara: Primeiro Secretário Geral e Idealizador do Projeto da CNBB," https://www.cnbb.org.br/dom-helder-camara-primeiro-secretario-geral-e-idealizador-do-projeto-da-cnbb/.

[38] Kenneth P. Serbin, "Dom Helder Camara: The Father of the Church of the Poor," in *The Human Tradition in Modern Brazil*, ed. Peter M Beattie, The Human Tradition Around the World, 7 (Wilmington, DE: Scholarly Resources, 2004), 249–266 (256).

[39] Câmara, *Essential Writings*, 47.

[40] Serbin, "Dom Helder Camara: The Father of the Church of the Poor," 256.

[41] Serbin, "Dom Helder Camara," 257.

Seeking to act in coherence with his discourse, Câmara often delegated responsibility to the laity, especially women.[42]

As early as the mid-1950s, Dom Hélder's work began to transcend Brazil. After cofounding CELAM in 1955 with Larraín, he was elected CELAM's first president, with Larraín serving as vice president. The work both men did at CELAM contributed to increase "awareness of the region's importance in the Catholic Church and provided support for the emerging Church of the Poor."[43] On July 17–24, 1955, Dom Hélder organized the International Eucharistic Congress in Rio de Janeiro. His leadership and organizing skills deeply impressed Monsignor Montini.[44] Assisted by Armando Lombardi (1905–1964), the Vatican nuncio in Brazil, he also organized the first Continental Conference of the Latin American Episcopate July 25 to August 4, 1955. As in the early years, CELAM's headquarters was situated in Rome; such a proximity to the Vatican would facilitate the articulation of the Latin American bishops prior to and during Vatican II.

CELAM became a key player in the efforts to "transform pastoral action in a response to the challenges of the economic development" of the region.[45] Starting in the early 1960s, Câmara's reformist tone, putting emphasis on the responsibility of the Church and of those in positions of privilege to stand in solidarity with those who were left out of the benefits of development, began to change. The lack of appropriate response on the part of those in a position of power to effect change, led him to be increasingly critical of the "social order" and of the passivity of the Church:

> The churchmen in this country and in this continent used to be so preoccupied with upholding authority and the social order that we were incapable of seeing the terrible injustices that were and still are perpetuated by this so-called social order. The Christianity we preached was too passive: patience, obedience, acceptance of suffering in union with Christ. Great virtues, of course: but in the context they merely reinforced oppression. And during all this

---

[42] Serbin, "Dom Helder Camara," 257.

[43] Serbin, "Dom Helder Camara," 256.

[44] Rampon, *O Caminho Espiritual de Dom Hélder Câmara*, 49.

[45] Rampon, *O Caminho Espiritual de Dom Hélder Câmara*, 49.

> time, the governments and the great lords were pleased and proud that the church guaranteed them support.[46]

That new tone provoked a reaction. Once "Catholic laymen, priests, nuns, and even bishops [like himself] began to denounce the injustices," those who formerly saw them as allies, "the proprietors of the established order," began to perceive them now as agitators and subversives.[47] Those individuals were then placed at the center of cataclysmic changes, which would have consequences not only for Christian theology and praxis but for the larger society. In Brazil, the sectors of the Church that chose to stand in solidarity with the oppressed quickly began to experience persecution. Dom Hélder, one of the best-known faces of the progressive Brazilian Catholic Church, suddenly had to deal with accusations of being an infiltrated Marxist trying to destroy the Church from the inside. This situation led him to utter one of his most famous phrases: "When I feed the poor, they call me a saint. When I ask why they are poor, they call me a communist."[48]

This was another conversion in Câmara's journey. He came to understand that charity was not enough. Those who have been impoverished, oppressed, dehumanized, and rejected need justice, as South African Dominican theologian Albert Nolan suggested. According to him, Dom Hélder urged Christians to become "justice Christians" while also personifying the meaning of the expression "the option for the poor."[49]

The conversion to the poor of bishops such as Dom Hélder and Dom Larraín helped create structures within the Church to support the base ecclesial communities (CEBs). Furthermore, progressive bishops in the region sought to put the resources of their dioceses and archdioceses at the service of the church of the poor. Therefore, they actively

[46] Câmara, *Essential Writings*, 48.

[47] Câmara, *Essential Writings*, 48–49.

[48] Albert Nolan, "Eles Me Chamam de Comunista," in *Hélder, o Dom*, 53–55 (53).

[49] Nolan, "Eles Me Chamam de Comunista," 54. Among other important bishops that also embraced radical solidarity with the poor, one can mention Leonidas Eduardo Proaño Villalba (1910–1988), bishop of Riobamba, Ecuador between 1954 and 1985, and Samuel Ruiz García (1924–2011), bishop of the diocese of San Cristóbal de Las Casas, Mexico between 1959 and 1999. Both of them were part of the Latin American delegation to Vatican II.

participated in the radical transformation that important sectors of the Latin American Church experienced during that period.

CELAM I demonstrated how the new structures emerging in the Latin American Church could support and enhance the work of the laity and contribute to raise awareness as for the centrality of the social question in the region. Among other things, CELAM I recommended the following:

a. that the superiors and members of the religious Orders and Congregations and secular Institutes seek to effectively favor the organization and progress of Catholic Action in the various countries;
b. that members of Catholic Action organizations study and disseminate the Christian principles and papal guidelines on social, economic and political problems, in order to effectively help form the conscience of the people in these very important aspects of the doctrine of the Church;
c. that Catholic Action devise ways to discover and inspire among its members true vocations to the social and civic activities, and encourage them to have optimal training, not only scientific and technical but also practical, for such important tasks for the common good;
d. and strongly urge that Catholic Action promote associations and works for the solution of the social problems that are most pressing today in Latin American countries.[50]

These developments aligned with the awareness raising already in course among participants of JAC, JEC, JOC, and JUC. Whereas a reformist approach remained the default position of these movements, they increasingly became convinced of the need to confront the structural causes of the dehumanizing living conditions in the region and the systemic nature of social injustice. The experiences some Latin American bishops—including Dom Hélder and Dom Larraín—had with the specialized sectors of Catholic Action informed their views and participation in Vatican II, contributing to their interpretation of the Council through the lens of the social, political, and cultural reality of Latin America. Based on that

[50] CELAM, "Declaración de los Cardinales, Obispos . . ."

experience, one can speak of the Latin American impact on the Council's legacy. Furthermore, one can say that what prepared the Latin American Church for Vatican II was the interpellation from those at the margins of church and society mediated by the Church's pastoral presence among the oppressed.

The Church of the Poor and the Pact of the Catacombs

After the death of Pius XII in 1958, Italian Cardenal Angelo Giuseppe Roncalli (1881–1963) was elected pope at the age of 76, taking the name John XXIII. To the surprise of many, shortly after his coronation the new pope called for an ecumenical council. The Second Vatican Council met in four sessions between 1962 and 1965, having 2,908 attendants between voting participants and observers.[51] This was the most ecumenical council in the history of the Catholic Church, not only because of the presence of two hundred non-Catholic observers but also for its global representation (with a significant number of participants coming especially from the Americas, Africa, and Asia). Approximately six hundred bishops from Latin America participated in the Council—roughly one-fifth of the overall attendance. On November 23, 1965, the Latin American delegation to Vatican II secured Pope Paul VI's support of a second Latin American Episcopal General Conference, meant to consider the reception of the Council in the region:

> We will even say more: in certain aspects and for certain subjects it may also be useful and appropriate to study a plan at a continental level through your Episcopal Council, in its function as a body of contact and collaboration between the Episcopal Conferences of Latin America.[52]

With the pope's blessing, CELAM II took place in Medellin in 1968.

---

[51] Austin Flannery, "Introduction," in *Vatican Council II: Constitutions, Decrees, Declarations*, ed. Austin Flannery (Collegeville, MN: Liturgical Press, 1996), 13, Kindle.

[52] Pope Paulo VI, "Nel X anniversario del C.E.L.A.M., Esortazione Pastorale Per Il Lavoro Apostolico Nell'America Latina," in Insegnamenti di Paolo VI, III/1965, Tip. Poliglotta Vaticana, 1966, 661. As quoted in Beozzo, "Medellín: inspiração e raízes," *Koinonia*.

Another significant step taken by the Council was its efforts "to overcome the centuries-old rupture between the Christian East and West, consummated in 1054, inviting Orthodox and ancient Oriental Churches to participate in the Vatican II as observers." At the closing of the Council, on December 7, 1965, celebrations were held in Rome and Constantinople, with a joint declaration by Pope Paul VI and the Ecumenical Patriarch of Constantinople Athenagoras I lifting the mutual excommunications and anathemas leveled against each other by their predecessors.[53]

The opening session of the Council took place on October 11, 1962, with the presence of 2,540 council fathers (those with right to voice and vote).[54] Remarkably, only 1,041 of them were from Europe—a major shift, considering that since the Middle Ages Europe had dominated the Catholic councils. The Americas, not present in the Council of Trent, and only marginally represented in Vatican I, sent 956 representatives, while Asia sent over 300, and Africa 379.[55] Brazil, which had only 7 representatives attending the opening session of Vatican I, had 204 bishops participating in the opening session of Vatican II—the third largest national episcopate in the Council after Italy and the United States.[56]

Beyond numbers, Vatican II was ecumenical in its openness to other churches and traditions as attested in documents such as

---

[53] José Oscar Beozzo, "Padres Conciliares Brasileiros no Vaticano II: Participação e Prosopografia, 1959–1965" (PhD diss., Universidade de São Paulo–USP, 2001), 23. The joint declaration states, "Pope Paul VI and Patriarch Athenagoras I with his synod realize that this gesture of justice and mutual pardon is not sufficient to end both old and more recent differences between the Roman Catholic Church and the Orthodox Church. Through the action of the Holy Spirit those differences will be overcome through cleansing of hearts, through regret for historical wrongs, and through an efficacious determination to arrive at a common understanding and expression of the faith of the Apostles and its demands." Pope Paul VI and Patriarch Athenagoras I, "Joint Catholic-Orthodox Declaration of His Holiness Pope Paul VI and the Ecumenical Patriarch Athenagoras I," December 7, 1965, https://www.vatican.va/content/paul-vi/en/speeches/1965/documents/hf_p-vi_spe_19651207_common-declaration.html.

[54] Ney de Souza, "Contexto e Desenvolvimento Histórico do Concílio Vaticano II," in *Concílio Vaticano II: Análise e Prospectivas*, ed. Paulo Sérgio Lopes Gonçalves and Vera Ivanise Bombonatto, 2nd ed. (São Paulo: Editoras Paulinas, 2005), 17–67 (33).

[55] de Souza, "Contexto e Desenvolvimento Histórico do Concílio Vaticano II," 34.

[56] Beozzo, "Padres Conciliares Brasileiros," 32.

the Decree on Ecumenism (*Unitatis redintegratio*), the Decree on the Eastern Catholic Churches (*Orientalium Ecclesiarum*), and the Declaration on the Relationship of the Church to Non-Christian Religions (*Nostra Aetate*). While this last document focused on the Church's concern with other religions, the other two were representative of an old dream Pope John XXIII cultivated, "the reunion of all Christians."[57]

Both the Council's openness to dialogue with the world and its pastoral tone expressed its ecumenicity. Its opening words were called a "Message to Humanity;" a message directed to all people and nations (not to Christians alone). That opening message had as its central concern the triad well-being, love, and peace.[58] The Catholic Church that the Council shows to the world is truly global, with many representatives from peripheral areas of the modern world, giving voice to what Massimo Faggioli calls "the Church of the margins."[59]

Although not devoid of doctrinal concerns—expressed in the Council's emphases on guarding, preserving, and teaching the inherited truth—the focus of Vatican II on the renewal of the Church reinforced its predominantly pastoral nature.[60] Pope John XXIII's convocation of the Council did not indicate any urgent doctrinal concern. Above all, his was a pastoral concern for a world in crisis, which the Church was called to serve. The rapid changes taking place in the modern world called for the renewal of the Church.[61] Thus the Council's emphasis on *aggiornamento* was also an ecumenical concern. As Ney de Souza points out, "The most important contribution on the part of the Church for unity and the essential task of the Council would be the program John XXIII called *aggiornamento*—an

[57] Lawrence Cardinal Shehan, "Introduction," in *The Documents of Vatican II: With Notes and Comments by Catholic, Protestant, and Orthodox Authorities*, ed. Walter M. Abbott (New York: Guild Press, 1966), xv–xix (xvi).

[58] Vatican II, "Message to Humanity," in *The Documents of Vatican II: With Notes and Comments by Catholic, Protestant, and Orthodox Authorities*, 3–8 (3).

[59] Massimo Faggioli, *A Council for the Global Church: Receiving Vatican II in History* (Minneapolis: Fortress Press, 2015), 165.

[60] Santiago Madrigal Terrazas, *Protagonistas del Vaticano II: Galería de Retratos y Episodios Conciliares* (Madrid: Biblioteca de Autores Cristianos, 2016), 24–25.

[61] Pope John XXIII, "Pope John Convokes the Council," in *The Documents of Vatican II: With Notes and Comments by Catholic, Protestant, and Orthodox Authorities*, 703–709 (705).

update of the Church, an insertion in the modern world, where Christianity should be present and active."[62]

This is the third dimension of the ecumenicity of the Council. Vatican II was not exclusively concerned with the unity of the Church but with human society as a whole, emphasizing themes such the peace of the world and the dignity and well-being of all people.[63] While such a concern with the world was already present in the papacies of Pius XI and Pius XII, those previous popes viewed the world through the lenses of the Church's task to Christianize it, whereas John XXIII seemed to understand the irreversible plurality of the modern age and the need for the Church to move into a new reality with an unreserved "acceptance of the modern democracy."[64] Pope John XXIII's encyclical *Pacem in Terris* (1963) sought to place the Church "on the side of democracy."[65] Whereas this was not a document produced by the Council, it represented its spirit. Vatican II brought the Church once and for all into the twentieth century, forcing it to face its new reality in a new world order. Its tone cannot be other but pastoral, and its authority in relation to the world is now dependent on its public witness, and its incarnational practices rather than on its ontological morals.

For Latin American bishops such as Câmara and Larraín, this is exactly what made the Council so relevant for Latin America. Pope John XXIII won the enthusiasm of these Latin American bishops especially when he referred to the Church of the Poor before the Council. *Pacem in Terris* would add to the enthusiasm among many Latin American Christians about the need for the Church to pay concerted attention to the most vulnerable. *Pacem in Terris*'s emphasis on the attainment of the common good, its view of human society as guided by respect for justice and the rights and duties of all its members, the inclusion of "decent standard of living" as a right to be protected for the preservation of life, and its acknowledgment of the natural rights of women and their rise in political life, also resonated

62 Ney de Souza, "Contexto e Desenvolvimento Histórico do Concílio Vaticano II," 24.

63 John F. Cronin, *The Social Teaching of Pope John XXIII* (Milwaukee, WI: The Bruce Publishing Company, 1963), 40.

64 Cronin, *The Social Teaching of Pope John XXIII*, 43.

65 Cronin, *The Social Teaching of Pope John XXIII*, 43

with the social changes Latin American bishops like Câmara, Larraín, and Proaño envisioned the Church would work toward.[66]

In its discussion of the common good, *Pacem in Terris* underscores the centrality of justice and equity, demanding "that those in power pay more attention to the weaker members of society, since these are at a disadvantage when it comes to defending their own rights and asserting their legitimate interests."[67] This could be seen as a foreshadow of the emphasis on the preferential option for the poor that would emerge later in Latin America. For the Latin American participants in Vatican II, *Gaudium et Spes: The Pastoral Constitution on the Church in the Modern World*, one of the important documents coming out of the final batch of deliberation of the Council on December 7, 1965, was also critical due to the deep pastoral solidarity it attaches to the task of the Church. Its preamble of the document is often cited in Latin America:

> The joys and hopes, the grief and anguish of the people of our time, *especially of those who are poor or afflicted*, are the joys and hopes, the grief and anguish of the followers of Christ as well. Nothing that is genuinely human fails to find an echo in their hearts. For theirs is a community of people united in Christ and guided by the holy Spirit in their pilgrimage towards the Father's kingdom, bearers of a message of salvation for all of humanity. That is why they cherish a feeling of deep solidarity with the human race and its history.[68]

While not of a common mind (there were important differences and tensions among the Latin American bishops), the sizeable Latin American delegation attended Vatican II with certain expectations. Pope John XXIII's preparatory work for the Council reinforced those expectations.

In advance of the Council, the Pope established the Secretariat for the Promotion of Christian Unity (SPCU), in 1960, appointing

[66] See Pope John XXIII, *Pacem in Terris*, Encyclical of Pope John XXIII on Establishing Universal Peace in Truth, Justice, Charity, and Liberty, Vatican website, April 11, 1963, https://www.vatican.va/content/john-xxiii/en/encyclicals/documents/hf_j-xxiii_enc_11041963_pacem.html.

[67] Pope John XXIII, *Pacem in Terris*.

[68] In Flannery, ed. *Vatican Council II: Constitutions, Decrees, Declarations*, 177–178.

German Jesuit Cardinal Augustin Bea (1881–1968) as its president. That secretariat became one of the most dynamic organisms of the curia in the following years and decades;[69] a watershed in respect to Catholic participation in ecumenical interactions. This organism coordinated the invitation for other churches to send observers to the Council and helped shape the ecumenical documents of Vatican II. Furthermore, it also sparked a new era of Catholic ecumenical commitment. Following Vatican II, the Roman Catholic Church took other important ecumenical initiatives, including the formation of the Joint Working Group with the World Council of Churches, "full partnership in Faith and Order, presence of individuals in some departments of Faith and Order," and the restoration of relationship with the Eastern Orthodox Churches, initiating "a common walk towards full sacramental unity." As Fr. Tillard put it, "This was the first official actualization of the Council."[70]

Also, in preparation for the Council, Cardinal Domenico Tardini, the Vatican Secretary of State, sent out a questionnaire to bishops, seminaries, and religious orders around the world, asking questions related to five topics to be discussed in the future Council: the holy custody of the truth, the sanctity and apostolate of clerics and the faithful, ecclesiastical discipline, schools, and the unity of the Church. He received 2,109 responses, which were synthesized by the commission and made available for the participants of the council in advance of it.[71] Whereas many of those responses focused on canonical and administrative concerns, others expressed an ecumenical solicitude that resonated with the spirit of the Council, with significant interest shown, particularly, in the idea of *aggiornamento*. Hélder Câmara was one of those who mailed his answers to the

---

[69] Souza, "Contexto e Desenvolvimento Histórico do Concílio Vaticano II," 25. As Fr Jean-Marie Tillard points out, those observers were not merely passive guests. They were consulted and even asked to criticize initial drafts of the documents of the council. Jean-Marie Tillard, "Rome and Ecumenism," August 11, 1995, https://www.oikoumene.org/resources/documents/rome-and-ecumenism.

[70] Tillard, "Rome and Ecumenism." The many bilateral dialogues the SPCU started and the joint declarations that have emanated from them are remarkable contributions that the Vatican engagement of ecumenism has offered to the worldwide Christian community.

[71] Souza, "Contexto e Desenvolvimento Histórico do Concílio Vaticano II," 28.

questionnaire back. Unsurprisingly, he expected greater focus on "the social question."[72]

The social question was a common concern among Global South bishops who expected the Council to take a clearer instance on the matter of the Church's solidarity with the impoverished masses around the world. For instance, talking about cooperation with "our separate brothers," [sic], Cardinal Valerian Gracias (1900–1978), Archbishop of Bombay, spoke about the need for Christian unity for social action, tying the Decree on Ecumenism to the service of the poor.[73] For him, when facing a common enemy, people are inclined to work together. Otherwise, they might perish. The common enemy to be faced, according to him, was "the well-nigh universal phenomenon of poverty and misery," which Christians can help defeat if they unite.[74] His words were representative of an emerging understanding of an ecumenism of life that informed several delegates to the Council, especially those coming from formerly colonized nations. Dom Hélder was one of the enthusiasts of that idea as well as of the formation of a coalition among bishops representing the "Third World" to address the theme of poverty.

John XXIII's announcement of the Council in 1959 had led Dom Hélder to dream "of a more evangelical and ecumenical church, closer to the poor, committed to the development of the peoples and to mutual understanding, capable of promoting dialogue between the north and south of the world, of collaborating for peace and international cooperation, as an interlocutor with the channels of social communication and modern culture."[75] Inspired by those dreams, Câmara participated in the creation of an informal working group initially composed of twenty-two representatives of "the main episcopal conferences to exchange information and points of

[72] Souza, "Contexto e Desenvolvimento Histórico do Concílio Vaticano II," 29. Câmara was one of 132 Brazilians who responded to the preliminary questionnaire. See José Oscar Beozzo, "Presença e Atuação dos Bispos Brasileiros no Vaticano II," in *Concílio Vaticano II: Análise e Prospectivas*, 117–162 (131).

[73] Cardinal Valerian Gracias, "Serving the Poor Together," in Hans Küng, Yves Congar, and Daniel O'Hanlon, eds., *Council Speeches of Vatican II* (New York: Paulist Press, 1964), 202–205 (203).

[74] Valerian Gracias, "Serving the Poor Together," 202–205 (203).

[75] José Oscar Beozzo, "Dom Hélder Câmara e o Concílio Vaticano II," in *Hélder, o Dom*, 102–111 (102).

view, coordinate among themselves, and propose initiatives to speed up the progress of the Council."[76] The role Câmara played in the articulation of the Domus Mariae group, which met regularly and became one of the most eclectic informal group in the Council, was characteristic of his quiet behind-the-scenes influence, which helped shape the Council.[77] As José Comblin pointed out, despite never using the floor, Câmara "was involved in everything in the corridors, and knew how to use the service of others to get his ideas across."[78]

Taking advantage of his platform as the CNBB president and the vice-president of CELAM, Câmara used the discussions in that working group, also known as "the ecumenical group," to advance south-north and south-south conversations, connecting specifically with bishops from Africa and Asia.[79] Another informal group he helped create was the Church of the Poor.[80] This group, which began to meet in the initial session of the Council in 1962, was inspired by the words John XXIII pronounced prior to the Council: "Confronted by the underdeveloped countries, the Church presents herself as she is and as she wants to be; the Church of all men and in particular the Church of the Poor."[81] Rallying on the phrase "The Church of the Poor," the group, which, besides Dom Hélder, also counted with the participation of individuals such as Pierre-Marie Gerlier (1880–1965), the cardinal of Lyon and a supporter of the priest-workers, and his auxiliary, and Monsignor Alfred Jean Félix Ancel (1898–1984), the founding chaplain of the JOC in Lyon, who also founded a worker-priest community in an area known as Prado, Gerland, a working class area of Lyon.

The group included Father Paul Gauthier, founder of the Companions of Jesus the Carpenter, in Nazareth,[82] Bishop Georges-Louis

---

[76] Beozzo, "Dom Hélder Câmara e o Concílio Vaticano II," 105.

[77] Rocco Caporale, *Vatican II: Les Hommes du Concile. Etude sociologique sur Vatican II* (Paris: Editions du Cerf, 1965), 88, as quoted in Beozzo, "Dom Hélder Câmara e o Concílio Vaticano II," 105.

[78] José Comblin, "Prefácio," in Marcelo Barros, *Dom Hélder Câmara: Profetas para os nossos dias* (São Paulo: Paulus, 2011), 8.

[79] Beozzo, "Dom Hélder Câmara e o Concílio Vaticano II," 106.

[80] Beozzo, "Presença e Atuação dos Bispos Brasileiros no Vaticano II," 147.

[81] John McComarck, "The Church of the Poor," *The Furrow* 17/4 (1996): 211–221 (215).

[82] Gauthier, a theologian who left his teaching position in Dijon, France, to become a construction worker in Nazareth, was, with the Carmelite nun Marie-Thérèse Lescase, an invitee of Monsignor Georges Hakim, bishop of Nazareth, Galilea,

Mercier from Laghouat, Algeria, and would grow in later sessions to a total of eighty-six participants from different parts of the world, the majority, though, from the Global South. That group helped shape the awareness of the Council about the problem of mass poverty and informed several of its decrees.[83] Yet, it failed to convince the Council as a whole to include a decisive commitment to the poor in its documents.

In the Council's third and final session, thirty-nine of those bishops met in the Catacombs of Saint Domitila to seal a commitment to a life of poverty and at the service of the poor.[84] In a discreet ceremony, they celebrated the Eucharist together at the underground basilica near the tombs of the holy martyrs Nereo and Achilleo.[85] At that ceremony, the bishops forming that group signed a document that became widely known as the "Pact of the Catacombs," a pledge through which they committed themselves "to walk with the poor and be not only a Church for the poor, but also of the poor, since it is the poor who embody and carry out the Gospel's highest mission."[86] To achieve that goal, they pledged "to adopt a simple style of life, characteristic of the poor, renouncing not only the symbols of power, but all outward power, as a way of recovering, with the help of the Triune God and the Spirit of Christ, the original missionary impulse of the Church for the contemporary world [. . .], marked by the harsh economic struggle and general oppression of the poor."[87] Whereas there is no formal list of all signatories of the pact, twenty-two of the bishops that signed it were from Latin America, eight from Brazil.[88] As Xabier Pikaza and José Antunes da Silva note,

---

to the Council. The three of them played a key behind-the-scenes role in advocating for a turn to a servant and poor Church. See José Oscar Beozzo, *O Pacto das Catacumbas: Por uma Igreja Servidora e Pobre* (São Paulo: Paulinas, 2015), 10.

83 McComarck, "The Church of the Poor," 217.

84 Beozzo, "Presença e Atuação dos Bispos Brasileiros no Vaticano II," 149.

85 Beozzo, *O Pacto das Catacumbas*, 11–12.

86 Xabier Pikaza and José Antunes da Silva, eds., *The Pact of the Catacombs: The Mission of the Poor in the Church* (Navarre, Spain: Editorial Verbo Divino, 2015), 11.

87 Pikaza and da Silva, eds., *The Pact of the Catacombs*, 11.

88 Pikaza and da Silva, eds., *The Pact of the Catacombs*, 19. That list included bishops Manuel Larraín, Hélder Câmara, and Leonidas Proaño. Curiously, although a signatory of the pact, and considered an animator of the initiative, backed by the example of a life championing "the downtrodden poor and oppressed," Dom Hélder did not attend the gathering in the Catacombs of Saint Domitila because he was at

> The spirit of the Pact of the Catacombs has guided some of the best Christian initiatives of the last fifty years, not only in Latin America, where it had particular impact, but throughout the Catholic Church, so that its witness (its inspiration and its text) have become one of the most influential and important signs of twentieth-century Catholicism.

That pact continues to inform the life and practice of many Christians around the world, having received renewed attention since Pope Francis's election, since he has used his platform to renew the call for the Church to be for and of the poor.[89] Rohan Curnow is right to affirm that the work of the Church of the Poor group sowed the seeds of the preferential option for the poor.[90] To be clear, the cry for the Church to radically identify with the poor already existed prior to Vatican II. It emerged in the outskirts of the world, from Palestine to Brazil, impacting priests and bishops who themselves were converted to the poor. The persistent work of these bishops at the Council impacted important sectors of the Church, creating a global platform for change in Christian praxis and theology through a new conversion to the poor.[91]

From the perspective of its participants, though, the group did not achieve its goals at Vatican II. Despite its persistent pleas, neither Pope Paul VI, who became the head of the Catholic Church with the death of Pope John XXIII in 1963, nor the Council as a whole, made the turn toward an unambiguous conversion to the poor that many in that group wished for.

---

a meeting discussing a late draft of *Gaudium et Spes*. See Hector Scerri, "The Pact of the Catacombs: An Early Harbinger of Pope Francis's Vision of the Church," *Journal of Cultural and Religious Studies* 7/6 (2019): 325–331 (326).

[89] Scerri, "The Pact of the Catacombs," 327.

[90] Rohan Curnow, "Stirrings of the Preferential Option for the Poor at Vatican II: The Work of the 'Group of the Church of the Poor,'" *Australasian Catholic Report* 89/4 (2012): 420–432.

[91] As Beozzo aptly put it, "It was precisely among bishops from these underdeveloped countries of Asia, Africa and Latin America, to whom some Europeans and Canadians were added, that concern arose over the issue of the Church of the poor and the commitment to raise awareness among the other Council Fathers of the needs and anxieties of the world's disinherited, who made up more than two thirds of humanity."

Beozzo, *O Pacto das Catacumbas*, 10.

The efforts of the group to make the poor central to the Council were numerous. In addition to seeking to sensitize the Council delegates to the problem of poverty and how it affected the evangelical announcement to the poor, the group supported the intervention of Giacomo Lercaro, archbishop of Bologne, who urged that the problem of poverty be "assumed as a central and hegemonic theme of the Council," stating that "this was the hour of the poor, of the millions of poor people across the face of the earth," and consequently, "the hour of Christ, especially in the poor." Lercaro did not want that to be just one of the themes mentioned in the Council, "but rather 'the only theme of the entire Vatican II.'" That should be the "unifying and vivifying principle" of the Council.[92] While effusively applauded, Cardinal Lercaro's discourse was only scarcely integrated into the documents of the Council.

Dom Hélder made his own efforts to guarantee a more central place to the theme of poverty both in the Council and in the Vatican's ongoing structure. He urged Paul VI to create a special secretariat to address the matter of hunger and impoverishment around the world. While the Pope made no commitment to create such a secretariat, two years after the end of Vatican II he created the Pontifical Commission for Justice and Peace. In response to Dom Hélder's appeal, the pope also committed to address the economic inequalities in the world in a post-Council encyclical—which came to be *Populorum Progressio*.[93]

While focusing on development (the development of the peoples), this document is considered a landmark in the evolution of the social teaching of the Catholic Church. It starts with an emphasis on the cry of "the hungry nations" as heard in Vatican II. In it, the pope makes references to his visits to Latin America (1960) and Africa (1962) before his election as pope, and to Palestine and India afterward, highlighting "the perplexing problems that vex and besiege these continents, which are otherwise full of life and promise." This firsthand knowledge of the struggles of "these age-old civilizations" for further development supported his appeal for "the case of the impoverished

[92] Beozzo, *O Pacto das Catacumbas*, 22.

[93] Pope Paul VI, *Populorum Progressio*, Encyclical of Pope Paul VI on the Development of Peoples, Vatican website, March 26, 1967, https://www.vatican.va/content/paul-vi/en/encyclicals/documents/hf_p-vi_enc_26031967_populorum.html. See also David Abalos, "The Medellin Conference," *Cross Currents* 19, no. 2 (1969): 113–32 (113–14).

nations," reinforcing what he had also voiced in his address to the United Nations Assembly prior to the end of Vatican II.[94] One of the key goals of the new Pontifical Commission was to "further the progress of poorer nations and international social justice."[95]

Paul VI saw poverty as a problem pertinent to all humans, thus urging all nations to pool their resources and ideas together in the common effort to overcome it. His commitment to social justice was ecumenical as he addressed all people, calling for a united effort to combat it that went far beyond Catholic Christianity.

Referring to John XXIII and his visit to Assisi shortly before the beginning of the Council, Dom Hélder highlighted the need for an ecumenical referential for that conversation, pointing to Saint Francis as the role model to be emulated: "Francis is rightly called Homo Catholicus. His ecumenism was open to everything and everyone. No one was excluded."[96] Similarly, Paul VI showed concern with the widening "disparity between rich and poor nations," and named colonialism as one of its causes. He called on all individuals to see themselves as members of the broader human community, urging for wide alliances "to further the development of human society as a whole."[97]

Populorum Progressio denounced social inequality as a problem that needed to be solved and called for the development of the whole person and all human beings. Considered a socially progressive encyclical, it became a reference for Latin American Christians on the front of the rise of liberation theology. Yet, due to its reformist and developmentalist tone, it was insufficient for a programmatic action aimed to impact the dehumanizing conditions of the most impoverished populations around the world.

Since the Council, a sentiment of frustration began to form among the Global South bishops who expected a more drastic change in the Church toward a more radical solidarity with the poor. Speaking of the Church of the Poor group and the Pact of the Catacombs, Dom

---

[94] Paul VI, *Populorum Progressio.*

[95] Paul VI, *Populorum Progressio.*

[96] Hélder Câmara, "49ª Circular - Roma, 23/24.11.1963," in *Vaticano II: Correspondência Conciliar: Circulares à Família do São Joaquim*, vol. 1/Tomo I, ed. Hélder Câmara, 954–959 (954).

[97] Paul VI, *Populorum Progressio.*

Antônio Fragoso (1920–2006), bishop of the Diocese of Crateús, expressed some of that frustration:

> [The Council] allowed me to discover [. . .] that the poor were not in the hearts and horizons of the bishops. Therefore, the Council did not pay greater attention to the topic. The Council allowed me to get out of that pessimism about nature and gave me joy, but I didn't see it reconciling itself with the poor.[98]

As Beozzo aptly noted, the impact of the Church of the Poor on the Council was above all spiritual. It informed some of its documents and impacted the commitment made by several bishops at the Council to help the Church become a poor and servant Church. Yet, the hope of those who thought that they would convince the whole Council to embrace the cause of the poor was frustrated.[99] Despite the fact that Vatican II was the first truly universal council, it was still dominated by European bishops and theologians.[100] The significant presence of Latin American bishops and theologians was a sign of hope. But their impact would only be felt in the long run.

While hoping to make the best possible impact on the Council, the Latin American bishops and theologians in Vatican II kept their focus on Latin America and what the Council could bring to it. Like other groups participating in the Council, they had their own internal disagreements. Nevertheless, there was a significant impetus within CELAM to reflect together on the significance of Vatican II for Latin America in light of the transformative experiences the Latin American Church had been experiencing since before the Council. In exercising their interpretative efforts, Latin American bishops and theologians contributed to the dispute of narratives about "the truth" of the Council, which continues to this day.[101]

---

[98] Dom Antônio Fragoso's interview to Beozzo, cited in *O Pacto das Catacumbas*, 13.

[99] Dom Antônio Fragoso's interview to Beozzo, cited in *O Pacto das Catacumbas*, 13.

[100] José Oscar Beozzo, "A Recepção do Vaticano II na Igreja do Brasil," Centro Teológico Manuel Larraín, https://centromanuellarrain.uc.cl/images/pdf/BeozzoJoseOscar.ArecepcaodoVaticanoII.pdf.

[101] The issue of continuity and rupture with a pre-Vatican II mentality is one of the focuses of that dispute. See João Batista Libânio, *Concilio Vaticano II: Em Busca de Uma Primeira Compreensão* (São Paulo, Brazil: Edições Loyola, 2005), 14.

The Reception of Vatican II in Latin America: The Joint Pastoral Program in Brazil

Due to the creation of CELAM years before Vatican II and the coordination of the Latin American bishops attending Vatican II to organize its reception in Latin America, the region became a "fertile soil for the seeds of the Council."[102] The two top leaders of CELAM, Dom Larraín and Dom Hélder, were extremely active in coordinating the next steps for the renewal of the Church in Latin America. As indicated earlier, the Latin American Church was already undergoing a process of renewal prior to the Council. That process needed to be more thoroughly understood and implemented as praxis. In the case of Brazil, a formal plan for the renewal of the Church initially conceived as a Plan of Emergency (1962), with support from John XXIII, was already in course. By the end of the Council (1965), the transitory plan, now supported by Paul VI, was turned into the more permanent Joint Pastoral Plan.[103]

The Joint Pastoral Plan (JPP) was elaborated in an extraordinary general assembly of the CNBB in 1965, still in Rome. Its main lines of action were structured in connection with the main documents of Vatican II:

> 1) Visible unity of the Catholic Church (*Lumen Gentium, Christus Dominus, Presbyterorum Ordinis, Optatam Totius, Perfectae Caritatis, Apostolicam Actuositatem*); 2) Missionary Action (*Lumen Gentium, Ad Gentes*); 3) Catechetical action, doctrinal deepening, theological reflection (*Dei Verbum*); 4) Liturgical Action (*Sacrosanctum Concilium*); 5) Ecumenical Action (*Unitatis Redintegratio*); 6) Action of the Church in the world (*Gaudium et Spes, Dignitatis Humanae, Nostra Aetate, Gravissimum Educationis, Inter* Mirifica).[104]

---

[102] Hosffman Ospino and Rafael Luciani, "Como a América Latina influenciou toda a Igreja Católica?" *CEBs do Brasil*, August 29, 2018, https://cebsdobrasil.com.br/como-a-america-latina-influenciou-toda-a-igreja-catolica-por-hosffman-ospino-e-rafael-luciani/.

[103] Conferência Nacional de Bispos do Brasil (CNBB), *Plano de Pastoral de Conjunto - 1966–1970* (Rio de Janeiro: CNBB, 1966). 2004 edition available at the PUC Minas portal, https://portal.pucminas.br/imagedb/documento/DOC_DSC_NOME_ARQUI20130906183626.pdf.

[104] Conferência Nacional (CNBB), *Plano de Pastoral*, 2.

These six emphases would inform the actions and structures of CNBB in the next three decades. In 1995, the CNBB Guidelines "began to be oriented according to the four "requirements" of evangelization: service, dialogue, proclamation, and communal testimony.[105] The plan responded to a deficiency of organic coordination in the Church's pastoral activity. Aware of the important transformations Latin America was undergoing, the motivation behind the JPP was to make the existing structures of the Church efficient and capable to respond to the drastic changes taking place in the continent. As the JPP stated,

> The Church exists, has solid and respectable secular structures: if it moves it is still widely followed; if it speaks, its voice is still widely heard. It must, therefore, manifest its vitality, and explore its great possibilities for action to the fullest, with a dynamic pastoral approach, suited to the pace of ongoing transformations. In this way, the Church will never find itself alienated and separated from the life of the society in which, by divine mandate, it is called to act. It must testify, with facts, that it was not only an integral part in the process of formation of each country in Latin America, but that today it also wants to be a ray of light and salvation in the process of current transformations.[106]

The plan attempted to balance its contrasting concerns with efficacy and unity, calling for an organic union among all participants in the Church's pastoral action—laity, religious orders, priests, bishops, and the episcopal conferences, including CELAM—whereas reaffirming the personal freedom and responsibility of each agent. The overall goal of the JPP was to "Create the means and conditions for the Church in Brazil to adapt, as quickly and fully as possible, to the image of the Church of Vatican II."[107] To promote the renewal of the Brazilian Church, two strategic steps were critical: (1) "the formulation applied to Brazil of the Church's action goals as made explicit in Vatican II;" and (2) raise awareness "of the situation of the Church in Brazil (its needs, demands and possibilities) in the light of the Council and the real data we have at the moment."[108]

---

105 Conferência Nacional (CNBB), *Plano de Pastoral*, 2.

106 Conferência Nacional (CNBB), *Plano de Pastoral*, 8.

107 Conferência Nacional (CNBB), *Plano de Pastoral*, 20.

108 Conferência Nacional (CNBB), *Plano de Pastoral*, 21.

Among the renewing proposals the JPP sought to advance was the decentralization of the parish.

> There is an urgent need for decentralization of the parish, not necessarily in the sense of creating new legal parishes, but of raising and dynamizing, within the parish territory, *base communities* (such as rural chapels) where Christians are not anonymous people who just seek a service or fulfill an obligation, but feel welcomed and responsible, and form an integral part of them, in communion of life with Christ and with all their brothers.[109]

The first *Comunidades Eclesiais de Base* (CEBs) emerged in Brazil in 1965. The JPP is one of the earliest official documents to mention them, even though in an embryonic manner. The CEBs are referred to when the document turns to the insufficiency of the parish and its traditional instruments for the Church's pastoral task, calling for its decentralization, the renewal of priestly ministry, and the need to reformulate the relation of the priests "with the bishop, other priests, lay people, non-Catholics, and non-Christians."[110] Thus the JPP seeks to rethink the Church's pastoral mission in light of the larger community, inserting the religious communities within an encompassing pastoral care on the diocesan, regional, and national levels to create "solid ecclesiological bases [. . .] vital for the action of the Church in Brazil."[111]

This joint pastoral care is bidirectional. First, it invites fuller participation of lay Christians into the pastoral care the Church provides to the entire community—which includes both non-Catholics and non-Christians. Second, it expands the Church's presence in the world, since it is manifested not only through its hierarchy or professional priests, but in its entirety, as the people of God—in the spirit of the Council. The Church becomes, thus, servant and welcoming of all, "assuming the values and the rhythms of their history and purifying and elevating them."[112]

While the Church intends to be present in different areas of concrete human existence, that presence does not resemble the

---

109 Conferência Nacional (CNBB), *Plano de Pastoral*, 29. Italics are mine.

110 Conferência Nacional (CNBB), *Plano de Pastoral*, 30.

111 Conferência Nacional (CNBB), *Plano de Pastoral*, 31.

112 Conferência Nacional (CNBB), *Plano de Pastoral*, 31.

early Catholic action model that focused on the Christianization of society, when the Church placed itself in a position of superiority, with little to learn from its immersion in the world. Now, the idea of presence in the world resembled the image of a witness. As the JPP shows, there is greater awareness on the part of the Church that the human community has assumed "its responsibilities more adultly, and the Church, preserving certain tasks of civilization, progressively takes on the role of witness, animation and leavening."[113]

The base communities emerged in that context of pastoral integration involving the entire Church and local communities made "visible through the presence of a cooperator of the bishop."[114] The use of the expression "base communities" at this point still referred basically to the various local communities that composed each parish. The JPP calls for the "creation or dynamization of these base communities," which "must develop, as far as possible, the six fundamental lines of action of the Church. Each parish should gradually "become one of these communities and the parish priest will preside over all that are in the portion of the flock entrusted to him." In accordance with this proposed model "all members of the people of God, responsible for the presence of the Church in a given area; and, in particular, the priests, as the bishop's collaborators, assume co-responsibly global and common tasks," being responsible "for their insertion into the diocesan community."[115] This coordinated pastoral work included a call for intentional mobilization of lay leadership through the formation of "teams of Catholic Action movements and lay activists [. . .] in base communities, who are better equipped to give missionary witness in temporal engagements."[116]

The JPP is a singular example of the mutual influence of local and global forces of change in the Church, including collaboration among bishops, priests, and lay pastoral agents. The document acknowledges that bilateral dynamics, highlighting, on one hand, how the Emergency Plan of 1962 "prepared the Church in Brazil for the application of conciliar decisions," and, on the other hand, how the Vatican II

[113] Conferência Nacional (CNBB), *Plano de Pastoral*, 32.

[114] Conferência Nacional (CNBB), *Plano de Pastoral*, 41.

[115] Conferência Nacional (CNBB), *Plano de Pastoral*, 41.

[116] Conferência Nacional (CNBB), *Plano de Pastoral*, 47.

"created the climate, means and conditions for the pastoral action undertaken by the Emergency Plan."[117]

As José Oscar Beozzo underscores, Pope John XXIII asked CELAM in 1958 to come up with a joint pastoral plan for the entire region.[118] In the absence of practical responses, he repeated the appeal in 1961, asking the diverse Latin American local churches to mobilize resources for a national pastoral plan. In response to this second appeal CNBB came up with the emergency plan in 1962.[119] While the dynamism of Dom Hélder and the preparatory articulation of CNBB—including during the Council, as the Brazilian bishops were hosted together at the *Domus Mariae*, the headquarters of the Italian Catholic Action—contributed to the prompt response on the part of the Brazilian Conference of Bishops to the Vatican II, this was only one aspect of the reception of Vatican II in Latin America. In addition to the coordination of similar responses in other Latin American countries, CELAM would organize its second conference in Medellin (1968), reaffirming the novelty of the CEBs as a revolutionary expression of the Church. Due to its widespread impact in the region, the Medellin gathering is considered the cradle of Latin American liberation theology (LALT).

117 Conferência Nacional (CNBB), *Plano de Pastoral*, 33.

118 Beozzo, "A Recepção do Vaticano II na Igreja do Brasil," 5. See also Pope John XXIII, "Discorso del Santo Padre Giovanni XXIII al Cardinali, Arcivescovi e Vescovi Partecipanti ala III Riunione del 'Consiglio Episcopale Latino-Americano," https://www.vatican.va/content/john-xxiii/it/speeches/1958/documents/hf_j-xxiii_spe_19581115_america-latina.pdf.

119 Beozzo, "A Recepção do Vaticano II na Igreja do Brasil," 6.

8

CEBs, MEDELLIN, AND THE DAWN OF LIBERATION THEOLOGY

The "Faithful, Creative, and Selective Reception" of Vatican II in Latin America

Whereas the Joint Pastoral Program was one of the most structured initiatives aiming at the practical implementation of the Vatican II reforms on the national level in Latin America,[1] other responses to the Council were formulated in the region.[2] The most significant of those came from CELAM itself. Still in Rome, prior to the closing session of Vatican II, CELAM started planning its second assembly, securing the pope's blessing to gather to discuss the reception of the Council in Latin America. The Second Episcopal Conference of Latin America (CELAM II) happened in Medellin, Colombia, in 1968, three years after the end of the Council. Sixteen committees and subcommittees were created to address specific emphases and themes stemming from each of the Vatican II documents.

The concerted efforts toward a Latin American interpretation and implementation of the Council's documents—prioritizing areas of specific significance for Latin American Christians—emphasized the Council's "insertion into the currents of the modern world, its

---

[1] I borrow the phrase in this chapter heading from historian José Oscar Beozzo.

[2] For contributions and responses to the Council from Argentina, Chile, Paraguay, Peru, Colombia, Venezuela, Mexico, Central America, and the Caribbean, see José Oscar Beozzo, ed., *Cristianismo y Iglesias de América Latina en Vésperas del Vaticano II* (San José, Costa Rica, DEI, 1992). On this topic, it is worth noting the cautionary words of Carlos Schickendantz, who brings attention to the limits of any uniform understanding of such reception, considering the Latin American and Caribbean people's diversity and differences, and the length of the region's territories. While acknowledging such plurality and complexity, it is possible to identify certain common emphases. Without ignoring its plurality, this chapter highlights the more concerted efforts organized by CELAM. See Carlos Schickendantz, "A Recepção do Vaticano II na América Latina e no Caribe: um panorama de alguns pontos relevantes," *in Concílio Vaticano II: experiencias e contextos*, ed. Rodrigo Coppe Caldeira (São Paulo: Paulus Editora, 2022), 71–102 (71), Kindle.

articulation with the ecumenical movement, its progressive de-westernization and its embodiment in the social, ethnic and cultural diversity of the different areas of the world."[3] While this chapter focuses on the movement unleashed by the interpreted embodiment of the Council in Latin America, it does not ignore the forces that have conspired against this particular "legacy of the Council, in a veiled or open way, and how many of its potentialities still remain as unfulfilled promises."[4]

To properly understand the impact of the Medellin conference in the region, it is important to take notice that Vatican II was only one of the sources and references for CELAM's reflections. Since its inception, CELAM had the religious, socioeconomic, political, and cultural situation of Latin America at the forefront of its concerns. Accordingly, the question to be asked of Vatican II was: what does the Council mean for the Latin American situation? Taking inspiration in *Gaudium et Spes*, Beozzo describes the roots of CELAM II as follows:

> The 2nd General Conference of the Latin American Episcopate, opened by Paul VI, in Bogotá, on August 24, 1968 and held in Medellin, from August 26 to September 6 of the same year, finds its roots and inspiration, on the one hand, in *the cries and hopes of the Latin American and Caribbean people* and, on the other, in the Second Vatican Council (1962–1965), and in the processes and dreams it triggered in the life of the church.[5]

In many ways, CELAM II expanded the pastoral approach that was characteristic of Vatican II, interpreting it through the lens of pastoral practices shaped in the region. The Church of the Poor group and the Third World project, which people like Câmara represented at Vatican II,[6] were key for such a reception.

CELAM II arose also from the awareness that some fundamental issues for the continent were not included in the conciliar agenda. Despite the inspiring preamble of *Gaudium et Spes*, "the underdeveloped countries of Latin America, Africa and Asia did not feel

[3] José Oscar Beozzo, "Introdución," in *Cristianismo y Iglesias de América Latina en Vésperas del Vaticano II*, 16.

[4] Beozzo, "Introdución," 16.

[5] Beozzo, "Medellín: inspiração e raízes."

[6] Terrazas, *Protagonistas del Vaticano II*, 380.

that their problems were understood and, finally, taken on by the already overloaded conciliar agenda."[7] As mentioned earlier, Paul VI promised to address those cries and concerns in his 1967 encyclical *Populorum Progression*. That encyclical became an important source for the Medellin conference as well.[8]

Although authorized to move forward with the plans for its second general conference, the leadership of CELAM had to diffuse tensions experienced with the Vatican to move ahead with its plans for the conference. While negotiations continued with the Vatican to resolve the regulations of the conference and its shared responsibilities, CELAM scheduled seven smaller gatherings between 1966 and 1968, which were used to start conversations on topics such as education, lay apostolate and social action, Latin American development and integration, the presence of the Church in the reality of the Latin American universities, and the social pastoral work of the Church. Those smaller gatherings helped in the preparation of some of the documents that would inform the Medellin conference.[9]

Methodologically, Medellin followed the see-judge-act method. Inspired by a theology of the signs of time, the conference took "the attentive study of the economic, political, social and ecclesiastical reality of Latin America and the Caribbean" as its starting point, "identifying the questions that emerged from that reality and analyzing them in the light of the word of God, Vatican II and the magisterium and experience of the entire church," to then move to the third step; that is, proposing "paths for pastoral action, aiming to transform, towards the kingdom of God and the liberation of the poor, the reality crossed by structures of sin and the cries and hopes of the little ones."[10] The collective work of the various committees and subcommittees formed in connection with Medellin contributed to complement previously collected information. With all these local and regional structures in place, the Medellin conference "became a unique example of collegial

7 Beozzo, "Medellín: inspiração e raízes."

8 Beozzo, "Medellín: inspiração e raízes."

9 Beozzo, "Medellín: inspiração e raízes."

10 Beozzo, "Medellín: inspiração e raízes." As Beozzo highlights, the preparatory gatherings, along with the Center for Religious Statistics and Social Research (Centro de Estatística Religiosa e Investigações Sociais, CERIS) created by CNBB, provided the analysis of the surrounding reality, interpreting the "signs of the times" ahead of the conference.

reception of the Council by the churches of Latin America and the Caribbean." Such a reception, as Beozzo underscores, was faithful, selective, and creative.[11] As for its faithfulness, Beozzo highlights Medellin's pastoral character inspired by the example of Pope John XXIII and the raffirmation of the centrality of episcopal collegiality, also important in the Council.[12] As for its creativity, he underscores that the Council was neither the starting point nor the point of arrival for the Medellin conference. Due to its emphasis on the constant interpellation of the reality of the poor, the oppressed, the victims of systemic injustice, the Medellin Conference became distinctively Latin American, recentering the agenda many bishops from the Global South felt Vatican II had sidelined. Seeking to interpret that reality in the light of the word of God, Medellin 1968 culminated with the affirmation of a necessary pastoral action.[13]

For many Latin Americans, Pope John XXIII's pre-Vatican II radiophonic speech of the "Church of the poor" offered great hope for meaningful change in a self-centered Church hierarchy. That hope, however, turned into frustration when they felt that the words of the Pope were largely ignored in the actual work of the Council. The Church of the Poor group was a significant and yet marginal initiative, which only engaged a small number of bishops. As Belgian-Brazilian historian Eduardo Hoornaert shows, the group stemmed from a meeting initiated by French priest Paul Gauthier and the Carmelite nun Marie-Thérèse Lescase, both actively involved in the fellowship of Companions of Jesus the Carpenter in Nazareth, Palestine. Accompanying Melkite bishop Georges Hakim to the Council in Rome, they started organizing meetings in the apartment Gauthier rented, which then began to attract some bishops, including Dom Hélder.[14] Although the focus on the poor continued to resurface

[11] Beozzo, "Medellín: inspiração e raízes."

[12] Beozzo underscores the extension of that collegiality, which included not only bishops but also experts (mostly theologians), priests, members of religious orders (men and women), lay men and women, as well as non-Catholic observers, "all actively participating in the elaboration of the texts." See Beozzo, "Medellín: inspiração e raízes."

[13] Beozzo, "Medellín: inspiração e raízes."

[14] Eduardo Hoornaert, "Medellín: 1968 não caiu do céu," *Espaços - Revista de Teologia e Cultura* 26/1(2019):5–21(9). https://espacos.itespteologia.com.br/espacos/article/view/35.

throughout the Council, it never became a central priority. Medellin aimed at correcting that problem, making both the Latin American reality and the poor central to its deliberations.

Beozzo draws attention to the selectivity of Medellin's reception of the Vatican II documents by pointing to the neglect of documents such as the *Christus Dominus* decree, which dealt with the office of pastoral care of the bishops, *Ad Gentes*, which focused on the missionary activity of the Church, and *Unitatis Redintegratio*, which addressed the Catholic principles regarding ecumenism.[15] Medellin did not produce a formal document on ecumenism. Despite that, it sparked a renewed ecumenical vigor among Latin American Christians. CELAM II counted with eleven non-Catholic Christian observers in attendance, among them Methodist theologian José Miguez Bonino. While Medellin's pronounced silence on *Unitatis Redintegratio* cannot be ignored, it must be considered in light of the pastoral urgency that dominated the conference at a time when the repositioning of the Church in relation to the grim socioeconomic and political realities in the continent became its most urgent priority. Regardless of that silence, much of the reception of Medellin in Latin America would be ecumenical in nature.[16]

Medellin took place in 1968, a year of profound social unrest not only in Latin America but around the world. The opening message of the conference not only addressed Christians but all Latin American peoples. In that message, the bishops acknowledged the unique cultural and social conditions in which those peoples existed and committed to stand with them and participate in the search for solutions to their multiple problems.

> Latin America seems to still live under the tragic sign of underdevelopment, which not only separates our brothers [sic] from the enjoyment of material goods, but from their own human fulfillment. Despite the efforts made, hunger and misery, illnesses and marginality, deep inequalities in income and tensions between social classes, outbreaks of violence and little participation of the people in the management of the common good are combined [. . .] As Pastors, with a common responsibility, we want to commit

15 Beozzo, "Medellín: inspiração e raízes."

16 Barreto, "Vatican II, Medellin, and Ecumenism."

> ourselves to the lives of all our people in the anxious search for adequate solutions to their multiple problems. Our mission is to contribute to the integral promotion of man [sic] and the communities of the continent.[17]

CELAM II's message to the Latin American peoples positioned the Church as a participant in the Latin American struggles, acknowledging, though, its limits and contradictions, since it has paradoxically participated "with our peoples" in "the process of colonization, liberation, and organization." Therefore, the Church does not present itself as competing with other national, Latin American, or international organisms, neither does it "reject what we do not know." The message reaffirmed the value of the Church's societal participation in the pervasive purpose of encouraging efforts, accelerating achievements, deepening their content, and penetrating "the entire process of change with evangelical values."[18]

Liberation and human flourishing were identified as the aspiration of the people.[19] Seeking to discern the signs of time, the Catholic bishops acknowledged the Latin American peoples' vocation for liberation and their determination to reach it "at the cost of any sacrifice." Such a vocation for liberation is not an end in itself but aims at an openness to unite with others in the world in an exchange of solidarity.[20] Thus, the Medellin message expressed a broader dialogical aspiration, similar to that of the Third World movement, especially with other peoples experiencing similar pain: "In particular, we consider the dialogue with sibling peoples from other continents who find themselves in situations similar to ours to be decisive in this task. United on the paths of difficulties and hopes, we can make our presence in the world definitive for peace."[21]

---

17 CELAM, "Mensaje a los Pueblos de América Latina," in *Documentos Finales de Medellín*, 6th ed., II Conferencia General del Episcopado Latinoamericano (Buenos Aires: Ediciones Paulinas, 1986), 8–9.

18 CELAM, "Mensaje a los Pueblos de América Latina," 9.

19 CELAM, "Mensaje a los Pueblos de América Latina," 10.

20 CELAM, "Mensaje a los Pueblos de América Latina," 14.

21 CELAM, "Mensaje a los Pueblos de América Latina," 14

Justice, Peace, and the Poverty of the Church in the Medellin Documents

Following the Vatican II pattern, the Medellin deliberations resulted in sixteen documents. The themes of those documents, though, do not necessarily reflect all Vatican II documents, despite being clearly produced in dialogue with the Council. The sixteen Medellin documents are the following: Justice, Peace, Family and Demography, Education, Youth, Popular Pastoral, the Pastoral of the Elites, Catechesis, Liturgy, Lay Movements, Priests, Religious Orders, Training of the Clergy, the Poverty of the Church, Joint Pastoral (pastoral en conjunto), and the Means of Social Communication. Whereas discussing each of these documents is beyond the scope of this book, in this section, it is worth highlighting three emphases present in those documents of particular significance for the topic of this book.

Justice

It should not surprise anyone that the first document among the sixteen produced in Medellin focused on justice. In a certain way, Medellin represented a moment of conversion of the Latin American Church to the Latin American peoples. As such, the bishops meeting in Medellin issued a *mea culpa*, acknowledging their distance from the common people in the past, and even the contradiction of the Church's participation in their suffering, then using the opportunity to turn their faces to them, "conscious that 'to know God, it is necessary to know man [sic].'"[22] Such a turn to the common people could not take place only through words or reflection. Instead, "It is necessary to act."[23] Thus the documents were divided into three areas of pastoral demands, connected with a process meant to change the situation of the continent: (1) the demand to promote the values of justice, peace, education, and family; (2) the need for an adapted evangelization and maturation in the faith of the people and their elites through catechesis and liturgy; and (3) the intensification of the Church's unity and pastoral action through visible structures, also adapted to the new conditions of the continent.[24]

[22] CELAM, *Documentos Finales de Medellín*, 16.

[23] CELAM, *Documentos Finales de Medellín*, 17.

[24] CELAM, *Documentos Finales de Medellín*, 20.

Justice was considered critical to the flourishing of humanity. The roots of the injustice that has impacted millions in the region was identified with a lack of solidarity, which leads to the crystallization of unjust structures. The message the bishops gathered in Medellin wanted to proclaim in response to such an injustice was the imperative of conversion from that lack of solidarity. Such a conversion, understood as a turn to God's reign of justice, love, and peace, demanded immediate change in those unjust structures.[25] Such a view discouraged any dualism between temporal and spiritual tasks. Love of Christ and neighbor must go together, functioning as "the great force of social justice, understood as a conception of life and as a drive towards the integral development of our people."[26]

In such a context, the pastoral mission of the Church was interpreted as offering inspiration and education to help believers understand the personal and social responsibilities of the faith. This orientation for social change implied the participation of the Church in the mobilization of several sectors of society—family, students, workers, rural workers, and others both nationally and internationally.[27] Furthermore, it saw the work for justice in Latin America as aiming to political reform, since the diagnostics stemming from that analysis of the social reality in anticipation of Medellin underscored the concentration of power and wealth in the hands of a few and the lack of popular participation in decision-making. Political reform was needed to "secure efficaciously and permanently through juridical norms, the inalienable rights and freedoms of all citizens and the free functioning of the intermediate structures," and to strengthen the mechanisms of political participation.[28] Another goal of the Church's political action was the formation of social consciousness and the strengthening of social structures.

On the practical level, Medellin recommended the creation of Commissions of Justice and Peace by the Episcopal Conferences in all Latin American countries. Through the work of those commissions, the Medellin final document stated, "The Church, the People of God, will provide help to those who are devoid of any type of

[25] CELAM, *Documentos Finales de Medellín*, 27.

[26] CELAM, *Documentos Finales de Medellín*, 29.

[27] CELAM, *Documentos Finales de Medellín*, 34.

[28] CELAM, *Documentos Finales de Medellín*, 35.

social means, so that they know their own rights and know how to make use of them."[29] Each Commission of Justice and Peace had the freedom to coordinate on the national level with other organisms of the civil society broader services of solidarity and advocacy. These national Justice and Peace Commissions, which continue to exist, occasionally meet, support each other, exchange information, and work together on issues of common concern.

During the peak of the COVID-19 pandemic, for instance, in response to the science denial of the Jair Bolsonaro administration, which contributed to more than 700,000 deaths, the Brazilian Commission for Justice and Peace (CBJP) played an active role forming a coalition with the National Council of Christian Churches in Brazil (CONIC), the Ecumenical Service Coordination (CESE), Fundação Luterana de Diaconia (FLD), the Ecumenical Forum ACT-BRASIL, Instituto Humanitas Unisinos (IHU), the Social Pastorals of the CNBB, and other networks such as #RespiraBrasil, Institute of Religious Studies (ISER), Processo de Articulação e Diálogo (PAD), Conferência dos Religiosos do Brasil (CRB) and Rede Eclesial Pan-Amazônica (REPAM Brasil) to cosponsor a major international seminar titled "The Brazilian Tragedy: A Risk for the Common Home." Having as its declared goal "to analyze the current scenario of collapse in health systems and disregard for health policies referenced by science," the seminar invited domestic and international partners, including the Vatican, the United Nations, and the World Council of Churches (WCC), to explore the risks "the present situation may represent (or not) for the planet as a whole—our Common Home," and look for coordinated responses to the crisis.[30] Likewise, the Commission of Justice and Peace, along with the Brazilian Bar Association, the Commission for the Defense of Human Rights Dom Paulo Evaristo Arns, the Brazilian Academy of Sciences, the Brazilian Press Association, and the Brazilian Society for the Progress of Science worked with bereaved families to debunk

---

[29] CELAM, *Documentos Finales de Medellín*, 37.

[30] Conselho Nacional de Igrejas Cristas do Brasil (CONIC), "Seminário Internacional: Tragédia Brasileira: Risco Para a Casa Comum?," May 4–6, 2021, https://conic.org.br/portal/conic/noticias/resumo-seminario-internacional-tragedia-brasileira-risco-para-a-casa-comum. For full disclosure, I facilitated one of the panels of that seminar, which included speakers representing Brazilian Indigenous communities, Quilombola communities, and the Vatican.

misinformation campaigns disseminated during the pandemic. Along with other civil society organizations, the Commission on Justice and Peace of the CNBB lobbied the National Congress to investigate the public management of the pandemic crisis. Furthermore, those organizations vigorously launched a campaign, which, considering the expansion of the pandemic and its consequences, demanded that the conduction of public affairs be "guided by the most absolute transparency, supported by the best science and conditioned by the fundamental principles of human dignity and the protection of life."[31]

This is just one among many examples that could be possibly mentioned of the vast work that the several Commissions on Justice and Peace spread throughout Latin America have been doing for over five decades. Their work attests to the lasting impact Medellin has on the continent and to how these commissions have become deeply ingrained in the fabric of the civil society.[32]

Peace

Describing persisting conditions of injustice as sin, Medellin examined structural violence in the region, which constituted an obstacle for true peace. Among the structural causes of violence, Medellin named all forms of marginality (socioeconomic, political, cultural, racial, and religious in urban and rural settings), excessive class inequality, growing frustrations due to the postponed satisfaction of legitimate aspirations of those in situation of disadvantage, oppression from dominant sectors that label all intent to change a system that favors the permanence of its privileges subversive action, and the unjust exercise of power.[33]

---

[31] Conferência Nacional de Bispos do Brasil (CNBB), "Pacto pela Vida e pelo Brasil," April 7, 2020, https://www.cnbb.org.br/pacto-pela-vida-e-pelo-brasil-01/.

[32] In some cases, Interecclesial Commissions on Justice and Peace have emerged, as in the case of Colombia, where for more than twenty-nine years an Interecclesial Commission on Peace and Justice "has promoted, defended and supported the demand and affirmation of the economic, social, cultural, environmental, psychological, gender, civil and political rights of people and rural and urban organizational processes before State and private actors." See Comision Intereclesial de Justicia y Paz, "Comisión Intereclesial de Justicia y Paz," https://www.justiciaypazcolombia.com/quienes-somos/.

[33] CELAM, *Documentos Finales de Medellín*, 42–43.

In addition to that, Medellin also addressed tensions generated by extreme neocolonialism. That form of oppression directly contributes to the economic impoverishment of Latin America, which is treated as merely a producer of raw materials whose value is made inferior to that of manufactured products that they need to purchase from those same countries that exploit their natural resources. That distortion generates a flight of economic and human resources, reinforcing the empire of capital. The document also denounces all sorts of ideological imperialism which seek to control Latin American societies through direct or indirect interventions.[34]

According to Medellin, the theological response Christianity can offer to this state of injustice and structural violence is peace, which is "the work of justice."[35] There cannot be real peace without justice. True peace presupposes and demands the instauration of a just order, in which human beings are not objectified. They become, instead, "the agents of their own history."[36] The persistence of unjust inequalities is, therefore, not only sinful but also an attack on peace.

Echoing the words of Martin Luther King Jr.,[37] the Medellin document states, "Peace in Latin America is not, therefore, the simple absence of violence and blood shedding. The oppression exerted by the powerful can give the impression that it keeps peace and order; however, in reality, it is nothing but 'the continuous and inevitable germ of rebellions and wars.'"[38] Finally, peace is also a fruit of love, an expression of real human fellowship.[39] In light of persistent injustice and violence, Medellin reaffirmed its Christian

---

34 CELAM, *Documentos Finales de Medellín*, 45–46.

35 CELAM, *Documentos Finales de Medellín*, 47.

36 CELAM, *Documentos Finales de Medellín*, 47.

37 "True peace is not merely the absence of tension; it is the presence of justice. The tension we see in Montgomery today is the necessary tension that comes when the oppressed rise up and start to move forward toward a permanent, positive peace." Martin Luther King Jr., *Stride Towards Freedom: The Montgomery Story* (New York: Harper and Row Publishers, 1958), 40. Slightly differently from King, Medellin talked about permanent peace not as an achievement but as a continuous construction. For the Medellin document, "peace is a permanent task," it is continuously constructed. Therefore, the Christian is described as an "artisan of peace." CELAM, *Documentos Finales de Medellín*, 48–49.

38 CELAM, *Documentos Finales de Medellín*, 48.

39 CELAM, *Documentos Finales de Medellín*, 49.

commitment to the creation of a more just order by raising awareness about the need for a life guided by justice and denouncing persisting systemic injustices.

The Poverty of the Church

A third and final emphasis that deserves attention in the Medellin conference is its fourteenth document, which is titled "The Poverty of the Church." From the perspective of what happened in the wake of CELAM II with the birth of a full-fledged liberation theology, this is probably the most cited document that came out of Medellin. The document expands the concept of the "Church of the poor" discussed at Vatican II. The preamble of the document makes a clear statement, which resembles the Pact of the Catacombs:

> The Latin American Episcopate cannot remain indifferent to the tremendous social injustices that exist in Latin America, which keep most of our people in painful poverty, close in many cases to inhumane misery.[40]

The words of Paul VI to rural workers in Mosquera, Colombia, prior to his opening of CELAM II, are cited in the document: "We are now listening in silence; however, we hear the cry that comes from your suffering."[41]

Document fourteen discusses three types of poverty: a) poverty as a voluntary commitment for the sake of love; b) spiritual poverty, which is a state of openness to God and the disposition of those who wait in God; and c) poverty as lack of goods and means to live with dignity in this world. In contrast to the first two types, the third kind of poverty is contrary to the will of God, the fruit of injustice and sin.[42] This is the context in which the Latin American Church is called to be a Church of the poor. As such, the Church must do the following: a) denounce the unjust lack of means to live in the world by so many and the causes of mass poverty; b) preach and live in

---

[40] CELAM, *Documentos Finales de Medellín*, 185.

[41] Pope Paul VI, "Discurso a los Campesinos em Mosquera, Colombia, on August 23, 1968," as cited in CELAM, *Documentos Finales de Medellín*, 185.

[42] Pope Paul VI, "Discurso a los Campesinos, 187.

spiritual poverty; that is, humbly and open to God; and c) commit to live in poverty, as close as possible to the dispossessed.[43]

The document also calls all Christians to live in evangelical poverty as "a sign of the inestimable value of the poor in God's eyes; a commitment to those who suffer."[44] Furthermore, given the situation of poverty and underdevelopment in the continent, the Latin American Church "experiences the urgency to translate this spirit of poverty into gestures, attitudes, and norms that make it a more lucid and authentic sign of its Lord." That sign must clearly translate into acts of justice, testimony, commitment, and efforts to fulfill its salvific mission.[45]

Although the phrase "preferential option for the poor" would only be adopted years later, the word "preference" appears as the title of a section of the document focusing on the solidarity with the poor.[46] Among other things, this preferential solidarity is expressed in two paragraphs. Paragraph ten explains what it means as follows: "We must sharpen our awareness of the duty of solidarity with the poor, to which charity leads us. This solidarity means making their problems and struggles our own, knowing how to speak for them." Then, paragraph eleven makes a commitment to support those in the Church who are already closer to the poor, who are often attacked and depicted as communists for doing so: "We express our desire to always be very close to those who work in the selfless apostolate with the poor, so that they feel our encouragement and know that we will not listen to voices interested in disfiguring their work."[47]

To follow through on that call for a preferential solidarity with the poor, Medellin points to the way the Church must structure its work in the region:

> Human promotion must be the line of our action in favor of the poor, so that we respect their personal dignity and teach them to help themselves. To this end, we recognize the need for the rational

[43] Pope Paul VI, "Discurso a los Campesinos, 187–188.

[44] Pope Paul VI, "Discurso a los Campesinos, 189.

[45] Pope Paul VI, "Discurso a los Campesinos, 188.

[46] Pope Paul VI, "Discurso a los Campesinos, 189.

[47] Pope Paul VI, "Discurso a los Campesinos," 190.

> structuring of our pastoral work and the integration of our efforts with those of other entities.[48]

To some extent, this line of action was already being implemented through the Joint Pastoral Plan in Brazil. In fact, the title of the fifteenth document coming out of Medellin was "pastoral *de conjunto*," or joint pastoral work. That document lays out the need to integrate the pastoral action of the Church on the national and the continental levels, referring to the *comunidades cristianas de base* as one of the aspects of renewal of the pastoral structures of the Church.[49]

The still incipient CEBs were already becoming one of the most dynamic innovations of Latin American Christianity. They were not a clergy's invention but a concrete sign of the irruption of the poor. As I will discuss the CEBs' origins later, it suffices for now to say that they already existed at the time CELAM met in Medellin. The significance of Medellin, though, is that not only did it acknowledge their existence, but it also affirmed those communities as significant for the pastoral renewal of the Church at a very early stage. As in the case with CNBB, the description of the base communities that one finds in the Medellin documents is embryonic. Yet, it is significant to note that Medellin presented the CEBs as a sign of renewal for the Latin American Church. As Medellin's Joint Pastoral document states, "The base Christian community is, then, the first and fundamental ecclesial nucleus, which must, on its proper level, be responsible for the wealth and expansion of the faith, as well as for the worship, which is its expression."[50] After exhorting both priests and bishops to work together in the formation of leaders for those communities, the conference recommended serious theological, sociological, and historical study of the CEBs in the region.

The central theme of Medellin was "The Church in the Current Transformation of Latin America, in the light of the Second Vatican Council." In his opening message, Brazilian cardinal Avelar Brandão Vilela, who replaced Larraín as president of CELAM, reminded the participants of the urgency of the task at hand, describing Latin

48 Pope Paul VI, "Discurso a los Campesinos," 190.

49 Pope Paul VI, "Discurso a los Campesinos," 199. In Latin America, the Base Christian communities are alternatively known as *comunidades eclesiales de base* (CEBs) or, simply, *comunidades de base*.

50 Pope Paul VI, "Discurso a los Campesinos," 199.

America as a continent in which change was transpiring at an accelerated pace. The anxieties of the Latin American people had become the yearnings of their pastors. The Church was, therefore, undergoing a moment of "total reflection," a new stage of "renovation, dialogue, and theological reflection."[51]

In response to such a dynamic context, the conference elected a liberating education as the key to effect actual liberation for all peoples facing all sorts of slavery, elevating them from dehumanizing social conditions to more humane situations. That kind of education should occur on all levels, taking on creative forms, thus anticipating "the new kind of society that we seek in Latin America."[52] The CEBs played a renewing role in such a context, not simply as pastoral and educative communities of renewal but also as eschatological anticipations of the sort of communitarian, self-determined and dialogical spaces of the society Christians should hope to build. Thus, from the perspective of the popular Church (the Church of poor), "Medellín is the founding event of the Latin American and Caribbean Church."[53] It is the birthplace of a Church conceived on Latin American terms. As Marcos Sassatelli aptly demonstrates, Medellin validates the CEBs not as simply another movement, such as the Church often thought of youth, students, workers, and others, but as "the Church at the base and, at the same time, the base of the Church."[54]

Comunidades de Base and the Rebirth of the Church in Latin America

Medellin 1968 was a turning point in the history of Latin American Christianity. It offered the earliest continental interpretation of the Vatican II and a starting point for a new understanding of Christian witness in the region. Employing the inductive see-judge-act method,

---

[51] Avelar Brandão Vilela, "Disccurso de Abertura," in *A Igreja na Atual Transformação da América Latina à Luz do Mundo: Conclusões de Medellín*, ed. Conselho Episcopal Latino-Americano (CELAM) (Petrópolis, Brazil: Vozes, 1985), 30–31.

[52] Conselho Episcopal Latino-Americano (CELAM), *A Igreja na Atual Transformação da América Latina à Luz do Mundo: Conclusões de Medellín*, 74.

[53] Marcos Sassatelli, "Medellin: As CEBs e seu lugar na estrutura eclesial," *CEBs do Brasil*, https://cebsdobrasil.com.br/medellin-as-cebs-e-seu-lugar-na-estrutura-eclesial-fr-marcos-sassatelli/.

[54] Sassatelli, "Medellin: As CEBs e seu lugar na estrutura eclesial."

Medellin provided an attentive and creative response to changes rapidly taking place in Latin American societies. In its response to the cry of the oppressed, Medellin assessed the situation of injustice in the continent with the aid of sociological and theological tools.[55] The result of its theological reflection was a deliberate move toward a more radical solidarity with the poor, as priests, theologians, and some bishops joined in the struggle for the transformation of the dehumanizing conditions in which they lived.[56]

Furthermore, Medellin woke to the reality that the poor made up most of the Catholic Church in the region and to the need of treating them as historical subjects. Therefore, while it did not initiate the significant transformations taking place in Latin America during that period, Medellin represented the first concerted effort on the part of the Latin American Church to respond to that effervescent social, political, and cultural situation pastorally and theologically. Among the important contributions Medellin offered to an already changing Latin American Church, it reaffirmed the theological concept of the people of God discussed in Vatican II, giving it a more concrete form. In Medellin, amid the turn toward the assertion of an unequivocally Latin American identity of the Church, the idea of the people of God was associated with the Church of the poor, the popular Church, and a popular pastoral action.

One of the novelties of the Medellin Conference was its acknowledgment of the CEBs as a new expression of the Church as the people of God. Leonardo Boff calls that phenomenon a "new ecclesiological experience," a "renaissance" of the Church, and "an action of the Spirit on the horizon of the matters urgent for our time."[57] For him,

---

[55] For more on the theology of CELAM II, see Mario de França Miranda, "A Teologia de Medellín," in *Medellín: Memoria, Profetismo e Esperança na América Latina*, ed. Ney de Souza & Emerson Sbardelotti (Petrópolis, Brazil: Editora Vozes, 2018), 41–52.

[56] As Agenor Brighent points out, Medellin embraced the poor and their social location, denouncing institutional injustice and social sin. It set the tone for the promotion of social justice and for the rise of liberation theology. Yet, its documents did not go as far as developing such a theology. Medellin functioned as a Moses figure, pointing the way from the top of the mountain, and, yet, not entering the promised land. See Agenor Brighenti, "A Justiça em Medellín e as Categorias da Tradição Eclesial Libertadora," in *Medellín: Memoria, Profetismo e Esperança na América Latina*, 151–166 (156).

[57] Boff, *Ecclesiogenesis*, 1.

the renewal the CEBs brought about was not as smoothly accepted as one might think when one reads the Medellin documents. In fact, he notes, the rise of the base communities resulted from a crisis of the institutional Church. In Boff's own words, "We are not dealing with the expansion of an existing ecclesiastical system, rotating on a sacramental, clerical axis, but with the emergence of another form of being church, rotating on the axis of the word and the laity."[58]

Elsewhere, Boff contrasts this new Church model that is born of the faith of the poor with other Church templates from the past such as the encompassing model of the "Church as the city of God," which was essentially clerical, "the colonial model of the Church" as mother and master (an alliance between Church and state through the patronage system) and the "Church as a salvific sacrament," which, for him, was the model advanced in the Vatican II, with its openness to relate to other sectors of society committed to the transformation of the world. The limits of this last model, Boff argues, is its accommodation to the status quo since it approaches the poor from the optic of the wealthy. As such, while it calls the rich to help the cause of the poor, that call does not demand any change in the social status or bourgeois practices of the wealthy.[59]

Therefore, the image that Boff uses, "the birthing of the church,"[60] expresses the joy and the pain involved in the birth of something new. The base communities, according to him, emerged not as something apart from the Church but as an expression of it. As the Medellin documents state, they are the first and most fundamental level of the Church. The new challenges that the CEBs posed to the hierarchy of the Church and to the social status quo provoked some resistance among many in positions of power. At the same time, the CEBs contributed to expand the presence of the Church in the world in ways not previously anticipated.

Filling a gap left by the scarcity of priests in Latin America and by the limits of Catholic Action, the CEBs became the face of the Church among the hundreds of thousands impacted by the process of rural migration to rapid-growing urban centers, functioning

[58] Boff, *Ecclesiogenesis*, 2.

[59] Leonardo Boff, *Igreja, Carisma e Poder: Ensaios de Eclesiologia Militante*, 2nd ed. (Lisboa, Portugal: Editorial Inquerito, 1991), 22.

[60] Boff, *Ecclesiogenesis*, 2.

as a new pastoral model to aggregate rural migrants into new communal urban structures.[61] Although initially dependent on the clergy, these communities began to grow more autonomous. Their growth and pastoral effectivity during the urban boom in the region won the sympathy of some bishops who saw them as a new and effective pastoral model furthering the see-judge-act method previously used in Catholic action.[62] In Brazil, and later elsewhere, as the military repressed left-wing movements and other popular organizations, the CEBs became a haven for those involved in different popular movements and a relatively safe space for political mobilization.

Although first and foremost religious communities, as the CEBs began to ask vital questions about the subsistence of impoverished multitudes and the causes of their struggle, they were also inevitably political. Resisting the oppression of authoritarian regimes, they found allies in other sectors of society also striving to overcome the nightmare of political repression.

Adopting Paulo Freire's pedagogy, the CEBs became communities of the poor and for the poor struggling for liberation. As such, they ended up becoming embryos of popular movements such as, in the case of Brazil, the Movimento contra a Carestia (Movimento against the high living costs), in 1973, the Workers' Party, founded in 1980, and the Landless Workers' Movement (Movimento dos Trabalhadoes Sem-Terra, MST), created in 1984. Many of the founders of these and other popular movements had been through the ranks of the CEBs.[63]

Having rapidly spread throughout Latin America, the CEBs took different shapes and forms. Yet, some characteristics remain common to them. Focusing on the Brazilian experience, Betto describes the CEBs as follows:

---

[61] Frei Betto, "Fermento de marca boa: Comunidades Eclesiais de Base - Entrevista com Frei Betto," *Sem Fronteiras* 252 (1997): 5, https://ospiti.peacelink.it/zumbi/news/semfro/252/sf252p05.html.

[62] Betto, "Fermento de marca boa," 5.

[63] Betto, "Fermento de marca boa," 5. See also, interview by the author with Frei Betto in São Paulo, Brazil, October 11, 2023. Betto cites, among others, Vicentinho, Luiza Erundina, José Rainha, João Pedro Stédile, who became important leaders in organizations such as CUT—Central Única dos Trabalhadores (United Workers Central), the Workers' Party and the MST.

> Base ecclesiastical communities are small groups organized around the parish (urban) or the chapel (rural) by lay people, priests, or bishops [. . .] In peripheral parishes, communities can be distributed in small groups or form a single larger group called base ecclesial community.[64]

They can be found, for the most part, in impoverished urban or rural neighborhoods. Their leaders or facilitators, normally called pastoral agents, live in the neighborhood and can be a priest, a member of a religious order or a lay person.[65] While urban CEBs tend to be smaller, with as few as fifteen members, in rural areas they can gather as many as one hundred people to celebrate worship on Sundays in a chapel. As Betto puts it,

> They are communities, because they bring together people who have the same faith, belong to the same church [parish], and live in the same region. Motivated by faith, these people live a common union around their problems of survival, housing, struggles for better living conditions and liberating desires and hopes. They are ecclesial, because they are congregated in the Church, as basic nuclei of the faith community. They are grassroots [social location] because they are made up of people who work with their own hands (popular classes): housewives, workers, underemployed people, retirees, young people, and employees in the service sectors, on the urban periphery; in rural areas, agricultural workers, squatters, small landowners, tenants, farmhands, and their families. There are also indigenous communities.[66]

While the CEBs can be understood in multiple ways, Betto's description explains the basic elements of these communities. They are primarily religious communities of people who gather to read the Bible vis-à-vis their day-to-day struggle for life. In other words, they do not separate life from worship. Adapting the see-judge-act method, they take their reading of the world around them as the starting point for their reading of the biblical text in search of discernment to act upon the world.

---

[64] Frei Betto, *O Oue é Comunidade Eclesial de Base*, 3rd ed. (São Paulo: Editora Brasiliense, 1981), 16.

[65] Betto, *O Oue é Comunidade Eclesial de Base*, 18.

[66] Betto, *O Oue é Comunidade Eclesial de Base*, 17.

In the decades following Medellin, the base communities got attention from all over the world, emerging in various countries. They are mostly known, though, in connection with the experience of the Latin American Church, where in the 1970s and 1980s they became one of the most vibrant popular movements in the region. As Faustino Luiz Couto Teixeira asserts, "the experience of the Base Ecclesial Communities (CEBs) constitutes the great and original contribution of the Latin American Church to the entire universal Church."[67]

The earliest expressions of embryonic CEBs can be traced back to the 1950s in Brazil. Some authors connect the origins of the CEBs, for instance, to the *Movimento de Natal*, in the state of Rio Grande do Norte.[68] In accord with this narrative, incipient CEBs emerged in Natal in the late 1950s and early 1960s. The Natal Movement, in the state of Rio Grande do Norte, started in 1948, even though it only gained national attention after the first regional gathering of the CNBB in 1959. Working closely with Dom Hélder Câmara, then representing the CNBB and the Brazilian Catholic Action, Monsignor Eugênio Sales, bishop of Natal, founded the first Rural Workers' union in that area in 1961. Through the work of specialized sectors of Catholic Action, the Church became involved in the mobilization of rural workers in Natal. That same year, in partnership with the Ministry of Education of the Brazilian Government, CNBB created the *Movimento de Educação de Base* (MEB), which, as Ferraro asserts, was "articulated as a literacy and registration activity of citizenship, aimed at dismantling traditional domination of northeastern oligarchies, counting on the regimentation of new voters disconnected from the traditional practices." MEB was also one of the earliest movements experimenting with Paulo Freire's literacy method. Due to the national network created through *Pastoral de Conjunto* (the JPP), the new ideas emerging from the Natal experience reverberated throughout the country, marking the rise of a Brazilian Catholic left, which gave birth to "some of the progressive currents and actions that would influence Catholicism in the following decades," including

[67] Faustino Luiz Couto Teixeira, *Os Encontros Intereclesiais de CEBs no Brasil* (São Paulo: Edições Paulinas, 1996), 9.

[68] Margaret Hebblethwaite, *Base Communities: An Introduction* (Mahwah, NJ: Paulist Press, 1994), 12.

Popular Action, Ecclesial Base Communities (CEBs) and liberation theology."[69]

While these scattered memories focus on incipient experiences leading to the formation of the first CEBs, their national spread is also associated with the emergency plan of the CNBB in 1962 and the subsequent Joint Pastoral Plan (JPP) in 1966.[70] Sensing the need to decentralize the parish and make its presence in the world more dynamic, the JPP proposed, as part of its national pastoral action, the creation of the CEBs as a national movement. That was, in Beozzo's words, JPP's most important resolution:

> The most important resolution of the JPP was to propose a new model of the Church that would facilitate the full participation of all the baptized at the base of society and the Church. The gateway to the thematization of CEBs in the PPC is the dynamization of parishes, but the proposal soon gains in practice autonomy of flight and its own configuration [. . .] The implementation of the CEBs, as the normal way of being a Church, was, in my opinion, the crucial decision for the future of the Church in Brazil. CEBs became the place and occasion for new lay ministries and popular ecclesial leadership to flourish. They also facilitated the participation of all the baptized as members of the only "people of God" in the life of the Church and in many of its decision-making spheres. The

[69] Ferraro, *Igreja e Desenvolvimento: O Movimento de Natal*, 9–10. Some authors alternatively place the origins of the CEBs in Rio de Janeiro and other parts of Brazil. Father José Marins, who accompanied the CEBs from the beginning, states that they began "in Brazil in the 1950s, with some pioneering experiences in the Northeast, Maranhão, Rio Grande do Norte, a little in Paraíba and then, in the state of São Paulo." See José Marins, "Ainda há lugar para as comunidades eclesiais de base na Igreja?" *CEBs do Brasil*, https://cebsdobrasil.com.br/ainda-ha-lugar-para-as-comunidades-eclesiais-de-base-na-igreja-jose-marins/. Frei Betto, on the other hand, mentions the initiative of Angelo Rossi in Volta Redonda, Rio de Janeiro, in the early 1960s. There is a certain consensus, however, around the idea of multiple origins in different parts of Brazil between the late 1950s and early 1960s. The phenomenon would only be consolidated, though, in the years following Medellin 1968. See Marilza J. L. Schuina, "As Comunidades Eclesiais de Base rumo ao seu 15º Intereclesial," *A Caminho: Informativo das Comunidades Eclesiais de Base do Brasil* 1 (2020), https://cebsdobrasil.ofertorio.com/comunidades-eclesiais-de-base-15o-intereclesial/#_edn1. See also William César de Andrade, *O Código Genético das* CEBs (São Leopoldo: Oikos, 2005), 12.

[70] Thomas C. Bruneau, *The Church in Brazil: The Politics of Religion* (Austin, TX: The University of Texas Press, 1982), 156.

> CEBs shaped a form of ecclesiastical experience that facilitated the link between faith and daily life; liturgical celebration and social and political commitment. The CEBs also opened the way for a silent revolution in order to overcome the exclusion of women within ecclesiastical structures traditionally dominated by men and clearly marked by their marginalization. Within the CEBs there was no more structural obstacle to women's participation and leadership in all aspects of community life.[71]

Only when this coordinated plan (JPP) was put in place, the CEBs began to flourish as a nationwide movement. Once that happened, its impact on the entire Brazilian Catholic Church and throughout Latin America was huge, at the point that non-ordained Catholic leaders formed in those base communities began to play crucial leadership roles in their parishes and in the pastoral work of the Church. One sign of that impact was the changes implemented in the liturgical practices of Catholic communities, which, using the vernacular and centering their weekly celebrations in service of the word, stopped depending as much on the presence of ordained priests to conduct their lives. According to the CNBB, seventy percent of the Sunday celebrations in the Church of Brazil are presided over not by ordained ministers but by lay leaders of the communities, in most cases women.[72] The CEBs became the foremost embodiment of the concept of the Church as the people of God. As Francisco de Aquino Júnior underscores,

> This new understanding of the Church found in the Ecclesial Base Communities (CEBs) in Latin America its most basic, creative, and fruitful expression. The Church as the people of God with its charisms and ministries is carried out primarily in base communities that constitute themselves as a place of prayer, fraternal life and commitment to the poor and marginalized, a place where they exercise and develop important and necessary charisms and ministries for the life of the community and the exercise of its mission in the world. These base communities are in themselves and

[71] Beozzo, "A Recepção do Vaticano II na Igreja do Brasil," 13–14.

[72] Judinei Vanzeto, "Leigos e Leigas são chamados pelo batismo ao ministério da palavra, lembrou Dom Bucciol" Regional Sul 3 da CNBB, https://www.cnbb.org.br/leigos-e-leigas-sao-chamados-pelo-batismo-ao-ministerio-da-palavra-lembrou-dom-bucciol/. See also Teixeira, *Os Encontros Intereclesiais de CEBs no Brasil*, 9.

> simultaneously "signs" (expressions) and "instruments" (mediations) of salvation or the reign of God in the world.

The rise of the CEBs proved to be the most creative reception of the Vatican II in Latin America, as it was in that process of reception that they acquired institutional acknowledgment and found the supportive environment they needed to thrive.[73]

As a popular expression of the Church driven by a deep sense of solidarity, "the CEBs have advanced a new ecumenical spirit, seeking to reconcile what was split." As Reynaldo Ferreira Leão Neto asserts, this is what makes them inherently ecumenical. In his words,

> It is the religious spirit, of *religare*, in its most positive light. The unity it seeks demands wideness and questions narrowness of mind. The dogmatism that a strict religious identity fosters can only be denied by an equally religious spirit firm in its ecumenical and beyond boundaries solidarity. In the case of the CEBs, religious identity feeds on the understanding of, identification with and service to the other.[74]

Javiér Jiménez Limón refers to them as an ecumenism from the perspective of the crucified, which starts with the crucifixion and resurrection of the poor.[75] Accordingly, "the Church of the poor is not a schismatic alternative to the great Church, but rather the evangelizing [. . .] and restructuring vocation of the entire Church. The poor can proclaim solidarity without hypocrisy; the reproach of Christ without shame; the parenthood of God, without opium. And they are evangelizing many bishops and lay people."[76]

In Latin America, the rise of the CEBs took place at one of the most difficult junctures in the history of the continent, a time when most countries in the region had to fight for autonomy amid civil wars or military dictatorships in the context of US imperialism. In the case of Brazil, it was at the heightening of the military regime

---

[73] Aquino Júnior, "Comunidades Eclesiais de Base (CEBs)," 94–105 (96).

[74] Reynaldo Ferreira Leão Neto, "Ecumenism of Permeability: The Base Ecclesial Communities in Brazil," (PhD Diss. The University of Birmingham: Birmingham, UK, 2009) 49.

[75] Javiér Jiménez Limón, "Ecumenismo desde los crucificados," *Estúdios Eclesiásticos* 55 (1980): 267–295 (278).

[76] Limón, "Ecumenismo desde los crucificados," 291.

that the CEBs became a national movement, emerging as one of the important forces of resistance. In contrast to the growing authoritarianism in the region, the CEBs were a democratizing force, which encouraged participation of its members in the betterment of their communities. When many were facing the pain imposed by the scourge of mass poverty, the CEBs pointed to the power of solidarity and community as a viable response to adversity. And, in a period when suppression and silencing of dissenting voices was the order of the day, the CEBs instilled self-awareness, autonomy, liberation, and hope.

As Lucília de Almeida Neves and Mauro Passos remind us, "During the military regime, the CEBs resisted impositions and became meeting spaces for groups to express themselves religiously and politically." They embodied the shift proposed at Medellin from an abstract Christ to one who put them back in touch with their humanity and concrete living situations.[77] Especially in the years of military authoritarianism, the CEBs became a voice for those who did not have a voice. As Frei Betto once noticed, though, this was not a natural move. It resulted from the fact that CEBs' members developed a high level of political consciousness. Betto attributes it to the conjuncture of the country in the 1960s and 1970s. The military regime forced people to look for new spaces to regroup and organize their resistance efforts. As the Catholic Church, at least initially, was one of the few spaces free from military surveillance, the popular classes turned to the Church for help. The renewed focus on the vocation of the laity and the reforms advanced in both Vatican II and the CELAM conferences in Medellin and Puebla helped create alternative spaces in the Church, also preparing priests, members of religious orders, and bishops to take necessary risks to stand with the poor and oppressed.[78]

The solidarity of the CEBs with the popular movements stems from the fact that the social issues they advocate for are not only relevant for Christians but also for the larger community. As Betto deftly points out, if they mobilize to get piped water to the community, that

---

[77] Lucília de Almeida Neves and Mauro Passos, "Silêncios e diálogos: o catolicismo e a defesa dos direitos sociais e humanos ante à intolerância política da ditadura militar no Brasil (1964–1985)," *Horizonte* 3/5 (2004): 67–81 (77).

[78] Betto, *O Oue é Comunidade Eclesial de Base*, 22.

is a matter of interest to everyone. Thus, the propensity to engage the popular movements is natural in the CEBs.[79]

Between the second CELAM conference in Medellin and its third conference, in Puebla, Mexico, 1979, the CEBs multiplied exponentially, also spreading its impact around the world. By 1980, it was estimated that in Brazil alone there were between sixty thousand and eighty thousand CEBs.[80] Their boom revitalized a Church that despite previous attempts to mobilize the laity, had not yet been able to deliver the promise of becoming a Church of the poor.

As the CEBs rapidly spread throughout Brazil, they started organizing national inter-ecclesial gatherings, which became themselves important signposts to the broader church and the Brazilian society. In those encounters, CEBs representatives from all over the country exchanged experiences, sharing their challenges and hopes. Over the years, these encounters created a national memory of the journey of the base communities. The first interecclesial gathering took place in the city of Vitória, Espírito Santo, in 1975. Ever since, fifteen interecclesial gatherings have been held in Brazil only. The first interecclesial gathering gathered seventy participants, including seven bishops, five theologians, and a number of priests and members of diverse religious orders, along with lay people representing eleven dioceses and seven states.[81] The theme of that first national gathering was "CEBs: A Church Born of the People by the Spirit of God." Reports on the experiences of eleven communities were shared with the participants in advance of the gathering. In response, some documents analyzing and reflecting on those experiences were prepared for discussion during the encounter. The event included small-group discussions, plenaries, and panels with the participation of invited theologians. At the end, the participants prepared a final document, highlighting "the reality of the people of God," based on political, cultural, and methodological analyses. Amaury Castanho, a bishop who accompanied the CEBs from their inception and who

---

79 Betto, *O Oue é Comunidade Eclesial de Base*, 24.

80 Betto, "Fermento de marca boa: Comunidades Eclesiais de Base," *Sem Fronteiras*. See also Teixeira, *Os Encontros Intereclesiais de CEBs no Brasil*, 10.

81 Amaury Castanho, *Caminhos das CEBs no Brasil*, 2nd ed. (Rio de Janeiro: Marques Saraiva Gráficos e Editores S/A, 1988), 12.

attended the interecclesial gatherings, summarized the findings of that first meeting as follows:

1. "'The People of God must organize in communities of faith and life.' These communities must be free to create their own paths. Yet, the communities, 'in accord with their concrete needs and the demands of the Gospel,' must live 'in communion with the other communities and with their bishop.
2. The whole Church must participate in the struggle for the liberation of the people, collaborating for the same people to realize the root causes of the oppression in which they live, denouncing all sorts of injustice; advancing a society without walls and privileges; a society in which the means of production and service and the collective goods are not concentrated in the hands of a few.
3. Popular religiosity must be respected and embraced, with the valorization of its gestures and signs. The Church (the bishops, priests, and all pastoral agents) 'must overcome the attitude of both exploiting popular religiosity and the indifferent and destructive behavior it often had [towards it] in the past.'
4. 'The common priesthood of the faithful must be valued.' All who were consecrated through baptism to the worship of the living God and the service of God's Kingdom must not only celebrate the day-to-day events, but also fully participate in liturgical celebrations and in all sacramental expressions of faith."[82]

The egalitarian impetus of the CEBs was a mark of the first interecclesial gathering. The gathering's take on popular religiosity was also significant, and would help inform future conversations around that topic in Latin America. In its inception, liberation theology had for the most part neglected the need to make grassroots religious expressions and practices a central part of the process of liberation. Medellin itself did not have much to say about that topic. The next CELAM conferences, though, would make that topic a more prominent part of their agendas.

[82] Castanho, *Caminhos das CEBs no Brasil*, 12–13.

The language of common priesthood used in that gathering, though, sounded threatening to some in the Catholic hierarchy, becoming the alleged reason for the suppression of the CEBs in some dioceses and parishes. Despite the obstacles faced in the journey, the CEBs continued to embody the idea of the church as the people of God. Combining liturgical practices and service to the larger community, they kept inspiring and mobilizing people for the creation of popular movements that responded to particular community needs.

In her study of the Movement for Collective Transportation and the Movement of Construction Workers in the late 1970s, in the city of Vitória, Ana Maria Doimo shows how the pastoral work of the Church through the CEBs was at the root of those two social movements. Among other things, the CEBs of Vitória produced a document titled "Christian Exigencies of a Public Order," which was published by the archdiocese. That document was the propulsor of the struggle for rights that culminated with the creation of those two movements.[83] In that context of pastoral participation, the CEBs represented a change in a Church where previously "the people did not participate; the priest turned his back to the people, wore a robe and spoke Latin." In this new way of being church, the people participated, including in liturgical celebrations, and the priest was with the people, not above them.[84]

Each of the fifteen interecclesial gatherings in the past five decades have focused on particular emphases and made specific contributions to church and society. Collectively, they serve as a map of the CEBs's national journey in Brazil. The most recent interecclesial gathering took place on July 18–22, 2022, in the diocese of Rondonópolis-Guiratinga, state of Mato Grosso.[85] Its theme was "CEBs: Igreja em

---

[83] Ana Maria Doimo, "Os Rumos dos Movimentos Sociais nos Caminhos da Religiosidade," in *A Igreja nas Bases em Tempo de Transicao (1974–1985)*, ed. Paulo Krische and Scott Mainwaring (Porto Alegre: L&PM/CEDEC, 1986), 101–130 (102–103).

[84] Doimo, "Os Rumos dos Movimentos Sociais," 107.

[85] Solange dos Santos Rodrigues et al., *15º Encontro Intereclesial das Comunidades Eclesiais de Base* (Cuiabá, Brazil: Editora dos Autores, 2022), 11.

Saída na Busca para a Vida Plena de Todos e Todas."[86] The inspiration for this title comes from a passage in *Evangelii Gaudium*, the Joy of the Gospel, Pope Francis's Apostolic Exhortation from 2014:

> Let us go forth, then, let us go forth to offer everyone the life of Jesus Christ. Here I repeat for the entire Church what I have often said to the priests and laity of Buenos Aires: I prefer a Church which is bruised, hurting and dirty because it has been out on the streets, rather than a Church which is unhealthy from being confined and from clinging to its own security. I do not want a Church concerned with being at the centre and which then ends by being caught up in a web of obsessions and procedures.[87]

The Brazilian CEBs have deeply identified with that vision of the Church, seeing themselves as an incarnation of that mandate. Due to the influence of theologians such as Juan Carlos Scannone and his theology of the people (one of the various branches of Latin American liberation theology) on Pope Francis's pastoral practice,[88] many in the CEBs see him as an ally who understands and cares for the plight of the poor.

---

[86] "CEBs: The Outgoing Church in Search of Full Life for All." The title borrows an expression that Pope Francis often uses, *Iglesia en salida* (Spanish) or *Igreja em saída* (Portuguese), which is best translated in English as "the outgoing church" a church turned outward, to the world, in contrast to an introvert church, turned to itself. See Allan Figueroa Deck, "Pope Francis and the Challenge of Ecclesial Introversion: Where is He Coming From? Where is He Going?" *Perspectiva Teológica* 54/3 (2022): 703–717. https://doi.org/10.20911/21768757v54n3p703/2022.

[87] Pope Francis, "Apostolic Exhortation *Evangelii Gaudium* of the Holy Father Francis to the Bishops, Clergy, Consecrated Person and the Lay Faithful on the Proclamation of the Gospel in Today's World" (Vatican City: Vatican Press, 2013), https://www.vatican.va/content/dam/francesco/pdf/apost_exhortations/documents/papa-francesco_esortazione-ap_20131124_evangelii-gaudium_en.pdf.

[88] See, for instance, Rafael Luciani, *Pope Francis and the Theology of the People* (Maryknoll, NY: Orbis Books, 2017). The late Juan Carlos Scannone (1931–2019) defined the theology of the people as one that "turns to the religion of the 'faithful people of God' as a key source for theological reflection." That influence on Francis is explicit since Francis's first encyclical, *Evangelii Gaudium*, first apostolic exhortation in 2013. Juan Carlos Scanonne, "Pope Francis and the Theology of the People," *Theological Studies* 77/1: (2016): 118–135. (118).

In the tradition of the CEBs, Francis has voiced solidarity with social movements. At the beginning of his papacy, he held three meetings with social movements in Rome and La Paz, Bolivia (2014, 2015, and 2016), uniting his voice to theirs to affirm what in Spanish and Portuguese is known as the three t's: *terreno, techo y trabajo* (land, roof, and work), while reinforcing the importance of their role in tasks he sees as key to the future of the world: (a) make the economy work in the service of the people, (b) unite the people on the path of justice and peace, and (c) protect Mother Earth.[89] Francis is not only a pope informed by the Latin American popular reception of the Vatican II but also a leader who, despite any flaws, takes the popular Church (the Church of the poor), its journey, values, and voice seriously. His persistent critique of an economy of exclusion and inequality that leads millions of people to die of hunger-related causes is a moral judgment influenced by a tradition that emphasizes the primacy of the human and the need to change the "'structural roots' of the social and environmental drama of the contemporary world."[90]

The interecclesial gatherings have brought to the fore the fact that the CEBs remain alive and active—despite what some people in the North Atlantic may think. The message they convey in each gathering continues to be important not only for the Latin American church but for the global church and for the world. Those gatherings not only offer an opportunity for exchange and mutual encouragement among representatives from different CEBs but also for regular assessment of the progress and challenges the CEBs face in their journey. The ecclesial base communities are still a relatively recent phenomenon in the life of the Church and have not exhausted their potential. Among other things, they remain important to help keep the Church's ears on the ground, being among the most outward stations of the Church; in particular, in the world of the poor.

---

[89] See Francisco de Aquino Junior, Mauricio Abdalia and Robson Sávio, eds. *Papa Francisco com os Movimentos Populares* (São Paulo: Edições Paulinas, 2018), 7–8.

[90] Manfredo Araújo de Oliveira, "O Papa Francisco e o Mundo de Hoje," in *Papa Francisco com os Movimentos Populares*, 15–32 (29).

As communities organized among the poor, they have been able to respond in practical ways to the challenges the poor face to survive and continue to fight for their rights and dignity. In the recent COVID-19 pandemic crisis, for example, the CEBs played an important role through their word-centered, small-group oriented, and solidarity-based communal faith, keeping the Church present among the people when the temples were closed.

The networks the CEBs form in impoverished neighborhoods were crucial to help the victims of the pandemic.[91] The COVID-19 outbreak started right after the Eleventh Continental Gathering of the CEBs, in Guayaquil, Ecuador.[92] The network of Latin American CEBs had just spent time together discussing Pope Francis's Post-Synodal Exhortation *Querida Amazonia* (2020), and the youth gathered in Guayaquil was talking about their ability to dream of a future as an act of resistance. As Leonardo Boff reminds us, the CEBs network functioned "as a dependable system of mutual aid, organizing food distribution and facilitating access to assistance coming from the state."[93] They were already present among the most vulnerable, and their leaders were important in the articulation with other religious and non-religious communities of concerted responses to the suffering of their neighbors. Furthermore, they also countered disinformation about the pandemic, which, often disseminated from Christian pulpits and even the highest government offices, caused too many unnecessary deaths.[94]

---

[91] Eduardo C. Lima, "As Covid-19 crisis grows, Latin America's basic ecclesial communities step up tohelp," *America: The Jesuit Review*, https://www.americamagazine.org/politics-society/2020/05/04/covid-19-crisis-grows-latin-americas-basic-ecclesial-communities-step.

[92] The XI Encuentro Latinoamericano de CEBs took place on March 9–12, 2020, right at the time the world was shutting down to face one of its most distressing global crises this century. The gathering, which was preceded by a meeting of youth CEBs, revolved around the theme "Listening to God in the Cries of the Earth and of the Poor, We Defend Life and Build God's Reign."

[93] Lima 2020. See also Raimundo C. Barreto, "The COVID-19 Pandemic and the Ongoing Genocide of Black and Indigenous Peoples in Brazil," *International Journal of Latin American Religions* 4 (2020): 417–439.

[94] See Rede de Comunicadores das CEBs, "4ª Carta às Comunidades: As CEBs em tempos de pandemia da COVID-19," *CEBs do Brasil*, June 2, 2020, https://cebsdobrasil.com.br/4a-carta-as-comunidades/. This letter was sent to all CEBs by the secretariat planning the 15º Encontro Intereclesial.

The interecclesial gatherings have contributed, above all, to remind the Church of the continuous value and vitality of the CEBs. Celebrating the resilience of the CEBs as communities of solidarity with a missionary spirit that embodies a communal dimension of life, and considering the role they play in the processes of evangelization and human promotion, Faustino Teixeira highlights that the CEBs remain "important and indispensable for the life of Church and society."[95]

Furthermore, bringing together bishops, priests, lay people, and theologians, those national and continental encounters have contributed to the construction of a genuinely Latin American theology. Theologians have played a consulting or advisory role in the interecclesial gatherings, reflecting on the reports received from panels and plenaries formed by CEBs' representatives. For instance, in the Fourth Interecclesial Gathering, in 1981, whose theme was "Church, oppressed people who organize for liberation," Leonardo Boff served as theological advisor, while Frei Betto was a participant listening carefully and writing his own report of the event.[96] This participatory role of theologians in the life of the CEBs has been key for the continuous development and self-assessment of Latin American liberation theology "as critical reflection on historical praxis," reinforcing the idea of a theology informed by the Christian praxis of and with the poor.[97]

Leão Neto, on the other hand, points to an aspect often neglected in the studies of the CEBs, that is, its mystical orientation, which is intrinsically ecumenical and even interreligious, as it is informed by the spirituality of the people. He calls that ecumenical spirit an "ecumenism of permeability," not only because of the exchange that happens on the ritual level with Indigenous and African-derived religions, but also because of the participation of practitioners of those religions in the CEBs mystical rituals.[98]

---

[95] Teixeira, *Os Encontros Intereclesiais de CEBs no Brasil*, 210.

[96] Frei Betto, *O Fermento na Massa: O 4º encontro intereclesial das Comunidades Eclesiais de Base* (Petrópolis: Vozes, 1981).

[97] Gutierrez, *A Theology of Liberation*, 12.

[98] Leão Neto, "Ecumenism of Permeability," 7. Leão Neto describes permeability as being distinct from syncretism, and involving "shared attitudes towards social and political issues from the standpoints that are spiritually and doctrinally distinct." (8) While there is no room for proper discussion of the topic here, it is important to highlight that syncretism should not be merely reduced to mixture of elements of

The acknowledgment of other religious traditions in the life of the CEBs is an outcome of relationships based on mutual solidarity at the base. There are places in the world where Base Christian Communities deliberately include non-Christian participation. Studying the district of Kanyakumari, in the state of Tamil Nadu, India, for instance, A. Maria David examines the impact of the CEBs, which he calls "Basic Christian Communities," on Christian-Hindu relations in a multireligious setting with a long and complex history. Describing how the Basic Christian Communities live out their faith in that multireligious context, "communities of love," David underscores their openness and inclusivity, even though they often have to respond to past and current conflicts. Despite the volatility of their situation, these base communities have not only developed a significant level of tolerance toward difference but have also explicitly worked to transcend "the barrier of religion," doing their best "to promote inter-religious harmony and in particular the Hindu-Christian relationship through their activities and programs."[99]

In Sri Lanka, as Aloysius Pieris has shown, one can find similar examples of the magisterium of the poor and its "liberational thrust," which also impacts their broader multireligious community. Those efforts are socially located in the Basic Human Communities (BHC).[100] While Christian identity remains part of their experience, it no longer makes sense to call those communities exclusively Christian, since their existence and action are for the sake of the entire community and involve participants from different faith traditions.

different religious traditions. As Jørgensen puts it, syncretism among other things, can be considered as "the mediation of borders and context in relation to the central value of the religious system." Jonas Adelin Jørgensen, "Indigenization, Syncretism, and the Assumed Boundedness of Christianity: A Critique," in *Religion on the Move: New Dynamics of Religious Expansion in a Globalizing World*, ed. Afe Adogame and Shobana Shankar (Leiden: Brill, 2013), 99–112 (108).

[99] A. Maria David, *Beyond Boundaries: Hindu-Christian Relationship and Basic Christian Communities* (Delhi, ISPK, 2009), 235. Another study of base communities in India points to their role in the process of inculturation. See Joseph Prasad Pinto, *Inculturation through Basic Communities: An Indian Perspective* (Bangalore: Asian Trading Corporation, 1985).

[100] Aloysius Pieris, "Interreligious Dialogue and Theology of Religions: An Asian Paradigm," *Horizons* 20/1 (1993): 106–114 (108). The Basic Human Communities are an interfaith version of the Latin American Christian or Ecclesial Base Communities.

Despite the immense diversity one can find in the experiences of the CEBs in Latin America and elsewhere, the spirituality informing the base communities often combines practice of popular religion with an emphasis on discipleship, that is, the discernment of the meaning of following Jesus in the broader world.[101] In Latin America, that trait reflects the impact of Black and Indigenous pastoral agents and their hermeneutical contributions to the interpretation of their relationship with the word and the world, affirming "[a]midst so much suffering [. . .] the certainty of our faith in a liberating God, who walked with our ancestors and walks with us."[102]

If popular spirituality and the deep experience of solidarity with people of other faith traditions have opened the CEBs to be inclusive of people from other faiths, they have also made room for Protestant participation. As discussed earlier, relationships between Catholics and Protestants in Latin America were rare prior to Vatican II. The dominant attitude between Catholics and Protestants was apologetic and conflictive. José Miguez Bonino was the first Latin American Protestant to attend a Catholic global gathering as an observer. In Vatican II, he was the only of two hundred non-Catholic observers coming from Latin America.[103]

In the post-Vatican II years, ecumenical collaboration involving Catholics and Protestants slowly improved within more progressive circles. Medellin 1968 sought to contextualize the Vatican II openness for ecumenical collaboration, which would continue to be sedimented in the following decades, being, therefore, a turning point on that front.[104] Protestant observers participated in Medellin and were even asked to read drafts of its documents and offer

---

[101] Faustino Teixeira, "A Espiritualidade nas CEBs," in *As Comunidades de Base em Questão*, ed. Clodovis Boff et al. (São Paulo: Edições Paulinas, 1997), 207–250.

[102] Obertal Xavier Ribeiro, "Black Pastoral Agents and the Bible in the Afro Context: A Hermeneutic of Years of Enchantment," *Crosscurrents* 67/1 (2017): 74–85 (74).

[103] As Elias Wolff points out, the first meeting in which Catholics and Protestants participated together in Latin America was a gathering of the WSCF in Bolivia, in 1954. However, only in 1969, there would be an official Catholic presence in a Protestant gathering in Buenos Aires. Isolated encounters and collaborative efforts happened between these two events, as the earlier discussion of ISAL showed. See Elias Wolff, "O Contexto Ecumênico de Medellín e o Posicionamento Católico sobre a Unidade Cristã na América Latina," *Encontros Teológicos* 33/2 (2018): 243–262 (245).

[104] María Teresa Porcile Santiso, "Ecumenismo en América Latina," *Medellín* 6/22 (1980): 186–199 (190).

suggestions. In the eleven years separating it from CELAM III, in Puebla, several Catholic-Protestant initiatives, although mostly happening on the margins of the churches, took shape in the region. In 1968, for instance, CELAM discussed an ecumenical project of Bible translation with the United Bible Societies, and, in 1967, it created an ecumenical section to oversee cooperation with non-Catholics.

Gradually, the CEBs themselves began to discern their ecumenical vocation as including Protestants. Even prior to naming their ecumenical nature, the CEBs opened themselves to the participation of members of other churches. In Brazil, the first inter-ecclesial gathering counted with the participation of the Taizé community, whose presence in Brazil since the 1960s was already an ecumenical outcome of Vatican II.

According to Brother Michel,[105] Dom Hélder Câmara, Dom Manuel Larraín, and Brother Roger (1905–2005), a Swiss Calvinist who founded the ecumenical Taizé community in France in 1940 and attended the Vatican II as an observer, met regularly during the Council. Sharing common dreams, Dom Hélder visited the Taizé community a few times in his travels to the Vatican. In those visits, as he and Brother Roger discussed their common passion for the poor, he invited the Taizé brother to visit Brazil. In 1966, Brother Michel visited Dom Hélder in Recife. At the latter's request, he established a Taizé fellowship in Olinda. That community included three Benedictine monks from the Olinda monastery. After working closely with Dom Hélder during some of the worst moments of the dictatorship, they moved the fellowship to the city of Vitória in 1972, and then to Alagoinhas, state of Bahia, in 1978, where it remains to this day.

For more than half a century, the Taizé brothers have been actively involved in the Brazilian ecumenical scene, mainly working with impoverished communities in a peripheral neighborhood in Alagoinhas. The small Taizé fellowship in Brazil, composed of four brothers working side-by-side with a number of Brazilian volunteers and partners, is currently located in one of the poorest communities in the also peripheric municipality of Alagoinhas. Whereas the Taizé Center

[105] Brother Michel, "Don Helder Camara et Taizé: Témoignage de frère Michel, de Taizé," February 22, 1999. Author's personal files. Unpublished document received via email from Sabine Laplane, Communauté Saint-François-Xavier, on June 12, 2018. Brother Michel wrote this testimony after Dom Hélder's passing in 1999. Two days after writing it, on February 24, he died at the age of 73 during a trip to Australia.

is located in a piece of land that belongs to the Catholic Church, it is immersed in a predominantly Black and religiously plural community, which has experienced a Pentecostal boom in the past few decades. In such a context, the Taizé community in Brazil has collaborated with popular sectors of the Brazilian Catholic Church on a number of projects, seeking to counter the high indices of violence against the impoverished Black population in the area where they live. Claudio Vereza, one of the participants of the Brazilian People's Council, another post-Vatican II development, explains the impact of the *convivência* (the experience of coexistence) with the Taizé community as follows:

> The Taizé brothers gave us the opportunity to leave a very homely, local vision-experience, to enter headfirst into the Latin American world, allowing us to see ourselves as Latin American, in all its reality and experience of faith! They introduced us to an internationalist vision, in terms of faith, and social and political concerns. Ultimately, we learned the sense of humanity through coexistence, celebration, and reflection.[106]

As a Catholic-Protestant community, the Taizé community has contributed to sow the seeds of grassroots or base ecumenism, especially through the collaborative work with religious and non-religious popular movements and civil society organizations in efforts to protect impoverished Black children from the violence of drug cartels and the police, and to promote racial justice, women's, youth, and human rights. In the words of Vereza, "As the Taizé community is eminently an ecumenical experience, this dimension has constituted us as experiencers of an embodied faith, in fellowship with other Christian denominations."[107]

A number of Protestants have participated in the CEBs and their interecclesial gatherings. Since 1986, Protestant pastors, theologians, and lay individuals have attended the CEBs national gatherings.[108] Methodist pastor and theologian Cláudio de Oliveira Ribeiro, for

---

[106] Comunidade Taizé de Alagoinhas, *50 Anos da Presença dos Irmãos de Taizé no Brasil: Caminhos Percorridos e a Percorrer* (Alagoinhas: Comunidade Taizé de Alagoinhas, 2017), 21.

[107] Comunidade Taizé de Alagoinhas, *50 Anos da Presença*. See also Comunidade Taizé de Alagoinhas, https://taize.org.br/helix/index.php/comunidade.

[108] Teixeira, *Os Encontros Intereclesiais de CEBs no Brasil*, 216.

instance, served as theological/pastoral adviser for the eighth inter-ecclesial gathering in 1992, and since then has participated in those gatherings several other times.[109]

Besides the gradual ecumenical participation that the CEBs have integrated into their practice over the decades, they have also inspired the rise of other grassroots ecumenical initiatives based on the communal reading of the world and the word (the Bible).[110] As Ribeiro rightly noted following the eighth inter-ecclesial gathering, Protestant participation was not only consolidated but "pointed to the possibility of new forms of ecclesial and religious unity."[111] One of these new forms of unity advancing a base-oriented ecumenicity emerged with a movement known as the Popular Reading of the Bible in the 1970s.

---

[109] Cláudio de Oliveira Ribeiro, "CEBs e Ecumenismo: Uma Discussão a Partir da Dimensão Ecumênica do Oitavo Intereclesial," *Revista Eclesiástica Brasileira* 52/208 (1992): 846–855. The adviser is "an expert in a given field of knowledge who provides occasional or sporadic services to a community or a set of communities. Their services can be in the field of reflection or formation (theology, Bible, liturgy, analysis of reality, history, sociology, etc.) or in the field of methodology (pedagogy, basic education, spirituality, planning, art, etc.). Advisory services can be also provided by lay people, members of religious orders, deacons, priests, and bishops, as long as they have a good command of the respective area of knowledge. This does not mean that they must have a high level of education, as the knowledge that comes from practice is also valuable." The adviser plays a "technical" function, as an expert. Therefore, they "do not necessarily need to be someone of the same religious confession and not even, at the limit, a person of Christian faith." Their dedication and service to the cause of liberation is more indispensable than their faith confession, even though "the Christian faith is [. . .] a valuable source of energy and communion with the community receiving the advisory service." Nelito Dornelas, Pedro A. Ribeiro de Oliveira, Tereza P. Cavalcanti, "O papel da assessoria pastoral nas CEBs," *Vida Pastoral* 51/272 (2010): 29–34. Online version available at https://www.vidapastoral.com.br/artigos/temas-pastorais/o-papel-da-assessoria-pastoral-nas-cebs/.

[110] That is, the application of the see, judge, act method on the grassroots level. The intereccIesial gatherings always start with a concrete theme, stemming from the "reading" of the world to the focus on a theological-biblical reflection aiming toward informing ongoing action.

[111] Ribeiro, "CEBs e Ecumenismo," 855.

9

THE RISE OF BASE ECUMENISM

CEBI and the Popular Reading of the Bible

In chapter five, I briefly mentioned the rise of the *Centro de Estudos Bíblicos* (CEBI) in 1979 and its meaningful work training lay leaders and producing hundreds of publications to support a reading of the Bible that takes the social reality of the poor and their struggle for life as its point of departure. This method has been disseminated throughout Latin America and in other parts of the world.

CEBI emerged, as mentioned earlier, from conversations among two Catholics (Carlos Mesters and Agostinha Vieira de Mello) and two Protestants (Jether Pereira Ramalho and Lucilia Ramalho) during an ecumenical gathering of theologians, biblical scholars, and pastoralists in the difficult years of the military dictatorship. It drew inspiration from Paulo Freire's popular education and the CEBs, also benefitting from Vatican II and Medellin 1968 insights. The popular reading of the Bible (one emerging from the grassroots, the base) is not only concerned with putting the Bible back in the hands of the people—which is something Protestantism has done for almost two centuries in Latin America—but also with "recognizing the presence of God in the struggles for the liberation of Latin American peoples, following Jesus in his commitment to the impoverished."[1] It reflects the "way of being church" seen in the CEBs, which follows "Jesus in the commitment to the impoverished." In tandem with the see-judge-act method, the Popular Reading of the Bible (PRB) "is based on a context-text-pretext hermeneutic triangle" through which the "Bible is read from a specific ecclesial experience and social reality that informs the type of questions we ask it." According to such a

[1] Joilson de Souza Toledo, "Textos que Abrem Portas: Leitura Popular da Bíblia apresentada a partir de textos bíblicos," *Interações* 15/1 (2020), https://www.redalyc.org/journal/3130/313064676011/html/.

method, the "sacred literature is read not separately from life, but to illuminate it."[2]

Differently from the CEBs, which, as discussed earlier, exist primarily within the Catholic Church structures, CEBI, as an association formed by individuals from various Christian denominations, works with Christian communities—both Catholic and Protestant—offering services such as formation, publication, exchanges, without depending on the churches' institutional structures or hierarchies. In its relation to the churches, CEBI seeks to remind them that they should serve the poor. It stands in line with the self-perception of the CEBs, which see themselves as "a church born of the poor."[3]

As a movement stemming from the practice of communities, CEBI promotes a communal interpretation of the Bible. CEBI is aware of the fact that it did not create the popular reading of the Bible. Popular communities such as the CEBs already approached the Bible that way. Carlos Mesters, the Carmelite friar and biblical scholar who cofounded CEBI participated in Inter-Ecclesial Gatherings of the CEBs in an advisory role prior to the formation of CEBI. He and his ecumenical companions borrowed important elements from the CEBs in the development of a biblical hermeneutics based on the Latin American reality, including regular national gatherings and the placing of scholars and other experts in advisory roles. As Rafael Rodrigues da Silva, a national advisor of CEBI, points out, Mesters' hermeneutics is based on five pillars:[4]

a. the readers of the Bible are the people, communities (not isolated individuals).[5]
b. The Bible is a mirror of life since God is amid life and history. Thus, in a critical manner, PRB presents a way to better

[2] Souza Toledo, "Textos que Abrem Portas."

[3] Antonio Alvimar Souza, "CEBS: Uma Igreja que Nasce do Povo," *Cadernos Cajuína* 3/3 (2018): 3–16.

[4] Rafael Rodrigues da Silva, "Frei Carlos Mesters- Uma Vida dedicada à LPB e aos pobres," *Portal do CEBI*, https://cebi.org.br/artigos-e-reflexoes/frei-carlos-mesters-uma-vida-dedica-a-lpb-e-aos-pobres/.

[5] In Mesters' own words, "We are God's people, not isolated individuals. Thus, the passage from life to the Bible and from the Bible to life takes place in community." Carlos Mesters & Equipo Bíblico CRB, *Lectura Orante de la Biblia* (Estella (Navarra), Spain: Editorial Verbo Divino, 1997), 9.

understand the present reality and the word of God in the world. It is important not only to interpret the Bible but also to interpret the lives that live it out.[6]

c. The Bible is a book written by the people (containing popular traditions and memories) and for the people.[7]
d. People read the Bible with faith: God speaks through the book and without this faith there is no light to penetrate the meaning of its pages.
e. PRB leads to engagement with the oppressed (praxis dimension). Therefore, it must lead to the transformation of life (liberation).

The popular reading of the Bible starts with the reality of life from the perspective of the poor. As Mesters underscores, "The poor bring their real-life problems with them into the Bible," meeting their own lives in the mirror of the Bible. They engage the text with deep respect, seeking to listen to what God is saying to them. Then, they go out in the world to practice what they have learned.[8] According to Mesters, this approach that connects the Bible to life is the most ecumenical element in PRB. God-given life, in general, "is being threatened, destroyed." An ecumenical reading of the Bible in a context where oppression and injustice prevails brings people together to interpret the Bible as they struggle for life and liberation.[9] The revolutionary

[6] In approaching the Bible from their experiences of suffering and oppression, the poor discover a truth that was hidden from them, that is, "1. a history of oppression like their own today, with the same conflicts; and 2. A liberation struggle for the same values they pursue today in Brazil: land, justice, sharing, fraternity, a decent life." Carlos Mesters, "'Listening to What the Spirit is Saying to the Churches.' Popular Interpretation of the Bible in Brazil," in *The Bible and Its Readers*, ed. Wim Beuken et al., Concilium 1991/1 (London: SCM Press, 1991), 100–111 (103).

[7] That is, "The Bible was written in community, from the community and for the community. The sacred books have their origin in the people of Israel. The author or authors of each book were aware that they belonged to a people and wrote to record their experience of a God who acts in the people and through people or events. These books were left in the memory of the community as an expression of its faith and from there they were reread and updated. The Christian Community inherits these traditions and interprets them in light of the founding event: the resurrection of Jesus." Mesters & Equipo Bíblico CRB, *Lectura Orante de la Biblia*, 9.

[8] Mesters & Equipo Bíblico CRB, *Lectura Orante de la Biblia*, 107–108.

[9] Mesters & Equipo Bíblico CRB, *Lectura Orante de la Biblia*, 108.

nature of this method resides in the fact that the professional exegete is no longer the primary interpreter. The interpretation of the Bible takes place in the community, with the participation of all, including the exegete who is in dialogue with the community.[10]

Of equal significance is the change this way of reading the Bible provokes in the social (and epistemic) location from where interpretation is carried out; that is, the perspective of the poor and marginalized.[11] When the popular church becomes the interpreter of the Bible, and the lives and sociocultural location of the impoverished inform that interpretation, one can see a decolonial turn taking place to restore knowledges, interests, and perspectives that have been concealed under the garment of coloniality.[12] This shift in the theological and hermeneutical loci of enunciation based on a communal and analectic praxis of biblical interpretation caused by the interpellation of the poor in hegemonic Christian theologizing was one of the most significant events in the life of the Christian churches in Latin America in the second half of the twentieth century.[13] Such a radical social, cultural, and epistemic turn continues to be significant to ecumenical praxis and theology today.

This is not to say that there are not limits in the praxis of the CEBs or CEBI. In fact, there has never been a time since the beginning of the liberation turn in Latin American Christianity when assessment and self-criticism of these ecclesial movements have not existed. In his early assessment of the inter-ecclesial gatherings, for instance, Teixeira critically examined the extent to which the CEBs were actually touching the most marginalized. He was aware that poverty and exclusion are not homogeneous. They affect individuals and

---

[10] Mesters & Equipo Bíblico CRB, *Lectura Orante de la Biblia*, 108.

[11] Mesters & Equipo Bíblico CRB, *Lectura Orante de la Biblia*, 108.

[12] Juan José Tamoyo, *Teologías del Sur: El Giro Descolonizador* (Madrid: Editorial Trotta, 2017), 26–27.

[13] According to Enrique Dussel, analectics is juxtaposed to dialectics as follows: "Dialectics is the logic of the thinking that grounds itself out of itself and that assimilates everything to itself without leaving a remainder. Analectics is the thought that thinks from the distinctness of the other without assimilating the alterity of the other to mere difference. Analectical logic opens itself to the radical otherness of the other in such a way that it can never ground itself." See Amy Allen and Eduardo Mendieta, "Introduction," in *Decolonizing Ethics: The Critical Theory of Enrique Dussel*, ed. Amy Allen and Eduardo Mendieta (University Park, PA: Penn State University Press, 2021), 7.

communities differently. There are multiple levels of exclusion and invisibility to be considered. The methods of the Popular Church must examine why the number of those pushed to the margins continues to increase and who the oppressed are, based more specifically for instance, on gender, sexuality, race, religion, etc.[14] Teixeira also saw the need for greater openness to take the religiosity of the people as a challenge to liberationist praxis. Even though the religiosity and culture of the marginalized have received greater attention more recently, further work is needed on that front.

Finally, the tension between the internal unity of the Church and the autonomy of the CEBs has always been a focus of critical reflection. Eduardo Hoornaert asked this very question more than three decades ago, as he reflected on the CEBs vis-à-vis Comblin's critical considerations of Catholic Action in the early 1960s. Looking at the numerical decline of the CEBs in Brazil in the early 1990s, Hoornaert asked if it was not the case that the ecclesiastical system itself was suffocating the CEBs and, therefore, would not ineluctably cause "the death of this experience that was born within it, but which rather called for broader frontiers, new 'models,' as we say today." Hoornaert was particularly concerned with the lack of "autonomous lay leadership in CEBs, the permanence of 'pastoral agents' in positions of command, the issue of money that comes from abroad, the proposal of 'awareness' without much connection with the lived cultural world of the people, and the dangers of a new 'Christendom,' even if from the left." Although born within the Church, the question is whether it was not time for the CEBs to break free from it to preserve their revolutionary novelty. These important questions are not only relevant for the future of the CEBs but also for the future of Christianity in Latin America.[15]

Some of the very mechanisms Hoornaert named have contributed to neutralize, coopt, or even dismantle grassroots liberative efforts both within the Catholic Church and among Protestants. Those tensions and concerns, however, are not new, as discussed earlier in the case with the specialized Catholic Action sectors. Popular initiatives such as CEBs and CEBI concomitantly contribute to the renewal of

---

[14] Teixeira, *Os Encontros Intereclesiais de CEBs no Brasil*, 211. This is a topic I will return to in the next chapter.

[15] Hoornaert, "The Future of the CEBs," 162.

the church and bring risks with them, especially to those more protective of the status quo. The way these tensions and challenges are resolved or balanced out is key to determine what Latin American Christianity will look like in the coming decades.

The nationalization of the base communities' movement in Brazil and its articulation with other pastoral sectors of the Church, like the Brazilian Commission on Justice and Peace, have expanded the influence of the CEBs, creating new spaces for leaders formed in the movement to play leadership roles in a broader public witness, expanding the network of cooperation in the struggle for justice. The rise of popular movements such as CEBI also contributed to expand the social impact CEBs brought to other Christian traditions and beyond.

National meetings such as the inter-ecclesial gatherings are now held in various Latin American countries. Furthermore, since 1980, CEBs' representatives from all over Latin America have held eleven continental gatherings to share their experiences, challenges, and hopes, and learn from one another. The Eleventh Continental Gathering, in Guayaquil, in 2020, counted with the participation of "225 women and men who lived our faith in the CEBs of 16 countries in Latin America, the Caribbean and the United States."[16] In its final message, this gathering responded to the challenge posed by Pope Francis in the Amazon Synod, urging for a renewed commitment "to carry out a social, cultural, ecological and ecclesiastical conversion." Such a call for an integral conversion of the Church takes the turn to the poor to a new level, acknowledging both different voices and social locations and the common concern with the well-being of the earth, the Common Home:

> Listening, speaking with parrhesia, the decisive presence and influence of women and indigenous peoples, taking care of the Common Home, bringing together all experiences, adopting new logics and languages, taking care of life, understanding that problems are global, [and] that it is essential to proclaim and have missionary ardor.[17]

---

[16] Rede de Comunicadores das CEBs, "Mensagem final do XI Encontro Continental das CEBs," *CEBs do Brasil,* March 13, 2020, https://cebsdobrasil.com.br/mensagem-final-cebs-continental-guayaquil/.

[17] Rede de Comunicadores das CEBs, "Mensagem final."

The call in *Querida Amazonia* which the Latin American CEBs responded to in Guayaquil stems from the analectic interaction between the Pope, the synod of the Amazon—its bishops, priests, experts, and observers from other faith traditions—and hundreds of marginalized communities living in the Amazon Rainforest, including CEBs that participated in two years of preparatory conversations prior to the synod. Their collective voices not only made it into the final document of the Amazon Synod but were also reflected in the Post-Synodal Apostolic Exhortation of Pope Francis, *Querida Amazonia*. As Francis himself put it, this document resulted from his attentive listening to the reports resulting from those ongoing conversations and presented a synthesis of those concerns.

> During the Synod, I listened to the presentations and read with interest the reports of the discussion groups. In this Exhortation, I wish to offer my own response to this process of dialogue and discernment. I will not go into all of the issues treated at length in the final document. Nor do I claim to replace that text or to duplicate it. I wish merely to propose a brief framework for reflection that can apply concretely to the life of the Amazon region a *synthesis* of some of the larger concerns that I have expressed in earlier documents, and that can help guide us to a harmonious, creative and fruitful reception of the entire synodal process.[18]

Throughout this book, the reader has encountered complex local, regional, and global networks of forces mutually impacting one another to promote change. Very often such influences tend to be seen only from the perspective of the global to the local, from the North to the South, from the West to the East, and from the center to the peripheries. The alternative focus on the Indigeneity of world Christianity, on the other hand, sometimes limits the understanding of transcultural, transnational, and transcontinental mutual influences. The stories shared throughout this book complicate such narratives. It is impossible to trace the formation of Indigenous forms of Christian experience in Latin America without situating them

[18] Pope Francis, "Post-Synodal Apostolic Exhortation of the Holy Father Francis 'Querida Amazonia,'" https://press.vatican.va/content/salastampa/en/bollettino/pubblico/2020/02/12/200212c.html#.

within more complex dynamics involving national, regional, and global exchanges. Likewise, it is not possible to imagine a history of the ecumenical movement in the twenty-first century that does not pay attention to the impact that the experience of *ecumenismo de base*, as seen in the examples of the CEBs and CEBI, on the broader ecumenical movement.

The Ecumenism of the CEBs

The *Comunidades Eclesiais de Base* not only took the Latin American Catholic Church by storm in the 1970s but also modeled a community-based ecclesial life that began to be emulated by other Christians—not only Catholics—throughout the world. The grassroots participatory paradigm of a church born of the poor and active in the world served as a parameter for a number of new ecumenical initiatives that followed. One of those was CEBI and the *leitura popular da bíblia*. That grassroots approach to the reading of the Bible forming new communities of worship and action has made its way also among Latin American Protestants.

For some Protestants, the base (impoverished, popular, and nuclear) ecclesial communities resemble ecclesiological roots they are familiar with. The idea of small communities meeting outside of formal liturgical spaces (temples) is not strange especially to Protestants from free church traditions. That is why some Protestants have been attracted by the CEBs and began to take part in their annual national gatherings. Cláudio Ribeiro, a Methodist pastor and theologian who has served as an advisor in CEBs' national encounters, has reflected on the communal nature of the Methodist tradition, especially through the motto *ecclesiolae in ecclesia* (little churches within the church) in an attempt to develop a Brazilian Methodist ecclesiology, which can expand the meaning of the CEBs experience.[19]

The CEBs have also inspired Latin American Protestant churches working with the poor. Although having some previous insertion in poorer neighborhoods, non-Pentecostal Protestants, with their focus

[19] Cláudio de Oliveira Ribeiro, "Por uma eclesiologia metodista brasileira," *Revista Caminhando* 9/13 (2004): 43–64 (47).

on methods of literacy that are not as meaningful for impoverished communities, tend to have greater appeal to the middle-class and more educated sectors of the population than to the poor. Despite their familiarity with small-group strategies, many of these churches lack tools to fully engage the bases. The concern some Protestants had to develop a Latin American Protestant identity in the mid-twentieth century resulted exactly from their lack of identification with the daily realities experienced by the large number of impoverished Latin Americans.

During that period, a group of young ecumenical Protestants experimented with living among blue-collar working communities in Campinas, São Paulo and Rio de Janeiro, providing an example of what a commitment to the working classes could look like. Yet, those experiments were marginal in the overall Protestant landscape and short-lived due to the opposition the church and society movement faced within Protestant ecclesiastical structures. Furthermore, they still reached mostly literate urban lower-class workers (and students), not those experiencing the direst consequences of exclusion and poverty. While resembling some Protestant ecclesial arrangements, the CEBs pointed the way for a deeper engagement with the world and the struggle of the poor.

On the other hand, Brazilian Benedictine monk Marcelo Barros reminds us that as early as the 1940s the antecessors of the CEBs found inspiration in Martin Luther and the reformers for the renewal of the Catholic Church. Likewise, they found inspiration in eighteenth-century Methodist communities in England "characterized by having as the center of their lives the Word of God and the service to the poor."[20] Barros equally attributes to the rise of the ecumenical movement post-Edinburgh 1910 a motivating factor for the rise of Catholic Action, which emerged in response to an ecumenical call for Christians of all stripes to "witness the Reign of God."[21] By highlighting these points, he affirms that ecumenical vocation of the CEBs is based on the centrality

[20] Marcelo Barros, "Comunidades Ecumênicas de Base: A vocação ecumênica das CEBs e seus desafios," in *Ecumenismo e Evangelização Inculturada: Comunidades Eclesiais de Base*, ed. Nelito N. Dornelas (São Leopoldo, Brazil [???]: CEBI, 2005), 50–63 (50).

[21] Barros, "Comunidades Ecumênicas de Base," 51.

of the Word, their openness to welcome everyone regardless of church affiliation and their emphasis on God's Reign, which is larger than any church and "relativizes the differences that exist among them."[22]

In Brazil, over the past forty years the base communities have contributed to intensify relations of collaboration and dialogue between Catholics, Lutherans, and Anglicans, among others.[23] Other points of collaboration can be found in the association of the CEBs with the Catholic Pastoral Commissions, especially the Land Pastoral Commission,[24] which works with rural workers' settlements in coordination with the Landless Workers' Movement (MST), which increasingly counts with Protestants, including Pentecostals, in its midst.

In addition to welcoming Protestant participation in all levels of coordination of its national and local encounters, Barros also draws attention to the fact that the CEBs were among the first spaces within the Latin American Catholic Church to welcome interfaith engagement—known in Latin America as macro-ecumenism.[25] Such an openness has allowed the CEBs to cooperate with practitioners of Indigenous and African-derived religious traditions, also making room for multiple religious practices in their midst. As Gilvander Moreira puts it, "the spirituality of the CEBs is fundamentally dialogical and ecumenical, inculturated and open to all people, churches, religions, situations and realities, seeing those who are horizontally different not as enemies but as siblings, an element that adds and can effectively contribute to the Reign of love and justice."[26] Consequently, it is inclusive of women, Indigenous peoples, children, persons with substance use disorders, persons with disabilities, people of all genders and sexual orientations, sex workers, and other excluded and marginalized people.[27] The significance of such inclusive and open spirituality is even greater once one considers the "culture of silence"

---

22 Barros, "Comunidades Ecumênicas de Base," 51.

23 Barros, "Comunidades Ecumênicas de Base," 55.

24 Barros, "Comunidades Ecumênicas de Base," 56.

25 Barros, "Comunidades Ecumênicas de Base," 52.

26 Gilvander Moreira, "As CEBs estão vivas e atuantes," in *Ecumenismo e Evangelização Inculturada*, 32–49 (44).

27 Moreira, "As CEBs estão vivas e atuantes," 45.

and the impact of authoritarianism and persecution of minoritized communities in the continent.[28]

Contributions from Puebla

The Third Assembly of CELAM, in Puebla, Mexico, 1979, was more contentious than its predecessor. Polish Pope John Paul II (1978–2005) had a different approach to liberation theology than his predecessor Paul VI. In his opening address in Puebla, he made a point to clarify the priorities of the pastoral work of Church: "To watch the purity of the doctrine, the basis of the edification of the Christian community, is, therefore, along with the annunciation of the Gospel, the first and irreplaceable task of the pastor, the master of faith."[29] In his diaries of Puebla, Frei Betto mentions the work done by conservative sectors of the Church and the press to turn the pope's words into a condemnation of liberation theology.[30]

The tensions between anti-communists and supporters of liberation theology was palpable at the assembly. Pedro Arnoldo Aparicio, president of the Episcopal Conference of El Salvador, went as far as calling the Jesuits working in his country communists.[31] Brazilian theologian João Batista Libânio, who was also in Puebla, described those divergencies as pertaining to the understanding of the nature of the reality of injustice in the continent. While more conservative bishops accepted it as a stage in the process of development, those informed by the rising liberation theology viewed such a reality of massive poverty not as a transitory stage of development but as "the product of economic, social, and political national structures that support and sustain this state of poverty."[32]

---

[28] Guillermo Cook, *The Expectation of the Poor: Latin American Base Ecclesial Communities in Protestant Perspective* (Maryknoll, NY: Orbis Books, 1985), 21.

[29] João Paulo II, "Discurso Inaugural," in Conferência Geral do Episcopado Latino-Americano (CELAM), *Conclusões da Conferência de Puebla—Texto Oficial: Evangelização no Presente e no Futuro da América Latina* (São Paulo: Edições Paulinas, 1979), 15–34 (17).

[30] Frei Betto, *Diário de Puebla*, 2nd ed. (Rio de Janeiro: Editora Civilização Brasileira, 1979), 56.

[31] Betto, *Diário de Puebla*, 96.

[32] Betto, *Diário de Puebla*, 102. Interview during the Puebla conference.

Despite those tensions, acknowledging the progress made in the previous decade, Puebla 1979 produced some remarkable moments, including the formulation of the expression "the preferential option for the poor,"[33] which is often mistakenly attributed to Medellin 1968. This phrase, which became widely used in connection with liberation theology (the body of theological literature that since the 1970s has stemmed from an evolving liberation Christianity), represented a decisive pastoral option made by a number of bishops in Puebla to place the Church—which for so long identified with the status quo—on the side of the poor.[34] That pastoral option did not end with the conflicts within the Church. However, it became a consequential identifying mark of the Catholic Church in the continent—one that remains important to this day.

While Medellin sought to translate the idea of the Church of the Poor into the Latin American context, in Puebla, eleven years later, the reality of the irruption of the poor, especially through the CEBs, was established as a renewed face of the Church, pressing the hierarchy to take a clearer position in the struggle of the poor for life. Despite the controversies between adherents of liberation theology and conservative sectors of the Church, at the end of the day Puebla reaffirmed the same pastoral commitments that had been informing the journey of the Latin American church since 1968.[35] As such, Puebla can be understood as part of an ongoing dialogue, in response to important developments that had been taking place not only within the Catholic Church but, more broadly, in the Latin American societies.

Compared to Medellin, Puebla paid greater attention to the cultural plurality of Latin America, acknowledging the variety of races and cultures as "a common cultural heritage," while also sounding the alarm about the lack of knowledge, marginalization and destruction of "values belonging to the ancient and rich tradition of our people."[36] That kind of warning opened the door for

---

[33] Antonio Manzatto, "A Opção Preferencial pelos Pobres," in *Puebla - Igreja na América Latina e no Caribe: Opção pelos pobres, libertação e resistência*, ed. Ney de Souza and Emerson Sbardelotti (Petrópolis: Vozes, 2019), 451–462 (451).

[34] Manzatto, "A Opção Preferencial pelos Pobres," 451–462 (451).

[35] Manzatto, "A Opção Preferencial pelos Pobres," 455.

[36] Conferência Geral do Episcopado Latino-Americano (CELAM), *Conclusões da Conferência de Puebla*, 99.

further consideration of the place of women, Indigenous peoples, people of African descent and popular religiosity that followed in the making of Latin American theology. The main novelty Latin American liberation theology (LALT) had brought to theological discourse was the shift in the starting point of theologizing, taking the situation and praxis of the poor as its starting point. Such a move turned the poor into new theological subjects, thus promoting a shift in the theological locus of enunciation. However, the existing diversity and nuances of the complicated reality in which the dispossessed existed were not fully considered in the initial years. As the new theology continued to relate to the development of a certain pastoral praxis, though, those nuances began to gradually emerge, contributing to problematize any hegemonic understanding of the poor.

In the introduction of Gustavo Gutiérrez's revised edition of *A Theology of Liberation*,[37] he highlighted the deep connection between the rise of LALT and Medellin 1968, recalling that the name and reality of "liberation theology" emerged in a meeting in Peru, only a few months before Medellin.[38] Ever since, he noted, "we have entered a new stage in the life of our peoples." Appealing to liberation theology's dual fidelity "to the God of our faith and to the peoples of Latin America," he reinforced, "we cannot separate our discourse about God from the historical process of liberation."[39]

Fifteen years after the book's first print, the parameters of liberation theology had to take into consideration all that took place between Medellin and Puebla. Among other things, it was no longer sufficient to speak of the poor as if they were a hegemonic category. The irruption of the poor Gutiérrez had foreseen had far-reaching consequences. It could be seen in the rise of new independent nations in Africa and Asia, of "racial minorities" and women as a diverse movement, drawing particular attention to those Puebla called "doubly oppressed and marginalized."[40] In fact, it was in recognition of this reality that Puebla affirmed "the need for a conversion of the whole Church to a preferential option for the poor, aiming for their

[37] Gutierrez, *A Theology of Liberation*, xvii.

[38] Gutierrez, *A Theology of Liberation*, xviii.

[39] Gutierrez, *A Theology of Liberation*, xviii.

[40] Gutierrez, *A Theology of Liberation*, xx.

full liberation."[41] Such a theological move derived from the liberating praxis among the poor.

Puebla talked about the scandal of extreme poverty, condemning the increasing distance between the rich and the poor, while noticing how that egregious situation specifically affected different sectors of the population: children, youth, women, Indigenous peoples, people of African descent, peasants, urban workers, under- and unemployed people, and the elderly, among others.[42] Such a reality demanded not only personal conversion, but "deep transformation in the structures that correspond to the legitimate aspirations of the people for an authentic social justice."[43] Some people saw Puebla's categorization of Indigenous and Black people as the "poorest of the poor" as ambiguous, since such a socioeconomic identification with the most dispossessed could prevent the appreciation of the rich values from those cultures, demanding a more adequate pastoral practice to address cultural difference.[44]

On the other hand, the acknowledgment of subjects that, as Gutiérrez noticed, had been "'absent' from our society and from the church" was a refreshing addition to the class-based focus that predominated in Medellin and the early years of Latin American liberation theology,[45] making room for increased attention to specific experiences of suffering, aspiration, hope, and praxis, and to the rise of new theological voices. Base-oriented pastoral practices that emerged from these distinct but interwoven realities would not only expand the impact of liberation theology but also widen the meaning of ecumenicity as it included previously excluded subjects.

The poor were no longer described as a faceless category but as embodied individuals and communities whose voices mattered. A consequence of that shift can be seen in the rise of Latin American

---

[41] Conferência Geral do Episcopado Latino-Americano (CELAM), *Conclusões da Conferência de Puebla*, 352.

[42] Conferência Geral do Episcopado Latino-Americano (CELAM), *Conclusões da Conferência de Puebla*, 95–96.

[43] CELAM, *Conclusões da Conferência de Puebla*, 95.

[44] Paulo Suess, "Relevância e Ambiguidade para a Causa dos Povos Indígenas," in *Puebla - Igreja na América Latina e no Caribe*, 131–142 (132).

[45] Gutierrez, *A Theology of Liberation*, xx. By absent, he meant, "of little or no importance, and without the opportunity to give expression themselves to their sufferings, their comraderies, their plans, their hopes."

feminist theologies, Indigenous and Black theologies and eco- and ecofeminist theologies in the 1980s and 1990s.[46] These emerging theologies have contributed to deepen and problematize some early assumptions of liberation theology, reflecting the implications of the epistemological turn to multifaced impoverished peoples during that period. While this shift was not exclusively a product of Puebla, CELAM III acknowledged the irruption of the poor in their multiple faces, as embodied theological subjects who collectively produced popular culture and religiosity.[47] The popular pastoral work that emerged in the Catholic parishes and of ecumenical popular initiatives after Medellin also contributed to produce new theological voices.

According to the CNBB, the popular pastoral presence of the Church in Brazil embodies "the set of activities through which the Church carries out its mission of continuing the action of Jesus Christ among different groups and realities."[48] That increased pastoral presence has brought the Catholic Church significantly closer to the struggles of the poor, making it also a significant player in the formation of important social movements in the region, including the Landless Workers Movement (*Movimento dos Trabalhadores Rurais Sem Terra*, MST), the Homeless Workers Movement (*Movimento dos*

---

[46] María Pilar Aquino, *Aportes para una Teología desde la Mujer* (Madrid: Biblia y Fe, 1988); María Pilar Aquino and Elsa Tamez, *Teología Feminista Latinoamericana* (Quito: Ed. Abya-Yala, 1998); Leonardo Boff, *Cry of the Earth, Cry of the Poor* (Maryknoll, NY: Orbis Books, 1997); Quince Duncan et al. *Cultura negra y teología* (San José, Costa Rica: DEI, 1986); Ivone Gebara, *Longing for Running Water: ecofeminism and liberation* (Minneapolis, MN: Fortress Press, 1999); Agustín Herrera Quiñones, *Teología afroamericana: conceptualizacion para una propuesta de elaboración* (Quito: Centro Cultural Afroecuatoriano, 1994); Paulo Suess, *Desarrollo histórico de la teología India* (Quito: Abya-Yala, 1998); Elsa Tamez, ed., *Through Her Eyes: Women's Theology from Latin America* (Maryknoll, NY: Orbis, 1989). Nicanor Sarmiento Tupayupanqui, *Caminos de la teología India* (Buenos Aires: Editorial Verbo Divino, 2000).

[47] Despite the conservative backlash under the papacies of John Paul II and Benedict XVI, important sectors of CELAM have continued to engage the popular praxis of marginalized Christian communities in the continent. See Robert S. Pelton, ed., *Aparecida: Quo Vadis?* (Scranton and London: University of Scranton Press, 2008).

[48] Conferência Nacional de Bispos do Brasil (CNBB), "Pastorais," https://www.cnbb.org.br/pastorais/. There are various pastoral actions linked to CNBB. Among them, the Afro-Brazilian Pastoral Action, the Prison Pastoral Action, the Children Pastoral Action, the Human Mobility Pastoral Action, the Pastoral Service to the Immigrant, Pastoral Action for Marginalized Women, the National Workers' Pastoral Action, the National Health Pastoral Action, and the Pastoral Action to the Deaf.

Trabalhadores Sem Teto, MTST), the *Central Única dos Trabalhadores* (CUT), and the Workers Party (*Partido dos Trabalhadores*, PT), just to cite some of the major social movements created with support and participation of the progressive popular church (*igreja popular*).[49]

These social movements brought together Marxists, Catholics, and Protestants such as Benedita da Silva. One of the founders of PT in 1980 and a black militant in the Favela Association of the State of Rio de Janeiro, she was elected to the city council of Rio de Janeiro in 1982 and to congress in 1986, participating in the 1987 National Constituent Assembly. In 1994, Silva won a senate seat. She would also later serve as governor of the state of Rio de Janeiro, and currently represents that state, once again, in the Brazilian House of Representatives. Although an evangelical (Baptized in the Assemblies of God and currently a Presbyterian), due to her involvement in the Black and feminist movements, Silva has worked closely with progressive Catholics in the CEBs and Catholic pastoral commissions, while also promoting dialogue between the Workers Party and progressive evangelicals.[50]

Many participants in the Land Pastoral Commission (*Comissão Pastoral da Terra*, CPT) have also been involved in the MST and MTST. Founded in 1975, the CPT supports pastoral agents working among rural workers, thus contributing to the formation of numerous rural social movements. The CPT found its inspiration in a letter published by Pedro Casaldáliga (1928–2020) on October 10, 1971, 13 days prior to his inauguration as bishop of São Felix, Araguaia. In an iconic thirty-page-long letter, Casaldáliga, who would become a widely known exponent of liberation theology, addressed the situation of the church in the Amazon, the continuous conflict with large estates and the social marginalization that deeply affected the local population.[51] His letter denounced, in particular, "the reality

---

[49] Many other popular movements throughout the continent emerged in conjunction with the popular church. For a more comprehensive analysis of such a connection, see Luiz Eduardo W. Wanderley, *Democracia e Igreja Popular* (São Paulo: educ, 2007). The popular movements (and political party) mentioned here are among the largest social movements in the continent, with millions of constituents.

[50] Benedita da Silva, "'Lula sempre ouviu evangélicos,' destaca Benedita da Silva," PT na Câmara, https://ptnacamara.org.br/lula-sempre-ouviu-evangelicos-destaca-benedita-da-silvaores/. Also, interview by the author (and João Chaves) with Benedita da Silva on May 3, 2023.

[51] Pedro Casaldáliga, "Uma Igreja da Amazônia em Conflito com o Latifúndio e a Marginalização Social," Available at Servicios Koinonia: https://servicioskoinonia.

of Indigenous people, squatters and farmhands in a portion of the Amazon, a new stage for Brazil's colonial expansion."[52]

This prophetic cry at the peak of the military dictatorship produced important reactions. Among other things, "prompted by the need to create bonds of solidarity between churches in times of repression," an informal group of bishops started meeting regularly to produce documents that revealed the reality of the people through pastoral eyes, including the spoliation of Indigenous peoples.[53] As Antônio Canuto, one of the founders of the CPT recalls, during that time, some of the bishops "provoked the CNBB to sponsor a Meeting of Bishops and Prelates of the Amazon." That effort, also supported by pastoral agents, resulted in the realization of the "Gathering of Bishops and Prelates of the Amazon" in Goiânia, on June 19–22, 1975. The meeting convened by the CNBB Commission on Justice and Peace had sixty-seven participants from twenty-seven dioceses. The exposure to "the reality experienced by workers in the Legal Amazon" amid tense moments of debate resulted in the creation of the "Land Commission," in connection with the missionary stream of the CNBB.[54] Among its concrete tasks, the CPT would "translate the Land Statute and Rural Labor Legislation into popular language so that workers are aware of the rights that the law guarantees them," and "promote a campaign in favor of the rights of the landless people."[55]

---

org/Casaldaliga/cartas/1971CartaPastoral.pdf. Pedro Casaldáliga arrived in São Félix do Araguaia in 1968. In July 1971, the Vatican nominated him as the Bishop of the Prelacy of São Félix do Araguaia. His ordination took place on October 23, 1971, just thirteen days after his famous letter. Due to his courageous and prophetic stand, as well as his radical solidarity with the oppressed, especially the Indigenous people of the Amazonia, he faced an assassination attempt right before his ordination. He lived with constant threats from the beginning of his bishopric.

[52] Antônio Canuto, "Há 40 anos nascia a Comissão Pastoral da Terra," https://mst.org.br/2015/06/08/ha-40-anos-nascia-a-comissao-pastoral-da-terra/.

[53] Antônio Canuto, "Há 40 anos nascia a Comissão Pastoral da Terra," https://mst.org.br/2015/06/08/ha-40-anos-nascia-a-comissao-pastoral-da-terra/.

[54] Canuto, "Há 40 anos nascia a Comissão Pastoral da Terra." The CPT also works closely with the Indigenous Missionary Council (CIMI), created in 1971 with the goal of "interconnecting, advising and energizing those who work in favor of landless people and rural workers, and establishing links with other similar organizations."

[55] Canuto, "Há 40 anos nascia a Comissão Pastoral da Terra." Landless is a reference to rural workers dislodged from their means of subsistence either due to natural disasters or as a direct consequence of the unfair competition imposed on them by the latifundia-based system in the region.

The CPT, which expanded its reach to become an ecumenical pastoral action over the years, not only contributed in the long run to the foundation of the Landless Workers Movement (MST), but also has continued to work for the rights of rural workers and the rights of the earth, serving as a formation center for new generations of rural workers as they become increasingly aware of their rights as citizens and as humans. In these five decades, the CPT has reaffirmed its commitment to popular spirituality and its pastoral character, supporting the communities they partner with and their social, political, and cultural agency. Its national structure plays a critical role in giving visibility to depredatory actions that "privilege capital to the detriment of the rights of peasant communities," inhibiting the construction of just power and gender relations, and "the valorization and liberation of peasant women and the strengthening of peasant youth initiatives."[56]

In a non-binary combination of spirituality and action, the CTP has promoted since 1978 the "Romarias da Terra e das Águas" (Pilgrimages of Land and the Waters), which in the spirit of Vatican II seek to end "the rupture between people, word, and altar."[57] While bringing attention to important social issues, the *romarias* are also mystical events that build on popular spiritual practices. As Dirceu Fumagalli, a CPT agent in the state of Paraná, highlights, "Earth Pilgrimages are the sacrament of the journey. They are the temple of the encounter between the divine and the human."[58] While building on traditional/popular spiritual practices, these *romarias* serve as spiritual wells for those acting in the world while dealing with violence and threats of harm.

One of the plenaries in the 2023 pilgrimage focused on "the resistance of the Pataxó people from the extreme south of Bahia against the occupation of their lands" and how it "has triggered retaliation

---

[56] Comissão Pastoral da Terra (CPT), "Histórico," https://www.cptnacional.org.br/sobre-nos/historico.

[57] Forty-six *romarias* have taken place between 1978 and 2023, drawing attention to a number of different issues. The 2023 romaria focused on the theme "To end hunger on this earth: Land, Water, Roof, Work and Bread." CPT Bahia, "46ª Romaria da Terra e das Águas leva milhares de romeiros a Bom Jesus da Lapa entre 7 e 9 de julho," https://cptba.org.br/46a-romaria-da-terra-e-das-aguas-leva-milhares-de-romeiros-a-bom-jesus-da-lapa-entre-7-e-9-de-julho/.

[58] CPT, "Romarias da Terra e Água," https://www.cptnacional.org.br/romarias.

from wealthy landowners, who hire gunmen and private militias to attack the indigenous people." In the months leading to the *romaria*, three young Pataxós (aged 14, 16, and 25) were murdered, and there was a general insecurity and fear that more people would be massacred "in their homes."[59] In addition to remembering the young lives lost in the conflict and bringing public attention to the significance of ongoing violence and land conflicts for the Indigenous peoples in Brazil, the *romarias* offered inspiration for the continuation of the journey. Mass celebration, popular music and devotion, and mutual pastoral care contribute to the renewal of hope and strength among both pastoral agents and the entire community. In other words,

> The Land Pilgrimages value the religious, and do not fail in their prophetic contribution. They seek more than comfort the heart; they seek the transformation of society, the construction of the Kingdom of God. Traditional pilgrimages are centered on individuality, promise, the transcendent and earth pilgrimages focus on the collective and the reality of the people.[60]

Continuing the grassroots-oriented mobilization seen in earlier movements such as JOC, JUC, Popular Action, and the CEBs, CPT brings popular religion and the preferential option for the poor together, reflecting the cultural emphasis seen in CELAM III (1979), IV (1992), and V (2007).

Other ecumenical expressions of the popular church from this period have equally contributed to expand the notion of ecumenicity in Latin America, making it increasingly inclusive of practices, beliefs and worldviews associated with the base, the organized poor. One of them is CESEEP (Centro Ecumênico de Serviços à Evangelização e Educação Popular). Founded in 1982, CESEEP was one of the first ecumenical centers to focus on popular education in Latin America. Its main goal is to serve the leadership of popular movements and communities through the pastoral work of Christian churches.

Based in São Paulo, CESEEP "is connected to a widespread network of Ecumenical Centers. These centers, known as social

[59] CPT Bahia, "Os Ataques contra o Povo Pataxó no Extremo Sul da Bahia," March 13, 2023. https://cptba.org.br/os-ataques-contra-o-povo-pataxo-no-extremo-sul-da-bahia/.

[60] CPT, "Romarias da Terra e Água."

animation centers, offer training services and mutual support, embracing the diversity of cultures and social experiences found on the Latin American and Caribbean continent."[61] It offers a number of courses, equipping lay participants with tools for social analysis, while envisioning their engagement with the broader society.

In addition to the publication of numerous resources for participating communities, CESEEP is widely known for its *Cursos de Verão* or Summer Institutes, which focus on themes of interest for the communities and movements with whom CESEEP engages. The first of those encounters took place in 1988, focusing on the pastoral agents and the aspiration for them to multiply and transmit what they learned to their communities. With support from some Protestant churches and blessings from CONIC, CESEEP initiated its Summer Institutes with three main goals in mind: (1) to respond to the demand for training of pastoral agents, pastors, and nuns who consecrate their energies and pastoral commitment to that kind of context; (2) to dedicate special attention to lay people, as the possibilities of formation are fewer for them, considering that a large part of the Christian witness in today's world depends on them; and (3) to support young people, a growing sector of the life of the churches with increasingly greater responsibilities in the social apostolate, the animation of singing and liturgy, and the formation and transmission of faith.[62]

In its initial editions (1988–1991), *Curso de Verão* was divided into four sections (biblical, theological, pastoral, and church and society) that complemented each other. The pastoral section initially focused on lay ministries, being followed by the study of the religions of the people, the history of Christianity in Brazil, and ecumenism. The church and society section, by its turn, examined matters of faith and politics, with an emphasis on the past and present of the Black Brazilian community in light of the 1988 constitution, then turning to popular movements and their projects of society, and finally providing tools for critical analysis of the social situation in Latin

[61] Centro Ecumênico de Serviços à Evangelização e Educação Popular (CESEEP), "História," https://ceseep.org.br/missao-e-objetivos/.

[62] Gilberto Gorgulho et al., eds, *Curso de Verão: Ano I*, 2nd ed. (São Paulo: Edições Paulinas, 1988), 6.

America. In addition, that section also discussed popular education and what the planners coined "a theology of work."[63]

The Thirty-Seventh Summer Institute took place on January 4–13, 2024. Its theme was "Work as a Right: For a Dignified Life and Social Justice." Each Summer Institute is organized in collaboration with several partners. This time, the collaborators included the Pontifical Catholic University of São Paulo (PUC-SP), the Catholic University Theater (TUCA) and other entities, social movements, churches, communities, and families. It had three hundred twenty-eight participants.[64] Clergy and theologians participated as advisers, following the same model of popular education seen in both CEBI and the CEBs. The 2024 Summer Institute sought to respond to the flexibilization of work, passed as a change in Brazilian legislation, rolling back rights Brazilian workers had acquired since the 1950s, and the subsequent dehumanization of laborers, especially those who would end up jobless. Among other things, the Summer Institute generated a public petition standing in solidarity with homeless people in the city of São Paulo and repudiating the Parliamentary Commission of Investigation proposed by conservative politicians to "criminalize the entities that provide them with support, including Father Júlio Lancellotti, who leads the Pastoral of Homeless People of the Archdiocese of São Paulo."[65]

Father Júlio, an outspoken priest who in the late 1970s and early 1980s was part of monsignor Paulo Evaristo Arns's team working with juvenile offenders, has been a champion for the homeless population in São Paulo, where he assists more than thirty-five thousand people in a district pejoratively nicknamed "crack land."[66] His tireless advocacy seeking to give voice to the poorest of the poor and his radical solidarity with all those who are marginalized, including the LGBTQIA+ community in São Paulo, has turned him a target of right-wing Catholics and evangelicals. Not only has he received death threats and been physically attacked on the streets, but he has also become the target of public investigations initiated by far-right

[63] Gorgulho et al., eds, *Curso de Verão*, 8.

[64] Curso de Verão, "Carta Compromisso do Curso de Verão de 2024," https://cursodeverao.ceseep.org.br/arquivos/1769.

[65] de Verão, "Carta Compromisso do Curso."

[66] Júlio Lancellotti, interview with the author on October 4, 2023.

politicians who see his work with the poor as a threat. His risky situation led Pope Francis to give him a call, which he recalls as follows:

> Talking on the phone with Pope Francis [. . .] was a very emotional moment, very beautiful, full of enthusiasm. What perhaps has changed now is the visibility, because people came to know that Pope Francis calls those who are facing a challenge, a difficulty, or when he wants to convey an important message. What he has transmitted to me is: "Take care of the poor, be together with them." And what he said to me: "live with the poor like Jesus."[67]

Lancellotti is one of many priests and lay Christians seeking to practice a radical love for the poor in conversation with the experiences that liberation Christianity organisms such as CESEEP have contributed to shape.

In addition to the Summer Institute, CESEEP offers many other courses on popular and pastoral education, including a course on Latin American Pastoral and Gender Relations. Created in 1995, this course "seeks to respond to current challenges in the social, economic, political, cultural and religious fields, from a gender perspective," deepening the "reflection on the condition of women and the social issues in which they are involved, encouraging debate on gender inequalities, in the search for overcoming them."

In those courses, CESEEP draws on Freire's popular education to equip those "committed to the search for less asymmetrical, more egalitarian and mutually enriching relationships."[68] One of its focuses is the formation of women for leadership. Whereas women constitute more than 51 percent of all Christians in Latin America,[69] and increasingly carry the burden of keeping Christian institutions functioning, they are underrepresented in positions of leadership,

[67] Cited in Társila Elbert and Andressa Collet, "Living with the poor like Jesus: The example of Fr Júlio Lancellotti," *Vatican News*. https://www.vaticannews.va/en/church/news/2021-10/laudato-si-story-brazil-poverty-fr-lancellotti.html.

[68] Centro Ecumênico de Serviços à Evangelização e Educação Popular (CESEEP), "Curso Latino-Americano de Pastoral e Relações de Gênero," https://ceseep.org.br/curso-latino-americano-de-pastoral-e-relacoes-de-genero-2023/.

[69] For detailed information on these numbers, see Gina Zurlo, *Women in World Christianity: Building and Sustaining a Global Movement* (West Sussex, UK: Wiley Blackwell, 2023), 15.

while being disproportionately affected by the indexes of violence and poverty such as unemployment, lower income, domestic and sexual violence, among others.[70] In light of these situations, both CEBI and CESEEP have emphasized the popular education of women whose leadership as pastoral agents and rights advocates, among others, is of critical significance.

The Latin American Council of Churches (CLAI), formed in 1982, has also produced specific resources to strengthen the position of women through its Women and Gender Pastoral Commission. These resources are produced by women and primarily—although not exclusively—aimed at reaching and strengthening Christian women in the region.[71] Likewise, CEBI has produced ecumenical materials examining the challenges women and the feminist movement have brought to ecumenical conversations, including topics such as women's ordination, the laicity of the state, and sexual and reproductive rights. The issues these women initiatives raise from a

---

[70] According to the Economic Commission for Latin America and the Caribbean (known in the region as CEPAL), at least 4,473 women were victims of feminicide only in 2021. See United Nations, "CEPAL: Ao menos 4.473 mulheres foram vítimas de feminicídio na América Latina e no Caribe em 2021." https://www.cepal.org/pt-br/comunicados/cepal-menos-4473-mulheres-foram-vitimas-feminicidio-america-latina-caribe-2021. That situation was worsened during the COVID-19 pandemic. The *Observatório da Imprensa*, created by the Universidade Estadual de Campinas (UNICAMP) in 1998, not only highlights the femininization of poverty in Latin America and the Caribbean but also points to the impact of laws on the bodies of women, causing a double experience of suffering. Jean-Jacques Kourliandsky, "Mulheres latino-americanas: um contexto de duplo sofrimento," *Observatório da Imprensa*, edition 1129, March 16, 2021, https://www.observatoriodaimprensa.com.br/genero-e-inclusao/mulheres-latino-americanas-um-contexto-de-duplo-sofrimento/.

[71] See, for instance, Judith van Osdol, ed., *Mujer, levántate: Porque no será fácil . . . Pero será posible* (Quito: Consejo Latinoamericano de Iglesias, 2006). Leading female theologians such as Maritze Trigos Torres, Ofelia Ortega, and Elsa Tamez have contributed to this project. The 1980s also saw the rise of a Latin American feminist theology, which took multiple forms. From the historiographical work of Ana Maria Bidegain to the rereading of the Bible "through her eyes" as seen in Elsa Tamez to the ecofeminism of Ivone Gebara, Latin American Christians were for the first time hearing women theologians reshaping not only the older theologies but even the newly founded liberation theology, which was still reflective of the male gaze. See, for instance, the collection of essays titled *Through Her Eyes*, published in connection with the first conference of women theologians in Latin America. In particular, read the final statement of that conference in Tamez, ed., *Through Her Eyes*, 150–154.

feminist perspective are critical to the ecumenical task.[72] Although these themes continue to face significant resistance in some settings, ecumenical organizations such as CESEEP have created spaces where women continue working to expand the ecumenical table.

CESEEP also offers annual courses on ecumenism, interfaith relations, pastoral formation, Christian activism, and Bible. Furthermore, it has created a course specifically for bishops, which, inspired by the Church of the Poor, offers information and training on popular education for "Catholic and evangelical bishops and pastors, from Latin America and the Caribbean, and even from other continents, regionally or nationally responsible for their churches."[73] A significant part of the resources CESEEP uses in these courses are easily accessible.

Puebla affirmed the preferential option for the poor and reaffirmed the ecumenical vocation of Latin American Christianity, among other things, by expanding the boundaries of the *oikoumenē* to include a wide range of impoverished and marginalized groups within the structures of the Church and in the larger society, which deserved specific attention. It also stimulated the rise of a number of popular ecumenical initiatives that contributed to the advancement of *ecumenismo de base* in the region.

---

[72] Romi Márcia Bencke & Sonia Gomes Mota, *Ecumenismo e Feminismo: Parcerias da Casa Comum* (São Leopoldo: CEBI, 2012), 25.

[73] Centro Ecumênico de Serviços à Evangelização e Educação Popular (CESEEP), "O que é o Curso para Bispos," https://ceseep.org.br/o-que-e-o-curso-para-bispo/.

10

THE GLOBAL IMPACT OF BASE ECUMENISM

Ecumenismo de Base: Globalization from Below

The expression "globalization from below" has been used to contrast what Richard Falk called "predatory globalization," the systemic and damaging impact of an economic world order largely dominated by the non-accountable powers of multinational corporations, transnational banks, and their collaborators, on those pushed to the margins of society. Despite its promises of a better future, such a globalized order has not contributed to resolve the increasing gap between the rich and the poor.[1]

Scholars like Robert C. Dash have called the alternative to predatory globalization, "globalization from below," a political project that involves popular mobilization and mass movements through consensual social control "from below" rather than by coercive means "from above."[2] This book has displayed a complex network of cross-cultural and transnational relationships, drawing attention to the impact of global influences on local developments, the impact of local developments on global events, and transnational relationships involving people and movements socially marginalized. In particular, this book highights ecumenical initiatives and networks which, formed among impoverished communities and oppressed peoples, have bounced back to impact the larger ecumenical movement. *Ecumenismo de base*, informed by Paulo Freire's popular education, became initially widely known due to the boom of *Comunidades Eclesiais de Base* (CEBs). Over the past five decades, base ecumenism has, taken different shapes and forms in Latin America, while also impacting global conversations. The CEBs exemplify the impact of globalization from below. Informed by epistemologies of the South, they embody the

[1] Falk used the metaphor of a global apartheid to describe this problem. See Richard Falk, *Predatory Globalization: A Critique* (Malden, MA: Blackwell, 2000), 13.

[2] Robert C. Dash, "Globalization: For Whom and For What," *Latin American Perspectives* 25/6 (1998): 52–54.

resilience of oppressed people who, despite experiencing the ugly face of the colonial/modern global order, do not give up on the possibility of collectively constructing another possible world.

In earlier chapters, I mentioned the rise of the Third World Movement in the 1950s as an inspiration for later initiatives among ecumenically minded Christians in the Global South. The Church of the Poor group formed in the Second Vatican Council was an early example of how "Third World" Christians sought to influence the global church and its agenda. This interdependence between the global and the local, often referred to as glocalization, glocalism, or global localization, advances a vision of globalization, which moves simultaneously in paradoxical directions, namely the universalization of the local and the particularization of the global.[3]

Despite its limitations and short existence, the Third World project left a legacy, which continues to impact popular movements and networks to this day. Even though the terms of the conversation have changed and the use of Global South, as discussed earlier, has replaced earlier references to the Third World it's spirit is not dead. It continues to influence transnational movements in the Global South and the aspiration of those impacted by a predatory global order who continue, nevertheless, to fight for emancipation and self-determination. On the ecumenical front, while the dream of a Christian Bandung, as expressed by Hélder Câmara during Vatican II, did not fully materialize, the efforts that he and others contributed to following the Council in Latin America have continued to inform new grassroots initiatives pointing to another possible world. A number of subsequent ecumenical initiatives have found inspiration in that dream. One of those initiatives was the Ecumenical Association of Third World Theologians (EATWOT), founded in 1976.

The Geneva Conference of Church and Society sponsored by the WCC in 1966 offered a unique opportunity for theologians and other Christians from the Global South to not only address the global church but also to stand face-to-face with one another to share their

---

[3] Roland Robertson, "Globalization and the Future of 'Traditional Religion,'" in *God and Globalization: Religion and the Powers of the Common Life*, vol. 1, ed. Max L. Stackhouse with Peter J. Paris (Harrisburg, PA.: Trinity Press International, 2009), 56, 64.

experiences and aspirations. Whereas since the formation of the WCC in 1948 a growing number of African and Asian voices were involved in the ecumenical movement, Latin America did not get enough attention until the creation of *ISAL*, the Latin American Commission on Church and Society, with financial support from the WCC Church and Society under the influence of Paul Albrecht.[4] Present on the global platform for the first time in Geneva 1966, ISAL made a strong case for the need of the churches to "serve as a voice for and defender of the poor, of those who are the victims of injustice due to the prevailing social order," drawing attention, in particular, to the complicity of the "Western, Christian civilization" whose structures maintained "a system of increasing exploration, which at the same time is extended to the 'developing' world by means of the nefarious action of the multinational corporations." Therefore, in the 'developing world,' "*agape* is expressed through political/social commitment and the practice of liberating action in its broadest and most inclusive sense."[5]

The Third Assembly of the World Council of Churches was the first one held outside the Europe–North America axis. The inaugural assembly of the WCC took place in Amsterdam (1948), followed by the second assembly in Evanston, Illinois, in 1954. The meeting in New Delhi in 1961 was the first in Asia or outside the North Atlantic axis. Although that move was meant to reflect the global nature of the newly founded Council, its rationale still represented the old church-mission divide, which inadvertently saw the non-Western world more as a mission field than as church per se. Churches from Africa, Asia, and Latin America were still treated as "new member churches."[6] The message coming out of that assembly was titled "The Light of the World," and the justification presented for the realization of the assembly in India was missionary. While affirming its commitment

[4] Willem Adolph Visser 't Hooft, "Oldham's Method in Abrecht's Hands," *Church and Society - Ecumenical Perspectives: Essays in Honor of Paul Abrecht* [*The Ecumenical Review* 37/1 (1985)], ed. Roger L. Shinn (Geneva: World Council of Churches, 1985), 3–9 (7).

[5] Luis E. Odell, "The Church and Society Explosion in Latin America," in *Church and Society - Ecumenical Perspectives*, 34–39 (38).

[6] Kenneth Slack, *Despatch from New Delhi: The Story of the World Council of Churches Third Assembly, New Delhi, 18 November–5 December 1961* (London: SCM Press, 1962), 9.

to "the mission of Christ's people to the whole inhabited earth," the assembly report cites *The Sunday Statesman*'s statement on November 19, 1961, which affirmed, "If the distinguished visitors from abroad can advance unity in their own countries, they will spread healthy influences far and wide . . . ," concluding with the following statement: "To expose ourselves to such words was surely part of the point to coming to Asia."[7] In other words, despite the efforts to see the WCC as a sign of the worldwide presence of Christianity, the perception of the West as the home of the movement and as distinguished visitors to Asia still informed the self-understanding of the Council. It would take the rise of several prophetic voices from Global South churches in the 1960s and 1970s to overcome that deeply seated Eurocentric prejudice.

New Delhi 1961 was also the WCC assembly where the merging of the IMC and the WCC was finalized. If, on the one hand, the new WCC Division of World Evangelism and Mission sought to integrate the missionary impetus of the IMC into the regular life of the WCC, it still brought with that a view of Africa, Asia, and Latin America as the primary areas where such mission should take place. Although mission would begin to take postcolonial sensibilities into consideration, the deep abyss cutting through the ecumenical movement, which saw those areas primarily as mission fields, had not yet been dispelled.[8]

A number of significant events happened between New Delhi and the next assembly in Uppsala (1968). Among them, Vatican II (1962–1965), which had a huge impact especially on faith and order conversations.[9] The Faith and Order WCC staff went to work during the Second Vatican Council. They joined the Vatican-initiated Joint Working Group created in 1965 to form a Joint Theological Commission in 1967 to study the theme "Catholicity and Apostolicity."[10] Also worth noting was the intense activity in the Department on Church and Society during that period, as this department advanced

[7] Slack, *Despatch from New Delhi*, 16–17.

[8] See, for instance, the report of the "Division of World Mission and Evangelism," in World Council of Churches, *New Delhi to Uppsala 1961–1968: Report of the Central Committee to the 4th Assembly of the World Council of Churches* (Geneva: World Council of churches, 1968), 24–47.

[9] "Division of World Mission and Evangelism," 54.

[10] "Division of World Mission and Evangelism," 58–59.

a "new conversation between the churches and the secular world on many issues of social ethics and policy."[11]

Equally significant was how the Department on Church and Society expanded the ecumenical table, adopting new criteria to invite participants for the 1966 Conference on Church and Society. Up to that point, participants in official ecumenical gatherings were appointed by member churches. The problem with that method was that it tended to result in the concentration of ecclesiastical leaders, thus producing a deficit in the representation of certain constituencies. Geneva 1966 was tasked with doing "the pioneering and creative thinking on the Church's responsibility in society." To achieve its goal, it altered the selection process of participants, seeking to reach a balance between theologians and lay specialists in different disciplines and regional representation "corresponding to their role in the world community." Such a move resulted in significant lay participation and a "relatively large representation from the non-western world."[12]

This Conference was the first ecumenical event with a greater number of lay participants than clergy and the first event of the WCC in which the combined number of participants from Africa, Asia, and Latin America was equivalent to those coming from Western Europe and North America.[13] Such a world perspective impacted the meeting's agenda and conversations. One of the critical topics discussed in that conference was the question about the role of "Christian witness in the face of revolutionary change," a topic that had been a part of conversations in the Global South since the early 1960s, and which would not take place on the world stage.[14] The goal of the conference was to bring topics of significance for Christians

---

[11] "Division of World Mission and Evangelism," 59.

[12] "Division of World Mission and Evangelism," 62. The Conference had 480 participants, including 38 observers and 18 guests from 80 countries and 164 churches. As for regional representation, 65 participants came from North America, 42 from Latin America, 76 from Western Europe, 45 from Eastern Europe, 42 from Africa, 46 from Asia, 17 from the Middle East, and 5 from Australia and New Zealand. Eight of the observers were Catholics who had participated in two Roman Catholic-WCC pre-consultations on Christian social thought today in March 1965 and February 1966. Ibid., 65.

[13] Ibid.

[14] Ibid., 64.

in the non-Western world to the worldwide ecumenical table, not as a point of arrival but as the beginning of a conversation that should continue in the following years.

The Secretariat on Racial and Ethnic Relations was deeply involved in the making of this conference, which also devoted critical attention to the issue of Christian practice and race relations, especially in South Africa.[15] These were also critical years in the Civil Rights Movement in the United States. All those events impacted the work of the Church and Society Department. Geneva 1966 marked the moment in which social themes began to pervade the ecumenical movement.

Another sign of the challenges the 1960s brought to ecumenical conversations on the way to Uppsala was the debate on the "admission of women to the organized ministry," which stemmed from a recommendation made by the New Delhi Assembly. Discussion about the participation of women in churches, councils, and governing bodies increased during that period. The WCC itself began to consider the impact of that conversation on its structures. In 1968, there were only five women in a Central Committee composed of one hundred people, and two women in its eighteen-member Executive Committee. Even the composition of the Church and Society Conference in 1966 was lacking on that front, with only twenty-three women among its four hundred ten participants.[16] In all these matters, the mid-1960s marked a moment when several justice-related themes started gaining greater prominence in ecumenical conversations, reflecting the rapid social changes taking place in the world at the time.[17]

---

[15] Ibid., 65.

[16] Ibid., 94.

[17] From its inception the WCC formed a Commission of Churches on International Affairs (CCIA), to deal with situations of concern in the international realm, including human rights, religious freedom, nuclear concerns, and issues of migration and refugees. These matters were seen as part of the public responsibility of the churches in the world and required collaborative witness from WCC members. The issues discussed in Geneva 1966, though, brought to the fore other sorts of divisions among the churches and within them, which required concerted attention in ecumenical conversations as those the Church and Society Department was conducting.

Those changes would become even more visible in the entire ecumenical movement in the Uppsala Assembly in 1968. The theme of the Assembly, held from July 4 to 20, 1968 was based on John 21: 5: "Behold, I make all things new." As Jürgen Moltmann asserts, this theme reflected the fears and hopes of turbulent times.[18] The Uppsala message began exactly by acknowledging that the council heard the cry of those suffering and seeking justice and peace: "We heard the cry of those who long for peace; of the hungry and exploited who demand bread and justice; of the victims of discrimination who claim human dignity; and of the increasing millions who seek for the meaning of life."[19] In its response to that cry, the theme of Christian unity was now placed within the framework of "a renewed human community." As such, the message stated, "Christians will manifest our unity in Christ by entering into full fellowship with those of other races, classes, age, religious and political convictions, in the place where we live. Especially we shall seek to overcome racism wherever it appears."[20]

Likewise, the key separation not only between Christians but dividing humanity as a whole was "The ever-widening gap between the rich and the poor, fostered by armament expenditure." This was "the crucial point of decision today." Such a separation needed to be overcome in a world that God makes new. In response to that, the assembly made the following commitment: "Therefore, with people of all convictions, we Christians want to ensure human rights in a just world community. We shall work for disarmament and for trade agreements fair to all. We are ready to tax ourselves in furtherance of a system of world taxation."[21] Whereas these commitments had no practical bearing on the responses Christians around the world would offer to those problems, they signaled a growing sensibility to the plight of the entire human race, especially the most vulnerable, in consonance with the discussions held in Geneva 1966.

---

[18] Jürgen Moltmann, "'Behold, I Make All Things New': The Unforgettable Message of the WCC Assembly in Uppsala in 1968," *The Ecumenical Review* 70/2 (2018): 357–369 (360).

[19] Moltmann, "Behold, I Make All Things New," 361.

[20] Moltmann, "Behold, I Make All Things New," 361.

[21] Moltmann, "Behold, I Make All Things New," 361.

Explaining half a century later how remarkable this message was, Moltmann pointed to the significance of Uppsala's connection between interpreting the "signs of the times" and listening to "the 'cry' of those suffering from the violence of war, of the hungry and exploited, of the despised, disadvantaged, and the disoriented." Thus, he identified in Uppsala an expanded view of ecumenicity:

> Christianity and humanity face the same dangers in the world, which is why Christian hope is universal and encompasses everyone. For the church foreshadows "a renewed human community." Its unity is geared toward the unity of the human race and thus toward overcoming its divisions into races, classes, generations, and sexes. The church of Christ is not a self-sufficient religious sect but the new humanity (1 Cor. 15:22).[22]

Unity was not only for the sake of Christians but for the whole human race. Christians worldwide were urged to advocate for "a just world community and the overcoming of war, the arms race, and the growing gap between the rich and poor."[23]

The journey from Uppsala 1968 to Nairobi 1975 would deepen that challenge. Between the two assemblies, the WCC elected a Caribbean as its third General Secretary. After the tenures of Dutch theologian Willem Adolf Visser 't Hooft (1948–1966) and American Presbyterian church leader Eugene Carson Blake (1966–1972), the Dominican Methodist pastor Philip Alford Potter was elected General Secretary in 1972. He was the first person from the Global South to hold that office. His tenure as general secretary lasted until 1984. To borrow an image from Michael Jagessar, Potter brought his Caribbean imagination to the world scene. In Jagessar's own words,

> He is quintessentially a Caribbean thinker, who comes from a region shaped by the "architectonic forces of conquest, colonization, slavery, sugar monoculture, colonialism, and racial and ethnic admixture." The region was "the testing ground of colonialism, imperialism, and capitalist racism." The stories of the Caribbean islands are essentially stories of the constant struggle for survival, cultural diversity/synthesis, subversion, nationalism, and black

[22] Moltmann, "Behold, I Make All Things New," 362.

[23] Moltmann, "Behold, I Make All Things New," 362.

> consciousness. All these factors are significant in understanding Potter's leadership of the WCC as they have shaped his thinking and the ways in which he negotiated working in a predominantly euro/western context.[24]

Criticized—mostly by people from the "dominant world"—for his "obsession with third-world problems and with issues like racism, liberation struggles (Southern Africa), development, human rights, and poverty/debt," Porter "intuitively grasped from his Caribbean heritage the incapacity of accompanying the 'master-race' narcissism to encompass the many sidedness of humanity."[25]

One of the important contributions he made to the ecumenical movement as WCC General Secretary was the emphasis he put on the universal dialogue of cultures. In an essay originally delivered as part of the Birks Lectures of McGill University, Canada, in 1977, Potter discussed the changes that took place in the previous decade in the life of the WCC, to show how the initial ecumenical vision based on "the call of the churches to unity, renewal and mission," had now been "extended to include the unity of mankind as the task of the ecumenical movement through one Church, renewed for mission."[26]

For Potter, the quest for unity (not only among the churches but among humans) was to be understood through the lenses of "the struggle for a just society in which barriers of class, race and sex are broken down, the divisions of peoples and nations are reconciled in peace, and the environment is made sustainable for the well-being of all."[27] Highlighting the theological contributions from Asia, Africa, Latin America, the Caribbean, and African-Americans in the US, he emphasized the significance of the dialogue with people of other living faiths and ideologies, which he called "the universal dialogue of cultures."[28] For him, the ecumenical movement was still to properly explore the ecumenical meaning of existence as part of a "community

---

[24] Michael Jagessar, "Introduction," in *At Home with God and in the World: A Phillip Potter Reader*, ed. Andrea Fröchtling, Michael Jagessar, Brian Brown, Rudolf Hinz, and Dietrich Werner (Geneva, WCC Publications, 2013), xiii–xx (xiv).

[25] Jagessar, "Introduction," xvii.

[26] Phillip Potter, "Toward a Universal Dialogue of Cultures," in *At Home with God and in the World*, 3–14 (4).

[27] Potter, "Toward a Universal Dialogue of Cultures," 5.

[28] Potter, "Toward a Universal Dialogue of Cultures," 5.

of peoples in all their variety of cultures."[29] He criticized the trend to regard Western civilization (which, "some still call Christian") as the norm for the *oikoumenē*, pointing to the reminiscences of "Western military, economic and political power through its scientific and technological process" in such a misplaced vision.[30]

The journey to Nairobi (1975) brought light to some of those emphases, highlighting (1) The relation between "the unity of the church and the unity of mankind [sic]," (2) a vision of "God's justice" that "manifests itself both in the justification of the sinner and in social and political justice," (3) the Church and Society follow-up of the 1966 conference, through a 1972 conference on the theme "Christians in the Technical and Social Revolutions of Our Time," and the creation of the Program to Combat Racism (PCR).[31] The study prepared by the Department on Church and Society on the future of humanity in a world of science-based technology brought to light a new set of ethical dilemmas to be considered, including the ecological challenges, seen through the lenses of the "Limits of Growth."[32] On all these fronts the seeds sowed in 1966 were generative of a new moment in the worldwide ecumenical movement.

Paulo Freire, the WCC, and the Globalization of the *Pedagogy of the Oppressed*

During those years, another Global South figure whose ecumenical influence is often neglected impacted the work of the WCC. The Central Committee Report compiled in 1975 makes a couple of direct references to Brazilian educator and philosopher Paulo Freire. First, he is mentioned by the CCIA in connection with his understanding of dialogue as "a means to ends of mutual understanding, reconciliation, justice and peace."[33] Then, the Program Unit on Education and

---

[29] Potter, "Toward a Universal Dialogue of Cultures," 6.

[30] Potter, "Toward a Universal Dialogue of Cultures," 7.

[31] Phillip Potter, "Introduction," in *Uppsala to Nairobi: 1968–1975. Report of the Central Committee to the Fifth Assembly of the World Council of Churches*, ed. David E. Johnson (London and New York: Friendship Press, 1975), 13–22 (13–14).

[32] David E. Johnson, ed., *Uppsala to Nairobi: 1968–1975. Report of the Central Committee to the Fifth Assembly of the World Council of Churches* (London and New York: Friendship Press, 1975), 113.

[33] Johnson, ed., *Uppsala to Nairobi*, 137.

Renewal uses terms such as "conscientization," "marginal church," and "liberation," in reference to the search for "ways to awaken the consciousness of people to situations in which their own silence and submissiveness contributed to their continued bondage," which indicated Freire's influence on its work. In the 1970s, that program unit saw liberation as an increasingly "significant theme of the work, whether it was with women, renewal movements, children, schools, lay people, church administrators or those seeking to stimulate awareness about development."[34]

Freire was one of the Brazilian intellectuals forced to leave the country after the military coup d'état of 1964. The military regime perceived his critical literacy method and his influence as coordinator of the National Plan of Education in the administration of João Goulart (1961–1964) as dangerous.[35] Persecuted, he left for Chile, where he became "an external advisor to the Chilean government, initially based at the Instituto Nacional de Desarrollo Agropecuario (INDAP, 1964–1966) and, later, at the Instituto de Capacitación e Investigación para la Reforma Agraria (1967–1969), a joint initiative of the Chilean Government, the United Nations Development Programme, the Food and Agriculture Organization, and UNESCO."[36] In Brazil, Freire's critical method of popular education had played a significant role in the development of popular movements such as the *Movimento de Educação de Base* (MEB), the *Centros Populares de Cultura* (CPC) and the *Movimentos de Cultura Popular* (MCPs).

A practicing Catholic, Freire had developed a pedagogical theory that united thought and action. The priority of practice and the urgency of the need to organize and coordinate the movement of democratization of culture throughout the country left Freire with less time than he would have liked for theoretical elaboration during that period.[37]

---

[34] Johnson, ed., *Uppsala to Nairobi*, 184.

[35] Marcela Gajardo, "Finding Paulo Freire in Chile," in *The Wiley Handbook of Paulo Freire*, ed. Carlos Alberto Torres (Hoboken, NJ: Wiley-Blackwell, 2019), 99–120 (101).

[36] Gajardo, "Finding Paulo Freire in Chile," 102.

[37] Francisco C. Weffort, "Educação e Política (Reflexões sociológicas sobre uma pedagogia da Liberdade)" in *Educação para a Prática da Liberdade*, ed. Paulo Freire (Rio de Janeiro: Paz e Terra, 1967), 1–26 (2). In the late 1960s and early 1970s, it was the ecumenical *Editora Paz e Terra* that published Freire's books in Portuguese.

The five years he spent in Chile were crucial for Freire's development of his pedagogical philosophy, as he sought to adapt his critical method to a new reality. He had moved from the local realities of Northeast Brazil where his first experiments originally took place to the Brazilian national education plan, and now to a new national context, in Chile. The next step would be to experiment with it on the global stage. He got that opportunity when he moved to Geneva in 1970, placing his liberative concept of education in conversation with different social and cultural contexts, including Guinea-Bissau in West Africa.[38]

It was in Chile that Freire wrote the first drafts of *Pedagogy of the Oppressed*, the book that would launch him to fame.[39] That book "resulted from Freire's reflections on his work with Chilean peasants in the reformed sector."[40] Among the many important insights in that

---

[38] See Paulo Freire, *Pedagogy in Process: The Letters to Guinea-Bissau* (New York: The Seabury Press, 1978).

[39] Paulo Freire, *Pedagogy of the Oppressed*, 30th anniversary edition, trans. Myra Bergman Ramos (New York, NY: Bloomsbury, [1970] 2000). *Pedagogy of the Oppressed* was Freire's first publication in English. Its Portuguese version was published that same year in Brazil by *Paz e Terra*. The English publication resulted from an encounter between Freire and Richard Shaull during a conference in Boston, in 1966. This is how Shaull recalled that unexpected encounter more than three decades later: "Perhaps my most significant contribution to this struggle for social transformation in the USA came as the result of something I had not planned. In 1966, I attended a meeting of Catholic Bishops from North and South America, held in Boston. As I was standing in line waiting for my overcoat, I noticed that the person directly ahead of me kept looking at me. Finally, he said, 'Are you Shaull?' When I answered affirmatively, he replied: 'I'm Paulo Freire.' And before I could say more, he disappeared and returned in a few minutes with a small bundle, what turned out to be a manuscript. He gave it to me and said, 'I'm living in exile in Chile. I've just completed a book which can't be published in Brazil. Since you are the only North American I know to whom I can entrust this manuscript, take it and get it translated and published. And since I'm not known in the USA, write an introduction to it.' I accepted the responsibility. As I read this manuscript, entitled *The Pedagogy of the Oppressed*, I was convinced that I had something in my hands which would be revolutionary in its impact on education and politics. I also realized that it would require a translation which would make the text more readable in English, and convinced Myra Bergmann and Jovelino Ramos to undertake this task. I wrote a short introduction pointing out what I considered to be the significance of this work and Bill Wipfler, at the National Council of Churches, got Seabury Press to publish the first edition of it." Richard Shaull, *Surpreendido pela Graça*, 263.

[40] Gajardo, "Finding Paulo Freire in Chile," 105.

book, Freire drew attention to the reigning "culture of silence" among the dispossessed, which resulted from the "situation of economic, social, and political domination—and of the paternalism—of which they were victims."[41] He realized that the "whole educational system was one of the major instruments for the maintenance of this culture of silence."[42] His humanizing intellectual vocation led him to a critical pedagogy, aimed at the realization of a "liberating awareness."[43]

After spending some time in 1969 as a consultant at the Harvard University School of Education, Freire accepted an invitation from the World Council of Churches to serve as a special consultant for its Office of Education. While in the United States, Freire feared that his absence from Latin America would remove him from the concrete contexts that were so important for his work. When he considered the WCC invitation, though, he understood that his work in Geneva would allow him to be in direct contact with diverse educational practices around the world.[44]

Even prior to the publication of *Pedagogy of the Oppressed*, Freire was already known in WCC circles. In a confidential document of the CCIA of November 28, 1969, which bore witness to the treatment of Indigenous peoples in Brazil by the military regime and to the risk that the government policy of "integration" could lead to genocide, Freire was mentioned as an important contact to keep in mind, considering that Darcy Ribeiro, the anthropologist known for his work on Brazilian indigenist politics, was imprisoned at that time.[45]

In the decade Freire lived in Geneva, he developed deep ties with Africa, highlighting the profound affinities between the African continent and Brazil. Speaking of his visits to Tanzania and Guinea-Bissau, Freire stated that he felt as if he was returning to a place he already knew (not visiting it for the first time), concluding that as he

[41] Freire, *Pedagogy of the Oppressed*, 23.

[42] Freire, *Pedagogy of the Oppressed*, 23.

[43] Adriana Puiggrós, "Paulo Freire's Place in Latin America's History and Future," in *The Wiley Handbook of Paulo Freire*, 121–132 (122).

[44] Balduino A. Andreola and Maria Bueno Ribeiro, *Andarilho da Esperança: Paulo Freire no CMI* (São Paulo: ASTE, 2005), 52.

[45] Letter from Baldwin Sjollema, first director of the WCC Programme to Combat Racism, to Leopoldo J. Niilus, Director of CCIA on November 28, 1969. WCC Archives, the Ecumenical Centre in Geneva. Accessed by the author on September 11, 2017.

felt at home on African soil, he was having an encounter with himself.[46] Freire's work as an educator in Africa was a time of meaningful learning. On the other hand, he saw his philosophy of education as a gift from Latin America to further the process of decolonization in the countries he engaged.[47] Seeking to develop collaborative educational projects deeply rooted in the local culture, Freire, once again, contributed to dismantle the culture of silence (the pedagogical, political, and sociocultural conditions) that hindered the voices of the dispossessed.[48]

In 1971, Freire and some of his Geneva colleagues created the Institute for Cultural Action (Institut d'action Culturelle—IDAC). Informed by Freire's concept of *conscientização* or consciousness-raising as a revolutionary factor in education systems, the work of this institute "aimed to offer educational services, especially to Third World countries struggling for their full independence."[49] Using his WCC platform, in collaboration with IDAC, Freire traveled to Africa, Asia, Australia, Europe, Latin America, the Middle East, and North America. While Freire himself found that the term *Third World* was tainted by the idea of a first world counterpart, his was a spirit nurtured in the postcolonial context that generated the Third World project as seen in Bandung, Cairo, and Havana in the late 1950s and early 1960s. Although a citizen of the world, Freire remained strongly connected to his native Recife. Deeply rooted in such a social and epistemic location, he established a profound empathy with the African peoples, developing a cosmopolitan sentiment, which, though, was only possible because of his deeply rooted emotional and intellectual location in Northeast Brazil.[50]

Freire's decade in the WCC contributed to the "universalization of the pedagogy of the oppressed."[51] In other words, his method and educational philosophy, despite being deeply localized in its origins, gained universal significance and applicability, even if, in order to be meaningful in different contexts, it had to be once again reimagined

---

46 Freire, *Pedagogy in Process*, 6.

47 Andreola and Ribeiro, *Andarilho da Esperança*, 71.

48 Andreola and Ribeiro, *Andarilho da Esperança*, 75.

49 Heinz-Peter Gerhardt, "Paulo Freire (1921–97)," *Prospects: the quarterly review of comparative education* 23/3–4 (1993): 439–458 (449).

50 Andreola and Ribeiro, *Andarilho da Esperança*, 82.

51 Andreola and Ribeiro, *Andarilho da Esperança*, 107.

in a given culture and society. In contrast to globalizing values that are imperially imposed on different cultures and societies, the universalization of Freire's humanizing pedagogical liberation can be properly understood through the lenses of what Orlando Espín calls "inter-trans-culturation," an approach that requires openness for another to "witness to me, in an open inter-discursive dialogue, what he or she understands and lives as truth."[52] The expected outcome of such an inter-discursive dialogue is for its participants to "move the process into an ever-deepening and continuing dialogue where truth is discovered and affirmed, over and over, through mutual witnessing, contrasting dialogue, and non-colonizing reflection."[53] In Freire, dialogue is also transformative. His is a "dialogical theory of action" in which "subjects meet in cooperation in order to transform the world."[54]

Freire embodied a humanizing ecumenical vision that emerged in Latin America in the 1950s and informed the rise of liberation theology years later. His popular education was critical for the rise of the base communities. While initially responding to local challenges, his liberative pedagogical method was gradually validated in other contexts around the world. In the 1960s, his philosophy of education shaped regional and national ecumenical networks, later making its way into international organisms, including the WCC. Furthermore, Freire's emphasis on the oppressed as a pedagogical subject shed light on the margins as spaces of production of knowledge, inviting those once deemed learned to listen and learn something anew from those experiences.[55] Freire's pedagogy brought the margins to the ecumenical table by shifting the locus of enunciation, breaking the silence of the dispossessed, and revealing their multiple faces.

How can the margins influence old self-proclaimed centers? Through the hopes and aspirations of Freire's humanizing and liberative call. As one can see throughout this book, in various instances, generative insights first formulated in the margins have spread

---

[52] Orlando O. Espín, *Idol and Grace: Traditioning and Subversive Hope* (Maryknoll: Orbis, 2014), loc. 1495 of 4388, Kindle.

[53] Espín, *Idol and Grace*.

[54] Freire, *Pedagogy of the Oppressed*, 126.

[55] Edla Eggert, "Qual a Contribuição e os Desafios da Educação Popular para a Transformação Social?" in *Teologia da Libertacao e Educacao Popular a Caminho*, ed. Fernando Torres et al (São Paulo: CEBI, 2006) 93–101.

through multiple transnational networks. While Freire's decade in Geneva is seldom discussed, further investigation is needed for instance to establish the extent to which his dialogical pedagogy influenced Porter's emphasis on the dialogue of cultures during his tenure as general secretary.

Latin America was one of those marginal sites whose insights informed global developments. In a letter to Porter's predecessor, WCC General Secretary Eugene Carson Blake, Eber Fernandes Ferrer, who had temporarily assumed the position of General Secretary of ULAJE (the Latin American Youth Union) in 1968, laid out a five-year strategic plan of action to advance a liberative ecumenicity that valued humanity and its integral development. The ecumenical network ULAJE aimed to bring together involved local and national Christian youth movements, multiple national church councils, the International Movement of Catholic Agrarian Youth (MIJARC), Youth Christian Workers (JOC), International Youth Catholic Students (JECI), the International Movement of Catholic Students (MIEC), YMCA, YMCA, the World Student Christian Federation (WSCF) and national Student Christian Movements (MECs), Church and Society in Latin America (ISAL), the Latin American Commission for Christian Education (CELADEC), the Provisional Committee for Latin American Unity (UNELAM), the International Christian Youth Exchange (ICYE), the Youth Department of the WCC, and "similar movements in Asia, Africa, Europe and the U.S.A."[56]

Informed by Freire's work in Latin America, such a program focused on youth education "for the formation of a political consciousness"[57] through which Latin American young Christians could organize locally, nationally, and transnationally. While it is difficult to measure the concrete impact, or even if there was any serious consideration in the WCC of the implementation of that plan, the fact that similar ideas are still alive and represented on different instances of the ecumenical movement demonstrates the significance of such initiatives.

---

[56] Letter from Eber Fernandes Ferrer to Eugene Carson Blake on November 25, 1986. WCC Archives, the Ecumenical Centre in Geneva. Accessed by the author on September 11, 2017.

[57] Letter from Eber Fernandes Ferrer to Eugene Carson Blake.

Whereas past and present ecumenical instruments such as the IMC in the first decades of the twentieth century and the WCC since 1948 are of critical importance, they can never be confused with the ecumenical movement as such. The word *movement* conveys the idea of something dynamic, which remains on the move.[58] Focusing on the ecumenical spirit rather than ecumenical institutions, Rubem Alves defined ecumenism as "a theological and ethical orientation and a commitment to the transformation of society," affirming that "only in a secondary sense does it refers to ecumenical bodies." The ecumenical spirit is present in ideas, movements, and events such as the Vatican II, Medellin, or Uppsala.[59] The study of ecumenism needs to pay greater attention to the developments that made each of those events extraordinary. In part, what made those gatherings significant was the way they pushed the boundaries of ecumenism through the open and critical interaction with realities and movements in different contexts around the world, as this chapter has shown it was the case with Latin America.

[58] See Dietrich Werner's reflection on the 11th Assembly of the WCC in Karlsruhe, Germany, 2022. Dietrich Werner, "'And Yet It Moves': Dream and Reality of the Ecumenical Movement," *Ecumenical Review* 75/1 (2023): 16–32.

[59] Cited in the report of the Secretariat for Relationships with Christian Councils: Report 43. August 1970. WCC Archives, the Ecumenical Centre in Geneva.

11

THE GLOBALIZATION OF THE THIRD WORLD PROJECT AND THE ECUMENICAL MOVEMENT

EATWOT AND THE WORLD FORUM ON THEOLOGY AND LIBERATION (WFTL)

The Third World project, which played an influential role in the various developments examined in previous chapters, continues to live through transnational ecumenical networks that emerged amid exchanges among emerging theologies and epistemologies of the South at the end of the twentieth century. As M. P. Joseph asserts, the starting point of the irruption of the Third World in the ecumenical movement was the conversation among the margins, among "the theologies of the non-person."[1] Such conversations began to take place in spaces such as the Second Vatican Council and the Church and Society Conference in 1966, where participants from the Global South started nourishing their common dream of a Christian Bandung.

Another ecumenical space that created opportunities for those at the margins to meet face to face was the Consultation on Theology and Development held by SODEPAX in Cartiny, Switzerland, in November of 1969.[2] SODEPAX was a liaison body established in 1968 in the spirit of the Vatican II and the Geneva Conference on Church and Society (1966), connecting the Committee on Society, Development, and Peace of the Programme Unit Justice and Service of the WCC with the Pontifical Commission *Justice and Peace* of the Holy See. Its mandate was "to awaken the Christian churches and their members to a realization of their obligation to make the problems of international social injustice a matter of conscience."[3] In

[1] Joseph, *Theologies of the Non-Person: The Formative Years of EATWOT.*

[2] An acronym for Société, Développement, and Paix.

[3] George H. Dunne, "Foreword" in *In Search of a Theology of Development: Papers from a Consultation on Theology and Development held by Sodepax in Cartiny, Switzerland, November, 1969*, ed. Committee on Society, Development, and Peace (Geneva: Committee on Society, Development and Peace, 1969), i–ii.

1969, SODEPAX put together a major consultation, which included towering figures such as John C. Bennett and Jürgen Moltmann among its participants, along with emerging Latin American theologians Rubem Alves and Gustavo Gutiérrez. At the time, the two theologians had independently been developing a new way of theologizing in Latin America, which would be known as liberation theology. The Brazilian Protestant theologian had just published his first book, *A Theology of Human Hope*,[4] which stemmed from his PhD dissertation successfully sustained at Princeton Theological Seminary. Alves's dissertation was the first book-length treatise to explicitly name a "theology of liberation."[5] The Peruvian Catholic theologian, on the other hand, had served as a theological consultant for the Latin American episcopate in the Medellín CELAM Assembly of 1968. The consultation in Switzerland created the first opportunity for these Latin American theologians to meet face-to-face.

The paper Alves presented at the consultation was titled "Theology and the Liberation of Man." In his address, Alves asked whether one should speak of a theology of development or of "a theology for the liberation of man," expressing the hope "that a new language of faith can be created which can become an effective tool for the transformation of the earth in a site of recovery." Furthermore, he also hoped for a theological language that could be spoken by the Christian communities themselves, because, he argued, "the power of words is totally derived from the power of those communities which sustain and utter them."[6] Therefore, according to him, the task before the consultation was "to create a theological language that can actually be spoken by real communities."[7] The practical implication of that, Alves stated, was to formulate a new theological language that could consciously articulate "the already existing existential conditions of the community."[8] According to him, "language becomes power when

[4] Rubem Alves, *A Theology of Human Hope* (Washington, DC: Corpus Books, 1969).

[5] Rubem Alves, "Toward a Theology of Liberation: An Exploration of the Encounter between the Languages of Humanistic Messianism and Messianic Humanism" (PhD diss., Princeton Theological Seminary, 1968).

[6] Rubem Alves, "Theology and the Liberation of Man," in *In Search of a Theology of Development*, 75–92 (75).

[7] Alves, "Theology and the Liberation of Man," 76.

[8] Alves, "Theology and the Liberation of Man," 76.

it serves to express the unconscious striving, protest, and hope of concrete communities."[9] Alves called, then, for a theology of praxis, which "articulates an ongoing activity which mediates a new future to man."[10]

Gutiérrez's address, on the other hand, had a title apparently more in line with the overall title of the consultation, "The Meaning of Development," which was, though, complemented by a provocative subtitle: "Notes on a Theology of Liberation." Like Alves, Gutiérrez also interrogated "the classic task of theology," pointing to a new way of theologizing, which saw theology "as critical contemplation of the pastoral action of the Church."[11] In a long and detailed essay, Gutiérrez criticized the concept of development, laying out some key tenets of liberation theology such as the primacy of action, the critical contemplation of action, the theory of dependence, and the "conscious awakening to a situation of 'alienation,'" which called Christians to a committed involvement in a completely "mundane world."[12] For him, the situation of Latin America urged the Church "to assume more responsibility in the present situation of injustice and in the tasks of today."[13]

His call for a deep commitment of solidarity to the poor, his expansion of the concept of salvation to include human "emancipation in the course of history," and his "eschatological conscience of humanity, opening the door for a universal understanding of salvation"[14] pushed the boundaries of Christianity, making room for a church without walls or fences, which informs the pastoral praxis of liberation Christianity in Latin America.

SODEPAX provided an international platform to bring these two emerging theologians together, as they worked independently to create a new theological language to engage the liberating practices of their communities. SODEPAX not only created the space where these two theologians would meet but also forged a space where they could speak to Euro-American theologians and representatives

9 Alves, "Theology and the Liberation of Man," 77.

10 Alves, "Theology and the Liberation of Man," 81.

11 Gustavo Gutiérrez, "The Meaning of Development," in *In Search of a Theology of Development*, 116–179 (118).

12 Gutiérrez, "The Meaning of Development," 131.

13 Gutiérrez, "The Meaning of Development," 140.

14 Gutiérrez, "The Meaning of Development," 145, 150.

of key ecumenical bodies, reversing roles in pre-established center-periphery dynamics.

In 1975, another important theological encounter took place, this time in Detroit, to promote dialogue between North and South American theologies. The main interest in that conversation on the North American end was to engage the emerging Latin American liberation theology and interrogate what kind of cross-cultural learning could happen in that exchange. While "Theology in the Americas: 1975" was a scholarly conversation, its planners decided that they would not invite only professional theologians but also "Christian activists committed to social change."[15] Those representing Latin America in that conversation included well-known theologians such as Gustavo Gutiérrez, Juan Luís Segundo, Enrique Dussel, Leonardo Boff, Hugo Assmann, and José Míguez Bonino. There were, however, less-known names such as Javier Inguíñiz, a young Peruvian sociologist, and Diego Irarrazával, who would some years later help propagate Indigenous theologies emerging in Abya Yala. Participating in that gathering was also Argentinean theologian Beatriz Melano Couch, credited as a forerunner of Latin American feminist theologies. The only woman in the Latin American group, Couch not only spoke as a representative of that delegation but also took part in the feminist theology panel with North American theologians Sheila Collins, Beverly Harrison, Rennie Golden, and Rosemary Radford Ruether. Black theologians such as J. Deotis Roberts and Michele Russel participated in a black theology panel. Likewise, Native American, Asian American, and Latine theologians participated in a panel devoted to "Other Minorities in America."[16] Despite its particular focus on the Americas, this event saw itself as global in scope. In the preface of the collection of statements that came out of this theological dialogue, Robert McAfee Brown states,

> Theology in the Americas' must be a combination of particularity and global vision. We must continue to stress the need for particularity, taking with utmost seriousness the context in which theology is done [. . .] But sooner or later (and at least sooner, if not concurrently), such varied contextual situations will need to

---

[15] Sergio Torres and John Eagleson, eds., *Theology in the Americas* (Maryknoll, NY: Orbis Books, 1976), 3.

[16] Torres and Eagkeson, *Theology in the Americas,* 357.

> relate *to one another*, for none of them ultimately exists in isolation. As Detroit made clear, each group helps to deliver other groups from parochialism. Furthermore, the final Christian vision does not point to a tightly circumscribed context for some only, but to a context that is inclusive of all.[17]

Theology in the Americas was not merely an encounter but a purposeful dialogue started a year earlier to explore the meaning of liberation theology for North America. That experiment became a foretaste for other efforts like the one that would result in the creation of the Ecumenical Association of Third World Theologians (EATWOT) in 1976. Differently from Theology in the Americas, EATWOT included theologians from Africa and Asia. In contrast to it, though, EATWOT would adopt a strict position about the participation of North Atlantic theologians to make sure that "Third World" theologians could articulate their own independent voices. While Black US theologians and other minoritized groups from the North Atlantic were welcome to participate in its gatherings, European and Anglo-American theologians were not invited to attend the opening EATWOT gathering in Dar es Salaam, Tanzania, in August 1976.[18]

After two years of planning, EATWOT's opening gathering counted with the participation of twenty-seven theologians,

---

[17] Robert McAfee Brown, "A Preface and a Conclusion," in *Theology in the Americas*, ix–xxviii (xiv).

[18] As Sergio Torres and Virginia Fabella documented, in the preparations for and at the meeting in Dar es Salaam, there was an intense conversation about who belonged in the Third World, since EATWOT was supposed to articulate Third World theological perspectives. Some people still saw the term as defined geographically. Thus, they did not think that Black Americans were part of the Third World. African theologians, however, sustained that there was only one Black world, whether Black people lived in Africa, the United States, or the Caribbean. Other participants reminded the planners that the Third World implied a certain kind of commitment, highlighting that there are people who may live in Hong Kong or Bolivia and who are not ideologically identified with the Third World. The same happened the other way around. That view ended up prevailing, thus favoring the inclusion of Black US theologians. The absence of white Northern theologians, though, had a negative impact on the representation of women at the meeting, which was noted as one of the weaknesses of the project. See Sergio Torres and Virginia Fabella, "Introdução," in *O Evangelho Emergente*, ed. Sergio Torres and Virginia Fabella (São Paulo: Edicoes Paulinas, 1982), 5–22 (7–8).

including "seven from Africa, seven from Asia, seven from Latin America and the Caribbean, and one from the Black minority in the United States." Its participants included Gustavo Gutiérrez, Enrique Dussel, Sergio Torres, Hugo Assman, Tissa Balassuriya, Virginia Fabella, Mercy Amba Oduyoye and James Cone.[19] The goal was to gather Catholic, Protestant, and Orthodox theologians from the Third World,

> with the aim of scrutinizing the "signs of the times" and fostering "new models of theology which would interpret the gospel in a more meaningful way to the peoples of the Third World and promote their struggle for liberation." (Article 2, EATWOT Constitution). Among these new models were Latin America Theology of Liberation, Black Theology of Liberation, Minjung Theology of Korea, Dalit Theology in India, and the Theology of Struggle in the Philippines.

The 1976 global gathering was followed by regional meetings such as the Pan-African Conference of Third World Theologians, on December 17–23, 1977, in Accra, Ghana, which included the participation of theologians such as José Miguez Bonino, Gustavo Gutiérrez, and Enrique Dussel, Mercy Amba Oduyoye, Ogbu U. Kalu, Desmond Tutu, Allan Boesak, John S. Pobee, and John Mbiti to support ongoing efforts for the development of African theologies, bringing to the attention of the ecumenical world important African theological questions and insights such as the value of African religious beliefs and practices for Christian theology.[20]

Highlighting the distinctiveness of African cultures and the contextuality of African theologies, that gathering did not escape internal tensions between, for instance, South African Black Theology and other Sub-Saharan African theologies, or between the latter and Latin American theologies. Yet, those voices from the Third World came together in the conference's final communiqué to protest colonialism and all forms of dehumanization:

---

19. EATWOT, "Eatwot Global—History," https://eatwotglobal.com/history.html.

20. For a selection of the papers presented at that gathering, see Kofi Appiah-Kubbi and Sergio Torres, eds., *African Theology en Route: Papers from the Pan-African Conference of Third World Theologians, December 17–23, 1977, Accra, Ghana* (Maryknoll, NY: Orbis Books, 1979).

> Because oppression is found not only in culture but also in political and economic structures and the dominant mass media, African theology must also be liberation theology. The focus on liberation in African theology connects it with other Third World theologies. Like black theologians in North America, we cannot ignore racism as a distortion of the human person. Like Latin American and Asian theologians, we see the need to be liberated from socio-economic exploitation. A related but different form of oppression is often found in the roles set aside for women in the churches. There is the oppression of Africans by white colonialism, but there is also the oppression of blacks by blacks. We stand against oppression in any form because the Gospel of Jesus Christ demands our participation in the struggle to free people from all forms of dehumanization.[21]

This declaration highlights some of the themes articulated in liberation theology since Medellin 1968, which, under the umbrella of Third World ecumenical solidarity, connects theological subjects from Africa, Asia, and Latin America and their diasporas. Forums like EATWOT have contributed to place distinct liberationist perspectives into conversation, underscoring the "multiple, intersecting systems of oppression that include race, gender, and ethnicity among many interwoven systems."[22]

Following this regional Pan-African conference, EATWOT sponsored other regional gatherings in Asia and Latin America. The Asian Conference took place in Wennappuwa, Sri Lanka, on January 7 20, 1979, around the theme "Asia's Struggle for Full Humanity." That regional conference emphasized the craft of an Asian theology that could contribute "to transform the society in which we live so that it may increasingly allow the Asian person to experience what it means to be fully alive."[23] Such a theology critically addressed the ways colonialism, economic exploitation, and political violence deprived many Asians "of their basic civil and human rights."[24]

Reinforcing the notion that the presence of Christianity in Asia preceded by centuries the arrival of Western missionaries, while

---

[21] Appiah-Kubbi and Torres, eds., *African Theology en Route*, 189–95 (194).

[22] Joseph, *Theologies of the Non-Person*, 204.

[23] Joseph, *Theologies of the Non-Person*, 75.

[24] Joseph, *Theologies of the Non-Person*, 76.

at the same time understanding the resistance of many Asians to a religion that in modern times has often been associated with the West, Asian theologians underscored the Christian identification with the "collective search and struggle for fullness of life for Asian peoples through a radical transformation of Asian reality."[25] In search for theological language that identified with the people and the struggles of the Asian social movements, those theologians specified the meaning of the term *people*, focusing on "those who are deprived, the oppressed, and the poor."[26] Such a view, with due nuance, has informed important Asian theological movements such as *Minjung*, Dalit, and Asian feminist theologies. An ongoing theme in the development of Asian theologies is interreligious cooperation and dialogue. Thus, the emerging Asian theologies advanced a triple dialogue, which ever since has been influential in the ecumenical movement: a dialogue "with Asian religions, Asian cultures, and Asia's poor."[27]

A third regional EATWOT meeting took place in São Paulo, Brazil, on February 20–March 2, 1980. The regional circumstances surrounding that conference included the fact that the host country, Brazil, was still dealing with a civil-military dictatorship, which although weakened, remained repressive. By that time, the popular struggle for redemocratization was gaining momentum. The rise of an organized Workers' Party along with the articulation of many other social movements made change inevitable.

The overall situation in Latin America, though, was grim. The doctrine of national security disseminated by the United States had spread throughout the continent. Military repression was increasing in many places. Countries such as Guatemala and El Salvador had become worst-case scenarios, with the fatal victims of military repression amounting to hundreds of thousands—including scores of Indigenous peoples.

In El Salvador, threats to the life of Oscar Arnulfo Romero, Archbishop of San Salvador, who, like Hélder Câmara and other Latin

[25] Joseph, *Theologies of the Non-Person*, 76.

[26] Joseph, *Theologies of the Non-Person*, 78.

[27] S. Wesley Ariarajah, "The Ecumenical Movement in Asia in the Context of Asian Socio-political Realities," in *Christian Theology in Asia*, ed. Sebastian C. H. Kim (Cambridge, UK: Cambridge University Press, 2008), 227–249 (237).

American bishops, had experienced a conversion to the poor, were intensifying.[28] As a result of his tireless denunciation of what he called the mortal sin of the concentration of wealth and the systemic violence against the poor, Romero was finally gunned down while celebrating mass at a hospital on March 24, 1980, three weeks after the end of the EATWOT gathering. The need to articulate a new understanding of Christian martyrdom in connection with the suffering of the poor, and the rise of a theology of the crucified people, originally developed in the Salvadorean context, was largely engaged by EATWOT during that period.[29]

On the other hand, the spread of the base communities throughout the continent was also a central topic at the gathering. One hundred eighty people from forty-two countries in Africa, Asia, Latin America, and the Caribbean gathered in São Paulo, eager to meet the CEBs many of them had only heard about. This was by far the largest EATWOT meeting up to that point. The participation of women also significantly increased in comparison with previous gatherings.[30]

Furthermore, it was becoming increasingly clear that theology was not the exclusive realm of professional theologians. In Latin America, the understanding that theology emerged from the struggles of the poor was consolidated. This was the message conveyed in the opening of the gathering by Cardinal Paulo Evaristo Arns, Archbishop of Sao Paulo. As Joseph points out,

> In contrast to the other EATWOT conferences, organizers discouraged so-called scholarly presentations—presentations of position papers that occupy the major attention of the participants during a conference—in favor of reflection and contributing a response. Cardinal Arns, in his opening address, expressed the concern through a different logic. He invited the participants to pay close attention to the fact that the conference was not a congress of theologians but a congress of theology. It was also a reminder

[28] Joseph, *Theologies of the Non-Person*, 115.

[29] A whole publication of EATWOT was devoted to this emerging liberating Christology. See José María Virgil, ed., *Getting the Poor Down from the Cross: Christology of Liberation*, Second English Digital Edition (International Theological Commission of the Association of Third World Theologians, 2007). https://drive.google.com/drive/folders/1vxdDbzNlC91ncZa9vVHx_EAyBqDIJn9H.

[30] Joseph, *Theologies of the Non-Person*, 110.

> that theology is not done by theologians who are alienated from the daily realities of the people. Instead, theology stems from the struggles of the people to ensure the gift of life. As he put it, "We come here to meet people from the grassroots, indigenous peoples, farmers, and workers who in their communities make theology in the measure that, in their theological life, they reflect the faith-commitment relation as a requirement of love. . . . In this sense, this congress should constitute a space in which the clamor of the oppressed can be heard."[31]

Inspired by the phenomenon of the CEBs, the conference followed the guidance of Puebla 1979, using the see-judge-act method with a view toward representing a vision of a "church that is trying to incarnate itself in the ranks of the common people on our continent, and that therefore arises out of their response in faith to the Lord."[32]

Among other things, the conference discussed the ecclesiology emerging from the CEBs and the increasing Christian participation in popular movements, which had been critical to the development of Latin American liberation theology. At the same time, that conversation also reflected on other social and cultural differences, including, gender, race, and ethnicity. Gustavo Gutiérrez, who attended the gathering, highlighted that the poor is never an individual but collective "groups, races, classes, cultures, sexes." Consequently, the irruption of the poor is always perceived as "tough and aggressive."[33] Another participant, Miguel Concha, defined the poor as exploited people who "possess special ethnic characteristics, such as being Indigenous or Black."[34]

In line with that discussion, a seminar was organized to discuss the specific challenges and issues women faced. From that point on, women's perspectives would increasingly inform EATWOT's agenda. The New Delhi EATWOT Assembly, on August 17–29, 1981, for instance, included a reflection by Mercy Amba Oduyoye, who, from a "Third World Woman's Perspective," drew attention to the experience

---

31 Joseph, *Theologies of the Non-Person*, 110.

32 Joseph, *Theologies of the Non-Person*, 111, citing John Eagleson and Philip Scharper, eds., *Puebla and Beyond* (Maryknoll, New York: Orbis Books, 1980), 157.

33 Joseph, *Theologies of the Non-Person*, 113.

34 Joseph, *Theologies of the Non-Person*, 113.

of women vis-à-vis liberation theologies.[35] In her address, Oduyoye defended the use of the term "Third World" against its critics, sharing an anecdote about someone she met in Germany who, opposing the term, said that there is only "one world." Her response was,

> We do have one *earth*, granted, but it is also true to say that we live in *different* worlds. The world of the rural woman in Ghana has little in common with that of the rural woman in Germany, nor does the world of the white women in South Africa bear comparison with that of her black compatriot.[36]

She used that analogy also to challenge the idea of any unified Third World Theology and to draw attention to the particularity of women's experiences as social location for their reading of the Bible and theological enunciation.

In a gathering that focused on the "Irruption of the Third World" and its challenge to theology, Oduyoye spoke of the irruption of Third-World women theologians as "the irruption within the irruption," challenging EATWOT to come to terms "with the fact that the community of women and men, even in the church and among 'liberation theologians,' is not as liberating as it could be." Thus, the irruption discussed in New Delhi "could have only come from a woman."[37]

Oduyoye's prophetic voice calling for an EATWOT that welcomes feminist theologians "as persons who seek to define more realistically what it means to be human" and her challenge for a way forward to form a "new community of men and women" had a deep impact on the conversation about the irruption of the Third World, putting

[35] Mercy Amba Oduyoye, "Reflections from a Third World Woman's Perspective: Women's Experience and Liberation Theologies," in *Irruption of the Third World: Challenge to Theology*, ed. Virginia Fabella and Sergio Torres, Papers from the Fifth International Conference of the Ecumenical Association of Third World Theologians, August 17–29, 1981, New Delhi, India (Maryknoll, NY: Orbis Books, 1983), 246–255. See also Mercy Amba Oduyoye, "The Passion Out of Compassion: Women of the EATWOT Third General Assembly," *International Review of Mission* 81 (1992): 313–318.

[36] Oduyoye, "Reflections from a Third World Woman's Perspective," 246.

[37] Oduyoye, "Reflections from a Third World Woman's Perspective," 247. This is a reference to the work of Virginia Fabella, who became the first woman to be program coordinator in EATWOT.

"women's experience, hitherto marginalized," on the center stage in the "community of interpretation" not only of Scriptures but of the entire Christian tradition.[38] While much work on that front is still needed, that gathering sparked a number of EATWOT meetings and publications organized by and centered on women.[39]

The São Paulo regional meeting also highlighted "the Indigenous question," which had also been the focus of a seminar in San Cristobal de las Casas, Mexico, September 3–7, 1979, and the "race question," which had likewise been discussed in a separate seminar in Kingston, Jamaica, on December 27–31, 1979, with a focus on the theme "Race, Class, and Liberation Theology."[40] These conversations reflected changes in liberationist thinking taking place on the ground in Latin America and beyond, while also anticipating theological movements that would soon come to the fore.

The process that started with those regional gatherings became a critical part of the 1981 EATWOT Assembly in New Delhi, which sought to identify power structures dividing humanity, taking on a liberative instance not only to examine them but also to develop liberating practices meant to dismantle those asymmetries. The conversations in New Delhi led to the creation of an EATWOT Women's Commission, forming "a sisterhood of resistance to all forms of oppression, [while] seeking creative partnership with men of the

---

[38] Oduyoye, "Reflections from a Third World Woman's Perspective," 255. See also Dorothea Erbele-Küster, "Rereading the Bible: A Dialogue with Women Theologians from Latin America, Africa and Asia," Voices 27/1 (2004): 53–67.

[39] A group of women also created a Latin American Women's Commission of EATWOT to advance that work, also benefiting from the Circle of Concerned African Women Theologians, a pan-African ecumenical organization that Oduyoye created with other African women. This work was key to diffuse women and feminist theologies from Asia, Africa, Latin America and their diasporas in ecumenical circles and beyond. For more on the work of the Latin American Women's Commission, see Maria Pilar Aquino (ed.). *Aportes para una Teologia desde la Mujer. Colaboraciones de teólogas latinoamericanas en la Conferencia Intercontinental de mujeres teólogas del Tercer Mundo, celebrada del 1 a 16 de diciembre de 1986, en Oaxtepec, México* (Madrid: Editorial Biblia y Fe, 1988). See also the 2016 issue of the EATWOT jornal *Voices*, "Feminist Theology Reaching New Borders," featuring theologians such as Meehyun Chung, Ivone Gebara, and Luiza Tomita. All *Voices* issues from 1999 to 2020 are available online: https://drive.google.com/drive/folders/1dVwApfESZaRd5H0z3tDuT6fN7UBYTFLf.

[40] Joseph, *Theologies of the Non-Person*, 107–108.

Association."[41] On December 1–6, 1986, the commission organized an Intercontinental Women's Conference in Oaxtepec, Mexico. That meeting was preceded by national meetings in Africa, Asia, and Latin America.[42] Ever since, EATWOT women have made valuable contributions to ecumenical spirituality and theology. Among other things, they have contributed to expand the notion of lived theology—by viewing theology as embodied, specifically, in women's lives and practices. They have also enriched EATWOT's theological method by intertwining religious-cultural and socioeconomic realities into a "living dialogue," "a dialogue of life which forms part of our experiences."[43] EATWOT women's authoritative theological work has challenged unspoken assumptions in a predominantly male theological association, significantly expanding the ecumenical horizons of the association. Furthermore, as Global South women started speaking in their own voices, they began to challenge monolithic approaches from women's movements that were predominantly Eurocentric and white, contributing an intersectional approach to conversations about gender and sexuality. As Oduyoye states,

> Women of the third world theologize out of situations that include the global effort to control the movement of Black and Asiatic people the world over, shuttling the Haitian and Vietnamese boat people, while attempting to expropriate land that was "reserved" for Native Americans at the time of European invasions of the Americas; while systematically utilizing Black land in Africa and elsewhere for the economic and leisure needs of Euro-American and Japanese peoples.[44]

Over the years, EATWOT has not only continued to promote and publish important South-South theological exchanges, as it has also sprung a number of other dialogues, including the continuation of theology in the Americas to examine more specifically the

---

[41] Virginia Fabella and Mercy Amba Oduyoye, "Introduction," in *With Passion and Compassion: Third World Women Doing Theology*, ed. Virginia Fabella and Mercy Amba Oduyoye (Maryknoll, NY: Orbis Books, 1990) ix–xv (ix–x).

[42] Fabella and Oduyoye, "Introduction," x.

[43] Fabella and Oduyoye, "Introduction," xi. The EATWOT women and their contribution to ecumenical praxis and thought remains under-examined and demands greater scholarly attention.

[44] Oduyoye, "The Passion Out of Compassion," 314.

relationship between US black liberation theology and Latin American liberation theology, which were born independently from each other in the heat of the 1960s. The proposed conversation envisioned to expand theological horizons and look for ways as these theologies could contribute with one another in the broader struggle for "religio-cultural, socio-economic and political liberation for Latin America and the United States."[45]

The New Delhi Conference represented a come-of-age moment in the EATWOT journey. It sought to not only develop a theological synthesis that incorporated critical elements from two major orientations in Third World theologies, but it also understood that it was time to engage "First World theologians" in dialogue so they could understand how the liberation struggles around the world could contribute "to a better understanding of God in different contexts."[46]

As stated earlier, EATWOT has never intended to build a homogeneous "third world theology." On the contrary, as its Second General Assembly in Oaxtepec, Mexico (1986) stated, this is a movement that seeks to identify commonalities amidst divergences. The theme of that assembly was "Commonalities, Divergencies, and Cross-Fertilization among Third-World Theologies." In her preface to the collection of documents and papers from the Oaxtepec assembly, Brazilian Catholic theologian Maria Clara Lucchetti Bingemer acknowledged that the task to find commonalities among differences is never smooth, explaining that the papers collected in that volume represented the "common desire to resolve the tensions so as to achieve a fruitful exchange," representing a stage in the growth of EATWOT.[47] One of those commonalities was the fact that Third World theologies were born out of the spirituality of peoples living in contexts marked by injustice and oppression. Their language emerged from "within the

---

45 George Cummings, *A Common Journey: Black Theology (USA) and Latin American Liberation Theology* (Maryknoll, NY: Orbis Books, 1993), xi.

46 "The Irruption of the Third World. Final Statement of the Fifth EATWOT Conference, New Delhi, August 17–29, 1981," in Fabella and Torres, eds., *The Irruption of the Third World*, 191–206 (205).

47 Maria Clara Lucchetti Bingemer, "Preface," in *Third World Theologies: Commonalities and Differences*, ed. K. C. Abraham. Papers and Reflections from the Second General Assembly of the Ecumenical Association of Third World Theologians, December, 1986, Oaxtepec, Mexico (Eugene, OR: Wipf & Stock Publishers, 2004 [1990]), vii–xiii (vii).

movement of peoples organizing themselves for their liberation."[48] Furthermore, these theologies are "ecclesial theologies;" that is, they are rooted in specific ecclesial praxes. This explains their necessary plurality, as they are connected to specific life struggles and identity quests.[49]

Such differences exist not only between African, Asian, and Latin American theologies, but also within each region and Christian tradition represented in the conversation. In the case of Latin America, Bingemer highlights the emergence of three groups with specific voices and experiences as representive of that theological diversity: Black Latin Americans and Caribbeans, Indigenous peoples, and women. In addition, she underscores minoritized groups in North America, which also include Black and Indigenous peoples, in addition to diasporic communities such as Latine Christians.[50]

In such a plural context, EATWOT promotes the cross-fertilization of experiences and perspectives, identifying methodological contact zones. For instance, the fact that these theologies do not offer "great principles to be applied to reality, but an orientation to clarify our commitment and practice, to establish new relationships and a new lifestyle" illustrates that.[51] Speaking from places of vulnerability and powerlessness, these theologies are called to a persistent "movement of conversion to others," [. . .] "daring to devise and create something new."[52] The final document of the Oaxtepec assembly reinforces that view, naming liberation one of the commonalities, and adding the urge to continue the dialogue between theologies developed not in academia but "by the communities of the poor."[53]

In all of this, the image invoked by Mercy Amba Oduyoye in New Delhi of the multiple worlds in one earth remains critical for EATWOT's ecumenical vision. The cross-fertilization among distinct experiences and social loci prevents the dominance of one particular

---

48 Bingemer, "Preface," viii–ix.

49 Bingemer, "Preface," ix.

50 Bingemer, "Preface," xi.

51 Bingemer, "Preface," xii.

52 Bingemer, "Preface," xii.

53 "Commonalities, Divergences, and Cross-fertilization among Third World Theologies: A Document Based on the Seventh International Conference of the Ecumenical Association of Third World Theologians, Oaxtepec, Mexico, December 7–14, 1986," in *Third World Theologies: Commonalities and Differences*, 195–213 (200).

voice. In Oaxtepec, women's theological perspectives and the importance of the living dialogue among multiple cultural and religious traditions were prominent. Latin American participants, in particular those of *mestizo* background, listened with attention to Black and Indigenous cultures that have often been marginalized in the region.[54] Furthermore, the gathering pointed to an increased sense of the importance of the poor in the singularity of their experiences and practices as theological and pastoral subjects.[55] Despite all theological differences among its participants, Oaxtepec reaffirmed the persistence of the collective struggle for justice and full humanity, which unifies "Third World peoples" as those who refuse to succumb.[56] In recent years, EATWOT has been describing itself as "a global union of theologians." As such, "We are united with the aim of scrutinizing the 'Signs of the times' and fostering 'New models of theology which would interpret the gospel in a more meaningful way to the peoples of the third world and promote their struggle for liberation.'"[57]

Despite its challenges, EATWOT remains alive, especially through its publications, which continued to appear online even during the COVID-19 pandemic. The EATWOT journal *Voices*, now an open access electronic publication, also continues to publish issues on a yearly basis, remaining an important platform for Third World theological voices. Furthermore, EATWOT has partnered with journals such as *Exchange* (Brill) and *Horizonte* (PUC Minas, Brazil) for relevant publications. Among the many challenges it faces, scarcity of funds for its activities seems to be the most serious one. Without a fixed headquarters, EATWOT moves around, usually housed by its General Secretary, which is elected every five years, along with a steering committee. EATWOT occasional gatherings currently take place in conjunction with the World Social Forum (WSF), a gathering of civil society organizations from all over the world. Many EATWOT members participate in that world forum. Furthermore, since 2003, EATWOT has had the company of the World Forum on Theology and Liberation (WFTL), which also meets in connection with the WSF. Several EATWOT theologians are also involved in the WFTL.

---

[54] "Commonalities, Divergences, and Cross-fertilization, 203–204.

[55] "Commonalities, Divergences, and Cross-fertilization, 202.

[56] "Commonalities, Divergences, and Cross-fertilization, 203.

[57] As found on EATWOT's website: https://eatwotglobal.com/about-us.html#.

The WFTL emerged from conversations between Leonardo Boff and Sergio Torres in the third edition of the World Social Forum (WSF) in Porto Alegre, Brazil (2003).[58] Boff and Torres began to explore "the possibility of a connection between the World Social Forum and a forum of liberation theologies organized in a global manner and inserting itself into the new world context of ecological sensibility, religious pluralism, and social movements."[59] The first edition of the WFTL took place at the Fifth World Social Forum, in Porto Alegre (2005). Whereas EATWOT is composed mostly by theologians involved in academia—despite their engagement with local communities and popular movements—the WFTL, from its inception, has intentionally created a mixed space for activists, pastoral agents, and academic theologians to meet in connection with the agenda of the social movements gathering in the WSF. In that sense, the WFTL fulfills EATWOT's expressed aspirations of a theology that emerges from the struggles of the people—those struggling for justice vis-à-vis oppressive and unjust social structures. The WFTL is intentional about its worldwide composition. While building on the contributions from multiple liberation theologies, it includes in its toolkit religious and cultural pluralism, ecological and planetary perspectives, migration studies, and decolonial approaches.[60]

---

[58] As Agenor Brighenti underscores, "The World Social Forum (WSF) emerged in Brazil from a network of grassroots anti-globalization activists and campaigners as an alternative to the World Economic Forum held in Davos, Switzerland each year. Davos provides an opportunity to discuss the role of the economy in promoting human well-being, but its participants tend to represent the agenda of the richer nations. The WSF focuses on human development in the more holistic sense of social capital and provides a forum for Southern perspectives to be heard. From its birth, faith-based organizations have been prominent in promoting the goals of, and offering support to, the WSF." The World Forum on Theology and Liberation arose in connection with that development, aspiring to provide a new space for a Christian ecumenicity committed to the making of another possible world, the motto that has inspired the WSF. See Agenor Brighenti. "Cries from Africa: The Second World Forum of Theology and Liberation," *Political Theology* 9/4 (2008): 513–524 (513).

[59] Luiz Carlos Susin, "Introdução: Um fórum mundial para uma teologia de libertação global," in *Teologia para Outro Mundo Possível*, ed. Luiz Carlos Susin (São Paulo: Edicoes Paulinas, 9–11 (9).

[60] The author participated in the Eighth Forum on Theology and Liberation, in Salvador, Brazil, on March 12-16, 2018. The WFTL was preceded by the Eighth EATWOT General Assembly, also held in Salvador, on March 10–11, 2018, and took place concomitantly with the sixteenth edition of the World Social Forum (WSF), held

Southern epistemologies have been particularly influential in both WSF and WFTL circles.

The first meeting of WFTL focused on the place of theology in the building of another possible world as a move signaling the different places from which theology can participate in the struggles of the social movements—an epistemically humble approach, which understands that the social movements were the ones setting the agenda (the terms of the conversation), and that Christian theologians would engage it as interpreters and conversation partners. The WFTL is a dialogical space, not interested in forming hegemonies. As such, its participants sense an increasing need to articulate collectively and dialogically the new challenges and horizons informing theological language and agendas in the contemporary world. Such new theological horizons include, as Spanish Jesuit theologian Juan José Tamayo underscores, the transition from the theological discourse on inculturation to "an intercultural theology in a symmetrical dialogue among cultures;" the transition from a privileged religious locus to "a theology of religions from the perspective of the victims and with a practice of liberation;" a move from androcentric religious and theological structures to the "incorporation of a gender outlook from the perspective of the experience of suffering and emancipatory struggles of women;" a move from a modern anthropocentric theology to theologies in ecological perspective; and an ethical-practical horizon that considers "ethics as first theology," in which theology is built and rebuilt "through historical processes and from the perspectives of new subjects: marginalized women, subjugated races and ethnicities, submersed cultures, suffocated religions, and entire peoples,

---

on March 13–17, 2018. EATWOT members were involved in the broader conversations and networks represented at the WSF and the WFTL. Whereas the EATWOT assembly was limited to its members, the WFTL gathering involved broader participation of scholars and activists attending the WSF. Its schedule included organized participation in activities of the WSF. Local, national, and international ecumenical organizations present at the WFTL were thoroughly involved in the WSF—among them, the *Coordenadoria Ecumênica de Serviço* (CESE), CEBIC (the Ecumenical Council of Churches of the State of Bahia, Brazil), Act Alliance (the ecumenical global faith-based coalition formed by 140 organizations working in long-term development, advocacy, and humanitarian assistance), and Koinonia—Presença Ecumenica e Serviço.

countries, and continents inundated by the hurricane of neoliberal globalization."[61]

Among the new subjects disrupting the order of the day in popular efforts for the construction of a theology for another world, voices such as Marcella M. Althaus-Reid and Andre S. Musskopf at the WFTL meeting challenged models of liberation that remain complicitous to ideologies of sexual oppression, advocating for full inclusivity on the liberationist ecumenical table. In her contribution, Althaus-Reid denounced the problems in Latin American liberation theology's discourse on gender and sexuality.

> Liberationists, due to a lack of reflection on their discourse on power, systematically denied seats around the table to poor people, whether women or non-heterosexuals. However, even worse than that, they managed to theologically malnourish an entire generation of Latin American Christians who should have been well prepared to continue questioning the influence of hegemonic ideologies of a political or gender nature on our continent.[62]

The reduced focus of Latin American liberation theology on the economically poor prevented it, with very few exceptions, from tackling colonial heteropatriarchy. Despite all its problems, Althaus-Reid still seemed to believe in the possibility of change, uttering a conversion call to liberation theology:

> I am calling on liberation theology to become, once again, an honest theology, that is, a theology that can reflect on people's lives and the manifestation of God in our communities, beyond the dogma of a sexual ideology like heterosexuality. Without this, we run the risk of continuing to betray the gospel of justice, making God a prisoner of issues of sexuality and power in the Church, and reducing the Kingdom project to an ideological apparatus.[63]

---

[61] Juan José Tamayo, "Teologia para outro mundo é possível," in *Teologia para Outro Mundo Possível*, 437–453 (444–447).

[62] Marcella M. Althaus-Reid, "Demitologizando a teologia da libertação. Reflexoes sobre poder, pobreza e sexualidade," in *Teologia para Outro Mundo Possível*, ed. Luiz Carlos Susin, 455–470 (460–461).

[63] Althaus-Reid, "Demitologizando a teologia da libertação," 469.

Likewise, Brazilian queer theologian André S. Musskopf published an open letter to the WFTL giving voice to similar concerns. While the forum discussed themes related to the economy, politics, and interreligious dialogue, among others, Musskopf felt that the queer matters brought to the forum by people like him had not made "a significant impact on the theology that uses liberation as its central hermeneutical principle."[64] He then urged liberation theologians to look to the poor and see their concrete faces, which include gender identities and sexual orientation, since these are also "aspects that sustain the systems we want to overcome to build liberation and another possible world."[65] At the end of the day, Musskopf demanded a seat for queer theologians around the liberation table. While the inclusion of queer theologians would not solve all problems for the actual realization of liberation, it is an important step toward that, since "the solution to these problems and the journey towards the closest to liberation we can get are not possible without the queer community."[66]

If the first WFTL focused on a theology for another possible world, the second one reflected on a spirituality for another possible world. This gathering took place in Nairobi, Kenya, on January 16–19, 2007, and counted with 300 participants from five continents, most of them from Africa.[67] Most of the participants in the Nairobi gathering were "people involved in faith-based practice."[68] The examination of the African religious reality, the reclaiming of the African heritage of Christian spirituality, a reflection on interreligious dialogue from a liberation perspective, pastoral challenges in Africa and beyond, and the relationship between spirituality and

[64] André S. Musskopf, "Até onde estamos dispostos (as) a ir? Carta aberta ao Fórum Mundial de Teologia. Libertação," in *Teologia para Outro Mundo Possível*, 471–474 (471).

[65] Musskopf, "Até onde estamos dispostos (as) a ir?" 473.

[66] Musskopf, "Até onde estamos dispostos (as) a ir?" 474.

[67] Brighenti, *Cries from Africa*, 514.

[68] Brighenti, *Cries from Africa*, 515. As Agenor Brighenti, a member of the WFTL's organizing committee, highlights, some of the theologians attending the Nairobi gathering felt that its focus on the praxis of liberation needed to be balanced with more theological reflection, underscoring that the challenge for the WFTL is to find the right balance in promoting "the interaction between popular practices and theological reflection, pastoral agents and professional theologians."

respect for religious and cultural diversity were among the topics discussed in Nairobi.[69]

In recent WFTL gatherings, local organizations have played a more prominent role in introducing the local situation, its peoples, challenges, political structures, cultures, human rights violations, and the local voices, movements, articulations, and networks of resistance fighting for liberation and the transformation of those realities to the forum participants. The forum's program includes a moment for the analysis of the social situation, which corresponds to the first stage of the see-judge-act method, now applied to the context of a world forum that seeks to be always connected with local practices.

Being an intentional open space, the WFTL is fluid and ready to adapt to new circumstances, challenges, and scenarios. In the eighth WFTL gathering, for instance, in the state of Bahia, which has a significant presence of Afro-Brazilian religions, religious intolerance and racism received significant attention. Among other activities on those topics, Brazilian feminist theologian Odja Barros, led a WSF workshop on the topic "Breads and Crumbs: Who owns the Sacred? Intolerances yesterday and today." This workshop offered perspectives based on the words of women from the Bible as resources and instruments to face contemporary situations of religious intolerance.[70]

Likewise, Lutheran pastor Romi Márcia Bencke, General Secretary of CONIC (the Brazilian National Council of Churches), spoke about the connections between religious intolerance in Brazil, racism, patriarchy, and the economic interests of agrobusiness. Her presentation titled "For a heretical theology" stated,

> The persecution of religious traditions of African origin, in addition to expressing religious intolerance, also points to racism, which is quite strong in the country, and to patriarchy, since these traditions feature a significant role for women as religious leaders. On the other hand, attacks on Indigenous religious traditions are

[69] For the papers of the second WFTL, see Mary N. Getui, Luiz Carlos Susin, Beatrice W. Churu, eds., *Spirituality for Another Possible World* (Nairobi: Twawezza Communications, 2008).

[70] Author's personal notes and files. Salvador, Brazil, March 10–17, 2018.

> strongly anchored in the dispute over land. In this case, it is possible to relate religious intolerance and agribusiness.[71]

Highlighting those connections, Bencke denounced the use of "an effective instrument for territorial disputes in agribusiness and mining," especially in cases affecting sacred spaces of Indigenous and African-based religions.[72]

The program of the eighth WFTL also included an interreligious celebration led by CEBIC and Koinonia, an opening session on Political Economy titled "Resistance and Transformation Spaces of Contestation: Theological Activity of Resistance, Creation and Transformation," and sessions on themes such as "Gender, Feminisms, and Resistance," "African-American Challenges in the Struggle of Resistance to Colonialism," "Ecology and Integrity of Creation," "Aboriginal/Indigenous Peoples," "Religion, Politics, and Liberation," "Youth and Culture," "Liberation and Interreligious/Interfaith Dialogue," and "Human Rights, Human Dignity." These sessions engaged biblical, historical, theological, and pastoral perspectives from theologians and pastoral agents from multiple Christian traditions from all over the world, especially Latin America, Africa, and Asia.[73]

Planetary life and ecology was the focus of the third WFTL, whose theme was "Water and Land for Another Possible World." This issue has become increasingly central to liberation theology and practice in the past few decades.[74] Such a concern has been voiced in Latin America especially through the work of ecofeminist theologian Ivone Gebara, also associated with EATWOT, who combines the critical feminist political struggle with the antiracist, antisexist, and anti-elitist struggles for the preservation and dignity of life—no longer

---

[71] Romi Márcia Bencke, "Por uma teologia herética," unpublished paper generously shared with the author on March 14, 2018. Author's personal files. A published version of this paper appeared in the following year in the bulletin *Tempo e Presença Digital*. For that slightly modified version, see Romi Márcia Bencke, "Notas para uma teologia herética," *Tempo e Presença Digital*, 32/2019, http://www.koinonia.org.br/tpdigital/detalhes.asp?cod_artigo=594&cod_boletim=32&tipo=Artigo.

[72] Bencke, "Por uma teologia herética."

[73] FMTL—Programa Salvador, Bahia, 12–16 de março de 2018. Author's personal files.

[74] Luiz Carlos Susin and Joe Marçal Gonçalves dos Santos, eds., *Nosso Planeta, Nossa Vida: Ecologia e Teologia* (São Paulo: Paulinas, 2011).

considered through an anthropocentric lens, but as a planetary life, which is intrinsically interdependent and relational.[75]

Addressing issues of religious pluralism, interreligious relations, migration, and human trafficking, the fourth edition of the WFTL promoted discussions involving the Permanent Secretary of WFTL and the International Theological Commission of EATWOT about the joint work envisioning the preparation of an "agenda for a planetary theology for the coming years." The result of that conversation was published in a double of *Voices* (34/3–4: 2012), which, starting with the proposals and reflections from Dakar, went on to offer new contributions to that planetary agenda.[76]

That document advances a view on behalf of "contextual liberating theologies that work for 'another world that is possible.'"[77] As such, it sees the task at hand as twofold: (1) to "challenge the neoliberal cultural hegemony that weighs down on the poor" and (2) to "accompany more closely and more efficiently the popular initiatives and movements, and even those coming from governments, which currently offer resistance."[78]

On the contextual dimension, "each theology has to better grasp the needs proper to its own context and in this way its local or regional operative agenda." The World Social Forum encompasses concerns

---

[75] Ivone Gebara, *Ecofeminismo: Desafios para Repensar a Teologia* (Edições Terceira Via, 2017), 9.

[76] EATWOT's International Theological Commission and WFTL Permanent Secretariat, "Presentation," *Voices* (Towards a Work Agenda for Planetary Theology) 35/3-4 (2012): 9–10 (9).

[77] International Theological Commission of EATWOT, "Towards a Work Agenda for Planetary Theology," *Voices* 35/3–4 (2012): 15–24 (15). By liberating theologies, the document meant those theologies "motivated by the 'principle of liberation' that conceives reality as history as a utopian-liberating process on the basis of the option for the poor (which includes very different 'poverties')." By contextual theologies it referred to "incarnated in their local contexts, based on reality and that return to it with a militant commitment with a practice of historic transformation, both locally and globally." And by theologies of "another possible world," also called axial theologies, it meant theologies that "find their center of gravity more on the side of the future than of the past, that consciously accept that we are in an axial time of ruptures and of new dimensions, and that attempt realistically to construct that other theology that is possible in the midst of the cultural and paradigmatic tsunamis that we are experiencing."

[78] International Theological Commission of EATWOT, "Towards a Work Agenda for Planetary Theology," 16.

with the victims of the world economic crisis, the victims of climate disaster, the victims of intercultural and interreligious conflicts, and the victims of wars and armed conflict. All these different forms of violence and their connections must be addressed.[79]

Finally, on the axial dimension, the task is "to adopt a vision that is more clearly determined in favor of this new time that we are already living in."[80] Based on those three dimensions, the proposed agenda is grouped into five paradigmatic nodes:

1. The gender paradigm already present in feminist movements and theologies (including womanist, *mujerista* and African and Asian women theologies), which use specific instruments (gender analysis) to examine a range of thematic issues such as "corporality, sexuality, sexual orientation, racism, ethno-racism, gender violence, the marginalization of women, the feminization of poverty, the cross between ecology and feminism, and so forth."[81]
2. The pluralist paradigm, which, seeking a planetary inter-religious approach, "abandons exclusivisms, superiorities, self-attributions of uniqueness and absoluteness and the accompanying vision of proselytizing the world."[82]
3. The ecological paradigm advances a theological agenda that is in dialogue with deep ecology and that "goes beyond anthropomorphism in favor of an oiko-centrism."[83]
4. The post-religional paradigm invites theology to "reevaluate religion (a new theological reflection on religion, a new 'theology of religion'), a need to study explicitly and deeply the possibility, as announced, of it being surpassed." Such a paradigm advances not necessarily the abandonment of the dimension of

[79] International Theological Commission of EATWOT, "Towards a Work Agenda for Planetary Theology," 17.

[80] International Theological Commission of EATWOT, "Towards a Work Agenda for Planetary Theology," 18.

[81] International Theological Commission of EATWOT, "Towards a Work Agenda for Planetary Theology," 18.

[82] International Theological Commission of EATWOT, "Towards a Work Agenda for Planetary Theology," 19.

[83] International Theological Commission of EATWOT, "Towards a Work Agenda for Planetary Theology," 20–21.

faith but a reevaluation of certain religious modalities, which is already taking place with the growth of religiously unaffiliated persons in different parts of the world, to explore, for instance, possible veins of spirituality beyond religions.[84]

5. The epistemological paradigm. With the growing cultural and religious pluralism in our societies, interculturality becomes an important dimension to this new epistemological perspective. Exclusivist and monocultural models, which are hegemonic in nature, are being left behind in favor of interculturalism or pluriculturalism, which invites a dialogical theology engaged in a historic praxis of liberation.[85] This new historical juncture is promoting an epistemological revolution that urges us "to reevaluate the securities of objectivity," and reinterpret religion through a more relational lens.[86]
6. The urge for such a radical paradigmatic shift stems from the awareness of the urgency to redirect humanity's path toward self-destruction. A reevaluation of religion is seen as necessary to make such a drastic correction of course. The concept paper prepared for the 2012 EATWOT Assembly in Yogyakarta, Indonesia, concluded, "We will only stop destroying nature and ourselves when we take up a new vision that makes us conscious of the divine dimension of nature and of our full and inevitable identity."[87]

Forums such as EATWOT and WFTL are not a Latin American creation. However, they have evolved in conversation with important theological and ecclesial developments in Latin America in the past sixty years or so. On the other hand, as pluri-theological forums, they are informed by the experiences and struggles of the victims of structural oppression (as the contextual dimension in the construction

[84] International Theological Commission of EATWOT, "Towards a Work Agenda for Planetary Theology," 22.

[85] International Theological Commission of EATWOT, "Towards a Work Agenda for Planetary Theology," 23.

[86] International Theological Commission of EATWOT, "Towards a Work Agenda for Planetary Theology," 24.

[87] International Theological Commission, "Ecological Vision and Planetary Survival: A Concept Paper for EATWOT's General Assembly at Yogyakarta, Indonesia, 2012," https://drive.google.com/drive/folders/1v-CgolPOplklQbl2eJGJlFoyHQu0M_Mj.

of a planetary theological agenda highlights). Furthermore, they promote encounters and conversations that expand the horizons of each particular theological and ecclesial movement engaged in these forums, including Latin American liberation theology (LALT).

Although part of the expansion and changes taking place in the Latin American theological agenda in the past few decades has to do with the rise of new pastoral and theological subjects—women, queer communities, Indigenous peoples, black communities, and other religious traditions—that process has been significantly enriched by sustained conversations with other theologies and epistemologies of the South through forums such as EATWOT and WFTL. A quick look at the theological agenda and language these forums have advanced shows how the universal aspirations of liberation-orientated theologies originated in Latin America in the 1960s, privileging the experiences and perspectives of the impoverished, have become part of theological movements based on other realities, and how these forums create the space for necessary exchange and mutual influence among these contextual theological movements.

Both EATWOT and WFTL have been deeply influenced by LALT's legacy, which largely stems from the work of the CEBs and other popular movements. On the other hand, those spaces of theological interaction from the margins have brought to the fore unique and important contributions African, Asian, Latin American, and other liberating Christianities and theologies (including women, queer, and Indigenous/aboriginal theologies) have made to the epistemic revolution that is taking place in ecumenical circles in connection with the irruption of the Third World. What has transpired in the movements associated with these two forums cannot be considered in isolation, though. Many of the same individuals and networks linked to these forums are also involved in other ecumenical networks locally, nationally, regionally, and globally.

These theological conversations from the margins informed by the epistemologies of the South, have impacted important ecumenical voices and platforms with a global reach. I will conclude this chapter by discussing two examples of that impact, first on the World Council of Churches and then on Francis's papacy.

The Third World agenda has influenced many facets of the work of the World Council of Churches (WCC). The WCC has a worldwide membership and, in thesis, should embody theological contributions made by different sectors of its constituency. In its inception, however, the WCC represented mostly the vision of its European and North American members who saw the churches from the Global North as the core of the council and treated the churches from the Global South as "younger churches" whose development was molded in accordance with ecclesial patterns and theological principles developed in the north.[88] Over time, with the growing participation of leaders from the Global South, the WCC gradually incorporated language and theological emphases originally developed in the churches of the South. The leadership of two general secretaries from the Global South, Philip Potter (1972–1984) and Emilio Castro (1985–1992) certainly contributed to that influence, as did the work of individuals such as M. M. Thomas, Mercy Amba Oduyoye, Oscar L. Bolioli, José Míguez Bonino, Julio de Santa Ana, Zwinglio Dias and many others who have served as bridges between the WCC and the epistemologies of the South. Some concrete examples can help one see the extent to which the Third World project contributed to the WCC agenda.

One of those instances was the creation of the Ecumenical Group on the Church and the Poor (EGCP) by the Commission on the Churches' Participation in Development (CCPD) of the World Council of Churches following the Fifth WCC Assembly in Nairobi (1975). During a hearing on "Justice and Development," members of the assembly tasked the CCPD with aiding "the poor and oppressed in their struggles, and at the same time help[ing] the churches to manifest their solidarity with the poor and to second their efforts for a more just and participatory society."[89] Referring to those Christians who have joined the struggles of the poor, Julio de Santa Ana rejoiced for their encounter with the CEBs, which he defined as new ecclesial communities pointing to "a new action of the Holy Spirit in our time to renew his Church and to transform it into a home for the poor and oppressed, 'the weary and the heavy laden.'" In short, for Santa Ana,

[88] This was the case with the notion of the responsible society and of God's design for the world that informed the opening assembly of the World Council of Churches in 1948. See World Council of Churches, *The Church's Witness to God's Design: An Ecumenical Study Prepared under the Auspices of the World Council of Churches*, Man's Disorder and God's Design: The Amsterdam Assembly Series, vol. 2 (London: SCM Press, 1949).

[89] Santa Ana, *Towards a Church of the Poor*, ix.

the encounter with the CEBs pointed the ecumenical movement to "the direction of the Church of the Poor."[90]

Using examples of the church of the poor emerging in places as different as among the Aymara people in Bolivia, the Appalachian mountains in the US, and churches in Bangalore (India), Indonesia, and Nampula (Mozambique) as signs of hope in the plight of the poor, the EGCP sent a letter to all WCC member churches, urging them to "reconsider their organized structures to permit maximum deployment of their resources to the struggles for a just, participatory, liberated and sustainable society."[91] The cry of the poor, the letter stated, is a call for change and the poor the heralds of "a new world, that of the Kingdom and its justice."[92]

The letter, then, invites the churches to give priority to the poor, not only by designing programs for them but by drawing up projects and programs from their perspective—which demands to do the work with them, so the projects are theirs, not simply for them.[93] This transformative message resembles that which was initially heard in Geneva 1966, Medellin 1968, and Puebla 1979. It also indicates a radical departure from previous understandings of the nature of the church. The churches are called to be churches of the poor, and Jesus is depicted as being among them.

The Nairobi gathering was, in the words of David M. Paton (1913–1992), a different assembly, especially in terms of its worldwide makeup.

> Both membership and agenda were more genuinely worldwide, and more representative of the human race. Of 676 voting delegates, 107 were Africans, 92 Asians, 147 West Europeans, 97 East Europeans, 137 North Americans, 21 Latin Americans, 9 from the Caribbean, 42 from Australasia and the Pacific, and 20 from the Middle East. Of the 676, 152 were women (22%; Uppsala 9%), 62 under 30 years of age (9%; Uppsala 25%) and 287 lay. For about 80% of delegates Nairobi was their first WCC Assembly.[94]

---

[90] Santa Ana, *Towards a Church of the Poor*, xxiv.

[91] Santa Ana, *Towards a Church of the Poor*, 202.

[92] Santa Ana, *Towards a Church of the Poor*, 209.

[93] Santa Ana, *Towards a Church of the Poor*.

[94] David M. Paton, ed., *Breaking Barriers: Nairobi 1975* (London: SPCK, 1975), 4.

The first assembly in Africa, Nairobi 1975 held a plenary session on the topic "Women in a Changing World," which not only featured the work of women in the life of the WCC but also shared with the assembly the findings of a consultation held in Berlin in June of 1974 in which 160 women from 49 countries explored together the theme "Sexism in the 70s," sharing their "experience of discrimination in society and church," while reaffirming their hope in "the promise of a new humanity."[95]

Another significant plenary session in that assembly was the address delivered by Michael Manley, Primer Minister of Jamaica, who described himself as a "humanist by instinct, an egalitarian in social philosophy, a Christian by faith, a democratic socialist by political commitment, a member and spokesman of the Third World by force of circumstances and by active involvement."[96] His address included a shattering critique of the economic order, which should be democratized, challenging the churches to participate in the process of liberation.

> Churches have a clear duty to make common cause with the Third World in the search for a new world order. Christendom cannot cease from struggle until outrages that violate our faith are ended. The Third World needs to be clear about its moral foundations and set its own house in order by tackling the internal injustices among its members.[97]

Mainley concluded his address with "an eloquent appeal for action to liberate the victims of oppression now," receiving a standing ovation in response.[98]

Several assembly reports addressed similar concerns. Emphasizing an understanding of Christ as someone who frees and unites, the assembly addressed "structures that obscure the confession of Christ," including "structures of racist oppression," "structures of sexism," and economic structures that obscure the confession of Christ. Together, Nairobi 1975 admitted the contrast Christians experienced: "While

---

[95] Paton, ed., *Breaking Barriers*, 20.

[96] Paton, ed., *Breaking Barriers*, 21–22.

[97] Paton, ed., *Breaking Barriers*, 22.

[98] Paton, ed., *Breaking Barriers*.

we confess a Christ who frees and unites, the economic structures in which we live tend to enslave to wealth and divide."[99]

The Nairobi Assembly made numerous references to the Third World. These few examples are sufficient, though, to show how Third World theologies and concerns made their way into the heart of the ecumenical movement in the 1970s. That WCC assembly signaled a new moment in the ecumenical movement when the mobilizations of the Third World base began to impact ecumenical spirituality, pastoral action, and theology.

In its confession and proclamation, Nairobi 1975 affirmed its embracing of the whole gospel, described as "the announcement of God's Kingdom and love through Jesus Christ," committing to "the responsibility to participate in the struggle for justice and human dignity, the obligation to denounce all that hinders human wholeness." Consequently, the gospel needed to speak specifically to multiple contexts of oppression.

> In our time, to the oppressed the gospel may be new as a message of courage to persevere in the struggle for liberation in this world as a sign of hope for God's inbreaking Kingdom. To women the gospel may bring good news of a Christ who empowered women to be bold in the midst of cultural expectations of submissiveness. To children the gospel may be a call of love for the "little ones" and to the rich and powerful it may reveal the responsibility to share the poverty of the poor.[100]

The Nairobi assembly affirmed a commitment to the whole person, the whole world, and the whole church, engaging the voices from the Global South on a new level. Churches in consumer societies were called to form countercultural communities and to stand in solidarity with the victims of discrimination and oppression in their struggle for change.[101] In many ways, Nairobi reflected a spirituality based on the lived experiences of people seeking to follow Jesus in the heat of the struggle for life and justice, which, as Faustino Teixeira underscores, was also the case with the liberation movements in Latin America. Based on the example of Jesus, and having the reign of God

---

[99] Paton, ed., *Breaking Barriers*, 47.

[100] Paton, ed., *Breaking Barriers*, 52.

[101] Paton, ed., *Breaking Barriers*, 57.

at its horizon, such a spirituality is rooted in a deep immersion in the world and in participation in its transformation.[102]

This sort of world-oriented spirituality has impacted the ecumenical movement on numerous occasions. The emphasis on social responsibility in the 1950s was gradually adjusted to become a more overarching concern with justice, peace, and integrity of creation, which although grounded on concrete local experiences and communities, moved outwardly in the aspiration for a more just world order, which takes seriously the cry of the poor and the cry of earth.

Paul Abretch, a key behind-the-scenes figure in the development of ecumenical social thought between the 1950s and the early 1980s called the years from 1969 to 1987 the "period of liberation ecumenism." According to him, in that period a new approach to ecumenical social witness stemming from the struggles for freedom and justice not only in Africa, Asia, and Latin American and the Caribbean, but everywhere in the world, including the Civil Rights Movement in the United States, took shape in the ecumenical movement.[103]

The increased presence of Third World voices in multiple departments in the World Council of Churches enriched the global ecumenical agenda in meaningful ways. Among other things, the contributions from numerous liberative theologies—Latin American, black American/South African, mujerista, womanist, Dalit, Minjung, Indigenous/Native American, Palestinian, and Islander, among others—have provided a renewed understanding of Christian relations with the poor, the earth, and other religious traditions. Those experiences and perspectives, for instance, have helped the ecumenical movement see interreligious dialogue through a situated lens, which makes the dialogue of life central, reimagining liberative insights from an interfaith perspective and thus contributing to the development of new interreligious liberative theologies.[104]

---

[102] Faustino Luiz Couto Teixeira, *A Espiritualidade do Seguimento* (São Paulo: Edições Paulinas, 1994), 13.

[103] Paul Abretch, "From Oxford to Vancouver: Lessons from Fifty Years of Ecumenical Workfor Economic and Social Justice," *The Ecumenical Review* 40/2 (1988): 147–168.

[104] See, for instance, Peniel Jesudason Rufus Rajkumar, ed., *Faith(s) Seeking Justice: Dialogue and Liberation* (Geneva: WCC Publications, 2021). See, especially, Rakjumar's introduction and S. Wesley Ariarajah's chapter "The Promise of an Interreligious Theology of Liberation." The essays in this volume converge in the same

This sort of engagement has expanded the meaning of both liberation and dialogue, contributing new theological insights to a dialogical praxis. In his tenure as Programme Executive for Interreligious Dialogue and Cooperation with the World Council of Churches, Peniel Rajkumar held consultations in different parts of the world to examine the experience of multiple religious belonging or complex/hybrid religious identities. Since this is a phenomenon that has been more visible in the experience of formerly colonized peoples and Christians living in religiously plural contexts, most of the participants in those conversations were either from the Global South or from minoritized ethnic and racial communities in the Global North. Yet, the fact that these conversations were now taking place on the world stage led those who were not even aware of the existence of those conversations to include that topic on their radar.

The first consultation happened in Chennai, India (2014), the second in Cleveland, Ohio (2015), and the third Matanzas, Cuba (2017).[105] The agenda they sought to advance was brought to the attention of ecumenical circles by people from formerly colonized nations[106] or living in diasporic communities which enact a decolonial praxis that demands a different logic to navigate religious

direction as the emerging Latin America and in the contexts of EATWOT, although a significant number of the publications emerging on those fronts are not in English. See, for instance, Luiza E. Tomita et al., eds., *Pluralismo e Libertacao: Por uma Teologia Latino-Americana Pluralista a partir da Fé Cristã* (São Paulo: EATWOT/ Edições Loyola, 2005); José Maria Virgil, *Teologia do Pluralismo Religioso: para uma releitura pluralista do Cristianismo* (São Paulo: Paulus, 2006); and Luiza E. Tomita et al., eds., *Teologia Latino-Americana Pluralista da Libertação* (São Paulo: EATWOT/ Edições Paulinas, 2006).

105 The author participated in the 2017 symposium in Havana (2017) and in a North American consultation in Seattle (2016) on the theme "Charting New Frontiers: Multiple Religious Participation and the Changing Religious Landscape" on October 23–26, 2016. The North American gathering was sponsored by the UCC, the WCC, and Seattle University. These efforts have led to publications such as Peniel Jesudason Rufus Rajkumar and Joseph Prebhakar Dayam, eds., *Many Yet One? Multiple Religious Belonging* (Geneva: WCC Publications, 2016) and a special issue of *Current Dialogue* on multiple religious belonging (December 2015).

106 This is not to say that such demands come exclusively from non-Western contexts. But the recent insertion of this conversation in ecumenical interreligious dialogue programs results from the provocation made by people who have seen and/ or experienced complex religious identity in Global South nations or in their diaspora.

boundaries, opening up the possibility of embracing multiple ways of being, thus unsettling binary thinking patterns.[107]

In the United States, Karen Georgia Thompson, currently the UCC General Minister and President, brought this topic to the agenda of the interreligious convening table of the National Council of Churches (NCCUSA), underscoring that the experience of multiple religious belonging or hybrid religious identity is common especially in contexts where popular religiosity preserved suppressed traditional practices in Christianized asymmetrical contexts.[108] One of the responses to the asymmetrical evangelization of Native Americans, Haitians, or Afro-Brazilians, for instance, was the acceptance of the new faith without the rejection of the previous one—adding values and practices associated with the new faith to an already existing "spiritual experience of knowing the divine, the self, and the world."[109]

This recent attention to hybrid religious identities in ecumenical conversations is an acknowledgment of a way of being religious that has existed (even when not acknowledged) among Christians from different traditions around the world. Its addition to the ecumenical agenda on interfaith/interreligious relations represents one of the instances in which the epistemologies of the South have impacted notions of *oikoumenē* and ecumenism.

In her address to the Seattle consultation, HyeRan Kim-Cragg underscored the decolonial element in this sort of conversation, reminding the participants that we were exploring a "suppressed territory," drawing attention to the agency of those who have been navigating such experiences.

> Though the conversation around multiple religious belonging, religious syncretism and religious hybridity has been silenced and

---

[107] Furthermore, as Rajkumar deftly states, "multiple religious belonging unsettles the sure foundations of Christian identity, mission and interreligious dialogue where identity is often understood in rigid and binary terms vis-à-vis other religions." Peniel Jesudason Rufus Rajkumar. "Editorial," *Current Dialogue* 57 (2015): 2–3 (2). Under the editorial auspices of Rajkumar, this entire issue of *Current Dialogue* was dedicated to the theme "Multiple Religious Belonging: Exploring Hybridity, Embracing Hospitality."

[108] Karen Georgia Thompson, "Multiple Religious Belonging: Erasing Religious Boundaries, Embracing New Ways of Being," in *Many Yet One?*, ed. Rajkumar and Dayam, 45–61 (47).

[109] Thompson, "Multiple Religious Belonging," 56.

> unnoticed, it is not new; it has always existed. Thus, I think we must clearly state that multiple religious belonging is not a new conversation. What we are doing is charting a "suppressed" territory. That is my first thought. We must lift up the agency of those of us who have been navigating this experience. We must disclose the silences; we must reveal the suppressed reality of religious multiplicity that has existed ever since the birth of Christianity, and I would assume, all religions.[110]

Kim-Cragg is right. The conversation is about silenced religious experiences that have never ceased existing. Salvador, the capital city of the state of Bahia, Brazil, where I was born and raised, is known for its many Catholic temples—including the Church of Our Lady of the Rosary of the Black People—where African deities are also honored.[111] African and Indigenous experiences of conversion to Christianity in Latin America and the Caribbean have as background "the spiritual conquest."[112]

With the creation of the *reducciones* in colonial Latin America, conversion became part of what William Hanks calls *conquista pacífica* (or peaceful conquest).[113] Yet, the oppressive situation in which

---

[110] Author's notes on HyeRan Kim-Cragg's presentation "Challenging the Logic of the One: A Theological Exploration," Charting a New Frontier Multiple Religious Belonging, October 26, 2016, Seattle University.

[111] See David Lindenfeld and Miles Richardson, "Introduction. Beyond Conversion and Syncretism," in *Beyond Conversion and Syncretism: Indigenous Encounters with Missionary Christianity, 1800–2000*, ed. David Lindenfeld and Miles Richardson (New York/Oxford: Berghahn Books, 2011), 1–23 (3). The emphasis on religious identity in this type of conversation moves the focus from the intermixing of practices and traditions to the subjects and communities that relate to those traditions, sometimes intermixing them, other times choosing to practice both, while remaining able to differentiate between them.

[112] Enrique Dussel, *The Invention of the Americas: Eclipse of "the Other" and the Myth of Modernity* (New York, NY: Continuum Publishing Company, 1995), 49.

[113] William F. Hanks, *Converting Words: Maya in the Age of the Cross* (Berkeley and Los Angeles: University of California Press, 2010), 1. The author contrasts the *conquista pacífica* to the military conquest. While the latter was conducted through the use of military power, the former was conducted by missionaries and relied for the most part on "persuasion, habituation, and discipline." These two models, however, were never fully separated. The fear factor and other coercive mechanisms meant to "convince" and convert must be factored in along with the overall perception on the part of the European invaders of their spirituality and morality as superior to those of natives and Africans.

conversion happened remained violent. Conversion demanded a "turning away from past and current ways, to take on different, better ways."[114] Whereas Indigenous peoples often accepted the principle of coexistence, believing in the multiple expressions of the divine, Iberian missionaries perceived Indigenous culture as pagan and in need to be Christianized. Even when not explicitly stated, the ultimate goal, as Guillermo Cook points out, was to eradicate "indigenous culture and religion."[115] Yet, either due to the lack of personnel or to the continuous resilience and resistance on the part of the Africans who were enslaved and the original peoples who survived genocide, such an eradication was never completed. The persistence of Indigenous and African ways of being and knowing in Latin America took different shapes and forms. Some Indigenous communities moved out of the reach of the colonizers, completely isolating themselves in the jungle, while others learned ways to coexist without giving up their values and traditions, even though they were often Christianized.

Whenever coexistence happened, the appropriation and reinterpretation of aspects of the new faith through the lens of older traditions was common, especially among the poor, who relied on oral traditions for the transmission of memories and knowledges. This process of appropriation and reinterpretation of traditional values into Christian language and symbols is at the root of popular Christian devotions such as the one around Our Lady of Guadalupe, in Mexico. The myth of the origins of that devotion has Our Lady of Guadalupe appearing to Juan Diego, a Nahua peasant, in 1531, on the hill of Tepeyac, present-day Mexico City. That hill had previously housed a shrine for the female Azteca deity Tonantzin. In that revelatory event, Saint Mary, a major Christian figure brought to the land by the Spaniards, appeared to a young Nahua peasant as a brown woman dressed in Indigenous clothes. Indigenous spirituality contributed to the reinterpretation of Christian devotion, expanding its meaning for the impoverished Indigenous masses. According to Judith Gleanson,

---

[114] Hanks, *Converting Words: Maya in the Age of the Cross*, 5.

[115] Guillermo Cook, "Introduction: Brief History of the Maya Peoples," in *Crosscurrents in Indigenous Spirituality: Interface of Maya, Catholic & Protestant Worldviews*, ed. Guilhermo Cook (Leiden: E. J. Brill, 1997), 1–33 (15).

> The Virgin of Guadalupe came to life in response to the putting down of her Nahuatl predecessor, Tonantzin, whom she continues in mysterious ways to embody.[116]

On the hill where the Azteca mother goddess had been worshipped, a brown Catholic Saint emerged to remind the Nahua that she was still the mother of her people.[117] Similar expressions of popular religion abound in Latin America, the Caribbean, and in other parts of the formerly colonized world, representing an important aspect of the faith of the people.

Drawing on the work of Gloria Anzaldúa, Mara Medina uses the Nahuatl word *nepantla*, which means the middle or in-between space, to refer to the experience of living on cultural borderlands.[118] As a colonial Christian order imposed by the Iberian conquistadores was in the process of full implementation, many Indigenous peoples were caught in between worlds, being challenged to survive, whereas also adapting to an overwhelming new reality. As Medina points out, indigenous responses went beyond outright resistance.

> Indigenous peoples did not merely resist the imposition of Christianity, but they responded to the foreign tradition by crafting their religiosity, developing unsanctioned traditions, reinforcing their community networks, and ultimately asserting their religious autonomy. They became Christian on their own terms and in that process, Christianity was changed.[119]

According to Medina, the word *nepantla* was first recorded in Spanish writings by a Dominican Friar in the sixteenth century to describe an Indigenous new convert who was still in the middle, not yet firmly rooted in the Christian faith. From that perspective, *nepantla* described the trauma one was forced to face living between

---

[116] Judith Gleanson, "Oya in the Company of the Saints," *Journal of the American Academy of Religion* 68/2 (2000): 265–292 (265).

[117] See Robert Orsi, "She Came, She Saw, She Conquered," book review of *Goddess of the Americas: Writings on the Virgin of Guadalupe*, ed. Ana Castillo (New York : Riverhead Books, 1996), *Commonwealth* 124/5 (1997): 24–25 (24).

[118] Lara Medina, "Nepantla Spirituality: Negotiating Multiple Religious Identities Among U.S. Latinas," in *Rethinking Latino(a) Religion and Identity*, ed. Miguel A. de La Torre & Gaston Espinosa (Cleveland, Ohio: Pilgrim Press, 2006), 248–266.

[119] Medina, "Nepantla Spirituality," 251.

ancient institutions and new, incomprehensible, ones brought by the colonizers. That in-between space encompassed multiple manifestations of the divine, which coexisted without losing their distinctiveness.[120] *Nepantla* thus represents the complexity of that space of discomfort in ways that the word *syncretism* may not be enough to describe, allowing for that multiple or hybrid existence to take numerous and even conflictive forms.

The experience of many Black communities in Latin America and the Caribbean has some parallels with that of Indigenous peoples. In the context of a violent evangelization, enslaved Africans continued to practice their faith in a strange and hostile land by associating their Orishas with Catholic Saints. In that process, though, many of them ended up practicing two religions, not one, relating to the two traditions as complementary, when not combining some elements of both.

For instance, in the 1980s some leaders of Candomblé, an African-derived traditional religion in Brazil, decided to reject outright syncretism (even though complete avoidance of that after centuries of coexistence was practically impossible) in favor of a re-Africanization of the tradition. In their efforts to distinguish Catholic symbols and beliefs from those of Candomblé, those leaders sought to de-syncretize the *terreiros* (Candomblé's houses of worship), removing Catholic images and symbols that used to be there. Yet, this movement did not interfere with the members of the *terreiros* who identify as both Christians and Candomblecists. For the faithful who practice both religions, these two religious traditions are perceived as complementary to one another. As Afonso Soares explains, "If someone continues to attend Mass and the sacraments without giving up anti-harm passes and orders at crossroads, this could mean that their pragmatic reading recognizes the effectiveness of both rituals, Catholic and Candomblé, for example."[121]

At the end of the day, not only have Indigenous and African-derived religious traditions survived cultural genocide in the course of five centuries but the survival of their wholistic and inclusivist worldview has led to changes in the dominant religion, Christianity. Whereas European and North American Christian missions in Latin

---

120 Medina, "Nepantla Spirituality," 253–254.

121 Afonso M. L. Soares, "Sincretismo Afro-Católico no Brasil: lições de um povo em exílio," *Revista de Estudos da Religião* 3(2002): 45–75 (71).

America saw Christianity as superior to the traditional religious practices they encountered on the occupied land, the persistence of Indigenous and African-derived spirituality and traditions has changed the landscape of Latin American Christianity, pointing to the possibility of a more equitable coexistence among multiple religious traditions and cultures.

This situation has provoked renewed attention to popular religion, Indigenous and African religious traditions, and religious pluralism and culture, which were almost completely overlooked in the early days of the ecumenical movement,[122] along with an ecumenism of solidarity, focused on the accompaniment of vulnerable communities, which tend to be Indigenous and Black in countries like Brazil. This kind of ecumenical spirituality has moved a long way from the early ecumenical conversations about the Christian message in the non-Christian world, as seen in chapter one.

Pope Francis and the Globalization of Hope from Below

Francis, previously Cardinal Jorge Mario Bergoglio, is the first Latin American pope. Since his election, he has proposed a spirituality that is inspired by ecclesiological insights that can be traced back to

---

[122] See, for instance, the book by late Catholic theologian Afonso M. L. Soares, *Interfaces da Revelação: Pressupostos para uma teologia do sincretismo religioso no Brasil* (São Paulo: Edições Paulinas, 2003). The development of *teologia índia* and liberationist pluralist theologies mentioned earlier also emerged in response to those pastoral conversations and encounters. Most of those theological developments emerged in connection with the commemorations of the 500th anniversary of the European occupation. The year 1992 became a symbolic moment when Indigenous peoples rose to remind the continent that they were still alive, despite the genocide. Instead of commemorating five centuries of evangelization as Pope John Paull II was inclined to do, the pople from Abya Yala commemorated five hundred years of resistance, joined by other popular movements and the popular Church. The CELAM 4th conference that same year, which took place in Santo Domingo, the Island where Christopher Columbus arrived five centuries earlier, acknowledged the problems of the first evangelization, the inhumane conditions in which most people in the continent lived, and the need for a new evangelization marked by "Human Promotion" in response to "the delicate and difficult situation in which Latin American countries find themselves." CELAM, "Documento de Santo Domingo," https://www.celam.org/documentos/Documento_Conclusivo_Santo_Domingo.pdf.

Vatican II.[123] As Allan Deck puts it, Francis's ecclesiology stresses a creative fidelity, which is considerably more open and inclusive than that of his two immediate predecessors, reaching "a better balance between orthodoxy and orthopraxis, and developing "a dynamic vision of the Church as *siempre en salida*, always reaching out, as a 'field hospital on the battlefield.'"[124]

His ecclesiological vision, however, is not only inspired by the Second Vatican Council. It takes a cue also from the meeting of Latin American bishops in Aparecida 2007 (the fifth Latin American Episcopal Conference) "who were convinced that the old paradigm of Christendom that held the medieval, baroque and Tridentine Catholicism of Latin America together for five centuries was simply exhausted and needed to be replaced by something more agile." In his remarks in Aparecida, then Cardinal Bergoglio "stressed the need to move beyond a complacent and self-referential, even narcissistic, mindset that holds the Church paralyzed."[125]

The model offered by the Church of the Poor group in Vatican II, which informed the rise of liberation theology in Latin America, has deeply impacted the trajectory of Pope Francis. That vison has, however, been refined by subsequent developments that continued to take place in the region after Medellin and Puebla. On his first trip after being elected Pope (four months after the conclave), Francis visited Brazil for the commemoration of the Youth World Day. He included in his itinerary a visit to the Favela of Manguinhos, Rio de Janeiro. Speaking to that impoverished community, Francis stated,

> And the Brazilian people, especially the simplest people, can give the world a great lesson in solidarity, which is a word—this word solidarity—that is often forgotten or silenced, because it is uncomfortable. It almost seems like a curse word . . . solidarity! I would like to launch an appeal to all those who have more resources, public authorities, and all people of good will committed to social justice: Don't get tired of working for a fairer and more supportive world! No one can remain insensitive to the inequalities that still exist in the world! Each person, according to their own possibilities

[123] Deck, "Pope Francis and the Challenge of Ecclesial Introversion," 707.

[124] Deck, "Pope Francis and the Challenge of Ecclesial Introversion," 707–708.

[125] Deck, "Pope Francis and the Challenge of Ecclesial Introversion," 708.

> and responsibilities, make sure to contribute to putting an end to so many social injustices![126]

In that address, Francis invoked the Aparecida Final Statement, affirming that the Church, described as "advocate for justice and defender of the poor before intolerable social and economic inequalities that cry out to heaven," also intends to take part in those initiatives aiming at the development of all humans and the whole human person.[127]

This line of thought, clearly stemming from post-Vatican II developments in Latin America, including the *teologia del pueblo*, the Argentinean version of liberation theology, has informed Pope Francis's actions and thought. Juan Carlos Scannone (1931–2019), one of the most influential professors Bergoglio had and a leading articulator of the theology of the people, describes his social ethics as focusing on five critical pillars: (1) A Christological understanding of the social dimension of the Gospel as good news of mercy; (2) a preferential option for and solidarity with the poor, inspired in a vision of a poor Church for the poor; (3) the social protagonism of the poor and excluded; (4) care for the common house; and (5) discernment of the signs of God in the world and personal history.[128] On different levels, all these pillars are present in post-Vatican II theological developments in Latin America as in different strands of liberation theology and in the pastoral work of the Church as reflected in the episcopal conferences of Medellin (1968), Puebla (1979), Santo Domingo (1992) and Aparecida (2007).

Rooted in the Latin American reception of Vatican II, Pope Francis envisions a renewal of the Church inspired in the model of the church of the poor and a call to participate in the struggle for justice, as seen in *Gaudium et Spes* (1965) and expanded through the lenses of Medellin (1968) and Puebla (1979). In that spirit, Francis's 2013 apostolic exhortation *Evangelii Gaudium* fearlessly criticizes the naiveté of those who blindly "trust in the goodness of those wielding economic power and in the sacralized workings of the prevailing

---

[126] Papa Francisco, *Pronunciamentos do Papa Francisco no Brasil* (São Paulo: Paulus/Edições Loyola, 2013), 20.

[127] Francisco, *Pronunciamentos do Papa Francisco no Brasil*, 21.

[128] Juan Carlos Scannone, *La Ética Social del Papa Francisco: El Evangelio de la Misericordia em episitu de discernimento* (Buenos Aires: Agape Libros, 2018).

economic system," keeping the excluded waiting. He also denounced the globalization of indifference, which perpetuates injustice, sustaining a selfish lifestyle that excludes others.[129]

By calling out the indifference of the powerful to the cry of the poor, Francis draws on the preferential option for the poor. That option is also at the root of his call for the Church "to go out to the peripheries of existence."[130] Francis represents the full circle of an ecumenical vision open to the world that started with the rebirth of the Catholic Church in its opening to the world in Vatican II. Such a rebirth continued through the radical interpretation of this message in Latin America, leading to the rise of the base communities and the rise of various streams of liberation theology, including the *theology of the people*, returning from the base to the center of the Church with Francis's election in 2013. Francis now urges the Church to "get back to the people."[131]

In his openness to God and to the world, Francis advances a theology of love, which, in contrast with rigid interpretations of Christian tradition, sees it as dynamic, flourishing, progressing over time, deepening with age.[132] Tradition seen as fidelity represents growth. By contrast, rigidity crystalizes tradition, leading to traditionalism and fundamentalism. Pope Francis's understanding of the non-rigidity of love and of creative fidelity keeps him open to the dynamic and untamed action of God's love in the world, which invites openness to others and deep solidarity with the vulnerable, the oppressed, the poor. On the level of interchurch ecumenicity, such an emphasis keeps him committed to ecumenical dialogue and to a reconciled diversity among Christians of all stripes.[133] On the level of a broader humanistic ecumenism, he advances an ecumenicity based on the dignity of all people, a life-giving bridge connecting all peoples, in

---

129 Pope Francis, *Evangelii Gaudium*. See also Kristin Heyer and Bryan Massingale. "*Gaudium et Spes* and the Call to Justice: The U.S. Experience," in *From Vatican II to Pope Francis: Charting a Catholic Future*, ed. Paul Crowley (Maryknoll, NY: Orbis Books, 2014), 81–100 (98).

130 Pope Francis and Antonio Spadaro, *Open to God, Open to the World* (London: Bloomsbury, 2018), 23.

131 Pope Francis and Spadaro, *Open to God*, 42.

132 Pope Francis and Spadaro, *Open to God*, 51.

133 Eduardo J. Echeverria, *Pope Francis: Legacy of Vatican II* (Hobe Sound, Florida: Lection Publishing, 2015), 146.

contrast to "wall-projects" and the selfishness and insensibility the capitalist system promotes.[134]

If, on the one hand, Pope Francis prophetically condemns "the structural causes of poverty," and an economic system that puts profit above people,[135] on the other, he is committed to promote a network of solidarity in response to the need for an alternative economic system. He sees that alternative system emerging from "the struggle of the excluded against the globalized system."[136] This struggle for the construction of hope from the bottom up is pan-ecumenical, since it demands an ample fellowship that includes Christians and non-Christians committed to the practice of love, justice, and solidarity.[137] For Francis, the popular movements are among those human groups that congregate different people in actions of popular insurgency. They also represent a "revitalization of our democracies."[138]

Pope Francis's commitment to the social movement became evident as he helped form the World Meeting of Popular Movements (WMPM), with the purpose of promoting "an 'encounter' between Church leadership and grassroots organizations working to address the 'economy of exclusion and inequality.'"[139] The participants in that global network are the "popular movements," that is "grassroots organizations and social movements established around the world by people whose inalienable rights to decent work, decent housing, and fertile land and food are undermined, threatened or denied outright."[140]

---

134 Mauricio Abdalla, "O 'projeto-ponte' dos povos x o 'projeto-muro do dinheiro," in *Papa Francisco com os Movimentos Populares*, ed. Francisco de Aquino Junior et al (São Paulo: Edições Paulinas, 2018), 43–62 (43).

135 Abdalla, "O 'projeto-ponte' dos povos x o 'projeto-muro do dinheiro," 50, 52.

136 Abdalla, "O 'projeto-ponte' dos povos x o 'projeto-muro do dinheiro," 57, 58.

137 Carlos Rodrigues Brandão, "'Vós sois semeadores de esperança: Três mensagens de Francisco a pessoas e coletivos de Movimentos Populares," in *Papa Francisco com os Movimentos Populares*, 63–84 (77).

138 Brandão, "'Vós sois semeadores de esperança," 77, 79.

139 This last phrase comes directly from his *Evangelii Gaudium*. Information available at WMPM, "World Meeting of Popular Movements," http://popularmovements.org/about/.

140 WMPM, "World Meeting of Popular Movements." These movements are composed of workers who are at risk or lack job security, landless farmers, family farmers, Indigenous people and those at risk of being driven off the land by large

In his address to the first World Meeting of Popular Movements in Rome (2014), Francis explained the significance of grassroots movements as signs of transformation and renewal: "This meeting of grassroots movements is a sign, it is a great sign, for you have brought a reality that is often silenced into the presence of God, the Church, and all peoples. The poor do not only suffer injustice; they also struggle against it!"[141] Mentioning that solidarity sometimes is a "dirty word," Francis legitimized the social movements as networks of solidarity that ecumenically gather people in need to act in community.

> Solidarity is a word that is not always well received. In certain circumstances it has become a dirty word', something one dares not say. However, it is a word that means much more than an occasional gesture of generosity. It means thinking and acting in terms of community. It means that the lives of all take priority over the appropriation of goods by a few. It also means fighting against the structural causes of poverty and inequality; of the lack of work, land and housing; and of the denial of social and labour rights. It means confronting the destructive effects of the empire of money: forced dislocation, painful emigration, human trafficking, drugs, war, violence and all those realities that many of you suffer and that we are all called upon to transform. Solidarity, understood in its deepest sense, is a way of making history, and this is what the popular movements are doing.[142]

Francis also addressed the Second World Meeting of Popular Movements in Santa Cruz de la Sierra, Bolivia (2015). In that address, he acknowledged the need for change, adding his voice to advocate "for the three "L's" for all our brothers and sisters: land, lodging and labor."[143] The pope mentioned the urgent need for

---

agribusiness corporations and violence; and the marginalized and forgotten, including persons who are homeless and persons living in communities without adequate infrastructure.

[141] Pope Francis, "Address of Pope Francis to the Participants in the World Meeting of Popular Movements," Old Synod Hall Tuesday, 28 October 2014, https://www.vatican.va/content/francesco/en/speeches/2014/october/documents/papa-francesco_20141028_incontro-mondiale-movimenti-popolari.html.

[142] Francis, "Address of Pope Francis to the Participants in the World Meeting."

[143] Pope Francis, "Participation at the Second World Meeting of Popular Movements: Address of the Holy Father." Expo Feria Exhibition Centre, Santa Cruz de la Sierra (Bolivia) Thursday, 9 July 2015, https://www.vatican.va/content/francesco/

structural change: "This system is by now intolerable: farmworkers find it intolerable, laborers find it intolerable, communities find it intolerable, peoples find it intolerable. . . . The earth itself—our sister, Mother Earth, as Saint Francis would say—also finds it intolerable."[144]

The changes he calls for are practical. Changes that "can affect the entire world, since global interdependence calls for global answers to local problems." Thus, he urges for a "globalization of hope" which "springs up from peoples and takes root among the poor." Such a globalization from below "must replace the globalization of exclusion and indifference!"[145] Then he turns to the social movements and calls them "sowers of change." They are the ones bringing about processes of change because they are close enough to those in need.

> As members of popular movements, you carry out your work inspired by fraternal love, which you show in opposing social injustice. When we look into the eyes of the suffering, when we see the faces of the endangered campesino, the poor laborer, the downtrodden native, the homeless family, the persecuted migrant, the unemployed young person, the exploited child, the mother who lost her child in a shootout because the barrio was occupied by drug dealers, the father who lost his daughter to enslavement . . . when we think of all those names and faces, our hearts break because of so much sorrow and pain. And we are deeply moved, all of us. . . . We are moved because "we have seen and heard" not a cold statistic but the pain of a suffering humanity, our own pain, our own flesh. This is something quite different than abstract theorizing or eloquent indignation. It moves us; it makes us attentive to others in an effort to move forward together. That emotion which turns into community action is not something which can be understood by reason alone: it has a surplus of meaning which only

---

en/speeches/2015/july/documents/papa-francesco_20150709_bolivia-movimenti-popolari.html.

[144] Pope Francis, "Participation at the Second World Meeting of Popular Movements."

[145] Pope Francis, "Participation at the Second World Meeting of Popular Movements."

> peoples understand, and it gives a special feel to genuine popular movements.[146]

Francis concludes the address by naming three key tasks to effect the change mentioned earlier: 1) "To put the economy at the service of peoples;" 2) "to unite our peoples on the path of peace and justice;" and 3) "to defend Mother Earth." In contrast to the belief that such major changes need to come from above, Francis affirms that "the future of humanity does not lie solely in the hands of great leaders, the great powers and the elites." On the contrary, it "is fundamentally in the hands of peoples and in their ability to organize. It is in their hands, which can guide with humility and conviction this process of change. I am with you."[147] No pope has spoken like that before. Here is not only the pope but the Argentine Catholic bishop who learned from the theology of the people on the Medellin and Puebla trail.

Pope Francis would also address the third world gathering of popular movements in Rome (2016). The three emphases named in the meeting in Bolivia would remain the focus of that gathering. Repeating the words of *Evangelii Gaudium*, "Inequality is the root of social ills," and reaffirming that the future of humanity does not lie solely in the hands of the powerful and the elites, Francis exhorted the popular movements to remain on course:

> As organizations of the excluded and many organizations from other sectors of society, you are called to revitalize and recast the democracies, which are experiencing a genuine crisis. Do not fall into the temptation of the straitjacket, which reduces you to being extras off-stage, or worse, to mere administrators of existing misery. In these times of paralysis, disorientation and destructive formulas, the active participation of peoples who seek the common good can triumph, with God's help, over the false prophets who exploit fear and despair, who peddle magic formulas of hatred and callousness, or a selfish prosperity and an illusory security.[148]

---

[146] Pope Francis, "Participation at the Second World Meeting of Popular Movements."

[147] Pope Francis, "Participation at the Second World Meeting of Popular Movements."

[148] Pope Francis, "Participation at the Second World Meeting of Popular Movements."

In his conclusion, he encouraged them to "continue combating fear by a life of service, solidarity and humility on behalf of peoples, and especially those who suffer most."[149]

After two papacies which did all they could to contain what some feared to be excesses of the Vatican II, Pope Francis has sought to restore the more expansive interpretation of the Council based on an radical openness to God and to the world. His initiative to create a forum for church leaders and vulnerable workers from all over the world points to his commitment to turn the prophetic words of *Evangelii Gaudium* into actions. Even more telling is the fact that in search for change he turns to the apparently weak and powerless as those with the greatest potential and capacity to lead the major changes the world urgently needs.

Let me end this chapter going back to *Querida Amazonia*, Francis's Post-Synodal Apostolic Exhortation following the 2019 Synod of Bishops for the Pan-Amazon region, mentioned in chapter nine. This was another significant initiative from Francis. This synod, like the WMPM, was part of Francis's intent to embody the words of *Laudato si'*, his encyclical on the care for and defense of the earth, our common home, and the Indigenous people in 2015. Among other things, *Laudato Si* makes a direct reference to Leonardo Boff's *Cry of the Earth, Cry of the Poor*.[150] The formation of Red Eclesial Pan-Amazonica (REPAM) in 2014 and the Amazon Synod, after

---

[149] Pope Francis, "Participation at the Second World Meeting of Popular Movements."

[150] Without naming Boff, Pope Francis cites the title of his book *Cry of the Earth, Cry of the Poor* (1997), "Today, however, we have to realize that a true ecological approach *always* becomes a social approach; it must integrate questions of justice in debates on the environment, so as to hear *both the cry of the earth and the cry of the poor*." Pope Francis, "Encyclical Letter *Laudato Si'* of the Holy Father Francis on Care for Our Common Home," https://www.vatican.va/content/dam/francesco/pdf/encyclicals/documents/papa-francesco_20150524_enciclica-laudato-si_en.pdf. Around the time the encyclical was published, I met with Leornardo Boff during a congress in Vitoria, Brazil. In a conversation over lunch at the home of historian Wanderley Pereira da Rosa, Boff confided that he had been consulted by Francis as he prepared that encyclical. Harvey Cox and Shanta Premawardhana were also part of that conversation. Ironically, Boff, who had been silenced by the previous pope, then the prefect of the Congregation for the Doctrine of the Faith in the papacy of John Paul II, was now consulted by his successor as he wrote one of his most important encyclicals.

two years of wide mobilization until its execution in 2019, were initiatives through which Francis hoped to turn the words of *Laudato Si'* into transformative action. REPAM promotes Indigenous rights, amplifying Indigenous leaders' voices on the global stage.[151] *Querida Amazonia* (2020) was Francis's response to the Synod. This post-synodal apostolic exhortation is still to receive the attention it deserves as one of the boldest documents Francis has produced.

The document stems from his listening to various presentations and reports in the synod, being also his response to the final document of the synod, which, according to him, "profited from the participation of many people who know better than myself or the Roman Curia the problems and issues of the Amazon region, since they live there, they experience its suffering and they love it passionately."[152] In *Querida Amazonia*, Francis discusses four dreams, which emanate from the final document of the synod.

1. A social dream: "Our dream is that of an Amazon region that can integrate and promote all its inhabitants, enabling them to enjoy 'good living.'"[153]
2. A cultural dream: In contrast to the colonizing process, Francis calls for the acknowledgment and care for the cultural identity of each people that survived colonization. In a context where peoples and cultures are endangered, the Pope calls for intercultural relations and the preservation of ancestral cultures.
3. An ecological dream: "In a cultural reality like the Amazon region, where there is such a close relationship between human

[151] Caritas, "The Work of REPAM," https://www.caritas.org/what-we-do/development/repam/. REPAM was inspired by Francis, whereas the Amazon Synod was his own initiative.

[152] Francis explained that he did not cite the Synod's final document in his exhortation directly, because he would "rather encourage everyone to read it in full." Pope Francis, "Post-Synodal Apostolic Exhortation of the Holy Father Francis, '*Querida Amazonia*.'"

[153] Pope Francis, "Post-Synodal Apostolic Exhortation of the Holy Father Francis, '*Querida Amazonia*.'" The social dream embodies the prophetic words from *Evangelii Gaudium*, denouncing the crimes and injustices committed against the poor and vulnerable people in the region. Among those crimes, Francis mentions "colonizing interests that have continued to expand—legally and illegally—the timber and mining industries, and have expelled or marginalized the indigenous peoples, the river people and those of African descent, are provoking a cry that rises up to heaven."

beings and nature, daily existence is always cosmic. Setting others free from their forms of bondage surely involves caring for the environment and defending it."[154]

4. Finally, a common dream: Inspired by the privileged expressions of the Church's presence alongside the people at the Bishops' Conference in Medellin (1968) and its application to the Amazon region at Santarem (1972), followed by Puebla (1979), Santo Domingo (1992), and Aparecida (2007), Francis reaffirms the call of the Church "to journey alongside the people of the Amazon region. Not only that, but this journey also aims at developing "a Church with an Amazonian face," which needs "to grow in a culture of encounter towards 'a multifaceted harmony.'"[155]

While examining these four dreams is outside the scope of this chapter, my goal here is simply to draw attention to the sharpening of Francis's insights regarding Indigenous peoples and ecology. In this document, once again, he connects the cry of the earth and the cry of the poor. However, the poor in this apostolic exhortation have a very concrete face: (1) Indigenous people in the Amazonia, (2) *quilombolas* (Black-Brazilian communities originally formed by enslaved Africans and Afro-Brazilians who escaped slavery), and (3) *ribeirinhos* (traditional rural communities living by the shore of the many Amazon rivers).

In addition to drawing attention to the suffering of these communities who, along the rainforest, have been on the receiving end of environmental destructive practices done by big agribusiness, miners, and other companies responsible for the catastrophe of deforestation, the poisoning of waters, and the continuous genocide of the peoples of the forest, Francis highlights their cultural agency and capacity to show the way to alternative values in line with the well-being of the earth, his version of another possible world. Then, Francis turns to the cry of the Amazon region, which includes the forest, the rivers, and the people of the Amazonia. The pope resorts to poetry to refer

[154] Pope Francis, "Post-Synodal Apostolic Exhortation of the Holy Father Francis, '*Querida Amazonia.*'"

[155] Pope Francis, "Post-Synodal Apostolic Exhortation of the Holy Father Francis, '*Querida Amazonia.*'"

to the pain shared by many in the region, citing Colombian poet Juan Carlos Galeano, natural of the Amazon region, who voices that wide-sweeping connection between the cry of the earth and the cry of the poor:

> *Those who thought that the river was only a piece of rope,*
> *a plaything, were mistaken.*
> *The river is a thin vein on the face of the earth . . .*
> *The river is a cord enclosing animals and trees.*
> *If pulled too tight, the river could burst.*
> *It could burst and spatter our faces with water and blood.*[156]

One of the most impressive moves Francis makes in this document is to tie the cry of the Amazon to "the conquest and exploitation of resources . . . [which] has today reached the point of threatening the environment's hospitable aspect," our common home. Thus, the health of the Amazon becomes the equilibrium of the world. How to cure the earth from the destruction imposed by greed?

Francis claims that contemporary technological knowledge is not enough to change course. He argues that it must be combined with "ancestral wisdom." In other words, reaching "sustainable management of the land" is just one part of the task. The other is to preserve "the lifestyle and value systems of those who live there."[157]

At this point, Francis restates what he said earlier to the WMPM. The powerful cannot solve the problem because of their greed. That is also the reason why technology is not the answer: "The powerful are never satisfied with the profits they make, and the resources of economic power greatly increase as a result of scientific and technological advances." New power structures based on a different set of values are required. Thus, he boldly points to the original peoples as those from whom "we" (the West) can learn:

> From the original peoples, we can learn to *contemplate* the Amazon region and not simply analyze it, and thus appreciate this precious

[156] Pope Francis, "Post-Synodal Apostolic Exhortation of the Holy Father Francis, '*Querida Amazonia*.'" Citation from Juan Carlos Galeano, "Los que creyeron," in *Amazonia y otros poemas* (Bogotá: ed. Universidad Externado de Colombia, 2011), 44.

[157] Pope Francis, "Post-Synodal Apostolic Exhortation of the Holy Father Francis, '*Querida Amazonia*.'"

> mystery that transcends us. We can *love* it, not simply use it, with the result that love can awaken a deep and sincere interest. Even more, we can *feel intimately a part of it* and not only defend it; then the Amazon region will once more become like a mother to us. For "we do not look at the world from without but from within, conscious of the bonds with which the Father has linked us to all beings."[158]

At this point, Indigenous peoples, their cultures, traditions, and ways of life gain a significance in the exhortation that does not depend on their relationship with Christianity. They become the teachers and "we" the learners. Francis acknowledges the sinful attitude of "the missionaries [who] did not always take the side of the oppressed," expressing shame and humbly asking for forgiveness "not only for the offenses of the Church herself, but for the crimes committed against the native peoples during the so-called conquest of America as well as for the terrible crimes that followed throughout the history of the Amazon region."[159] Besides that, he also points to a strong sense of human fellowship that permeates the work, rest, relationships, rites, and celebrations of the original peoples of the Amazon region as crucial for the efforts to "build a just society" because such an endeavor requires "a capacity for fraternity."[160]

Francis's invitation to social, cultural, ecological, and ecclesial dialogue thus not only favors "the preferential option on behalf of the poor, the marginalized and the excluded, but also respect[s] them as having a leading role to play." As a region that has been exploited, colonized and missionized, the Amazon is portrayed in the exhortation as a cultural polyhedron, and its peoples as survivors with inherent cultural values, which not only were important for their own survival of five centuries of genocide but which remain important for the survival of the planet today. Acknowledging the plural nature of existence, Francis asserts,

---

158 Pope Francis, "Post-Synodal Apostolic Exhortation of the Holy Father Francis, '*Querida Amazonia*.'"

159 Pope Francis, "Post-Synodal Apostolic Exhortation of the Holy Father Francis, '*Querida Amazonia*.'"

160 Pope Francis, "Post-Synodal Apostolic Exhortation of the Holy Father Francis, '*Querida Amazonia*.'"

> Each of the peoples that has survived in the Amazon region possesses its own cultural identity and unique richness in our multicultural universe, thanks to the close relationship established by the inhabitants with their surroundings in a non-deterministic symbiosis which is hard to conceive using mental categories imported from without.[161]

Francis's remarkable recommendation for the young people of the Amazon who are being constantly uprooted is to nurture their own roots. "I urge the young people of the Amazon region, especially the indigenous peoples, to 'take charge of your roots, because from the roots comes the strength that will make you grow, flourish and bear fruit.'"[162]

In *Querida Amazonia*, Pope Francis, himself a product of the theology of the people, after listening to the cry of the Amazon people and of the forest, not only reestablishes the preferential option for the poor but, in Freirean fashion, turns the Indigenous and other impoverished peoples of the Amazon into the teachers of another possible world, and reinforcing the value of their knowledge, wisdom, and lifestyle as critical for the renewal of life in a planet at risk of catastrophic death.

This is the full circle of a liberating Christianity that stems from Christian encounters with the poor in colonialized contexts, moves toward the rise of consciousness among the poor who irrupt as new historical and theological subjects, and whose prophetic claims affect established ecclesial and societal structures from the bottom up, as a movement of globalization from below. Then, attention is turned back to the poor, no longer merely as exploited and excluded subjects or as recipients of charity and mission, but as cultured beings and knowledge producers. Their experiences and knowledge become

---

161 Pope Francis, "Post-Synodal Apostolic Exhortation of the Holy Father Francis, '*Querida Amazonia*.'"

162 Pope Francis, "Post-Synodal Apostolic Exhortation of the Holy Father Francis, '*Querida Amazonia*.'" Those roots are Indigenous cultures, oral traditions, wisdom, myths, legends, and tales they learned from their elders, because those are the roots that keep a community alive. Thus, "without the umbilical cord of those stories, distance and lack of communication would have fragmented and dissolved." While those roots might include Christian stories for those who are baptized, those stories are only part of it, and not necessarily the roots that those who are not Christians are called to preserve.

liberating as they challenge death-oriented, egotistic, and self-destructive patterns of thinking with a resilient collective wisdom that has for centuries resisted annihilation. By bringing the focus back to the Indigenous peoples of the Americas, the main victims of the vicious violence of conquest and colonization, Francis calls for the integral conversion of Christianity to the other, to those who, once victimized by Christian subjects, are now in the position to become their teachers, including the earth.

12

FOR AN *OIKOUMENĒ* IN WHICH MANY WORLDS COEXIST[1]

I started this book with a reference to Dale Irvin's claim that the modern ecumenical movement was originally shaped under the influence of powerful "lingering memories of Christendom East and West," haunted by the specter of Constantine. Irvin also argued that a new ecumenism is emerging, one that "resembles the fluid assemblages and cross-border flows of globalization and exile."[2] In previous chapters, I examined those contrasting developments through the lenses of the Latin American ecumenical experiment and the mutual influence it has experienced in connection with other ecumenical developments worldwide. The two apparently contrasting realities are not detached. On the contrary, they continue to be part of the ecumenical movement. Christianity is both a religion haunted by the specter of Constantine and colonial Christendom and the fluid assemblages of the experiences of dislodged, colonized, enslaved, and other oppressed peoples from all parts of the world. Such a paradoxical nature remains part of the Christian experience in today's world, being, consequently, present in the ecumenical movement: thus the tensions this book has alluded to on many occasions.

Emancipatory, anticolonial, antiracist, and antipatriarchal liberatory movements have never been able to create any sort of definitive reality. While many modern ecumenical leaders have talked about the ecumenical movement as marked by "reconciled differences," it would be more accurate to say that this is a movement of differences in search for reconciliation. Whether full reconciliation will

[1] This title takes a cue from an essay I recently published. See Raimundo Barreto, "'A World in Which Many Worlds Fit': Ecumenism and Pluriversal Ontologies," in *Decolonial Horizons: Reimagining Theology, Ecumenism and Sacramental Praxis*, ed. Raimundo Barreto and Vladimir Latinovic (New York: Palgrave MacMillan, 2023), 79–100.

[2] Irvin, "Specters of a New Ecumenism," 24–25.

ever be possible is not clear. But there is a remarkable elasticity in the ecumenical movement, which allows for pull and push forces to coexist.[3] The origins of the ecumenical movement are in the modern missionary movement, which was basically a European and Euro-American enterprise. Search for unity in that context was tainted by imperial and colonial interests. Yet, as members of churches formed in colonized and formerly colonized territories started seeking a seat around the ecumenical table, they realized that there were other forms of ingrained division separating Christians and other humans that went beyond denominational and doctrinal borders. Especially since the rise of the Third World in the 1950s, it has become increasingly clearer for many Christians in the Global South that most of the critical divisive issues today have to do with the line of the human and the non-human, the racialized hierarchization of the human created in connection with the rise of modernity/coloniality, starting in the end of the fifteenth century and consolidated between the seventeenth and the nineteenth century. A critical component of that new world order was a Europeanized Christendom, which contributed with moral and theological justifications for the European expansionism at the root of a colonial world built on the backs of the genocide and enslavement of Native American/Amerindian and African peoples. The lingering memories of Constantine that Irvin mentions are, from the perspective of the Global South, lingering memories of colonialism. Since the late 1990s, Latin American and Latine scholars have used the term *coloniality* to speak of those lingering memories, which still divide the line of the human and the nonhuman today. Those lines of separation are determined by the hierarchization of human groups through class, race, ethnicity, gender, and sexuality.

Ecumenical contributions inspired by the Third World project and the epistemologies of the South form, as M. P. Joseph called it, an ecumenism of the nonperson, of those struggling to reclaim their

[3] I want to thank my former student Nina Laubach (Spring 2024) for helping me see the significance of using the word *elasticity* in this conversation. Whereas, throughout this narrative there is a push toward the margins and the local, the ecumenicity of the human (more recently a planetary ecumenicity) driving the movements in question functions as an important pull force, bringing them back to a sense of unity and mutual belonging that characterizes what was earlier known as globalization from below.

personhood. That is the reason why in the Global South, without demeriting faith and order concerns, ecumenism has been more about life, humanity, and, more recently, the planet than about churches. Consequently, one can say that the epistemologies of the South contribute to expand the notion of the *oikoumenē*, overcoming the imperial contours associated with previous readings of this term, and reinterpreting it through the lenses of a more plural understanding of the world, as the notion of "our common home" in Francis's *Querida Amazonia* or the Andean concept *buen vivir* (good living) seem to imply. The latter, especially, means not only the ability to live in harmony with the earth and in solidarity with other beings but also to coexist in plural realities where the dialogue among peoples and cultures is informed by notions of equality and social justice.[4]

In the past half-century, Christians in Africa, Asia, and Latin America have drastically increased in numbers, now comprising most Christians in the world. Accordingly, they are taking more leadership roles in church, academia, and society not only in their own nations but also on the international level, bringing to those roles both their cultural identities and ways of worshipping and their knowledges and ways of knowing, which consequentially impact ecumenical theology and praxis.

The popular spirituality developed in the context of Latin American liberation Christianity has impacted the church worldwide, as communal experiences that emerged in that context have been shared through broader ecumenical networks. The spread of alternative forms of ecumenism challenges ecumenical models that still reflect modern/colonial hierarchizations, thus expanding the possibilities of renewal in the ecumenical movement as it enters a new era.

Influences from the Global South on the ecumenical movement can be traced back to as early as Edinburgh 1910, when V. S. Azariah voiced the powerful appeal, "Give us friends!" to a predominantly European and North American gathering.[5] The rise of a Latin American Protestant leadership in the Panama Congress in 1916 and the incipient involvement of "younger churches" in the IMC enlarged meetings of Jerusalem (1928) and Tambaram (1938) are

---

[4] Catherine Walsh, "Development as Buen Vivir: Institutional Arrangements and (De)colonial Entanglements," *Development* 53/1(2010): 15–21 (19).

[5] Stanley, *The World Missionary Conference*, loc. 1186.

other examples of that early impact. However, it was only with the rise of the Third World project and of liberation Christianity from the 1950s on that voices from the Global South began to impact the ecumenical agenda more significantly.

The networks formed around ideals inspired by the Third World project, informed emerging Christian leaders in the Global South, including Latin America, who dreamed of a "Christian Bandung." The Church of the Poor group in the Second Vatican Council (1962–1965) and the Third World impact on the WCC World Conference on Church and Society in Geneva (1966) exemplify the rise of Third World Christian voices who influenced the theological agenda of the world Christian movement on the global stage in the second half of the twentieth century. More than that, those international forums generated fresh opportunities for South-South interactions, which kept the dream of a Christian Bandung alive.

Not only were those emerging leaders determined to impact the global ecumenical agenda, but they were also committed to immerse back into the daily struggles of their own people and support each other in the creation of spaces where they could exchange experiences and expand the impact of their struggle for justice and human dignity in a "glocalized" manner—that is, they remained committed to local transformations while dreaming of and contributing to global thought and action. That determination resulted in a number of local movements such as the popular reading of the Bible in Brazil and the organization of a resilient resistance to the authoritarian regimes that emerged in Latin America between the 1960s and the 1980s, leading to the creation of forums such as EATWOT, the World Forum on Theology and Liberation, the Global Christian Forum, and, more recently, the World Meeting of Popular Movements.

This book has also shown that Latin American liberation theology and other liberative theologies that appeared ever since cannot be treated only as intellectual movements. In all the cases discussed in previous chapters, context-based theologies were often a product of organic intellectual activity ingrained in the praxis of liberation in particular situations. Theology in those cases becomes indeed a second act preceded by liberating praxis. In Latin America, the rise of the base ecclesial communities (CEBs), grassroots Christian communities seeking to live their faith often in hostile situations of oppression, struggling to read the word (the Bible) and the world to find guidance for their continuous resistance against systemic exclusion and impoverishment, provide the community basis for the emancipatory praxis of most liberation theologians in the region.

Such a community-oriented praxis committed to social transformation and liberation from all sorts of violence, deprivation, and injustices has inspired many other movements around the world. One can see its visible impact by the way its vocabulary has been integrated into the parlance of the ecumenical movement. As shown in chapter eleven, key language and assumptions developed by liberative theologies can be found in WCC and Vatican documents, informing ecumenical language at large in ways that are often taken for granted. The expansion in ecumenical vocabulary, understanding and practices in connection with the struggle for justice through the lenses of liberation and postcolonial thinking is an undeniable proof of the global impact of these movements.

Although the paradox between the imperial memories haunting the ecumenical movement and the assemblages of cross-border networks creating opportunities for its renewal remains alive, it is important to acknowledge how far popular (base-organized) struggles have come since the days of Popular Action and the rise of the ecclesial base communities in the 1960s, so one can appreciate the impact these movements have made on ecumenical language and praxis around the world. Taking a cue from Boaventura de Sousa Santos, one can speak of the epistemic dimension of the struggle for justice, which resists epistemicide, the erasure of knowledges and ways of knowing from peoples pushed to the margins. This epistemic struggle for emancipation shows a critical face of liberatory movements, considering that knowledge and knowledge production are often weaponized as instruments of regulation of the masses.[6] Thus the impact of base ecumenism should not be measured only in terms of its numbers or lasting social impact but also in terms of how it has impacted the terms of the conversations we have today in ecumenical circles, and the agenda and language of the ecumenical movement.

---

6 Boaventura Sousa Santos, *Epistemologies of the South: Justice against Epistemicide* (London and New York: Routledge, 2016).

Toward an Ecumenism of the Spirit

Since the late 1970s, people like Carlos Mesters began to highlight the role of the Spirit as the interpreter of the word.[7] In recent decades, the World Council of Churches also started paying greater attention to pneumatology, as seen in its seventh assembly in Canberra (1991), which focused on the theme "Come Holy Spirit—Renew the Whole Creation."[8] The growth of pneumatological references in ecumenical circles reflects the impact Pentecostalism has had on Christianity worldwide as a global movement.[9] In his reflections on the official report of the ninth WCC assembly in Porto Alegre (2006), Puerto Rican historian Luis N. Rivera-Pagán highlighted the fact that the six hundred ninety-one delegates representing three hundred forty-eight member churches from one hundred twenty countries, the two thousand seventy-nine participants in the *mutirões*, and the journalists, stewards, delegated representatives, and observers who filled up the grounds of the *Pontifícia Universidade Católica do Rio Grande do Sul*, the site of the assembly, represented "a kaleidoscope of nations, cultures, races, languages and ecclesiastical traditions, a striking demonstration of the demographic shift from the West and the North to the South and the East taking place in world Christianity."[10] Part of the transformation that world Christianity has brought to the global stage is the pentecostalization in large scale of Global South Christian expressions.

Latin America is one of those landscapes where Pentecostalism has experienced an expressive boom in the past few decades. Likewise, Latin America has also seen the pentecostalization of other forms of Christianity—both Protestant and Catholic. For the most part, Latin American Pentecostals have been suspicious of both ecumenism and liberation theology. Part of that suspicion has its origins in the

---

[7] Carlos Mesters, "'Listening to What the Spirit is Saying to the Churches,'" 100–111.

[8] Michael Kinnamon, ed., *Signs of the Spirit: Official Report—Seventh Assembly, Canberra, Australia, 7–20 February 1991* (Geneva: WCC Publications, 1991), 1.

[9] See Veli-Matti Kärkkäinen, *Pneumatology: The Holy Spirit in Ecumenical, International, and Contextual Perspective* (Grand Rapids, MI: Baker Publishing Group, 2018).

[10] Luis N. Rivera-Pagán, "Porto Alegre 2006: A Polycentric World Christianity," in *God, in Your Grace. . . Official Report of the Ninth Assembly of the World Council of Churches*, ed. Luis N. Rivera-Pagán (Geneva: WCC Publications, 2007), 5–54 (5).

propaganda disseminated, starting in the 1960s, by US conservative evangelical missionaries who associated both movements with communism in their Cold War anti-communist crusades, labeling them a threat to the churches. Despite that sort of campaign, a few Latin American Pentecostal Churches have been involved in the ecumenical movement since its inception. The Chilean *Misión Iglesia Pentecostal* (MIP) is one of the Pentecostal churches that has continued to devise ways to identify as both a Pentecostal and ecumenical church, despite the challenges it faced during the Chilean military regime (1973–1990), "when the official propaganda equaled ecumenism with communism."[11]

As Juan Sepúlveda aptly notes, Pentecostal involvement in ecumenical initiatives Chile can be traced back to as early as 1941, when a visit by John Mott, on behalf of the IMC, and W. Stanley Rycroft, on behalf of the CCLA, to promote Christian unity in Latin America led to the creation of the Chilean Committee on Cooperation, later replaced by the Chilean Evangelical Council (CEC), which comprised twenty-six churches, including some that were Pentecostal.[12] Through CEC, those Pentecostal churches participated in the CELA gatherings in Buenos Aires (1949), Lima (1961), and Buenos Aires again (1969). Two of those churches, the already mentioned MIP and *Iglesia Pentecostal de Chile*, became members of the WCC in the New Delhi Assembly, in 1961. Likewise, in 1973, Pentecostal leaders contributed to the formation of the Chilean Ecumenical Fellowship (*Fraternidad Ecuménica de Chile*, FRAECH) in the company of other Protestant, Catholic, and Orthodox Christians.[13]

The perception of Pentecostalism as intrinsically anti-ecumenical is misplaced. As Wolfgang Vondey rightly argues, Pentecostalism is itself an ecumenical melting pot. In contrast with other denominations, "Pentecostal communities worldwide did not organize or institutionalize in conscious reaction to particular ecclesiastical patterns." On the contrary, they emerged "in both continuity and discontinuity with various existing doctrines, practices, rituals, disciplines,

[11] World Council of Churches, "Pentecostal Mission Church," Member Churches. https://www.oikoumene.org/member-churches/pentecostal-mission-church.

[12] Juan Sepúlveda, "Another Way of Being Pentecostal," in *Pentecostal Power: Expressions, Impact and of Latin American Pentecostalism*, ed. Calvin L. Smith (Leiden/Boston: Brill, 2011), 37–61 (51).

[13] Sepúlveda, "Another Way of Being Pentecostal," 51–52.

spiritualities, and organizational forms," therefore, not forming a homogeneous coalition.[14]

Likewise, Vondey underscores the early ecumenical impulse of the Pentecostal movement, which was later frustrated by the rise of restorationism, leading to a sharp distinction between church and world and a strong emphasis on a piety that prevented broader alliances with other Christians. Also, the fact that many Pentecostal churches originated as splits from other churches generated a sentiment of rejection that did not encourage ecumenical relations.[15] On the other hand, over time, Pentecostals have engaged in interdenominational and ecumenical organizations in different parts of the world. Several Latin American Pentecostals, for instance, participate in the Latin American Theological Fellowship (Fraternidad Teologica Latinoamericana, FTL), the InterVarsity Christian Fellowship, the World Evangelical Alliance, and other interdenominational organizations.

In Brazil, the first Pentecostal to participate in the ecumenical movement was Manoel de Mello (1929–1990) founder of the church *O Brasil para Cristo* (OBPC) in 1956.[16] By the early 1970s, OBPC was one of the fastest-growing churches in Brazil, having a new temple in São Paulo that seated 25,000 people. Mello participated in the Uppsala WCC Assembly in 1968. His human rights concerns and fierce opposition to the authoritarian military regime in Brazil led him to embrace the ecumenical movement.

OBPC became a member of the WCC in 1968. Locally, Mello also affiliated the church with CESE, Brazil's chief ecumenical agency for community service and advocacy, chairing CESE's inaugural meeting in 1973.17 A Northeastern migrant in São Paulo with firsthand knowledge of poverty, Mello developed a social reading of the gospel, which informed his ministry and his engagement with CESE and the WCC.18 Resisting the abuses of the military regime, he formed alliances with people such as Catholic archbishops Hélder Câmara

[14] Wolfgang Vondey, "Pentecostalism and Ecumenism."

[15] Vondey, "Pentecostalism and Ecumenism."

[16] Brazil for Christ.

[17] Lucyvanda Moura, ed., *Coordenadoria Ecumênica de Serviço CESE: uma trajetória de luta por direitos humanos, desenvolvimento e justiça* (São Leopoldo: CEBI, 2013), 125.

[18] Moura, ed., *Coordenadoria Ecumênica de Serviço CESE*, 127.

and Paulo Evaristo Arns, in addition to Presbyterian pastor Jaime Wright and other ecumenical leaders in Brazil and beyond. Due to his opposition to the authoritarian regime, Mello was imprisoned several times. In explaining the reasons his church was joining the WCC, he affirmed,

> The World Council of Churches concerns itself with the contemporary life of people. "Brasil para Cristo" will join the World Council of Churches because of its social mission in today's world. But there is another reason, namely, that we must get rid of the small-mindedness that divides men into denominations. The World Council is accomplishing this. Ecumenism is another good thing the World Council of Churches offers us.[19]

Mello saw evangelism as the spread of good news, which opposed the status quo. He preached a "Gospel of the Kingdom of God" which is "here and now."[20] Curiously, he attended the Uppsala assembly in response to negative comments he had heard about the WCC in Brazilian Pentecostal circles. In his own words, "I needed to know the Council which came under such attack." Once he got to the assembly, he encountered a paradoxical reality: "We are in the jet age and, from the religious point of view, the World Council of Churches is riding a bicycle. However, it is doing tremendous work such as we are not able to do with all our religiosity: a gigantic work of social action."[21] The opportunity to join that worldwide network of churches serving the needs of people was appealing to him: "The Church here on earth must get into its head that it is a part of society. It cannot think only of numerical growth. The Church is reaching a point where it cannot grow within these structures. If it fails to open up new frontiers, the time will come when intelligent men will no longer join it."[22]

Prior to developing a good relationship with WCC general secretary Philip Potter, Mello approached Potter's predecessor, Eugene

---

[19] Manoel de Mello, "Participation is Everything: Evangelism from the point of view of a Brazilian Pentecostal," *International Review of Mission* 60/238 (1971): 245–248 (248).

[20] Mello, "Participation is Everything," 247.

[21] Mello, "Participation is Everything," 247.

[22] Mello, "Participation is Everything," 248.

C. Blake, who had announced his plans to attend CELA III, inviting the WCC General Secretary to visit his church. The initial invitation made orally in Uppsala (1968) was formalized in a letter on behalf of OBPC on November 29, 1968. Interested in strengthening the WCC ties with Latin America, Blake expressed the desire to visit Mello's church and to talk with other Pentecostals.[23] In a letter to Blake on October 18, 1968, Mello offered his church as a venue for CELA III. In that letter, he expressed enthusiasm about his ecumenical experience in Uppsala, stating that while he did not agree "with everything in the WCC" he appreciated the work it "has done in the ecumenical, social, and educational fields."[24] On the other hand, Blake was encouraged by the interest from an important Brazilian Pentecostal church to join the council.

Equally impressed by that possibility, the editors of the *Centro Evangélico de Informação* (later *Centro Ecumênico de Informação*, CEI) sent a note to the *International Review of Mission*, along with a translation of an interview with Mello, which read: "With this ecumenical consciousness directed towards renewal, the Pentecostals should become the greatest revolutionary force in Protestant thought in Brazil."[25]

Although OBPC did not remain affiliated with the ecumenical movement after Mello's death, his leadership and years of relationship with the WCC and CESE in Brazil show the potential for Pentecostal ecumenical engagement. Pentecostals have a dynamic spirituality, which is directly connected to the *cotidiano*, the day-to-day life of the people, especially those who are impoverished. As such, they can contribute to "the new paradigm of faith and Christian life" that base ecumenism and liberation-oriented Christians, sensitive to the cry

---

[23] Correspondence between Eugene C. Blake, Manoel de Mello, José Coelho Ferraz (General Secretary of the Confederação Evangélica do Brasil), and Ver. Karl Gottschald, president of the Igreja Evangélica de Confissão Luterana do Brasil (IECLB) between October of 1968 and January of 1969. On January 7, 1969, Blake wrote a letter to Robert Lodwick, of Missão Presbiteriana do Brasil Central, to inform him of the cancellation of his trip to Latin America due to the cancellation of the CELA gathering in São Paulo due to the political situation in Brazil.

[24] Letter from Manoel de Mello to Eugene C. Blake on October 18, 1968. WCC Archives, the Ecumenical Centre in Geneva. Accessed by the author on September 11, 2017.

[25] In Mello, "Participation is Everything," 245.

of the poor and the cry of the earth, have advanced through organic ecumenical initiatives rooted in the practices of the poor.[26]

That message has been equally embraced by many other Christians, as seen in the II Continental Congress of Theology on the occasion of the fiftieth anniversary of the Vatican II in October of 2015. Inspired by Pope Francis's call in *Evangelii Gaudium* for "discernment, purification and reform" as ways to renew the announcement of the liberating presence of God's reign in history, the congress focused on the need for the Christian community to walk with the *Ruah*, the Spirit, from the perspective of the poor, describing the Spirit as the symbol of God's presence amid "the cries, resistances, and victories of the subjects made invisible."[27] Looking at the challenges placed by the fundamentalism of hegemonic Western reason and the extremisms stemming from it, Leonardo Boff argues that it is by treating each other humanely and cultivating the life of the spirit—one marked by justice, solidarity, love, care, and togetherness—that the fear posed by terrorism and exclusionary fundamentalisms can be overcome so a future for our threatened planetary life can exist.[28]

Even though a significant number of Pentecostal churches and leaders remain distant from the ecumenical movement, the examples mentioned above point to promising signs of another way of being Pentecostal, to borrow a phrase from Juan Sepúlveda, that is ecumenically open to the work of the spirit beyond the churches and Christianity, being consequently socially and ecologically engaged. In Latin America, a group of Pentecostal scholars created a Latin American Network of Pentecostals Studies (Red Latinoamericana de Estudios Pentecostales, RELEP), which is producing significant Pentecostal theological contributions to Latin American theology.

Stepping on the shoulders of liberation theology and the revolutionary epistemological turn to the margins, these Pentecostal

---

26 André Corten, "Prefácio," in *Pentecostalismo e Futuro das Igrejas Cristãs: Promessas e Desafios*, ed. Waldo César and Richard Shaull (Petrópolis: Vozes, 1999), 9–16 (10, 12).

27 Socorro Martinez Maqueo and Pablo Bonavía "Presentación," in *Iglesia que Camina com Espiritu y desde los Pobres*, ed. Oscar Elizalde Prada et al (Montevideo: Fundación Ameríndia, 2016), 7–9 (9).

28 Leonardo Boff, "El Factor Religioso en el Contexto de la Conflictividad Global y el Futuro de la Vida," in *Iglesia que Camina com Espiritu*, 21–37 (37).

theologians see themselves as theologizing from the margins, recentering the Pentecostal experience in the study of Christian praxis and theology. In a recent RELEP publication, Pentecostal and non-Pentecostal scholars jointly address topics of concrete significance for societal and planetary life. The topics addressed in the volume *Pentecostal Experience in Latin America* span from ecotheology to migration, urbanization, the expansion of the meaning of the baptism in the Holy Spirit, spirituality and economy, consumerism, ecumenical dialogue, Catholic-Pentecostal exchanges, gender equity, the work of evangelical women in the *Coletivo Evangélicas pela Igualdade de Gênero* (EIG),[29] and Pentecostal epistemology and political presence.[30]

Even though not all RELEP members are Pentecostals, most of them are, with many being pastors and leaders in their churches. Their work, for the most part, is rooted in ecclesial praxis. Founded in 1999, RELEP has held several continental meetings and numerous national gatherings.[31] Most of these gatherings have led to publications, which are mostly available in Portuguese and Spanish.[32] RELEP is one of the recent ecumenical developments in Latin America that deserves greater attention because it points to new possible paths for the future of Christian theology and the ecumenical movement. Among other things, the Pentecostal theology RELEP is producing has a strong emphasis on social transformation, based on the reinterpretation of the prophetic tradition through a Pentecostal lens.[33] In addition to their collective work, RELEP members are individually producing important literature on a variety of topics, including

[29] Evangelical Collective of Women for Gender Equality.

[30] David Mesquiati de Oliveira and Kenner Terra, eds., *Experiência Pentecostal na América Latina* (São Paulo: Editora Recriar, 2023).

[31] I participated in the eighth Continental Congress of RELEP (Latin American Network of Pentecostal Studies) held in Brazil, in the city of Vitória, state of Espiríto Santo, on October 25–27, 2018. In addition to its Latin American participants, the gathering had the participation of representatives from Asia, Africa, and North America.

[32] In addition to those volumes, the series *Pentecostalismos* done in partnership with Editora Reflexão, for instance, had ten published volumes by 2017.

[33] See, for instance, David Mesquiati de Oliveira, ed., *Pentecostalismo e Transformação Social* (São Paulo: Fonte Editorial, 2013).

gender and domestic violence,[34] ecumenism and Pentecostalism,[35] and mission and intercultural dialogue,[36] to mention a few.

RELEP is not the only Latin American Pentecostal network working in ecumenical fashion. The Latin American and Caribbean Pentecostal Forum (Foro Pentecostal Latinoamericano y Caribeño, FPLyC) is another important ecumenical forum. Formed in connection with the Global Christian Forum, an ecumenical initiative stemming from a proposal made by former WCC General Secretary Konrad Raiser in 1998 aimed to create "a place, independent of existing structures, for the growing unity of the global church,"[37] the FPLyC gathers Pentecostal representatives from the entire continent.

Entrusted with an autonomous continuation committee and aspiring to enlarge the ecumenical table, the GCF held its first general assembly in Limuru, Kenya, on November 6–9, 2007. As a result of its creation, regional and national forums with the similar goal of creating an independent space for further dialogue "across denominational, regional, national, ethnic and cultural boundaries" were also formed.[38]

The FPLyC was created during a meeting in Costa Rica (2010) that included representatives from the GCF in Latin America, CELAM, CLAI, FTL, World Vision, and FIDE (Foro Iberoamericano de Diálogo Evangélico).[39] Following the steps of the GCF, FPLyC aimed at creating "a space of encounter, dialogue and reflection among Pentecostal church leaders, theologians and social scientists committed to the study of the Pentecostal movement in the Latin

[34] Valeria Cristina Vilhena, *Uma Igreja sem Voz: Análise de Gênero da Violência entre Mulheres Evangélicas* (São Paulo: Fonte Editorial, 2011).

[35] Gedeon Freire de Alencar, *Ecumenismos e Pentecostalismos: A Relação entre o Pescoço e a Guilhotina?* (São Paulo: Editora Recriar, 2018).

[36] David Mesquiati de Oliveira, *Diálogo e Missão nos Andes: Um Estudo de Teologia da Missão Latino-Americana* (Rio de Janeiro: Editora PUC Rio, 2017).

[37] Global Christian Forum, "Our History," https://globalchristianforum.org/about-us/our-history/.

[38] Global Christian Forum, "Our Purpose," https://globalchristianforum.org/about-us/about-the-gcf-introduction/.

[39] Ibero-American Forum for Evangelical Dialogue. See David Mesquiati de Oliveira, "Instituições Pentecostais Latino-Americanas para a Unidade Eclesial e para a Produção Acadêmica: O Caso do FPLyC e da RELEP," in *As Vozes da Cooperação I: FPLyC, RELEP, FCM* (São Paulo: Reflexoa Editorial, 2017), 19–46 (26).

American and Caribbean continent; as well as also seek to promote relationship with the other Christian families in the region and in the world."[40]

Among its activities, FPLyC convened a Conesur Pentecostal Forum in Santiago (2012) to reflect specifically on the theme of Pentecostalism and Christian unity, examining the relationship between Pentecostal churches and other Christian traditions in Latin America, while also interrogating theological and sociological understandings of Christian unity from a Pentecostal perspective.

Bernardo Campos, a pastor, seminary professor, and director of Peruvian Institute of Religious Studies (IPER), led the theological reflection, underscoring that Christian unity is a mark of the early church. Consequently, the search for the unity of the church is a Christian mandate, not an option. According to him, whereas the Holy Spirit works on the invisible side of unity, it is our task to work on the visible aspects of that unity.[41] Furthermore, the disposition for dialogue with other traditions is important to prevent Pentecostals from absolutizing their own experience. Such a dialogue is a step toward a *universal pentecostality*, a term he uses to describe the "experience of all Christianity with the Holy Spirit."[42] In short, Campos demonstrates that the conversations that Latin American Pentecostals are advancing on Christian unity provide a mediating space for "the matters of the Kingdom of God that are common to all members of the Christian faith." In other words, repeating the pattern seen in other Latin American ecumenical initiatives, the ecumenism advanced in these conversations is not about church

---

[40] Oliveira, "Instituições Pentecostais Latino-Americanas para a Unidade Eclesial e para a Produção Acadêmica," 31. "Visão e Missão do FPLyC," document attached to Oliveira's essay.

[41] Bernardo Campos, "Pentecostalismo y Unidad en América Latina. 'Aspectos teológicos,'" in *Fuego que Une: Pentecostalismo y Unidad de la Iglesia*. Documentos del III y IV Foro Pentecostal Latinoamericano y Caribeño, Santiago de Chile 2012 y Bogotá, Colombia 2013, ed. Bernardo Campos and Luis Orellana (Lima: Foro Pentecostal Latinoamericano y Caribeño, 2014), 33–39 (33).

[42] Campos, "Pentecostalismo y Unidad en América Latina, 33–34. This is one of the important contributions Campos makes to this conversation, as he portrays pentecostality not as an exclusive trait of Pentecostalism but as an expression of a universal spirituality rooted in the resurrection of Jesus, and, therefore, pertinent to all Christians.

only (ecclesiocentric, inward) but about the reign of God (outward, mission-oriented).[43]

Another important aspect that forum highlighted was the emphasis on the nature of the unity it seeks, which, Campos insisted, "should not remain solely in a border configuration, of territorial, continental, or linguistic demarcation compared to other latitudes such as Asia, Africa, etc." On the contrary, "it also has an identity dimension, of cultural ethos, idiosyncratic, of political project, of unity as a great country."[44] In other words, this Pentecostal forum conceives of a Latin American project composed of many faces, while affirming a common trajectory that allows its different counterparts to recognize each other despite their differences. Such a pentecostality sees the Spirit as the mediator, making it possible to see "the community of the Kingdom as a community of solidarity that merges . . . with the people." [45] Such a view conveys the idea of a cosmic promise for all flesh, which can help humans overcome shortcomings, weaknesses, and threats limiting the horizon of hope.[46]

Whereas the deficit in Pentecostal participation in ecumenical efforts in Latin America is still significant, these recent developments signal a promise of renewed hopes about the contributions Pentecostals can make to the ecumenical movement as the CEI editors foresaw in Mello's ecumenical involvement in the early 1970s. These developments also help dismantle the myth of the antagonism between Pentecostalism and ecumenism. The Pentecostal tradition has a wealth of resources that must be tapped by those working to expand the reach of the current ecumenical instruments.

Latin American Pentecostalism is growing fast and becoming increasingly diverse. The emphasis on the plural "pentecostalisms" seen in RELEP and FPLyC publications captures that internal plurality, which prevents the absolutization of certain Pentecostal models or the reduction of Pentecostalism to certain stereotypes. On the other hand, it acknowledges the forms of Pentecostalism which, despite not being the largest or most powerful ones, remain critical

43 Campos, "Pentecostalismo y Unidad en América Latina, 34.

44 Campos, "Pentecostalismo y Unidad en América Latina, 35.

45 Campos, "Pentecostalismo y Unidad en América Latina, 36.

46 Campos, "Pentecostalismo y Unidad en América Latina, 37.

in the dynamic and ongoing formation of this important Christian tradition.

Latin American Pentecostalism, in its multifaceted constitution, is today a critical mass impacting important theological conversations, including reflections on race, ecology, gender and sexuality, and interfaith/intercultural relations.

In Brazil, two initiatives in which Pentecostals have assumed more prominent roles deserve note. The Black evangelical movement, which I discuss elsewhere, has counted with a number of Pentecostal leaders.[47] While, for a long time, Pentecostals seemed to be absent from conversations about race and racism in Latin America, a growing number of Pentecostals are currently challenging white supremacy and its manifestation in whitewashed forms of Christianity.

In recent years some Brazilian evangelicals have raised their voices to reject the depiction of Jesus as white, claiming, instead, that Jesus is black.[48] Amid various initiatives, the Black Evangelical Movement (Movimento Negro Evangélico, MNE), formed in connection with the the *Sociedade Cultural Missões Quilombo*, is the most widely known. Its founder, Hernani Francisco da Silva, is a member of the Pentecostal Church *O Brasil para Cristo* (OPBC), who, converted from Catholicism at the age of fifteen, and went through a process of awakening to his *negritude*, which he has depicted as a second conversion.[49] This movement formed by individuals who identify as both Black and evangelical aims to change the perception of Brazilian Black culture in evangelical and Pentecostal circles and combat racism in all its forms.[50] The movement also underscores the African roots of Christianity and uses its platforms to debunk what it describes as an "evangelical racist theology."[51] Despite the resistance it faces among many evangelical leaders, the MNE continues to offer an alternative narrative that is increasingly appealing to younger

[47] Raimundo Barreto, "Black and Evangelical: Reimagining Faith and Race Relations in Brazil," *Perspectives in Religious Studies* 49/4 (2022): 357–368.

[48] See, for instance, Henrique Vieira—"Jesus é negro," https://www.youtube.com/watch?v=ZPvF6j-hwhc, July 4, 2017.

[49] Rosenilton Silva de Oliveira, "'Hoje eu orei, Ele é negro': A Gêneses do Movimento Negro Evangélico no Brasil," *Religião e Sociedade* 41/3(2021): 169–191 (172).

[50] Oliveira, "Hoje eu orei, Ele é negro," 173.

[51] Oliveira, "Hoje eu orei, Ele é negro," 173.

Black and brown evangelicals who, like Silva, are also awakening to their *negritude*.

A similar movement taking shape within Pentecostal communities is challenging dominant narratives on gender and sexuality in Latin American evangelical circles. Valéria Cristina Vilhena, a member of RELEP, founded the collective Evangelical Women for Gender Equality (EIG), a women's network that brings unheard voices of evangelical women to speak from the margins on a variety of matters of public interest, including topics such as gender violence; Christianity and misogyny; the connection between racism, misogyny, and racism; abortion; HIV/AIDS; and other themes related to a woman's body, life, and well-being.[52]

Several other developments taking place within Latin American Pentecostalism deserve scholarly scrutiny. One of them is the rise of welcoming and affirming Pentecostal churches in different Latin American countries. Brazil has been an epicenter of that phenomenon. While several churches and Christian communities like that have emerged in recent years, the rise of *Igreja Cidade de Refúgio,* a Pentecostal church self-identified as "apostolic, prophetic, and made up of plural people," is one of the most visible developments of this sort of Pentecostalism in the past twenty years. Central to this church's mission is the evangelization of LGBTQIAPN+ people.[53] Even when considering the entire Christian landscape in Brazil, only a few Christian communities are inclusive of this important sector of the Brazilian population.

Cidade de Refúgio's founding pastors Lanna Holder and Rosania Rocha were already leading successful ministries in the Brazilian Pentecostal scene when they came out as queer. The two ended up marrying each other. Convinced of God's love for them and undergoing a spiritual reaffirmation of their apostolic ministry, they founded *Cidade de Refúgio* church in 2011 in São Paulo. The church today is present in nineteen cities across the country and in Lisbon, Portugal and continues to grow, offering a spiritual home for people who otherwise would not have a community of faith.

---

52 EIG, "Mulheres EIG," https://mulhereseig.wordpress.com/. March 3, 2024.

53 See Lanna Holder and Rosania Rocha, eds., *Anunciando Jesus: Reflexões sobre o Evangelismo de LGBTQIAPN+ na Contemporaneidade* (São Paulo: Plúrima Editora, 2023). This is a book produced by the pastors of Cidade Refúgio.

Igreja Betesda is another church of Pentecostal origin in São Paulo, which recently changed its traditional approach to gender and sexuality, adopting a welcoming and affirmative position towards the LGBTQIAPN+ community. Founded in 1981, this church was initially influenced by *teologia de misión integral* (wholistic mission theology), which became widely known for its influence on the emphasis on social responsibility in the 1974 Lausanne Covenant (1974).[54] In the past decade or so, the Betesta leaders have developed a post-evangelical pastoral theology, which, also influenced by insights coming from liberation theology, challenges predetermined understandings of God, reading the Bible anew from the location of the human experiences of suffering and injustice. Such an experience has renewed the church's theology, opening it to embrace and affirm those whose gender and sexuality do not conform to dominant patterns.

Similar experiences can be found in other Latin American countries, including Colombia and Mexico. Although there is much that can be discussed on this topic,[55] for the purpose of the argument of this book, it suffices to highlight that the Pentecostal movement is dynamic, effervescent, plural and maliable. It cannot be defined homogeneously, and certainly not in opposition to ecumenism. It is crucial, though, for those in leadership in ecumenical structures to pay closer attention to and be more interested in what is going on in the vast Pentecostal universe. By doing that, they may find out that the renewal of creation voiced in the invocation of the Spirit in the Canberra 1991 litany, "Come, Holy Spirit, renew the whole creation," is taking place in those spaces.[56]

A World in Which Many Worlds Fit

Acknowledging imperial lingering memories that continue to haunt the ecumenical movement, this book has brought to the fore efforts, voices, and concerns from those who, having been victims of structural violence in a variety of forms, are striving for a place around the

[54] See Barreto, *Protesting Poverty*, chapter 4.

[55] I will devote more attention to this phenomenon in my forthcoming book, *Christians in the City of São Paulo: The Shaping of World Christianity in a Brazilian Megacity* (Bloomsbury Publishing Plc. Forthcoming).

[56] Kinnamon, *Signs of the Spirit*, vii.

ecumenical table as historical subjects who deserve full citizenship in the making of the ecumenical movement. Their persistence in finding their voice around the ecumenical table had transformative impact on ecumenical discourse and practices.

The rise of the downtrodden—the wretched, those whose voices have often been silenced—as new theological subjects in the past five decades or so has already contributed to a renewed understanding of ecumenicity. In Latin America, what began as the irruption of the poor has led to the rise of Indigenous people as a collective historical subject since the early 1990s, adding to that mix a nonbinary way of reasoning, which makes room for the coexistence of plural knowledges, worlds, and ways of being and knowing that point to the possibility of an ecumenicity based on a pluriversal view of the world. Such an ecumenicity is not primarily concerned with resolving differences. Instead, it devises ways to live in more harmonic and respectful terms with different ways of knowing and being in the world.[57] Such a view seeks to understand the fundamental plurality of existence. In his well-known address to the Indigenous Clandestine Revolutionary Committee in January of 1996, insurgent Subcomandante Marcos stated:

> Many words walk in the world. Many worlds are made for us. Many worlds make us. There are words and worlds which are lies and injustices. There are words and worlds that are truth and truthful. [. . .] In the world of the powerful there is no space except for anyone but themselves and their servants. The Nation which we construct is one where all communities and languages fit, where all steps may walk, where all may have laughter, where all may live the dawn.[58]

Words create worlds, and many worlds make us. This is an antihegemonic statement, which affirms the necessary plurality of existence. If all worlds are created, and we emanate from various worlds, no world is superior to other worlds.

[57] For the idea of pluriversal politics, see Arturo Escobar, *Pluriversal Politics: The Real and the Possible* (Durham and London: Duke University Press, 2020).

[58] Subcomandante Marcos, *Our Word is Our Weapon*, ed. Juana Ponce de León (New York: Seven Stories Press. Kindle Edition), 88.

This statement that arises from the Zapatista struggle for the creation of a pluri-ethnic and pluri-cultural nation in Mexico, continues to inspire popular movements in the continent and around the world. Extrapolating its immediate context, one can find in it an alternative logic for an understanding of *oikoumenē* that can contribute to an ecumenicity for the twenty-first century. In contrast to the one-world logic[59] that prevailed in the modern world in which the ecumenical movement was initially shaped, the Indigenous wisdom of the Zapatista movement advances a heterogeneous understanding of *oikoumenē*, a world that is made of many coexisting worlds—ways of knowing and being.

The liberationist turn to the poor as historical subjects in Latin America in the 1960s started an epistemic revolution, opening a range of new possibilities. First, the poor (a faceless mass in the 1960s and early 1970s) gained concrete faces, taking different shapes and forms—Black, Indigenous, queer, women. Thus, the turn to the poor not only contributed to enable them as subjects with rights, but allowed them, for the first time, to be heard speaking in their own theological voices. They were no longer simply economic subjects but also subjects of knowledge, capable of reimagining the world through another possible logic.

Having experienced dislodging and relearned to exist anew under imposed circumstances, formerly colonized peoples have lived in what Chicana cultural theorist Gloria Anzaldúa identifies as a fractured, traversed existence that, although seemly inescapable, can paradoxically become a place in which open wounds turn into creative spaces of reinvention, *entremedios* (in-between spaces) in which those impacted by the colonial matrix of power constantly experience the discomfort of dislocation, disorientation, and reorientation.[60]

Subjects living in existential *entremedios* reject essentializing identities and the binary reasoning of the one-world logic. The borderlands, originally a place of violence and separation, can also produce renewed consciousness. Anzaldúa's borderlands, just like Marcos's

---

[59] John Law, "What's Wrong with a One-World World," *Heterogeneities*, http://www.heterogeneities.net/publications/Law2011WhatsWrongWithAOneWorldWorld.pdf.

[60] Gloria Anzaldúa, *Light in the Dark: Rewriting Identity, Spirituality, Reality*, ed. Analouise Keating (Durham and London: Duke University Press, 2015), 81.

world in which many worlds fit, gives us a way to speak of "intersectional conditions of language, gender, religion, sexuality, class, culture and space,"[61] and to "recreate spaces in which the multiple worlds we inhabit and the various identities we have developed mesh and blend with/out conforming to no/one in particular."[62]

This new conscience emerging from in-between spaces may be exactly where the future of ecumenism dwells. Ecumenism is no longer about hegemonic understandings of unity. In fact, that sort of universalistic modern design at the origins of the modern ecumenical movement contributed to dehumanizing those subjected to the colonial mind, limiting the possibilities of existence outside the grip of modernity/coloniality. In response to such a crisis, Arturo Escobar calls for a new design, a new world-making that can move us beyond "the dualist ontology of separation, control and appropriation" prevalent in "patriarchal capitalist modernity" to explore models of being that emphasize profound "relationality and connectedness."[63] The overarching argument running through the pages of this book is that such a design does not need to be reinvented. It can already be found around the world, especially in popular movements such as those that gave birth to base ecumenism. Redesigning ecumenical structures on the basis of openly engaging ways of knowing and being that are resurfacing through the irruption of the poor as plural historical and epistemic subjects seems to be a critical challenge before the ecumenical community at this historical juncture. The way as existing and future ecumenical instruments respond to such a challenge will determine how significant the ecumenical movement will remain to the emancipatory struggles of this century.

Liberation is an unfinished business, since, despite its new faces, the lingering imperial and colonial memories that created the existing disparities in a racialized and gendered hierarchized global order continue to divide, separate, oppress, and dehumanize scores of human beings, this time with real capacity not only to erase their

---

[61] Margaret Cantú-Sánchez et al., "Introduction," in *Teaching Gloria E. Anzaldúa: Pedagogy and Practice for Our Classrooms and Communities*, ed. Margaret Cantú-Sánchez (Tucson, AR: University of Arizona Press, 2020), 3.

[62] Cantú-Sánchez, "Breaking the Mold: Redesigning Curricula for the 'Planetary Citizen,'" in *Teaching Gloria E. Anzaldúa*, 16.

[63] Arturo Escobar, *Designs for the Pluriverse* (Durham and London: Duke University Press, 2018), 19–20.

dignity and humanity, but also to, in their greed, destroy Mother Earth. Whereas the ecumenical ideal remains relevant, ecumenical instruments, and even language created in the early to mid-twentieth century, no longer speak as effectively to the urges of this new reality. The challenge ahead is not to begin something new from scratch but to pay closer attention to the renewal movements, which, from the margins, continue to infuse the ecumenical movement with new life and possibilities.

BIBLIOGRAPHY

Collections

The Burke Library Archives. Columbia University Libraries. Union Theological Seminary. New York Missionary Research Library Archives: Section 9. Committee on Cooperation in Latin America (CCLA) and Congress on Christian Work in Latin America (CCWLA) Records. 1914–1956 Primary Sources.

CEDIC, Centro de Documentação e Informação Científica. Virtual Collection.

Departamento Ecuménico de Investigaciones, digital library. https://www.deicr.org/biblioteca-en-l%C3%ADnea.

IDHeC, Instituto Dom Hélder Câmara. http://www.acervocepe.com.br/acervo/idhec---instituto-dom-helder-camara.

Memorial da Democracia, virtual museum. Instituto Lula. http://memorialdademocracia.com.br/museu.

SIAN, Sistema de Informações do Arquivo Nacional. Arquivo Nacional. Digital Archive.

World Council of Churches Archives. Ecumenical Centre, Geneva.

Wright Library. Princeton Theological Seminary. Latin American Collection. Digital Collections.

Wright Library. Princeton Theological Seminary. Special Collections: John A. Mackay Collection, Series IV. Princeton Theological Seminary Presidency.

Wright Library. Princeton Theological Seminary. Special Collections: The M. Richard Shaull Papers.

Primary Sources

Abbott, Walter M., ed. *The Documents of Vatican II: With Notes and Comments by Catholic, Protestant, and Orthodox Authorities*. New York: Guild Press, 1966.

Abraham, K. C., ed. *Third World Theologies: Commonalities and Differences*. Papers and Reflections from the Second General Assembly of the Ecumenical Association of Third World Theologians, December, 1986, Oaxtepec, Mexico. Eugene, OR: Wipf & Stock Publishers, 2004 [1990].

Acción Católica Peruana. *Primer Congreso Nacional*. Lima/Huampaní: Acción Católica Peruana, 1955.

Appiah-Kubbi, Kofi and Sergio Torres, eds. *African Theology en Route: Papers from the Pan-African Conference of Third World Theologians, December 17–23, 1977, Accra, Ghana*. Maryknoll, NY: Orbis Books, 1979.

Aquino, Maria Pilar, ed. *Aportes para una Teologia desde la Mujer*. Colaboraciones de teólogas latinoamericanas en la Conferencia Intercontinental de mujeres teólogas del Tercer Mundo, celebrada del 1 al 6 de diciembre de 1986, en Oaxtepec, México. Madrid: Editorial Biblia y Fe, 1988.

Arns, Paulo Evaristo. *Brasil: Nunca Mais*. 10th ed. Petrópolis: Editora Vozes, 1985.

Báez-Camargo, Gonzalo. *Hacia la Renovación Religiosa en Hispanoamérica*. Mexico City: Casa Unida de Publicaciones, 1930.

Bencke, Romi Márcia & Sonia Gomes Mota. *Ecumenismo e Feminismo: Parcerias da Casa Comum*. São Leopoldo: CEBI, 2012.

Braga, Erasmo E. *Pan-americanismo: Aspecto Religioso*. New York: Missionary Education Movement of the United States and Canada, 1916.

Braga, Erasmo and Kenneth Grubb. *The Republic of Brazil: A Survey of the Religious Situation* London: World Dominion Press, 1932.

Calvimonte, Luis Q. *Orígenes de la Acción Católica en Córdoba: sus primeros diez años 1931–1941*. Cuadernos de Historia. Córdoba, Argentina: Junta Provincial de Historia de Córdoba, 1994.

Câmara, Hélder. *Vaticano II: Correspondência Conciliar: Circulares à Família do São Joaquim*. Vol. 1/Tomo I. With an introduction and notes by Luiz Carlos Luz Marques. Recife, Brazil: Instituto Dom Hélder Câmara, 2004.

Casaldáliga, Pedro. "Uma Igreja da Amazônia em Conflito com o Latifúndio e a Marginalização Social," Available at Servicios Koinonia: https://servicioskoinonia.org/Casaldaliga/cartas/1971CartaPastoral.pdf.

Castro, Emilio, ed. *El Rol de la Mujer en la Iglesia y en la Sociedad*. Montevideo: UNELAM, 1968.

CELAM. *Documentos Finales de Medellín*. 6th ed. II Conferencia General del Episcopado Latinoamericano. Buenos Aires: Ediciones Paulinas, 1986.

César, Waldo, ed. *Presença da Igreja na Evolução da Nacionalidade*. Rio de Janeiro: CEB, 1960.

Cirvadi, Luis. *Manual de Acción Católica: Volume I – Teoria*. 3rd ed. Monterrey, Mexico: Pablo Cervantes, PBRO, 1935.

Cólon, Cristóbal. *Textos y Documentos Completos*, edited by Consuelo Varela. *Nuevas Cartas*, edited by Juan Gil. Madrid: Alianza Editorial, 1995.

Columbus, Christopher. "Letter of Columbus describing the results of his first voyage." In *The Journal of Christopher Columbus*, translated by Cecil Jane. New York: Clarkson N. Potter Inc., 1960

Committee on Cooperation in Latin America. *Christian Work in Latin America*. Vol. 1–3. New York: The Missionary Education Movement, 1917.

Committee on Cooperation in Latin America. *Report of Committee on Cooperation in Latin America, Representing the American and Canadian Mission Boards Working in Latin America*. New York: Committee on Cooperation in Latin America, 1919.

Committee on Cooperation in Latin America. *Committee On Cooperation in Latin America: Report for 1921*. New York: Committee on Cooperation in Latin America, 1921.

Committee on Society, Development, and Peace, ed. *In Search of a Theology of Development: Papers from a Consultation on Theology and Development held by Sodepax in Cartiny, Switzerland, November, 1969*. Geneva: Committee on Society, Development and Peace, 1969.

Comunidade Taizé de Alagoinhas. *50 Anos da Presença dos Irmãos de Taizé no Brasil: Caminhos Percorridos e a Percorrer*. Alagoinhas: Comunidade Taizé de Alagoinhas, 2017.

Confederação Evangélica do Brasil. *Relatórios: Biênio 1934–1936*. Rio de Janeiro: CEB, 1936.

Confederação Evangélica do Brasil. *Relatórios: Biênio 1948–1950*. Rio de Janeiro: CEB, 1951.

Confederação Evangélica do Brasil. *Relatórios: Biênio 1952–1954*. Rio de Janeiro: CEB, 1955.

Confederação Evangélica do Brasil. *Relatórios: Biênio 1955–1956*. Rio de Janeiro: CEB, 1958.

Conferência Geral do Episcopado Latino-Americano (CELAM). *Conclusões da Conferência de Puebla—Texto Oficial: Evangelização no Presente e no Futuro da América Latina*. São Paulo: Edições Paulinas, 1979.

Conferencia Evangélica Latinoamericana. *Cristo la esperanza para América Latina. Ponencias—informes—comentarios de la Segunda Comisión II Conferencia Evangélica Latinoamericana*. 2nd ed. Lima, Perú: Conferencia Evangélica Latinoamericana, 1962.

Conselho Episcopal Latino-Americano (CELAM). *A Igreja na Atual Transformação da América Latina à Luz do Mundo: Conclusões de Medellín*. Petrópolis, Brazil: Vozes, 1985.

Fabella, Virginia and Sergio Torres, eds. *Irruption of the Third World: Challenge to Theology*. Papers from the Fifth International Conference of the Ecumenical Association of Third World Theologians, August 17–29, 1981, New Delhi, India. Maryknoll, NY: Orbis Books, 1983.

Flannery, Austin, ed. *Vatican Council II: Constitutions, Decrees, Declarations*. Collegeville, MN: Liturgical Press, 1996. Kindle Edition.

Francisco, Papa. *Pronunciamentos do Papa Francisco no Brasil*. São Paulo: Paulus/Edições Loyola, 2013.

Getui, Mary N., Luiz Carlos Susin, Beatrice W. Churu, eds. *Spirituality for Another Possible World*. Nairobi: Twawezza Communications, 2008.

Holder, Lanna and Rosania Rocha, eds. *Anunciando Jesus: Reflexões sobre o Evangelismo de LGBTQIAPN+ na Contemporaneidade*. São Paulo: Plúrima Editora, 2023.

Inman, Samuel Guy. *Christian Cooperation in Latin America: Report of a Visit to Mexico, Cuba and South America, March-October, 1917*. New York: CCLA, 1917.

Inman, Samuel Guy. *Problems in Pan Americanism*. New York: George H. Doran Company, 1921.

Inman, Samuel Guy. *Evangelicals at Havana*. New York: CCLA, 1929.

International Theological Commission of EATWOT. "Towards a Work Agenda for Planetary Theology." *Voices* 35/3–4 (2012): 15–24.

International Missionary Council. *Addresses on General Subjects*. The Jerusalem Meeting of the International Missionary Council, March 24–April 8, 1928. Vol. 8. New York/London: International Missionary Council, 1928.

International Missionary Council. *The Christian Mission in the Light of Race Conflict*. The Jerusalem Meeting of the International Missionary Council, March 24–April 4, 1928. Vol. 4. New York: International Missionary Council, 1928.

International Missionary Council. *The Christian Mission in Relation to Industrial Problems.* The Jerusalem Meeting of the International Missionary Council, March 24–April 4, 1928. Vol. 5. New York: International Missionary Council, 1928.

International Missionary Council. *The Relation Between the Younger and the Older Churches.* The Jerusalem Meeting of the International Missionary Council, March 24–April 4, 1928. Vol. 3. New York: International Missionary Council, 1928.

International Missionary Council. *The Authority of the Faith.* The Madras Series. Presenting Papers Based Upon the Meeting of the International Missionary Council, at Tambaram, Madras, India. December 12–29, 1938. New York/London: International Missionary Council, 1939.

International Missionary Council. *The International Missionary Council: What It Is, What It Does.* New York: International Missionary Council, 1951.

International Missionary Council. *Minutes of the Assembly of the International Missionary Council,* Ghana, December 28, 1957 to January 8, 1958. London, IMC, 1958.

International Missionary Council. *Minutes of the Assembly of the International Missionary Council,* November 17–18, 1961 and the First Meeting of the Commission on World Mission and Evangelization of the World Council of Churches, December 7–8, 1961 at New Delhi. Delhi: IMC, 1961.

ISAL, *Encuentro y Desafío: La acción cristiana evangélica latinoamericana ante la cambiante situación social, política y económica.* Montevideo: ISAL, 1961.

Jack, Homer A. *Church and Society: Special Report.* Boston, MA: Department of Social Responsibility, Universalist Unitarian Association, 1966.

Johnson, David E., ed. *Uppsala to Nairobi: 1968–1975. Report of the Central Committee to the Fifth Assembly of the World Council of Churches.* London and New York: Friendship Press, 1975.

Kinnamon, Michael, ed. *Signs of the Spirit: Official Report – Seventh Assembly, Canberra, Australia, 7–20 February 1991.* Geneva: WCC Publications, 1991.

Küng, Hans, Yves Congar, and Daniel O'Hanlon, eds. *Council Speeches of Vatican II.* New York: Paulist Press, 1964.

Liggett, Thomas J. *The Latin American Evangelical Church in Inter-church Relationships: The Wider Responsibilities of the Evangelical Churches in Latin America.* Study Conference of the Committee on Cooperation in Latin America. Buck Hill Falls, PA. November 12–14, 1959. New York: The Committee on Cooperation in Latin America, 1959.

Mackay, John A. "The Church's Task in the Realm of Thought: Reflections on the Oxford Conference." *Princeton Seminary Bulletin* 31/3 (1937): 2–9 (4).

Mackay, John A. "Significant Trends Today in the Younger Churches of Mission Lands," Dec. 6, 1939, 1–4 (1). Introduction to Ecumenics – General Material (1938–1954). John Mackay Collection. Series IV – Princeton Theological Seminary Presidency, box 26.

Marcos, Subcomandante. *Our Word is Our Weapon,* edited by Juana Ponce de León. New York: Seven Stories Press. Kindle Edition.

Marques, Luiz Carlos Luz and Roberto de Araújo Farias, eds. *Dom Helder Camara: Circulares Conciliares.* Vol. 1. Recife, Brazil: Companhia Editora de Pernambuco, 2008.

Mello, Manoel de. "Participation is Everything: Evangelism from the point of view of a Brazilian Pentecostal," *International Review of Mission* 60/238 (1971): 245–248.

Michel, Brother. "Dom Helder Camara et Taizé: Témoignage de frère Michel, de Taizé," February 22, 1999. Author's personal files.

Mott, John R., ed. *International Missionary Cooperation*. The Jerusalem Meeting of the International Missionary Council, March 24–April 4, 1928. Vol. 7. New York: International Missionary Council, 1928.

Oldham, J. H. *Christianity and the Race Problem*. London: The Student Christian Movement, 1924.

Oldham, J. H. *Church, Community and State: A World Issue*. New York & London: Harper and Brothers Publisher, 1935.

Page, Joseph A. "The Little Priest Who Stands UP To Brazil's Generals," *New York Times*. March 23, 1971. NYT Archives. https://timesmachine.nytimes.com/timesmachine/1971/05/23/91286597.pdf?pdf_redirect=true&ip=0.

Paton, David M., ed. *Breaking Barriers: Nairobi 1975*. London: SPCK, 1975.

Pereira, Carlos E. *O Problema Religioso na América Latina: Estudo Dogmático Histórico*. São Paulo: Empresa Editora Brasileira, 1920.

Portocarrero Costa, J. B. *Ação Católica: Conceito, Programa, Organização*. Rio de Janeiro: Empresa Editora ABC Limitada, 1937.

Rapp, Robert S. *A Confederação Evangélica do Brasil e o Evangelho Social*. São Paulo, Brazil: Missão Bíblica Presbiteriana do Brasil, 1965.

Rivera-Pagán, Luis N., ed. *God, in Your Grace . . . Official Report of the Ninth Assembly of the World Council of Churches*, edited by Luis N. Rivera-Pagán. Geneva: WCC Publications, 2007.

Rocha, Zildo & Daniel Sigal, eds. *Dom Hélder Câmara: Circulares Pós-Conciliares*. Vol. III/Tomo I. Recife, Brazil: CEPE, 2012.

Rodrigues, Solange dos Santos et al. *15º Encontro Intereclesial das Comunidades Eclesiais de Base*. Cuiabá, Brazil: Editora dos Autores, 2022.

Scopes, Wilfred, ed. *The Christian Ministry in Latin America and the Caribbean*. Report of a survey of the Evangelical Churches undertaken February–May, 1961 on behalf of the International Missionary Council (now the Commission on World Mission and Evangelism of the World Council of Churches). Geneva/London/New York: Commission on World Mission and Evangelism of the World Council of Churches, 1962.

Slack, Kenneth. *Despatch from New Delhi: The Story of the World Council of Churches Third Assembly, New Delhi, 18 November–5 December 1961*. London: SCM Press, 1962.

Susin, Luiz Carlos and Joe Marçal Gonçalves dos Santos, eds. *Nosso Planeta, Nossa Vida: Ecologia e Teologia*. São Paulo: Paulinas, 2011.

Torres, Sergio and John Eagleson, eds. *Theology in the Americas*. Maryknoll, NY: Orbis Books, 1976.

Torres, Sergio and Virginia Fabella, eds. *O Evangelho Emergente*. São Paulo: Edicoes Paulinas, 1982.

Universal Council for Life and Work. *The Message and Decisions of Oxford on Church, Community and State*. New York: Universal Christian Council, 1937.

WCC Central Committee. *Evanston to New Delhi, 1954–1961: Report of the Central Committee to the Third Assembly of the World Council of Churches*. Geneva: World Council of Churches, 1961.

World Council of Churches. *The World Council of Churches: Its Process and Formation*. Geneva: World Council of Churches, 1946.

World Council of Churches. *The Church's Witness to God's Design: An Ecumenical Study Prepared under the Auspices of the World Council of Churches*. Man's Disorder and God's Design: The Amsterdam Assembly Series. Vol. 2. London: SCM Press, 1949.

World Council of Churches. *Evanston Speaks: Reports from the Second Assembly of the World Council of Churches, Evanston, Ill., U.S.A., August 15–31, 1954*. Geneva: WCC/SCM Press, 1954.

World Council of Churches. *Christians in the Technical and Social Revolutions of Our Time: World Conference on Church and Society, Geneva, July 12–26, 1966*. Geneva: WCC, 1967.

World Council of Churches. *New Delhi to Uppsala 1961–1968: Report of the Central Committee to the 4th Assembly of the World Council of Churches*. Geneva: World Council of churches, 1968.

World Missionary Conference, 1910. *The History and Records of the Conference Together with Addresses Delivered at the Evening Meetings*. Edinburgh and London: Oliphant, Anderson & Ferrier/Fleming H. Hevel Company, 1910.

World Missionary Conference, 1910. *Report of Commission I: Carrying the Gospel to All the Non-Christian World*. Edinburgh and London: Oliphant, Anderson & Ferrier/Fleming H. Hevell Company, 1910.

Secondary Sources

Abalos, David. "The Medellin Conference." *Cross Currents* 19, no. 2 (1969): 113–32 (113–14).

Albright, L. S. *The International Missionary Council: Its History, Functions and Relationships*. New York: The International Missionary Council, 1946.

Alencar, Gedeon Freire de. *Ecumenismos e Pentecostalismos: A Relacao entre o Pescoco e a Guilhotina?* São Paulo: Editora Recriar, 2018.

Allen, Amy and Eduardo Mendieta, eds. *Decolonizing Ethics: The Critical Theory of Enrique Dussel*. University Park, PA: Penn State University Press, 2021.

Alves, Marcio Moreira. *A Igreja e a Política no Brasil*. São Paulo, Brasil: Editora Brasiliense, 1979.

Alves, Rubem. "Toward a Theology of Liberation: An Exploration of the Encounter between the Languages of Humanistic Messianism and Messianic Humanism." PhD diss., Princeton Theological Seminary, 1968.

Alves, Rubem. *A Theology of Human Hope*. Washington, DC: Corpus Publications, 1969.

Alves, Rubem. *Dogmatismo e Tolerância*. São Paulo: Ed. Loyola, 2004.

Alves, Rubem et al., eds. *De la Iglesia y la Sociedad*. Montevideo: Tierra Nueva, 1971.

Amestoy, Norman Rubén. "De la crisis del modelo liberal a la irrupción del movimiento Iglesia y Sociedad en América Latina (ISAL)." *Teología y Cultura* 8/13 (2011): 7–26.

Andrade, William César de. *O Código Genético das* CEBs. São Leopoldo: Oikos, 2005.

Andreola, Balduino A. and Maria Bueno Ribeiro. *Andarilho da Esperança: Paulo Freire no CMI*. São Paulo: ASTE, 2005.

Anzaldúa, Gloria. *Light in the Dark: Rewriting Identity, Spirituality, Reality*. Edited by Analouise Keating. Durham and London: Duke University Press, 2015.

Aquino Júnior, Francisco de. "Comunidades Eclesiais de Base (CEBs): de Medellín-Puebla aos nossos dias," *Cuestiones Teológicas*, 47/107 (2020): 94–105.

Aquino Júnior, Francisco de, Mauricio Abdalia, and Robson Sávio, eds. *Papa Francisco com os Movimentos Populares*. São Paulo: Edições Paulinas, 2018.

Aquino, María Pilar, ed. *Aportes para una Teología desde la Mujer*. Madrid: Biblia y Fe, 1988.

Aquino, María Pilar and Elsa Tamez. *Teología Feminista Latinoamericana*. Quito: Ed. Abya-Yala, 1998.

Araújo, João Dias de. *O Cristo Brasileiro: A Teologia do Povo*. São Paulo: ASTE, 2012.

Ariarajah, S. Wesley. "The Ecumenical Movement in Asia in the Context of Asian Socio- political Realities." In *Christian Theology in Asia*, edited by Sebastian C. H. Kim. Cambridge, UK: Cambridge University Press, 2008, 227–249.

Barreto, Raimundo C. "Vatican II, Medellin, and Ecumenism: A Brazilian Protestant Perspective." *Journal of World Christianity* 9/2 (2019): 187–202.

Barreto, Raimundo C. "The COVID-19 Pandemic and the Ongoing Genocide of Black and Indigenous Peoples in Brazil." *International Journal of Latin American Religions* 4 (2020): 417–439

Barreto, Raimundo C. "Black and Evangelical: Reimagining Faith and Race Relations in Brazil." *Perspectives in Religious Studies* 49/4 (2022): 357–368.

Barreto, Raimundo C. "The International Missionary Council: From Lake Mohonk 1921 to New Delhi 1961." In *Together in the Mission of God: Jubilee Reflections on the International Missionary Council*, edited by Risto Jukko. Geneva: WCC Publications, 2022, 31–58.

Barreto, Raimundo C. *Protesting Poverty: Protestants, Social Ethics, and the Poor in Brazil*. Waco, TX: Baylor University Press, 2023.

Barreto, Raimundo and Roberto Sirvent, eds. *Decolonial Christianities: Latin American and Latinx Perspectives*. Cham, Switzerland: Palgrave MacMillan, 2019.

Barreto, Raimundo and Vladimir Latinovic, eds. *Decolonial Horizons: Reimagining Theology, Ecumenism and Sacramental Praxis*. New York: Palgrave MacMillan, 2023.

Barros, Marcelo. *Dom Helder Câmara: Profetas para os nossos dias*. São Paulo: Paulus, 2011.

Barros, Odja. *Flores que Rompem Raízes: Leitura Popular e Feminista*. São Paulo: Editora Recriar, 2020.

Bastian, Jean-Pierre. *Breve Historia del Protestantismo en América Latina*. Mexico City: Casa Unida de Publicaciones, 1986.

Bennett, John. "The Geneva Conference of 1966 as a Climactic Event." *The Ecumenical Review* 37/1 (1985): 26–33.

Beozzo, José Oscar, ed. *Cristianismo y Iglesias de América Latina en Vésperas del Vaticano II*. San José, Costa Rica, DEI, 1992.

Beozzo, José Oscar. "A Igreja no Brasil." In *A Igreja Latino-Americana às Vésperas do Concilio*, edited by José Oscar Beozzo. São Paulo, Brazil: Edições Paulinas, 1993, 46–75.

Beozzo, José Oscar. "Padres Conciliares Brasileiros no Vaticano II: Participação e Prosopografia, 1959–1965." PhD diss., Universidade de São Paulo–USP, 2001.

Beozzo, José Oscar. *O Pacto das Catacumbas: Por uma Igreja Servidora e Pobre*. São Paulo: Paulinas, 2015.

Berríos, Fernando. "Manuel Larraín y la conciencia eclesial latino-americana: Visión y legado de un precursor." *Teología y Vida* 50 (2009): 13–40.

Betiato, Mário Antônio. *Da Ação Católica à Pastoral da Juventude*. Petrópolis, Brazil: Vozes, 1985.

Betto, Frei. *Diário de Puebla*. 2nd ed. Rio de Janeiro: Editora Civilização Brasileira, 1979.

Betto, Frei. *O Fermento na Massa: O 4º encontro intereclesial das Comunidades Eclesiais de Base*. Petrópolis: Vozes, 1981.

Betto, Frei. *O que é comunidade eclesial de base*. 3rd ed. São Paulo, Brazil: Editora Brasiliense, 1981.

Bittencourt Filho, José. *Caminhos do Protestantismo Militante: ISAL e a Conferência do Nordeste*. Vitória: Editora Unida, 2014.

Boff, Leonardo. *Igreja, Carisma e Poder: Ensaios de Eclesiologia Militante*. 2nd ed. Lisboa, Portugal: Editorial Inquerito, 1991.

Boff, Leonardo. *Ecclesiogenesis: The Base Communities Reinvent the Church*. Maryknoll, NY: Orbis, 1992.

Boff, Leonardo. *Cry of the Earth, Cry of the Poor*. Maryknoll, NY: Orbis Books, 1997.

Bonino, José Miguez. "The Reception of Vatican II in Latin America," *Ecumenical Review* 37/3 (1985): 266–274.

Briggs, John, Mercy Amba Oduyoye, and Georges Tsetsis, eds. *A History of the Ecumenical Movement, 1968–2000*. Vol. 3. Geneva: World Council of Churches, 2004.

Brighenti, Agenor. "Cries from Africa: The Second World Forum of Theology and Liberation." *Political Theology* 9/4 (2008): 513–524.

Brugaletta, Federico. "Cristianismo y Sociedad (1963–1973). Protestantismo de Izquierda en la História Reciente de América Latina," *Catedral Tomada* 6/11 (2018): 236–263.

Bruno-Jofré, Rosa. "To Those in 'Heathen Darkness': Deweyan Democracy and Education in the American Interdenominational Configuration—The Case of the Committee on Cooperation in Latin America." In *Democracy and the Intersection of Religion: The Reading of John Dewey's Understanding of Democracy and Education*, edited by Rosa Bruno-Jofré et al. Montreal and Kingston: McGill-Queen's University Press, 2010, 131–170.

Burrows, William R., Mark R. Gornic, and Janice A. McLean, eds. *Understanding World Christianity: The Vision and Works of Andrew F. Walls*. Maryknoll, NY: Orbis Books, 2011.

Byrnes, Robert F. "The French Priest-Workers." *Foreign Affairs* 33/2 (1995): 327–331.

Cáceres Mateus, Sergio Armando. "La Acción Católica en la organización y puesta en marcha del Segundo Congreso Nacional Mariano de Colombia (1939–1946)." *Anuario de Historia Regional y de las Fronteras* 22/2(2017): 217–245.

Caldeira, Rodrigo Coppe. *Concílio Vaticano II: experiencias e contextos.* São Paulo: Paulus Editora, 2022.

Câmara, Hélder. *Les Conversions D'un D'UN Évêque.* Paris: Editions L'Harmattan, [1977] 2002.

Câmara, Hélder. Essential Writings. Selected with an Introduction by Francis McDonagh. Maryknoll, NY: Orbis Books, 2009.

Campos, Bernardo. "Pentecostalismo y Unidad en América Latina 'Aspectos teológicos.'" In *Fuego que Une: Pentecostalismo y Unidad de la Iglesia.* Documentos del III y IV Foro Pentecostal Latinoamericano y Caribeño, Santiago de Chile 2012 y Bogotá, Colombia 2013, edited by Bernardo Campos and Luis Orellana. Lima: Foro Pentecostal Latinoamericano y Caribeño, 2014, 33–39.

Cantú-Sánchez, Margaret. *Teaching Gloria E. Anzaldúa: Pedagogy and Practice for Our Classrooms and Communities.* Tucson, AR: University of Arizona Press, 2020.

Castanho, Amaury. *Caminhos das CEBs no Brasil.* 2nd ed. Rio de Janeiro: Marques Saraiva Gráficos e Editores S/A, 1988.

César, Waldo. "Um Ecumenismo Voltado Para o Mundo: Esboço Para uma História do Movimento Ecumênico no Brasil." *Contexto Pastoral* 26 (1995): 3–8.

César, Waldo. "Church and Society or Society and Church?" In *Revolution of Spirit: Ecumenical Theology in Global Context,* edited by Nantawan B. Lewis. Grand Rapids, MI: Eerdmans, 1998: 133–48.

César, Waldo and Richard Shaull. *Pentecostalismo e Futuro das Igrejas Cristãs: Promessas e Desafios.* Petrópolis: Vozes, 1999.

Cheng, C. Y. "An Interpretation of the Five-Year Movement in China." *International Review of Missions* 20/2 (1931): 173–188.

Christo, Carlos Alberto Libânio. *Against Principalities and Powers: Letters from a Brazilian Jail.* Maryknoll, NY: Orbis Books, 1977.

Chuji, Monica, Grimaldo Reginfo, and Eduardo Gudynas. "Buen Vivir." In *Pluriverse: A Post-Development Dictionary,* edited by Ashish Kothari et al. New Delhi, India: Tulika Books, 2019, 111–114.

Comblin, Joseph. *Échec de l'Action catholique?* Paris, Éditions Universitaires, 1961.

Committee on Society, Development, and Peace. *In Search of a Theology of Development: Papers from a Consultation on Theology and Development Held by Sodepax in Cartigny, Switzerland, November 1969.* Geneva: Committee on Society, Development, and Peace, 1969.

Consejo Latinoamericano de Iglesias, ed. *Oaxtepec 1978: Unidad y Misión en América Latina.* San José, Costa Rica: CLAI, 1980.

Cook, Guillermo. *The Expectation of the Poor: Latin American Base Ecclesial Communities in Protestant Perspective.* Maryknoll, NY: Orbis Books, 1985.

Cook, Guillermo. *Crosscurrents in Indigenous Spirituality: Interface of Maya, Catholic & Protestant Worldviews,* edited by Guilhermo Cook. Leiden: E. J. Brill, 1997.

Couch, Beatriz Melano. *La Mujer y la Iglesia.* Buenos Aires: Publicaciones El Escudo, 1973.

Cronin, John F. *The Social Teaching of Pope John XXIII*. Milwaukee, WI: The Bruce Publishing Company, 1963.

Cuevas, Luis Vaccaro. "Monseñor Manuel Larraín, profeta desde el sur de Chile." *Revista Universum* 25/1 (2010): 188–202.

Cummings, George. *A Common Journey: Black Theology (USA) and Latin American Liberation Theology*. Maryknoll, NY: Orbis Books, 1993.

Cunha, Magali do Nascimento. "A Revista Paz e Terra: um lugar da memória da comunicação religiosa, ecumênica e política no Brasil." *Horizonte*, 18/56 (2020): 513–541.

Curnow, Rohan. "Stirrings of the Preferential Option for the Poor at Vatican II: The Work of the 'Group of the Church of the Poor.'" *Australasian Catholic Report* 89/4 (2012): 420–432.

Cury, Carlos Roberto Jamil. *Alceu Amoroso Lima*. Recife, Brazil: Fundação Joaquim Nabuco, 2010.

Dash, Robert C. "Globalization: For Whom and For What," *Latin American Perspectives* 25/6 (1998): 52–54.

Dasilio, Derval. *Jaime Wright: O Pastor dos Torturados*. Rio de Janeiro: Metanoia, 2012.

David, A. Maria. *Beyond Boundaries: Hindu-Christian Relationship and Basic Christian Communities*. Delhi, ISPK, 2009.

Davis, Mike. *Late Victorian Holocausts: El Niño Famines and the Making of the Third World*. London/New York: Verso, 2001.

Deck, Allan Figueroa. "Pope Francis and the Challenge of Ecclesial Introversion: Where is He Coming From? Where is He Going?" *Perspectiva Teológica* 54/3 (2022): 703–717. https://doi.org/10.20911/21768757v54n3p703/2022.

Della Cava, Ralph. "Catholicism and Society in Twentieth-Century Brazil." *The Latin American Research Review* 11/ 2 (1976): 7–50.

Di Gregorio, Maria de Fátima. *História das Memórias do Movimento Social da Juventude Universitária Católica/JUC no Brasil dos Anos 50/60*. Curitiba, Brazil: Editora CRV, 2014.

Dias, Zwinglio Mota. *Krisen und Aufgaben im brasilianischen Protestantismus: e. Studie zu d. sozialgeschichtl. Bedingungen u. volkspädag. Möglichkeiten d. Evangelisation*. Bern, Frankfurt am Main, Las Vegas: Lang, 1978.

Dias, Zwinglio Mota. *Reencantamentos da Graça numa Favela Carioca: Memórias e Vivências de Zwinglio Mota Dias*, edited by Moisés Abdon Coppe. Juiz de Fora, MG: Editora Siano, 2021.

Dias, Zwinglio M., ed. *Memórias Ecumênicas Protestantes: Os Protestantes e a Ditadura, Colaboração e Resistência*. Rio de Janeiro: KOINONIA Presença Ecumênica e Serviço, 2014.

Dietz, James L. "Destabilization and Intervention in Latin America and the Caribbean." *Latin American Perspectives* 11/3 (1984): 3–14.

Doimo, Ana Maria. "Os Rumos dos Movimentos Sociais nos Caminhos da Religiosidade." In *A Igreja nas Bases em Tempo de Transicao (1974–1985)*, edited by Paulo Krische and Scott Mainwaring. Porto Alegre: L&PM/CEDEC, 1986, 101–130.

Dornelas, Nelito N., ed. *Evangelização Inculturada: Comunidades Eclesiais de Base*. São Leopoldo: CEBI, 2005.

Dornelas, Nelito, Pedro A. Ribeiro de Oliveira, Tereza P. Cavalcanti. "O papel da assessoria pastoral nas CEBs," *Vida Pastoral* 51/272 (2010): 29–34. https://www.vidapastoral.com.br/artigos/temas-pastorais/o-papel-da-assessoria-pastoral-nas-cebs/.

Dubalen, Marie T. *The Worker Priests*. New York: Student League for Industrial Democracy, 1955.

Duncan, Quince et al. *Cultura negra y teologia*. San José, Costa Rica: DEI, 1986.

Dussel, Enrique. *História da Igreja Latino-Americana* (1930–1983). 2nd ed. São Paulo, Brazil: Paulus, 1989.

Dussel, Enrique. *The Invention of the Americas: Eclipse of "the Other" and the Myth of Modernity*. New York: Continuum Publishing Company, 1995.

Eagleson, John and Philip Scharper, eds. *Puebla and Beyond*. Maryknoll, New York: Orbis Books, 1980.

Eggert, Edla. "Qual a Contribuição e os Desafios da Educação Popular para a Transformação Social?" In *Teologia da Libertacao e Educacao Popular a Caminho*, edited by Fernando Torres et al (São Paulo: CEBI, 2006) 93–101.

Erbele-Küster, Dorothea. "Rereading the Bible: A Dialogue with Women Theologians from Latin America, Africa and Asia," Voices 27/1 (2004): 53–67.

Escobar, Arturo. *Pluriversal Politics: The Real and the Possible*. Durham and London: Duke University Press, 2020.

Escobar, Arturo. *Designs for the Pluriverse*. Durham and London: Duke University Press, 2018.

Escobar, Samuel. "The Legacy of John Alexander Mackay." *International Bulletin of Missionary Research* 16/3 (1992): 116–122.

Espín, Orlando O. *Idol and Grace: Traditioning and Subversive Hope*. Maryknoll: Orbis, 2014.

Fabella, Virginia and Mercy Amba Oduyoye, eds. *With Passion and Compassion: Third World Women Doing Theology*. Maryknoll, NY: Orbis Books, 1990.

Faggioli, Massimo. *A Council for the Global Church: Receiving Vatican II in History*. Minneapolis, MN: Fortress Press, 2015.

Falk, Richard. *On Human Governance: Toward a New Global Politics*. University Park: Penn University Press, 1995.

Falk, Richard. *Predatory Globalization: A Critique*. Malden, MA: Blackwell, 2000.

Faria, Eduardo G. *Fé e Compromisso: Richard Shaull e a Teologia no Brasil*. São Paulo, Brazil: ASTE, 2002.

Feierstein, Daniel. "National Security Doctrine in Latin America: The Genocide Question." In *The Oxford Handbook of Genocide*, edited by Donald Bloxham and A. Dirk Moses. Oxford, UK: Oxford University Press, 2010, 489–508.

Ferraro, Alceu Ravanello. *Igreja e Desenvolvimento: O Movimento de Natal*, edited by Renato Amado Peixoto. 2nd ed. Natal, Brazil: Jovens Escribas, 2015.

Ferreira, Julio Andrade. *O Profeta da Unidade: Erasmo Braga, Uma Vida a Descoberto*. Petrópolis, Brazil: Vozes, 1975.

Fischer-Tine, Harald, Stefan Huebner, and Ian Tyrrell, eds. *Spreading Protestant Modernity: Global Perspectives on the Social Work of the YMCA and YWCA, 1889–1970*. Honolulu: University of Hawaii Press, 2021.

Flower, J. E. "Forerunners of the Worker-Priests." *Journal of Contemporary History* 2/4 (1967) 183–199.

Freire, Paulo. *Educação para a Prática da Liberdade*. Rio de Janeiro: Paz e Terra, 1967.

Freire, Paulo. *Pedagogy in Process: The Letters to Guinea-Bissau*. New York: The Seabury Press, 1978.

Freire, Paulo. *Pedagogy of the Oppressed*, translated by Myra Bergman Ramos. 30th anniversary edition. New York: Bloomsbury, [1970] 2000.

Freire, Ana Ester Pádua. "Marginal Desire and Unsubmissive Transit Between the Center and the Margin of Christianity: Two Brazilian Cases." In *Alterity and the Evasion of Justice*, edited by Deanna Womack and Raimundo C. Barreto. World Christianity and Public Religion Series. Minneapolis, MN: Fortress Press, 2023. Kindle Edition.

Fröchtling, Andrea et al, eds. *At Home with God and in the World: A Phillip Potter Reader*. Geneva, WCC Publications, 2013.

Gaines, David P. *The World Council of Churches: A Study of Its Background and History*. Peterborough, NH: Richard R. Smith, 1966.

Galeano, Juan Carlos. "Los que creyeron." In *Amazonia y otros poemas*. Bogotá: ed. Universidad Externado de Colombia, 2011.

Gebara, Ivone. *Longing for Running Water: ecofeminism and liberation*. Minneapolis, MN: Fortress Press, 1999.

Gebara, Ivone. *Ecofeminismo: Desafios para Repensar a Teologia*. Edições Terceira Via, 2017.

Gerhardt, Heinz-Peter. "Paulo Freire (1921–97)." *Prospects: the quarterly review of comparative education* 23/3–4 (1993): 439–458.

Gleanson, Judith. "Oya in the Company of the Saints." *Journal of the American Academy of Religion* 68/2 (2000): 265–292.

Gonçalves, Leandro Pereira and Odilon Caldeira Neto. *Fascism in Brazil: From Integralism to Bolsonarism*. Routledge Studies in Fascism and the Far Right. London and New York: Taylor and Francis, 2022.

Gonçalves, Paulo Sérgio Lopes and Vera Ivanise Bombonatto. *Concílio Vaticano II: Análise e Prospectivas*, 2nd ed. São Paulo: Editoras Paulinas, 2005.

González, Juan. *Harvest of Empire: A History of Latinos in America*. Second revised and updated edition. New York: Penguin Books, 2022.

González, Justo L. *The Changing Shape of Church History*. St. Louis, MO: The Chalice Press, 2002.

González, Justo L. and Ondina E. González. *Christianity in Latin America*. New York: Cambridge University Press, 2008.

Gorgulho, Gilberto et al., eds. *Curso de Verão: Ano I*. 2nd ed. São Paulo: Edições Paulinas, 1988.

Grosfoguel, Ramon. "What is Racism?" *Journal of World-Systems Research* 22 (1): 9–15.

Guisolphi, Anderson José. "Os rosários precederam os coturnos: o anticomunismo nas Cruzadas do Rosário em Família na América Latina e os golpes civil-militares (1960–1964)." *Cadernos de História*, 21/33 (2019): 158–184.

Gutierrez, Gustavo. *A Theology of Liberation: History, Politics, and Salvation*. 15th Anniversary Edition. Maryknoll, NY: Orbis Books, 2019 [1988]. Kindle Edition.

Hanks, William F. *Converting Words: Maya in the Age of the Cross*. Berkeley and Los Angeles: University of California Press, 2010.

Hebblethwaite, Margaret. *Base Communities: An Introduction*. Mahwah, NJ: Paulist Press, 1994.

Hogg, William Richey. *Ecumenical Foundations: A History of the International Missionary Council and Its Nineteenth-Century Background*. New York: Harper, 1952.

hooks, bell. "Choosing the Margin as a Space of Radical Openness." *Framework: The Journal of Cinema and Media* 36 (1989): 15–23.

Hoornaert, Eduardo. "The Future of the CEBs." *Revista Eclesiástica Brasiieira* 51/201 (1991): 161–162.

Hoornaert, Eduardo. "Medellín: 1968 não caiu do céu." *Espaços - Revista de Teologia e Cultura* 26/1(2019):5–21(9). https://espacos.itespteologia.com.br/espacos/article/view/35.

Horn, Gerd-Rainer. *Western European Liberation Theology: The First Wave (1924–1959)*. Oxford, UK: Oxford University Press, 2008.

Irvin, Dale. "Specters of a New Ecumenism: In Search of a Church 'Out of Joint.'" In *Religion, Authority, and the State: From Constantine to the Contemporary World*, edited by Leo D. Lefebure. New York: Palgrave Macmillan, 2016, 3–32.

Irvin, Dale. "World Christianity: An Introduction." *The Journal of World Christianity* 1:1 (2008): 1–26.

Jackson, Eleanor M. "Paton, William." In *Biographical Dictionary of Christian Missions*, edited by Gerald H. Anderson. New York: Simon & Schuster Macmillan, 1998, 519.

Jenkins, Philip. *The Next Christendom: The Coming of Global Christianity*. 3rd ed. New York: Oxford University Press, 2011.

Johnson, Todd M. & Kenneth R. Ross. *Atlas of Global Christianity*. Edinburgh: Edinburgh University Press, 2009.

Jørgensen, Jonas Adelin. "Indigenization, Syncretism, and the Assumed Boundedness of Christianity: A Critique." In *Religion on the Move: New Dynamics of Religious Expansion in a Globalizing World*, edited by Afe Adogame and Shobana Shankar. Leiden: Brill, 2013, 99–112.

Joseph, M. P. *Theologies of the Non-Person: The Formative Years of EATWOT*. New York: Palgrave MacMillan, 2015.

Joshi, Khyati Y. *White Christian Privilege: The Illusion of Religious Equality in America*. New York: NYU Press, 2020.

Jukko, Risto. *Together in the Mission of God: Jubilee Reflections on the International Missionary Council*. Geneva: WCC Publications, 2022.

Kalapati, Joshua. "Tambaram International Missionary Council Conference, 1938." In *The Oxford Encyclopaedia of South Asian Christianity*, edited by Roger E. Hedlund, Jesudas M. Athyal, Joshua Kalapati, and Jessica Richard. Oxford, UK: Oxford University Press, 2011.

King Jr, Martin Luther. *Stride Towards Freedom: The Montgomery Story*. New York: Harper and Row Publishers, 1958.

Kinzer, Stephen. *The Brothers: John Foster Dulles, Allen Dulles, and Their Secret World War*. New York: Times Books, 2013.

Klinken, Adrian van. *Kenyan, Christian, Queer: Religion, LGBT Activism, and Arts of Resistance in Africa*. University Park: Pennsylvannia State University Press, 2019

Kloß, Sinah Theres. "The Global South as Subversive Practice: Challenges and Potentials of a Heuristic Concept," *The Global South* 11/2 (2017): 1–17.

Kollman, Paul. "Understanding the World-Christian Turn in the History of Christianity and Theology." *Theology Today*, 2014. Vol. 71(2), 164–177.

Koschorke, Klaus. "New Maps of the History of World Christianity," *Theology Today* 71/2 (2014): 178–191

Koschorke, Klaus, Frieder Ludwig, Marian Delgado, and Roland Spliesgart, eds. *A History of Christianity in Asia, Africa, and Latin America, 1450–1990: A Documentary Sourcebook*. Grand Rapids, MI: Wm. Eerdmans Publishing Co., 2007.

Kraemer, Hendrik. *The Christian Message in a Non-Christian World*. New York: Harper & Brothers, 1938.

Larraín Errázuriz, Manuel. *La Voz Profética de Don Manuel Larraín E. recopilación de discursos y escritos, textos íntegros*. Santiago: Ediciones Mundo, 1976.

Larraín Errázuriz, Manuel. "Carta Pastoral: Desarrollo: éxito o fracasso em América Latina," *Veritas* 37 (2017): 205–232.

Leão Neto, Reynaldo Ferreira. "Ecumenism of Permeability: The Base Ecclesial Communities in Brazil." PhD Diss. The University of Birmingham: Birmingham, UK, 2009.

Levenson-Estrada, Deborah. *Trade Unionists Against Terror Book: Guatemala City, 1954–1985*. Chapel Hill, NC: The University, 2008.

Libânio, João Batista. *Concilio Vaticano II: Em Busca de Uma Primeira Compreensão*. São Paulo, Brazil: Edições Loyola, 2005.

Lima, Alceu Amoroso. *Revolução, Reação ou Reforma?* 2nd ed. Petrópolis, Brazil: Vozes, 1999.

Lima, Alceu Amoroso. *Memórias Improvisadas: diálogos com Medeiros Lima*. Petrópolis, Brazil: Vozes, 1973.

Lima, Alceu Amoroso. *Pela Cristianização da Idade Nova*. Rio de Janeiro, Brazil: Agir, 1946.

Lima, Eduardo C. "As Covid-19 crisis grows, Latin America's basic ecclesial communities step up to help." *America: The Jesuit Review*. https://www.americamagazine.org/politics-society/2020/05/04/covid-19-crisis-grows-latin-americas-basic-ecclesial-communities-step. Accessed 7 Nov 2020.

Lima, Haroldo and Aldo Arantes. *História da Ação Popular: da JUC ao PCdoB*. São Paulo, Brazil: Editora Alfa-Omega, 1984.

Limón, Javiér Jiménez. "Ecumenismo desde los crucificados." *Estúdios Eclesiásticos* 55 (1980): 267–295.

Lindenfeld, David F. and Miles Richardson, eds. *Beyond Conversion and Syncretism: Indigenous Encounters with Missionary Christianity, 1800–2000*. New York/Oxford: Berghahn Books, 2011.

Longuini Neto, Luiz. *O Novo Rosto da Missão*. São Paulo, Brazil: Ultimato, 2002.

Löwy, Michael. *The War of Gods: Religion and Politics in Latin America*. London/New York: Verso, 1996.

Löwy, Michael. *O Que é Cristianismo da Libertação: Religião e Política na América Latina*, 2nd ed. São Paulo, Brazil: Editora Fundação Perseu Abramo/Expressão Popular, 2016.

Luciani, Rafael. *Pope Francis and the Theology of the People*. Maryknoll, NY: Orbis Books, 2017.

Mackay, John A. *El Otro Cristo Español*, translated by Gonzalo Báez-Camargo. México: Casa Unida; Buenos Aires: La Aurora, 1952.

Maduro, Otto. *Maps for a Fiesta: A Latina/o Perspective on Knowledge and the Global Crisis*. New York: Fordham University Press, 2015.

Maldonado, Beatriz Carrera and Zara Ruiz Romero, eds. *Abya Yala Wawgeykun. Artes, saberes y vivencias de indígenas americanos*. Madrid, Spain: Acer-vos, 2016.

Maldonado-Torres, Nelson. "On the Coloniality of Human Rights." *Revista Crítica de Ciências Sociais* [online] 114 (2017), DOI: https://doi.org/10.4000/rccs.6793.

Marini, Ruy Mauro. "Os movimentos estudantis na América Latina." *Cadernos Cemarx* 9 (2016): 89–104.

Marques, Luiz Carlos Luz & José Oscar Beozzo. "A Igreja do Brasil na Preparação do Vaticano II." *Horizonte* 9/24 (2011): 986–1009.

Mata, Maria Cristina. "La Experiencia del Programa de Comunicación de CELADEC." *Chascqui: Revista Latinoamericana de Comunicación* 8 (1983): 76–79.

Mateus, Odair Pedroso. "A Century of World Conferences on Faith and Order." *The Ecumenical Review* 75/2 (2023): 154–171.

Mattos, André Luiz Rodrigues de Rossi. *Uma História da UNE: 1945–1964*. Campinas: Pontes Editores, 2014.

Mays, Benjamin. "The Second Assembly of the World Council of Churches." *Journal of Religious Thought* 10, no. 2 (1953): 144–148.

McComarck, John. "The Church of the Poor." *The Furrow* 17/4 (1996): 211–221.

Medina, Lara. "Nepantla Spirituality: Negotiating Multiple Religious Identities Among U.S. Latinas." In *Rethinking Latino(a) Religion and Identity*, edited by Miguel A. de La Torre & Gaston Espinosa. Cleveland, Ohio: Pilgrim Press, 2006, 248–266.

Mendes, Murilo. "O Catolicismo e os Integralistas." *Anuário de Literatura* 9 (2001): 33–36.

Mesters, Carlos. *Defenseless Flower: A New Reading of the Bible*. Maryknoll, NY: Orbis Books, 1989.

Mesters, Carlos. "'Listening to What the Spirit is Saying to the Churches.' Popular Interpretation of the Bible in Brazil." In *The Bible and Its Readers*, edited by Wim Beuken et al. Concilium 1991/1. London: SCM Press, 1991, 100–111.

Mesters, Carlos & Equipo Bíblico CRB. *Lectura Orante de la Biblia*. Estella (Navarra), Spain: Editorial Verbo Divino, 1997.

Metzger, John Mackay. *The Hand and the Road: The Life and Times of John A. Mackay*. Louisville, KY: Westminster John Knox Press, 2009.

Mignolo, Walter D. "Introduction: Coloniality of power and de-colonial thinking." *Cultural Studies* 21:2–3 (2007): 155–167.

Mignolo, Walter D. *Local Histories/Global Designs: Coloniality, Subaltern Knowledges, and Border Thinking*. Princeton Studies in Culture/Power/History. Princeton, NJ: Princeton University Press. Kindle Edition.

Mignolo, Walter D. and Catherine E. Walsh. *On Decoloniality: Concepts, Analytics, Praxis*. Duke University Press, 2018. Kindle Edition.

Miguez Bonino, José. *Faces of Latin American Protestantism*, translated by Eugene L. Stockwell. Grand Rapids, MI: Eerdmans, 1995.

Miguez Bonino, José. "A Latin American Attempt to Locate the Question of Unity." Consultation on Faith and Order, Salamanca, 1973. In *The Ecumenical Movement: An Anthology of Key Texts and Voices*. 2nd ed. Edited by Michael Kinnamon. Geneva: WCC Publications, 2016, 95–98.

Míguez, Néstor O. "Latin America." In *The Oxford Handbook of Ecumenical Studies*, edited by Geoffrey Wainwright and Paul McPartlan. Oxford, UK: Oxford University Press, 2021, 527–535.

Moltmann, Jürgen. "'Behold, I Make All Things New': The Unforgettable Message of the WCC Assembly in Uppsala in 1968." *The Ecumenical Review* 70/2 (2018): 357–369.

Moura, Lucyvanda, ed. *Coordenadoria Ecumênica de Serviço CESE: uma trajetória de luta por direitos humanos, desenvolvimento e justiça*. São Leopoldo: CEBI, 2013.

Neely, Alan. "Protestant Antecedents of the Latin American Theology of Liberation." PhD diss., American University, 1977.

Neely, Alan. "Liberation Theology in Latin America: Antecedents and Autochthony." *Missiology: An International Review* 6/3 (1978): 343–370.

Neves, Lucília de Almeida and Mauro Passos. "Silêncios e diálogos: o catolicismo e a defesa dos direitos sociais e humanos ante à intolerância política da ditadura militar no Brasil (1964–1985)." *Horizonte* 3/5 (2004): 67–81.

Odell, Luis E. "Fifty Years of Ecumenism in Latin America." In *The Growth of Interreligious Dialogue 1939–1989: Enlarging the Circle*, edited by Franklin H. Littell. Lewiston/Queenston/Lampeter: The Edwin Mellen Press, 1989, 95–111.

Oduyoye, Mercy Amba. "The Passion Out of Compassion: Women of the EATWOT Third General Assembly." *International Review of Mission* 81 (1992): 313–318.

Okihiro, Gary Y. *Third World Studies: Theorizing Liberation*. Durham and London: Duke University Press, 2016.

Oliveira, David Mesquiati de., ed. *Pentecostalismo e Transformação Social*. São Paulo: Fonte Editorial, 2013.

Oliveira, David Mesquiati de. *Dialogo e Missao nos Andes: Um Estudo de Teologia da Missao Latino-Americana*. Rio de Janeiro: Editora PUC Rio, 2017.

Oliveira, David Mesquiati de and Kenner Terra, eds. *Experiência Pentecostal na América Latina*. São Paulo: Editora Recriar, 2023.

Oliveira, Rosenilton Silva de. "'Hoje eu orei, Ele é negro': A Gêneses do Movimento Negro Evangélico no Brasil." *Religião e Sociedade* 41/3(2021): 169–191.

Orlandi, Carlos F. Cardoza. "From Christian Continent to Mission Field: The Missional Discourse of the Committee on Cooperation in Latin America and Protestant Latin Americans Concerning the Missional Needs of Latin America (1910–1938)." PhD diss., Princeton Theological Seminary, 1999.

Orsi, Robert. "She Came, She Saw, She Conquered." Book review of *Goddess of the Americas: Writings on the Virgin of Guadalupe*, edited by Ana Castillo. New York: Riverhead Books, 1996, *Commonwealth* 124/5 (1997): 24–25.

Pelton, Robert S., ed. *Aparecida: Quo Vadis?* Scranton and London: University of Scranton Press, 2008.

Piedra, Arturo. *Evangelización Protestante en América Latina: Análisis de las razones que justificaron y promovieron la expansión protestante 1830–1960*. Tomo I. Quito: CLAI, 2001.

Pieris, Aloysius. "Interreligious Dialogue and Theology of Religions: An Asian Paradigm." *Horizons* 20/1(1993):106–114.

Pierson, Paul E. *A Younger Church in Search of Maturity: Presbyterianism in Brazil from 1910 to 1959*. San Antonio: Trinity University Press, 1974.

Pikaza, Xabier and José Antunes da Silva, eds. *The Pact of the Catacombs: The Mission of the Poor in the Church*. Navarre, Spain: Editorial Verbo Divino, 2015.

Pinto, Joseph Prasad. *Inculturation through Basic Communities: An Indian Perspective*. Bangalore: Asian Trading Corporation, 1985.

Potter, Philip and Thomas Wieser. *Seeking and Serving the Truth: The First Hundred Years of the World Student Christian Federation*. Geneva: WCC Publications, 1997.

Prada, Oscar Elizalde et al., eds. *Iglesia que Camina com Espiritu y desde los Pobres*. Montevideo: Fundación Ameríndia, 2016.

Prashad, Vijay. *The Darker Nations: A People's History of the Third World*. The New People's History. New York/London: The New Press, 2007, Kindle Edition.

Quijano, Anibal. "Coloniality and Modernity/Rationality." *Cultural Studies* 21:2–3 (2007): 168–178.

Quiñones, Agustín Herrera. *Teología afroamericana: conceptualizacion para una propuesta de elaboración*. Quito: Centro Cultural Afroecuatoriano, 1994.

Rajkumar, Peniel Jesudason Rufus. "Editorial." *Current Dialogue* 57 (2015): 2–3.

Rajkumar, Peniel Jesudason Rufus and Joseph Prebhakar Dayam, eds. *Many Yet One? Multiple Religious Belonging*. Geneva: WCC Publications, 2016.

Ramalho, José Ricardo, ed. *Uma Presença no Tempo: A Vida de Jether Ramalho*. São Paulo: Oikos Editora, 2021.

Rampon, Ivanir A. *O Caminho Espiritual de Dom Helder Camara*. São Paulo: Editora Paulinas, 2013.

Ribeiro, Cláudio de Oliveira. "CEBs e Ecumenismo: Uma Discussão a Partir da Dimensão Ecumênica do Oitavo Intereclesial." *Revista Eclesiástica Brasileira* 52/208 (1992): 846–855.

Ribeiro, Cláudio de Oliveira. "Por uma eclesiologia metodista brasileira." *Revista Caminhando* 9/13 (2004): 43–64.

Richard, Pablo, ed. *Raízes da Teologia-Latino Americana*. São Paulo: Edições Paulinas, 1988.

Rivera-Pagán, Luís. *A Violent Evangelism: The Political and Religious Conquest of the Americas*. Louisville, KY: Westminster-John Knox, 1992.

Rivera-Pagán, Luís. *Essays from the Diaspora*. Mexico City: Publicaciones El Faro, 2002.

Robertson, Roland. "Globalization and the Future of 'Traditional Religion.'" In *God and Globalization: Religion and the Powers of the Common Life*, edited by Max L. Stackhouse with Peter J. Paris. Vol. 1. Harrisburg, PA: Trinity Press International, 2009.

Rocha, Zildo, ed. *Hélder, o Dom: Uma Vida que Marcou os Rumos da Igreja*. 2nd ed. Petrópolis, Brazil: Editora Vozes, 1999.

Rosa, Wanderley Pereira da. *Por uma Fé Encarnada: Uma Introdução à História do Protestantismo no Brasil*. São Paulo: Editora Unida/Editora Recriar, 2020.

Rosa, Wanderley Pereira da & José Adriano Filho, eds. *Cristo e o Processo Revolucionário Brasileiro: A Conferência do Nordeste 50 Anos Depois (1962–2012)*. Rio de Janeiro: Mauad X, 2012.

Rouse, Ruth and Stephen Charles Neil, eds. *A History of the Ecumenical Movement 1517–1948*, 4th ed. Geneva: World Council of Churches, 1993.

Sabanes Plou, Dafne. *Caminhos de Unidade: Itinerário do Diálogo Ecumênico na América Latina*. São Leopoldo: CLAI/Editora Sinodal, 2002.

Salinas, Daniel. *Latin American Evangelical Theology in the 1970's: The Golden Decade*. Leiden/Boston: Brill, 2009.

Sanfelice, José Luís. "A UNE na Resistência ao Golpe de 1964 e à Ditadura Civil-Militar." *Revista Simbio-Logias* 8/11 (2015): 127–143.

Sanneh, Lamin. *Disciples of All Nations: pillars of World Christianity*. New York: Oxford University Press, 2008.

Sanneh, Lamin and Michael McClymond, eds. *The Wiley Blackwell Companion to World Christianity*. Hoboken, NJ: John Wiley & Sons, 2016.

Santa Ana, Julio de. *Towards a Church of the Poor: The Work of an Ecumenical Group on the Church and the Poor*. Geneva: World Council of Churches, 1981.

Santa Ana, Julio de. "The Ecumenical Movement at the Crossroads." *Student World*, 2003/1: 11–23.

Santiso, María Teresa Porcile. "Ecumenismo en América Latina." *Medellín* 6/22 (1980):186–199.

Santos, Boaventura de Sousa. "Beyond Abyssal Thinking: From Global Lines to Ecologies of Knowledges," *Review (Fernand Braudel Center)* 30/1 (2007): 45–89.

Santos, Boaventura de Sousa. *Epistemologies of the South: Justice against Epistemicide*. London and New York: Routledge, 2016.

Santos, Boaventura de Sousa. *The End of Cognitive Empire: The Coming of Age of Epistemologies of the South*. Durham and London: Duke University Press, 2018.

Scannone, Juan Carlos. "Pope Francis and the Theology of the People," *Theological Studies* 77/1: (2016): 118–135.

Scannone, Juan Carlos. *La Ética Social del Papa Francisco: El Evangelio de la Misericordia em espiritu de Discernimento*. Buenos Aires: Agape Libros, 2018.

Scerri, Hector. "The Pact of the Catacombs: An Early Harbinger of Pope Francis' Vision of the Church," *Journal of Cultural and Religious Studies* 7/6 (2019): 325–331.

Schelling, T. C. "The Global Dimension." In *Rethinking American Security*, edited by Graham Allison and Gregory F. Treverton. New York: Norton, 1992.

Schmidt, Bettina E. and Steven Engler, eds. *Handbook of Religions in Brazil*. Leiden, NL: Brill, 2016.

Sepúlveda, Juan. "Another Way of Being Pentecostal." In *Pentecostal Power: Expressions, Impact and of Latin American Pentecostalism*, edited by Calvin L. Smith. Leiden/Boston: Brill, 2011, 37–61.

Serbin, Kenneth P. "Dom Helder Camara: The Father of the Church of the Poor." In *The Human Tradition in Modern Brazil*, edited by Peter M Beattie. Series: The

Human Tradition Around the World, 7. Wilmington, DE: Scholarly Resources, 2004, 249–266.

Shaull, M. Richard. *Encounter with Revolution*. New York: Association Press, 1955.

Shaull, M. Richard. "The Form of the Church in the Modern Diaspora." *The Princeton Theological Bulletin* 57/1 (1963): 3–18.

Shaull, M. Richard. *De Dentro Do Furacão: Richard Shaull e Os Primórdios Da Teologia Da Libertação*. São Paulo, Brazil: Editora Sagarana/CEDI/CLAI/Programa Ecumênico de Pós-Graduação em Ciências da Religião, 1985.

Shaull, M. Richard. "Responding to the Challenge: Renewal and Re-Creation." *Freedom and Discipleship: Liberation Theology in an Anabaptist Perspective*, edited by Daniel S. Schipani. New York: Orbis Book, 1989, 147–158.

Shaull, M. Richard. *The Reformation and Liberation Theology: Insights for the Challenges of Today* Louisville, KY: Westminster/John Knox Press, 1991.

Shaull, M. Richard. *Surpreendido Pela Graça: Memórias de Um Teólogo*. Rio de Janeiro: Record, 2003.

Shinn, Roger L., ed. *Church and Society - Ecumenical Perspectives: Essays in Honor of Paul Abrecht* [*The Ecumenical Review* 37/1 (1985)], Geneva: World Council of Churches, 1985.

Shor, Ira and Paulo Freire. "What is the 'Dialogical Method' of Teaching?" *The Journal of Education* 169/3: (1987): 11–31.

Sinclair, John H. and Arturo Piedra Solano. "The Dawn of Ecumenism in Latin America: Robert E. Speer, Presbyterians, and the Panama Conference of 1916." *The Journal of Presbyterian History* 77/1 (1999): 1–11.

Sintado, Carlos A. and Manuel Quintero Perez. *Emilio Castro: A Legacy of Passionate Ecumenism*. Geneva: WCC Publications, 2018.

Soares, Afonso M. L. "Sincretismo Afro-Católico no Brasil: lições de um povo em exílio," *Revista de Estudos da Religião* 3(2002): 45–75.

Soares, Afonso M. L. *Interfaces da Revelação: Pressupostos para uma teologia do sincretismo religioso no Brasil*. São Paulo: Edições Paulinas, 2003.

Souza, Antonio Alvimar. "CEBS: Uma Igreja que Nasce do Povo." *Cadernos Cajuína* 3/3 (2018): 3–16.

Souza, Ney de. "Ação Católica, Militância Leiga no Brasil: méritos e limites." *Revista de Cultura Teológica* 14/55 (2006): 39–59.

Souza, Ney de. *História da Igreja na América Latina*. Petrópolis: Vozes, 2022.

Souza, Ney de & Emerson Sbardelotti, eds. *Medellín: Memoria, Profetismo e Esperança na América Latina*. Petrópolis, Brazil: Editora Vozes, 2018.

Souza, Ney de & Emerson Sbardelotti, eds. *Puebla - Igreja na América Latina e no Caribe: Opção pelos pobres, libertação e resistência*. Petrópolis: Vozes, 2019.

Souza, Ricardo Luiz de. *A Reação Católica no Brasil: Instituição e Pensamento (1899–1945)*. Porto Alegre, Brazil: Editora da UFCSPA, 2023.

Souza, Rodrigo Augusto de. "A trajetória das ideias políticas de Alceu Amoroso Lima: da contrarrevolução ao modernismo católico (1928–1938)." *Cadernos de História da Educação* 20 (2021): 1–18.

Stanley, Brian. *The World Missionary Conference, Edinburgh 1910*. Studies in the History of Christian Missions. Grand Rapids, MI: W.B. Eerdmans, 2009.

Stolte, Carolien. "'The People's Bandung': Local Anti-imperialists on an Afro-Asian Stage." *Journal of World History* 30/1–2 (2019): 125–156.

Suess, Paulo. *Desarrollo histórico de la teología India*. Quito: Abya-Yala, 1998.

Tamez, Elsa, ed. *Through Her Eyes: Women's Theology from Latin America*. Maryknoll, NY: Orbis, 1989.

Tamoyo, Juan José. *Teologías del Sur: El Giro Descolonizador*. Madrid: Editorial Trotta, 2017.

Teixeira, Faustino Luiz Couto. *A Espiritualidade do Seguimento*. São Paulo: Edições Paulinas, 1994.

Teixeira, Faustino Luiz Couto. *Os Encontros Intereclesiais de CEBs no Brasil*. São Paulo: Edições Paulinas, 1996.

Teixeira, Faustino Luiz Couto. "A Espiritualidade nas CEBs." In *As Comunidades de Base em Questão*, edited by Clodovis Boff et al. São Paulo: Edições Paulinas, 1997, 207–250.

Temple, William. *The Church Looks Forward*. New York: Macmillan, 1944.

Tesfai, Yacob. "Ecumenism and 'the South': The Irruption of the Third World and Its Impact on the Ecumenical Movement." *Journal of Ecumenical Studies* 31/3–4 (1994): 332–344.

Thomas, M. M. "An Assessment of Tambaram." *International Review of Mission*, 77/307 (1988): 390–397.

Thomas, M. M. and Paul Albrecht. "The Structure and Work of the Conference: An Introduction to the Report." In *Christians in the Technical and Social Revolutions of Our Time: World Conference on Church and Society, Geneva, July 12–26, 1966*. World Council of Churches. Geneva: WCC, 1967.

Thompson, Michael G. *For God and Globe: Christian Internationalism in the United States between the Great War and the Cold War*. Ithaca, NY: Cornell University Press, 2016.

Tiel, Gerhard. *Ecumenismo na Perspectiva do Reino de Deus: Uma análise do movimento ecumênico de base*. São Leopoldo: Editora Sinodal, 1998.

Tomita, Luiza E. et al., eds. *Pluralismo e Libertação: Por uma Teologia Latino-Americana Pluralista a partir da Fé Cristã*. São Paulo: EATWOT/Edições Loyola, 2005.

Tomita, Luiza E. et al., eds. *Teologia Latino-Americana Pluralista da Libertação*. São Paulo: EATWOT/Edições Paulinas, 2006.

Torres, Carlos Alberto, ed. *The Wiley Handbook of Paulo Freire*. Hoboken, NJ: Wiley-Blackwell, 2019.

Trindade, Helgio. "A Legalidade e o Movimento Estudantil Brasileiro." *Anos 90*, 18/33 (2011): 129–164.

Tupayupanqui, Nicanor Sarmiento. *Caminos de la teología India*. Buenos Aires: Editorial Verbo Divino, 2000.

van Osdol, Judith, ed. *Mujer, levántate: Porque no será fácil . . . Pero será posible*. Quito: Consejo Latinoamericano de Iglesias, 2006.

Vilhena, Valeria Cristina. *Uma Igreja sem Voz: Análise de Gênero da Violência entre Mulheres Evangélicas*. São Paulo: Fonte Editorial, 2011.

Virgil, José Maria. *Teologia do Pluralismo Religioso: para uma releitura pluralista do Cristianismo*. São Paulo: Paulus, 2006.

Visser' t Hooft, W. A. *The Ecumenical Movement and the Racial Problem*. The Race Question and Modern Thought. Paris: UNESCO, 1954.

Wanderley, Luiz Eduardo W. *Democracia e Igreja Popular.* São Paulo: educ, 2007.

Walls, Andrew F. *The Cross-Cultural Process in Christian History: Studies in the Transmission and Appropriation of Faith*. Maryknoll, NY: Orbis Books, 2001.

Walls, Andrew F. "Eusebius Tries Again: The Task of Reconceiving and Re-visioning the Study of Christian History." In *Enlarging the Story: Perspectives on Writing Christian World History*, edited by Wilbert R. Shenk. Maryknoll, NY: Orbis Books, 2002.

Walsh, Catherine. "Development as Buen Vivir: Institutional Arrangements and (De) colonial Entanglements," *Development* 53/1(2010): 15–21.

Werner, Dietrich. "'And Yet It Move's: Dream and Reality of the Ecumenical Movement." *The Ecumenical Review* 75/1 (2023): 16–32.

Williamson, Edwin. *The Penguin History of Latin America*. Revised Edition. London, UK: 2009 [1992].

Wolff, Elias. "O Contexto Ecumênico de Medellín e o Posicionamento Católico sobre a Unidade Cristã na América Latina." *Encontros Teológicos* 33/2 (2018): 243–262.

Womack, Deanna F. "A View from the Muslim Arabic Press, 1928: The International Missionary Conference in Jerusalem." *Exchange* 46 (2017): 180–205.

Womack, Deanna F. and Raimundo C. Barreto, eds. *Alterity and the Evasion of Justice: Race, Gender, Sexuality, and Explorations of the "Other" in World Christianity.* World Christianity and Public Religion Series, vol. 5. Minneapolis, MN: Augsburg Fortress Press, 2023.

Zurlo, Gina. *Women in World Christianity: Building and Sustaining a Global Movement*. West Sussex, UK: Wiley Blackwell, 2023.

Online Resources

Bencke, Romi Márcia. "Notas para uma teologia herética." *Tempo e Presença Digital* 32/2019. http://www.koinonia.org.br/tpdigital/detalhes.asp?cod_artigo=594&cod_boletim=32&tipo=Artigo.

Beozzo, José Oscar. "A Recepção do Vaticano II na Igreja do Brasil." Centro Teológico Manuel Larraín. n.d. https://centromanuellarrain.uc.cl/images/pdf/BeozzoJoseOscar.ArecepcaodoVaticanoII.pdf.

Betto, Frei. "Fermento de marca boa: Comunidades Eclesiais de Base - Entrevista com Frei Betto." *Sem Fronteiras* 252 (1997): 5. https://ospiti.peacelink.it/zumbi/news/semfro/252/sf252p05.html.

Bidegain, Ana Maria. "From Catholic Action to Liberation Theology: The Historical Process of the Laity in Latin America in the Twentieth Century." *Working Paper # 48*. The Helen Kellogg Institute for International Studies, University of Notre Dame, 1985, 2. https://kellogg.nd.edu/sites/default/files/old_files/documents/048_0.pdf.

Brasil: Nunca Mais. https://bnmdigital.mpf.mp.br/pt-br/.

Brizola, Leonel. "Conferência na UNE em 1961 – o Brasil, os EUA e o Caso Cubano." Conference delivered on June 16, 1961, reprinted in *Hora do Povo*,

January 20, 2022. https://horadopovo.com.br/brizola-conferencia-na-une-em-1961-o-brasil-os-eua-e-o-caso-cubano/.

Canuto, Antônio. "Há 40 anos nascia a Comissão Pastoral da Terra." https://mst.org.br/2015/06/08/ha-40-anos-nascia-a-comissao-pastoral-da-terra/.

CEBI. https://cebi.org.br/historia/.

CEBs, Rede de Comunicadores das. "Mensagem final do XI Encontro Continental das CEBs." *CEBs do Brasil,* March 13, 2020. https://cebsdobrasil.com.br/mensagem-final-cebs-continental-guayaquil/.

CEBs, Rede de Comunicadores das. "4ª Carta às Comunidades: As CEBs em tempos de pandemia da COVID-19," *CEBs do Brasil,* June 2, 2020. https://cebsdobrasil.com.br/4a-carta-as-comunidades/.

CELAM. "Declaración de los Cardinales, Obispos y demás Prelados Representantes de la Jerarquia de America Latina Reunidos em la Conferencia Episcopal de Rio de Janeiro (1955). https://www.celam.org/documentos/Documento_Conclusivo_Rio.pdf.

CELAM. "Documento de Santo Domingo," https://www.celam.org/documentos/Documento_Conclusivo_Santo_Domingo.pdf.

Centro Ecumênico de Serviços à Evangelização e Educação Popular (CESEEP). "História." https://ceseep.org.br/missao-e-objetivos/.

Centro Ecumênico de Serviços à Evangelização e Educação Popular (CESEEP). "Curso Latino-Americano de Pastoral e Relações de Gênero." https://ceseep.org.br/curso-latino-americano-de-pastoral-e-relacoes-de-genero-2023/.

Centro Ecumênico de Serviços à Evangelização e Educação Popular (CESEEP). "O que é o Curso para Bispos." https://ceseep.org.br/o-que-e-o-curso-para-bispo/.

CNBB Sul 3. "Fraternidade e Diálogo: Compromisso de Amor." Formação, Campanha da Fraternidade Ecumênica 2021. https://anec.org.br/wp-content/uploads/2020/10/CAMPANHA-DA-FRATERNIDADE- 2021.pdf.

Comissão Pastoral da Terra (CPT). "Histórico." https://www.cptnacional.org.br/sobre-nos/historico.

Comisión Intereclesial de Justicia y Paz. "Comisión Intereclesial de Justicia y Paz." https://www.justiciaypazcolombia.com/quienes-somos/.

Comunidade Taizé de Alagoinhas. https://taize.org.br/helix/index.php/comunidade.

Conferência Nacional de Bispos do Brasil (CNBB). *Plano de Pastoral de Conjunto - 1966–1970.* Rio de Janeiro: CNBB, 1966. 2004 edition available at the portal of PUC Minas. https://portal.pucminas.br/imagedb/documento/DOC_DSC_NOME_ARQUI20130906183626.pdf.

Conferência Nacional de Bispos do Brasil (CNBB). "Dom Hélder Câmara: Primeiro Secretário Geral e Idealizador do Projeto da CNBB." https://www.cnbb.org.br/dom-helder-camara-primeiro-secretario-geral-e-idealizador-do-projeto-da-cnbb/

Conferência Nacional de Bispos do Brasil (CNBB). "Pastorais." https://www.cnbb.org.br/pastorais/.

CPT. "Romarias da Terra e Água." https://www.cptnacional.org.br/romarias.

CPT Bahia. "46ª Romaria da Terra e das Águas leva milhares de romeiros a Bom Jesus da Lapa entre 7 e 9 de julho." https://cptba.org.br/46a-romaria-da-terra-e-das-aguas-leva-milhares-de-romeiros-a-bom-jesus-da-lapa-entre-7-e-9-de-julho/.

Curso de Verão. "Carta Compromisso do Curso de Verão de 2024." https://cursodeverao.ceseep.org.br/arquivos/1769.

de França Belém, Euler. "Dom Helder Camara, de fascista a esquerdista, deve se tornar santo católico." Jornal Opção. https://www.jornalopcao.com.br/colunas-e-blogs/imprensa/dom-helder-camara-de-fascista-esquerdista-deve-se-tornar-santo-catolico-87535/.

EATWOT. "Eatwot Global – History." https://eatwotglobal.com/history.html.

EIG. "Mulheres EIG." https://mulhereseig.wordpress.com/.

Elbert, Társila and Andressa Collet. "Living with the poor like Jesus: The example of Fr Júlio Lancellotti." *Vatican News*. https://www.vaticannews.va/en/church/news/2021-10/laudato-si-story-brazil-poverty-fr-lancellotti.html.

Fishman, Andrew et al., "'Keep it confidential': The Secret History of U.S. Involvement in Brazil's Scandal-Wracked Operation Car Wash." *Intercept* March 12, 2020. https://theintercept.com/2020/03/12/united-states-justice-department-brazil-car-wash-lava-jato-international-treaty/.

Francis, Pope. "Apostolic Exhortation *Evangelii Gaudium* of the Holy Father Francis to the Bishops, Clergy, Consecrated Person and the Lay Faithful on the Proclamation of the Gospel in Today's World." Vatican City: Vatican Press, 2013. https://www.vatican.va/content/dam/francesco/pdf/apost_exhortations/documents/papa-francesco_esortazione-ap_20131124_evangelii-gaudium_en.pdf.

Francis, Pope. "Post-Synodal Apostolic Exhortation of the Holy Father Francis 'Querida Amazonia.'" https://press.vatican.va/content/salastampa/en/bollettino/pubblico/2020/02/12/200212c.html#.

Friends of the MST. "What is the MST?" https://www.mstbrazil.org/content/what-mst.

Gil, Theodore. "CMI relembra a contribuição de Rubem Alves ao movimento ecumênico." *WCC News*, July 24, 2014. https://www.oikoumene.org/pt-pt/news/the-ecumenical-movement-remembers-rubem-alves-1933-2014.

Global Christian Forum. "Our History." https://globalchristianforum.org/about-us/our-history/.

International Theological Commission. "Ecological Vision and Planetary Survival: A Concept Paper for EATWOT's General Assembly at Yogyakarta, Indonesia, 2012." https://drive.google.com/drive/folders/1v-CgolPOplklQbl2eJGJlFoyHQu0M_Mj.

ISER. "Linha do Tempo ISER 50 anos." https://www.iser.org.br/linha-do-tempo/.

John XXIII, Pope. *Pacem in Terris*. Encyclical of Pope John XXIII on Establishing Universal Peace in Truth, Justice, Charity, and Liberty. April 11, 1963. https://www.vatican.va/content/john-xxiii/en/encyclicals/documents/hf_j-xxiii_enc_11041963_pacem.html.

John XXIII, Pope. "Discorso del Santo Padre Giovanni XXIII al Cardinali, Arcivescovi e Vescovi Partecipanti ala III Riunione del 'Consiglio Episcopale Latino-Americano." https://www.vatican.va/content/john-xxiii/it/speeches/1958/documents/hf_j-xxiii_spe_19581115_america-latina.pdf.

Koinonia—Presença Ecumênica e Serviço. https://kn.org.br/quem-somos/sobre-koinonia.

Latin Link. "History." https://latinlink.org.uk/about-us/history.

MacDonald, Gary B. "The Church and Social Responsibility: Contributions to Contemporary Social Ethics from the Ecumenical Social Method of the Oxford

Conference on Church, Community, and State of 1937" (2019). *Religious Studies Theses and Dissertations.* 12. https://scholar.smu.edu/religious_studies_etds/12.

King Jr., Martin Luther. "Nobel Lecture." December 11, 1964. The Nobel Prize. https://www.nobelprize.org/prizes/peace/1964/king/lecture/.

Kourliandsky, Jean-Jacques. "Mulheres latino-americanas: um contexto de duplo sofrimento." *Observatório da Imprensa* edition 1129, March 16, 2021. https://www.observatoriodaimprensa.com.br/genero-e-inclusao/mulheres-latino-americanas-um-contexto-de-duplo-sofrimento/.

Law, John. "What's Wrong with a One-World World." *Heterogeneities.* http://www.heterogeneities.net/publications/Law2011WhatsWrongWithAOneWorldWorld.pdf.

Marins, José. "Ainda há lugar para as comunidades eclesiais de base na Igreja?" *CEBs do Brasil.* https://cebsdobrasil.com.br/ainda-ha-lugar-para-as-comunidades-eclesiais-de-base-na-igreja-jose-marins/.

Movimento de Educação de Base (MEB). *Viver é Lutar.* Rio de Janeiro: MEB, 1963. https://www4.pucsp.br/cedic/meb/nas-salas-de-aula/arquivos-pdf/2-2-cartilha-viver lutar.pdf.

Ordorika, Imanol. "Student Movements and Politics in Latin America: A Historical Reconceptualization." *Higher Education* 83 (2022): 297–315. https://doi.org/10.1007/s10734-020-00656-6.

Ospino, Hosffman and Rafael Luciani. "Como a América Latina influenciou toda a Igreja Católica?" *CEBs do Brasil,* August 29, 2018. https://cebsdobrasil.com.br/como-a-america-latina-influenciou-toda-a-igreja-catolica-por-hosffman-ospino-e-rafael-luciani/

Paul VI, Pope. *Gaudium et Spes: Pastoral Constitution on the Church and the Modern World.* Vatican, December 7, 1965. https://www.vatican.va/archive/hist_councils/ii_vatican_council/documents/vat-ii_const_19651207_gaudium-et-spes_en.html.

Paul VI, Pope. "*Populorum Progressio*: Encyclical of Pope Paul VI on the Development of Peoples (March 26, 1967)." https://www.vatican.va/content/paul-vi/en/encyclicals/documents/hf_p-vi_enc_26031967_populorum.html.

Paul VI, Pope and Patriarch Athenagoras I. "Joint Catholic-Orthodox Declaration of His Holiness Pope Paul VI and the Ecumenical Patriarch Athenagoras I." December 7, 1965. https://www.vatican.va/content/paul-vi/en/speeches/1965/documents/hf_p-vi_spe_19651207_common-declaration.html.

Pew Research Center. "Religion in Latin America: Widespread Change in a Historically Catholic Region." Nov. 13, 2014. https://www.pewresearch.org/religion/2014/11/13/religion-in-latin-america/#:~:text=in%20the%20priesthood.-,History%20of%20Religious%20Change,from%20the%20World%20Religion%20Database. Accessed on Oct. 20, 2022.

Pius XIII, Pope. "Carta Apostolica 'Ad Ecclesiam Christi' Pio XII a los Obispos Latinoamericanos." Iª Conferencia General del CELAM, Rio de Janeiro (1955). https://www.celam.org/documentos/Documento_Conclusivo_Rio.pdf.

Sassatelli, Marcos. "Medellin: As CEBs e seu lugar na estrutura eclesial." *CEBs do Brasil.* https://cebsdobrasil.com.br/medellin-as-cebs-e-seu-lugar-na-estrutura-eclesial-fr-marcos-sassatelli/.

Schuina, Marilza J. L. "As Comunidades Eclesiais de Base rumo ao seu 15º Intereclesial." *A Caminho: Informativo das Comunidades Eclesiais de Base do Brasil* 1 (2020). https://cebsdobrasil.ofertorio.com/comunidades-eclesiais-de-base-15o-intereclesial/#_edn1.

Silva, Benedita da. "'Lula sempre ouviu evangélicos', destaca Benedita da Silva," PT na Câmara. https://ptnacamara.org.br/lula-sempre-ouviu-evangelicos-destaca-benedita-da-silvaores/.

Silva, Rafael Rodrigues da. "Frei Carlos Mesters- Uma Vida dedicada à LPB e aos pobres." *Portal do CEBI*. https://cebi.org.br/artigos-e-reflexoes/frei-carlos-mesters-uma-vida-dedica-a-lpb-e-aos-pobres/.

The Holy See. "Address of His Holiness Pope Francis to the Joint International Commission for Theological Dialogue between the Catholic Church and the Oriental Orthodox Churches." Wednesday, June 23, 2022. https://www.vatican.va/content/francesco/en/speeches/2022/june/documents/20220623-dialogo-teologico.pdf.

The Holy See. *Mater et Magistra*. Encyclical of Pope John XXIII on Christianity and Social Progress. https://www.vatican.va/content/john-xxiii/en/encyclicals/documents/hf_j-xxiii_enc_15051961_mater.html. Accessed on Oct. 6, 2022.

The Holy See. *Ubi Arcano Dei Consilio*: Encyclical of Pope Pius XI on the Peace of Christ in the Kingdom of Christ to our Venerable Brethren the Patriarchs, Primates, Archbishops, Bishops, and Other Ordinaries in Peace and Communion with the Apostolic See. https://www.vatican.va/content/pius-xi/en/encyclicals/documents/hf_p-xi_enc_19221223_ubi-arcano-dei-consilio.pdf.

The Nobel Peace Prize. "John R. Mott – Facts." NobelPrize.org. Nobel Prize Outreach AB 2023. Wed. 29 Nov 2023. https://www.nobelprize.org/prizes/peace/1946/mott/facts/.

Tillard, Jean-Marie. "Rome and Ecumenism." August 11, 1995. https://www.oikoumene.org/resources/documents/rome-and-ecumenism.

Toledo, Joilson de Souza. "Textos que Abrem Portas: Leitura Popular da Bíblia apresentada a partir de textos bíblicos. *Interações* 15/1 (2020). https://www.redalyc.org/journal/3130/313064676011/html/.

Tooley, Mark. "John Foster Dulles, God & America." *Providence*. January 15, 2021. https://providencemag.com/2021/01/john-foster-dulles-god-america/.

UNESCO. *Youth and Adult Literacy in Brazil: Learning from Practice*. Brasilia, Brazil: UNESCO, 2009, 18. https://unesdoc.unesco.org/ark:/48223/pf0000162640.

União National de Estudantes (UNE). "História da UNE." https://www.une.org.br/2011/09/historia-da-une/.

União National de Estudantes (UNE). "História." https://www.une.org.br/memoria/historia/.

United Nations. "CEPAL: Ao menos 4.473 mulheres foram vítimas de feminicídio na América Latina e no Caribe em 2021." https://www.cepal.org/pt-br/comunicados/cepal-menos-4473-mulheres-foram-vitimas-feminicidio-america-latina-caribe-2021.

Vanzeto, Judinei. "Leigos e Leigas são chamados pelo batismo ao ministério da palavra, lembrou Dom Bucciol." Regional Sul 3 da CNBB. https://www.cnbb.org.br/leigos-e-leigas-sao-chamados-pelo-batismo-ao-ministerio-da-palavra-lembrou-dom-bucciol/.

Vieira, Henrique. "Jesus é negro." July 4, 2017. https://www.youtube.com/watch?v=ZPvF6j-hwhc.

Virgil, José María, ed. *Getting the Poor Down from the Cross: Christology of Liberation*. Second English Digital Edition. International Theological Commission of the Association of Third World Theologians, 2007. https://drive.google.com/drive/folders/1vxdDbzNlC91ncZa9vVHx_EAyBqDIJn9H.

World Council of Churches. "Pentecostal Mission Church." Member Churches. https://www.oikoumene.org/member-churches/pentecostal-mission-church.

WSCF. "Senior Friends rejoice in WSCF renewal." *Federation News*. Nov. 2008. https://www.wscf.ch/docs/resources/federation-news/WSCF_Federation_News_2008-11.pdf.

INDEX

Abya Yala, 50, 318
Ação Católica Brasileira (ACB; *see also* Brazilian Catholic Action), 179, 214
Ação Integralista Brasileira (AIB), 180
Ação Popular (AP - Popular Action), 132, 188, 192, 193, 200–2, 257, 291, 371
Acción Social Ecuménica Latinoamericana (ASEL - Latin American Ecumenical Social Action), 155n
Afro-Brazilians, 125, 347, 362
Aggiornamento, 77, 221, 224
Albrecht, Paul, 121–24, 148, 299
Aliança de Batistas do Brasil (ABB - Alliance of Brazilian Baptists), xxxi
Althaus-Reid, Marcella M., 333
Alves, Rubem, 93, 105, 111–13, 115, 130–38, 138–41, 153–54, 201, 313, 316–17
Amazon, 14, 279, 288–89, 360, 361–65
Amazon Synod, 278–79, 360
American Baptist Churches (ABCUSA), xxiii, xxv, xxxi
Amoroso Lima, Alceu, 179–83, 196
Amsterdam (1948), 73, 78, 119, 299
Ancel, Alfred Jean Félix, 226
Anglican, 18, 35, 282
Anglo-Saxon, 47, 56
Antunes da Silva, José, 227
Anzaldúa, Gloria, 350, 386
Aparecida (2007), 353–54, 362
Arantes, Aldo da Silva, xx, 193, 200
Araújo, João Dias de, 113, 128
Assmann, Hugo, 93, 173, 318
Associação de Cristãos Acadêmicos (ACAS -Association of Academic Christians), 106–7
Azariah, V. S., xv, 369

Báez-Camargo, Gonzalo, 46, 64, 66
Balassuriya, Tissa, 320
Bandung, 88–90, 298, 310, 315, 370
Barbieri, Sante Uberto, 157
Barros, Marcelo, 281–82
Barros, Odja, 138, 335
Barth, Karl, 29, 130
base ecumenism, 10, 12–3, 114, 116, 165, 167–68, 271, 273, 297, 371, 377, 387
base communities (ecclesial/ Christian), 59, 94, 137, 144, 204, 217, 234–35, 250, 253, 256–58, 261, 265, 268–69, 278, 282, 311, 323, 355
Basic Human Communities (BHC), 268
Bastian, Jean-Pierre, 52, 57
Bea, Augustin, 224
Beato, Joaquim, 128–29, 131
Bencke, Romi Márcia, 335–36
Bennett, John, 91, 108, 316
Beozzo, José Oscar, 201–2, 208, 231, 236, 238–41, 257
Betto, Frei, 93, 254–55, 260, 267, 283
Bible societies, 3, 55, 97, 270
Bible society, 61
Bidegain, Ana Maria, 172
Billy Graham Evangelistic Association (BGEA), 164
Black Evangelical Movement (Movimento Negro Evangélico, MNE), 382
Boegner, Marc, 157
Boesak, Allan, 320
Boff, Clodovis, 93

Boff, Leonardo, 93, 116, 252–53, 266–67, 318, 331, 360, 377
Bolioli, Oscar, 100, 341
Bolsonaro, Jair, 245
Bonhoeffer, Dietrich, 71
Braga, Erasmo, 46, 52, 54–57, 60–63
Brandão Lopes, Juarez Rubens, 129
Brandão Vilela, Avelar, 250
Brazilian Ecumenical Fellowship Campaign, xxix
Brazilian Social Action (ACB), 182–84, 195–96, 214
Brizola, Leonel de Moura, 189
Brother Roger, 270
Broucker, José de, 205, 208
buen vivir, 9, 369
Buenos Aires, 53, 97, 99, 157, 161–63, 264, 373
Burakumin theologies, xx

Cáceres Mateus, Sergio Armando, 178
Câmara, Hélder, 90, 183–84, 195–98, 205, 208–10, 213–18, 222, 224–30, 238, 256, 270, 298, 322, 374
Câmara, Jaime, 195, 214
Campinas, 81, 111–12, 115, 124, 130
Campos, Bernardo, 380–81
Canberra (1991), 372, 384
Canuto, Antônio, 289
Cardijn, Joseph, 172–73, 184
Carey, William, 14–15
Carson Blake, Eugene, 304, 312, 376
Casaldáliga, Pedro, 288
Castanho, Amaury, 261
Castillo, Gonzalo, 77
Castro, Emilio, 69, 72, 76, 153–54, 161, 164, 341
Catholicism, 12, 37, 40, 43, 50, 63, 96, 159, 163, 167–69, 176–82, 193, 228, 256, 353, 382
Catholic Action, 12, 94, 167–206, 208, 210–15, 218, 235–36, 253–54, 256, 277, 281
Catholic Church in the National Council of Education, 214
Central Única dos Trabalhadores (CUT), 288
Centro Ecumênico de Documentação e Informação (CEDI - Ecumenical Center of Information and Documentation), 134–35, 137, 155
Centro Ecumênico de Informação (CEI - Ecumenical Center of Information), 134, 137, 147, 155, 376, 381
Centro Ecumênico de Serviços à Evangelização e Educação Popular (CESEEP - Ecumenical Center for Services to Evangelization and Popular Education), 137, 291–96
Centros Populares de Cultura (CPC - Popular Cultural Centers), 194, 307
César, Waldo A., 81, 99–100, 120, 122–23, 126, 129, 132–34, 140, 144–49
Chao, T. C., 31–32
Chilean Ecumenical Fellowship (Fraternidad Ecuménica de Chile, FRAECH), 373
Ching-Yi, Cheng, 27
Christendom, 1–6, 21, 35, 277, 343, 353, 367–68
Christus Dominus, 232, 241
Church and Society Movement, xxii, 81, 100, 118, 130, 132–33, 154–56, 168, 195, 204, 281
Church of the Poor, 13, 168, 207–36, 238, 240, 248, 252, 259, 261, 265, 284, 296, 298, 342, 353–54, 370
Cold War, 73, 101–2, 104, 107, 164, 373
Coletivo Evangélicas pela Igualdade de Gênero (EIG), 378
colonialism, 2–3, 39, 85–86, 89, 152, 187, 230, 247, 304, 320–21, 336, 368
coloniality, 2–5, 276, 386
Comblin, José, 201, 226, 277

Comisión Provisional pro Unidad Evangélica Latinoamericana (UNELAM - Provisional Commission for Latin American Evangelical Unity), 69, 76, 155, 161, 163–65, 312
Comissão Pastoral da Terra (CPT - Pastoral Land Commission), 126, 288–91
Commission on World Mission and Evangelism (CWME), 70, 84, 144–45
Committee on Co-operation in Latin America (CCLA), 36, 79, 86, 97–99, 147–49, 156–57, 159, 373
communism, 102, 107–10, 126, 164, 186, 194, 373
communist, 88, 102, 108, 175, 177–78, 180, 188–89, 191, 194–96, 198, 202, 217, 249, 283
anti-communist, 283, 373
Comunidades Eclesiais de Base (CEBs - Ecclesial Base Communities), xxix, 94, 114, 116, 130, 204–5, 217, 234, 236, 237–72, 274, 276–84, 288, 291, 293, 297, 323–24, 340–42, 370, 371
Comunidades Universitárias de Base (CUBs), 203
Cone, James, 320
Conesur Pentecostal Forum, 380
Confederação Evangélica do Brasil (CEB - Protestant Confederation of Brazil), 77, 79, 81, 106, 117, 137, 146
Conferencia Evangélica Latinoamericana (CELA - Latin American Evangelical Conference), 59, 127, 156–65
  CELA I, 68, 156–60
  CELA II, 59, 127, 147, 155–61
  CELA III, 161–65, 376
Comisión Evangélica Latinoamericana de Educación Cristiana (CELADEC - Evangelical Latin American Commission on Christian Education), 59–60, 312
Conferência Nacional dos Bispos do Brasil (CNBB - National Conference of Bishops of Brazil), 200, 202–3, 208–9, 213–15, 226, 232–36, 245–46, 250, 256–58, 287–89
Congreso Latinoamericano de Evangelización (CLADE - Latin American Evangelization Congress), 165
conscientização, 60, 310
Consejo Episcopal Latinoamericano (CELAM - Latin American Episcopal Council),
  Latin American Episcopal Council, 76, 162–63, 208–11, 213–16, 226, 231–39, 250, 260–62, 270, 379
  CELAM I, 210, 218
  CELAM II, 219, 237–38, 241–48, 316
  CELAM III, 270, 283, 287, 291
  CELAM IV, 291
  CELAM V, 291
Consejo Latinoamericano de Iglesias (CLAI - Latin American Council of Churches), 69, 155, 295, 379
Conselho Nacional de Igrejas Cristãs do Brasil (CONIC - National Council of Christian Churches), xxxi, 245, 292, 335
Conteris, Hiber, 77
Continental Conference of the Latin American Episcopate, 216
Coordenadoria Ecumênica de Serviço (CESE - Ecumenical Coordination of Social Service), xxxi, 135, 155, 245, 374, 376
Costas, Orlando, 162–64
cotidiano, 376
coup d'état, 140, 155, 188–89, 198, 205, 307
COVID-19 pandemic, 245, 266, 330
Cristero War, 63

Cristianismo y Sociedad, 142, 146, 149
Curso de Verão, 292

da Silva, Hernani Francisco, 382
Dalits, xx
Dalit theology, xix, 320, 322, 339, 345
de Souza, Herbert, 144
de Vries, Edgar, 123
Deck, Allan, 353
decolonial, 2–3, 10, 87, 276, 331, 346–47, 367
Departamento Ecuménico de Investigaciones (DEI - Ecumenical Research Department), 138, 155
Dias, Ivan Mota, 133, 142
Dias, Zwinglio Mota, 133, 141, 154
diaspora, 94, 163
Diego, Juan, 349
Dietz, James L., 103
Di Gregorio, Maria de Fátima, 183
Diretas Já, 139, 192
Division of World Mission and Evangelism, 84–85
Dom Vital Center, 179–81
Domus Mariae, 226, 236
dos Santos, Almir, 128, 145
Dri, Ruben, 93
Dulles, Allen, 102
Dussel, Enrique, 93, 318, 320

Eastern Orthodox, xvii, 224
Ecumenical Association of Third World Theologians (EATWOT), 13, 86, 90, 298, 315–40, 370
Ecumenical Group on the Church and the Poor (EGCP), 341–42
Ecumenismo de base, xxviii, xxix, 2, 280, 296–97
Edinburgh (1910), xv–xvi, 1–7, 11–20, 26, 35–43, 83, 167, 281, 369
Edinburgh (1937), 70–71, 78
Edinburgh Continuation Committee, 16, 19, 42
Eisenhower, Dwight D., 102
Ellacuría, Ignacio, 93
entremedios, 386
Errázuriz, Manuel Larraín, 208–13, 216–18, 222–23, 227, 232, 250, 270
Escobar, Arturo, 387
Espín, Orlando 311
Eurocentric, xix, 21, 23, 74, 86, 151, 300, 327
Evangelical Union of South America (EUSA), 40
Evangélicas pela Igualdade de Gênero (EIG - Evangelical Women for Gender Equality), 378, 383
Evangelii Gaudium, 264, 354–56, 359–61, 377
Evanston (1954), 72, 73, 81–2, 117–22, 148, 299
Evaristo Arns, Paulo, 135–36, 245, 293, 323, 375

Fabella, Virginia, 319n, 320. *See also*, EATWOT
Faith and Order, xv, 61, 70, 71, 78, 224, 369
Falk, Richard, 297
Fals Borda, Orlando, 72, 77
feminist, 138, 287–88, 295–96, 318, 322, 325, 335, 338
Fernandes Ferrer, Eber, 312
Ferreira Leão Neto, Reynaldo, 259, 267
Fisher, Galen M., 25
Foreign Missions Conference of North America, 36
Forum Ibero-Americano de Diálogo Evangélico (FIDE), 379
Fragoso, Antônio, 231
Fraternidad Teológica Latinoamericana (FTL - Latin American Theological Fellowship), 138, 165, 374, 379
Freire, Paulo, xxiv, 13, 60, 136–38, 143, 197n, 199, 254, 256, 273, 294, 297, 306–12, 365
Frente de Mobilização Popular (FMP - Front of Popular Mobilization), 188

Freyre, Gilberto, 129
Furtado, Celso, 129–31

Galilea, Segundo, 93
Gallant, Valdo, 105
Gandhi, Mahatma, 32
Gaudium et Spes, 223, 232, 238, 354
Gauthier, Paul, 226, 240
General Secretariat of the Brazilian Catholic Action, 215
Geneva, 13, 136, 148, 308, 309–12
Geneva Conference on Church and Society (1966), 12, 72–74, 78, 82, 86, 91, 147, 153, 165, 298–99, 301–3, 315, 342, 370
Gerlier, Pierre-Marie, 226
Global South, xix, xx, 3, 7, 7n, 12, 18, 27, 34, 83, 85, 87, 89, 165, 208, 225, 227, 230, 240, 298, 300–1, 304, 306, 315, 327, 341, 344, 346, 368–70, 372
globalization, 20, 297–98, 306, 315, 317, 319, 333, 352, 355, 358, 365, 367
González, Justo and Ondina, 39
Goulart, João, 182, 188, 190–91, 200, 307
Gracias, Valerian, 225
Gutiérrez, Gustavo, 86, 93, 173, 285–86, 316–24
Guzmán, Jacobo Arbenz, 101–2

Havana Congress, 57, 64–69, 78–79, 86, 97
heathendom, 3, 35
Heckel, Theodor, 71
Hogg, William Richey, 19, 24, 27, 31–32
Homeless Workers Movement (MST - Movimento dos Trabalhadores Sem Teto), 287
hooks, bell, 140
Hoornaert, Eduardo, 201, 240, 277
Huampaní, 75, 127, 147–50, 161
Hurtado, Alberto, 212

Iglesia y Sociedad en América Latina (ISAL - Church and Society in Latin America), 72, 78, 96, 105, 117–37, 142, 145–55, 161, 299, 312
Igreja Betesda, 384
Igreja Cidade de Refúgio, 383
Igreja Presbiteriana do Brasil (IPB - Presbyterian Church of Brazil), 53
Igreja Presbiteriana Independente do Brasil (IPI - Independent Presbyterian Church of Brazil), 53
Indigenous Clandestine Revolutionary Committee, 385
Indigenous people, 14, 50, 126, 278, 282, 286–91, 309, 322, 324, 329, 336, 340, 349–52, 360, 362–66
Inguíñiz, Javier, 318
Inman, Samuel Guy, 40–47, 57, 65, 67
Institute for Cultural Action (IDAC - Institut d'action Culturelle), 310
Instituto Superior de Estudos Teológicos (ISET - Higher Institute of Theological Studies), 138
Instituto Superior de Estúdios Teológicos (ISEDET - Higher Institute of Theological Studies), 113
International Mission Council (IMC), 11, 14–33, 61–62, 70, 79, 83–85, 157, 300, 313, 369, 373
Interreligious Dialogue, 334, 345–47
InterVarsity Christian Fellowship, 374
intervention, 38–9, 101–4, 229, 247
Irarrazával, Diego, 318
Irvin, Dale, 1, 367

Jagessar, Michael, 304
Jerusalem (1928), 20–27, 29, 46, 61, 66, 369
Jeunesse Ouvrier Catholique (JOC - Youth Catholic Workers, Juventude Operária Católica), 171–76, 182, 184, 197, 214, 218, 226, 291

Joint Pastoral Plan (JPP), 232, 236, 250, 257
Juventude Agrária Católica (JAC – Catholic Agrarian Youth), 171, 182, 184, 197, 214, 218,
Juventude Católica Brasileira (JCB – Brazilian Catholic Youth), 170
Juventude Estudante Católica (JEC – Catholic Student Youth), 171, 182
Juventude Independent Católica (JIC – Catholic Independent Youth), xii
Juventude Universitária Católica (JUC – Catholic University Youth), 133, 171

Kagawa, Toyohiko, 27
Kalapati, Joshua, 29
Kalu, Ogbu U., 320
Kim-Cragg, HyeRan, 347–48
King Jr., Martin Luther, 247
koinonias, 94–96, 115
Kraemer, Hendrik, 28–31
Kubitschek, Juscelino, 124, 215

La Democracia, 99
Lake Mohonk, 19
Lancellotti, Júlio, 293–94
Land Pastoral Commission (CPT - Comissão Pastoral da Terra), 126, 282, 288–91
Latin America
  Latin American and Caribbean Pentecostal Forum (FPLyC - Foro Pentecostal Latinoamericano y Caribeño), 379
  Latin American Congress on Christian Work, 12
  Latin American Episcopal General Conference, 219
  Latin American liberation theology (LALT), 12–13, 68, 82, 97, 105, 114, 172, 236, 264, 267, 285–86, 318, 324, 328, 333, 370
  Latin American Network of Pentecostals Studies (RELEP - Red Latinoamericana de Estudios Pentecostales), 377–83
  Latin American Protestant Federation, 69
  Latin Americanidad, 65
  Latin-Americanization, 52, 56, 66–67, 75, 95, 157
Latourette, Kenneth Scott, 18, 28
Laudato Si', 360–61
Lausanne Covenant, 384
Lay Apostolate Commission, 212
leitura popular da bíblia, 136, 138, 280
Leme da Silveira Cintra, Sebastião, 171, 179, 182
Lercaro, Giacomo, 229
Lescase, Marie-Thérèse, 240
LGBTQIAPN+, 293, 383–84
Life and Work Conference, xv, 61–62, 71, 73, 78, 105, 119
Life and Work Movement, 70, 72
Ligget, Thomas J., 156
Lima, 50, 53, 58, 99, 147, 158–59, 373
Literatura Evangélica Latinoamericana (LEAL – Latin American Evangelical Literature), 97
Lombardi, Armando, 216
Longuini Neto, Luiz, 57, 157, 162
Löwy, Michael, 93–94, 96
Lucchetti Bingemer, Maria Clara, 328–29

Machado, Orlando, 199
Mackay, John A., 46, 58, 60–62, 74, 157, 163
Maldonado-Torres, Nelson, 2
Manifest Destiny, 38–39, 52
Maritain, Jacques, 182, 196
Marseille, 168, 175
Martins, Figueiredo, 179
Marx, Karl, 199
Marxism, 108–10, 124, 151
Marxist, 126, 134, 184, 199, 205, 217, 288

Marxist-Leninist, 202
Marxist-Leninist Popular Action (APML), 203
Mater et Magistra, 168, 173
Maury, Phillip, 108
Mbiti, John, 320
McAfee Brown, Robert, 318
Medina, Mara, 350
Melano Couch, Beatriz, 154, 318
Mello, Manoel de, 374–76, 381
Mendes de Almeida, Candido, 77
Mercier, Georges-Louis, 227
Mesters, Carlos, 93, 273–76, 372
Mexico City, 63, 97, 349
Miguez Bonino, José, 70, 93, 105, 154, 159–61, 241, 269, 318, 320, 341
Minjung theology, xx, 320, 322, 345
Missiens en Roulette, 174
Misión Iglesia Pentecostal (MIP), 373
mission/missions, 14–16, 19, 20, 23, 25, 29–30, 35–37, 39, 41–45, 49, 51–57, 70, 83–84, 95, 97, 118, 124, 156, 159, 162, 163, 165, 169, 174–76, 194–95, 203–4, 207, 214, 227, 234, 242, 244, 249, 258, 287, 299, 300, 305, 351, 365, 375, 379, 381, 383
mission agencies, 3, 11–12, 17, 40–45, 51
mission board, 41 42, 46, 50, 52, 57, 65, 68, 156–57
mission field, 3, 6, 17, 20, 39, 84, 299, 300
missionary/missionaries, 1–6, 12, 14–18, 19–21, 26–28, 30, 31, 33, 36–37, 39, 41–48, 51–57, 60, 65–69, 81–84, 98, 106–9, 121, 140, 146, 148, 154, 164, 212, 227, 232, 235, 241, 267, 278, 289, 300, 321, 349, 364, 368, 373, 384
missionized, 364
missionizing, 4, 44
modernity, 3, 6, 90, 169, 387
modernity/coloniality, 3, 368, 387
Moltmann, Jürgen, 303–4, 316
Mondey, Herbert, 164
Monroe Doctrine, 38–9, 45, 54, 103
Montevideo Congress, (1925) 57, 60
Montini, Giovanni Batista, 209, 216
Moraes, Benjamin, 123, 160
Mott, John, 20–23, 26, 39, 43, 104, 373
Motu Proprio, 169
Movement of Popular Culture, 201
Movimento de Educação de Base (MEB – Movement of Base Education), 201, 214, 256, 307
Movimento dos Trabalhadores Rurais Sem Terra (MST – Landless Workers' Movement) 125, 254, 282, 287, 290
Movimentos de Cultura Popular (MCP – Movements of Popular Culture), 195, 307
mujerista theology, 338, 345
Muñoz, Ronaldo, 93
Musskopf, Andre S., 333–34

Nairobi, 13, 165, 304, 306, 334, 335, 341–44
Natal Movement, 256
National Council of Churches, USA (NCCUSA), xxxi, xxxiii, 102n
Neely, Alan, 105, 146, 148
negritude, 382–83
nepantla, 350–51
New Delhi, xv, xvii, 73, 84, 299–300, 302, 324–26, 328–29, 373
Niebuhr, H. Richard, 108, 119
Niles, D.T., xxi
Nolan, Albert, 217
non-Western, xv, xx, 3–7, 11, 14, 17–18, 22, 28–31, 33, 84, 86, 299, 301, 302,
nonpersons, xxvii
North Atlantic, xxi, 26, 83, 87, 119, 154, 265, 299, 319
Nostra Aetate, 221, 232

O Brasil para Cristo (OPBC), 374, 382
Odell, Luis E., 146, 149, 153, 161
Oduyoye, Mercy Amba, 320, 324–27, 329, 341

oikoumenē, xix, xxviii, 14, 296, 306, 347, 367, 369, 386
Okihiro, Gary Y., 86–87
Oldham, J. H., 20, 23, 26, 28, 71
Organization of the American States (OAS), 100, 102
Orientalium Ecclesiarum, 221
Orlandi, Carlos F. Cardoza, 46
Orthodox Church, 22, 69, 76, 181, 220, 320, 353, 373
Our Lady of Guadalupe, 349
Oxford (1937), 71–74, 78, 105, 119

Pacem in Terris, 222–23
Pact of the Catacombs, 219–31, 248
Padilha, Anivaldo, 132–33, 154, 202
pagan, 22, 50, 349
paganism, 40
paganization, 178
Pan-Americanism, 45, 50, 53
Panama Canal, 38, 41, 44
Panama Congress, 40–54, 155, 369
Partido Comunista Brasileiro (PCB), 186, 200
Partido Comunista do Brasil (PCdoB), 202
Partido Social Democrático (PSD), 186
Partido Trabalhista Brasileiro (PTB), 186
Pastoral Universitária, 202–3
Paton, David M., 342
Paton, William, 28
Pax Americana, 38
Paz e Terra, 134
peasant leagues, 126, 129, 131, 188, 201, 214
Pedroso Mateus, Odair, 70, 154
Pentecostalism, 14, 37, 164, 372–73, 379–83
  Pentecostal 126, 157–58, 164, 271, 280, 282, 372–76, 378–84
  pentecostalization, 372
  universal pentecostality, 380
Pepper, Charles M., 49
Pereira, Anthony, 125
Pereira, Carlos Eduardo, 53–54
Pereira de Matos, Domício, 132
Pereira da Rosa, Wanderley, 80, 127
Pereira de Souza, Francisco, 132
Pereira Ramalho, Jether, 132, 137, 273
Peruvian Institute of Religious Studies (IPER), 380
Piedra, Arturo, 39
Pieris, Aloysius, 268
Pierson, Paul, 61
Pikaza, Xabier, 227
Pobee, John S., 320
Pope Francis, xviii, 13, 176, 228, 264, 266, 278–79, 294, 352–66, 369,
Pope John Paul II, 283
Pope John XXIII, 168, 173, 219–23, 225–26, 228, 230, 232, 236, 240
Pope Leo XIII, 169
Pope Paul VI, 209, 219–20, 228–30, 232, 238–39, 248, 283
Pope Pius X, 169, 178
Pope Pius XI, 169, 171, 178–79, 183, 204, 222
Pope Pius XII, 184, 219, 222
Popular Reading of the Bible (PRB), xxii, 136–38, 272, 273–75, 370
Populorum Progressio, 229–30, 239
Potter, Phillip, xix, 304–5, 341, 375
Prashad, Vijay, 88–89, 100, 190
Proaño, Leonidas, 223
Program Unit on Education and Renewal, 306
Puebla, 13, 260–61, 270, 283–96, 324, 342, 353, 359, 362

Querida Amazonia, 13, 266, 279, 360–65, 369
quilombolas, 362

race, 20–26, 56, 73, 87, 152, 158, 223, 277, 284, 302, 303–5, 321, 324, 326, 332, 342, 368, 372, 382
  supra-racial, 22
racism, 25, 118, 303–6, 321, 335, 338, 382
racial discrimination, 21, 23, 25, 73
Rajkumar, Peniel, 346
Ramos, Jovelino and Miriam, 132, 154

Recife, 127, 129, 132, 196, 208, 270, 310
Red Eclesial Pan-Amazonica (REPAM), 245, 360, 361
Rerum Novarum, 169, 177
Revista de Interpretación Bíblica Latinoamericana (RIBLA - Latin American Journal of Biblical Interpretation), 138
revolution, 75, 77, 82, 86, 94, 109–11, 122, 128, 131, 147, 161, 182–83, 191, 202, 258, 306, 339–40, 386
  Brazilian Revolution, 199
  Cuban Revolution, 126, 195
  Christianity and Revolutionary Change in Latin America, 77
  Haitian Revolution, 38
  Mexican Revolution, 64
  counterrevolution, 182–83
ribeirinhos, 362
Ribeiro, Cláudio de Oliveira, 271, 280
Ribeiro, Darcy, 309
Richard, Pablo, 93
Rio de Janeiro, 53, 115, 120, 130, 139, 143–44, 170, 185, 189, 192, 208–9, 214, 216, 281, 288, 353
Rivera-Pagán, Luis N., 4, 372
Rocha, Rosania, 383
Rodrigues da Silva, Rafael, 274
Roman Catholic Church (RCC), 37, 53, 78, 224
Romero, Oscar Arnulfo, 322–23
Rouse, Ruth, 105
Rural Unions, 201
Rycroft, W. Stanley, 148, 373

Sabanes Plou, Dafne, 100
Salazar, António de Oliveira, 180, 186
Sales, Eugênio, 256
Salgado, Plínio, 180, 214
Santa Ana, Julio de, 6, 72, 105, 113–14, 137, 146, 154, 341–42
Santo Domingo (1992), 354, 362
São Paulo, 54, 81, 107, 115–16, 123, 129–30, 135–40, 281, 291, 293, 322–23, 326, 374, 383–84
Scannone, Juan Carlos, 93, 264, 354
Schelling, Thomas C., 9–10
Secretariat for the Promotion of Christian Unity (SPCU), 223
  see, judge, act / *see-judge-act* 172–73, 182, 184, 194, 239, 251, 254, 255, 324, 335
Segundo, Juan Luis, 93, 173, 318
Sepúlveda, Juan, 373, 377
Setor de Responsabilidade Social da Igreja (SRSI - Church's Sector of Social Responsibility), 77, 117, 120, 123–40, 145–48, 150, 152, 198
setores populares, 59
Shaull, M. Richard, 77, 81, 94, 107–15, 120–23, 130, 132, 140, 146–47, 154
Silva, Benedita da, 288
Silva Gotay, Samuel, 93
Singer, Paul, 129
Skiles, Jacqueline, 131
Soares, Afonso, 351
Sobel, Henry Isaac, 135
Sobrino, Jon, 93
Société, Développement, and Paix (SODEPAX), 315–17
Solidarity Conference of the Peoples of Africa, Asia, and Latin America, 75
Sousa Santos, Boaventura, 85, 371
Souza, Ney de, 188, 221
Spanish-American War, 38
Speer, Robert E., 36, 41–42, 46, 57
Stanley, Brian, 3, 18, 35
Student Christian Movement, 12, 26, 94, 98, 104–16, 146, 153, 312
Subcomandante Marcos, 385

Taizé, 270–71
Tamayo, Juan José, 322
Tambaram, 7, 27
Tambaram International Missionary Council Conference, 27–34
Tardini, Domenico, 224
Teilhard de Chardin, Pierre, 182
Temple, William, 18, 78, 85
teologia de misión integral, 384

terreiros, 351
terreno, techo y trabajo, 265
Tesfai, Yacob, 83, 86
theology of the people, 13, 264, 354–55, 359, 365
Third World, 7n, 13, 18, 69, 83, 86–91, 190, 211, 225, 298, 305, 310, 315, 319–28, 330, 340, 343–45, 359, 368, 370
Third World Conference in Bandung, 75
Third World Movement, 12, 188, 242, 298
Third World project, 13, 75, 87–91, 95–96, 238, 298, 310, 315–70
Third World theologies, 321, 328, 344
Thomas, M. M., 30, 91, 341
Thompson, Karen Georgia, 347
Torres, Sergio, 319n, 320, 331
Tutu, Desmond, 320

Ubi Arcano Dei Consilio, 169
União Cristã de Estudantes do Brasil (UCEB – Christian Student Union of Brazil), 81, 106–8, 113, 116–17, 133–40
União de Estudantes para o Trabalho de Cristo (UETC – Union of Students for the Work of Christ), 106
União Democrática Nacional (UDN), 186
União National de Estudantes (UNE – National Student Union), 98, 107, 133, 186–94, 199–200
Unión Latinoamericana de Juventudes Evangélicas (ULAJE – Latin American Evangelical Youth Union), 99, 100, 104, 109, 312
Unitatis Redintegratio, 232, 241
United Fruit Company (UFCO), 38, 101–2
United Nations, 80, 88, 139, 230, 245, 307
United Nations High Commissioner for Refugees (UNHCR), 80
Uppsala (1968), 91, 165, 300, 302–4, 313, 374–76
Urban and Rural Missions Group, 145

Vargas, Getúlio, 180, 182, 185
Vatican II / Second Vatican Council, 13, 76, 82, 89, 163, 167–68, 175, 182, 204, 206, 207–48, 250–53, 258–60, 265, 269–71, 273, 290, 298, 300, 313, 315, 353–55, 360, 370–71, 377
Vieira de Mello, Agostinha, 137, 273
Visser' t Hooft, Willem Adolph, 22
Voices, 330, 337
Vondey, Wolfgang, 373–74

Wagner, C. Peter, 164
Womack, Deanna, 23
womanist, xx, 338, 345
Women's Union Missionary Society, 49
Worker–Priest Movement, 115, 168, 177
Workers Party (PT - Partido dos Trabalhadores), 254, 288, 322
world Christianity, 8, 10–11, 18, 19, 33, 62, 85, 279, 294, 372
World Conference on Church and Society (1966), 12, 73, 76, 78
World Council of Churches (WCC), xv, xvi, xviii, xxiii, xxv, 11, 13, 22, 28, 34, 70, 72–76, 78, 83, 85, 118, 122, 136, 138, 146, 157, 224, 245, 299, 309, 313, 340–41, 345–46, 372, 375
World Evangelical Alliance, 374
World Forum on Theology and Liberation (WFTL), 13, 315, 330–37, 339–40, 370
World Meeting of Popular Movements (WMPM), 357, 360, 363, 370
World Missionary Conference, 1–5, 14–18, 35, 37, 41
World Missionary Conference in Edinburgh (1910), *see* Edinburgh

World Missionary Conference in London (1888), 15
World Missionary Conference in New York (1900), 15
World Social Forum (WSF), xxxii, 330–32, 335, 337
World Student Christian Federation (WSCF), 16, 103–9, 312
World War I, 19
World War II, 73–4, 78, 88, 95, 101, 157, 185, 211
World Vision, 379
Young Men's Christian Association (YMCA), xv, 16, 21, 25, 42, 55, 106, 312
Young Women's Christian Association (YWCA), xv, 16
younger churches, 6, 11, 17–19, 23–24, 26–28, 33, 66, 83–84, 341, 369

Zapatista, 386
zeitgeist, 14, 89, 96